The Insider's Guide to

THE GMAT CAT®

KARL WEBER

**Author of nearly 20 books offering frank
and impartial test-preparation advice**

www.petersons.com

PETERSON'S™

THOMSON LEARNING

Australia • Canada • Mexico • Singapore • Spain • United Kingdom • United States

About Peterson's

Founded in 1966, Peterson's, a division of Thomson Learning, is the nation's largest and most respected provider of lifelong learning online resources, software, reference guides, and books. The Education Supersite^{SM} at petersons.com—the Web's most heavily traveled education resource—has searchable databases and interactive tools for contacting U.S.-accredited institutions and programs. CollegeQuest^{SM} (CollegeQuest.com) offers a complete solution for every step of the college decision-making process. GradAdvantage^{TM} (GradAdvantage.org), developed with Educational Testing Service, is the only electronic admissions service capable of sending official graduate test score reports with a candidate's online application. Peterson's serves more than 55 million education consumers annually.

Thomson Learning is among the world's leading providers of lifelong learning, serving the needs of individuals, learning institutions, and corporations with products and services for both traditional classrooms and for online learning. For more information about the products and services offered by Thomson Learning, please visit www.thomsonlearning.com. Headquartered in Stamford, Connecticut, with offices worldwide, Thomson Learning is part of The Thomson Corporation (www.thomson.com), a leading e-information and solutions company in the business, professional, and education marketplaces. The Corporation's common shares are listed on the Toronto and London stock exchanges.

For more information, contact Peterson's, 2000 Lenox Drive, Lawrenceville, NJ 08648; 800-338-3282; or find us on the World Wide Web at: www.petersons.com/about

ISBN 0-7689-0593-1

Printed in Canada

10 9 8 7 6 5 4 3 2 1   02 01 00

Acknowledgments

Creating this edition for *The Insider's Guide to the GMAT CAT* has been a team effort. I've been fortunate enough to have the assistance of a very talented group of educators and writers who skillfully crafted significant portions of the manuscript, drawing on both their considerable knowledge and their notable literary skills to complement my abilities beautifully. In particular, I wish to acknowledge and thank:

Dr. Harold D. Shane
Peter Lanzer
Nancy J. Brandwein
Robert A. Kaplan
Laura A. Weber

Naturally, any errors or inadequacies that the book may contain are mine alone.

I also want to thank Bob Schaeffer of FairTest and John Nelson and Andrea Wilson of Kaplan Educational Centers for their helpful responses to my many inquiries. Thanks, too, to Charles A. Wall, an old and valued friend, Linda Bernbach, Cindy Kitchel, and Bob Sehlinger.

And my gratitude especially, and always, to Mary-Jo Weber, my wife, whose love makes it all worthwhile.

Karl Weber
Chappaqua, New York

About the Author

Karl Weber has been helping students to prepare for the GMAT CAT and other standardized exams for twenty years. He was a teacher, writer, and editor for Stanley H. Kaplan Educational Centers and later designed and taught the verbal test-preparation programs at Mathworks, a school in New York City. Weber is featured on a popular series of test-preparation videos published by Video Aided Instruction, a producer of educational materials located in Roslyn Heights, New York.

Weber is also well known in the publishing industry as an editor, literary agent, and book developer. He was the editor of two of the best investment books of all time, as selected in 1997 by *Worth* magazine, and also worked with former president Jimmy Carter on two best-selling books about the Christian religion, *Living Faith* and *Sources of Strength*. He lives with Mary-Jo Weber, his wife of twenty-five years, in Chappaqua, New York.

Contents

Contents

Learn about the best business school options
with the **QuickStart Counselor–**
real-time, online education advice you can trust.

Are you looking for

- An alternative to expensive independent counseling?

- Personalized attention from a qualified professional?

- Valuable advice to help you reach your educational goals?

Chat online with a trained education counselor!

- 60 minutes of unlimited sessions

- Immediate feedback from an actual human being

- Access to high-quality educational resources from the leader in education information

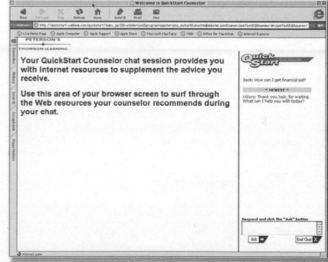

Register today at www.petersons.com/counselor

The Insider's Guide Declaration of Independence

In an America where advanced educational credentials are growing more and more important, the GMAT CAT has become one of the crucial hurdles in the lives of business people. Your performance on the GMAT CAT plays a major role in determining whether or not you'll be able to attend the graduate business school of your choice.

Furthermore, the GMAT CAT covers an arbitrary and slightly weird collection of skills. In addition to questions on high-school math topics something like those you may remember from the SAT or ACT (way back when), the GMAT CAT includes questions that require you to correct grammar errors in other people's sentences, determine the kinds of data needed to solve hypothetical mathematical problems, and detect logical fallacies in short persuasive passages. What does it all add up to? No one knows. Does it make sense as a prerequisite for B-school? Not much. Do you have a choice? Not really.

To survive the process—and to make it work for you—you need help.

YOU CAN'T DEPEND ON THE TEST-MAKERS

Unfortunately, it seems that almost everyone involved in the standardized testing industry (and make no mistake, it *is* an industry—a big one) has some kind of ax to grind.

The test-makers themselves—the Graduate Management Admission Council, a consortium of business schools which sponsors the GMAT CAT program, and the Educational Testing Service, which writes and administers the test—have a huge vested interest in the survival and credibility of the exam. Both GMAC and ETS are not-for-profit organizations. That doesn't make them immune to the pressures felt by every organization in a competitive industry. They make their living by producing the GMAT CAT for use by universities as part of the student admission process. The fine salaries and nice offices enjoyed by the executives at ETS are dependent on having university admission officers and the general public continue to believe that the GMAT CAT is a useful, accurate, and basically fair tool for measuring student abilities. If that belief were to vanish, business schools would stop asking students to take the GMAT CAT, and the people who work for ETS would have to find new jobs.

Therefore, everything the test-makers say publicly about the GMAT CAT must serve the purpose of sustaining public confidence in the accuracy and fairness of the exam. They must be careful to avoid any suggestion that the GMAT CAT, or any part of the GMAT CAT, can be successfully negotiated by mastering a handful of relatively simple techniques. If students can score higher on the GMAT CAT by using a few easy-to-learn "tricks," then the exam begins to appear more like a gimmick than a serious educational tool. From the test-makers' point of view, that would never do.

Thus, the test-makers have a vested interest in stressing how difficult, time-consuming, and intellectually challenging it is to prepare for the GMAT CAT. They need desperately to bolster the image of the GMAT CAT as an "unbeatable" exam. It's understandable. In their shoes, most of us would feel—and behave—the same.

Don't misunderstand. We don't consider the GMAC or ETS crass, unprofessional, or venal. They are highly competent specialists in test design and administration, and, undoubtedly, they sincerely believe in the value of their work. But the nature of that work makes it impossible for them to offer you the kind of disinterested, unbiased, and completely honest advice you need about the best and easiest ways to really prepare for the GMAT CAT.

TEST-PREP SCHOOLS HAVE THEIR OWN AGENDA

What about the other sources of test-taking advice and information? Aren't they immune to these kinds of biases?

Yes—but most of them have other biases of their own. For example, over the last two decades, several nationwide chains of test-preparation schools have sprung up. They offer classroom courses, supplemented with printed and electronic study material, to help students prepare for the GMAT CAT and other exams. Some of these have become big businesses in their own right, owned by or affiliated with major media conglomerates. You can find books and software bearing the names of these schools and containing some of the techniques and strategies taught in their classroom programs.

Naturally, like any business people, the executives who manage these schools are interested in keeping profits high. To do this, they must funnel as many students as possible through their classroom programs.

Given a choice, they'd much rather have you buy one of their ambitious, multi-week courses than a book or even a piece of software. (The profit on a book that costs around $15 can't begin to compare with the profit on a $500 class.) Thus, they must view their books primarily as promotional vehicles for their schools. They hope that some of the students who buy their books will be sufficiently impressed—and perhaps sufficiently intimidated—to sign up for a class.

In their case, the vested interest lies in making the GMAT CAT appear scary enough to drive you into a a $500 classroom program—and in making the test-taking strategies and techniques you need to learn appear complicated and arcane enough to demand weeks of work with a teacher or tutor.

Again, don't misunderstand. Some of the test-preparation schools offer fine programs. And some of the books and software they produce can be quite helpful in preparing for an exam. But, just as with the test-makers themselves, we think the inherent self-interest in how the test-prep schools do business inevitably colors the kind of advice they give you and the kinds of preparation they recommend.

OUR PLEDGE

We have no such bias. We have no vested interest in the reputation or image of the GMAT CAT, and we are not selling classroom courses for any exam. Our only concern is to offer you the most efficient, accurate, and useful guidance for earning your highest possible score on the GMAT CAT. If a particular type of math question can be solved without performing any calculations, or a certain kind of logic question can be answered even if you don't recognize the fallacy, or some parts of a reading passage can be safely ignored, we're free to say so, thus letting you focus your time and energy in more effective ways—and earn a higher score in the process.

That's why we proudly bear the banner of the *Insider's Guides*. Authorized and controlled by no one, we serve only one master—you, our reader.

How This Guide Was Researched and Written

The authors of this book are specialists in test-preparation, teaching, and the writing of educational materials. We've followed the development of the GMAT (now GMAT CAT) for close to twenty years, tracking and analyzing the changes in the kinds of questions used and the skills tested. We've also worked with students (and teachers) in various settings, helping them to develop the test-taking abilities and the self-confidence needed to do well on the exam.

Based on these years of experience, we've developed a keen awareness of what the GMAT CAT is like and what techniques the test-makers use to measure the strengths and weaknesses of individual students. Equally important, we've developed a strong sense as to what kinds of test-taking strategies most students find really beneficial and which ones, frankly, are more complicated or confusing than helpful. This expertise has helped to shape both the contents and the style of this guide.

The individual chapters are each based on extensive analysis of actual GMAT CAT exams. Take, for example, Chapter 12, "The Insider's GMAT CAT Writer's Manual." This chapter is designed to help you prepare for sentence correction questions on the GMAT CAT, which focus on grammar and usage errors in English. Rather than simply create a grammar manual based on instinct or on the recommendations of English teachers, we started by compiling a list of all the grammar and usage rules tested on recent GMAT CAT exams. We then selected the rules that turned up most frequently on the exam, discovering, to our delight, that the number of rules you *really* need to master is even smaller than we'd expected.

To increase the value of the chapter as a learning tool, we then added clear, accurate explanations of the rules and sample sentences, illustrating how these rules are actually tested on the GMAT CAT. The result, we believe, is the most up-to-date, complete, and truly useful GMAT CAT grammar review currently available. And we've applied a similar approach to every topic on the exam.

SPECIAL FEATURES

To help you get the most out of this book quickly and easily, the text is enhanced with FYI sidebars that provide you with:

- tips and shortcuts that save you time

- cautions and warnings about pitfalls to avoid

- strategies that offer an easier or smarter way to do something

- statements from real people that can give you valuable insights

- an insider's fact or anecdote

We also recognize you need to have quick information at your fingertips and thus have provided the following helpful Appendices at the back of the book:

A. The Insider's GMAT CAT Word List
B. The Insider's GMAT CAT Math Review
C. The Insider's GMAT CAT Writer's Manual
D. The Insider's Stress-Busting Guide

The Newest Wrinkles

What to Expect on the GMAT CAT for 2001–02

ESSAYS TO BE GRADED BY COMPUTER: ETS INTRODUCES "E-RATER"

The Educational Testing Service announced in February, 1999, that one of the two graders of the Analytical Writing Assessment essays on the GMAT CAT will now be a computer program—the so-called E-rater. (Think "e-mail" or "e-commerce.") It's all part of the test-makers' never-ending quest to remove the fallible, the unpredictable, and the human from the testing process.

Until now, the essays you wrote for the Analytical Writing Assessment were read and scored by two humans, generally moonlighting college teachers or graduate students specially trained by ETS. Each essay was read quickly (usually in about two minutes) and assigned a score from 0 to 6. Your final score was an average of the two readers' scores. If there was a score difference of more than one point between the two readers' scores, a third reader would settle the discrepancy.

Now, the E-rater will substitute for one of the human readers. As in the past, a score discrepancy of greater than one point will be settled by having a third (human) reader give an additional grade.

How will the E-rater affect your essay scores? It's hard to provide a detailed answer, since ETS is *not* releasing specific information about the design of the E-rater software. However, based on the test-makers' public statements, we recommend the following:

- Pay special attention to the stylistic tips outlined in Chapter 9 of this book, especially these three: "Guide the Reader Using Signpost Words," "Vary the Length of Your Sentences," and "Make Concessions as Needed."

- Use the paragraph as a structural device for organizing your essay. Give each main idea in your essay a separate paragraph of its own, and use the four, five, or six paragraphs of your essay as obvious stepping-stones in your argument.

- Be careful about basic errors in grammar, usage, and spelling. If in doubt about the proper way to use a particular word, choose another. (Appendix C, "The Insider's GMAT CAT Writer's Manual," reviews the most common errors in grammar and usage that you should be certain to avoid.)

These steps should help ensure that your essay will have the *obvious* features of logic, clarity, and correctness that a computer is capable of recognizing. More subtle and sophisticated elements of writing skill will be detected by your human reader only—if at all.

Read Chapter 9 for more detailed instructions about how to perform well on the GMAT CAT Analytical Writing Assessment.

"FATAL ERROR" MESSAGES PLAGUE SOME TEST-TAKERS

Since the introduction of the GMAT CAT, test-takers have complained from time to time about computer glitches that hampered their testing experience. The Educational Testing Service has now conceded that some 400 GMAT CAT test-takers suffered software problems during October, 1998, in what appears to be the most significant outbreak of GMAT CAT computer glitches to date.

The students affected were shown a "Fatal Error" message on their monitors at the conclusion of the computerized GMAT CAT, just before being shown their test scores. Obviously, these students were left feeling uncertain as to whether or not their test scores were accurate.

ETS claims to have remedied the problems that caused the "Fatal Error" messages, and we have no reason to doubt this. However, if you encounter any kind of computer error during the administration of your GMAT CAT, you should take the following steps:

- Immediately notify the test center administrator of the problem.

- As soon as possible, note in writing what happened, the date and location, and how your test-taking experience was affected.

- Contact ETS promptly and explain what happened. If you feel that your test score may not be valid, ask that you be permitted to retake the exam at no cost to you.

- If the computer error invalidates your test score, ask ETS not to handle the test administration as a routine "score cancellation," which would indicate that you took the exam and asked to have your score deleted. Instead, ask that they remove from their records all indications that you ever took the exam.

- Keep written notes of all your conversations with ETS, in case it ever becomes necessary to lodge a formal complaint.

See Chapters 11 and 12 in this book for more information about how to protect your rights when dealing with ETS before, during, and after the GMAT CAT.

Part I

First Things First

Chapter 1

An Insider's Look at the GMAT CAT: The Insider's GMAT CAT Diagnostic Test

INSTRUCTIONS

The following Insider's GMAT CAT Diagnostic Test will provide your first look at the format, contents, and difficulty levels of the GMAT CAT. It will also allow you to diagnose your strengths and weaknesses and help you focus on the skills and test areas where you have the greatest opportunity to boost your GMAT CAT scores.

This test is about the same length as the real GMAT CAT. Take it under true testing conditions. Complete the entire test in a single sitting. Eliminate distractions (TV, music) and clear away notes and reference materials.

Time each section of the test separately with a stopwatch or kitchen timer, or have someone else time you. If you run out of time before answering all of the questions, stop and draw a line under the last question you finished. Then, go on to the next test section. When you are done, score yourself based only on the questions you finished in the allotted time. Later, for practice purposes, you should answer the questions you were unable to complete in time.

The answer key, explanatory answers, and information about interpreting your test results appear at the end of the test.

SECTION 1

ANALYTICAL WRITING 1

Time—30 Minutes

ANALYSIS OF AN ISSUE

In this section, you will need to analyze the issue presented and explain your views on it. There is no "correct" answer. Instead, you should consider various perspectives as you develop your own position on the issue.

WRITING YOUR RESPONSE
Take a few minutes to think about the issue and plan a response before you begin writing. Be sure to organize your ideas and develop them fully, but leave time to reread your response and make any revisions that you think are necessary.

EVALUATION OF YOUR RESPONSE
College and university faculty members from various subject-matter areas, including management education, will evaluate the overall quality of your thinking and writing. They will consider how well you

- organize, develop, and express your ideas about the issue presented
- provide relevant supporting reasons and examples
- control the elements of standard written English

Directions: Read the statement and the instructions that follow it, and then make any notes that will help you plan your response. Write your response on scrap paper or type it on a word processor.

"The use of surveillance cameras to monitor activity in public places is a valuable tool for fighting crime and poses no threat to the privacy of law-abiding citizens. After all, a person who is doing nothing wrong has nothing to fear from being observed."

To what extent do you agree or disagree with the opinion expressed above? Support your views with reasons and examples drawn from your own experiences, observations, or reading.

SECTION 2

ANALYTICAL WRITING 2

Time—30 Minutes

ANALYSIS OF AN ARGUMENT

In this section, you will be asked to write a critique of the argument presented. *You are NOT being asked to present your own views on the subject.*

WRITING YOUR RESPONSE

Take a few minutes to evaluate the argument and plan a response before you begin writing. Be sure to organize your ideas and develop them fully, but leave time to reread your response and make any revisions that you think are necessary.

EVALUATION OF YOUR RESPONSE

College and university faculty members from various subject-matter areas, including management education, will evaluate the overall quality of your thinking and writing. They will consider how well you

- organize, develop, and express your ideas about the argument presented
- provide relevant supporting reasons and examples
- control the elements of standard written English

Directions: Read the statement and the instructions that follow it, and then make any notes that will help you plan your response. Write your response on scrap paper or type it on a word processor.

The following appeared in the editorial section of a local newspaper.

"More than half of the households in Citrus City are childless, and almost all of the voters in these households voted against this year's school budget bill, forcing dramatic reductions in public school spending. These voters, however, were shortsighted. Although childless people do not benefit directly from high-quality public schools, a strong educational system will make Citrus City an attractive place for families to live and help keep home values in the area high."

Discuss how well reasoned you find this argument. In your discussion, be sure to analyze the line of reasoning and the use of evidence in the argument. For example, you may need to consider what questionable assumptions underlie the thinking and what alternative explanations or counterexamples might weaken the conclusion. You can also discuss what sort of evidence would strengthen or refute the argument, what changes in the argument would make it more logically sound, and what, if anything, would help you better evaluate its conclusion.

SECTION 3

QUANTITATIVE

37 Questions

Time—75 Minutes

Directions (Problem Solving): Solve the problem and indicate the best of the answer choices given.

Numbers: All numbers used are real numbers.

Figures: A figure accompanying a problem solving question is intended to provide information useful in solving the problem. Figures are drawn as accurately as possible EXCEPT when it is stated in a specific problem that its figure is not drawn to scale. Straight lines may sometimes appear jagged. All figures lie in a plane unless otherwise indicated.

Directions (Data Sufficiency): This data sufficiency problem consists of a question and two statements, labeled (1) and (2), in which certain data are given. You have to decide whether the data given in the statements are *sufficient* for answering the question. Using the data given in the statements *plus* your knowledge of mathematics and everyday facts (such as the number of days in July or the meaning of *counterclockwise*), you must indicate whether

- statement (1) ALONE is sufficient, but statement (2) alone is not sufficient to answer the question asked;
- statement (2) ALONE is sufficient, but statement (1) alone is not sufficient to answer the question asked;
- BOTH statements (1) and (2) TOGETHER are sufficient to answer the question asked; but NEITHER statement ALONE is sufficient;
- EACH statement ALONE is sufficient to answer the question asked;
- statements (1) and (2) TOGETHER are NOT sufficient to answer the question asked, and additional data specific to the problem are needed.

Numbers: All numbers used are real numbers.

Figures: A figure accompanying a data sufficiency problem will conform to the information given in the question, but will not necessarily conform to the additional information given in statements (1) and (2).

Lines shown as straight can be assumed to be straight and lines that appear jagged can also be assumed to be straight.

You may assume that the positions of points, angles, regions, etc., exist in the order shown and that angle measures are greater than zero.

All figures lie in a plane unless otherwise indicated.

Note: In data sufficiency problems that ask for the value of a quantity, the data given in the statements are sufficient only when it is possible to determine exactly one numerical value for the quantity.

---

1. Morton earns 20% more than Caroline, and Caroline earns $\frac{2}{3}$ of what Sasha earns. What percent of Sasha's earnings are Morton's earnings?

   (A) 80%
   (B) 90%
   (B) 100%
   (D) 120%
   (E) 167%

2. If $y - 9 = 3 - y$, then $y =$

   (A) 12
   (B) 9
   (C) 6
   (D) 3
   (E) -6

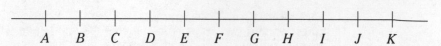

3. On the number line above, if all the points shown are equidistant, what is the coordinate of *H*?

   (1) The coordinate of *A* is 3.72.
   (2) The coordinate of *F* is 3.82.

   (A) Statement (1) ALONE is sufficient, but statement (2) alone is not sufficient.
   (B) Statement (2) ALONE is sufficient, but statement (1) alone is not sufficient.
   (C) BOTH statements (1) and (2) TOGETHER are sufficient, but NEITHER statement ALONE is sufficient.
   (D) EACH statement ALONE is sufficient.
   (E) Statements (1) and (2) TOGETHER are NOT sufficient.

4. If $\dfrac{RST}{K^2}$ is a positive number, and *R* is negative, which of the following CANNOT be true?

   I.   *K* is negative, and *S* and *T* are negative.
   II. *K* and *S* are negative, and *T* is positive.
   III. *S* and *T* are positive.

   (A) I only
   (B) II only
   (C) I and II only
   (D) I and III only
   (E) I, II, and III

5. If $a \neq 2$, then what is the value of $\dfrac{b + 3}{2 - a}$?

    (1) $\dfrac{12}{a} = 2$

    (2) $\dfrac{b}{3} = -1$

(A) Statement (1) ALONE is sufficient, but statement (2) alone is not sufficient.

(B) Statement (2) ALONE is sufficient, but statement (1) alone is not sufficient.

(C) BOTH statements (1) and (2) TOGETHER are sufficient, but NEITHER statement ALONE is sufficient.

(D) EACH statement ALONE is sufficient.

(E) Statements (1) and (2) TOGETHER are NOT sufficient.

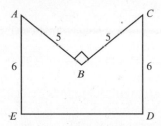

6. What is the area of *ABCDE* in the figure above?

    (1) The perimeter of *ABCDE* is 30.

    (2) The length of *ED* is 8.

(A) Statement (1) ALONE is sufficient, but statement (2) alone is not sufficient.

(B) Statement (2) ALONE is sufficient, but statement (1) alone is not sufficient.

(C) BOTH statements (1) and (2) TOGETHER are sufficient, but NEITHER statement ALONE is sufficient.

(D) EACH statement ALONE is sufficient.

(E) Statements (1) and (2) TOGETHER are NOT sufficient.

7. The ratio of broken to unbroken eggs in a box of a dozen could be any of the following EXCEPT

    (A) 1:1

    (B) 1:2

    (C) 1:3

    (D) 1:5

    (E) 1:6

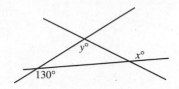

8. In the figure above, what is the relationship between x and y?
    (A) $x + y = 130$
    (B) $x + y = 50$
    (C) $y = 50 - x$
    (D) $x = y - 50$
    (E) $y = x - 50$

9. What is the value of x^2?

    (1) $(x - 3)^2 = (x + 7)^2$
    (2) $2x + 5 = 1$

    (A) Statement (1) ALONE is sufficient, but statement (2) alone is
         not sufficient.
    (B) Statement (2) ALONE is sufficient, but statement (1) alone is
         not sufficient.
    (C) BOTH statements (1) and (2) TOGETHER are sufficient, but
         NEITHER statement ALONE is sufficient.
    (D) EACH statement ALONE is sufficient.
    (E) Statements (1) and (2) TOGETHER are NOT sufficient.

10. A rectangle has one side with a length of 12 and a diagonal with a
    length of 20. What is the area of the rectangle?
    (A) 60
    (B) 72
    (C) 96
    (D) 144
    (E) 192

11. Maria has 77¢ in a combination of pennies, nickels, and dimes. If
    she has 2 more dimes than she has nickels, what is the least
    number of pennies that she can possibly have?
    (A) 42
    (B) 27
    (C) 17
    (D) 12
    (E) 2

12. What is the area of a triangle with vertices at $P(0, -1)$, $Q(0,5)$, and $R(a,b)$?

   (1) $a = 4$
   (2) $b = 3$

   (A) Statement (1) ALONE is sufficient, but statement (2) alone is not sufficient.
   (B) Statement (2) ALONE is sufficient, but statement (1) alone is not sufficient.
   (C) BOTH statements (1) and (2) TOGETHER are sufficient, but NEITHER statement ALONE is sufficient.
   (D) EACH statement ALONE is sufficient.
   (E) Statements (1) and (2) TOGETHER are NOT sufficient.

13. A full bottle of milk that is 5% butterfat by volume is mixed with a full bottle of milk that is 3% butterfat by volume. What percent of the resulting mixture is butterfat?

   (1) The first bottle holds 12 ounces.
   (2) The second bottle holds 8 ounces.

   (A) Statement (1) ALONE is sufficient, but statement (2) alone is not sufficient.
   (B) Statement (2) ALONE is sufficient, but statement (1) alone is not sufficient.
   (C) BOTH statements (1) and (2) TOGETHER are sufficient, but NEITHER statement ALONE is sufficient.
   (D) EACH statement ALONE is sufficient.
   (E) Statements (1) and (2) TOGETHER are NOT sufficient.

14. A car that averages m miles per gallon of gas in city traffic gets 25% better mileage on the highway. In terms of m, how many gallons of gas will it use if driven for 100 miles in city traffic and 200 miles on the highway?

   (A) $150m$

   (B) $\dfrac{260}{m}$

   (C) $\dfrac{350}{m}$

   (D) $\dfrac{300}{2.25m}$

   (E) $\dfrac{420}{m}$

15. In the set of positive integers less than 100, how many are NOT evenly divisible by either 3 or 4?

    (A) 25
    (B) 42
    (C) 48
    (D) 50
    (E) 58

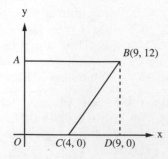

16. In the figure above, $AB \parallel OC$. What is the perimeter of the quadrilateral $ABCO$?

    (A) 38
    (B) 40
    (C) 44
    (D) 46
    (E) 48

17. Is $xy > \dfrac{x}{y}$?

    (1) $y = \dfrac{1}{3}$

    (2) $x = 0$

    (A) Statement (1) ALONE is sufficient, but statement (2) alone is not sufficient.
    (B) Statement (2) ALONE is sufficient, but statement (1) alone is not sufficient.
    (C) BOTH statements (1) and (2) TOGETHER are sufficient, but NEITHER statement ALONE is sufficient.
    (D) EACH statement ALONE is sufficient.
    (E) Statements (1) and (2) TOGETHER are NOT sufficient.

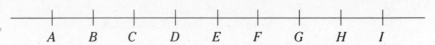

18. On the number line shown above, if all the labelled points are equidistant, which point represents the number that is greater than *E* and one third as far from *E* as *G* is from *A*?

    (A) *F*
    (B) *G*
    (C) *H*
    (D) *I*
    (E) Not a labelled point

19. In △*ABC*, ∠*B* is 30° more than twice ∠*A*, and the measure of ∠*C* is equal to the sum of the other two angles. What is the degree measure of the smallest angle?

    (A) 10
    (B) 15
    (C) 20
    (D) 25
    (E) 30

20. If *k* is a positive integer, what is the remainder when $7k + 2$ is divided by 14?

    (1) *k* is greater than 7.
    (2) *k* is even.

    (A) Statement (1) ALONE is sufficient, but statement (2) alone is not sufficient.
    (B) Statement (2) ALONE is sufficient, but statement (1) alone is not sufficient.
    (C) BOTH statements (1) and (2) TOGETHER are sufficient, but NEITHER statement ALONE is sufficient.
    (D) EACH statement ALONE is sufficient.
    (E) Statements (1) and (2) TOGETHER are NOT sufficient.

21. What is the largest integer less than $\frac{x}{2}$?

    (1) $2 < x$
    (2) $x < 4$

(A) Statement (1) ALONE is sufficient, but statement (2) alone is not sufficient.

(B) Statement (2) ALONE is sufficient, but statement (1) alone is not sufficient.

(C) BOTH statements (1) and (2) TOGETHER are sufficient, but NEITHER statement ALONE is sufficient.

(D) EACH statement ALONE is sufficient.

(E) Statements (1) and (2) TOGETHER are NOT sufficient.

22. If $14 = 3x - 1$ and $B = 6x + 4$, what is the value of B?

    (A) 12
    (B) 14
    (C) 24
    (D) 30
    (E) 34

23. For what values of x is $12 - x = 3x + 8$?

    (A) $x = 4$
    (B) $x = 3$
    (C) $x = 0$
    (D) $x = 2$
    (E) $x = 1$

24. What is the length of a rectangular solid of height 6 that is twice as long as it is wide, if its volume is the same as that of a cube with total surface area of 864 square inches?

    (A) 12
    (B) 14
    (C) 24
    (D) 30
    (E) 36

25. What is the value of $x + 3y + 7$?
    (1) $x - 3y = 0$
    (2) $x^2 + 4y^2 = 0$

    (A) Statement (1) ALONE is sufficient, but statement (2) alone is not sufficient.
    (B) Statement (2) ALONE is sufficient, but statement (1) alone is not sufficient.
    (C) BOTH statements (1) and (2) TOGETHER are sufficient, but NEITHER statement ALONE is sufficient.
    (D) EACH statement ALONE is sufficient.
    (E) Statements (1) and (2) TOGETHER are NOT sufficient.

26. If $\dfrac{2x}{3} + 2 = a$, and $y = 2x + 6$, what is the value of y in terms of a?

    (A) $2a - 3$

    (B) $\dfrac{3}{a}$

    (C) $3 + a$

    (D) $3a$

    (E) $\dfrac{a}{3}$

27. If $a\P b = \dfrac{a}{a + b}$, and $x \neq 0$, which of the following must be true?

    I. $x\P y = y\P x$
    II. $x\P 0 = 1$
    III. $x\P(1 - x) = x$

    (A) I only
    (B) I and II only
    (C) II and III only
    (D) I, II, and III
    (E) Neither I, II, or III

2   a   b

28. The vertical marks are equally spaced on the number line shown
     above. What is value of *a*?
     (1) *b* = 3.4
     (2)   The average of *a* and *b* is 3.
     (A) Statement (1) ALONE is sufficient, but statement (2) alone is
          not sufficient.
     (B) Statement (2) ALONE is sufficient, but statement (1) alone is
          not sufficient.
     (C) BOTH statements (1) and (2) TOGETHER are sufficient, but
          NEITHER statement ALONE is sufficient.
     (D) EACH statement ALONE is sufficient.
     (E) Statements (1) and (2) TOGETHER are NOT sufficient.

29. What is the value of *A*?

     (1) $A = \dfrac{3 + B}{4 \cdot 3 - 3B}$

     (2) *B* = 3
     (A) Statement (1) ALONE is sufficient, but statement (2) alone is
          not sufficient.
     (B) Statement (2) ALONE is sufficient, but statement (1) alone is
          not sufficient.
     (C) BOTH statements (1) and (2) TOGETHER are sufficient, but
          NEITHER statement ALONE is sufficient.
     (D) EACH statement ALONE is sufficient.
     (E) Statements (1) and (2) TOGETHER are NOT sufficient.

30. In how many ways can 3 men and 3 women be seated in 6 theater
     seats if a woman must be seated in the first seat and men and
     women must be seated in alternate seats?
     (A) 36
     (B) 24
     (C) 12
     (D) 9
     (E) 6

31. What is the perimeter of a triangle with vertices at $(-2,6)$, $(3,6)$,
     and $(3,-6)$?
     (A) 60
     (B) 50
     (C) 40
     (D) 30
     (E) 24

32. At an art show, Eleanor sold ten paintings. The first six sold at an average price of $70 each. What was the overall average price of the ten paintings?

    (1)   The last four paintings sold for an average price of $100 each.

    (2)   The most expensive painting sold for $180.

(A) Statement (1) ALONE is sufficient, but statement (2) alone is not sufficient.

(B) Statement (2) ALONE is sufficient, but statement (1) alone is not sufficient.

(C) BOTH statements (1) and (2) TOGETHER are sufficient, but NEITHER statement ALONE is sufficient.

(D) EACH statement ALONE is sufficient.

(E) Statements (1) and (2) TOGETHER are NOT sufficient.

33. The point $(t, -1)$ lies on a circle with a radius of 5 and its center at $(4,2)$. Which of the following is a possible positive value of t?

(A) 4

(B) 5

(C) 6

(D) 7

(E) 8

34. On a number line, A has coordinate -2 and B has coordinate 3. C is as far from B as A is from B. Which of the following is a possible coordinate of C?

(A) -5

(B) -3

(C) 5

(D) 7

(E) 8

35. By what percent was the cost of a coat marked down?

    (1)   The coat was marked down $30.

    (2)   The cost after the markdown was $170.

(A) Statement (1) ALONE is sufficient, but statement (2) alone is not sufficient.

(B) Statement (2) ALONE is sufficient, but statement (1) alone is not sufficient.

(C) BOTH statements (1) and (2) TOGETHER are sufficient, but NEITHER statement ALONE is sufficient.

(D) EACH statement ALONE is sufficient.

(E) Statements (1) and (2) TOGETHER are NOT sufficient.

36. In $\triangle ABC$, $\angle B$ is 20° more than three times $\angle A$. How many degrees are there in the smallest angle of the triangle?

    (1)   The measure of $\angle C$ is equal to sum of the other two angles.

    (2)   The measure of $\angle C = 90°$.

  (A) Statement (1) ALONE is sufficient, but statement (2) alone is not sufficient.

  (B) Statement (2) ALONE is sufficient, but statement (1) alone is not sufficient.

  (C) BOTH statements (1) and (2) TOGETHER are sufficient, but NEITHER statement ALONE is sufficient.

  (D) EACH statement ALONE is sufficient.

  (E) Statements (1) and (2) TOGETHER are NOT sufficient.

37. If $(x - 5)^2 = (x + 5)^2$, then $x =$

  (A) -10

  (B) -5

  (C) 0

  (D) 5

  (E) 10

SECTION 4

VERBAL

41 questions

Time—75 Minutes

Directions (Reading Comprehension): The questions in this group are based on the content of a passage. After reading the passage, choose the best answer to each question. Answer all questions following the passage on the basis of what is *stated* or *implied* in the passage.

Directions (Critical Reasoning): For this question, select the best of the answer choices given.

Directions (Sentence Correction): The following questions present a sentence, part of which or all of which is underlined. Beneath the sentence you will find five ways of phrasing the underlined part. The first of these repeats the original; the other four are different. If you think the original is best, choose the first answer; otherwise choose one of the others.

Questions 1–5 refer to the following passage.

Line When epidemiologists study clusters of cancer cases and other noncontagious conditions, such as birth defects or miscarriage, they take several variables into account, such as background rate (the number of people affected in the general population), cluster size, and specificity (any notable characteristics of the
(5) individual affected in each case). If a cluster is both large and specific, it is easier for epidemiologists to assign blame.

Not only must each variable be considered on its own, but it must also be combined with others. Lung cancer is very common in the general population. Yet when a huge number of cases turned up among World War II shipbuilders
(10) who had all worked with asbestos, the size of the cluster and the fact that the men had had similar occupational asbestos exposures enabled epidemiologists to assign blame to the fibrous mineral.

Furthermore, even if a cluster seems too small to be analyzed conclusively, it may still yield important data if the background rate of the condition is low
(15) enough. This was the case when a certain vaginal cancer turned up almost simultaneously in a half-dozen young women. While six would seem to be too small a cluster for meaningful study, the cancer had been reported only once or twice before in the entire medical literature. Researchers eventually found that

(20) the mothers of all the afflicted women had taken the drug diethystilbestrol (DES) while pregnant.

Although several known carcinogens have been discovered through these kinds of occupational or medical clusters, only one community cancer cluster has ever been traced to an environmental cause. Health officials often discount a community's suspicion of a common environmental cause because citizens (25) tend to include cases that were diagnosed before the afflicted individuals moved into the neighborhood.

Add to this the problem of cancer's latency. Unlike an infectious disease like cholera, which is caused by a recent exposure to food or water contaminated with the cholera bacterium, cancer may have its roots in an (30) exposure that occurred ten to twenty years earlier. Citizens also conduct what one epidemiologist calls "epidemiologic gerrymandering,"—finding cancer cases, drawing a boundary around them, and then mapping this as a cluster.

1. The case of the World War II shipbuilders with lung cancer (lines 9–12) is an example of

   (A) an occupational cluster.
   (B) a medical cluster.
   (C) a radiation cluster.
   (D) an environmental cluster.
   (E) an inconclusive cluster.

2. The passage suggests that the fact that "only one community cancer cluster has ever been traced to an environmental cause" (lines 22–23) is most likely due to the

   (A) methodological difficulties in analyzing community cancer clusters.
   (B) general absence of carcinogenic agents from most communities.
   (C) reluctance of epidemiologists to investigate environmental factors in cancer.
   (D) lack of credibility of citizen activists in claiming to have identified cancer agents.
   (E) effectiveness of regulations restricting the use of carcinogens in residential areas.

3. The reference to cancer's "latency" in line 27 refers to the tendency of cancer to

   (A) be linked to several underlying causes.
   (B) exist in a dormant or hidden form.
   (C) spread through the body at a surprisingly rapid rate.
   (D) pass through phases of apparent cure and recurrence.
   (E) be masked by other, unrelated illnesses.

4. The "epidemiological gerrymandering" that the author describes in line 31 is most closely analogous to

(A) a toddler's declaring that all the toys in one area of the school playground are now his property.

(B) a school principal's redistributing students in two classrooms so that each classroom has the same number of gifted students.

(C) a politician's drawing of election district boundaries so as to give one political party control of a majority of districts.

(D) a nurse's erasing information on a patient's chart and substituting false data.

(E) a cartographer's mistakenly redrawing the border between two counties so as to make the smaller county appear larger.

5. Studies over the last 20 years have shown that virtually all babies born to drug-addicted mothers are themselves addicted to drugs. No such correlation, however, has been shown between drug-addicted fathers and their newborn children. It would appear, then, that drug addiction is a genetically inherited trait that is gender-linked and passed through the mother.

All of the following, if true, would weaken the argument above EXCEPT

(A) Although some biological conditions have been shown to be genetically based, drug addiction is not among them.

(B) Drug addiction is an acquired condition that cannot be passed on from a mother to her children.

(C) Prior to the recent development of DNA testing, while maternity was unquestionable, paternity could not be positively determined.

(D) There have been instances in which drug-addicted babies have been born to addicted fathers and non-addicted mothers.

(E) Very few studies regarding fathers of drug-addicted babies have been conducted.

6. Stationery, envelopes, and the business card are an important business tool that send a message to those you deal with about your company and yourself.

(A) Stationery, envelopes, and the business card are an important business tool

(B) Stationery, the envelope, and business cards can be important business tools

(C) Stationery, envelopes, and business cards are important business tools

(D) Stationery, envelopes, and business cards is an important business tool

(E) Stationery, the envelopes, and the business card are important business tools

7. Those who have difficulty remembering the names or faces of the people they meet would be well advised to take a course or read a book designed to help them improve their memory.

(A) would be well advised to take a course

(B) would do well if they were to take a course

(C) should consider the possibility to take a course

(D) would be well advised in taking a course

(E) should do well if they were to take a course

8. The major issue of the 1860 American presidential campaign was the extension of slavery into the territories. Of that year's four candidates, Republican Abraham Lincoln was against extension; Northern Democrat Stephen A. Douglas, Southern Democrat John C. Breckinridge, and Constitutional Union candidate John Bell all favored it. Lincoln won the popular vote with 1,800,000, but his opponents together garnered more than 2,850,000 votes. Lincoln was named president by the electoral college.

All of the following conclusions can be reasonably drawn from the information above EXCEPT

(A) Lincoln won the election largely because voters who opposed his political views were split among the other three candidates.

(B) Despite—or due to—his stand on slavery extension, Lincoln was the most popular single candidate in the presidential election.

(C) None of the other issues in the campaign contributed significantly to the final result of the election.

(D) The Democratic party failed to win the election because its supporters were split between Douglas and Breckinridge.

(E) The extension of slavery was a crucial issue in the presidential election of 1860.

9. The minuscule print on train schedules can be very difficult to read, particularly if <u>one doesn't have their</u> reading glasses.

   (A) one doesn't have their
   (B) they don't have their
   (C) you don't have your
   (D) someone doesn't have their
   (E) you don't have one's

10. When the three original *Star Wars* films were re-released in 1996 and 1997, their producer, George Lucas, expected them to enjoy respectable revenues at the nation's movie box offices. In fact, however, each of the three films had a commanding lead in ticket sales during the first weekend on which it was shown.

    Which of the following statements, if true, would be LEAST likely to help account for the information presented above?

    (A) None of the other films released on the same weekends as the *Star Wars* films featured a major box-office star.
    (B) Despite his expertise in the movie industry, Lucas seriously misjudged the extent of the public's interest in his films.
    (C) The announced release of three new *Star Wars* movies helped rekindle the public's interest in the original films.
    (D) It had been so long since the original *Star Wars* films had been released that there was a whole generation of movie-goers that had never seen them in theaters.
    (E) Several actors from the original *Star Wars* films had recently appeared in highly-touted but unsuccessful films.

11. In 1962, when the Pennsylvania Railroad announced plans to tear down New York's Pennsylvania Station, an architectural gem completed in 1910 and designed by one of America's preeminent architectural firms, civic groups rose in protest. Nevertheless, the building was demolished the following year. In 1965, New York City established its Landmarks Preservation Commission, which was followed by the establishment of similar commissions around the country.

All of the following conclusions, if true, would help account for the events described above EXCEPT

(A) Only the razing of a building as famous as Pennsylvania Station was sufficient to rouse the public's interest in landmark preservation.

(B) There was no public interest in preserving America's architectural heritage prior to 1962.

(C) Several other significant urban landmarks had been torn down in the years just prior to the railroad's announcement.

(D) New York City is considered by other cities to be a leader in cultural affairs.

(E) Civic groups are, on occasion, able to bring about important changes in the urban policies of American cities.

Questions 12–14 refer to the following passage.

Line Do women tend to devalue the worth of their work? Do they apply different standards to rewarding their own work than they do to rewarding the work of others? These were the questions asked by Michigan State University psychologists Lawrence Messe and Charlene Callahan-Levy. Past experiments
(5) had shown that when women were asked to decide how much to pay themselves and other people for the same job, they paid themselves less. Following up on this finding, Messe and Callahan-Levy designed experiments to test several popular explanations of why women tend to shortchange themselves in pay situations.
(10)   One theory the psychologists tested was that women judge their own work more harshly than that of others. The subjects for the experiment testing this theory were men and women recruited from the Michigan State undergraduate student body. The job the subjects were asked to perform for pay was an opinion questionnaire requiring a number of short essays on
(15) campus-related issues. After completing the questionnaire, some subjects were given six dollars in bills and change and were asked to decide payment for themselves. Others were given the same amount and were asked to decide payment for another subject who had also completed the questionnaire.
        The psychologists found that, as in earlier experiments, the women paid
(20) themselves less than the men paid themselves. They also found that the women paid themselves less than they paid other women and less than the men paid the women. The differences were substantial. The average paid to women by themselves was $2.97. The average paid to men by themselves was $4.06. The average paid to women by others was $4.37. In spite of the differences, the

(25) psychologists found that the men and the women in the experiment evaluated their own performances on the questionnaire about equally and better than the expected performances of others.

On the basis of these findings, Messe and Callahan-Levy concluded that women's attachment of a comparatively low monetary value to their work *(30)* cannot be based entirely on their judgment of their own ability. Perhaps, the psychologists postulated, women see less of a connection than men do between their work (even when it is superior) and their pay because they are relatively indifferent to receiving money for their work.

12. According to the passage, the work of Messe and Callahan-Levy tends to weaken the notion that

   (A) people will tend to overreward themselves when given the opportunity to do so.
   (B) women are generally less concerned with financial rewards for their work than are men.
   (C) men are willing to pay women more than women are willing to pay themselves.
   (D) payment for work should generally be directly related to the quality of the work.
   (E) women judge their own work more critically than they judge the work of men.

13. According to the passage, how is the research of Messe and Callahan-Levy related to earlier experiments in the same field?

   (A) It suggests a need to discard methods used in earlier experiments.
   (B) It tends to weaken the assumptions on which earlier experiments were designed.
   (C) It suggests that the problem revealed in earlier experiments may be more widespread than previously thought.
   (D) It helps to explain a phenomenon revealed in earlier experiments.
   (E) It calls into question the accuracy of the data obtained in earlier experiments.

14. The experiment designed in the passage would be most relevant to the formulation of a theory concerning the
   (A) generally lower salaries received by women workers in comparison to men.
   (B) reluctance of some women to enter professions that are traditionally dominated by men.
   (C) low prestige given by society to many traditionally female-dominated professions.
   (D) anxiety expressed by some women workers in dealing with male supervisors.
   (E) discrimination often suffered by women in attempting to enter the workforce.

15. Many a father of the 1950s took home movies of their children, but stopped doing so once they began to approach adulthood.
   (A) a father of the 1950s took home movies of their children,
   (B) fathers of the 1950s took home movies of their children,
   (C) fathers of the 1950s took home movies of his children,
   (D) a father took home movies of their children in the 1950s,
   (E) fathers took home movies of the children of the 1950s,

16. If you run your own business, trying to organize your activities, finances, and personal contacts are some of the most difficult things you'll ever have to do.
   (A) are some of the most difficult things you'll ever have
   (B) is one of the most difficult things one ever has
   (C) are some of the hardest things you're likely to ever have
   (D) is among the most difficult things a person ever has
   (E) is one of the most difficult things you'll ever have

17. Anatole France's often-quoted statement, "The only books I have in my library are those which people have lent me," would seem to justify the fear of those who love books that, once lent, they are unlikely to be returned.

Which of the following, if true, most strengthens the argument above?

(A) France was considered by those who knew him to be unusually remiss in returning books.

(B) Most people who borrow books return them after a reasonable period of time.

(C) Only a small percentage of borrowed books are ever returned to their owners.

(D) Many book lovers are eager to share their pleasure in particular books with others.

(E) France made his statement because he thought it would be entertaining rather than because it was true.

18. Despite Paul's efforts at persuasion, in the end he had to admit that <u>neither his friends, nor his family, or his co-workers</u> really accepted the validity of his arguments.

(A) neither his friends, nor his family, or his co-workers

(B) not his friends, nor his family, nor his co-workers

(C) neither his friends, nor his family, nor his co-workers

(D) his friends, his family, and his co-workers alike never

(E) neither his friends, or his family, or his co-workers

19. From the time they burst onto the music scene in England in 1962 until they disbanded in 1969, the Beatles were the most popular rock group the world had ever seen. They were also the best because, while their music retained its characteristic style, each new album was different and exhibited a steadily increasing depth and sophistication.

    The argument above requires all of the following assumptions EXCEPT

    (A) Prior to 1962, there had never been a rock group with as large a following as the Beatles.
    (B) Each member of the Beatles was individually more talented than his counterparts in other popular rock groups.
    (C) Prior to the Beatles, no other rock group had retained its unique style while exhibiting the same degree of musical growth.
    (D) Increasing depth and sophistication are evidence of a musical group's extraordinary talent.
    (E) To attain true greatness in music, it is essential that a group develop and retain a recognizable style.

20. Until the sinking of the *Titanic*, ships were not required to <u>carry enough lifeboats for all on board or maintaining</u> 24-hour radio contact.

    (A) carry enough lifeboats for all on board or maintaining
    (B) carry sufficient lifeboats for all on board or the maintenance of
    (C) carry enough lifeboats for all on board or to maintain
    (D) carry enough lifeboats for all of those on board or else to maintain
    (E) be carrying sufficient lifeboats for all those on board or maintaining

21. During the past ten years, as the population of the northern suburbs of Metropolis has grown, commuter traffic on the highways leading from the suburbs into the city has more than doubled. In an effort to relieve the resulting traffic jams, local officials have decided to double the highway tolls, which should encourage commuters to travel into the city by train instead.

Which of the following, if true, casts the most doubt on the effectiveness of the solution proposed above?

(A) For most commuters, highway tolls represent only a small percentage of the overall cost of traveling to and from work.

(B) When highway tolls have been increased in and around other cities, the volume of traffic on local roads has generally dropped between five and ten percent.

(C) Many commuters say that the convenience of traveling to work by private automobile outweighs the expense of highway tolls.

(D) Several of the largest employers in Metropolis have adopted staggered work hours in an effort to relieve traffic jams during the most popular time periods for commuting to and from work.

(E) During the morning and evening rush hours, trains between Metropolis and the northern suburbs are already filled to capacity, and no expansion of train services is planned.

Questions 22–25 refer to the following passage.

(The article from which this passage was taken appeared in 1987.)

Line   A major goal of the Viking spacecraft missions was to determine whether the soil of Mars is dead, like the soil of the moon, or teeming with microscopic life, like the soils of Earth. Soil samples brought into the Viking lander were sent to three separate biological laboratories to be tested in different ways for the presence of
(5)   life.

The tests were based on two assumptions. First, it was assumed that life of Mars would be like life on Earth, which is based on the element carbon and thrives by chemically transforming carbon compounds. Second, on Earth, where there are large life-forms (like human beings and pine trees), there are also small
(10)   ones (like bacteria), and the small ones are far more abundant, with thousands or millions of them in every gram of soil. To have the best possible chance of detecting life, an instrument should look for the most abundant kind of life.

The Viking instruments were designed, therefore, to detect carbon-based Martian microbes or similar creatures living in the soil. The three laboratories in
(15)   the lander were designed to warm and nourish any life in the Martian soil and to detect with sensitive instruments the chemical activity of the organisms.

One characteristic of earthly plants is that they transform carbon dioxide in the air into the compounds that make up their roots, branches, and leaves. Accordingly, one Viking experiment, called the carbon assimilation test, added

(20)   radioactive carbon dioxide to the atmosphere above the soil sample. The
sample was then flooded with simulated Martian sunlight. If any Martian
life-forms converted the carbon dioxide into other compounds, the compounds
could be detected by their radioactivity.

(25)   Living organisms on Earth give off gases. Plants give off oxygen, animals
give off carbon dioxide, and both exhale water. A second experiment on each
lander, the gas exchange test, was designed to detect this kind of activity.
Nutrients and water were added to the soil, and the chemical composition of the
gas above the soil was continuously analyzed for changes that might indicate
life.

(30)   A third experiment on each lander was based on the fact that earthly
animals consume organic compounds and give off carbon dioxide. The labeled
release test added a variety of radioactive nutrients to the soil and then waited
to see whether any radioactive carbon dioxide would be given off.

22. According to the passage, the tests conducted on the Viking
lander were designed to search for microbes in the Martian soil
because

(A) the gas exchange activities of microbes would be readily
detectable.
(B) previous exploratory missions had suggested the presence of
microbes on Mars.
(C) microbes were assumed to be the most abundant form of life
on Mars.
(D) microbes are the most primitive form of life on Earth.
(E) the small size of microbes would make them easily transport-
able.

23. According to the passage, the Viking instruments were designed to
detect possible life-forms on Mars by their

(A) chemical activity.
(B) motion.
(C) radioactivity.
(D) reproductive patterns.
(E) purposeful activity.

24. It can be inferred from the passage that radioactive carbon dioxide was used in the carbon assimilation test primarily because

(A) radioactive carbon dioxide is commonly found in the Martian atmosphere.
(B) the chemical changes induced by radioactivity would be a certain indication of the presence of life on Mars.
(C) radioactivity is found on Earth only in areas where life also exists.
(D) radioactive carbon dioxide was considered likely to be absorbed more readily than nonradioactive carbon dioxide.
(E) radioactivity would be detectable by the Viking instruments.

25. It can be inferred from the passage that the Viking experiments would be LEAST likely to detect life-forms

(A) that thrive only in warm temperatures.
(B) of microscopic size.
(C) that require sunlight similar to that found on the surface of Mars.
(D) based on chemical processes differing from those on which earthly life-forms are based.
(E) that give off carbon dioxide.

26. Through the mid-1960s, most city children were required to wear jackets and ties or skirts to school, but from that time and afterward they were allowed to attend school without them.

(A) from that time and afterward they were
(B) from afterward on they were
(C) from the mid-1960s until now they are
(D) since then they have been
(E) since then they had been

27. Which of the following best completes the passage below?

Census figures show that Hispanic Americans represent the single fastest-growing ethnic group in the United States. Historically, as the numbers of any group of Americans increased, so did their political power, including their ability to elect public officials from their own community. However, the "Hispanic" designation disguises the fact that Spanish-speaking Americans are more disparate than they are alike, with racial and geographic roots in dozens of cultures and countries. Consequently,

(A) we can expect serious cultural and political clashes among Hispanic Americans in the coming years.

(B) the growth of population among Hispanic Americans is likely to slow significantly in the near future.

(C) no single political party is likely to command the allegiance of a clear majority of Hispanic Americans.

(D) it's unlikely that Hispanic Americans will soon wield political influence commensurate with their numbers.

(E) Hispanic Americans are more likely to amass economic and social influence than political power.

28. Company Spokesperson: Charges that our corporation has discriminated against women in its hiring and promotion practices are demonstrably untrue. In fact, statistics show that over 60 percent of the people employed by our corporation are women.

Which of the following challenges indicates the most serious weakness in the argument offered above?

(A) What is the average tenure among women employees of the company?

(B) What percentage of company employees in higher-level management positions are women?

(C) What percentage of employees in competing companies are women?

(D) How has the percentage of women employees at the company changed over time?

(E) Is the chief executive officer of the company a man or a woman?

29. Computer technology is generally considered to be a great advantage to mankind, but <u>it's not necessary that everyone wants</u> to take advantage of it.

    (A) it's not necessary that everyone wants
    (B) everyone necessarily does not want
    (C) not everyone necessarily wants
    (D) everyone does not want necessarily
    (E) all people necessarily do not want

30. As we get older, we often find it increasingly difficult to remember recent events, <u>but we generally have less trouble</u> recalling those of the distant past.

    (A) but we generally have less trouble
    (B) but we've generally had less trouble
    (C) though we often are having less trouble
    (D) but as a rule we generally have less trouble
    (E) but we frequently are more troubled by

31. Between 1985 and 1995, the annual budget of the U.S. armed forces shrank by over 20 percent, with no apparent diminution in the level of security enjoyed by the nation. Thus it is clear that the level of spending on the U.S. military in 1985 was unnecessarily high.

    The argument above is flawed in that it ignores the possibility that

    (A) military budgets are determined as much by political factors as by actual need.
    (B) a low rate of inflation between 1985 and 1995 reduced the need for increased military spending.
    (C) a change in presidential administrations affected the government's willingness to spend money on military purposes.
    (D) increased efficiency made it possible for the military to provide the same level of security with lower spending.
    (E) changes in the world situation between 1985 and 1995 affected the military requirements of the U.S.

Questions 32–34 refer to the following passage.

Line   In the early 1980s, Wang represented the preeminent office automation
capability in the world—so much so that in many offices the name "Wang" had
become a synonym for "office automation," the same way "Xerox" was used to
mean "photocopier." Wang dominated every step of the process, from research
(5)   and development through manufacturing and sales to customer service and the
aftermarket. With a reputation for quality and with proprietary hardware and
software that guaranteed the uniqueness of its product, Wang had built a market
position that seemed unassailable.

Yet in less than a decade, Wang faded to near obscurity, contracting
(10)   dramatically and surviving only by transforming itself to leverage its software
and engineering strengths in completely different ways. In place of Wang's
proprietary, closed systems, versatile personal computers linked together in
networks had become the dominant office appliance. With their open
architecture, interchangeable software, and integrated communications, per-
(15)   sonal computers first transformed the market for office automation networks
and then obliterated the old market.

Wang had seen itself as a specialized kind of computer company, providing
service via a central processor with distributed workstations. Its excellence and
leadership in innovation were highly respected, and it was important to Wang
(20)   not to lose that position. That view led it to stick to its business until it was too
late. It failed to see the opportunity presented by the personal computer and the
potential to network smaller, distributed computers. Eventually, Wang did
attempt to move into personal computers as a basis of integrated office systems,
but by this time the company's opportunity to move forward by leveraging its
(25)   strengths was gone. Wang had been badly outflanked and was left with no
market.

Sometimes a business leader stumbles into this kind of trap by waiting to
see what develops, trading time for the prospect of more information and less
uncertainty. Sometimes the leader is simply so averse to losing that he or she is
(30)   incapable of the bold action required for success. In either case, the leader is
operating with limited vision, and comes out a loser as a result.

32. According to the passage, the business decline suffered by Wang
during the 1980s may be attributed primarily to the company's

(A)   inability to maintain its reputation for high-quality products.
(B)   unwillingness to invest significant funds in research and
development.
(C)   failure to respond promptly to the challenge posed by
personal computers.
(D)   refusal to allow computer manufacturers to license Wang's
proprietary software systems.
(E)   neglect of customer service and consequent loss of major
clients.

33. The passage implies that customers for office automation systems turned away from Wang mainly because other products offered greater

    (A) reliability.
    (B) central control.
    (C) capacity for expansion.
    (D) cost efficiency.
    (E) flexibility.

34. Which of the following best describes the relation of the last paragraph to the passage as a whole?

    (A) It offers two possible explanations for the events recounted.
    (B) It suggests a remedy for the problem described.
    (C) It outlines a process other business can use to avoid similar difficulties.
    (D) It shows why the events recounted were probably inevitable.
    (E) It explains two alternative courses of action that could have changed the outcome.

35. Even the second and third editions of a book often contain typographical errors which were overlooked not only by the book's proofreader but also, in addition, by its editor and author.

    (A) which were overlooked not only by the book's proofreader but also, in addition,
    (B) that were overlooked not only by the book's proofreader but also, in addition,
    (C) which were overlooked by the book's proofreader and as well
    (D) which were overlooked not only by the book's proofreader but also
    (E) that was overlooked not only by the book's proofreader but also

36. In general, obesity is caused not by the ingesting of foods with a high fat content but rather by eating foods that contain too much sugar. For proof, consider this: over the past ten years, even as sales of low-fat meals, snacks, and desserts have skyrocketed in the United States, the percentage of Americans who are obese has reached a new high.

   Which of the following, if true, would most support the claims above?

   (A) Ninety percent of the low-fat foods sold in the U.S. are purchased by just 10 percent of the population.
   (B) Sales of foods with a high sugar content have increased significantly during the past ten years.
   (C) Government-approved standards of obesity have changed several times during the past ten years.
   (D) Some foods labeled as "low-fat" actually contain relatively high levels of fat.
   (E) Most physicians consider regular exercise to be an important component of any effective weight-loss program.

37. The disagreement over slavery was one of the basic causes of the Civil War, although it <u>was neither named or recognized as such</u> by those responsible for initiating the war.

   (A) was neither named or recognized as such
   (B) were not named nor recognized as such
   (C) was neither named nor recognized as such
   (D) was not so named or recognized
   (E) was not named nor recognized in that way

38. Some carpenters enjoy building duck decoys. All those who enjoy building duck decoys will appreciate these fine wood-carving tools.

   Which of the following is the most reasonable conclusion based on the statements above?

   (A) All of those who will appreciate these fine wood-carving tools are carpenters.
   (B) Some of those who will appreciate these fine wood-carving tools will use them to build duck decoys.
   (C) All carpenters who will appreciate these fine wood-carving tools enjoy building duck decoys.
   (D) These fine wood-carving tools will be appreciated by all carpenters.
   (E) Some carpenters will appreciate these fine wood-carving tools.

39. The original *Star Wars* films <u>were among the most popular movies of all time, and the new movies in the series are</u> expected to be equally, if not more, successful.

    (A) were among the most popular movies of all time, and the new movies in the series are
    (B) were among the most popular films of all time, and the new movies in the series will be
    (C) were most popular among all-time movies, and the new movies in the series will be
    (D) have been among the most popular movies ever, and, in the series, the new movies are going to be
    (E) were highly popular as compared to the movies of all time, and the new movies in the series are

40. A proposed law would forbid any individual who has been employed as a lobbyist on behalf of a particular industry from serving as the director of a government agency charged with regulating that same industry. The intention of those promoting the law is to prevent conflicts of interest. However, if passed, the law will prove counterproductive, since it will prevent individuals who are knowledgeable about industries from serving as government regulators.

    The conclusion drawn in the argument above depends most directly on which of the following assumptions?

    (A) Those who have served as lobbyists on behalf of an industry are capable of objective, unbiased decisions as regulators.
    (B) Government has a legitimate role to play in the regulation of most industries.
    (C) Those who direct government regulatory agencies are appointed by the president and must be approved by Congress.
    (D) Only those who have served as lobbyists on behalf of an industry are knowledgeable about that industry.
    (E) The primary objective of government regulation of industry should be to strengthen and support that industry.

41. There are times when the only three things teenage boys seem to be interested in are <u>driving cars, playing computer games, and the effort to get girls</u>.

    (A) driving cars, playing computer games, and the effort to get girls
    (B) cars, playing computer games, and getting girls
    (C) driving cars, computer games, and girls
    (D) cars, playing computer games, and getting girls
    (E) diving cars, playing computer games, and getting girls

Answer Key

SECTIONS 1 AND 2—ANALYTICAL WRITING

On the real GMAT CAT, your essays will be graded on a scale of 0 (lowest) to 6 (highest) by the "holistic" method—that is, a single score will be assigned to each essay based on the overall impression it makes on the reader. See chapter 9 for more information on the holistic scoring system and how to evaluate your own writing in light of the GMAT CAT scoring criteria.

Section 3 Quantitative			Section 4 Verbal		
1. A	14. B	26. D	1. A	15. B	29. C
2. C	15. D	27. C	2. A	16. E	30. A
3. C	16. A	28. D	3. B	17. C	31. E
4. D	17. E	29. C	4. C	18. C	32. C
5. B	18. B	30. A	5. D	19. B	33. E
6. D	19. C	31. D	6. C	20. C	34. A
7. E	20. B	32. A	7. A	21. E	35. D
8. E	21. C	33. E	8. C	22. C	36. B
9. D	22. E	34. E	9. C	23. A	37. C
10. C	23. E	35. C	10. E	24. E	38. E
11. D	24. C	36. D	11. B	25. D	39. A
12. A	25. B	37. C	12. E	26. D	40. D
13. C			13. D	27. D	41. E
			14. A	28. B	

Scoring Guide

COMPUTING YOUR QUANTITATIVE SCALED SCORE

Step 1. Count the number of correct answers you chose for the questions in Section 3. Write the total here: _____

Step 2. Count the number of incorrect answers you chose for the questions in Section 3. (Do not count questions you did not answer.) Write the total here: _____

Step 3. Divide the total from Step 2 by 4. (The result may include a fraction.) Write the result here: _____

Step 4. Subtract the result from Step 3 from the total in Step 1. Write the result here: _____

Step 5. Round off the result from Step 4 to the nearest whole number. Round a number ending in *down*; for example, 28 rounds to 28. Write the result here: _____ This is your Quantitative Raw Score.

Step 6. Look up your Quantitative Raw Score on the Score Conversion Table. Find the corresponding Quantitative Scaled Score and write it here: _____

COMPUTING YOUR VERBAL SCALED SCORE

Step 1. Count the number of correct answers you chose for the questions in Section 4. Write the total here: _____

Step 2. Count the number of incorrect answers you chose for the questions in Section 4. (Do not count questions you did not answer.) Write the total here: _____

Step 3. Divide the total from Step 2 by 4. (The result may include a fraction.) Write the result here: _____

Step 4. Subtract the result from Step 3 from the total in Step 1. Write the result here: _____

Step 5. Round off the result from Step 4 to the nearest whole number. Round a number ending in *down*; for example, 28 rounds to 28. Write the result here: _____ This is your Verbal Raw Score.

Step 6. Look up your Verbal Raw Score on the Score Conversion Table. Find the corresponding Verbal Scaled Score and write it here: _____

Score Conversion Table

Insider's GMAT CAT Sample Test

Raw Score	Verbal Scaled Score	Quantitative Scaled Score
41	50	
40	50	
39	49	
38	48	
37	47	50
36	46	49
35	45	48
34	44	47
33	43	46
32	42	45
31	41	44
30	40	43
29	40	42
28	39	41
27	38	40
26	37	40
25	36	39
24	36	38
23	35	37
22	34	36
21	33	35
20	32	34
19	31	34
18	30	33
17	30	32
16	29	31
15	28	30
14	28	30
13	27	29
12	26	28
11	25	27
10	24	26
9	23	25
8	22	24
7	21	23
6	20	22
5	20	21
4	18	20
3	16	17
2	14	14
1	12	12
0 or less	10	10

Computing Your Total Scaled Score

Add your Quantitative Raw Score and your Verbal Raw Score from Step 5. The result is your Total Raw Score. Find this number on the Total Score Conversion Table to determine the corresponding Total Scaled Score.

Total Score Conversion Table
Insider's GMAT CAT Sample Test

Total Raw Score	Total Scaled Score	Total Raw Score	Total Scaled Score
78	800	65	690
77	780	64	690
76	770	63	680
75	760	62	680
74	750	61	670
73	750	60	660
72	740	59	660
71	730	58	650
70	730	57	650
69	720	56	640
68	710	55	640
67	710	54	630
66	700	53	630
52	620	25	470
51	620	24	460
50	610	23	460
49	600	22	450
48	600	21	450
47	590	20	440
46	590	19	440
45	580	18	430
44	580	17	430
43	570	16	420
42	570	15	410
41	560	14	400
40	560	13	390
39	550	12	390
38	550	11	380
37	540	10	370

Total Raw Score	Total Scaled Score	Total Raw Score	Total Scaled Score
36	540	9	360
35	530	8	350
34	520	7	340
33	510	6	330
32	500	5	310
31	500	4	300
30	490	3	280
29	490	2	250
28	480	1	220
27	470	0	200
26	470		

Explanatory Answers

SECTION 3—QUANTITATIVE

1. **The correct answer is (A).** Let M, C, and S be the earnings of the three people. M is 20% more than C, which means $M = 1.2C$. $C = \frac{2}{3}S$. Therefore, $M = (1.2)\frac{2}{3}S = 0.8S$. That is, M is 80% of S.

2. **The correct answer is (C).** Adding $y + 9$ to both sides of the equation:

$$\begin{array}{r} y - 9 = 3 - y \\ y + 9 = y + 9 \\ \hline 2y \quad\;\; = 12 \end{array}$$

   Dividing by 2 yields $y = 6$.

3. **The correct answer is (C).** There are five spaces between A and F, but knowing A or F alone is not sufficient, since we would not know the size of each space. The answer is thus choice (C) or (E). However, knowing both A and F, we know that the tick marks must be in units of 0.02. Hence, $G = 3.84$ and $H = 3.86$.

4. **The correct answer is (D).** K^2 cannot be negative, so this possibility can be ignored. Since R is negative, the only way the fraction can be positive is if exactly one of S or T is negative. This corresponds only to case II. However, the questions asks for those cases that are *not* possible: that is, cases I and III, which is choice (D).

5. **The correct answer is (B).** From (1), we can calculate the value of the denominator of the fraction, but that is not sufficient to find the value of the fraction. So the answer is choice (B), (C), or (E). However, (2) tells us that $b = -3$, so the numerator is zero and so is the fraction.

6. **The correct answer is (D).** From (1), we can calculate that $DE = 8$, which is the same information given in (2). Connecting A to C forms a rectangle $ACDE$ with an area of $6 \times 8 = 48$. The right triangle ABC has an area of $\frac{1}{2}(5)(5) = 12.5$. Subtracting this area from that of the rectangle leaves $48 - 12.5 = 35.5$.

7. **The correct answer is (E).** One dozen, of course, is 12. Letting the number of broken eggs be k, then, the ratio 1:2 leads to $k + 2k = 12$, or $k = 4$. So 1:2 is a possible ratio. Try the same with each of the answer choices, and you'll find that only the case 1:6, which yields $k + 6k = 12$, has no integer solution. The number of unbroken eggs must be a whole number, so choice (E) is the only impossible ratio given.

8. **The correct answer is (E).** The three angles in the triangle are 50°, $y°$, and $180° - x°$. These must total 180°. Thus, $50 + y + 180 - x = 180$, which leads to $50 + y = x$, or $y = x - 50$.

9. **The correct answer is (D).** It is easiest to look at (2) first. From (2), we have $2x + 5 = 1$, which means $2x = -4$ and $x = -2$. Thus, $x^2 = 4$. Thus, the answer is choice (B) or (D). Expanding the binomials in (1):

$$x^2 - 6x + 9 = x^2 + 14x + 49$$

Subtracting x^2 from both sides and combining like terms:

$$20x = -40; x = -2,$$

which also answers the question.

10. **The correct answer is (C).** Since the diagonal and the sides form a right triangle, we can call the unknown side x and use the Pythagorean Theorem to get $x^2 + 12^2 = 20^2$; $x^2 = 256$; $x = 16$. Or we can recognize that 12:20 is a multiple of 3:5, so the other leg must be the appropriate multiple of 4, namely, 16. The area, then, is $\frac{1}{2}(12)(16) = 96$.

11. **The correct answer is (D).** Using P, N, and D to stand for pennies, nickels, and dimes, we have:

$$P + 5N + 10D = 77$$

Since $D = N + 2$, this gives us:

$$P + 5N + 10(N + 2) = 77$$
$$P + 15N + 20 = 77$$
$$P + 15N = 57$$

which means that $(57 - P)$ must be a positive number divisible by 15. The choices for $(57 - P)$ are 15, 30, or 45, which give us $P = 42$, 27, or 12. The least of these is 12.

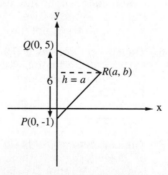

12. **The correct answer is (A).** From the diagram above, we see that we can think of the base of the triangle as PQ, which has a length of 6. The height is the perpendicular distance from the y-axis to point R, that is, the x-coordinate of R. (1) gives us that information, but (2) tells us nothing of use. The area is $\frac{1}{2}(6)(4) = 12$.

13. **The correct answer is (C).** Using either (1) or (2) alone is not sufficient. Hence, the choice is between choices (C) or (E). Using both statements, 5% of 12 is $(.05)(12) = 0.6$, and 3% of 8 is $(.03)(8) = 0.24$. Therefore, we have a total of 0.84 oz. of butterfat in 20 oz. of liquid. $0.84 \div 20 = 0.042 = 4.2\%$.

14. **The correct answer is (B).** The total mileage is given by (miles per gallon) $\times$ (number of gallons). Letting m = miles per gallon in the city, then $1.25m$ gives us the miles per gallon on the highway. Thus, we have:

$$100 = mg_c \text{ and } 200 = 1.25mg_h.$$

Thus, $g_c = \dfrac{100}{m}$ and $g_h = \dfrac{200}{1.25m} = \dfrac{160}{m}$.

So the sum is $\dfrac{100}{m} + \dfrac{160}{m} = \dfrac{260}{m}$.

15. **The correct answer is (D).** Of all the positive integers that are less than 100, 33 are divisible by 3 ($99 \div 3$). Only 24 are divisible by 4 ($99 \div 4$, ignoring the remainder). Of the total of 57, we have counted the 8 numbers divisible by 12 twice. Hence, the number of digits divisible by 3 or 4 is $57 - 8 = 49$. The number not divisible by either is $99 - 49 = 50$.

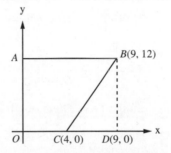

16. **The correct answer is (A).** Dropping a vertical line from B to D (9,0) on the x-axis creates a right triangle with side $CD = 5$ and side $BD = 12$ (see the figure above). Therefore, $BC = 13$. Consequently, $OA = 12$, $AB - 9$, $BC = 13$, and $CO = 4$. The perimeter is $12 + 9 + 13 + 4 = 38$.

17. **The correct answer is (E).** From (1) alone, substituting $y = \dfrac{1}{3}$ we are comparing $\dfrac{x}{3}$ to $3x$. But $\dfrac{x}{3} < 3x$ only if x is positive. Hence, we have choices (B), (C), or (E). (2) alone allows for the possibility that $x = 0$, for which both sides are zero and thus equal; if x is not zero, the answer would depend upon the value of y. If we could say definitely that x is definitely either positive or negative, we could answer the question. However, x could be zero, and we cannot answer it. Hence, the best answer is choice (E).

18. **The correct answer is (B).** The distance from A to G is 6 units, one third of which is 2. Thus, the point we want is 2 units to the right of E, that is, point G.

19. **The correct answer is (C).** Calling the measure of $\angle A$ in degrees x, we have the following:

$$x = \text{number of degrees in } \angle A$$
$$2x + 30 = \text{number of degrees in } \angle B$$
$$x + (2x + 30) = 3x + 30 = \text{number of degrees in } \angle C$$

Summing, we have $x + 2x + 30 + 3x + 30 = 180$. Combining like terms:

$$6x + 60 = 180$$
$$6x = 120$$
$$x = 20$$

Clearly, $2x + 30$ and $3x + 30$ are larger than x, so the smallest angle is 20 degrees.

20. **The correct answer is (B).** Knowing that k is greater than 7 tells us very little about divisibility. The decision is choices (B), (C), or (E). From (2) alone, k is even, so you can write $k = 2m$ and $7k + 2 = 14m + 2$, leaving a remainder of 2 when divided by 14.

21. **The correct answer is (C).** From (1), $2 < x$ tells us that $1 < \dfrac{x}{2}$, but there may be other integers that are also less than $\dfrac{x}{2}$. The choices are (B), (C), or (E). (2) tells us only that $\dfrac{x}{2} < 2$. The choices are now (C) or (E). From the two statements together, $\dfrac{x}{2}$ is between 1 and 2, and the largest integer less than $\dfrac{x}{2}$ must be 1. Therefore, the best answer is choice (C).

22. **The correct answer is (E).** From the first equation, $3x - 1 = 14$. Adding 1 to both sides:

$$3x = 15$$

Dividing both sides by 3:

$$\frac{3x}{3} = \frac{15}{3}$$
$$x = 5$$

Of course, the question asked for B, not x. So we substitute $x = 5$ into $B = 6x + 4$ and get $B = 6(5) + 4 = 34$, which is choice (E).

23. **The correct answer is (E).** We solve this just like an equation. Start by adding the like quantity $(x - 8)$ to both sides in order to group the x terms on one side and the constants on the other; thus:

$$\begin{array}{r} 12 - x \geq 3x + 8 \\ \underline{x - 8 = x - 8} \\ 4 \geq 4x \end{array}$$

Now, divide by 4, which does not change the sense of the inequality, yielding:

$$1 \geq x$$

which is the same as choice (E), $x \leq 1$.

24. **The correct answer is (C).** Let $x =$ the width. Now, $2x =$ length. The volume of the rectangular solid is $V = 6(x)(2x) = 12x^2$. Since the cube has six faces, its total surface area is 6 times the area of one face. In symbols, $6s^2 = 864$. Dividing by 6, $s^2 = 144$; $s = 12$. Hence, the volume of the cube is $12^3 = 1,728$. Since the two solids have the same volume:

$$12x^2 = 1728;\ x^2 = 144;\ x = 12$$

Thus, the length, which is twice the width, is 24.

25. **The correct answer is (B).** (1) tells us only that $x = 3y$, so $x + 3y + 7 = 6y + 7$, but y could be anything. The choices are (B), (C), or (E). (2) actually tells us that both x and y are zero. (How else could the sum of their squares sum to zero?) Hence, $x + 3y + 7 = 7$. The best answer is (B).

26. **The correct answer is (D).** We want to solve $\dfrac{2x}{3} + 2 = a$ for x. Multiply by 3 to clear the fractions. You should now have:

$$2x + 6 = 3a$$

Now add -6 to both sides of the equation:

$$\begin{array}{r} 2x + 6 = 3a \\ \underline{-6 = -6} \\ 2x = 3a - 6 \end{array}$$

Divide by 2:

$$\frac{2x}{2} = \frac{3a - 6}{2};\ x = \frac{3a - 6}{2}$$

Substituting:

$$y = 2\left[\frac{3a - 6}{2}\right] + 6y = 3a - 6 + 6$$

Therefore, $y = 3a$, which is choice (D).

27. **The correct answer is (C).** For I: $x\P y = \dfrac{x}{x+y}$, but $y\P x = \dfrac{y}{x+y}$. The two are not equal unless $x = y$.

   For II: $x\P 0 = \dfrac{x}{x+0} = 1$, which is true.

   For III: $x\P (1-x) = \dfrac{x}{x+(1-x)} = \dfrac{x}{1} = x$, which is true.

   Hence, choice (C): only II and III are true.

28. **The correct answer is (D).** Since b is the seventh tick mark from 2, knowing that $b = 3.4$, we know that each space between tick marks = 0.2, and $a = 2.6$. This leaves choices (A) or (D). (2) tells us that the average of a and b is 3. Thus, we know that the tick mark halfway between them is 3. But that one is the fifth tick mark after 2. Again, this tells us that each space is 0.2 and answers the question. The best answer is (D).

29. **The correct answer is (C).** Since B could be any number, using (1) alone is not sufficient. The choices are (B), (C), or (E). Similarly, $B = 3$ tells us nothing about A if the only information we have is from (2). The choices are now (C) or (E). Using both pieces of information and remembering that the fraction bar in a fraction acts as a "grouping symbol" like parentheses, we should first calculate the numerator and denominator separately. That is, we should read this as $(3 + B) \div (4 \times 3 - 3 \times B)$. When $B = 3$, the numerator is $3 + 3 = 6$, and the denominator is $12 - 3 \times 3 = 12 - 9 = 3$. Therefore, the fraction is $\dfrac{6}{3} = 2$. Therefore, the best answer is (C).

30. **The correct answer is (A).** The 3 women can be arranged in $3! = 6$ ways (that is, $3 \times 2 \times 1$). However, for each of these ways, the 3 men can be also arranged in $3! = 6$ ways. Hence, there are really $6 \times 6 = 36$ ways altogether.

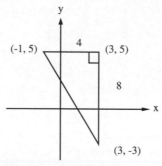

31. **The correct answer is (D).** Sketching the points on the xy-plane (as in the figure above), we see that they form a right triangle with one leg 5 and the other 12. Hence, the hypotenuse is 13, and the sum of the three sides is $5 + 12 + 13 = 30$.

32. **The correct answer is (A).** Using (1), the price of the first six paintings averaged \$70, the total received for the 6 was \$420. In the same way, the next 4 paintings must have brought in \$400 in order for them to average \$100 apiece. Therefore, we have a total of 10 paintings selling for \$420 + \$400 = \$820, and the average is $\dfrac{\$820}{10}$ = \$82. The choices are (A) or (D). Using only (2), we can conclude nothing about the total amount received for all ten paintings. The best answer is (A).

33. **The correct answer is (E).** Since every point on the circle must be 5 units from the center, we know that $(t,-1)$ must be 5 units from $(4,2)$. Using the distance formula,

$$\sqrt{(t-4)^2 + (2-(-1))^2} = 5$$

$$\sqrt{(t^2 - 8t + 16) + 9} = 5$$

$$\sqrt{t^2 - 8t + 25} = 5$$

Squaring both sides, we have:

$$t^2 - 8t + 25 = 25$$

We subtract 25 from both sides to yield:

$$t^2 - 8t = 0$$

which factors as:

$$t(t - 8) = 0$$

with two possibilities, $t = 0$ or $t = 8$. The positive solution is 8.

34. **The correct answer is (E).** The distance from A to B is the distance from -2 to $+3$, or 5 units. Since C is 5 units from B, C is either 5 units greater than 3 or 5 units less. That is, either -2 or 8.

35. **The correct answer is (C).** (1) alone is not sufficient, because we need to have a basis on which to calculate the fraction markdown. (2) alone is also not sufficient, because we need to know how much the markdown was. The choices are (C) or (E). Both together answer the question. The coat was marked down from \$200 to \$170, or 15%.

36. **The correct answer is (D).** Calling the measure of $\angle A$ in degrees x, we have the following:

$$x = \text{number of degrees in } \angle A$$
$$3x + 20 = \text{number of degrees in } \angle B$$
$$x + (3x + 20) = 4x + 20 = 180 - y$$

where y is the number of degrees in $\angle C$. Using (1), we have the number of degrees in $\angle C = 4x + 20$. Substituting for y:

$$4x + 20 = 180 - (4x + 20)$$
$$4x + 20 = 180 - 4x - 20$$
$$8x = 140$$
$$x = 17.5$$

The choices are either (A) or (D). From (2), we have the measure of $\angle C = 90°$, and thus $4x + 20 = 90$, which we can solve to get $x = 17.5$. Clearly, the other two angles are larger than x, so the smallest angle is $17.5°$.

37. **The correct answer is (C).** By just checking the choices, you see that substituting $x = 0$ gives $5^2 = (-5)^2$, which is correct. So choice (C) is correct. To solve algebraically, expand both sides to yield:

$$x^2 - 10x + 25 = x^2 + 10x + 25$$
$$-10x = 10x$$
$$0 = 20x$$
$$x = 0$$

SECTION 4—VERBAL

1. **The correct answer is (A).** Since the workers were all exposed to asbestos on the job, it seems clear that their cancers were an example of an occupational cluster.

2. **The correct answer is (A).** Paragraphs four and five are devoted to describing the difficulties experts have in gathering and interpreting information about cancer clusters with suspected environmental causes.

3. **The correct answer is (B).** As the last paragraph explains, cancer's "latency" is its tendency to break out as much as ten to twenty years after the exposure which caused it.

4. **The correct answer is (C).** The "gerrymandering" described in the passage involves community activists drawing boundaries to fit their preconceived ideas or wishes, just as a politician does when he draws an election district boundary to produce a particular electoral result.

5. **The correct answer is (D).** The statements in choices (A), (B), (C), and (E) all either undermine the notion that drug addiction is an inherited ailment or weaken the idea that drug addiction is a maternally linked trait. Choice (D), however, does not weaken the argument, since it's possible that a genetically transmitted trait may *also* be developed through other means, at least in a modest number of cases (as implied in the answer: "there have been instances . . . ").

6. **The correct answer is (C).** Since several tools are being mentioned, the phrase *an important business tool* must be made plural, *important business tools,* to be both consistent and logical. Choice (C) is better than choice (E) because it names the three "tools" in parallel grammatical form.

7. **The correct answer is (A).** The proper English idiom is *would be well advised to* do something. Each of the incorrect answer choices in some way mangles the idiom, producing a sentence that sounds wrong to native ears.

8. **The correct answer is (C).** Choice (C) *cannot* be logically inferred from the information presented because it is an overstatement. The first sentence of the passage tells us that slavery extension was "the major issue" of the campaign, but not that "none of the other issues . . . contributed significantly" to the outcome.

9. **The correct answer is (C).** The original phrasing is wrong, because it pairs the third-person *one* with the second-person pronoun *you*. Choice (C) fixes this error by making both words consistently second person, *you* and *your*. Choice (D) is wrong because *someone* is singular, but *their* is plural. The two pronouns need to match in number as well as in person.

10. **The correct answer is (E).** All of the answers except choice (E) help to explain the discrepancy between Lucas's expectations and the actual box-office results. Choice (E), however, makes the success of the rereleased movies *more*, not less surprising.

11. **The correct answer is (B).** What needs to be "accounted for" here is the fact that the razing of an important building, curiously, led to a surge of interest in landmark preservation. All of the answers help suggest possible explanations except choice (B), which merely emphasizes the degree of novelty in the concept of landmark preservation without helping to explain why it became popular.

12. **The correct answer is (E).** The first sentence of the second paragraph says that Messe and Callahan-Levy wanted to test the theory "that women judge their own work more harshly than that of others." Their experiment seemed to challenge this belief, since the women evaluated their own work as highly as men did (see the last sentence of the third paragraph).

13. **The correct answer is (D).** Previous experiments had suggested that women tend to pay themselves less than they paid others for the same work. The question Messe and Callahan-Levy tried to answer was *why*. Although their experiment didn't provide any definitive answer to this question, it suggested some plausible directions; hence, choice (D).

14. **The correct answer is (A).** Since the entire experiment focuses on the pay demanded and received by women and their perception of the value of their work, it seems clear that the most relevant social issue would be inequities in the pay of women vis-a-vis men.

15. **The correct answer is (B).** *A father* is singular, but *their* is plural, which makes the original phrasing incorrect. Choice (B) fixes the error by changing both to plural, so they match nicely. Choice (E) corrects this problem, but it obscures the meaning of the sentence by referring to "the children of the 1950s," as if they are being discussed as some sort of sociological or demographic grouping—which is obviously not the case.

16. **The correct answer is (E).** Choice (E) fixes the incorrect predication of the original; "trying to organize," which is the subject of the second verb, is singular, so it requires the singular verb *is* rather than the plural verb *are*. Choice (E) is better than choices (B) or (D), because it consistently maintains the pronoun *you* rather than arbitrarily shifting it.

17. **The correct answer is (C).** Choices (A) and (B) suggest that most people are actually pretty good about returning books they've borrowed; choice (E) suggests that France's original statement may have been false in itself, which certainly weakens the argument based on it. Choice (D) suggests a motive for book lending without strengthening the notion that borrowed books are never returned. Only choice (C) supports that idea.

18. **The correct answer is (C).** The paired words *neither . . . nor* must be used together consistently; it's not correct to change the latter word to *or,* even when three (or more) items are being listed, as in this question.

19. **The correct answer is (B).** For the group as a whole to be the world's best band needn't imply that each individual in the band was the best at his particular role; it's conceivable, for example, that the weakness of Ringo Starr on drums (as compared to, say, rival Ginger Baker) might have been more than offset by the songwriting talent of Lennon and McCartney.

20. **The correct answer is (C).** Parallelism requires the construction *to carry . . . or to maintain* in naming the two things that ships were not required to do. Choice (E) introduces parallelism, using the present participles *carrying . . . maintaining,* but the result is awkward when compared to choice (C).

21. **The correct answer is (E).** If true, this statement suggests that commuters may not have the option to switch from cars to trains, so despite the proposed toll increase, they may simply have to continue to drive into the city.

22. **The correct answer is (C).** The last two sentences of the second paragraph explain this point. Since microbes are the most common form of life on Earth, the Viking scientists assumed that the same would be true on Mars, so that looking for microbes would be the most likely way to find living things.

23. **The correct answer is (A).** See the last sentence of the third paragraph, which explains this point.

24. **The correct answer is (E).** Radioactive carbon dioxide was used because, if Martian life-forms converted it into other compounds (as living things on Earth would do), the radioactivity would be found on those compounds and would be detectable by the Viking instruments. The fourth paragraph explains this.

25. **The correct answer is (D).** The Viking tests were designed to detect chemical processes similar to those found among living things on Earth. So if Martian life operated through entirely different processes, the Viking tests would be likely to overlook them completely.

26. **The correct answer is (D).** Choices (A), (B), and (C) are all both non-idiomatic (weird-sounding) and verbose (wordy). Choices (D) and (E) both fix these problems, but the use of the past perfect tense (*they had been*) in choice (E) doesn't make sense, since what's being described is not a past event prior to some other past event—the only circumstance that calls for the past perfect.

27. **The correct answer is (D).** The passage, at first, appears to be building toward the point that Hispanic Americans will soon have considerable political power. But the word *However* strongly hints that the author intends to show the opposite—that Hispanics will be an exception to the rule that population = political clout. Hence, choice (D), which carries out the expected reversal of the logical conclusion, is correct.

28. **The correct answer is (B).** It's quite possible, of course, for a company to employ large numbers of women in menial or low-paying jobs, which would not necessarily absolve them of the charge of discriminating against women in their hiring and promotion practices—hence choice (B). Choice (E) focuses on an issue that may be relevant but is basically peripheral; even with a female CEO, a company could have a culture and practices that are unfair to women.

29. **The correct answer is (C).** Choice (C) is the only phrasing that is both idiomatic and clear.

30. **The correct answer is (A).** The original phrasing is perfectly correct, idiomatic, and understandable. In choices (B) and (C), the verb phrases used are inappropriate and awkward; in choice (D), the wording is clumsy and verbose; and choice (E) changes the meaning of the sentence.

31. **The correct answer is (E).** Assuming that the information in the passage is correct, the facts don't necessarily prove that military spending in 1985 was too high; the higher level in 1985 may have been appropriate given the nation's needs at that moment in history. (Don't try to answer this one based on your own opinions or knowledge of history; just go by the information and ideas presented in the passage.)

32. **The correct answer is (C).** The third paragraph makes it clear that Wang's major mistake was its failure "to see the opportunity presented by the personal computer."

33. **The correct answer is (E).** See the second half of the second paragraph, which mentions the advantages of the networked personal computers that came to dominate the market that Wang had formerly owned. These PCs are described as *versatile* and as having *open architecture, interchangeable software, and integrated communications.* Whether or not you are especially knowledgeable about information management, you can tell from this description that the main benefits derived from moving toward PCs had to do with flexibility.

34. **The correct answer is (A).** The last paragraph suggests two possible ways in which a business leader may "stumble into" the trap in which Wang was caught.

35. **The correct answer is (D).** The original phrasing is redundant; *also* and *in addition* mean the same thing, and either one can be eliminated without changing or weakening the meaning of the sentence.

36. **The correct answer is (B).** The information in the passage seems to suggest that low-fat foods don't help prevent obesity, but it doesn't necessarily indicate that sugar is the culprit. Choice (B) strengthens (without irrefutably proving) the case for that assertion by showing that, at least, the rise in obesity has coincided with an increase in the sales of high-sugar foods.

37. **The correct answer is (C).** *Neither . . . nor* must be paired together consistently. Choice (E) pairs *not . . . nor,* which isn't a "recognized" entry in the idiom sweepstakes.

38. **The correct answer is (E).** If all those who enjoy building duck decoys will appreciate the tools, and if some in that group are carpenters, then there are some carpenters who will appreciate the tools.

39. **The correct answer is (A).** The last underlined word should be *are,* since the "expectations" about the future movies are happening *currently,* not in the future. Choice (E) is verbose, awkward, and somewhat confuses the meaning of the first half of the sentence.

40. **The correct answer is (D).** The conclusion stated in the last sentence will be true only if it is true that the government *must* turn to former lobbyists if it wants to find knowledgeable regulators. If such people are available elsewhere—for example, among university professors—then the conclusion is faulty.

41. **The correct answer is (E).** Only choice (E) describes the three obsessions in grammatically parallel form.

Chapter 2

Making Your Plan

Get the Scoop On . . .

- The three levels of GMAT CAT skills, and how you can improve all three
- How to develop a personalized study plan that is focused on your current skill levels and needs
- How to tailor your study plan to the amount of time you have to prepare

---

HOW TO GET WHERE YOU WANT TO GO

Let's recap. You have a good idea about the role of the GMAT CAT in the business school admission process. And you've begun to consider the kinds of business school programs you're interested in applying to. As your choices become more specific and focused, your GMAT CAT goals will become more clear, based largely on the credentials that are necessary to win admission to the program(s) of your choice.

Now we come to the heart of this book. How can you make sure that your GMAT CAT scores will be a help rather than a hindrance to you when you apply to business schools? What steps can you take to close the gap that may exist between your current levels of GMAT CAT skills and the ones you'll need to earn your highest possible score?

The rest of this book will help you answer those questions.

THE INSIDER'S ROUTE TO TOP SCORES

There are three levels of skill that can help boost your GMAT CAT scores. Each requires a different kind of preparation. Most important, each requires a different time frame to be completely developed. If you want to reach your full potential on the GMAT CAT, you'll want to devote time and energy to all three levels of skill.

The following sections describe how the three levels work.

Level One—Testwiseness (30 to 150 points)

This first level of test-taking skill is the "low-hanging fruit" of test-preparation: skills that are relatively quick and simple to learn and that can rapidly boost your total GMAT CAT score from 30 to 150 points.

Level One includes such skills as:

- Familiarity with the format, structure, and question types found on the exam

- Ability to budget your time wisely as you work through each section of the exam

- Understanding of the Computer Adaptive Test format and how to make it work for you

Level One skills are specific to the computerized GMAT CAT. A student who'd never seen a standardized exam before and had done no preparatory reading about the GMAT CAT would lack these skills, and therefore would lose points through sheer ignorance of the game.

Fortunately, Level One skills are easy to learn. Many students pick up some of them just by taking a GMAT CAT. That's why, as the test-makers admit, most students increase their scores by 30 to 50 points when they take the exam a second time, even if they do not study between the two tests.

If your preparation for the GMAT CAT is condensed into just a couple of weeks, you'll need to focus especially on Level One skills. Chapters 3 and 10 through 12 in this book are particularly focused on Level One skills.

Level Two—Topic Strategies (75 to 250 points)

Some of the terms and topics in the explanation may not be famliar to you. Don't worry—you'll learn much more about them in Chapter 3.

Skills at this level are a bit more complex. They generally take longer to learn, but they have a correspondingly greater payoff. If you work to improve your Level Two skills (as well as your Level One skills), you can expect to boost your overall GMAT CAT score by anywhere from 75 to 250 points.

Level Two includes such skills as:

- Ability to recognize the logical connections between parts of a reading passage

- Understanding of the basic elements of a logical argument and how they are related to one another

- Awareness of how and when to use rounding off and guesstimating when working on math problems

- Knowing how to create a simple outline that will enable you to quickly write a well-organized essay in less than 30 minutes

Level Two skills relate specifically to particular question types on the GMAT CAT. However, they involve intellectual abilities that can be used in other contexts as well. For instance, if you're good at seeing the logical connections between parts of a reading passage, this will help you not only on the GMAT CAT but whenever you do any difficult reading—in a business report, a textbook, or a scholarly journal, for example.

You've probably developed some Level Two skills already, both in school and out. However, you probably aren't aware of how to directly apply these skills to answering GMAT CAT questions. Since these skills are somewhat complex (and because there are many of them), it'll take you a while to master them. But the rewards can be great.

If you have four weeks or more to prepare for the GMAT CAT, you'll have enough time to delve fairly deeply into Level Two skills. Chapters 4 through 9 of this book explain them in detail.

Level Three—Broad-Based Verbal and Math Abilities (150–600 points)

The test makers at ETS officially minimize the importance of Level One and Level 2 skills. They tend to consider them a kind of trick, and they imply in their public pronouncements that "short-term preparation" to develop these skills won't earn you many points. The fact is that these skills, which most students have never learned, are vital to handling GMAT CAT questions confidently and correctly.

These are the most general skills, and they take the longest amount of time to fully develop. In a sense, Level Three skills are the ones the test-makers originally intended the GMAT CAT to focus on, and your performance on the test will certainly be heavily affected by your Level Three skills. If you devote significant time and effort to improving your Level Three skills (along with Levels One and Two), you can aim for an increase of your overall GMAT CAT score of from 150 to 600 points.

Level Three includes such skills as:

- Knowledge of the meanings and correct usage of a large number of difficult English words

- Ability to read and understand complex passages that deal with challenging topics from science, the humanities, the social sciences, and business

- Familiarity with the basic facts, principles, and procedures of arithmetic, algebra, and geometry

- Knowledge of the basic rules of English grammar and usage and how to apply them to editing sentences

- Sophisticated understanding of logical reasoning and the fallacies that can undermine an argument

Level Three skills clearly go well beyond the requirements of the GMAT CAT. In fact, you probably learned and practiced skills like these in every high school and college class you ever took (well, maybe not gym).

You'll continue to develop and improve your Level Three skills in many ways between now and the time you take the GMAT CAT—through your ongoing college coursework, through challenging reading that you may do for school or any other purpose, and through the intellectual exercise you get whenever you take a test, including the sample GMAT CAT you use as part of your test-prep program.

The more time you have between now and the exam, the greater your chances of improving your Level Three skills. In this book, Appendixes A, B, and C specifically address these skills by offering help in building word knowledge, sharpening your understanding of mathematics, and strengthening your grasp of the rules of English grammar and usage.

In addition, you'll find that you are using and practicing your Level Three skills every time you work on an exercise or sample test from any chapter in this book. Just as regular, disciplined exercise improves your overall muscle tone and strengthens your heart, *mental workouts* are the key to strengthening your Level Three skills.

MAKING THE MOST OF THE TIME YOU HAVE

As with any form of learning, preparing for the GMAT CAT is an investment of time. The more time you have, the better your chances of boosting your scores significantly. Next, we'll walk you through three different study plans, each tailored to a specific amount of preparation time. Find the plan that fits your circumstances and adapt it to your needs.

If You Have Two Weeks to Prepare

Obviously, if you plan to take the GMAT CAT in two weeks or less and are just beginning your preparation program, your time is at a premium. You'll have to make the most of every available hour between now and the day of the test. As much as you can, cut back or eliminate nonessential activities over the next two weeks (work, travel, entertainment) and focus your energies on the exam.

You can still develop a plan, leaning heavily on Level One skills, that will make a significant difference in your test scores, but you need to make it your highest priority, starting *today*. The outline shown in Table 2.1 will help.

Table 2.1
Your Two-Week Plan—The Steps to Take

1. If you haven't already, take the Insiders GMAT CAT Diagnostic Test (Chapter 1). Set aside four hours and take the exam under true test conditions. Then, grade your performance using the Scoring Guide.

2. Based on the results of your Insider's GMAT CAT Diagnostic Test, identify the *three* question types on which you need the greatest improvement.

3. Turn to Part II of this book and read Chapter 3, Finding Your Way Around the Computer Adaptive GMAT CAT. It will give you an overview of the real exam and a number of important hints about test-taking strategy that will help boost your score.

4. Then, find the three chapters from Chapters 4 through 9 that cover the three question types you identified in Step 2. Study those chapters, and try your hand on at least two of the practice exercises in each one. If you achieve an above-average or excellent score on both practice exercises, move on. Otherwise, reread the chapter and do as many additional practice exercises as you can.

5. Turn to Appendix B, The Insider's GMAT CAT Math Review. This part of the book covers the fifty math topics that are most frequently tested on the GMAT CAT. Take 15 minutes to skim this appendix, pencil in hand. Circle the number of any topic you find new or unfamiliar. Then, set aside an afternoon or evening to read those topics in detail.

6. If you have time, read the chapters in Part II that you haven't already read.

7. Sometime in the week before the GMAT CAT, set aside 4 hours. Take the Insider's GMAT CAT Sample Test (Chapter 10) under true test conditions. Then, grade your performance using the Scoring Guide that follows the exam.

8. Compare your performance on the Insider's GMAT CAT Sample Test with your performance on the Insider's GMAT CAT Diagnostic Test. Is there any *one* question type where your performance still lags? If you have time, read or reread the chapter in Part II that covers that type of question.

9. Two days before the GMAT CAT, read Chapter 11 and follow the advice about how to approach the weekend of the exam.

10. After taking the GMAT CAT, read Chapter 12.

If You Have Four to Six Weeks to Prepare

With a month or more to get ready for the GMAT CAT, you can make some major improvements in your test-taking skills. You can delve rather deeply into Level Two skills and master all of the key Level One skills. It'll take some discipline and some hard work, of course. Try to

Table 2.2
Your Four- to Six-Week Plan—The Steps to Take

1. If you haven't done so already, take the Insider's GMAT CAT Diagnostic Test (Chapter 1). Set aside four hours and take the exam under true test conditions. Then grade your performance using the Scoring Guide.

2. Based on the results of your Insider's GMAT CAT Diagnostic Test, identify the *four* question types on which you need the greatest improvement.

3. Turn to Part II of this book and read Chapter 3, Finding Your Way Around the Computer-Adaptive GMAT CAT. It will give you an overview of the real exam and a number of important hints about test-taking strategies that will help boost your score.

4. As soon as possible, begin to set aside 15 minutes each day to study Appendix A, The Insider's GMAT CAT Word List. Plan to read the definitions and explanations of fifteen words from the word list each day. At this rate, you'll have been exposed to every word on the list within five weeks.

5. Now, find the four chapters from Chapters 4 through 9 that cover the four question types you identified in Step 2. Over the next two weeks, study those chapters, and try your hand on at least two of the practice exercises in each chapter. If you achieve an above-average or excellent score on both practice exercises, move on. Otherwise, reread the chapter and do as many additional practice exercises as you can.

6. Next, turn to Appendix B, The Insider's GMAT CAT Math Review. This part of the book covers the fifty math topics that are most frequently tested on the GMAT CAT. Over the next week, read this appendix thoroughly. With a pencil, circle the number of any topic you find difficult or confusing. Between now and the date of the exam, review the circled topics from time to time.

7. If you have time, read the chapters in Part II that you haven't already read.

8. Sometime in the week before the GMAT CAT, set aside 4 hours. Take the Insider's GMAT CAT Sample Test (Chapter 10) under true test conditions. Then grade your performance using the Scoring Guide that follows the test.

9. Compare your performance on the Insider's GMAT CAT Sample Test with your performance on the Insider's GMAT CAT Diagnostic Test. Is there any *one* question type where your performance still lags? If you have time, read or reread the chapter in Part II that covers that question type.

10. Two days before the GMAT CAT, read Chapter 11 and follow the advice about how to approach the weekend of the exam.

11. After taking the GMAT CAT, read Chapter 12.

Table 2.3
Your Three-Month Plan—The Steps to Take

1. If you haven't done so already, take the Insider's GMAT CAT Diagnostic Test (Chapter 1). Set aside 4 hours and take the exam under true test conditions. Then, grade your performance using the Scoring Guide.

2. Based on the results of your Insider's GMAT CAT Diagnostic Test, rank the six question types in order of priority, from the one in which you need the greatest improvement to the one in which you currently perform the best.

3. Turn to Part II of this book and read Chapter 3, Finding Your Way Around the Computer Adaptive GMAT CAT. It will give you an overview of the real exam and a number of important hints about test-taking strategies that will help boost your score.

4. As soon as possible, begin to set aside 15 minutes each day to study Appendix A, The Insider's GMAT CAT Word List. Plan to read the definitions and explanations of 15 words from the word list each day. At this rate, you'll have been exposed to every word on the list within five weeks. As suggested in the appendix, also start your own vocabulary notebook and add to it frequently.

5. Now, read Chapters 4 through 9 in the priority sequence you identified in Step 2. Also, try your hand on at least two of the practice exercises in each chapter. If you achieve an above-average or excellent score on both practice exercises, move on. Otherwise, reread the chapter and do as many additional practice exercises as you can.

6. Next, turn to Appendix B, The Insider's GMAT CAT Math Review. This part of the book covers the fifty math topics most frequently tested on the GMAT CAT. Over the next week, read this appendix thoroughly. With a pencil, circle the number of any topic you find difficult or confusing. Between now and the date of the exam, review the circled topics from time to time.

7. Get a copy of *The Official Guide for GMAT CAT Review*, a publication of ETS that contains a collection of recent actual GMAT CAT questions. During each of the four to six weeks prior to your scheduled test, use the sample test questions in this book for additional practice. As the weeks pass, keep track of your scores in each test area. They may rise and fall, but the overall trend should be upward.

8. Sometime in the week before the GMAT CAT, set aside 4 hours. Take the Insider's GMAT CAT sample test (Chapter 10) under true test conditions. Then, grade your performance using the Scoring Guide.

9. Compare your performance on the Insider's GMAT CAT sample test with your performance on the Insider's GMAT CAT Diagnostic Test. Is there any *one* question type where your performance still lags? If you have time, reread the chapter in Part II that covers that question type.

10. Two days before the GMAT CAT, read chapter 11 and follow the advice about how to approach the weekend of the exam.

11. After taking the GMAT CAT, read chapter 12.

cut back on nonessential activities between now and the day of the exam, and set aside significant blocks of time (evenings, weekends) to read, study, and practice. If you do this, following the steps we suggest in Table 2.2, you'll boost your scores noticeably.

If You Have Three Months or More to Prepare

Congratulations! Through astute planning, admirable self-discipline, or sheer good luck, you've positioned yourself so that you have ample time to prepare thoroughly for one of the most important challenges of your academic life. With three months or more to prepare, you can improve all three levels of your GMAT CAT skills and give yourself an excellent chance of achieving or surpassing your score goals.

Take advantage of your foresight by intelligently pacing yourself. Set aside time every week to pursue your test-prep program, preferably in major chunks—2 or 3 hours at a time on an evening or a weekday. An extended study program that is spread out over twelve weeks or more will boost your score more than an intensive, high-pressure program with the same number of study hours crammed into fewer weeks.

The steps in Table 2.3 will guide you through the planning process.

Once you've sketched your plan, turn to Chapter 3. There, you'll begin to develop your Level One skills by learning what to expect on the real GMAT CAT and some of the best test-taking strategies for every part of the exam.

JUST THE FACTS

- Level One skills involve Testwiseness, and can be developed quickly.

- Level Two skills involve Topic Strategies, and take more time to develop.

- Level Three skills involve broad-based Verbal, Quantitative, and Analytical Writing Abilities, and take the longest time to develop.

- Skills at all three levels can help boost your GMAT CAT scores.

- Depending on your schedule, your personal study program can delve more or less deeply into all three kinds of skills.

Part II

Getting Inside the GMAT CAT

Chapter 3

Finding Your Way Around the GMAT CAT

Get the Scoop On . . .

- The new computer-adaptive testing—a revolution in which *you* may be a pawn
- How the CAT differs from traditional paper-and-pencil tests in format, content, and scoring
- How to manage the mechanics of test-taking on the computer
- Test-taking strategies that will boost your GMAT CAT scores

---

GETTING THE BIG PICTURE

We are living through a revolution in standardized testing. In 1994, the test makers at ETS and the Graduate Management Admission Council, sponsors of the GMAT CAT, introduced the Computer-Adaptive Test (CAT) version of the GMAT. It seems likely that most other standardized tests, including ETS's famous and controversial college admission test, the SAT, will eventually be administered via computer. It's a whole new way of taking a standardized test, involving changes that go far beyond whether you mark your answers with a number two pencil or the click of a mouse. As you'll see, the changes have major implications for every test taker.

THE OFFICIAL DESCRIPTION

How the CAT Works

When you take the GMAT CAT, you'll be tested in the same subject areas that appeared on the traditional exam in the past. However, rather than reading questions from a printed test booklet and marking answers on a scannable sheet, you'll read questions from a computer monitor and select answers by clicking the button on a mouse.

The GMAT CAT questions are divided into three broad categories—Verbal, Quantitative, and Analytical Writing. There are three specific types of Verbal questions: reading comprehension, sentence correction, and critical reasoning. There are two types of Quantitative questions: multiple-choice problems and data sufficiency. There are two types of essays you'll be asked to write for the Analytical Writing Assessment: an analysis of an issue and an analysis of an argument. (You'll find a chapter in this book for each of these question types, filled with test-taking strategies and practice questions.)

The Map of the GMAT CAT (Table 3.1) gives a more detailed listing of the types and quantities of questions you'll probably encounter on the exam.

How the CAT Adapts to the Test-Taker

If the CAT were simply a matter of putting questions on a screen rather than printing them in a booklet, the change from paper-and-pencil to computerized format would be relatively insignificant. But the test makers have a far more ambitious agenda. They are using computer-adaptive testing to radically change the way standardized tests are written, administered, and scored. Here's how it works.

As you know, a standardized test like the GMAT CAT is intended to measure the level of your skills and knowledge in particular areas—in this case, what the test makers call Verbal, Quantitative, and Analytical Writing ability. Each test taker, in theory, has some "true" level of ability, represented by an overall score from 200 to 800 on the three-digit GMAT CAT scale and a score from 0 to 60 on the Verbal and Quantitative scales. (Analytical Writing is graded in a special way, which we'll explain in Chapter 9.) In order to determine with fair accuracy where your ability

Table 3.1
Map of the GMAT CAT

Verbal Section—75 minutes	Analytical Writing Assessment—60 minutes (2 sections)
13–14 reading-comprehension questions (based on three or four passages)	1 analysis of an issue topic
13–14 sentence-correction questions	1 analysis of an argument topic
13–14 critical-reasoning questions	2 TOPICS TOTAL
41 QUESTIONS TOTAL	
Quantitative Section—75 minutes	
22 multiple-choice problems	
15 data-sufficiency questions	
37 QUESTIONS TOTAL	

level falls, the traditional paper-and-pencil test included questions covering a wide range of difficulty levels, from very easy to very hard.

The number of questions you get right in a given test area is supposed to give a good indication of your "true" ability in that area. If your "true" Verbal ability, for example, is around 28—close to the average level among GMAT CAT test takers—then, when you take the paper-and-pencil exam, you will get nearly all of the easy questions right, nearly all of the very difficult questions wrong, and, on those questions that fall in the middle of the difficulty range, some right and some wrong. The number you get right overall determines your score.

On the old paper-and-pencil GMAT, you normally had to answer a total of 61 Verbal questions to cover this wide range of difficulties. On the GMAT CAT, however, there are fewer items. You'll have just one Verbal section with a total of only 41 questions to answer.

How is this possible? Here's how. In theory, when an average-level student takes the paper-and-pencil test, he is "wasting" a lot of his time on very easy questions (nearly all of which he answers correctly) and on very hard questions (nearly all of which he answers wrong). It's the middle-level questions—where his performance is more unpredictable—that really determine this student's score.

Because the CAT is tailored to each test taker, no two students will be given the same questions. This is the single most revolutionary feature of computer-adaptive testing. If every student takes a different test, can their performances really be fairly compared? ETS says that their statistical formulas make it possible; but whether the general public will accept this remains to be seen.

Ideally, then, the test makers would like to be able to give each student a test that is tailored to that student's specific skill level. Mr. Average would get a test made up almost entirely of middle-level questions, while Mr. Below-Average would get an easier test, and Mr. Above-Average would get a harder one. This would save the test taker's time and energy by focusing him on questions at the most relevant difficulty level. It would also, in theory, enable the test makers to zero in more precisely on the test taker's "true" skill level.

The GMAT CAT is designed to make this ideal a reality. It works like this. When you begin work on the Verbal section (for example), you'll be given a question of average difficulty, selected at random from an extensive bank of questions stored in the computer's software. If you get it right, you'll next be given a slightly harder question from the bank; if you get it wrong, you'll be given a slightly easier one. Depending on how you do with the second question, you'll be given either an easier or a harder question after that. As you continue through the section, the difficulty level of the questions will continue to be adjusted. If you're like most students, you'll eventually settle into a specific skill range that is appropriate for you, and most of the questions you'll be given should be in that difficulty range.

Navigating the Test Section

The adaptive nature of the computer-adaptive test, by which the questions are selected, one by one, while the test is actually in progress, gives rise to a number of interesting features in the test format.

- Question types are intermingled rather than presented in batches. In other words, when you tackle the Verbal section, you might start with a sentence correction item followed by a critical-reasoning question, a sentence correction, a reading comprehension passage, another critical-reasoning question, two sentence corrections, two reading comprehension items . . . you get the idea. By the time you finish the section, you'll have been given a fair assortment of every question type, but rather than getting them grouped in batches, you'll get them in a seemingly random order.

- You may not work on question types in any sequence that you choose. The items are presented in whatever order the software's algorithm (formula) dictates. If you prefer to start with reading comprehension, too bad; you must answer the questions as the computer picks them.

- You may not skip or go back to an earlier question. Once you've selected an answer for question 1 and moved on to question 2, you will never see question 1 again. If you decide later in the section that your answer to question 1 was wrong, you can't change it.

- You can see only one question at a time. It's not possible, as it was with the paper-and-pencil test, to compare two questions from different portions of the same test section. The software is set up to show one and only one item on the screen at any given time.

This scoring method is fair only if you trust ETS when they say, "Don't worry—our software knows how to pick the 'right' questions to score your abilities fairly." Is this a believable claim? You decide. Unfortunately, the procedure by which the questions for your test are selected is not subject to scrutiny or evaluation by anyone outside ETS.

As you can imagine, these features of the CAT have important implications for test-taking strategy. We'll discuss these in detail shortly.

How the CAT Is Scored

On the traditional (now obsolete) GMAT, each question was worth the same amount of points. Your three-digit scaled score was determined by a formula based on the number of correct answers you chose. The formula varied depending on the overall difficulty level of the test, but it didn't differentiate among questions.

Again, the CAT is different. Your exam will include a mixture of hard, easy, and middle-level items, but most of the questions will be at a difficulty level that the computer figures is approximately right for you. The score you end up with will take into account not only the number of right answers you chose but also the difficulty rating of the individual questions. In other words, if you get a batch of difficult questions right, you'll earn more points than you would by getting a batch of easy questions right.

Is there any way to outsmart the software by focusing particularly on the questions that will earn you the most points? Yes. We'll explain the system shortly.

THE INSIDER'S REPORT

Why the Test Makers Love the CAT

Although the folks at ETS will never admit it, the freedom from test disclosure benefits them in another way, too. It's much easier for the test makers to operate in secrecy than in the glare of publicity. When students can't review their test questions after the exam, at home, they can't easily detect or complain about errors or ambiguities in the items, and ETS is spared the expense, effort, and embarrassment of admitting and correcting their mistakes.

The CAT has several specific, powerful benefits for the folks at ETS.

- Because each computerized GMAT CAT requires fewer questions than the traditional test, ETS needn't write, edit, and pretest as many items, thereby saving a lot of money.

- Better still, because the test disclosure laws on the books in New York State and elsewhere apply only to test forms taken by a certain minimum number of individuals—and *no two people ever take the same CAT*—the computerized tests are exempt from disclosure. This means that ETS can use and reuse the same items over and over again. (Of course, a minimum number of new items must always be created, so that students who retake the exam don't run into a number of the same questions.)

- The fact that every student takes a different exam makes the risk of cheating—*test security*, in ETS parlance—absolutely minimal. As long as the GMAT CAT software that contains those banks of difficulty-graded questions is secure, it's almost impossible to imagine how anyone can compromise the integrity of the exam. (On the other hand, there's probably a lot of money waiting for the shrewd hacker who can crack those precious question banks. Any takers? *Note to the lawyers at ETS: Just kidding.*)

- Because the CAT is administered to one student at a time at centers around the country, GMAT CAT testing and score reporting is spread out through the year rather than concentrated around a few nationwide test dates. This makes the flow of paperwork much easier for ETS to manage.

- As with most automated processes, the computerization of the GMAT CAT reduces the number of relatively costly humans required to administer the exams—another cost saving.

- Finally, the fact that you can learn your score instantly, right off the computer screen, saves ETS the headache of fielding inquiries from anxious students during the weeks after the exam. And if instant feedback encourages more students to retake the exam once, twice, or even more often—at $96 a pop—the test makers won't mind a bit.

Making the GMAT CAT Work for You

It's easy to see why ETS likes the CAT. But is there anything in it for you?

Some of the advantages of the CAT can work in your favor, too. Ready availability of the test on most days of each month, rather than a handful of Saturdays a year, certainly adds to your convenience. So does being able to see your test scores immediately. And the fact that the number of test questions is smaller on the CAT than it is on the paper-and-pencil test probably strikes many test takers as a blessing. (But don't expect your time at the test center to be any shorter. Paperwork and the computer tutorial that walks you through the workings of the testing software all combine to make the CAT at least as time consuming overall as the traditional test.)

If you're computer literate or even a computerphile, someone who works with computers daily and enjoys using them, you may prefer the CAT to the traditional paper-and-pencil test. You may also like it if you prefer the idea of a highly intense, relatively *shorter* mental challenge as opposed to the longer, marathon-like endurance battle of the traditional exam.

In any case, there are definite steps you can take both to make the GMAT CAT experience relatively painless and to maximize your opportunity to score high under the special new conditions of computerized testing. On the next few pages, we'll outline these strategies and explain how and why they work.

FYI

Don't accept working conditions that are less than comfortable at the test center. If your carrel is too small, with inadequate room for you to work on your scrap paper; if the room is very hot, very cold, or noisy; or if your computer, keyboard, monitor, and mouse aren't working perfectly, speak up and insist on having the problem remedied. If this doesn't work, complain later to ETS (see Chapter 12 for details).

What to Expect at the Testing Center

Most students take the GMAT CAT at one of several hundred Sylvan Learning Centers around the country. A private company, Sylvan is the subcontractor that provides this service to ETS; they were chosen largely because they have an extensive network of computerized centers in which space is generally available for testing on weekday mornings.

The Sylvan facilities vary widely in size, quality, and amenities. Some are relatively spacious, clean, quiet, and well organized; others are not. If you have a choice of more than one location, you may want to visit both before choosing one at which to register.

On the day of your test, you'll be asked to show up early, bearing your photo I.D. (driver's license, passport, etc.), admission card from ETS, a pen, and a pencil. You may find that you can begin the GMAT CAT process right away, or you may have to sit in a waiting room half an hour or more, depending on how well run your Sylvan center is. The administrator should provide you with a small locker in which to store your jacket, bag, or other belongings; she's not supposed to let you bring any such item into the test room with you.

After being admitted to the test room—and possibly photographed for security purposes—you'll be assigned to a carrel with a desk, a chair, and a computer with keyboard, monitor, mouse, and mouse pad. You'll be given a few pages of scrap paper, too. The GMAT CAT software will be loaded and booted up, and you should be ready to go right away.

The GMAT CAT software begins with an extensive tutorial that explains how the test works, features of the testing interface (i.e., what the different items on the screen are for), how to use the mouse, and so forth. Make sure you understand exactly how the program works before you plunge into the first test section.

Managing the Mechanics of the CAT

FYI

Explanations from the pre-test tutorial remain available to you throughout the test, by clicking Help. However, any time you spend reviewing the tutorial during a test section comes out of the time you're given for answering questions. So avoid using the Help option.

If you're familiar with the conventions of Windows- or Mac-based computing, as most students are today, you won't find the GMAT CAT software complicated. If you're not, get familiar with them *before* you sit for the GMAT CAT. Visit your college computer center or talk a friend into letting you use her desktop for a few hours. Type a term paper, work up a personal budget, or manage some other mundane task using Windows- or Mac-style software. The idea is to be comfortable with computer basics such as pointing and clicking with the mouse; typing and editing an essay using common word-processing commands; scrolling up and down through a lengthy text; the use of Next, Help, Quit, and other specialized on-screen command buttons; selecting activities from a menu of choices; and the feel of reading or working with material in one window while other information appears elsewhere on the computer desktop.

There are a handful of crucial mechanical details you *must* pay attention to when you take the exam.

- **Understand how to choose, change, and confirm answer choices.** For each question that appears on the screen, you'll be given five answers to choose from. They are *not* labeled (A), (B), (C), (D), and (E), by the way; each is merely preceded by a little oval "bubble" not unlike the bubbles to be blackened in on the traditional paper-and-pencil answer sheet.

  To choose an answer, move the on-screen arrow to the bubble using the mouse and click either mouse button. The bubble will be filled in. To change the answer, just click on a different bubble.

  When you're satisfied with your answer, click on the Next arrow at the bottom of the screen. This will cause another box, labeled Answer Confirm, to be highlighted. Click there and your answer will be registered, and you'll move on to the next question.

  Be certain you check your answer before hitting the Answer Confirm button. Make sure, for one thing, that you've correctly clicked and highlighted the answer you really want! Remember, you'll have no opportunity to reconsider or change your answer once it has been confirmed and registered by the computer.

■ **Be aware of what happens when you exit a test section or quit the test.** At the bottom of each screen, you'll find buttons labeled Test Quit and Section Exit. Unless you become deathly ill, *don't use these.*

If you click on Test Quit, the exam will vanish, and your scores for that day will be canceled, including your scores on any previous test sections you completed. Similarly, if you click on Section Exit without having completed *every* question in the section, you will *not* receive a score for that section.

Rather than run the risk of wasting your time and effort in this way, simply ignore those two buttons. If you finish a section with 2 or 3 extra minutes to spare, use the time to rest and relax. This will reenergize you for the sections still to come.

■ **Keep track of the test item you are working on and the amount of time you have left.** Throughout the test, you'll see a bar across the top of the screen that contains three pieces of information: the time remaining for the section, the number of the section, and the number of the item you are working on. It will look something like this:

> 00:18   GMAT CAT Section 3   14 of 37

When 5 minutes remain, the time indicator will flash and change to read:

> 00:05:00

which means that 5 minutes and zero seconds are left. For the last 5 minutes, seconds are counted down along with the minutes.

Glance at this information bar from time to time as you work. It will help you follow the proper timing strategy, as we'll discuss in a moment.

■ **Use the scroll bar to read long passages.** In the Verbal section, full-length reading passages do not fit on the computer screen all at once. To read through the entire passage, you have to scroll through the material. The same may be true of graphs in the Quantitative section and, occasionally, other materials.

Long passages and graphs will normally be set up on the left-hand side of the screen, leaving a window on the right for a question to appear. This way, you can scan the passage while simultaneously looking at the question.

FYI

On Verbal items, for which no single "perfect" answer is calculated, try this technique: scroll with the mouse arrow down through the five bubbles as you read the corresponding answer choices, and click when you come upon an answer you like better than any preceding answer. After reading all five answers, the one best *answer should be highlighted.*

There are three different ways you can scroll through a long text: (1) by clicking on the Up and Down arrows at the top and bottom of the scroll bar; (2) by "pulling" the scroll tab up or down within the bar; or (3) by clicking anywhere within the bar to move the tab. We recommend method (1): it moves the text more smoothly and so makes for much easier reading.

Test-Taking Strategies for the CAT That Really Work

1. Above All, Get the First Five Questions In Each Section Correct

The single most important thing you can do to boost your score on the GMAT CAT is to answer the first five questions correctly. The difference this will make in your overall score—regardless of your performance on the remaining questions—is stunning.

Why is this so? Let's explain.

The theory of computer-adaptive testing, you'll recall, is that the program that selects questions for your customized test is supposed to zero in fairly quickly on your general skill level for a particular test area. Starting with a question of medium difficulty, the program rapidly shifts up or down based on how well you do, settling down after just a handful of questions at the level it "thinks" is approximately right for you.

Thereafter, the difficulty adjustments made by the program are much smaller. In effect, the program thinks it knows you by now: the issue now is not whether you'll earn a score of 300 or 700, but whether you'll earn 520, 540, or 560. The remaining questions will all be of roughly similar difficulty, and will be chosen with the goal of "fine- tuning" your score within a range that has already been determined.

How do we know that the test works this way? See the box labeled *One Test Taker's Story* for an account of an actual experiment. The results will surprise you.

What does this mean for you as a test taker? *You should do whatever it takes to answer the first five questions in each section correctly.* Throw out all test-taking strategies that are designed to save time. Instead, tackle the first five items with extra care, even if it takes more time. Read *and reread* the questions to make sure you understand what's being asked. Double-check your calculations. Solve the same problem twice, using two different methods or approaches, to make sure that the answers match. On Quantitative items, try checking not only the right answer but also each answer you think is wrong, to confirm that both direct solving and the process of elimination point to the same response. And on Verbal items, consider every answer choice carefully to make sure that one you've overlooked isn't subtly correct.

In short, treat those first five questions as if your entire test score depends on them. *To a large degree, it does.*

2. Start Slow; Speed Up Later
On a paper-and-pencil test, your best timing strategy is to tackle the easiest questions first, zip through them, then slow down as you try your hand at the harder items. On the CAT, *reverse* this approach. Take your time on the first few items so as to maximize your chance of getting them all right; then, gradually, speed up as you move into items that will affect your final score less significantly.

Table 3.2 shows our suggested timing pattern, based on the number of questions per section used on the typical GMAT CAT. We suggest you learn it and use it, at least roughly, as a guide when you take the exam.

Actually, the time allotments for each section of the GMAT CAT are fairly generous. If you practice the question types diligently between now and the day of the exam, you'll probably find that you have no difficulty in finishing all the questions on each section in the time permitted.

The Best Tips
1. Practice With the Test-Taking Tools As Long As You Need
The on-screen tutorial that precedes the first test section walks you through the various test-taking tools that are built into the CAT program. You're not allowed to skip this tutorial—there's no "early exit" button to click—but it's tempting to rush through it by simply clicking the "Next" button on each screen in rote fashion.

Table 3.2
Suggested Timing For CAT Sections

Verbal (41 questions, 75 minutes)	
Questions 1–5:	15–18 minutes
Questions 6–15:	15–18 minutes
Questions 16–24:	15–18 minutes
Questions 25–35:	15–18 minutes
Questions 36–41:	Time remaining
Quantitative (37 questions, 75 minutes)	
Questions 1–5:	15–18 minutes
Questions 6–14:	15–18 minutes
Questions 15–22:	15–18 minutes
Questions 23–30:	15–18 minutes
Questions 31–37:	Time remaining

One Test Taker's Story

By the time my appointment to take the GMAT CAT came along, I'd changed my mind about going to business school, but I decided to take the test anyway.

"I knew from practice tests that I could score high on both the Verbal and Quantitative sections, but I wanted to see what would happen to my scores if I handled the start of the sections differently. So I made a plan. I figured out how many questions would be 65 percent of the total and made that my target for the total number of questions I'd answer correctly.

Then, I decided to deliberately get the first five Verbal questions *wrong*, and the first five Quantitative questions *right*. After that, I'd get some wrong and some right, in the proper numbers to add up to 65 percent correct overall.

The results floored me. My Quantitative score came in at the 80th percentile, but my Verbal score at the 19th percentile.

Remember, on both sections I got about the same overall number correct! The only difference was how I did on the first five items. Getting them right put me in the penthouse; getting them wrong put me in the basement.

FYI

Bring both a pen and a pencil to the GMAT CAT. When creating diagrams on scrap paper for geometry problems, use the pen to note the basic information provided by the test makers. Then use the pencil to add your own deductions. This way, if you make a mistake or need to change your conclusions, you can erase what you've added without losing the basic, unchanging data.

Resist the temptation. You may be familiar with Windows- or Mac-style software, but the CAT program, like every other, has its small peculiarities of appearance and procedure. Take all the time you need to become fully comfortable with it before the test begins. It would be a shame to lose points on your GMAT CAT score because you hastily clicked the wrong button due to a misunderstanding or memory lapse.

2. Use Scrap Paper Freely

The test administrator should provide you with a small batch of scrap paper at the start of the test. You'll be warned that you may not carry this paper out of the center; ETS doesn't want students to copy the questions down and circulate them among future test-takers. However, you can and should use this paper freely during the exam. In fact, working back and forth between the monitor, the mouse, and your scrap paper is one of the key skills you'll need to use when you take the GMAT CAT.

In Chapters 4 through 9 of this book, we explain test-taking strategies for each question type that appears on the GMAT CAT. In those chapters, whenever we refer to making notes or sketches or jotting down information, we are talking about using your scrap paper. Here are some specific ways you should expect to use the scrap paper during the CAT.

- Briefly outline each long reading passage on the Verbal section, using key words and phrases to summarize the main ideas (see Chapter 4 for details).
- Perform all necessary math calculations during the Quantitative section (Chapters 7 and 8).
- Copy the diagrams that accompany geometry problems from the Quantitative section and add to or modify these as you develop new information based on the data provided (Chapters 7 and 8). If no diagram is provided, sketch your own.
- Create a simple outline for each of the essays you'll write for the Analytical Writing Assessment (Chapter 9).

As you can see, you may need a large amount of scrap paper. Use the short break between sections to ask the test administrator for more paper; the supply is unlimited, and there's no reason to take a chance on running out.

The Most Important Warnings

Guess Selectively

If you are faced with a question you can't answer, guess. Use elimination to rule out any answers you know or suspect are wrong, and then follow your best hunch in choosing from among the remaining answers. You *must* select an answer before you'll be allowed to move on to the next item, so obviously you have no option—you must guess.

Don't guess at random. Instead, take the time to examine each item. Eliminate answers that are clearly wrong; guesstimate, work backward from individual answer choices, experiment with possible solutions, and use any other techniques you know to try to zero in on a correct answer. (Many such techniques are covered in Chapters 4 through 8 of this book.) Only when you've picked the right answer, or narrowed the possible choices to two, should you choose and confirm an answer.

You'll help your score in the final moments more by approaching the last few questions carefully and thoughtfully than by rushing to select any old answer.

Remember—The Clock Never Stops

Once you begin work on a test section, the computer begins counting down the allotted time for that section. Time remaining appears on the upper left-hand corner of your screen, unless you choose to remove that number by clicking the Time box at the bottom.

Be aware that *nothing* that you or the test administrator can do will stop or slow the ticking of the software's internal clock. Removing the time indication from the screen, visiting the rest room or getting a drink of water, requesting extra scrap paper, opening the Help screen to refresh your memory about techniques for using the software—none of these has any effect on the inexorable march of time.

The point is obvious: don't waste your testing time on any of these activities. Instead, use the five-minute breaks between sections for any housekeeping you must do. If you're efficient (and if you make a pit stop *before* beginning work), those pauses will suffice.

Taming the CAT?

Having read this chapter, you know a lot about computer-adaptive testing as well as about the test-taking strategies that are necessary to score your highest on the GMAT CAT.

As advocates for test takers, we regret the demise of the paper-and-pencil exam. In part, this is for personal reasons: unfortunately, some of the test-taking strategies we've developed and taught through the years that rely on paper-and-pencil methods will have to be scrapped.

On the other hand, the CAT offers a host of opportunities for new strategies, which will keep us busy for years to come. So our work in helping students earn higher scores on the GMAT CAT won't really be dramatically affected by the change.

No, our regret over the passing of the paper-and-pencil text is really due to one fact:

> *On the paper-and-pencil exam, the student is (largely) in control. On the CAT, the software is in control.*

Earlier in this chapter, we explained some of the reasons the test makers love the CAT. Here's another, which may be the crucial factor: *For control freaks like the folks at ETS, computer-adaptive testing is a true joy.*

- The CAT replaces the familiar test booklet, which the student can flip through (section by section) at will, with a "black box" that presents only one question at a time, selected by a mysterious process that is completely hidden from the student.

- It supposedly tailors the test to the skills of the individual, creating the specter (a false one, of course) of a machine that can "read the mind" of the student.

- It forces the test taker to answer questions as presented, precluding the possibility of revisiting items, tackling questions in any preferred sequence, or changing his or her mind on later reflection.

FYI

Use the pauses between sections for a quick relaxation break. It will increase your alertness and efficiency as you start work on each new topic. We explain how in Chapter 11.

- And it eliminates—at least under current law—the test disclosure rules that have forced the test makers to make most past exams publicly available for scrutiny and criticism.

All of these changes, intentional or not, have the same psychological impact: they put the test taker in a one-down position, forced to respond passively to the agenda of a machine rather than actively managing the test-taking process. For a student who is computer illiterate or uncomfortable with machines, that effect is heightened.

As you can see, we're not fans of computer-adaptive testing. For now, however, it is the wave of the future. And there is no reason why you can't score high on the GMAT CAT if you prepare for it in a savvy fashion.

In the chapters that follow, we'll examine each of the question types that are used on every form of the GMAT CAT, and you'll learn test-taking strategies that will help you conquer each one.

JUST THE FACTS

- Every GMAT test taker must now cope with the new Computer-Adaptive Test (GMAT CAT).

- You need to master both the mechanics and the special strategy of computerized testing before taking the GMAT CAT.

- Above all, aim to answer the first five questions of each GMAT CAT section correctly; they're crucial to your score.

- Use scrap paper freely to solve problems, take notes, and otherwise assist you in tackling test items.

- When you're not sure about the answer to a question, eliminate as many answers as possible and then guess, following your best hunch.

Chapter 4

Reading Comprehension

Get the Scoop On . . .

- How the three-stage reading method can help you get more questions right
- How to separate main ideas from supporting details
- How to recognize the vital connections among ideas in the passages
- Why you should read with pencil in hand
- The kinds of deceptive wrong answers the test makers love to use—and how to avoid them

THE TEST CAPSULE

What's the Big Idea?

In reading comprehension, you'll be given a passage to read, that will read like an excerpt from a serious discussion of a topic from the natural sciences, the social sciences, or a business-related field. You'll then have to answer a group of questions about the passage, testing how well you've understood its content.

How Many?

Your GMAT CAT will probably have a total of 13 or 14 reading comprehension questions out of 41 total verbal questions.

How Much Do They Count?

Reading comprehension questions are 22 out of 76 total verbal questions. They count as 34 percent of your overall Verbal score.

How Much Time Should They Take?

You should spend about one minute per question on any group of reading passages. For example, when you tackle a passage with a total of 4 questions, plan to spend 4–5 minutes on the entire set. Expect to spend about half of that time on reading, the other half on answering the questions.

What's the Best Strategy?

Use the *three-stage method* when reading passages: previewing, reading, reviewing. With this approach, you'll gather much more information from the passage than with conventional one-step reading, and you'll be able to answer the questions that follow faster and more correctly.

What's the Worst Pitfall?

The worst pitfall is choosing answers merely because they sound familiar or are factually true. The answers you pick must not only be plausible and true but must also relate directly to the question and be drawn from the most relevant portion of the passage.

THE OFFICIAL DESCRIPTION

What They Are

Reading on the GMAT CAT involves two steps. The first step is to read a passage of nonfiction prose, usually between 150 and 350 words long, that may deal with almost any subject from the natural sciences, the social sciences, and business. The second step is to answer a group of 3 to 9 questions dealing with the content, form, and style of the passage.

Where They Are

In the typical GMAT CAT, you'll have a 75-minute Verbal section with a total of about 41 questions. Reading comprehension is one of the three types of questions that will appear in this section, intermingled in a seemingly random sequence. Reminder: the test makers claim the right to change the format at any time! However, the typical format we just described is what you're most likely to encounter.

What They Measure

Reading comprehension is designed to measure your ability to handle the various kinds of sophisticated, complex, and subtle reading that graduate business students are called upon to do. In order to answer the questions, it's not enough to understand the basic facts presented in the passage; you also need to notice the more elusive *implications* in the passage (that is, ideas that are suggested rather than directly stated) as well as the *form, structure, and style* of the passage (that is, how the author has chosen to present her ideas).

What They Cover

GMAT CAT reading passages consist of edited excerpts from scholarly or serious nonfiction-fiction books about almost any subject from the natural sciences (chemistry, biology, physics, geology, astronomy), the social sciences (history, sociology, psychology, anthropology), and the humanities (literature, art, music, architecture, philosophy). The four passages you'll probably be given on your GMAT CAT will normally include one passage from each category plus a second passage from one category that is quite different in style and approach from the other passage in that category. For example, if two natural science passages are presented, one may be a detailed account of a particular experiment and its ramifications, while the other is a description of the philosophical implications of the work of a certain scientist.

The Directions

Directions: The questions in this group are based on the content of a passage. After reading the passage, choose the best answer to each question. Answer all questions following the passage on the basis of what is *stated* or *implied* in the passage.

THE INSIDER'S REPORT: STRATEGIES THAT REALLY WORK

Read Each Passage in Three Stages: Previewing, Reading, Reviewing

FYI

If previewing quickly is a problem for you, try this: Sweep your index finger in a single, steady motion down the passage, taking about 30 seconds to scan the whole thing. Let your eyes follow your traveling finger as a guide. This will force you to keep moving as you preview rather than getting stuck with reading a sentence or paragraph that catches your attention.

Reading comprehension on the GMAT CAT poses a special time-management problem. Unlike the other verbal question types, reading comprehension requires you to spend a large chunk of time doing something *before* you look at the questions—namely, reading the passage itself. Under the circumstances, with time pressure a real concern for most students, it's easy to get impatient. The temptation to rush through the passage in your haste to start filling in answers may be very great.

Don't do it! Unless you invest some time in getting to know the passage well, your chances of answering most of the questions correctly are pretty slim. In fact, we'll go further. We'll recommend that you spend *more time* reading the passages than you normally would. Whereas most people ordinarily read anything once and once only, we suggest that you read (or at least scan) each passage on the GMAT CAT *three* times before answering a single question.

We have good reasons for this recommendation. The three-stage reading method is a proven technique long taught and used by skilled readers as the best way of getting the most possible information out of anything in writing. Paradoxically, you'll find—we can virtually guarantee it—that if you practice the three-stage method, you'll soon find that you're gathering more information out of what you read *more quickly than ever before.*

Here's how the three-stage method works.

- **Previewing:** First, preview the passage in one of two ways. You can skim its contents by letting your eyes quickly scroll down the screen, picking up as much information as you can. Or you can actually read selected sentences from the passage: specifically, the *first* sentence of each paragraph in the passage and the *last* sentence of the entire passage. Either of these methods works well; we suggest you experiment with both and choose the one you prefer.

  What's the point of previewing? It's to give you some idea of what the passage is about and, generally, how it is organized, before you actually read it. Think about it: when you know, in general, what a teacher will be teaching, don't you find it easier to understand and absorb the lesson? (Educational researchers have proven it's true.) The same idea applies here: if you know generally what the passage is about before reading it, you'll understand it better.

  Don't spend long on previewing. On the average GMAT CAT reading passage, this stage should take about 30 seconds. Practice with a watch until you get a feel for it.

- **Reading:** Having previewed the passage, go ahead and read it through, more or less in the conventional way. (Actually, we'll be suggesting some special reading techniques for this stage in a moment, but for now, just think of stage two as the familiar reading process you've always done.)

- **Reviewing:** The third stage involves scanning the passage one more time, reminding yourself of its main ideas, most important details, and overall structure. Like previewing, this should be a fast process—spend no more than 30 seconds reviewing an average GMAT CAT passage.

  Why bother with reviewing? There are three main reasons. First, by the time you finish reading a complex, subtle, or confusing GMAT CAT passage, you may find that you don't really remember how the passage began. Reviewing refreshes your memory of the structure of the entire passage, making it easier for you to "hold it in mind" as a unit.

  Second, reviewing can help you to understand the earlier parts of the passage better than you did when you first read them. Quite often, a point made in the first or second paragraph isn't fully explained until the third or fourth paragraph. Reviewing the whole thing ties together loose ends that otherwise might have remained slightly confusing.

  Third, reviewing helps you remember which topics are discussed in which parts of the passage. This will make it easier when you need a specific detail to answer a question. Rather than scanning the whole passage, you'll probably be able to zero in on the right paragraph quickly.

Here's how the timing of the three-stage method works. Let's say the reading passage is 350 words long (toward the high end for GMAT CAT passages). The average student reads about 250 words per minute. So the three stages would take a total of two and a half minutes:

Stage Number	Stage	Time
Stage 1	Previewing	½ minute
Stage 2	Reading	1½ minutes
Stage 3	Reviewing	½ minute
Total time		2½ minutes

You'll spend about the same amount of time on the questions that follow the passage, making a total of 5 minutes for the passage and questions. On the exam, you'll find that this kind of timing works well and will leave you with ample time for the other verbal questions in the section.

Focus on Big Ideas, Not Little Details

Almost everything you read—on the GMAT CAT or elsewhere—can be broken down into two kinds of information: *main ideas* and *supporting details*. It's important to distinguish between the two when reading for the exam. The main ideas are worth focusing on; the supporting details are usually not.

How can you recognize the main ideas in a passage? There are several clues to look for.

- Main ideas tend to be broad and general; supporting details tend to be narrow and specific.

- Often, each paragraph of a passage is centered on a single main idea that is explicitly stated somewhere in the paragraph.

- The main idea often appears first or last in the paragraph; supporting details usually appear in the middle of the paragraph.

Consider the following example. It's a paragraph excerpted from a reading passage on an actual exam.

The myth of the infallible scientist evaporates when one thinks about the number of great ideas in science whose originators were correct in general but wrong in detail. The English physicist John Dalton (1766–1844) gets credit for modern atomic theory, but his mathematical formulas for

FYI

The birth and death dates given for John Dalton in the passage about the mistakes made by scientists are a classic example of the kind of insignificant details reading passages contain. Don't waste energy trying to remember those dates. In the unlikely event that there's a question about them, you can find them in a flash.

calculating atomic weights were incorrect. The Polish astronomer Copernicus, who corrected Ptolemy's ancient concept of an Earth-centered universe, nevertheless was mistaken in the particulars of the planets' orbits.

There are three sentences in this paragraph. Of the three, which one expresses a broad, general idea rather than a narrow, specific detail? The answer: the first sentence. It makes a general point—that scientists, even great ones, are not infallible. The second and third sentences give details to support and explain this idea. The second sentence describes the example of John Dalton, and the third sentence adds the example of Copernicus. Both are interesting and help to clarify the overall theme, but neither is as important as the first sentence, which states the author's main point.

Here's another real example:

> "Popular art" has a number of meanings, impossible to define with any precision, which range from folklore to junk. The poles are clear enough, but the middle tends to blur. The Hollywood Western of the 1930s, for example, has elements of folklore but is closer to junk than to high art or folk art. There can be great trash, just as there is bad high art. The musicals of George Gershwin are great popular art, never aspiring to high art. Schubert and Brahms, however, used elements of popular music—folk themes—in works clearly intended as high art. The case of Verdi is a different one: he took a popular genre—bourgeois melodrama set to music (an accurate definition of nineteenth-century opera)—and, without altering its fundamental nature, transmuted it into high art. This remains one of the greatest achievements in music, and one that cannot be fully appreciated without recognizing the essential trashiness of the genre.

This paragraph starts with a broad, general idea—that "popular art" has a number of meanings. The next five sentences give a series of examples to illustrate this idea—Hollywood Westerns and the works of Gershwin, Schubert, and Brahms.

Then we see a shift. The author signals us, in the next sentence, that Verdi will be considered as more than just another example of the use of elements of popular art ("The case of Verdi is a different one"). He devotes the next two sentences to explaining what is unique about Verdi, and, in fact, the rest of the passage deals exclusively with Verdi. (A glance at the remaining paragraphs makes this obvious; just run your eye down the screen, and a host of capital Vs jump out at you!)

This paragraph is almost *two* paragraphs in one. The first half of the paragraph deals with various definitions of popular art and offers a number of examples—none of them very important in themselves, but they illustrate the ways popular art can be used by "fine" artists. All of this helps to introduce the *real* topic of the passage, which is Verdi's use of popular motifs and forms in his great operatic works. The second half of the paragraph (starting with "The case of Verdi") makes the transition into this idea.

In this paragraph, as in the paragraph about the "infallible scientist," the details are interesting, they certainly add to the experience of reading the passage, and they help make the author's point vivid and understandable. *But the details are of secondary importance.* Don't spend a lot of time struggling to understand the details of a passage if they are tricky, and certainly don't try to memorize them. Instead, read them quickly, and make a mental note of where they are in case a question is asked about them. *It probably won't happen.*

Look for the Connections Among the Parts of the Passage

Some students wonder whether they should learn "speed-reading" to improve their GMAT CAT performance. For most students, this is unnecessary. If you can read at an average rate of 250 words per minute, as most college students do, you'll have plenty of time for the passages on the exam.

Think of a reading passage as a *structure of ideas.* Most passages are devoted to conveying a number of ideas that are connected to one another in some way. If you understand these ideas *and* the connections among them, you truly understand the passage as a whole.

Quite often, the structure of ideas will be made very explicit, even obvious. Consider, for example, a reading passage that contains five paragraphs that begin with the following five sentences:

(1) Historians have long debated the reasons for the defeat of the Confederacy in the American Civil War.

(2) For decades, the dominant theory held that the North's victory was due primarily to the superior economic resources available to the Union armies.

(3) A second school of historians pointed instead to the geographic advantages enjoyed by the Northern generals.

(4) In recent years, however, more and more historians have begun to claim that, contrary to traditional Southern belief, the Northern generalship was consistently superior.

(5) In the end, perhaps the most likely explanation of the Northern victory is that it was caused by a combination of several factors.

By simply reading these five sentences, you can get a very good idea of the content and structure of the whole passage. The passage deals with the issue of why the North won the Civil War. Its structure is clear. Paragraph (1) sets forth the question to be discussed. Paragraphs (2), (3), and (4) each suggest a different answer to the question. And paragraph (5) concludes the passage by suggesting a possible resolution of the disagreement.

Why is it helpful to recognize the logical structure of a reading passage? It helps you in several ways.

- It makes it easy to see the main ideas of the passage. In this case, the main ideas are the three separate theories being presented and discussed.

- It tells you the *purpose* of the supporting details—even when you don't know what those details are. In this passage, for example, we've looked at only the first sentence of paragraph (2). Nonetheless, we can easily imagine what kind of supporting details will be given in the rest of the paragraph. The missing sentences will probably give examples of the superior economic resources enjoyed by the North (coal mines, factories, or railroad lines, for instance).

  If, in reading the complete passage, the actual details turned out to be complex or tricky, that would be okay. We'd still understand their purpose and basic thrust, even if the fine points were elusive. In most cases, that would be enough to answer any questions.

- The logical structure *organizes* all of the information in the passage, making it easy to locate any detail that may appear in a question. In this passage, if a question focuses on some detail that is related to the third of the three theories (Northern generalship), you'll be able to find the relevant paragraph quickly.

- The structure explains how the main ideas are related to one another. In this case, the main ideas are three different, conflicting explanations of the same historical event. One or more questions are likely to focus on the relationships among these ideas; for example, how they differ from one another, and why the earlier theories have been superseded by later ones.

GMAT CAT passages don't always boast such clear-cut, logical structures, but a structure of some kind is usually present. With practice, you can learn to recognize it.

Table 4.1 will help. It lists several of the most common types of logical structures found in GMAT CAT reading passages. Either alone or in combination, these structures underlie many of the passages you'll encounter on the exam. Practice looking for them whenever you read.

Make Notes on the Passage as You Read

When tackling reading comprehension on the GMAT CAT, read with your pencil in hand. Use it to note key points and logical connections as you find them by jotting a brief outline of the passage on your scrap paper.

Table 4.1
Types of Logical Structures Often Used in
GMAT CAT Reading Passages

1. Several theories or approaches to a single question or topic (often one theory or approach per paragraph)
2. One theory or idea illustrated with several detailed examples or illustrations (often one example or illustration per paragraph)
3. One theory or idea supported by several arguments (often one argument per paragraph)
4. Pro-and-con arguments presented on both sides of a single issue
5. A comparison or contrast between two events, ideas, phenomena, or people
6. A cause-and-effect sequence showing how one event led to another (presented either in chronological order or via "flashback," with later events named *before* the earlier ones)

This will help you in two ways: the physical act of noting particular words and phrases will strengthen your memory of the ideas you've highlighted, and the rudimentary outline you create will make it easier to find key parts of the passage if you need to locate them later.

Here are some specific suggestions about what to look for and note as you read.

■ **Look for the main idea of the passage as a whole.** This is one sentence that summarizes the central theme of the passage. Most passages contain such a sentence. It often appears near the beginning of the passage to introduce the key idea; in other cases, it appears near the end, as a kind of summary or conclusion. When you find it, jot down a few words that sum it up on your scrap paper outline.

■ **Look for the main idea of each paragraph.** Remember the idea of the topic sentence? You may have had a high school English teacher who taught you to include one in every paragraph you write. GMAT CAT paragraphs often contain such a sentence, which summarizes the central point of the paragraph. When you find one, jot down a couple words from it on your scrap paper.

■ **Look for the logical structure of the passage, and record it on your scrap paper in any appropriate style.** For example, if a passage is organized as a pro-and-con presentation of arguments on both sides of an issue, summarize each argument with the word pro or con alongside of it. If a passage presents a series of historical events by showing how one led to the next, jot the date of each key event and number the events in sequence—1, 2, 3, and so on.

Practice making notes on reading passages each time you work on critical reading between now and the day of the test.

The truth is, the *process* of making notes about the passage is more important than the marks themselves. It encourages an active approach to reading as opposed to a passive one. Using this as part of the three-stage reading method will help you delve more deeply into the meaning of a passage than you ever did with conventional ways of reading.

Keep your notes simple and very brief; only you need to understand them and only for the next few minutes. For example, for the passage we discussed above that dealt with the American Civil War, the paragraphs might be summarized with these key words:

- reason South lost?
- Northern economy
- N. geography
- maybe better generals?
- combination

These notes will help you remember the structure and main ideas of the passage, and they'll help you find key details when they're needed to answer a question.

THE INSIDER'S REPORT: THE BEST TIPS

Try Previewing the First Question Stems Along with the Passage

Remember, the question stem is the part of the question that precedes the answer choices: "The author of the passage includes the details concerning the funding of the Tennessee Valley Authority primarily in order to emphasize . . ." would be an example of a question stem.

By previewing the stem, some students feel they get an advance look at the main themes of the passage and one of the details the test makers plan to focus on. Other students, however, find this strategy more time-consuming than useful. Our recommendation: try this technique a couple of times and decide whether you find it helpful. If you do, use it.

Refer Back to the Passage as Often as You Need to

Most questions will focus on a particular paragraph or sentence of the passage. Many of the questions will contain explicit references to specific line numbers in the passage; others will simply mention particular details and expect you to locate them.

When this happens, you'll usually need to look back at the passage to answer the question correctly. Don't try to answer from memory. Quite often, the wrong answer choices will be *subtly* wrong; only a careful review of the specific detail that is being asked about will enable you to see which answer is correct and why the others are not.

THE INSIDER'S REPORT: THE MOST IMPORTANT WARNINGS

Don't Pick the First Answer Choice That Sounds Good

On all verbal questions, there are *degrees* of right and wrong. (In contrast, on math questions, correctness is much more black and white: if the right answer to a math problem is 16, then the answer 13 isn't "partially right" or "arguably right," it's just plain *wrong*.)

The grayness of verbal answer choices is especially noticeable on reading comprehension questions. The test makers are highly skilled at crafting wrong answer choices (distractors) that are plausible and attractive. So if you begin reading the answers to a reading comprehension question and find that choice (A) sounds good, *don't* just immediately select it. Read on. Choice (C) may sound even better, and choice (E) may be best of all. You always have to read all five answers to a reading comprehension item before making your choice.

Don't Pick an Answer Just Because it Sounds Familiar

One popular trick used by ETS in crafting distractors is to draw the information for wrong answers from the passage itself. This makes for distractors that are especially tempting because they sound (and are) familiar. Your reaction may be, "Oh, yes, it says that right here in paragraph 2. This must be the right answer."

Such reasoning may be flawed. The correct answer for the particular question may be found in paragraph 4, and paragraph 2 may simply be irrelevant. Don't fall for this.

The best way to avoid this trap is to refer back to the portion of the passage that is being asked about before you pick an answer. Make sure the answer you choose comes from *there*, not from some other part of the passage.

Don't Pick an Answer Just Because It's True

Most of the passages you'll read on the GMAT CAT will be about topics you know only a little about. That's okay. The test makers don't expect you to have any background knowledge, and none is needed to answer the questions.

Occasionally, however, you may encounter a passage on a topic you're familiar with. It may even be a topic you are fascinated by. This can be helpful—reading about something you like and care about is fun, and you'll probably find the passage easy to understand.

However, this situation can also be dangerous. The danger lies in bringing your own outside knowledge and opinions to the questions. You may be tempted to pick an answer choice because you happen to know it's true, or because you personally agree with it. Those aren't good reasons. The correct answer must be based specifically on the information in the passage, and it must reflect accurately the opinions and ideas expressed there—even if you happen to disagree with them.

So set aside your own knowledge and beliefs when reading a passage on a topic you care about. Pick answers based solely on what you find in the passage—not on anything else you happen to know.

JUST THE FACTS

- Use the three-stage method—previewing, reading, reviewing—to get the most out of every passage on the GMAT CAT.

- As you read, look for the main ideas in the passage and the connections among them.

- Read with pencil in hand and make notes about the main ideas and the structure of the passage on scrap paper.

- Learn the most common types of wrong answers used by the test makers and how to avoid choosing them.

PRACTICE, PRACTICE, PRACTICE: READING COMPREHENSION EXERCISES

Instructions

The following exercises will give you a chance to practice the skills and strategies you've just learned for tackling critical reading questions. As with all practice exercises, work under true testing conditions. Complete each exercise in a single sitting. Eliminate distractions (TV, music) and clear away notes and reference materials. Time yourself with a stopwatch or kitchen timer, or have someone else time you. If you run out of time before you answer all of the questions, stop and draw a line under the last question you finished. Then go ahead and tackle the remaining questions. When you are done, score yourself based only on the questions you finished in the allotted time.

Record your response by blackening the circle next to the answer of your choice.

Understanding Your Scores

- **0–2 correct:** A poor performance. Study this chapter again, and (if you haven't already), begin spending time each day on building your vocabulary using the Insider's GMAT CAT Word List in Appendix A.

- **3–4 correct:** A below-average score. Study this chapter again, focusing especially on the skills and strategies you've found to be the newest and most challenging.

- **5–7 correct:** An average score. You may want to study this chapter again. Also, be sure you are managing your time wisely (as explained in Chapter 3) and avoiding errors due to haste or carelessness.

- **8–9 correct:** An above-average score. Depending on your personal target score and your strength on other verbal question types, you may or may not want to devote additional time to reading comprehension.

- **10–11 correct:** An excellent score. You are probably ready to perform well on GMAT CAT reading comprehension questions.

EXERCISE 1

11 Questions

Time—15 Minutes

> **Directions (Reading Comprehension):** The questions in this group are based on the content of a passage. After reading the passage, choose the best answer to each question. Answer all questions following the passage on the basis of what is *stated* or *implied* in the passage.

Questions 1–5 are based on the following passage.

Line   The delegates to the Constitutional Convention were realists. They knew that the greatest battles would follow the convention itself. The delegates had overstepped their bounds. Instead of amending the Articles of Confederation by which the American states had previously been governed, they had proposed an
(5)   entirely new government. Under these circumstances, the convention was understandably reluctant to submit its work to the Congress for approval.

Instead, the delegates decided to pursue what amounted to a revolutionary course. They declared that ratification of the new Constitution by nine states would be sufficient to establish the new government. In other words, the
(10)   Constitution was being submitted directly to the people. Not even the Congress, which had called the convention, would be asked to approve its work.

The leaders of the convention shrewdly wished to bypass the state legislatures, which were attached to states' rights and which required, in most cases, the agreement of two houses. For speedy ratification of the Constitution,
(15)   the single-chambered, specially elected state ratifying conventions offered the greatest promise of agreement.

Battle lines were quickly drawn. The Federalists, as the supporters of the Constitution were called, had one solid advantage: they came with a concrete proposal. Their opponents, the Antifederalists, came with none. Since the
(20)   Antifederalists were opposing something with nothing, their objections, though sincere, were basically negative. They stood for a policy of drift while the Federalists were providing clear leadership.

Furthermore, although the Antifederalists claimed to be the democratic group, their opposition to the Constitution did not necessarily spring from a
(25)   more democratic view of government. Many of the Antifederalists were as distrustful of the common people as their opponents. In New York, for example, Governor George Clinton criticized the people for their fickleness and their tendency to "vibrate from one extreme to another." Elbridge Gerry, who refused to sign the Constitution, asserted that "the evils we experience flow from the
(30)   excess of democracy," and John F. Mercer of Maryland professed little faith in his neighbors as voters when he said that "the people cannot know and judge the character of candidates."

1. The best title for the passage would be
   (A) The U.S. Constitution: Its Strengths and Weaknesses
   (B) The Battle for Ratification of the Constitution
   (C) Divided Leadership at the Constitutional Convention
   (D) The Views of the Antifederalists on Democracy
   (E) How the Constitution Became Law

2. According to the passage, the delegates to the Constitutional Convention did not submit their work to Congress for approval because
   (A) they believed that Congress would not accept the sweeping changes they had proposed.
   (B) they knew that most members of Congress gave little weight to the concept of states' rights.
   (C) it was unclear whether Congress had the legal right to offer or withhold such approval.
   (D) they considered it more democratic to appeal directly to the citizens of the separate states.
   (E) Congress was dominated by a powerful group of Antifederalist leaders.

3. In stating that the Antifederalists "were opposing something with nothing" (line 20), the author suggests that the Antifederalists
   (A) based most of their arguments on their antidemocratic sentiments.
   (B) lacked leaders who were as articulate as the Federalist leaders.
   (C) were unable to rally significant support for their position among the populace.
   (D) had few reasonable arguments to put forth in support of their position.
   (E) offered no alternative plan of government of their own.

4. The words of John F. Mercer are quoted in lines 31–32 primarily to illustrate
   (A) the antidemocratic sentiments of some Antifederalist spokesmen.
   (B) the concern for states' rights shared by most leaders from the smaller states.
   (C) some of the weaknesses of the plan of government proposed by the Federalists.
   (D) the "policy of drift" advocated by the Antifederalists.
   (E) the kinds of arguments to which the Federalists were forced to reply.

5. The author implies that, by comparison with the position of the Antifederalists, the position of the Federalists was which of the following?

    I.   More decisive
   II.   More democratic
  III.   More sincere

(A) I only
(B) I and II only
(C) I and III only
(D) II and III only
(E) I, II, and III

Questions 6–11 are based on the following passage.

Line Although Alfred Wegener was not the first scientist to propose the idea that the continents have moved, his 1912 outline of the hypothesis was the first detailed description of the concept and the first to offer a respectable mass of supporting evidence for it. It is appropriate, then, that the theory of continental drift was
(5) most widely known as "Wegener's hypothesis" during the more than fifty years of debate that preceded its ultimate acceptance by most earth scientists.

    In brief, Wegener's hypothesis stated that, in the late Paleozoic era, all of the present-day continents were part of a single giant land mass, Pangaea, that occupied almost half of the earth's surface. About 40 million years ago, Pangaea
(10) began to break into fragments that slowly moved apart, ultimately forming the various continents we know today.

    Wegener supported his argument with data drawn from geology, paleontology, zoology, climatology, and other fields. So impressive was his array of evidence that his hypothesis could not be ignored. However, until the 1960s,
(15) most scientists were reluctant to accept Wegener's ideas. There are several reasons why this was so.

    First, although Wegener showed that continental movement was consistent with much of the geological and other evidence—for example, the apparent family relationships among forms of plants and animals now separated by vast
(20) expanses of ocean, once geographically united on the hypothetical Pangaea—he failed to suggest any causal mechanism for continental drift sufficiently powerful and plausible to be convincing.

    Second, while the period during which Wegener's theory was propounded and debated saw rapid developments in many branches of geology and an
(25) explosion of new knowledge about the nature of the earth and the forces at work in its formation, little of this evidence seemed to support Wegener. For example, data drawn from the new science of seismology, including experimental studies of the behavior of rocks under high pressure, suggested that the earth has far too much internal strength and rigidity to allow continents to "drift" across its
(30) surface. Measurements of the earth's gravitational field made by some of the early scientific satellites offered further evidence in support of this view as late as the early 1960s.

    Third, and perhaps most significant, Wegener's theory seemed to challenge one of the most deeply-held philosophical bases of geology—the
(35) doctrine of uniformitarianism, which states that Earth history must always be explained by the operation of essentially unchanging, continuous forces. Belief

in the intervention of unexplained, sporadic, and massive shaping events—known as catastrophism—was considered beyond the pale by mainstream geologists.

(40)   Wegener was not, strictly speaking, a catastrophist—he did not suggest that some massive cataclysm had triggered the breakup of Pangaea—but his theory did imply a dramatic change in the face of the Earth occurring relatively late in geologic history. Such a belief, viewed as tainted with catastrophism, was abhorrent to most geologists throughout the first half of this century.

6. According to the passage, Wegener believed that Pangaea

(A) was destroyed in a massive cataclysm occurring about 40 million years ago.

(B) consisted of several large land areas separated by vast expanses of ocean.

(C) was ultimately submerged by rising oceans at the end of the Paleozoic era.

(D) has gradually drifted from its original location into its current position.

(E) contained in a single land mass the basic material of all the continents that exist today.

7. It can be inferred from the passage that, by the end of the Paleozoic era,

(A) early human beings existed on earth.

(B) many forms of plant and animal life existed on earth.

(C) the land mass of Pangaea no longer existed.

(D) a series of unexplained catastrophes had changed the face of the earth.

(E) most of today's land forms had taken their current shape.

8. The passage provides information to answer which of the following questions?

I.   What geological forces caused the breakup of Pangaea?

II.   What evidence discovered in the 1960s lent support to Wegener's hypothesis?

III. When did Wegener's hypothesis win acceptance by most earth scientists?

(A) I only

(B) II only

(C) III only

(D) I and III only

(E) II and III only

9. The passage implies that the most significant reason for the opposition to Wegener's hypothesis on the part of many scientists was its

    (A) indirect challenge to a fundamental premise of geology.
    (B) lack of supporting evidence from fields other than geology.
    (C) impossibility of being tested by experimental means.
    (D) conflict with data drawn from the fossil record.
    (E) failure to provide a comprehensive framework for Earth history.

10. The author refers to the scientific information gathered by satellites in order to suggest the

    (A) philosophical changes that ultimately led to the acceptance of Wegener's hypothesis.
    (B) dramatic advances in Earth science during the 1960s.
    (C) differing directions taken by various Earth scientists in the decades following Wegener.
    (D) nature of the some of the evidence that appeared to refute Wegener.
    (E) need for experimental demonstration before any new geological theory can be accepted.

11. It can be inferred from the passage that the ultimate acceptance of Wegener's hypothesis by most geologists could not have occurred unless

    (A) the catastrophic event that destroyed Pangaea had been conclusively demonstrated.
    (B) Wegener had renounced his efforts to attack the doctrine of uniformitarianism.
    (C) uniformitarianism had been shown to be demonstrably false.
    (D) the general bias against catastrophism had moderated.
    (E) the empirical evidence in its favor had been uniform and overwhelming.

EXERCISE 2

11 Questions

Time—15 Minutes

> **Directions:** The questions in this group are based on the content of a passage. After reading the passage, choose the best answer to each question. Answer all questions following the passage on the basis of what is *stated* or *implied* in the passage.

Questions 1–4 are based on the following passage.

(The following passage was written in 1985.)

Line   The steady increase in world population complicates the problems of food production and distribution and the encouragement of self-reliance. The time to deal with world hunger, therefore, is now.

(5)   The time may have arrived when government development agencies, scientists, agronomists, construction engineers, and—yes—bankers need to borrow the environmentalists' slogan, "Small is beautiful." This means a toning down of the emphasis on grandiose development projects—vast irrigation schemes, power dams, new industrial establishments, and huge loans for "economic growth" or food imports by the poorest nations.

(10)   Instead, there would be a turn toward simpler but probably politically less popular approaches to world hunger and more emphasis on helping the hungry help themselves. World Bank economist Mahbub ul Haq says, bluntly, "The only convincing solution to the problem of world hunger is for the developing countries to grow their own food. What the poor and hungry need are

(15)   permanent incomes, not temporary handouts."

It remains to be seen whether donor countries will willingly forego continuation of the massive contributions bestowed ostensibly for the poor in the past, but with so little helpful impact. A new approach could include a decision by the United States to curtail its present gifts and subsidized exports

(20)   of surplus foodstuffs except in natural disasters or famine—a politically difficult move, since such gifts and exports are extremely popular with American agricultural interests.

It will be equally difficult to persuade private and public financial institutions to restrain their eagerness to extend credit (mostly guaranteed by

(25)   U.S. taxpayers) to poor nations, many already in debt. A considerable percentage of these loan dollars eventually purchase industrial world products for middle- or upper-income customers abroad, doing little to assuage hunger.

The same is often true of the Third World branches of plants of wealthy multinational corporations whose products are exported or sold to the affluent.

(30)   When they pay bare subsistence wages or worse, in luring the poor off the land and into city slums in search of nonexistent jobs they aggravate an already bad situation. Simple technology, agricultural extensive services or implements, with the requirement that they reach the poor, could be much more helpful. Underdeveloped societies must work out for themselves other urgent

(35) reforms—more equitable distribution of land and access to water, effective control of corrupt marketing practices, and an end to the exploitation of labor.

Finally, and perhaps most difficult, means must be found to make it contrary to anyone's interest to keep others poor. Movement in this direction may occur only as the Earth's resources become more scarce, population *(40)* pressures increase, and the starving become more desperate and articulate.

1. According to the passage, all of the following have a stake in continuing the current forms of aid to hungry nations EXCEPT

    (A) American financial institutions.
    (B) international corporations operating in the Third World.
    (C) upper-income groups in the poverty-stricken countries.
    (D) manufacturers in the industrial nations.
    (E) members of environmentalist groups in the U.S.

2. It can be inferred that the author would be most likely to favor a U.S. aid program to an impoverished nation that included

    (A) the building of a large irrigation system.
    (B) a provision of credit for purchasing consumer goods.
    (C) development of a hydroelectric plant.
    (D) construction of an automobile factory.
    (E) shipments of agricultural tools.

3. The author develops the central idea of the passage primarily by

    (A) attacking the powerful oligarchies that have deliberately perpetuated hunger among Third World peoples.
    (B) contrasting hunger relief programs that have proven effective with those that have proven ineffective.
    (C) listing a series of recommended changes to the current approach to world hunger.
    (D) recounting the history of failed past attempts to alleviate world hunger.
    (E) critically examining arguments for and against the most common approaches to the world hunger crisis.

4. The author's attitude toward future progress in combatting world hunger may best be described as

    (A) encouraging.
    (B) ambiguous.
    (C) enthusiastic.
    (D) coolly objective.
    (E) pessimistic.

Questions 5–11 are based on the following passage.

Line
    In the summer of 1904, the great Russian Empire was, unlike most of the
countries of Europe by that time, still under the control of one man, the
36-year-old Tsar Nicholas II, who had ruled since the death of his father,
Alexander III, ten years before. By many accounts a kind man with a genuine love
(5)   for his country, Nicholas was nevertheless beginning to be pictured as a ruthless
dictator by those who wished to see the empire democratized, and the
complaints of his people were very much in the Tsar's thoughts that summer.
One event, however, took Nicholas' mind away from his political difficulties. On
August 12, he wrote in his diary, "A great, never-to-be-forgotten day when the
(10)   mercy of God has visited us so clearly. Alix gave birth to a son at one o'clock.
The child has been called Alexis."
    Married to Nicholas since 1894, the former Princess Alix of Hesse-
Darmstadt and one of Queen Victoria's numerous grandchildren, the Tsarina
(called Alexandra after her marriage), had given birth to four daughters—Olga,
(15)   Tatiana, Marie, and Anastasia—between 1897 and 1901. But the laws of
succession decreed that only a male could succeed the Tsar, so the birth of
Alexis, which assured the continuation of the 300-year-old Romanov dynasty,
was a cause of great rejoicing for his parents as well as throughout the vast
empire.
(20)   But within a few months it became clear that the apparently healthy child
was not healthy at all—he had hemophilia, a disease he had inherited through
his mother from his great grandmother, Queen Victoria, many of whose other
descendants also had the disease. Hemophilia is a blood disorder in which the
blood not does clot properly. A small, external scratch or cut presents no real
(25)   problem as the bleeding can be stopped relatively quickly, but bumps and
bruises, such as children are prone to, create internal bleeding. This blood, in
turn, gathers in knee and elbow joints, causing excruciating pain and,
sometimes, permanent injury. Once Alexis' diagnosis was confirmed, however, it
was decided that, for the good of the dynasty and the country, the boy's illness
(30)   would remain a family secret. That decision may have changed history.
    Despite his joy at the birth of an heir, Nicholas' political problems
continued. Just a few months later, in January 1905, government troops fired on
a crowd of unarmed petitioners at the Winter Palace in St. Petersburg, killing
over one hundred and wounding hundreds more. This in turn, set off
(35)   countrywide demonstrations against the government. Despite halfhearted
efforts on Nicholas' part to satisfy the dissidents, notably the October Manifesto
of 1905, which converted Russia into a constitutional monarchy with an elected
parliament called the *Duma*, these problems would plague him for another
dozen years.
(40)   In the meantime, in her anguish over her son's illness, Alexandra turned to
religion, and to a newcomer to the Russian court, for help. Grigory Rasputin,
born in Siberia in 1871, was an Eastern Orthodox mystic who had been
introduced to the court by one of the Tsar's numerous relatives. Although it was
well known that he led a dissolute life, he had mesmerizing eyes that captivated
(45)   many of the Tsar's courtiers. More important, he was able—although to this day
no one knows how—to calm the young Alexis when he had hurt himself and,
apparently, to ease his pain considerably. For the Tsarovich's distraught mother,
this was sufficient, and for the rest of their lives Alexandra heeded Rasputin's
advice, both personal and, more important, political.
(50)   For nearly a decade after Alexis' birth, the political situation in Russia
grew worse. Even the great patriotic fervor that greeted the empire's entry into
the First World War took a downturn when the nation's early victories gave

(55) way to progressively greater defeats and the loss of hundreds of thousands of Russian lives. In an effort to stem the tide, Nicholas decided it was his duty to lead the army himself, and in 1915, he left St. Petersburg and took up residence at Army Headquarters, in effect leaving Alexandra to rule the country with Grigory Rasputin at her side.

(60) The increasingly dire situation at the front resulted in a repudiation of the war by many in Russia, which led to even more demonstrations at home by dissidents, most importantly the Bolsheviks, who wanted not a constitutional monarchy but, rather, a fully democratic state answering only to the people. The Tsar and Tsarina came increasingly under personal attack, as did Rasputin. The Russian people, not knowing of the Tsarovich's hemophilia, could not understand why the mystic seemed to have so much power over the imperial (65) family, and both he and Alexandra were much reviled in the press. Rasputin had also made important enemies at court. On December 16, 1916, he was assassinated by three courtiers.

Three months later, on March 15, 1917, the Tsar abdicated his throne, and on November 7th the Bolshevik Revolution brought the communists to power. (70) Less than a year later, on July 29, 1918, Nicholas and his family, including Alexis, who would have been the next Tsar, were executed on orders of Bolshevik authorities at Ekaterinburg in the Ural Mountains, ending the 300-year-old Romanov dynasty.

5. The passage implies that those who in 1904 regarded Nicholas II as a "ruthless dictator" (lines 5–6) primarily objected to

   (A)   the excessive influence of Rasputin over court affairs.
   (B)   his refusal to consider establishment of an elected parliament for Russia.
   (C)   the alliance between the Romanovs and the family of Queen Victoria.
   (D)   his maintenance of an autocratic form of government in Russia.
   (E)   the failure of the Tsar and his wife to produce a male heir to the throne.

6. The author implies that the October Manifesto of 1905 failed to placate those who advocated reform of the Russian government because it was

   (A)   never fully carried out as written into law.
   (B)   unaccompanied by religious, economic, and social changes.
   (C)   undermined by the continuing dictatorial behavior of Nicholas.
   (D)   unable to prevent the onset of the First World War.
   (E)   only a partial step toward the establishment of full democracy.

7. The author implies that the decision of Nicholas to assume personal leadership of the Russian army stemmed mainly from his

    (A) sense of responsibility.
    (B) political desperation.
    (C) inability to trust other leaders.
    (D) growing megalomania.
    (E) fear of popular revolt.

8. The "downturn" mentioned in line 52 refers most directly to

    (A) the growing popular concern over the political power of Rasputin.
    (B) personal attacks on the Tsar and Tsarina in the Russian press.
    (C) national disaffection with Russia's undemocratic form of government.
    (D) the Tsar's distraction from civic duties by his son's illness.
    (E) public dismay over Russian military failures.

9. The author implies that, if the Russian people had known of Rasputin's ability to ease the symptoms of the Tsarovich, they would have

    (A) demanded that Rasputin relinquish his authority over the imperial family.
    (B) insisted that the Romanov dynasty abdicate in favor of a more democratic regime.
    (C) sympathized with the motives of the Tsarina in relying on Rasputin.
    (D) renewed their support of the Tsar and the war effort he was leading.
    (E) been won over to the religious and mystical views Rasputin advocated.

10. It can be inferred from the passage that, during World War I, newspapers in Russia were

    (A) under the strict control of the imperial family and its supporters.
    (B) generally enthusiastic in their support of the war effort.
    (C) relatively free to criticize the government and its actions.
    (D) mainly opposed to the growing pacifism among some elements of Russian society.
    (E) severely restricted by military censors in order to protect state security.

11. The passage suggests that the murder of Rasputin was motivated primarily by
    (A) the growing demand among the Russian populace for true democracy.
    (B) disagreements over religious doctrine.
    (C) hostility in the popular press against both Rasputin and the imperial couple.
    (D) intrigues and jealousies among the Tsar's retinue.
    (E) increasing disaffection with the war among many Russians.

EXERCISE 3

11 Questions

Time—15 Minutes

> **Directions:** The questions in this group are based on the content of a passage. After reading the passage, choose the best answer to each question. Answer all questions following the passage on the basis of what is *stated* or *implied* in the passage.

Questions 1–5 are based on the following passage.

Line   In the early years of the twentieth century, astrophysicists turned their attention to a special category of stars, known as cepheid variables. A variable star is one whose apparent brightness changes from time to time. Among some variables, the change in brightness occurs so slowly as to be almost imperceptible; among
(5)   others, it occurs in sudden, brief, violent bursts of energy. Cepheid variables (which take their name from the constellation Cepheus, where the first such star was discovered) have special characteristics that make them a useful astronomical tool.

It was Henrietta Leavitt, an astronomer at the Harvard Observatory, who
(10)   first examined the cepheid variables in detail. She found that these stars vary regularly in apparent brightness over a relatively short period of time—from one to three days to a month or more. This variation in brightness could be recorded and precisely measured with the help of the camera, then still a new tool in astronomy.

(15)   Leavitt also noticed that the periodicity of each cepheid variable—that is, the period of time it took for the star to vary from its brightest point to its dimmest, and back to its brightest again—corresponded to the intrinsic or absolute brightness of the star. That is, the greater the star's absolute brightness, the slower its cycle of variation.

(20)   Why is this so? The variation in brightness is caused by the interaction between the star's gravity and the outward pressure exerted by the flow of light energy from the star. Gravity pulls the outer portions of the star inward, while light pressure pushes them outward. The result is a pulsating, in-and-out movement that produces increasing and decreasing brightness. The stronger
(25)   the light pressure, the slower this pulsation. Therefore, the periodicity of the cepheid variable is a good indication of its absolute brightness.

Furthermore, it is obvious that the apparent brightness of any source of light decreases the further we are from the light. Physicists had long known that this relationship could be described by a simple mathematical formula, known
(30)   as the inverse square law. If we know the absolute brightness of any object—say, a star—as well as our distance from that object, it is possible to use the inverse square law to determine exactly how bright that object will appear to be.

This laid the background for Leavitt's most crucial insight. As she had discovered, the absolute brightness of a cepheid variable could be determined
(35)   by measuring its periodicity. And, of course, the apparent brightness of the star when observed from the earth could be determined by simple measurement. Leavitt saw that with these two facts and the help of the inverse square law, it

would be possible to determine the distance from Earth of any cepheid variable.
If we know the absolute brightness of the star and how bright it appears from
(40)   the Earth, we can tell how far it must be.
　　　Thus, if a cepheid variable can be found in any galaxy, it is possible to
measure the distance of that galaxy from earth. Thanks to Leavitt's discovery,
astronomical distances that could not previously be measured became
measurable for the first time.

1. The primary purpose of the passage is to explain

　　(A) the background and career of the astronomer Henrietta
　　　　 Leavitt.
　　(B) how and why various categories of stars vary in brightness.
　　(C) the development of the inverse square law for determining
　　　　 an object's brightness.
　　(D) important uses of the camera as an atronomical tool.
　　(E) how a particular method of measuring astronomical dis-
　　　　 tances was created.

2. According to the passage, the absolute brightness of a cepheid
　　variable

　　(A) depends upon its measurable distance from an observer on
　　　　 Earth.
　　(B) may be determined from the length of its cycle of variation.
　　(C) changes from time to time according to a regular and
　　　　 predictable pattern.
　　(D) indicates the strength of the gravitation force exerted by the
　　　　 star.
　　(E) is a result of the periodicity of the star.

3. According to the passage, Leavitt's work provided astronomers
　　with the means of determining which of the following?

　　I.   The absolute brightness of any observable cepheid variable
　　II.   The apparent brightness of any object a given distance from
　　　　 an observer
　　III. The distance from Earth of any galaxy containing an observ-
　　　　 able cepheid variable

　　(A) I only
　　(B) III only
　　(C) I and II only
　　(D) I and III only
　　(E) I, II, and III

4. It can be inferred from the passage that a cepheid variable of great absolute brightness would exhibit

(A) a relatively rapid variation in brightness.
(B) a correspondingly weak gravitational force.
(C) brief, violent bursts of radiant energy.
(D) slow and almost imperceptible changes in brightness.
(E) a strong outward flow of light pressure.

5. The passage implies that Leavitt's work on cepheid variables would not have been possible without the availability of

(A) the camera as a scientific tool.
(B) techniques for determining the distances between stars.
(C) a method of measuring a star's gravitational force.
(D) an understanding of the chemical properties of stars.
(E) a single star whose distance from earth was already known.

Questions 6–11 are based on the following passage.

Line   From the opening days of the Civil War, one of the Union's strategies in its efforts to defeat the rebelling southern states was to blockade their ports. Compared to the Union, relatively little was manufactured in the Confederacy—either consumer goods or, more important, war material—and it was believed that a
(5)   blockade could strangle the South into submission. But the Confederacy had 3,500 miles of coastline and, at the start of the war, the Union had only 36 ships to patrol them.

Even so, the Confederate government knew that the Union could and would construct additional warships and that in time all its ports could be
(10)   sealed. To counter this, the Confederacy decided to take a radical step—to construct an ironclad vessel that would be impervious to Union gunfire. In doing so, the South was taking a gamble because, though the British and French navies had already launched experimental armor-plated warships, none had yet been tested in battle.

(15)   Lacking time as well as true ship-building capabilities, rather than construct an entirely new ship, in July, 1861, the Confederacy began placing armor-plating on the hull of an abandoned U.S. Navy frigate, the steam-powered *U.S.S. Merrimack*. Rechristened the *C.S.S. Virginia*, the ship carried ten guns and an iron ram designed to stave in the wooden hulls of Union warships.

(20)   Until then, Union Secretary of the Navy Gideon Welles had considered ironclads too radical an idea and preferred to concentrate on building standard wooden warships. But when news of the *Virginia* reached Washington, the fear it engendered forced him to rethink his decision. In October, 1861, the Union began construction of its own ironclad—the *U.S.S. Monitor,* which would
(25)   revolutionize naval warfare.

Designed by John Ericson, a Swede who had already made substantial contributions to marine engineering, the *Monitor* looked like no other ship afloat. With a wooden hull covered with iron plating, the ship had a flat deck with perpendicular sides that went below the waterline and protected the propeller
(30)   and other important machinery. Even more innovative, the ship had a round, revolving turret that carried two large guns. Begun three months after work

started on the conversion of the *Virginia,* the *Monitor* was nevertheless launched in January, 1862, two weeks before the Confederacy launched its ironclad.

(35)   On March 8th, now completely fitted, the *Virginia* left the port of Norfolk, Virginia, on what was expected to be a test run. However, steaming into Hampton Roads, Virginia, the Confederate ship found no fewer than five Union ships at the mouth of the James River—the *St. Lawrence, Congress, Cumberland, Minnesota,* and *Roanoke.* The first three of these were already-obsolete sailing ships, but the others were new steam frigates, the pride of the Union navy.

(40)   Attacking the *Cumberland* first, the *Virginia* sent several shells into her side before ramming her hull and sinking her. Turning next to the *Congress,* the southern ironclad sent broadsides into her until fires started by the shots reached her powder magazine and she blew up. At last, after driving the *Minnesota* aground, the *Virginia* steamed off, planning to finish off the other (45) ships the next day. In just a few hours, she had sunk two ships, disabled a third, and killed 240 Union sailors, including the captain of the *Congress*—more naval casualties than on any other day of the war. Although she had lost two of her crew, her ram, and two of her guns, and sustained other damage, none of the nearly 100 shots that hit her had pierced her armor.

(50)   The *Monitor,* however, was already en route from the Brooklyn Navy Yard, and the next morning, March 9th, the two ironclads met each other for the first—and only—time. For nearly four hours the ships pounded at each other, but despite some damage done on both sides, neither ship could penetrate the armor-plating of its enemy. When a shot from the *Virginia* hit the *Monitor's* pilot (55) house, wounding her captain and forcing her to withdraw temporarily, the Confederate ship steamed back to Norfolk.

Although both sides claimed victory, the battle was actually a draw. Its immediate significance was that, by forcing the withdrawal of the *Virginia,* it strengthened the Union blockade, enabling the North to continue its ultimately (60) successful stranglehold on the South. Even more important, it was a turning point in the history of naval warfare. Although neither ship ever fought again, the brief engagement of the *Monitor* and *Virginia* made every navy in the world obsolete, and, in time, spelled the end of wooden fighting ships forever.

6. According to the passage, the Confederacy wanted an ironclad vessel for all the following reasons EXCEPT

   (A) an ironclad vessel might be able to withstand Union attacks.
   (B) it needed open ports in order to receive supplies from overseas.
   (C) the British and French navies already had ironclads.
   (D) it knew that the Union would be building more warships.
   (E) without an ironclad, it would probably be unable to break the Union blockade.

7. The passage implies that the South was vulnerable to a naval blockade because of its

   (A) limited manufacturing capabilities.
   (B) relatively short coastline.
   (C) weak and ineffectual navy.
   (D) lack of access to natural resources.
   (E) paucity of skilled naval officers.

8. All of the following were unusual design features of the *Monitor* EXCEPT

   (A) armor plating.
   (B) perpendicular sides.
   (C) revolving gun turret.
   (D) flat deck.
   (E) wooden hull.

9. It can be inferred from the passage that, by comparison with the design of the *Monitor,* that of the *Virginia* was more

   (A) offensively oriented.
   (B) radical.
   (C) costly.
   (D) versatile.
   (E) traditional.

10. It can be inferred from the passage that the *Virginia* was able to sink or disable the *St. Lawrence, Congress,* and *Cumberland* for which the following reasons?

   (A) It carried more guns.
   (B) Its armor plating was virtually impervious to gunfire.
   (C) Its steam-powered engines made it highly maneuverable.
   (D) Its armor plating made it fireproof.
   (E) It was capable of greater speed than the Union warships.

11. The author suggests that the most important long-term result of the battle between the *Virginia* and the *Monitor* was that it

   (A) enabled the Union to maintain its blockade of southern ports.
   (B) demonstrated that ironclad ships represented the future of naval warfare.
   (C) saved the Union navy from destruction by the *Virginia.*
   (D) demonstrated the superior technological prowess of the North.
   (E) effectively ended the naval career of the captain of the *Monitor.*

EXERCISE 4

11 Questions

Time—15 Minutes

> **Directions:** The questions in this group are based on the content of a passage. After reading the passage, choose the best answer to each question. Answer all questions following the passage on the basis of what is *stated* or *implied* in the passage.

Questions 1–5 are based on the following passage.

(This passage is from an article published in 1976.)

Line The idea of building "New Towns" to absorb growth is frequently considered a cure-all for urban problems. It is erroneously assumed that if new residents can be diverted from existing centers, the present urban situation at least will get no worse. It is further and equally erroneously assumed that since European New
(5) Towns have been financially and socially successful, we can expect the same sort of result in the United States.

Present planning, thinking, and legislation will not produce the kind of New Towns that have been successful abroad. It will multiply suburbs or encourage developments in areas where land is cheap and construction profitable rather
(10) than where New Towns are genuinely needed.

Such ill-considered projects not only will fail to relieve pressures on existing cities but will, in fact, tend to weaken those cities further by drawing away high-income citizens and increasing the concentration of low-income groups that are unable to provide tax revenues. The remaining taxpayers,
(15) accordingly, will face increasing burdens, and industry and commerce will seek escape. Unfortunately, this mechanism is already at work in some metropolitan areas.

The promoters of New Towns so far in the United States have been developers, builders, and financial institutions. The main interest of these
(20) promoters is economic gain. Furthermore, federal regulations designed to promote the New Town idea do not consider social needs as the European New Town plans do. In fact, our regulations specify virtually all the ingredients of the typical suburban community, with a bit of political rhetoric thrown in.

A workable American New Town formula should be established as firmly
(25) here as the national formula was in Britain. All possible social and governmental innovations as well as financial factors should be thoroughly considered and accommodated in this policy. Its objectives should be clearly stated, and both incentives and penalties should be provided to ensure that the objectives are pursued. If such a policy is developed, then the New Town approach can play an
(30) important role in alleviating America's urban problems.

1. The passage implies that New Town projects are often considered a possible solution to the problem of

    (A) poverty in the central cities.
    (B) excessive suburban population.
    (C) urban crime.
    (D) declining property values.
    (E) uncontrolled urban growth.

2. It can be inferred from the passage that the author regards past and present New Town projects in the United States as

    (A) largely successful.
    (B) socially innovative.
    (C) hampered by government regulation.
    (D) financially sound.
    (E) poorly planned.

3. According to the passage, as compared with American New Towns, European New Towns have been designed with greater concern for

    (A) social needs.
    (B) typical suburban lifestyles.
    (C) the profits of developers and builders.
    (D) the needs of high-income residents.
    (E) financial conditions.

4. It can be inferred from the passage that the author considers present American New Town regulations to be

    (A) overly restrictive.
    (B) insufficiently innovative.
    (C) politically expedient.
    (D) unrealistically idealistic.
    (E) highly promising.

5. The author cites the British experience with the construction of New Towns as an example of

    (A) the difficulties New Town projects face in a socially traditional environment.
    (B) a New Town policy wisely tailored to national needs.
    (C) the economic weaknesses that have generally plagued New Town projects.
    (D) a political system in which New Town projects are likely to achieve success.
    (E) the use of both penalties and incentives in controlling New Town development.

Questions 6–11 are based on the following passage.

Line   For years, the contents of a child's sandbox have confounded some of the
nation's top physicists. Sand and other granular materials, such as powders,
seeds, nuts, soil, and detergent, behave in ways that seem to undermine natural
laws and cost industries ranging from pharmaceuticals to agribusiness and
(5)   mining billions of dollars.

Just shaking a can of mixed nuts can show you how problematic granular
material can be. The nuts don't "mix"; they "unmix" and sort themselves out,
with the larger Brazil nuts on top and the smaller peanuts on the bottom. In this
activity and others, granular matter's behavior apparently goes counter to the
(10)   second law of thermodynamics, which states that entropy, or disorder, tends to
increase in any natural system.

Mimicking the mixed-nut conundrum with a jar containing many small
beads and one large bead, one group of physicists claimed that vibrations
causing the beads to percolate open up small gaps rather than larger ones.
(15)   Thus, when a Brazil nut becomes slightly airborne, the peanuts rush in
underneath and gradually nudge it to the top. Another group of physicists color
coded layers of beads to track their circulation in the container and achieved a
different result. Vibrations, they found, drive the beads in circles up the center
and down the sides of the container. Yet downward currents, similar to
(20)   convection currents in air or water, are too narrow to accommodate the larger
bead, stranding it on top.

One industrial engineer who has studied the problem says that both the
"percolation" and "convection current" theories can be right, depending upon
the material, and that percolation is the major factor with nuts. Given the
(25)   inability of scientists to come up with a single equation explaining unmixing, you
can see why industrial engineers who must manage granular materials go a little,
well, "nuts." Take pharmaceuticals, for instance. There may be six types of
powders with different-sized grains in a single medicine tablet. Mixing them at
some speeds might sort them, while mixing at other speeds will make them
(30)   thoroughly amalgamated. One aspirin company still relies on an experienced
employee wearing a latex glove who pinches some powder in the giant mixing
drum to see if it "feels right."

Granular material at rest can be equally frustrating to physicists and
engineers. Take a tall cylinder of sand. Unlike a liquid, in which pressure exerted
(35)   at the bottom increases in direct proportion to the liquid's height, pressure at
the base of the sand cylinder doesn't increase indefinitely. Instead, it reaches a
maximum value and stays there. This quality allows sand to trickle at a nearly
constant rate through the narrow opening separating the two glass bulbs of an
hourglass, thus measuring the passage of time.
(40)   Physicists have also found that forces are not distributed evenly
throughout granular material. It is this characteristic that may account for the
frequent rupturing of silos in which grain is stored. In a silo, for instance, the
column's weight is carried from grain to grain along jagged chains. As a result,
the container's walls carry more of the weight than its base, and the force is
(45)   significantly larger at some points of contact than at others.

Coming up with equations to explain, much less, predict, the distribution
of these force chains is extremely difficult. Again, using beads, physicists
developed a simple theoretical model in which they assume that a given bead
transmits the load it bears unequally and randomly onto the three beads on
(50)   which it rests. While the model agrees well with experimental results, it doesn't
take into account all of the mechanisms of force transmission between grains of
sand or wheat.

(55)

(60)

In the struggle to understand granular materials, sand-studying physicists have at least have one thing in their favor. Unlike particle physicists who must secure billions of dollars in government funding for the building of supercolliders in which to accelerate and view infinitesimal particles, they can conduct experiments using such low-cost, low-tech materials as sand, beads, marbles, and seeds. It is hoped that more low-tech experiments and computer simulations will lead to equations that explain the unwieldy stuff and reduce some of the wastage, guesswork, and accidents that occur in the various industries that handle it.

6. Which of the following titles most accurately describes the above passage?

   (A) New Theories About the Physical Properties of Sand
   (B) The Behavior of Granular Matter in Motion and at Rest
   (C) The Percolation Theory Versus the Convection Current Theory of Unmixing
   (D) Theoretical and Practical Problems in Handling Granular Matter
   (E) How Physicists Are Helping to Solve Industrial Problems

7. The percolation theory of unmixing is best illustrated by which of the following examples?

   (A) Larger rocks rising to the surface in a garden after a period of frost
   (B) Currents of small beads blocking the upward movement of large beads in a shaken container
   (C) Contents settling in a bag of potato chips so that the package appears less full after handling
   (D) Large nuts blocking the upward movement of small nuts in a shaken container
   (E) A can of multi-sized beads sorting into layers of large and small beads upon shaking

8. In saying that the percolation and convection current theories may both be right (line 23), the industrial engineer means that

   (A) neither theory is supported by an adequate mathematical basis.
   (B) both theories are still unproven, since they have not been tested on a variety of material.
   (C) though the theories have different names, they describe the same physical mechanisms.
   (D) the mechanism causing unmixing varies depending upon the type of granular material.
   (E) both mechanisms are involved in all instances of unmixing.

9. Which of the following appears to be the best solution for combating the "unmixing" problem faced by pharmaceutical manufacturers that must prepare large quantities of powders?

   (A) To craft powders so that all the grains have similar sizes and shapes
   (B) To craft powders in which every grain weighs the same amount
   (C) To mix all the powders together at the same speed
   (D) To hire only engineers who have years of experience in powder mixing
   (E) To analyze and control the pattern of force chains in a vat of powder

10. The passage implies that, if the top bulb of an hourglass were filled with water instead of sand, the pressure pushing the water through the opening would

    (A) increase as water trickles through the opening.
    (B) decrease as water trickles through the opening.
    (C) remain constant as water trickles through the opening.
    (D) be directed at the walls of the container rather than the base.
    (E) make the water trickle down in drops rather than a stream.

11. In lines 53–54, the author implies that physicists studying granular material

    (A) are grappling with issues that are less complicated than those confronting particle physicists.
    (B) are fortunate in having available a selection of relatively easy means of crafting experiments.
    (C) are less likely to receive government funding than are particle physicists.
    (D) are likely to develop a complete predictive model for the behavior of granular material in the future.
    (E) know less about grains of sand than particle physicists know about infinitesimal forms of matter.

EXERCISE 5

11 Questions

Time—15 Minutes

> **Directions:** The questions in this group are based on the content of a passage. After reading the passage, choose the best answer to each question. Answer all questions following the passage on the basis of what is *stated* or *implied* in the passage.

Questions 1–4 are based on the following passage.

Line Urodeles, a class of vertebrates that includes newts and salamanders, have the enviable ability to regenerate arms, legs, tails, heart muscle, jaws, spinal cords, and other organs. Planaria, simple worms, can be sliced and diced in hundreds of pieces, with each piece giving rise to a completely new animal. However, while
(5) both urodeles and planaria have the capacity to regenerate, they use different means of accomplishing this feat.

In effect, urodeles turn back the biological clock. First the animal heals the wound at the site of the missing limb. Then various specialized cells at the site, such as bone, skin, and blood cells, lose their identity and revert to cells as
(10) unspecialized as those in the embryonic limb bud. This process is called dedifferentiation, and the resulting blastema, a mass of unspecialized cells, proliferates rapidly to form a limb bud. Ultimately, when the new limb takes shape, the cells take on the specialized roles they had previously cast off.

In contrast, planaria regenerate using cells called neoblasts. Scattered
(15) within the planarian body, these neoblasts remain in an unspecialized, stem-cell state, which enables them at need to differentiate into any cell type. Whenever planaria are cut, the neoblasts migrate to the site and form a blastema by themselves. It is interesting to note that this mechanism is similar to that following reproductive fission in these animals, and that species incapable of
(20) this form of asexual reproduction have poorly developed regenerative capacities.

1. The primary purpose of the passage is to
   (A) describe the roles of blastema in regenerating urodeles and planaria.
   (B) describe how urodeles use the process of dedifferentiation to regenerate.
   (C) contrast the mechanisms by which urodeles and planaria accomplish regeneration.
   (D) show how methods of cellular regeneration have evolved in different animal species.
   (E) explain the link between reproductive fission and regeneration in simple worms.

2. All of the following are true of dedifferentiation in regenerating urodeles EXCEPT

(A) the cells recover their specialized roles after the limb bud takes shape.

(B) it involves a regression by cells to an earlier stage of development.

(C) specialized cells migrate to the site of the blastema and proliferate rapidly.

(D) the healing of the wound at the site of the injury is the first step of the process.

(E) dedifferentiation is characterized by a loss and then recovery of cellular identity.

3. The author says that urodeles "turn back the biological clock" (line 7) because they can

(A) revert the cells in a severed part to a nearly embryonic state.

(B) regrow body parts from existing cells.

(C) produce a new limb bud from formerly differentiated cells.

(D) create a blastema from unspecified cells.

(E) develop specified cells from a blastema.

4. In the final sentence of the passage, the author implies that

(A) those planaria that reproduce by splitting themselves in two are more likely to regenerate using the same mechanism.

(B) planaria that reproduce sexually use the process of dedifferentiation to regenerate entirely new animals.

(C) asexual reproduction is related to regeneration in planaria but not in urodeles.

(D) the genetic makeup of planaria created through regeneration would be the same as in those created through reproductive fission.

(E) reproductive fission and regeneration in certain planaria differ solely in the quantity of new planaria produced.

Questions 5–11 are based on the following passage.

Line   As the climate in the Middle East changed beginning around 7000 B.C.E.,
conditions emerged that were conducive to a more complex and advanced form
of civilization in both Egypt and Mesopotamia. The process began when the
swampy valleys of the Nile in Egypt and of the Tigris and Euphrates rivers in
(5)   Mesopotamia became drier, producing riverine lands that were both habitable
and fertile, and attracting settlers armed with the newly developed techniques
of agriculture. This migration was further encouraged by the gradual
transformation of the once-hospitable grasslands of these regions into deserts.
Human population became increasingly concentrated into pockets of settlement
(10)   scattered along the banks of the great rivers.
        These rivers profoundly shaped the way of life along their banks. In
Mesopotamia, the management of water in conditions of unpredictable drought,
flood, and storm became the central economic and social challenge. Villagers
began early to build simple earthworks, dikes, canals, and ditches to control the
(15)   waters and reduce the opposing dangers of drought during the dry season
(usually the spring) and flooding at harvest time.
        Such efforts required a degree of cooperation among large numbers of
people that had not previously existed. The individual village, containing only a
dozen or so houses and families, was economically vulnerable; but when several
(20)   villages, probably under the direction of a council of elders, learned to share
their human resources in the building of a coordinated network of water-control
systems, the safety, stability, and prosperity of all improved. In this new
cooperation, the seeds of the great Mesopotamian civilizations were being sown.
        Technological and mathematical invention, too, were stimulated by life
(25)   along the rivers. Such devices as the noria (a primitive waterwheel) and the
Archimedean screw (a device for raising water from the low riverbanks to the
high ground where it was needed), two forerunners of many more varied and
complex machines, were first developed here for use in irrigation systems.
Similarly, the earliest methods of measurement and computation and the first
(30)   developments in geometry were stimulated by the need to keep track of land
holdings and boundaries in fields that were periodically inundated.
        The rivers served as high roads of the earliest commerce. Traders used
boats made of bundles of rushes to transport grains, fruits, nuts, fibers, and
textiles from one village to another, transforming the rivers into the central
(35)   spines of nascent commercial kingdoms. Trade expanded surprisingly widely;
we have evidence suggesting that, even before the establishment of the first
Egyptian dynasty, goods were being exchanged between villagers in Egypt and
others as far away as Iran.
        Similar developments were occurring at much the same time along the
(40)   great river valleys in other parts of the world—for example, along the Indus in
India and the Hwang Ho in China. The history of early civilization has been
shaped to a remarkable degree by the relationship between humans and rivers.

5. The primary purpose of the passage is to explain

    (A) how primitive technologies were first developed in the ancient Middle East.
    (B) how climatic changes led to the founding of the earliest recorded cities.
    (C) the influence of river life on the growth of early civilizations.
    (D) some of the recent findings of researchers into early human history.
    (E) the similarities and differences among several ancient societies.

6. According to the passage, the increasing aridity of formerly fertile grasslands in Egypt and Mesopotamia caused settlement patterns in those regions to become

    (A) less stable.
    (B) more sparse.
    (C) more concentrated.
    (D) less nomadic.
    (E) more volatile.

7. According to the passage, the unpredictability of water supplies in Mesopotamia had which of the following social effects?

    I.   It led to warfare over water rights among rival villages.
    II.   It encouraged cooperation in the creation of water-management systems.
    III. It drove farmers to settle in fertile grasslands far from the uncontrollable rivers.

    (A) I only
    (B) II only
    (C) III only
    (D) II and III only
    (E) Neither I, II, nor III

8. The passage implies that the earliest geometers were patronized primarily by

    (A) Mesopotamian monarchs.
    (B) mechanical artisans.
    (C) traders and merchants.
    (D) farm laborers.
    (E) landowners.

9. According to the passage, the earliest trade routes in the ancient Middle East

    (A)   were those between various centrally ruled commercial kingdoms.
    (B)   were those that linked villages in Egypt with others in Iran.
    (C)   were created to ease the transfer of technological and mathematical knowledge among villages.
    (D)   served to link the inhabitants of small villages with the dynastic kings who ruled them.
    (E)   connected villages that were scattered along the banks of the same river.

10. It can be inferred from the passage that the emergence of complex civilizations in the Middle East was dependent upon the previous development of

    (A)   basic techniques of agriculture.
    (B)   symbolic systems for writing and mathematical computation.
    (C)   tools for constructing houses quickly and easily.
    (D)   a system of centralized government.
    (E)   a method of storing and transferring wealth.

11. The author refers to emerging civilizations in India and China primarily in order to emphasize the

    (A)   importance of water transportation in the growth of early trade.
    (B)   relatively advanced position enjoyed by the Middle East in comparison to other regions.
    (C)   rapidity with which social systems developed in the Middle East spread to other places.
    (D)   crucial role played by rivers in the development of human cultures around the world.
    (E)   significant differences in social systems among various groups of early humans.

Answer Key

Exercise 1	Exercise 2	Exercise 3	Exercise 4	Exercise 5
1. B	1. E	1. E	1. E	1. C
2. A	2. E	2. B	2. E	2. C
3. E	3. C	3. D	3. A	3. C
4. A	4. E	4. E	4. B	4. A
5. A	5. D	5. A	5. B	5. C
6. E	6. E	6. C	6. D	6. C
7. B	7. A	7. A	7. D	7. B
8. C	8. E	8. E	8. D	8. E
9. A	9. C	9. E	9. A	9. E
10. D	10. C	10. B	10. B	10. A
11. D	11. D	11. B	11. B	11. D

Explanatory Answers

EXERCISE 1

1. **The correct answer is (B).** The passage focuses specifically on some of the key issues that arose during the early stages of the battle for ratification of the Constitution. All of the other answer choices are either off the point (choices A, C, and E) or too narrow (choice D).

2. **The correct answer is (A).** See the first paragraph. Having exceeded the mandate given them by Congress, the delegates to the convention naturally feared that Congress would not approve of the sweeping changes they were proposing.

3. **The correct answer is (E).** The fourth paragraph explains that the Federalists had the advantage of "a concrete proposal," i.e., the Constitution itself. The Antifederalists had no such specific plan to offer in its place.

4. **The correct answer is (A).** The Mercer quotation is one of several offered in the last paragraph to illustrate the general point that "Many of the Antifederalists were distrustful of the common people as their opponents."

5. **The correct answer is (A).** The author says that both the Federalists and the Antifederalists had doubts about the virtues of democracy, and he credits the Antifederalists with being just as "sincere" as the Federalists (see the fourth paragraph). However, the Federalists were more "decisive," since they offered a program, while the Antifederalists offered only "a policy of drift."

6. **The correct answer is (E).** The first sentence of the second paragraph makes this point clearly.

7. **The correct answer is (B).** In the fourth paragraph, the passage explains that Wegener used the existence of similar plants and animals on widely separated continents as evidence that all of the Earth's land masses were formerly connected in the supercontinent of Pangaea. For this evidence to be valid, it would have to mean that many plants and animals existed prior to the breakup of Pangaea, which paragraph two tells us began late in the Paleozoic era.

8. **The correct answer is (C).** The first paragraph tells us that Wegener's hypothesis was accepted some fifty years after it was first proposed in 1912; thus, in the early 1960s. This answers question III. Question I is not answered; the passage only says (at the end of paragraph four) that Wegener himself had no answer for this question. Question II is not answered; in fact, paragraph five refers to evidence from the 1960s that seemed to undermine, rather than support, Wegener's hypothesis.

9. **The correct answer is (A).** See the first sentence of the sixth paragraph. The "perhaps most significant" reason for many scientists' discomfort with Wegener's hypothesis was that it seemed to challenge their deep-seated belief in uniformitarianism.

10. **The correct answer is (D).** You'll find this stated in the last sentence of the fifth paragraph.

11. **The correct answer is (D).** Clearly, the discomfort felt by most geologists at the notion of accepting an idea "tainted with catastrophism" must have become less strong by the 1960s; otherwise, Wegener's hypothesis could never have been ultimately accepted. However, choices (A) and (C) are too strong; it's not necessary for uniformitarianism to have been utterly abandoned, merely that one exception to the principle should be considered plausible. Choice (E) is wrong because, as paragraph five explains, some of the new evidence in the 1960s seemed to undermine Wegener's theory, not support it.

EXERCISE 2

1. **The correct answer is (E).** The fourth, fifth, and sixth paragraphs of the passage explain how and why the various groups named in choices (A) through (D) have a stake in the current forms of aid. Environmentalists are not among them; in fact, in paragraph 2, the author implies that bankers, governments, and others should adopt the environmentalist philosophy of "small is better" in order to combat poverty more effectively.

2. **The correct answer is (E).** In the fifth paragraph, the author urges programs that provide "simple technology, agricultural extension services or implements," which nicely matches choice (E)—agricultural tools. The other answers sound like the massive development projects the author rejects as ineffective.

3. **The correct answer is (C).** Throughout the passage, the author describes the current ineffective programs and explains how, in his opinion, they ought to be changed in order to have a greater impact on the hunger problem.

4. **The correct answer is (E).** See the last paragraph. The author believes that the situation may have to get much worse before it gets better—a pessimistic outlook, surely.

5. **The correct answer is (D).** The first paragraph attributes the opposition to "those who wished to see the empire democratized," and it has already explained that Russia was, at this time, one of the few countries in Europe still ruled by a single individual—in other words, "an autocratic form of government."

6. **The correct answer is (E).** The fourth paragraph describes the October Manifesto as one of Nicholas's "halfhearted efforts . . . to satisfy the dissidents." There's no implication that the Manifesto was "never fully carried out," choice (A), only that it was an inadequate step toward full democracy.

7. **The correct answer is (A).** See paragraph six: "Nicholas decided it was his duty to lead the army himself."

8. **The correct answer is (E).** The sentence that mentions the "downturn" attributes it specifically to "progressively greater defeats" in the war.

9. **The correct answer is (C).** The latter portion of the seventh paragraph makes this clear. It says that Rasputin and Alexandra "were much reviled in the press" because the Russian people did not understand the health concerns that had driven the Tsarina to rely on Rasputin.

10. **The correct answer is (C).** Since we're told that the press harshly criticized the royal family, it's clear that a large measure of freedom—at least in this regard—was enjoyed by the Russian press.

11. **The correct answer is (D).** We're told in the last two sentences of the seventh paragraph that Rasputin's murder came about because he "had also made important enemies at court."

EXERCISE 3

1. **The correct answer is (E).** The last paragraph of the passage neatly summarizes the significance of Leavitt's work with cepheid variables.

2. **The correct answer is (B).** The third paragraph describes the important relationship Leavitt discovered: that the cepheid variable's periodicity (its cycle of variation) and its absolute brightness vary together. Thus, each one can be determined from the other.

3. **The correct answer is (D).** As the last sentence of paragraph four makes clear, statement I is true; from its periodicity (which is easily observable), we can determine the absolute brightness of a cepheid variable. Statement III is supported by the last paragraph of the passage. Statement II is false because the passage doesn't suggest that Leavitt developed the method by which astronomers measured stars' apparent brightness; in fact, in paragraphs two and six, Leavitt appears to take this method for granted and build upon it.

4. **The correct answer is (E).** Paragraph four explains that a star with a great absolute brightness is also a star with relatively stronger light pressure; hence, the slower in-and-out pulsation and the longer periodicity that Leavitt observed.

5. **The correct answer is (A).** See the last sentence of the second paragraph. It seems clear that the camera was a necessary tool for Leavitt's work to be possible.

6. **The correct answer is (C).** Although it's true that the British and French already had ironclad ships, the passage doesn't imply that this was a motivation for the Southern leaders; after all, neither the British nor the French were enemies of the South (as you can tell from the passage, even if your knowledge of Civil War history is a little shaky).

7. **The correct answer is (A).** This point is made in the second sentence of the passage.

8. **The correct answer is (E).** The last sentence of the third paragraph makes it obvious that wooden hulls were the rule, not the exception, among ships of the period.

9. **The correct answer is (E).** The *Virginia* was created simply by armor-plating a traditional wooden boat, whereas the *Monitor* had an entirely new design that "looked like no other ship afloat."

10. **The correct answer is (B).** See the last sentence of the seventh paragraph: "none of the nearly 100 shots that hit her had pierced her armor."

11. **The correct answer is (B).** Choice (B) restates the idea found in the last sentence of the passage.

EXERCISE 4

1. **The correct answer is (E).** The first two sentences of the passage imply that New Towns are viewed as a way of "diverting" population from existing cities and thereby preventing the problems of those cities from getting worse. Thus, uncontrolled growth appears to be the problem that New Towns are supposed to relieve.

2. **The correct answer is (E).** See the first sentence of the second paragraph, which summarizes the author's skepticism about American New Towns.

3. **The correct answer is (A).** The last paragraph and a half of the passage is devoted to praising European-style New Towns in contrast to American-style New Towns, because the European-style towns "consider social needs."

4. **The correct answer is (B).** The author criticizes U.S. regulations governing New Towns because they "specify virtually all the ingredients of the typical suburban community" (paragraph four). In other words, they contain no new ideas and instead merely replicate the problems of existing towns.

5. **The correct answer is (B).** In the last paragraph, the author holds up the British formula for New Towns as the kind of successful model American planners ought to imitate.

6. **The correct answer is (D).** Choices (A) and (C) are too narrow; choices (B) and (E) are too broad. Choice (D) is good because it brings out the *practical* slant of the passage, which, after all, focuses on the industrial use of granular matter and the role played by science in facilitating it.

7. **The correct answer is (D).** Review the first two sentences of the third paragraph. The percolation theory deals with how small and large objects interrelate when a mass of granular material is shaken, as in a can of nuts.

8. **The correct answer is (D).** See the first sentence of the fourth paragraph; the engineer says that both theories can be right, "depending on the material."

9. **The correct answer is (A).** As the fourth paragraph makes clear, the problem pharmaceutical firms face in dealing with granular materials is based mainly on the fact that different sized grains are present in a single product. Clearly, it would help matters if all the grains could be made the same size.

10. **The correct answer is (B).** The fifth paragraph explains that, unlike sand, the pressure in a liquid "increases in direct proportion to the liquid's height." In other words, the higher (or deeper) the mass of liquid, the greater the pressure at the bottom. Therefore, as the water trickled through (getting shallower, of course), the pressure would decrease.

11. **The correct answer is (B).** Notice the way the granular scientists' "low-cost, low-tech" experiments are contrasted with the complicated and expensive studies that particle physicists must somehow fund.

EXERCISE 5

1. **The correct answer is (C).** The last sentence of the first paragraph sets forth this central theme. The paragraphs that follow give the relevant details.

2. **The correct answer is (C).** As paragraph two explains, the specialized cells "lose their identity and revert" to being unspecialized cells, forming a blastema. *Only after this* do they proliferate; so it's wrong to say that the "specialized cells . . . proliferate rapidly," as choice (C) states.

3. **The correct answer is (C).** Urodeles "turn back the clock" because the specialized cells revert to the embryonic state of a limb bud. Choice (A) is wrong because it is not the cells "in a severed part" that revert but rather the cells near the site where the severed part formerly existed.

4. **The correct answer is (A).** The sentence says that those species of planaria that engage in "reproductive fission" (i.e., splitting) are the ones that are more likely to regenerate themselves in the same way.

5. **The correct answer is (C).** The last sentence of the passage neatly summarizes its main theme.

6. **The correct answer is (C).** The last two sentences of the first paragraph explain that the transformation of the grasslands into deserts made the human population "increasingly concentrated . . . along the banks of the great rivers."

7. **The correct answer is (B).** The third paragraph of the passage describes how the need for water-management systems encouraged cooperation among large groups of Mesopotamian villagers. Statement I is not supported by the passage, and Statement III is contradicted by the last sentence of the first paragraph.

8. **The correct answer is (E).** The last sentence of the fourth paragraph says that geometry was developed in response to "the need to keep track of land holdings and boundaries in fields."

9. **The correct answer is (E).** See the first sentence of the fifth paragraph.

10. **The correct answer is (A).** In the first paragraph, we're told that the development of great civilizations in the Middle East began when the river valleys attracted "settlers armed with the newly developed techniques of agriculture."

11. **The correct answer is (D).** The last paragraph, where India and China are mentioned, is used to make the point that life along river valleys has played a crucial role in the development of civilization in many parts of the world.

Chapter 5

Sentence Corrections

Get the Scoop On . . .

- Quick and accurate ways to tackle sentence correction items
- The kinds of grammar errors often tested on the GMAT CAT—and the kinds the test makers ignore
- How to focus on the only possible answer choices within just a few seconds
- How not to get bogged down in the confusing verbiage that clogs many questions
- Telltale signs of answer choices that look correct but aren't

THE TEST CAPSULE

What's the Big Idea?

Each sentence correction item presents a sentence that reads like an excerpt from a passage of serious nonfiction prose—an article from a magazine or journal, for example, or a passage from a book. Part or all of the sentence is underlined, and five answer choices are presented, four of which rephrase the underlined portion. You must decide which of the five alternatives is best from the standpoint of grammatical correctness, proper English usage, clarity, conciseness, and style.

How Many?

Your GMAT CAT will probably have 13 or 14 sentence correction questions out of 41 total Verbal questions.

How Much Do They Count?

Sentence correction questions are about 14 out of 41 total Verbal questions. They count as 34 percent of your overall Verbal score.

How Much Time Should They Take?

You should be able to answer sentence correction items at an average rate of about 90 seconds per question.

What's the Best Strategy?

Rather than simply reading all five versions of the sentence looking for the one that seems best, you should actively search for the error that has been inserted (80 percent of the time) in the original sentence.

Then, *before looking at the answer choices,* decide how you would correct that error. Finally, *scan* the answer choices, looking only at the part of the sentence in which the original error appeared, and eliminate any answer that does not correct the error. You can usually eliminate one, two, or three answer choices this way, allowing you to focus your attention strictly on the answers that fix the original mistake.

What's the Worst Pitfall?

The worst pitfall is getting bogged down in long, complex, hard-to-follow verbiage, much of which may be irrelevant to the grammatical or stylistic issue central to the question. Learn to *ignore* extraneous phrases and clauses that complicate the sentence without affecting its basic logical and grammatical structure.

THE OFFICIAL DESCRIPTION

What They Are

In the words of the test makers, sentence corrections "require you to be familiar with the stylistic conventions and grammatical rules of standard written English and to demonstrate your ability to improve or correct ineffective expressions." They test these skills through what might be called an *editing exercise.* You are given a sentence that may or may not contain a grammatical mistake, a stylistic weakness, or another writing flaw. You job is to decide whether or not the sentence contains such a flaw and, if so, to pick one of four alternatives that corrects the flaw without introducing any new flaws.

Where They Are

In the typical computerized GMAT CAT, you'll have a 75-minute Verbal section with a total of about 41 questions. Sentence corrections are one of the three types of questions that will appear in this section, intermingled in a seemingly random sequence. Reminder: the test makers claim the right to change the format at any time! However, the typical format we just described is what you will most likely encounter.

What They Measure

The test makers' phrase for the language tested on the GMAT CAT is *standard written English.* This means the language used in serious, "respectable" publications that feature works of nonfiction prose written in contemporary American English. What does this definition exclude? Slang, colloquialisms, technical jargon, geographic or ethnic dialects, archaic language (like Shakespeare's), and creative or experimental language (like James Joyce's)—all are excluded. To get a fix on GMAT

CAT English, think of the prose in which publications like the *Atlantic Monthly, Scientific American,* the *New Republic, National Review,* and the *New York Times* are written—or the style in which you probably wrote term papers in college. This is standard written English.

What They Cover

Sentence correction items are intended to test both *correctness* and *effectiveness* of expression. Correctness refers to the degree to which a sentence obeys the rules of English grammar and usage, including such specific principles as subject-verb agreement, proper use of pronouns, correct construction of verb tenses, parallel sentence structure, and accurate use of idioms. Effectiveness is a little more nebulous. An effective sentence, as defined by the GMAT CAT, is one that is clear and unambiguous, reasonably graceful, and concise, without needless repetition or wordiness. When you take the GMAT CAT, you'll encounter sentences that are guilty of sins against both correctness and effectiveness, and you'll be expected to know how to correct them without creating any new errors in the process. Subtle stylistic or esthetic considerations are *never* tested on the GMAT CAT, nor are rules of grammar and usage that are disputed or changing (we'll give examples of this later).

The Directions

> **Directions:** The following questions present a sentence, part of which or all of which is underlined. Beneath the sentence you will find five ways of phrasing the underlined part. The first of these repeats the original; the other four are different. If you think the original is best, choose the first answer; otherwise, choose one of the others.

THE INSIDER'S REPORT: STRATEGIES THAT REALLY WORK

Read the Whole Sentence, *Listening* for the Error

There are many ways in which people learn to use a language correctly. If you were raised in a non-English-speaking country, you probably first learned English in the same way most Americans learn Spanish, French, or German—from a teacher in a classroom. You studied grammar, vocabulary, and sentence structure from a textbook, and you practiced English through dialogues, exercises, quizzes, and compositions. At first, English was a collection of rules to be memorized and followed; only later, perhaps after you moved to the United States, did it become for you a living language about which you developed a feeling, an instinct.

Most Americans, however—as well as Canadians, Britons, Australians, and many others—learn English "at their mothers' knees," and the *feeling* for English as a living language comes long before any formal study of English grammar or word usage. In fact, nowadays many Americans hardly study grammar at all. Whatever knowledge of grammar rules they have was picked up almost by accident. An English teacher notes your error in the use of a verb in the margin of a term paper, a friend corrects you during a conversation ("Not 'If I *was*'; you mean, 'If I *were*'"), you hear some "language maven" on TV discussing who versus whom. That's the full extent of most people's "study" of English grammar these days.

If this describes you, *don't be concerned*. The GMAT CAT is designed to be friendly to people like you. Sentence correction items on the test do test your ability to apply the rules of English grammar and usage correctly. However, the test rewards the writer whose knowledge of the language is a matter of feeling or instinct. On the GMAT CAT, you never have to explain or identify a grammar error, no grammar terminology is used or tested, and you never have to diagram or otherwise analyze the structure of a sentence. Instead, you just have to pick the version of the sentence that *sounds right* from a collection of versions that sound, and are, wrong.

The first step, then, in tackling any sentence correction item is simply to read the entire sentence and *listen*, as if you were reading aloud, for any part of the sentence that sounds odd, weird, awkward, or wrong. In most of the sentences, you'll notice such a part—anything from one word to a whole phrase or clause that doesn't sound right. It's like tasting a dish in the kitchen before bringing it out to the table or giving the leg on a chair you're fixing one last shake before sitting on it: if something is wrong, you'll probably know it, whether or not you can name or describe it with words.

Let's consider an example—a sample sentence much like those you'll encounter on the GMAT CAT, though presented here *without* any answer choices:

1. Unlike Eisenstein, whose films clearly transcend any ideological purpose, Riefenstahl is generally dismissed <u>with merely being a propagandist</u> for a morally repugnant political cause.

Does any part of this sentence sound wrong to you? (Of course, the fact that certain words have been underlined by the test makers offers a significant clue as to which part of the sentence you should focus on.)

The "wobbly" piece of this sentence is the phrase "dismissed with merely being"; it's not the normal wording for the idea being expressed here.

Think about how you've seen the verb *dismissed* used in other sentences. Can you formulate, in your mind, the normal phrasing of the words that would follow dismissed? That's the first and crucial step you'd take in tackling this sentence if it appeared as a real GMAT CAT sentence correction item.

In a moment, we'll see how the rest of this item might look on the exam. But for now, note that the first step in analyzing the question is simply to read the sentence with care, trying to observe any part of it that sounds or feels wrong—any part that your instinct for English rebels against. Improving your skill at sentence correction questions on the exam is largely a matter of honing this instinct through practice, much as a musician sharpens her ear by listening to good music as often as she can.

Does this mean that it's pointless to study (or review) the rules of grammar? Not at all. Your instinct for correct English can be greatly enhanced by knowing the rules that linguists and grammarians have devised to explain how sentences are normally constructed.

In Appendix C, The Insider's GMAT CAT Writer's Manual, we've captured the thirty-six rules of grammar and usage that are most commonly tested on the GMAT CAT. You may want to pause right now in your reading of this chapter and skim the pages of that appendix. Do the contents look somewhat familiar, perhaps from a high school English course? Or are the rules explained there completely new to you? If the latter is the case, you should devote some time over the next week to reading the appendix to acquaint yourself with the basic principles of English grammar and sentence structure—what verbs and nouns are, how they relate to one another, and so on. We'll refer to these principles—though with a minimum of jargon—as we consider some sample GMAT CAT items in the rest of this chapter. You'll find it helpful to have at least a nodding acquaintance with them.

On the assumption that you know at least the rudiments of English grammar, or will pick up whatever knowledge you lack by studying Appendix C, we suggest you look at Table 5.1. It offers four basic principles for error spotting on GMAT CAT sentence correction items. These are techniques that can help you zero in on the grammar and stylistic errors that most GMAT CAT sentences contain—a useful supplement and aid to your instinctive ear for what's right and wrong in English. If any of the rules mentioned there, or the terms used, seem unfamiliar, you'll find them clearly explained in the appendix.

Table 5.1
Sentence Correction Error-Spotting Strategies

When in doubt as to where the error is located in a sentence correction item, follow these four steps in the sequence indicated. If there is an error, it will probably be uncovered through this process.

- Find the verb, then find its subject. Check subject-verb agreement, correct tense, and proper verb formation.

- Examine all pronouns. Make sure each has a clear antecedent with which it agrees in person and number.

- Look for wobbling of the sentence structure. Make sure modifiers are attached to what they modify, parallel ideas are grammatically parallel, and comparisons are clear and logical.

- Listen for awkwardness, verbosity, and incorrect use of idioms.

Once You Spot the Error, Consider How You'd Correct It

There are some kinds of writing errors you can safely forget about on the GMAT CAT— including certain types that many students find especially vexing. These include: vocabulary errors, spelling (including capitalization and hyphenation), and punctuation. None of these are tested on the exam. So if you think you've spotted an error of this sort on the GMAT CAT, you haven't! Ignore it and look else-where.

Approximately four out of five sentence correction sentences will contain an error in grammar, usage, or style, and, in most cases, you'll be able to "hear" that error by reading the sentence carefully.

Having done that, the next step is to consider how you'd correct the error if *you* had written the sentence. Do this before looking at any of the answer choices. Try rephrasing the faulty part of the sentence in your mind, figuring out what word or words you'd eliminate, change, move, or add, and imagine how the improved phrase or clause would read.

You may or may not find it easy to do this; it depends on the degree of writing skill you possess and how tricky the particular test item is. However, as you'll see in a moment, this is an important time-saving step as well as a way of avoiding the confusion and errors that can easily occur if you plunge immediately into the answer choices.

Let's see how this would work by first referring back to the sample item we saw a moment ago:

1. Unlike Eisenstein, whose films clearly transcend any ideological purpose, Riefenstahl is generally dismissed <u>with merely being a propagandist</u> for a morally repugnant political cause.

As we noticed before, the error here lies in the phrase that follows the verb *dismissed,* which is not worded as it would normally be. (The technical term for this error is *non-idiomatic usage.* It's frequently tested on the GMAT CAT.) Can you decide how you'd rephrase it? Having come up with your own version of those words, you're ready to move on to the next step in the process, which is to . . .

Scan Choices (B) Through (E), Looking for Answers That Correct the Error

Each GMAT CAT sentence correction item provides you with five versions of the underlined words from the original sentence. These are the five answer choices you'll to have to choose from. Here's how this item might look, complete with answer choices, on the real exam:

1. Unlike Eisenstein, whose films clearly transcend any ideological purpose, Riefenstahl is generally dismissed <u>with merely being a propagandist</u> for a morally repugnant political cause.

   (A)   with merely being a propagandist
   (B)   as being a propagandist merely
   (C)   for being merely a propagandist
   (D)   as a mere propagandist
   (E)   merely for being a propagandist

If you were able to anticipate how the error in the original sentence should be corrected, picking the best answer choice should be fairly easy. Just scan choices (B), (C), (D), and (E), *looking for the wording you thought would be correct.* If you find that wording in one of the answer choices, you've probably found the correct answer.

In this case, if you knew that the normal English idiom would be "to dismiss [someone] as a" propagandist (or whatever), without using the words "with" or "being," you could zero in quickly on answer choice (D)—which is the best version of the underlined words. Recognizing the error and anticipating how it should be corrected obviates the necessity of reading through all of the answer choices, let alone plugging them into the entire, lengthy sentence to hear how they sound in context.

Try this method with another example:

2. Due to current limitations in scientific methods, the age of many inorganic substances, including the minerals that largely constitute the inner layers of the earth, <u>are impossible to determine precisely.</u>

   (A)   are impossible to determine precisely.
   (B)   may precisely not be determined.
   (C)   is impossible to determine precisely.
   (D)   are not able precisely to be determined.
   (E)   is impossible for precise determination.

Can you "hear" the error in the original wording? If you're not sure, try using the error checklist from Table 5.1. One of the first hot spots to examine in any GMAT CAT sentence is the main verb; errors often focus on that word or phrase.

In this case, the verb is the first underlined word, *are,* and the error associated with it is one of the most common GMAT CAT error types: *faulty subject-verb agreement.* A detailed explanation of this topic, complete with examples, appears in Appendix C, but the gist is that the subject and verb of a sentence must agree in number; a singular subject requires a singular verb, while a plural subject requires a plural verb.

That rule is violated in this sentence. To find the subject of the verb *are,* ask yourself: "*What* are impossible to determine precisely?" The answer is, "the age of many" blah blah blah. (Exactly what doesn't matter. The key word is *age,* since it's the age that can't be determined, and, therefore, *age* is the subject of the verb. The complex words that follow "the age of many" don't affect the grammar of the sentence, and therefore we can safely ignore them, thinking of them merely as "blah blah blah.") Since *age* is a singular subject, a singular verb is needed rather than the plural *are.* The verb should be *is* instead.

With that in mind, scan—don't read—the answer choices. Two of them can be eliminated immediately. Choice (A) (of course) and choice (D) both contain the verb *are,* which caused the problem in the first place. However, choices (C) and (E) look promising; they use the correct singular verb *is* instead. And choice (B) is a possibility; it changes the verb altogether, to "may . . . be," which does agree with the subject *age.* So now you must choose among three potential answer choices. This requires you to read all three in full and leads to the next step in the process:

Pick an Answer That Corrects the Error Without Introducing Any New Errors

Scanning the answer choices to eliminate those that fail to correct the error will usually leave you with one, two, or three possible options. If there are two or more options to choose from, read them all carefully. Although each corrects the original error, you'll find that all but one introduce some new error. Your job is to "listen" for those new errors and find the answer choice that doesn't contain one.

In this case, choices (B) and (E) introduce new errors. Choice (B) moves the location of the adverb *precisely* into an awkward and unclear spot. (Generally speaking, an adverb should be as close as possible to the word it modifies. In this sentence, *precisely* should be as close as possible to *determine,* since that is the word whose meaning it affects.) And choice (E) uses the nonidiomatic, weird-sounding locution "impossible for precise determination." In normal English, one speaks of something as being "impossible to do," not "impossible for doing." Thus, both choice (B) and choice (E) are wrong, leaving choice (C) as the correct answer.

Try another example:

3. Once almost hidden under centuries of soot and grime, <u>skilled preservationists have now restored Michelangelo's famous frescoes on the ceiling of the Sistine Chapel</u>.

   (A)   skilled preservationists have now restored Michelangelo's famous frescoes on the ceiling of the Sistine Chapel

   (B)   Michelangelo's famous frescoes on the ceiling of the Sistine Chapel now have been by skilled preservationists restored

   (C)   the restoration of Michelangelo's famous frescoes on the ceiling of the Sistine Chapel has been done by skilled preservationists

   (D)   skilled preservationists on the ceiling of the Sistine Chapel have now restored Michelangelo's famous frescoes there

   (E)   Michelangelo's famous frescoes on the ceiling of the Sistine Chapel have now been restored by skilled preservationists

Can you spot the error in the original sentence? The mistake is another common GMAT CAT error known as a *misplaced modifier*. The opening phrase of the sentence, "Once almost hidden" blah blah blah, is a *modifying phrase* because it describes or gives more information about something else in the sentence. The rule is that a modifying phrase should be right next to the word or phrase that names what is being described.

Now, what is being described here? In other words, what was "Once almost hidden" blah blah blah? The answer is "Michelangelo's famous frescoes"; those frescoes are what was "Once almost hidden" blah blah blah. Therefore, in this sentence, the words "Michelangelo's famous frescoes" should follow the modifying phrase immediately, so as to make it clear that the frescoes are being modified or described by the words "Once almost hidden" blah blah blah. The way the original sentence is written, it almost sounds as through "the skilled preservationists" were "Once almost hidden" blah blah blah—a bizarre image, surely.

Now scan—don't read—the answer choices, looking for any that put "Michelangelo's famous frescoes" right at the start of the underlined portion, next to the modifying phrase. Only two answers qualify—choices (B) and (E)—so those are the only two you need to consider. And choice (B) can be eliminated, since it awkwardly moves the phrase "by skilled preservationists" in such a way as to separate the words "have been restored," which clearly belong together. The right answer is choice (E).

On the GMAT CAT, the underlined sentence portions—and the answer choices—will often be quite lengthy, as in this example. Focusing on the few words that need to be changed to correct the original error can save you a lot of time by making it unnecessary to read every answer choice in detail.

THE INSIDER'S REPORT: THE BEST TIPS

Expect Three or Four Grade A Sentences—Perfectly Correct

Generally speaking, the test makers will give you *roughly* equal numbers of each answer choice on any given test section. In other words, out of 41 verbal items, about one fifth will have the first choice, (A), as the correct response, one fifth will have the second choice, (B), and so on.

Therefore, out of the 14 sentence correction items that you'll probably have on the GMAT CAT, about one fifth—that is, three or four—should be answered with choice (A). This choice means that the original sentence contains *no* errors and is better than any of the variations offered. Think of these as "Grade A" sentences—perfectly correct as written and in no need of revision.

This simple fact has two consequences for your test-taking strategy.

- If you read a sentence that sounds perfectly okay, it probably is. Depending on where you are in the test section and on the time constraints you're feeling, you have two choices. If you are near the start of the section and have plenty of time to work with, go ahead and read the other answer choices so as to confirm that the original version is the best. If you are near the end of the section and are running low on time, don't bother: if the original sentence seems fine, simply pick choice (A) and move on.

- Keep count of the number of choice (A) answers, and adjust if the count is too high or too low. On your scratch paper, note the number of sentence corrections you encounter, as well how many you answer with choice (A). When you've done six or seven sentence corrections, check how many choice (A)s you've picked. If you've found no choice (A) items, you may be overanalyzing the sentences, finding "errors" where none actually exist. If you've found too many—say, three or more—you may be too forgiving, overlooking errors you should be spotting. Adjust accordingly.

All Things Being Equal, Choose the Shortest Answer

Occasionally, you'll find that eliminating all of the answers that contain errors does not narrow your options to a single choice. You may find that two (or rarely, three) answer choices all appear to be completely correct and equally clear, graceful, and unambiguous.

When this happens, choose the shortest answer. Generally speaking, the test makers regard a concise, tightly worded sentence as more "effective" than a wordy, loosely structured one. Therefore, when all other factors appear equal, the shortest sentence is the one that the test makers are most likely to consider correct.

THE INSIDER'S REPORT: THE MOST IMPORTANT WARNINGS

Don't Get Bogged Down in Mere Verbiage

Some of the grammar and usage rules most often discussed by teachers and others are not tested on the GMAT CAT. This is because, like many aspects of language, they are changing; as a result, some usages once considered wrong are now accepted by many speakers of English. Examples: the split infinitive, in which an infinitive verb ("to go") is divided by an adverb ("to boldly go"), is now generally accepted; so, too, is ending a sentence with a preposition ("This is the plan we came up with"). These "rules" will not be tested on the GMAT CAT—so forget your junior high school teacher's lectures about them!"

The sentences used on the GMAT CAT are fairly long. Most contain more than twenty words, and many are thirty to forty words in length. This makes for some complex, convoluted sentences with ideas that may be difficult to follow.

Don't let this throw you off. Remember, these are not reading comprehension passages; you won't be asked to explain the meaning of the sentences or to interpret the ideas they contain. You should focus only on the basic grammatical structure of each sentence and the connections among its main grammatical features. If you do this, you can spot any errors the sentence contains *even if you don't understand every detail of the long and convoluted verbiage.*

To illustrate, consider this sample sentence:

4. The average person's conception of scientific method is fundamentally flawed insofar as it assumes that theory develops
   automatically from observations of natural <u>events; which are</u>
   essentially unaffected by the preconceptions of the observer.

   (A) events; which are
   (B) events, which are
   (C) events, these being
   (D) events; themselves
   (E) events, such events being

This is a fairly long (thirty-two words) and complicated sentence. It includes phrases like "scientific method" and "the preconceptions of the observer," which most of us don't use every day (and consequently have to stop to think about when we read them). Furthermore, if you're slightly intimidated by the topic of science—as many people are—the very theme of the sentence may make you nervous.

Our advice: forget all that. The key things to notice about this sentence are the following:

■ Only a few words are underlined. Thus, the problem is localized
  in a small part of the sentence rather than being a sentence-wide
  structural problem.

- The underlined portion is near the end of the sentence. Thus, the error is likely to involve mainly or exclusively the latter half of the sentence rather than the first half of the sentence.

In combination, these features tell you that you don't need to worry too much about what appears near the start of the sentence. If you understand it, fine. If you don't, don't agonize over it. Read the sentence fairly quickly, make sure you recognize where its key features appear (verb, subject, direct object, or subject complement), and feel free almost to ignore phrases or groups of words that don't relate directly to the underlined part of the sentence.

Thus, you might read this sentence as follows:

> The average person's [blah blah blah] assumes that theory develops automatically from observations of natural events; which are essentially unaffected [blah blah blah].

Notice how this simplified version of the sentence makes the grammatical error more obvious. The last part of the sentence, following the semicolon, is an unconnected verbal phrase. This makes it wrong to use the semicolon. Only an independent clause—a clause that can stand alone as a sentence—may follow a semicolon. Read what follows the semicolon in this case, and you can probably "hear" that it cannot stand alone as a sentence.

(If you're familiar with this grammatical rule, fine. If not, you'll find it explained in more detail in Appendix C, The Insider's GMAT CAT Writer's Manual.)

To correct the sentence, the connection between the final clause and the rest of the sentence needs to be repaired. Changing the semicolon to a comma, as in choice (B), fixes the error. Choice (D) retains the error, and choices (C) and (E) introduce a new error by inserting the nonidiomatic *being* construction.

In any case, notice how *fundamentally irrelevant* most of the first half of the sentence is to the error and its correction. This pattern is found in many sentence correction items. That's why you mustn't let long, complex, hard-to-understand verbiage confuse or slow you down. Instead, mentally replace the toughest phrases with "blah blah blah" and focus on the grammatical connections rather than the overall meaning of the sentence.

Avoid Answers That Repeat Ideas

The test makers say that sentence correction tests both "correctness" and "effectiveness" of writing. It's pretty clear what "correctness" refers to: writing that doesn't break any of the basic rules of grammar, usage,

When a sentence contains phrases basically unconnected to the underlined error, especially phrases that are complex or hard to understand, mentally replace them with "blah blah blah." Rather than struggle to understand the difficult parts of the sentence, just focus on the grammatical structure of the sentence and how the "blah blah blah" verbiage is connected to it—if at all.

and sentence structure. "Effectiveness" is a little more vague. It includes such concepts as clarity, gracefulness, and conciseness.

One basic test of effectiveness used by the GMAT CAT test makers is *redundancy*. This is needless repetition of ideas in a sentence. When the same concept is stated twice or more in a given sentence, the test makers are sending you a broad hint that this is an ineffective sentence that needs to be simplified. Here's an example:

5. The remarkable growth in increased attendance currently being enjoyed by such formerly moribund sports franchises as baseball's Cleveland Indians shows that building a new stadium can have a powerful effect on the popularity of a team.

    (A) The remarkable growth in increased attendance currently being enjoyed
    (B) Remarkably, the growth in attendance that is currently enjoyed
    (C) The growth in attendance remarkably being enjoyed currently
    (D) The remarkable growth in increased attendance currently enjoyed
    (E) The remarkable attendance boom currently enjoyed

The original phrasing here contains not one, but two, examples of redundancy. The words *growth* and *increased* both convey the same idea concerning attendance at Indians games. And the word *being* tells you merely that this phenomenon is happening now—the same idea that the word *currently* expresses.

The best rephrasing is choice (E), which eliminates both redundancies without changing the meaning of the sentence (as choices (B) and (C) do by changing *remarkable* to *remarkably*).

Listen for redundancy when reading sentence correction items. It's a very straightforward and concrete type of "ineffectiveness," which makes it popular with the test makers.

Avoid Answers That Separate Basic Sentence Elements

Another form of "ineffective" writing is awkwardness. This, too, can be hard to precisely define. However, one strong clue often used by the GMAT CAT test makers is when basic sentence elements—subject and verb, verb and object, or verb and complement—are needlessly separated in a sentence. When words that appear naturally to belong together are separated by other words, the result is an awkward sentence that the test makers expect you to reject.

Here's an illustration:

6. <u>The Beach Boys, as other rock bands of the 1960s, considered the Beatles as</u> the preeminent innovators whose creativity and style they strove to emulate.

(A)   The Beach Boys, as other rock bands of the 1960s, considered the Beatles as

(B)   Like other rock bands of the 1960s, the Beach Boys considered the Beatles

(C)   The Beach Boys, as did other rock bands of the 1960s, considered the Beatles to be

(D)   As did other rock bands, the Beach Boys of the 1960s considered the Beatles as being

(E)   The Beatles were considered by the Beach Boys, like other rock bands of the 1960s,

The original sentence contains two flaws. One is a confusion between *as* and *like*. *As* is a conjunction that should be followed by a clause (a group of words containing a subject and a verb), which is not the case here. In this case, the preposition *like* should be used instead.

The second flaw lies in the fact that the sentence needlessly separates the subject—"The Beach Boys"—from the verb "considered." The best answer, choice (B), corrects both flaws (unlike choice (C), for instance).

JUST THE FACTS

- Sentence correction tests your knowledge of both grammar rules (correctness) and stylistic clarity and conciseness (effectiveness).

- Tackle each item by first reading the original sentence and looking for the error it probably contains.

- Anticipate how the error should be corrected and scan choices (B) through (E), looking for answers that fix the error.

- Don't get bogged down in complex verbiage; substitute "blah blah blah" for difficult but irrelevant phrases.

- All things being equal, choose the shorter answer.

PRACTICE, PRACTICE, PRACTICE: SENTENCE CORRECTION EXERCISES

Instructions

The following exercises will give you a chance to practice the skills and strategies you've just learned for tackling sentence correction questions. As with all practice exercises, work under true testing conditions. Complete each exercise in a single sitting. Eliminate distractions (TV, music) and clear away notes and reference materials.

Time yourself with a stopwatch or kitchen timer, or have someone else time you. If you run out of time before answering all the questions, stop and draw a line under the last question you finished. Then go ahead and tackle the remaining questions. When you are done, score yourself based only on the questions you finished in the allotted time.

Record your responses by blackening the circle next to the answer of your choice.

Understanding Your Scores

0–4 correct: A poor performance. Study this chapter again, and study Appendix C, The Insider's GMAT CAT Writer's Manual, for tips on the grammar and usage rules most often tested on the exam.

5–6 correct: A below-average score. Study this chapter again, and focus especially on the skills and strategies you've found newest and most challenging. Also read the sections from Appendix C that cover the grammar and usage rules you find most unfamiliar or difficult.

7–9 correct: An average score. You may want to study this chapter again. Also be sure you are managing your time wisely (as explained in Chapter 3) and avoiding errors due to haste or carelessness.

10–12 correct: An above-average score. Depending on your personal target score and your strength on the other verbal question types, you may or may not want to devote additional time to sentence correction study.

13–15 correct: An excellent score. You are probably ready to perform well on GMAT CAT sentence correction questions.

EXERCISE 1

15 Questions

Time—20 Minutes

> **Directions:** The following questions present a sentence, part of which or all of which is underlined. Beneath the sentence you will find five ways of phrasing the underlined part. The first of these repeats the original; the other four are different. If you think the original is best, choose the first answer; otherwise, choose one of the others.

1. In many nations around the Pacific Rim, the so-called overseas Chinese are more powerful, wealthy, and wield more influence as any ethnic group.
   - (A) wield more influence as any ethnic group
   - (B) more influential as any other ethnic group
   - (C) influential than any group ethnically
   - (D) wield influence greater than any other ethnic group
   - (E) influential than any other ethnic group

2. University presses, once strictly the province of scholarly books read only by an academic audience, are now publishing more and more works of interest to a general readership.
   - (A) of interest to a general readership
   - (B) generally interesting to readers
   - (C) that interest readers generally
   - (D) interesting to readers who are general
   - (E) of general interest to every reader

3. In 1929, nearly 90 percent of the U.S. population attended a movie once a week; and only 20 percent in 1990.
   - (A) week; and only 20 percent
   - (B) week; while 20 percent did so
   - (C) week, but only 20 percent
   - (D) week, a number that fell to 20 percent
   - (E) week; as compared to 20 percent

4. Since life is unpredictable and no one is gifted with perfect foresight or wisdom, <u>living life fully is to make mistakes and to accept</u> them as a natural part of experience.

    (A) living life fully is to make mistakes and to accept
    (B) to live life fully is making mistakes and accepting
    (C) living life fully is making mistakes and to accept
    (D) to live life fully is to make mistakes and to accept
    (E) life fully lived is making mistakes but accepting

5. Inscribed with the names of each of the thousands of Americans <u>who lost their lives in the war</u>, Maya Lin's Vietnam veterans' memorial in Washington, D.C., has become a favorite stop for visitors to the nation's capitol.

    (A) who lost their lives in the war
    (B) that lost their lives during the war
    (C) who lost his life in the war
    (D) whose life the war took
    (E) from whom the war took a life

6. Any of the stockholders <u>who disapproves</u> of the management-endorsed slate of candidates may offer an alternative slate under procedures established by the SEC.

    (A) who disapproves
    (B) who disapprove
    (C) that are disapproving
    (D) that do not approve
    (E) who are not in approval

7. Carrying with it a monetary award <u>greater than that associated with the Nobel Prize</u>, the Templeton Prize for Progress in Religion is one of the world's most prestigious prizes.

    (A) greater than that associated with the Nobel Prize
    (B) of greater size than is the one given along with the Nobel Prize
    (C) which is greater than the award given when the Nobel Prize is given
    (D) beside which the award associated with the Nobel Prize is less
    (E) greater than the Nobel Prize's award, also monetary,

8. <u>With</u> three decades of intensive research and experimentation, automotive engineers still find the goal of a practical, non-polluting electric car an elusive one.

   (A) With
   (B) Despite
   (C) Following
   (D) Having spent
   (E) As a result of

9. It is not enough to make vaccines against childhood diseases available; experience shows that it is also necessary for local governments to enact regulations <u>requiring that children should be immunized</u> before they attend school.

   (A) requiring that children should be immunized
   (B) that require children's being immunized
   (C) which require the immunization of children
   (D) to require immunization of the children
   (E) requiring that children be immunized

10. During the summer of 1998, the reason for virtually every unusual weather condition, from droughts and heat waves to floods and storms, was <u>said to be caused by</u> El Niño.

    (A) said to be caused by
    (B) blamed on
    (C) attributed to
    (D) supposed to be due to
    (E) said to be

11. Horbach's promotion to partner meant that she enjoyed the <u>more prestigious post</u> held by a woman in any of the leading leveraged buyout firms on Wall Street.

    (A) more prestigious post
    (B) post of greater prestige
    (C) most prestigious post
    (D) post highest in prestige
    (E) more highly prestigious post

12. Although advocates of charter schools claim that they do a better job of educating children than public schools, most comparisons <u>for</u> the two systems are misleading at best.

    (A) for
    (B) from
    (C) as to
    (D) between
    (E) regarding

13. Current rules regarding investment of state employee pension funds require money managers either to sell all stock in companies that market tobacco products by the end of the year or <u>that they file</u> a timetable for doing so within the next six months.
    - (A) that they file
    - (B) file
    - (C) be filing
    - (D) they should file
    - (E) to file

14. Cheaper yet more powerful than yesterday's desktop machines, <u>many consumers are finding today's laptop computers remarkably appealing</u>.
    - (A) many consumers are finding today's laptop computers remarkably appealing
    - (B) today's laptop computers are remarkably appealing to many consumers
    - (C) the laptop computers of today are found by many consumers remarkably appealing
    - (D) today's laptop computers appeal in remarkable fashion to many consumers
    - (E) many consumers find remarkably appealing the laptop computers of today

15. The Dead Sea Scrolls, which were found in a cave near the Dead Sea in the late 1940s, <u>have provided scholars with unprecedented information</u> about the Bible and about Judaism in Jesus' time.
    - (A) have provided scholars with unprecedented information
    - (B) has provided scholars with unprecedented information
    - (C) are providing scholars unprecedentedly with information
    - (D) has provided unprecedented information to scholars
    - (E) have provided to scholars information that is unprecedented

EXERCISE 2

15 Questions

Time—20 Minutes

> **Directions:** The following questions present a sentence, part of which or all of which is underlined. Beneath the sentence you will find five ways of phrasing the underlined part. The first of these repeats the original; the other four are different. If you think the original is best, choose the first answer; otherwise, choose one of the others.

1. On the verge of bankruptcy less than five years ago, many observers consider Gulfstream one of the most remarkable turnarounds in recent corporate history.

   (A) many observers consider Gulfstream
   (B) Gulfstream is considered by many observers
   (C) many observers regard Gulfstream to be
   (D) Gulfstream, according to many observers, is to be considered
   (E) it is considered by many observers that Gulfstream is

2. Although some people think of New York as the quintessential high-rise city, many of the most elegant examples of skyscraper architecture may be found in Chicago.

   (A) many of the most elegant examples of skyscraper architecture may be found in Chicago
   (B) Chicago is where may be found many of the most elegant examples of skyscraper architecture
   (C) it is in Chicago that one would find many of the most elegant examples of skyscraper architecture
   (D) you would in Chicago find many of the most elegant examples of skyscraper architecture
   (E) of the most elegant examples of skyscraper architecture, many are to be found in Chicago

3. Although we can infer, on the basis of surviving documents and works of art, that many Europeans during the Middle Ages believed that unicorns actually existed, <u>no one today believes that they are real</u>.

   (A) no one today believes that they are real
   (B) they are not believed in today by anyone
   (C) such belief in their reality does not any longer exist
   (D) this belief is today held by no one
   (E) today they are not believed in by anyone

4. Even without an official report, cigarette smokers should have known that smoking was bad for their health, but the first Surgeon General's report on the subject, released in the 1960s, <u>for some reason came as a surprise to the smoker</u>.

   (A) for some reason came as a surprise to the smoker
   (B) somehow came as a surprise to the smoker
   (C) for some reason was surprising to a smoker
   (D) for some reason came as a surprise to many smokers
   (E) somehow came as a surprise to many of the smokers

5. In its antitrust complaint, the Justice Department claimed that the software design employed by the company did not allow the consumer <u>neither to disable</u> the Internet browser provided with the software or to easily install a different browser.

   (A) neither to disable
   (B) either to disable
   (C) to either disable
   (D) the power of disabling
   (E) to either disable

6. The economics of book publishing more closely resembles that of live theatre <u>than</u> movies or television; both books and theatre are elite forms of entertainment with a relatively small, select audience.

   (A) than
   (B) than that of
   (C) rather than
   (D) than does
   (E) in comparison to

7. Because of the continuing crisis in Indonesia, most observers believe that the party currently in control of the government there are liable to be ousted in the forthcoming general election.

(A) are liable to be ousted
(B) is likely to be ousted
(C) will be ousted, most likely,
(D) is liable to lose
(E) are likely to lose

8. Despite the doubts expressed by most physicians, the theory that people ought to vary their diet based in large part on their blood type has won many new adherents in recent years.

(A) based in large part on their blood type
(B) as determined by their blood type for the most part
(C) owing to their blood type in large part
(D) in large part in accordance with their blood type
(E) because in large part of their blood type

9. The emergence of political parties, usually referred to as "factions," were anticipated and generally disapproved of by the first generation of American statesmen.

(A) were anticipated and generally disapproved of
(B) was anticipated and, in general, not approved,
(C) were anticipated, though with disapproval,
(D) had been anticipated and generally disapproved
(E) was anticipated and generally disapproved of

10. Discarding and replacing worn appliances may seem to be a wasteful thing to do, but in many cases, a new appliance is actually cheaper than fixing an old one.

(A) a new appliance is actually cheaper than fixing an old one
(B) a new appliance is actually cheaper than an old one is
(C) buying a new appliance is actually cheaper than fixing an old one
(D) it is actually cheaper to buy a new appliance than fixing an old one
(E) a new appliance is actually cheaper to buy than it is to fix an old one

11. Few novelists have ever rivaled Dickens in terms of human sympathy, imaginative curiosity, <u>and being morally generous</u>.

   (A) and being morally generous
   (B) or generosity of morality
   (C) as well as moral generosity
   (D) and moral generosity
   (E) moral, or being generous

12. Most of us can only imagine the sense of grief and desolation that a homeowner must feel <u>upon finding their house and all its contents</u> destroyed by flood or other natural disaster.

   (A) upon finding their house and all its contents
   (B) to find his house and all its contents
   (C) finding their house and all it contains
   (D) when he finds that his house and its contents is
   (E) in finding their house, with all its contents,

13. <u>Known for his autocratic style and shrewd political instincts, much of the landscape of postwar New York and its environs was profoundly shaped by Robert Moses.</u>

   (A) Known for his autocratic style and shrewd political instincts, much of the landscape of postwar New York and its environs was profoundly shaped by Robert Moses.
   (B) Robert Moses profoundly shaped much of the landscape of postwar New York and its environs, known for his autocratic style and shrewd political instincts.
   (C) Known for his autocratic style and shrewd political instincts, Robert Moses profoundly shaped much of the landscape of postwar New York and its environs.
   (D) Much of the landscape of postwar New York and its environs was shaped by Robert Moses; he was known for his autocratic style and shrewd political instincts.
   (E) The autocratic style and shrewd political instincts for which Robert Moses was known helped him profoundly shape much of the landscape of postwar New York and its environs.

14. Every collector cherishes stories <u>like the one about</u> the motor-cycle fan who discovered a vintage Harley-Davidson that had been custom-made for Elvis Presley on sale for a few dollars in a New England junkyard.

 (A) like the one about
 (B) such as the story in regard to
 (C) as the one concerning
 (D) like the story as to
 (E) as the story about

15. <u>While being a lawyer</u>, Van Susteren developed many of the communications skills that served her well in her later career as a broadcast journalist.

 (A) While being a lawyer
 (B) While in the practice of a lawyer
 (C) During her time as a lawyer
 (D) As she practiced law
 (E) As a lawyer

EXERCISE 3

15 Questions

Time—20 Minutes

Directions: The following questions present a sentence, part of which or all of which is underlined. Beneath the sentence you will find five ways of phrasing the underlined part. The first of these repeats the original; the other four are different. If you think the original is best, choose the first answer; otherwise, choose one of the others.

1. There is something strange about the notion of a theme park featuring wild animals, since "wild" means "uncontrolled," while the very essence of the theme park experience is the strict control of every variable.
   - (A)   is the strict control of every variable
   - (B)   being how strictly every variable is controlled
   - (C)   must be that every variable is strictly controlled
   - (D)   is that every variable is controlled strictly
   - (E)   is to control, and strictly, every variable

2. If you keep a rotary file for names, addresses, and phone numbers on your desk and maintain it on a regular basis, you will never have to worry about whether or not you are able to find any phone numbers you might need.
   - (A)   you will never have to worry about whether or not you are able to find
   - (B)   you will never have to worry about finding
   - (C)   you won't never have to worry that you'll find
   - (D)   you will never have to look around for or worry about finding
   - (E)   you won't ever need to go on a search for or worry about finding

3. In the days prior to the development of modern medicine, people often used roots, berries and other flora in their attempts to alleviating symptoms and curing diseases.
   - (A)   to alleviating symptoms and curing diseases
   - (B)   to cure diseases and alleviating symptoms
   - (C)   for alleviating symptoms and curing diseases
   - (D)   to alleviate symptoms and cure diseases
   - (E)   at the alleviation of symptoms and the curing of diseases

4. According to NASA officials, the decision concerning tomorrow's scheduled launch of the space shuttle will depend primarily <u>on if</u> the thunderstorms currently moving up the Florida coast continue north or instead drift out to sea.

   (A) on if
   (B) as to whether
   (C) from whether
   (D) on whether
   (E) on the question if

5. No other talent of the CEO is as crucial to the future of her business as her ability <u>to recognize, recruit, and to nurture</u> the best executive talent available.

   (A) to recognize, recruit, and to nurture
   (B) to recognize, recruit, and nurture
   (C) for recognizing, recruiting, and nurturing
   (D) at recognition, recruitment, and nurturing
   (E) in recognizing, recruiting, and the nurturing of

6. Both anecdotal evidence and survey results suggest that, of all the athletes on the global stage, basketball star Michael Jordan remains <u>the more widely known</u> and generally admired.

   (A) the more widely known
   (B) the most widely known
   (C) more widely known
   (D) known more widely
   (E) widely known

7. Stories about air travel mishaps are carefully edited out of news programs prepared for in-flight viewing, <u>since they</u> have no desire to increase the anxiety some passengers already feel about flying.

   (A) since they
   (B) because airlines
   (C) inasmuch as they
   (D) due to airlines
   (E) in that the airlines

8. <u>Recognizing, understanding, and adjusting to</u> changes in the global marketplace has become an increasingly complex task for most product managers.

   (A) Recognizing, understanding, and adjusting to
   (B) To recognize, understand, to adjust to
   (C) The recognition, understanding, and adjustment to
   (D) Recognizing, as well as understanding and adjusting to
   (E) That one recognize, understand, and adjust to

9. <u>Blinded by the sun's reflection, the crevasse was all but invisible until the climbers nearly stumbled into it.</u>

   (A) Blinded by the sun's reflection, the crevasse was all but invisible until the climbers nearly stumbled into it.

   (B) The climbers, blinded by the sun's reflection, nearly stumbled into the crevasse, which they had found until then all but invisible.

   (C) The crevasse was all but invisible to the climbers blinded by the sun's reflection, until they nearly stumbled into it.

   (D) Nearly stumbling into the crevasse, the climbers, blinded by the sun's reflection, found it all but invisible.

   (E) All but invisible, the climbers nearly stumbled into the crevasse, blinded by the sun's reflection.

10. Although Americans are accustomed to speaking of Jefferson as the progenitor of our modern democratic ideals, the views most Americans actually hold are significantly <u>closer to Madison.</u>

   (A) closer to Madison
   (B) closer to Madison's
   (C) more close to Madison
   (D) more like Madison
   (E) more close to those of Madison

11. While <u>not all children has artistic ability</u>, it's advisable for parents to provide encouragement to all who do.

   (A) not all children has artistic ability
   (B) all children doesn't have artistic ability
   (C) artistic ability is not had by every child
   (D) every child has no artistic ability
   (E) not every child has artistic ability

12. The chairman of the Federal Reserve Bank, along with his counter-parts from the leading industrial nations, <u>are expected to attend</u> next month's economic summit in Milan.

   (A) are expected to attend
   (B) will attend, so it is expected,
   (C) is expected to attend
   (D) are expecting to attend
   (E) is to attend, as expected,

13. After remaining constant for half a century, over the past forty years the number of major league baseball franchises in operation had increased almost fourfold.

   (A) had increased almost fourfold
   (B) has increased almost fourfold
   (C) have increased almost fourfold
   (D) are almost four times greater
   (E) is now almost four times as great

14. Most people today, if they have any image at all of newspaper magnate William Randolph Hearst, picture him as resembling the caricature portrayed in Orson Welles' classic film *Citizen Kane*.

   (A) picture him as resembling
   (B) picture him to resemble
   (C) imagine him to be like
   (D) would imagine him as
   (E) see him as being similar as

15. Earheart's athletic figure, her ebullient smile, and her striking resemblance to fellow aviation pioneer Charles Lindbergh all contributed to the rapid growth of her status as a popular heroine.

   (A) and her striking resemblance to fellow aviation pioneer Charles Lindbergh
   (B) as well as the fact that she strikingly resembled fellow aviation pioneer Charles Lindbergh
   (C) along with her striking resemblance to Charles Lindbergh, who was a fellow aviation pioneer
   (D) and Earheart's striking resemblance to Charles Lindbergh, fellow aviation pioneer
   (E) and striking resemblance to fellow aviation pioneer Charles Lindbergh

EXERCISE 4

15 Questions

Time—20 Minutes

Directions: The following questions present a sentence, part of which or all of which is underlined. Beneath the sentence you will find five ways of phrasing the underlined part. The first of these repeats the original; the other four are different. If you think the original is best, choose the first answer; otherwise, choose one of the others.

1. Despite the influx of pedestrian traffic that resulted from the establishment of the downtown mall, most Main Street store owners report little additional customers patronizing their businesses.

   (A) report little
   (B) are reporting little
   (C) say that few
   (D) say they have little
   (E) report few

2. Although Edison is often credited to have invented the modern motion picture, Edison's company did not play a decisive role in developing the commercial potential of the movies.

   (A) is often credited to have invented
   (B) often receives the credit for invention of
   (C) is often credited with inventing
   (D) has been often credited for inventing
   (E) is often said to have been inventing

3. If you wish to keep your lawn green and healthy-looking, it is necessary to maintain it throughout the year, not just in the summertime.

   (A) it is necessary to maintain it
   (B) you have to make sure that maintaining it is done
   (C) it is necessary that one maintain it
   (D) you have to be maintaining it
   (E) one needs to maintain it

4. Before accepting a competitor's offer to merge, the company has considered a leveraged buyout by several of its top managers, but that deal fell through.

   (A) has considered
   (B) were in consideration of
   (C) had considered
   (D) has been considering
   (E) was to consider

5. Despite the fact being that six of the cancer victims had drank water from the contaminated well, epidemiological experts doubt any connection between the pollution and the high rate of cancer in the community.

   (A) Despite the fact being that six of the cancer victims had drank
   (B) Although six of the cancer victims had drank
   (C) Regardless that six of the cancer victims had drunk
   (D) Despite the fact that six of the cancer victims drunk
   (E) Although six of the cancer victims had drunk

6. Paleontologists are revising their image of the family life of dinosaurs; many now believe that some dinosaurs lived in flocks, tending and feeding their young much like birds do.

   (A) tending and feeding their young much like birds do
   (B) and tended and fed their young much as birds
   (C) tending and feeding their young much like birds
   (D) and, much like birds, were tending and feeding their young
   (E) much as birds, tending and feeding their young

7. Though living as a recluse in her family's Amherst, Massachusetts home, Emily Dickinson's poetry reveals an astonishing breadth and depth of imaginative and intellectual experience.

   (A) Though living as a recluse
   (B) Although she lived as a recluse
   (C) Despite living reclusively
   (D) Though her life was that of a recluse
   (E) Regardless of the fact that she lived a recluse

8. Polls are useful tools for the politician, but they must never control policy; to lead is to direct public opinion, not simply reacting to it.

   (A) not simply reacting to it
   (B) more than simply reacting to it
   (C) rather than to react to it simply
   (D) not simply to react to it
   (E) not to react simply to it

9. Those who deny the authorship of "Shakespeare's" plays to the man from Stratford-on-Avon generally contend that he lacked both the classical education <u>or the experience of life at court that are</u> reflected throughout the plays themselves.

(A) or the experience of life at court that are
(B) and the experience of life at court that are
(C) or the experience of life at court that is
(D) as well as the experience of life at court
(E) and the experience of life at court one finds to be

10. When the space shuttle *Atlantis* returns to earth tomorrow, its crew <u>would have spent</u> over three months conducting experiments while orbiting the planet.

(A) would have spent
(B) will be spending
(C) shall spend
(D) have spent
(E) will have spent

11. <u>Fountain pens long ago replaced feather quills</u>, which were in turn replaced by ballpoint pens, which have now been largely replaced by felt-tipped writing instruments.

(A) Fountain pens long ago replaced feather quills
(B) Feather quills were long ago replaced by fountain pens
(C) Replacing feather quills long ago were fountain pens
(D) Long ago, fountain pens replaced feather quills
(E) Feather quills, replaced by fountain pens long ago

12. The euphoria of the stock market when Dunlap took over the company proved short-lived; <u>he failed to improve the firm's performance, and</u> within two years he was dismissed by a disappointed board of directors.

(A) he failed to improve the firm's performance, and
(B) the firm's performance was not improved by him; thus
(C) failing to improve the firm's performance, so
(D) having failed to improve the firm's performance, and
(E) he failed at improving the firm's performance; therefore

13. Everyone over the age of fifty <u>have become fair game for</u> a wide array of marketing ploys aimed at the burgeoning population of aging "baby boomers," one of the most affluent generations in history.

    (A) have become fair game for
    (B) has become fair game for
    (C) are becoming fair game to
    (D) have become fair game of
    (E) is becoming fair game in

14. Troubled scion of one of the most distinguished families in America, <u>Henry Adams was a noted historian as well as the author of one of the world's greatest works of autobiography.</u>

    (A) Henry Adams was a noted historian as well as the author of one of the world's greatest works of autobiography
    (B) one of the world's greatest works of autobiography was authored by the noted historian Henry Adams
    (C) as well as a noted historian, one of the world's greatest works of autobiography was authored by Henry Adams
    (D) Henry Adams was both a noted historian and in addition author of one of the world's greatest works of autobiography
    (E) a noted historian, and author of one of the world's greatest works of autobiography was Henry Adams

15. <u>Over one thousand years old, the medieval fortress on the Spanish island of Ibizia is the oldest such structure still extant in Europe.</u>

    (A) Over one thousand years old, the medieval fortress on the Spanish island of Ibizia is the oldest such structure still extant in Europe.
    (B) The medieval fortress on the Spanish of Ibizia is over one thousand years old but is the oldest such structure still extant in Europe.
    (C) Still extant, the medieval fortress on the Spanish island of Ibizia is over one thousand years old and the oldest such structure in Europe.
    (D) The oldest such structure still extant in Europe is over one thousand years, the medieval fortress on the Spanish island of Ibizia.
    (E) On the Spanish island of Ibizia, the medieval fortress, which is over one thousand years old, is the oldest such structure still extant in Europe.

EXERCISE 5

15 Questions

Time—20 Minutes

> **Directions:** The following questions present a sentence, part of which or all of which is underlined. Beneath the sentence you will find five ways of phrasing the underlined part. The first of these repeats the original; the other four are different. If you think the original is best, choose the first answer; otherwise, choose one of the others.

1. Neither the board of trustees nor the president of the university <u>were quite certain how</u> to respond to the lawsuit initiated by several of the school's most senior faculty.

   (A) were quite certain how
   (B) was sure as to the proper way
   (C) were certain exactly how
   (D) was quite certain how
   (E) were sure in what way

2. <u>As</u> the electronic synthesizer of today, in its time the pipe organ was remarkable as both a technological and an artistic innovation.

   (A) As
   (B) Like
   (C) Just as
   (D) Similar to
   (E) In the same way as

3. <u>The newest microchips operate so powerfully that</u> a typical laptop computer of today can perform more computations more quickly than the room-sized supercomputers of a generation ago.

   (A) The newest microchips operate so powerfully that
   (B) It is with such power that the newest microchips operate that
   (C) So powerfully operate the newest microchips that
   (D) Because the newest microchips are so powerful, it is so that
   (E) So powerful are the newest microchips that

4. According to a report issued by the Soviet air command, fighter pilots mistakenly identified the civilian airliner with a military jet intruding on Russian air space.

   (A) identified the civilian airliner with
   (B) confused the civilian airliner as being
   (C) identified the civilian airliner as
   (D) took the civilian airliner for being
   (E) considered the civilian airliner as

5. In the years after he left the White House, Richard Nixon strove to burnish his image for history more assiduously than did any former president.

   (A) more assiduously than did any former president
   (B) more assiduously than any other former president
   (C) with an assiduousness unmatched by any former president
   (D) with more assiduousness than did any other former president
   (E) more assiduously in comparison to any former president

6. In a revelation that was both embarrassing and deeply disturbing, a leading news magazine was recently forced to admit that one of its best-known writers had completely fabricated a number of his stories.

   (A) was recently forced to admit
   (B) recently was forced into admitting
   (C) had to admit in recent times
   (D) were forced recently to admit
   (E) admitted recently, having been forced,

7. The tallest peak in Maine, the weather on Mount Washington is notoriously unpredictable, with freezing temperatures common even during July and August.

   (A) the weather on Mount Washington
   (B) Mount Washington's weather
   (C) Mount Washington has weather that
   (D) the weather found on Mount Washington
   (E) Mount Washington is known for its weather being

8. When paint is to be added as part of the restoration process on an old picture, the new pigment must closely match the old in terms of color, texture, and even in chemical composition.

   (A) and even in chemical composition
   (B) as well as chemical composition
   (C) and even chemical composition
   (D) and in terms of chemical composition
   (E) and chemical composition in addition

9. As legal barriers against gambling continue to fall, new forms of wagering become available, intensifying competition in a basically stagnant market, <u>and also increase</u> the social costs associated with gambling.

    (A)   and also increase

    (B)   while it increases

    (C)   as well as increase

    (D)   and increases

    (E)   as well as increasing

10. Although the blimp is considered obsolete as a form of air transportation, <u>they are still common sights</u> in the skies above American cities.

    (A)   they are still common sights

    (B)   it is still a common sight

    (C)   they are still commonly seen

    (D)   a blimp may still commonly appear

    (E)   blimps are commonly still seen

11. Whereas the Soviet leadership opted for a kind of economic shock therapy that has produced significant suffering on the part of the average Russian citizen, China is moving toward capitalism <u>in a more gradual, and perhaps more humane, fashion</u>.

    (A)   in a more gradual, and perhaps more humane, fashion

    (B)   more gradually, and humanely perhaps

    (C)   in a fashion that is more gradual yet perhaps humane

    (D)   in gradual fashion, and perhaps in humane fashion

    (E)   perhaps more humanely and gradually

12. <u>Despite its status as the world's most popular sport, professional soccer</u> has never won the allegiance of more than a handful of fans in the United States.

    (A)   Despite its status as the world's most popular sport, professional soccer

    (B)   Professional soccer, though the world's most popular sport, nevertheless it

    (C)   The world's most popular sport, professional soccer however

    (D)   Although its status is that of the world's most popular sport, professional soccer

    (E)   It is the world's most popular sport, yet despite this fact professional soccer

13. Just as television once replaced radio for most forms of at-home entertainment and information, the Internet <u>is now begun to replace</u> television.

   (A) is now begun to replace
   (B) has now began to replace
   (C) has now begun to replace
   (D) is started replacing
   (E) now is started at replacing

14. Coca-Cola and Pepsi have been battling for years in their quest for dominance in the global soft drink market, but <u>despite its best efforts Pepsi was still</u> continuously falling behind its competitor.

   (A) despite its best efforts Pepsi was still
   (B) no matter how hard they try Pepsi is still
   (C) despite its best efforts Pepsi is still
   (D) its best efforts aside, Pepsi is still
   (E) although having made its best efforts, Pepsi still is

15. <u>Having swam in three events prior to</u> the 500-meter freestyle, Karen was nearly exhausted even before the race began.

   (A) Having swam in three events prior to
   (B) Having swum in three events in precedence of
   (C) Swimming in three events previous to
   (D) With three previous events having been swum before
   (E) Having swum in three events prior to

Answer Key

Exercise 1	Exercise 2	Exercise 3	Exercise 4	Exercise 5
1. E	1. B	1. A	1. E	1. D
2. A	2. A	2. B	2. C	2. B
3. C	3. A	3. D	3. A	3. E
4. D	4. D	4. D	4. C	4. C
5. A	5. B	5. B	5. E	5. B
6. B	6. B	6. B	6. C	6. A
7. A	7. B	7. B	7. B	7. C
8. B	8. A	8. A	8. D	8. C
9. E	9. E	9. C	9. B	9. E
10. E	10. C	10. B	10. E	10. B
11. C	11. D	11. E	11. B	11. A
12. D	12. B	12. C	12. A	12. A
13. E	13. C	13. B	13. B	13. C
14. B	14. A	14. A	14. A	14. C
15. A	15. E	15. A	15. A	15. E

Explanatory Answers

EXERCISE 1

1. **The correct answer is (E).** The sentence lists three things that the overseas Chinese "are more." For the sake of parallelism, all three qualities should be described in grammatically similar ways: "powerful, wealthy, and *influential.*" In addition, *than* should be used rather than *as,* and the word *other* must be included to make the comparison logical.

2. **The correct answer is (A).** The original sentence is perfectly correct. It contrasts "an academic audience" with "a general readership," which is logical both in terms of meaning and in terms of grammar.

3. **The correct answer is (C).** In this context, a semicolon (;) is incorrect, since what follows it is not an independent clause. Choice (C) uses the construction that is most parallel to the first half of the sentence, as well as the logical conjunction *but.*

4. **The correct answer is (D).** The verb *is* indicates that "living life fully" is being equated with "to make mistakes and to accept them." Therefore, these actions should be described in grammatically parallel forms: "to live life fully," "to make mistakes and to accept them."

5. **The correct answer is (A).** The original sentence is correct. Note that the plural pronoun *their* is correct, since its antecedent is "thousands of Americans," also plural.

6. **The correct answer is (B).** The plural verb *disapprove* is necessary here. The antecedent of the pronoun *who* is "any of the stockholders," which is plural (the pronoun *any* may be either singular or plural, depending on the context).

7. **The correct answer is (A).** The original version is the best. The other answer choices are wordy, awkward, or both.

8. **The correct answer is (B).** The meaning of the sentence requires a conjunction that brings out the contrast between the two halves of the sentence. It is surprising that the goal of a good electric car is still elusive, considering how much effort has gone into the concept; therefore, a word like *despite* is needed.

9. **The correct answer is (E).** Normal English verb construction calls for the phrase "require that" to be followed by the verb *be*. (Technically, this is the *subjunctive mood* of the verb *to be*; however, the terminology is not important. Just remember that you should say, "require that *they be*.")

10. **The correct answer is (E).** Since the words *the reason* appear earlier in the sentence, choices (A) through (D) are all redundant; each somehow refers to the concept of cause and effect, which is already included in the word *reason*. Choice (E) is logical: "the reason . . . was said to be El Niño."

11. **The correct answer is (C).** Since Horbach's post is being compared to the posts of all other women on Wall Street, the superlative form of the adjective is required rather than the comparative: "the most prestigious post" is correct.

12. **The correct answer is (D).** The idiomatic preposition here is *between;* one speaks of "comparisons *between*" two things, not *for* two things.

13. **The correct answer is (E).** Simplify the sentence, focusing just on the essential grammatical structure: "Rules [blah blah blah] require money managers either to sell [blah blah blah] or to file [blah blah blah]." The phrases naming the two options—"to sell" or "to file"—must be grammatically parallel, which is what makes choice (E) correct.

14. **The correct answer is (B).** The phrase that starts the sentence modifies "today's laptop computers," so only choices (B), (C), and (D) are possible. Of the three, choice (B) is the least awkward and most clear.

15. **The correct answer is (A).** The original sentence is perfectly correct. Note that the subject of the verb *have provided* is the plural "Dead Sea Scrolls," so the plural verb is appropriate.

EXERCISE 2

1. **The correct answer is (B).** Since the opening phrase of the sentence modifies or describes Gulfstream, the word *Gulfstream* should immediately follow that phrase; so only choices (B) and (D) are possible. Of the two, choice (B) is more graceful and less awkward.

2. **The correct answer is (A).** The first version of this sentence is grammatically correct and more effective than any of the other answer choices, all of which needlessly separate words and phrases that logically belong together.

3. **The correct answer is (A).** The original version of the clause is more idiomatic and graceful than any of the other versions.

4. **The correct answer is (D).** The original sentence errs by shifting needlessly from the plural *smokers* to the singular *smoker.* Choice (D) corrects this error more gracefully and idiomatically than choice (E).

5. **The correct answer is (B).** Since the word *not* has already been used in the clause (four words before *neither*), the word *neither* has the effect of a *double negative*, which is considered incorrect in English. The logical construction is: "the software design [blah blah blah] did not allow the consumer either to disable [blah blah blah] or to easily install [blah blah blah]."

6. **The correct answer is (B).** To make the comparison logical, the words *that of* are necessary; when they are inserted, "The economics of book publishing" is being compared to "that [i.e., the economics] of movies or television."

7. **The correct answer is (B).** Use *liable* only in the sense of *responsible* (e.g., "Whoever caused the accident is liable for the damages"). In this context, *likely* is the correct word.

8. **The correct answer is (A).** There's nothing wrong with the original sentence. The placement of the modifying phrase "in large part" next to the word "based" is appropriate, since that is the word whose meaning the phrase affects.

9. **The correct answer is (E).** The subject of the compound verb "were anticipated and . . . disapproved" is *emergence.* Since the subject is singular, the verb should be, too: "*was* anticipated" rather than "were."

10. **The correct answer is (C).** The two things being compared should be described in grammatically parallel ways: "buying a new appliance" and "fixing an old one."

11. **The correct answer is (D).** The sentence lists three qualities of Dickens, which should all be grammatically parallel. Choice (D) satisfies the parallelism by providing a third phrase made up, like the first two, of an abstract noun (*generosity*) preceded by an adjective (*moral*).

12. **The correct answer is (B).** The plural pronoun *their* is wrong, since its antecedent is the singular "a homeowner." Choice (D) introduces a new error by using the singular verb *is* with the plural subject "his house and its contents."

13. **The correct answer is (C).** The modifying phrase "Known for his autocratic style and shrewd political instincts" needs to be next to what it modifies, "Robert Moses," as is the case in choice (C). Choices (D) and (E) revamp the sentence more thoroughly while making its meaning and its structure a little less clear and coherent.

14. **The correct answer is (A).** The original version of this phrase is the most idiomatic and natural sounding.

15. **The correct answer is (E).** This version is the most concise of the five alternatives; it accurately expresses the meaning in the simplest and shortest way, and therefore is "effective" in GMAT CAT terms.

EXERCISE 3

1. **The correct answer is (A).** The original version is more idiomatic and clear than any of the four alternatives.

2. **The correct answer is (B).** Each of the other versions is verbose (wordy), unclear, or both. Choice (C) also commits the flaw of including a double negative ("won't never"), which is considered an error in English.

3. **The correct answer is (D).** Idiomatically, one speaks of "an attempt *to do*" something rather than "an attempt *to* [or *for*] *doing*" something.

4. **The correct answer is (D).** A decision "depends *on*" something else, so *on* is the idiomatic preposition for this context. In addition, the conjunction *whether* should be used here rather than the word *if.*

5. **The correct answer is (B).** Parallelism requires that the three items in the list be set up in the same fashion; either all three should have *to* attached, or it should be omitted (except at the start of the entire series). Choice (B) chooses the latter option, which is perfectly correct.

6. **The correct answer is (B).** The superlative rather than comparative form of the adjective is required, since Jordan is being compared not just to one other athlete but to all the athletes in the world.

7. **The correct answer is (B).** In the original phrasing, the pronoun *they* has no clear antecedent; you can't tell who or what "they" are. Answer (B) fixes this problem by eliminating the pronoun and inserting the word *airlines* instead.

8. **The correct answer is (A).** The original version is correct, since it sets up the three items in the list in properly parallel form.

9. **The correct answer is (C).** The modifying phrase "blinded by the sun's reflection" must be placed as close as possible to the words that name what it modifies—in this case, *the climbers.* Choice (C) does this in a more graceful and less awkward fashion than any of the alternative choices.

10. **The correct answer is (B).** To make the comparison clear and logical, the word "Madison's" must be used rather than "Madison." This shows that the two things being compared are "the views most Americans hold" and "Madison's [views]."

11. **The correct answer is (E).** The original phrasing is wrong because it attaches the singular verb *has* to the plural subject "not all children." Choice (E) fixes this by making the subject singular, too: "not every child."

12. **The correct answer is (C).** The problem here is subject-verb agreement. The subject of the verb *are expected* is the singular word *chairman*. (Contrary to appearances, "his counterparts blah blah blah" are not part of the subject; the phrase "along with . . . industrial nations" is a parenthetical, interrupting phrase that doesn't affect the grammatical structure of the sentence.) Therefore, the verb should be singular: *is expected*.

13. **The correct answer is (B).** Since the action being described is an action taking place in the past up to and into the future—namely, the increase in the number of baseball franchises in recent years—the proper tense is the present perfect tense, "has increased."

14. **The correct answer is (A).** The original sentence is quite correct. The other answer choices are either awkward or nonidiomatic (i.e., "weird" sounding).

15. **The correct answer is (A).** The original version is the most graceful and the most grammatically parallel in form.

EXERCISE 4

1. **The correct answer is (E).** Since "customers" are countable, the correct adjective to describe them is *few*. (*Little* would be used with a noun that names something one cannot count; "little additional business," for example, would be correct.)

2. **The correct answer is (C).** The proper idiom is to say that someone "is credited with doing" something, not "credited to have done" something as in the original sentence.

3. **The correct answer is (A).** The original version is the best.

4. **The correct answer is (C).** The action being described in the underlined verb phrase is one that took place prior to another action in the past (namely, the "falling through" of the leveraged buyout deal). In that situation, the correct verb tense to use is the past perfect: "had considered."

5. **The correct answer is (E).** In the original version, there are two errors. The word *being* is redundant and nonidiomatic, and "had drank" uses the wrong verb form; *drank* is the past tense, not the past participle. "Had drunk" is correct.

6. **The correct answer is (C).** Distinguish carefully between the use of *like* and *as* in comparisons. Use *like* when what follows is a noun or a noun phrase, not a clause; use *as* when a clause, including a subject and a verb, follows. In the original wording, like is wrong because it's followed by the clause "birds do." Choice (C) corrects this by eliminating the verb, leaving simply the noun "birds."

7. **The correct answer is (B).** The original sentence makes the first half of the sentence a modifying phrase, which ends up sounding wrong; it sounds as if "Emily Dickinson's poetry" was "living as a recluse," which makes no sense. Choice (B) fixes the problem by turning the first half of the sentence into a separate clause in its own right and inserting the word *she* to make it clear who "lived as a recluse."

8. **The correct answer is (D).** In the interest of parallelism, the last verb in this sentence should be in the infinitive form, as the others are: "to react" rather than "reacting."

9. **The correct answer is (B).** The word *both* should be followed by the word *and* rather than the word *or*: one speaks of "both X and Y," not "both X *or* Y."

10. **The correct answer is (E).** Use the future perfect tense, including the helping verbs *will have,* to describe an event happening in the future prior to some other future event. In this case, the landing of the space shuttle tomorrow is a future event; prior to that, the crew "will have spent over three months" blah blah blah.

11. **The correct answer is (B).** The first clause here must end with "fountain pens," since the next clause picks up with "which were in turn replaced." The parallel structure requires each clause in the series to take the general form, "X was replaced by Y."

12. **The correct answer is (A).** The original version is the best.

13. **The correct answer is (B).** The pronoun *everyone* is singular (as is every pronoun that ends in "-one"); therefore, it requires the singular verb "has become."

14. **The correct answer is (A).** The original version is perfectly correct. Note that the underlined portion of the sentence *must* begin with "Henry Adams," since he is what the modifying phrase at the start of the sentence refers to.

15. **The correct answer is (A).** The original sentence is correct and preferable to any of the other answer choices.

EXERCISE 5

1. **The correct answer is (D).** When the two parts of a compound subject are linked by *or* (or, in this case, *nor,* which is the equivalent), the verb should agree in number with the latter part (since that is closer to the verb). Therefore, the governing subject in this sentence is "president," and the singular verb "was" is correct.

2. **The correct answer is (B).** Since what follows is not a clause but a noun phrase ("the electronic synthesizer of today"), the preposition *Like* should be used rather than the conjunction *as.*

3. **The correct answer is (E).** The idiomatic construction is "So X is Y that . . ." etc. The other choices here are awkward or ambiguous in meaning.

4. **The correct answer is (C).** It is idiomatic to say that someone "identified X as Y," not "identified X with Y."

5. **The correct answer is (B).** Since Nixon was himself a former president, he is a member of the group with which he is being compared in the final part of the sentence. Therefore, the word "other" is essential to make the comparison logical.

6. **The correct answer is (A).** There are no errors in the original version of the sentence.

7. **The correct answer is (C).** Because the sentence begins with the modifying phrase "The tallest peak in Maine," what follows must be the words "Mount Washington," since that is what the phrase describes.

8. **The correct answer is (C).** Choice (C) creates the "most parallel" possible construction; the three things being listed are "color, texture, and [even] chemical composition."

9. **The correct answer is (E).** The gerund, *increasing,* is necessary in order to match the previous gerund, *intensifying.* The second half of the sentence is saying that, as "new forms of wagering become available," it is causing two things to happen: it is "intensifying competition" and "increasing" blah blah blah.

10. **The correct answer is (B).** In the original, the plural pronoun *they* has no sensible antecedent. Choice (B) changes it to the singular pronoun *it,* which matches nicely with the antecedent "the blimp."

11. **The correct answer is (A).** The original version of the sentence is completely correct.

12. **The correct answer is (A).** There are no errors in the original sentence. Note that it is best to end the underlined portion with the words "professional soccer," since this keeps the subject and the verb of the sentence together—generally a desirable state of affairs.

13. **The correct answer is (C).** The correct present perfect form of the verb "begin" is "has begun."

14. **The correct answer is (C).** Since the action being described is happening now, "is falling behind" is the correct form of the verb.

15. **The correct answer is (E).** The past participle of the verb *to swim* is *swum,* and that is the proper form to use with the helping verb *having.* (The past tense, swam, would only be used by itself, without a helping verb: "Karen swam all day.")

Chapter 6

Critical Reasoning

Get the Scoop On . . .

- Tested techniques for conquering critical reasoning questions
- How to recognize the three key elements in every logical argument
- The six types of logical fallacies most often tested on the GMAT CAT
- The four question types you'll encounter and how to answer each one
- The dangers of "creative" and "sophisticated" thinking and how to avoid them

THE TEST CAPSULE

What's the Big Idea?

You'll be given a short reading passage, 50–100 words long, that presents a logical argument designed to prove a point of some kind. You'll then have to answer a question that requires you to evaluate the logic of the passage.

How Many?

Your GMAT CAT will probably have 13 or 14 critical reasoning questions out of 41 total Verbal questions.

How Much Do They Count?

Critical reasoning questions are about 14 out of 41 total Verbal questions. They count as 34 percent of your overall Verbal score.

How Much Time Should They Take?

You need to answer critical reasoning questions at a rate of about 2 minutes per question. This includes the time you'll take both to read the argument and to answer the question about it.

What's the Best Strategy?

Learn to look for the six most common types of fallacies—logical errors—that are built into most critical reasoning passages. If you can recognize these, you'll be able to demolish the faulty arguments that turn up on the exam and ace the questions that are related to them.

What's the Worst Pitfall?

It's a mistake to respond to a critical reasoning passage or to the accompanying question on the basis of what you know or believe to be true. You may have strong opinions or extensive personal knowledge about some of the topics discussed in this part of the exam. Forget all of it! A worthy point of view may be defended ineptly in a critical reading passage, whereas a despicable position may be argued ably. All you should care about is the strength or weakness of the argument on the page—not the validity of the underlying opinions.

THE OFFICIAL DESCRIPTION

What They Are

Critical reasoning is a specialized kind of reading comprehension in which the emphasis is placed on your ability to understand and analyze the logic behind an argument. You'll be given a short passage to read, which may resemble an excerpt from a magazine article, a book, a newspaper editorial, a political speech, an advertisement, or even a snippet of conversation. In every case, the passage presents an argument—that is, an attempt to persuade the reader of the truth of some statement. You'll then be asked to answer a question that focuses in one way or another on the strength or weakness of the argument.

Where They Are

In the typical computerized GMAT CAT, you'll have a 75-minute Verbal section with a total of about 41 questions. Critical reasoning is one of the three types of questions that will appear in this section, intermingled in a seemingly random sequence. Reminder: The test makers claim the right to change the format at any time! However, the typical format we just described is what you're most likely to encounter.

What They Measure

You're not expected to bring any special background knowledge to critical reasoning questions. The passages contain all of the information necessary to answer the questions. Even if a passage deals with a topic you know absolutely nothing about (the second law of thermodynamics, say, or drunk driving laws in Oregon), don't be concerned; you'll be told everything you need to know.

In addition, formal logic is not tested on the GMAT CAT. You won't be required to solve a syllogism or use specialized terms or symbols from logic. If you've taken a logic course, fine—it won't hurt—but you're not at a disadvantage if you haven't. The key skill that is being tested is the ability to think clearly and to see the flaws in the fuzzy thinking of others.

The Directions

> **Directions:** For this question, select the best of the answer choices given.

THE INSIDER'S REPORT: STRATEGIES THAT REALLY WORK

Learn to Recognize the Key Elements of Any Argument

The word *argument* as used here may be a bit misleading. We don't mean a quarrel (the way "argument" is usually used in everyday life: "My aunt and uncle had another argument, and she threw his clothes all over the front lawn again"). Instead, we're using the word to mean any attempt to persuade you that a particular fact, idea, or opinion is correct.

In this sense, you encounter arguments by the dozens every day. Your spouse or best friend tries to talk you into taking a vacation in the mountains instead of by the shore; she marshals arguments to persuade you that her plan will be more fun, more affordable, more whatever. A commentator on the radio holds forth about the latest political controversy; he fires arguments at you in an attempt to convince you of his point of view. What is an advertisement if not an argument designed to persuade you that a certain product or service is the best available and that you'll be oh-so-happy if you buy it?

The fact is, you're constantly bombarded by arguments. Some are sound and valid (maybe a cabin in the Rockies *would* be a nice change this year); others are laughably inept (think of the last TV commercial whose idiocy made you snort). In most cases, however, you probably don't bother to carefully analyze the arguments you hear—nor should you. A quick "gut check" is often enough, in real life, to tell you whether you believe a particular argument, and, in most cases, you won't go too wrong making decisions on that basis.

Critical reasoning on the GMAT CAT attempts to test your ability to evaluate arguments in a more formal, rigorous fashion. The gut instinct for baloney that most of us develop through a lifetime of exposure to TV commercials, newspaper editorials, and political rhetoric will be your main weapon in tackling these questions. But it also helps to have at your disposal a few basic tools for analyzing and understanding arguments in a consistent, formal fashion. When the questions on the exam get tricky, subtle, or complicated, these tools can help you.

The first tool you need is a knowledge of the basic structure of any argument. As presented on the GMAT CAT, almost every argument has three elements: a *conclusion, evidence* to support the conclusion, and one or more *hidden assumptions* on which the argument rests. Let's consider each more closely.

The Conclusion

This is what the author of the argument is trying to get you to believe or agree with. It will normally be stated explicitly somewhere in the passage (although not always, as we'll discuss later). The conclusion may sound like a statement of fact ("One third of the physicians in the Denver area own foreign sports cars"); it may sound like an opinion ("The new Alberghetti convertible is fun to drive!"); it may even sound like a call to action ("You should test-drive the new Alberghetti today."). In each case, the conclusion is what the rest of the argument is intended to support or prove.

The conclusion is often signaled by one or more *clue words*, which are inserted specifically to alert the reader to the fact that the main point of the argument is coming. We've listed some of the most common examples in Table 6.1. Practice looking for them whenever you read.

The Evidence

This is the material that the author of the argument is using to convince you to agree with the conclusion. In GMAT CAT critical reasoning questions (as in real life), evidence isn't necessarily like evidence in a court of law. It may include all manner of ideas, statements, and information—relevant or irrelevant.

The evidence used in a critical reasoning passage may include facts ("The Alberghetti convertible goes from 0 to 60 in 1.2 milliseconds"), quotations ("Sports-car driver Jim Crashtest says, 'I love the new Alberghetti convertible!'"), statistics ("The Alberghetti is the fastest selling convertible in America"), emotional appeals ("The sleek lines of the Alberghetti ooze sex appeal!"), and so on. What they all have in

Table 6.1
Clue Words That Signal Conclusions

therefore
consequently
hence
thus
so
we can conclude
which shows that
it can be inferred that
it is apparent that
we must agree that

Table 6.2
Clue Words That Signal Evidence

Because
Since
As
Due to
Inasmuch as
Insofar as
Given the fact that
As demonstrated by

common is that they are intended to help win you over to the author's conclusion. Anything that plays this role in a GMAT CAT argument, we call evidence.

Sometimes, the evidence is also signaled by clue words. Table 6.2 lists some examples to watch for.

The Hidden Assumptions

These are facts or ideas, *not stated in the passage,* that must be true if the argument is to be considered valid. Hidden assumptions underlie every argument. This is inevitable because no argument can state explicitly every single fact or idea that's needed to support a particular conclusion. (Life is too short.) However, assumptions are the secret pitfall of many an argument. If they are true, the argument may be sound, valid, and convincing. If they are false, the argument is likely to break down completely. Because they are unstated—"hidden" in that sense—they are easy to overlook, although they are crucial.

Because assumptions don't actually appear in the passage, no clue words mark them. Instead, you must "read between the lines" to recognize what is not being said, but what *must* be true if the argument is valid.

Here's how it works. Suppose that an argument is being made to support the conclusion, "You should buy the new Alberghetti convertible." As we've already seen, many kinds of evidence could be presented on behalf of this conclusion. Almost every one involves one or more hidden assumptions.

> *Evidence:* "The Alberghetti convertible goes from 0 to 60 in 1.2 milliseconds."

> *Assumption:* You need or want a car that can accelerate obscenely fast.

FYI

Here's another way to think about assumptions: They are often necessary links between the evidence and the conclusion. If the assumption is sound, then the evidence leads inexorably to the conclusion. If the assumption is weak—like a crumbling footbridge—then there's no real connection between the evidence and the conclusion, and the argument collapses.

(If this assumption is true, then the evidence does support the notion that the Alberghetti is a good car to buy; if not, then the evidence is worthless.)

> *Evidence:* "Sports-car driver Jim Crashtest says, 'I love the new Alberghetti convertible!' "

> *Assumptions:* You should care what Jim Crashtest says. The opinion of a professional sports-car driver concerning which car is best is relevant to your needs as a driver.

(If you, too, are a sports-car driver, then Jim's opinion may actually be relevant to your driving needs. But if you spend most of your driving hours stuck in five-mile-per-hour traffic, or if you use your car mainly to shuttle a three-year-old to day care, then Jim's tastes may mean nothing to you.)

> *Evidence:* "The Alberghetti is the fastest selling convertible in America."

> *Assumptions:* If a car sells quickly, it must be good. If other people are buying a car, it must be right for you, too.

(Obviously, sheer popularity isn't proof of quality. After all, a lot of people bought Spice Girls albums, too.)

> *Evidence:* "The sleek lines of the Alberghetti ooze sex appeal!"

> *Assumption:* You want or need a car whose design is sexy.

(Whatever that means)

When you read a critical reasoning argument on the GMAT CAT, start by looking for the conclusion. You may want to mark it in some way on your scrap paper. The most important thing you can do is to be clear on exactly what the author is trying to convince you of.

Then, consider the evidence. How convincing is it? How strong is the connection between the evidence and the conclusion? What hidden assumptions underlie that connection? Are those assumptions plausible? These are the issues that determine whether or not the argument is logical, valid, and convincing. In almost every case, the question that follows the passage will focus on these issues.

Look for *Fallacies*—the Logical Weaknesses That Can Cripple an Argument

As we've already suggested, the arguments presented on the GMAT CAT aren't always watertight in their logic (to say the least). Like advertisements, political speeches, newspaper letters to the editor, and the dinner-table pronouncements of your father-in-law, they are often marred by lapses in reasoning, implausible assertions, and illogical connections. These, of course, are fodder for the questions that follow.

Logic is an ancient discipline, and philosophers dating back to classical Greece have studied, diagnosed, and catalogued dozens of specific types of logical flaws. These are often called *fallacies*. If you've ever taken a course in what's usually called "informal logic," you've learned about these. They're sometimes taught in English or writing classes, as well. However, if you've never studied the topic, no matter. As with every area on the GMAT CAT, the test is designed so that no particular college course is necessary to do well. Only a handful of the many types of fallacies studied by philosophers appear frequently on the exam.

In what follows, we'll explain the most common fallacies found in critical reasoning passages and give an example or two of each.

Scanty Evidence

The names we use for the common fallacies are not tested on the exam, nor is any other terminology from the study of logic. To do well on the GMAT CAT, you need to recognize when an argument is flawed; you don't *need to be able to classify the flaw according to any specific or formal system of logic.*

This is probably the single most common fallacy found on the GMAT CAT. In an argument with this fallacy, the amount of evidence offered in support of the conclusion is inadequate. The fallacy can take several forms:

> The conclusion may be a sweeping generalization, whereas the evidence may be one or two specific facts that fall short of justifying the broad conclusion.

> The evidence may consist of a few handpicked facts that tend to support the conclusion, whereas other facts that might tend to undermine the conclusion are (deliberately?) ignored.

> The evidence may involve statistics, a survey, or an experiment that is too limited in scope to justify the conclusion drawn.

Here are a couple of examples:

> Despite what people say, there are plenty of teaching opportunities for Ph.D.s in the humanities. Windsor College recently had to cancel plans to hire two teachers for their English department because of a lack of qualified candidates.

(One anecdote isn't sufficient evidence to support the general conclusion stated in the first sentence. Maybe Windsor College is an exceptionally unattractive employer—located in the Arctic tundra, for example.)

> Samothrace Shoes is deeply committed to fair treatment of all workers, including those in developing countries. The company recently announced a new policy of refusing to do business with any Asian supplier that hires children to work in its factories.

(Only one fact is mentioned, whereas facts that might reflect badly on the business methods of Samothrace Shoes aren't mentioned. Is it because they don't exist or because the author wants to bury them?)

Post Hoc Reasoning

The name of this fallacy comes from a Latin phrase, *post hoc, ergo propter hoc,* which means "After this, therefore because of this." The phrase describes the fallacy: It occurs whenever the author of an argument assumes that because one event occurs *after* another event, it therefore occurs *because of* that other event. (You might also call this fallacy "faulty cause-and-effect reasoning.")

Because the world is a complicated place, cause-and-effect relationships are rarely simple or obvious. Arguments that assume that one cause is the sole cause of one effect are often oversimplified or misleading; more often, a combination of factors lies behind any significant event or trend. Arguments that commit the post hoc fallacy ignore this reality.

Here are a couple of examples of the post hoc fallacy:

> Fifty years ago, American schools were safe havens for the young. Students' persons and property were rarely assaulted, and serious crimes of violence were almost unheard of. Over the past four decades, ever since the U.S. Supreme Court banned voluntary prayer in public schools, the rate of violent crime in schools has risen steadily. It's time to bring back prayer in schools to restore them to morality and safety.

(Undoubtedly, many factors have contributed to increasing crime in schools. Is the absence of prayer such a factor—even the major factor, as the author apparently believes? Maybe—but the argument presented certainly doesn't prove it.)

> In a study of 200 families with school-age children, those families that had received family counseling from a psychologist or social worker reported significantly higher rates of drug, alcohol, and sexual abuse than those that had not received such counseling. Clearly, family counseling does more harm than good.

(This argument has probably gotten cause and effect backwards. It seems more logical to assume that the families with problems are the ones who seek counseling rather than assume that the counseling *causes* the problems.)

The Straw Man

A logical argument sometimes must respond to opposing points of view by showing how and why they are wrong. Occasionally, however, an argument designed to respond to an opponent goes awry. In an argument with the *straw man fallacy,* the opposing point of view is presented in an unfairly simplified, exaggerated, or distorted form. (Hence the name of the fallacy: rather than battle a flesh-and-blood opponent, the author props up a "straw man" and beats *that* to a pulp.)

A simple version of this fallacy appears constantly in politics, where candidates on the right call their opponents "way-out liberals," whereas candidates on the left call their opponents "right-wing extremists." Here's a slightly more subtle version, taken from a real exam, complete with the accompanying question:

> Asserting that newspapers should reflect the needs of their readers, a group of newspaper publishers conducted a survey to determine how readers felt newspapers could be improved. The readers made two recommendations: newspapers should emphasize events closer to the readers' lives and should feature articles about the reporters. If we take the publishers and their survey seriously, readers will be asked which events in their own lives they wish to read about, and these articles, overlaid with autobiographical vignettes, will be produced by the reporters. In this closed world, writers and readers will hold forth in an uninterrupted one-to-one dialogue from which events of the larger world—what used to be called news—are shut out.

1. The author's response to the survey is flawed because the author
   - (A) fails to consider alternative explanations of the data.
   - (B) fails to define what he means by the term "news".
   - (C) considers only one of the recommendations made by the survey respondents.
   - (D) misinterprets the intention of the survey respondents' recommendations.
   - (E) assumes that newspapers do not need to be improved.

Whatever you may think about the survey described in the passage, the author's description of the "closed world" that would be created if newspapers followed the recommendations made is certainly exaggerated. The readers who asked for more coverage of events close to their lives and expressed an interest in knowing more about the reporters surely didn't mean to imply that "events of the larger world" should be completely *eliminated* from the news. Yet that is what the author seems to think. He is guilty of turning the point of view he dislikes into a straw man, as explained in other words by answer choice (D).

The Ad Hominem Argument

This is another Latin phrase borrowed from scholarly logicians; *ad hominem* means "against the person." An ad hominem argument attacks an opposing point of view not by pointing out logical or factual flaws in the opposing argument but by criticizing the opponent on personal grounds.

Again, politics is a fruitful source of examples. But an ad hominem argument can crop up in almost any field. Here's an example:

> The Energy Resources Council has issued a report advocating the use of ethanol as a fuel additive, claiming that it will help clean our atmosphere and reduce our reliance on fossil fuels. But the Council receives a portion

of its annual budget from a large grain-processing firm, which will benefit financially from the use of ethanol, so the claims in the report must be discounted.

Notice how one might respond logically to the information presented here. In the real world, we know that people *are* influenced by their pocketbooks, so an awareness of the Council's funding sources and any *possible* bias they might promote is important. Knowing that the Council's supporters might have a stake in promoting ethanol should prompt informed readers (especially those competent to judge the claims made in the report, such as scientists) to examine the data in the report with an especially skeptical eye.

However, to simply dismiss the report because of the Council's funding source is to go too far. It's not enough to show that an opponent *might* be biased; it's also necessary to refute the actual arguments raised by the opponent in order to demonstrate that that *possible* bias has become real. As written, the argument is guilty of the ad hominem fallacy because it assumes that merely attacking the credibility of the opponent is sufficient.

The Excluded Middle

Not some sort of flab-fighting exercise plan, the excluded middle is a fallacy that involves reducing disagreements to black-and-white terms. An excluded-middle argument assumes, literally, that there is no middle ground and tries to force anyone with a different position to occupy one of two diametrically opposed camps.

Debates over deeply held moral convictions often generate excluded-middle arguments: Think of abortion, for example, where opposing groups, both sincerely convinced of their moral rightness, seem unable to view one another in any light but the most uncompromisingly negative one.

Here's an example from a field that is only slightly less contentious:

> The U.S. Department of Justice has announced its intention to prosecute a leading software manufacturer for what it calls "anti-competitive" practices. Far from benefiting consumers, this action will, in the long run, harm them and our nation. The government has no business interfering in the operations of the free market, and when it does so, it inevitably produces a worse mess than the one it intended to "fix." One need only look at the disastrous effects of government-run markets in the former Soviet bloc to recognize this.

The author of this argument lumps together a Justice Department prosecution of a software company for anti-competitive practices with all the problems of the former Soviet economy—as if any government role in the economy is tantamount to communism. This is a classic example of excluded-middle reasoning—persuasive at a glance, but without nuance and, ultimately, divorced from reality.

The Dubious Assumption

As we've seen, every argument rests on one or more hidden assumptions. There's nothing sinister about this. Because there's never enough time to say *everything,* it's inevitable that any author must take for granted certain basic concepts. If these are valid, there's no problem. The trouble starts when an argument is based on assumptions that are logically flawed or factually dubious. When this is true, the entire argument is likely to collapse.

Here's a fairly obvious example from a real exam, complete with the accompanying question:

> Young people today have more formal education than their grandparents had. Wilma is young, so she must have had more formal education than her grandparents had.

1. The chief weakness of this argument is its

   (A) attempt to draw a conclusion by offering a reason for that conclusion.

   (B) attempt to assign a single cause to a phenomenon that might have multiple causes.

   (C) assumption that what is true for a group as a whole is true for each member of that group.

   (D) failure to define its terms adequately.

   (E) attempt to draw a conclusion from possibly incorrect evidence.

The correct answer is (C). The conclusion—that Wilma has had more formal education than her grandparents—is true only if the assumption stated in choice (C) is correct. If it is correct, then the connection between the evidence stated in the first sentence of the passage and the conclusion stated in the second sentence is a strong one.

But that assumption is obviously false. We all know that (virtually) every generalization has its exceptions—although we all forget this at times, like when we stereotype people on the basis of one characteristic. The problem with the logic in the passage is its reliance on a false assumption, and the question is designed to ferret this out.

Here's a more subtle example, also from a real exam:

> The essence of the United States president's relationship with members of the executive branch is that he must persuade them to believe that what the president wants of them is what their own appraisal of their own responsibilities requires them to do in their own interest, not the president's. For persuasion deals in the coin of self-interest, and people always have some freedom to reject what they find counterfeit.

2. The claim about the nature of persuasion advanced above is weakened if it is true that some members of the executive branch

    (A) are subject to persuasion not only by appeals to self-interest but also by reasoned argument.
    (B) are appointed by the president and therefore are likely to be like-minded agents who require no persuasion.
    (C) are appointed by the president and therefore are beholden to the president for their jobs.
    (D) do not appraise their own interests and responsibilities accurately.
    (E) do what they consider to be in their own interest regardless of the president's attempts at persuasion.

Notice that, in this case, neither the question nor the answer explicitly uses the word assumption. Nonetheless, this is a question about the faulty assumption underlying the argument. The author assumes—without offering evidence to prove it—that people only and always act in accordance with their self-interest. This *may* be true—it's a large philosophical question—but it depends, in large measure, on how you define self-interest and on what sorts of seemingly altruistic or unselfish acts one is willing to consider exceptions to the rule. In any case, it's a sweeping generalization that is certainly open to question, if not clearly erroneous.

Because this is the major flaw in the argument, the best way to weaken the claim it makes (as asked for in the question) is to expose that flaw—which choice (A) does by suggesting that the assumption may be false.

THE INSIDER'S REPORT: THE BEST TIPS

The six fallacies we've just discussed certainly don't exhaust the possibilities you'll encounter on the GMAT CAT, but you'll probably find that most of the critical reasoning passages on the exam do contain fallacies of one kind or another and that most of these are variations of our top six list.

Recognize and practice the four most common question types. As with every question type, critical reasoning items fall into definite patterns. We've found that the test makers generally use variations on four basic types of questions. If you understand what the test makers are looking for in a response to each of these four question types, none of the items on the exam are likely to mystify you.

■ **Pick the rebuttal.** As we've seen, most (not all) critical reasoning passages contain fallacies of some kind. A pick-the-rebuttal question asks you to recognize the kind of fallacy the passage exhibits and choose an answer that brings it clearly to the fore.

Here are some of the typical question stems that are used to introduce pick-the-rebuttal items:

Which of the following is the most serious weakness in the argument above?

All of the following are valid objections to the argument above EXCEPT

Which of the following is the best criticism of the argument above?

■ **Unearth the assumption.** This kind of question asks you to recognize one or more of the hidden assumptions that underlie the argument. You may have to recognize the difference between a truly crucial assumption—an idea that must be true to keep the entire argument from collapsing—and a minor assumption, whose falsehood would affect the argument only marginally.

Here are some of the typical question stems to expect for an unearth-the-assumption item:

> Which of the following assumptions is most pivotal to the argument above?

> Which of the following must be true if the conclusion of the argument above is valid?

> Which of the following is an assumption underlying the conclusion of the passage above?

■ **Weigh new evidence.** Here, the question presents you with one or more new pieces of evidence—facts, ideas, or other information. Your job is to decide how each piece of new evidence would affect the argument. Does it agree with or bolster the evidence given in the argument and thereby strengthen the conclusion? Or does it undermine or contradict the evidence presented and thereby weaken the conclusion?

Here are some of the ways that a weigh-new-evidence item may be worded:

> Which of the following, if true, most weakens (*or* strengthens) the argument above?

> The answer to which of the following questions would be most helpful in evaluating the argument above?

> Which of the following, if true, provides evidence to support (*or* refute) the claim made in the argument above?

■ **Draw your own conclusion.** Occasionally, you'll be presented with a passage that contains *no* conclusion. Instead, a number of facts, ideas, opinions, or other pieces of evidence will be offered, and your job will be to decide what kind of conclusion may logically be based on this evidence. The correct answer choice will be one that states a conclusion that grows naturally from the evidence; wrong answers will normally exhibit one or more logical fallacies such as the ones we illustrated previously.

THE INSIDER'S REPORT: THE MOST IMPORTANT WARNINGS

Forget What You Know; Forget What You Think

The passages appearing in the GMAT CAT for critical reasoning will deal with a wide variety of topics: social issues, business concerns, political and economic disputes, scientific theories, and purely personal matters. If you happen to know or care about a particular topic that pops up on the exam, *forget what you know or think.*

It's likely that the conclusion reached by the author of the argument on the exam will be different from your own opinion; it's quite possible that the evidence presented will be inaccurate, outdated, or completely fictitious. You mustn't let any of this bother you. Base your answer strictly on the logical strengths and weaknesses of the passage as written, and don't bring your personal knowledge or beliefs into the equation.

Don't Think Outside the Box

Remember that each passage on the GMAT CAT represents an argument as presented by an author, either real or fictitious. The argument may be valid, invalid, or a little of both; but in any case, your job is to respond to the question *in terms of the argument presented,* not in broader terms of right and wrong, truth and falsehood.

Consider this example, from a real exam:

> Between 1950 and 1965, the federal government spent one third more on research and development than industry did from its own funds. In 1980, for the first time, industry spent more on research and development than the federal government did. Representatives of industry claim that these statistics show an increased commitment on the part of industry to develop competitive products.

> Which of the following, if true, would help to refute the claim of the representatives of industry?

> (A) In 1980, the federal government spent half as much on research and development as it spent in 1965.
> (B) Between 1965 and 1980, industry in the United States experienced increasing competition from industry in other countries.
> (C) In 1979, the federal government shifted research allocations from pharmaceuticals to electronics.
> (D) Since 1965, industry has developed major product innovations, such as the personal computer.
> (E) Before 1985, money spent by industry on research and development was not taxed by the federal government.

Now, this passage reads like part of the ongoing debate over American business competitiveness. Is American industry doing enough to ensure its competitive strength versus foreign companies into the next century? What role should the government play in this effort? As a nation, are we investing enough in R&D, education, capital improvements, worker training, and other efforts to bolster the productivity and creativity of business? These issues have been argued about for years, and people with interests on all sides have traded criticisms and rebuttals freely.

In this context, we might read the claim made by "representatives of industry" in the passage as part of a larger defense of U.S. business interests against the attacks of those who consider American executives shortsighted, self-serving, or inept. This larger context actually exists in the real world. *However, it's completely irrelevant to the question as written* and is likely to mislead you when you try to answer the question. Here's why.

If you think of this passage as part of the ongoing pro and con debate about American business, you might be tempted to choose choice (B) or choice (E). Choice (B) could be relevant because it suggests that U.S. industry was under siege from foreign competition during the 1970s (as in fact it was) and that only because of this intense, unprecedented pressure did American business increase its R&D investments. Therefore, one might conclude that industrial leaders don't really deserve any credit for spending more on R&D; it was a "no-brainer" decision that may in any case have been too little, too late.

Similarly, choice (E) might seem relevant because it suggests an important secondary motive for business people in spending money on R&D—to get the tax breaks provided for such spending by Uncle Sam. Again, this statement, if true, could be regarded as taking away much of the credit the executives might otherwise deserve.

In a debate about the wisdom or foolishness of American business leadership, both of these ideas might well be relevant. In the context of the GMAT CAT question, however, both are irrelevant. The question does not ask about the larger issues of the quality of American business management, the proper role of government in the economy, laissez-faire versus government intervention, and so on. It simply asks for the best refutation of the *specific* claim in the passage.

That claim relates only to the argument cited by the "representatives of industry"—namely, the fact that, in 1980, industry spent more on R&D than government. What are the weaknesses in the use of this fact as evidence of an increased commitment to competitiveness by industry? It's simple. The fact that industry spent more than government may not reflect increased spending on the part of industry; rather, it may reflect *decreased* spending by the government. Industry's spending could have remained the same, or even fallen, as long as it fell by less than government spending. Without the actual numbers, we can't tell. The answer that focuses on this very narrow, specific issue is choice (A), and that's the only answer the test makers will accept.

The point? Be careful not to broaden the question by including it in a wider, more general, or more sophisticated intellectual, social, or conceptual context. The GMAT CAT doesn't reward creative or sophisticated thinking! Stick closely and single-mindedly to the specific question asked and the specific facts cited; that's what the test makers like to see.

JUST THE FACTS

- Every argument has three key elements—evidence, a conclusion, and hidden assumptions.

- Six types of fallacies are commonly found in critical reasoning passages; you should learn to recognize each.

- Each of the four question types featured on the exam focuses differently on the relationship among the key elements of the argument.

- Avoid interpreting the questions in a creative, sophisticated way or applying outside knowledge; stick closely to what's on the page.

PRACTICE, PRACTICE, PRACTICE: CRITICAL REASONING EXERCISES

Instructions

The following exercises will give you a chance to practice the skills and strategies you've just learned for tackling critical reasoning questions. As with all practice exercises, work under true testing conditions. Complete each exercise in a single sitting. Eliminate distractions (TV, music) and clear away notes and reference materials.

Time yourself with a stopwatch or kitchen timer, or have someone else time you. If you run out of time before answering all the questions, stop and draw a line under the last question you finished. Then, go ahead and tackle the remaining questions. When you are done, score yourself based only on the questions you finished in the allotted time.

Record your responses by blackening the circle next to the answer of your choice.

Understanding Your Scores

0–4 correct: A poor performance. Study this chapter again.

5–6 correct: A below-average score. Study this chapter again, focusing especially on the skills and strategies you've found newest and most challenging.

7–9 correct: An average score. You may want to study this chapter again. Also be sure you are managing your time wisely (as explained in Chapter 3) and avoid errors due to haste or carelessness.

10–12 correct: An above-average score. Depending on your personal target score and your strength on the other verbal question types, you may or may not want to devote additional time to critical reasoning study.

13–14 correct: An excellent score. You are probably ready to perform well on GMAT CAT critical reasoning questions.

EXERCISE 1

14 Questions

Time—25 Minutes

> **Directions:** For each question, select the best of the answer choices given.

1. Due, in part, to the success of African-American Alex Haley's book in 1976, and the popular television miniseries based on it, interest in genealogy has increased significantly in the United States over the past 20 years.

   Since the book's publication, the average age of Americans has also increased, due to the millions of Americans born during the "baby boom" who, by the mid-90s, were reaching middle age, and many of whom are now interested in discovering their own "roots."

   If the information in the statement above is true, which of the following must also be true?

   (A) African-Americans are more interested than other Americans in their family histories.

   (B) Prior to the publication of Haley's book, the American public had little interest in genealogy.

   (C) Middle-aged Americans are more likely to have an interest in genealogy than are younger people.

   (D) White Americans are more interested in genealogy than African Americans.

   (E) Television is chiefly responsible for the current increase in interest in genealogy.

2. In 1939, when the film *Gone with the Wind,* based on Margaret Mitchell's best-selling book, was about to be released, Hollywood's censors were very strict about permitting off-color language to be used in the movies. Nevertheless, David O. Selznick, the film's producer, was able to convince the censors to allow the film to close with Clark Gable's now-famous line, "Frankly, my dear, I don't give a damn."

Knowledge of all of the following would potentially be useful in explaining the events described above EXCEPT

(A) the status of Selznick in the film industry at the time.

(B) whether the line in question had appeared in the original best-selling book.

(C) the degree of Selznick's concern over public reaction to the use of the word "damn."

(D) whether the censors had banned the use of the word "damn" in other films.

(E) the popularity of Clark Gable among the movie-going public.

3. Neither archaeologists nor historians have found any written texts in the Hebrew language dating from before the tenth century B.C. This means that the story of the Israelites' exodus from Egypt as recorded in the Old Testament, which occurred before that date, must have been originally preserved not as a written text but by means of oral tradition.

All of the following are valid objections to the argument above EXCEPT

(A) the story of the exodus may have been originally written down in a language other than Hebrew.

(B) texts in Hebrew from before the tenth century B.C. may have existed at some time in the past.

(C) texts composed in an earlier form of Hebrew may have been found but not recognized as such.

(D) texts in Hebrew from before the tenth century B.C. may exist without having come to the attention of historians or archaeologists.

(E) oral tradition is not as reliable a means of preserving stories of the past as written accounts.

4. Arthur Conan Doyle's fictional detective Sherlock Holmes is renowned as a master of deductive reasoning. On more than one occasion, when Holmes was confronted with an apparently insoluble problem, he was quoted as saying, "When you have eliminated the impossible, whatever remains, *however improbable, must be the truth.*"

All of the following are valid criticisms of Holmes's argument EXCEPT

(A) "the truth" may involve a combination of possibilities rather than a single fact.

(B) the improbability of an explanation makes it unlikely to be the truth.

(C) there may be a possibility of which the reasoner is unaware.

(D) a reasoner may be unable to determine with certainty whether a particular explanation is possible.

(E) improbability is a subjective rather than objective criterion.

5. Many film critics have called Sir Laurence Olivier the greatest actor of the twentieth century. However, his participation in such ill-conceived and poorly executed films as *The Betsy, Clash of the Titans*, and *Bunny Lake Is Missing* seriously undermines his claim to any such exalted title.

All of the following assumptions underlie the conclusion of the passage above EXCEPT

(A) the three films cited were in fact ill-conceived and poorly executed.

(B) if a particular film was poor, then Olivier's performance in it must have been equally poor.

(C) the three films cited are representative of Olivier's acting career.

(D) film critics frequently make inflated claims about actors whom they admire.

(E) even a few poor performances by an otherwise fine actor can undermine his claim to true greatness.

6. Dr. O: Extensive clinical trials of the new drug Pilogro have demonstrated that Pilogro is effective in slowing the rate of hair loss associated with male pattern balding in men between the ages of 35 and 65 years old.

   Dr. T: I disagree. A recent study suggests that Pilogro is also useful in restoring hair growth among women who have suffered hair loss due to chemotherapy or other cancer treatments.

   Dr. T.'s response suggests that she has interpreted Dr. O.'s statement to mean that

   (A) Pilogro is effective only in treating male pattern balding.
   (B) not all men who suffer from male pattern balding should be treated with Pilogro.
   (C) Pilogro should be available to either men or women who suffer from hair loss.
   (D) women rarely suffer hair loss sufficient to justify the use of a drug like Pilogro.
   (E) Pilogro is the only drug that has been found effective in treating male pattern balding.

7. As a rule, those who work in the book publishing industry are underpaid, overworked, and subject to being fired without warning at any time. Moreover, as more and more people turn to computers for both information and entertainment, books are rapidly becoming outdated. It is accordingly inadvisable for young people to choose careers in book publishing.

   All of the following are valid objections to the argument above EXCEPT

   (A) Despite the recent increase in the use of computers, overall book sales have continued to grow.
   (B) Individuals in the publishing industry are no more subject to being fired than are those in many other industries.
   (C) There are numerous fields other than book publishing in which workers are underpaid and overworked.
   (D) For a significant minority, book publishing careers prove to be both enjoyable and lucrative.
   (E) Those interested in literary endeavors find book publishing to be an ideal working environment.

8. In 1861, the fossilized remains of an unknown and rather strange creature were discovered in a geological stratum dating from the latter years of the age of the dinosaurs. Although it resembled a small dinosaur, it was clear that the creature had wings and feathers. Consequently, it was named *archaeopteryx*, which means "ancient wing." Largely on the basis of this discovery, Thomas Henry Huxley, among others, argued that modern-day birds must be descended from dinosaurs.

Which of the following is NOT an assumption on which Huxley's argument was based?

(A) An animal that resembles a dinosaur is most likely related to dinosaurs.

(B) Modern-day animals have evolved from earlier forms of life.

(C) The biological connection between birds and dinosaurs is at best a tenuous one.

(D) *Archaeopteryx* lived during the age of the dinosaurs.

(E) An animal exhibiting features resembling those of birds is most likely related to birds.

9. Frank Lloyd Wright was the designer of such notable buildings as Fallingwater in Pennsylvania; his own homes in Spring Green, Wisconsin, and Scottsdale, Arizona; and the Guggenheim Museum in New York City. Based on this body of work, Wright is considered by most American architects, as well as many critics around the world, as the preeminent architect of the twentieth century.

Which of the following assumptions is most pivotal to the argument above?

(A) The buildings mentioned are outstanding examples of modern architecture.

(B) American architects generally agree with the critical assessments of architects from around the world.

(C) Architects put more care into designing their own homes than they put into other buildings.

(D) There are many twentieth-century architects who have designed notable buildings.

(E) The buildings mentioned are the best known of those Wright designed.

10. Many individuals take antihistamine medications to alleviate the symptoms of allergies. Although all antihistamines are essentially similar, there is sufficient variation among the available formulations to make some more effective for a particular individual than others. Therefore, if an allergy sufferer keeps trying different antihistamine formulations, she will eventually find one that is effective in her case.

All of the following assumptions underlie the conclusion of the passage above EXCEPT

(A) At least one antihistamine will relieve any individual's allergy symptoms.

(B) The effectiveness of an antihistamine is partially determined by an individual's unique characteristics.

(C) The effectiveness of an antihistamine is partially determined by the drug's specific formulation.

(D) No factors other than body chemistry and antihistamine formulation significantly alter the effectiveness of an antihistamine in alleviating allergy symptoms.

(E) Some allergy sufferers have symptoms that will not respond to any available antihistamine treatment.

11. Although the extent of the Holocaust, the murder of 6 million Jews by the Nazis during World War II, became apparent with the war's end in 1945, it wasn't until the early 1990s, due to the success of Steven Spielberg's film *Schindler's List* and the opening of the U.S. Holocaust Memorial Museum in Washington, D.C., that it became a topic of general conversation among Americans.

Which of the following conclusions can properly be drawn from the statement above?

(A) Prior to the 1990s, the American public was largely unaware of the Holocaust.

(B) *Schindler's List* would not have been a success if the Holocaust museum had not opened at the same time.

(C) Prior to the opening of the museum in Washington, D.C., the U.S. government had taken no official notice of the Holocaust.

(D) The museum would not be as popular as it has been if Spielberg's film had not been so successful.

(E) The success of Spielberg's film and the museum opening were instrumental in bringing the subject of the Holocaust to the public's attention.

12. Ernest Hemingway is considered by many literary critics to be one of the greatest American writers of the twentieth century, if not of all time. However, his sexist attitude toward women and his macho posturings have made him less popular than some of his contemporaries among today's readers.

If the statements above are true, all of the following must also be true EXCEPT

(A) Hemingway's more popular contemporaries do not exhibit his sexist and macho attitudes.

(B) Hemingway's outdated attitudes are a major reason for his relative lack of popularity.

(C) Many modern readers find Hemingway's sexist and macho attitudes distasteful.

(D) Most of Hemingway's contemporaries exhibited the same sexist and macho attitudes.

(E) Most of the general reading public does not agree with the critics' estimation of Hemingway's work.

13. Which of the following best completes the argument below?

In the nineteenth century, the "robber barons" who built many of America's greatest industries sought to maintain control of those industries—and increase their profits—by ownership of all the companies involved in the production and distribution of a given commodity. Thus, the owner of steel mills sought to control the mines that provided the iron, coal, and coke needed in steel manufacture as well as the railroads that shipped the finished steel products. In the same way, it is only natural that the television networks that broadcast programs today should want to _____.

(A) own the production companies that create the programs they broadcast.

(B) increase their profits by charging high rates for network advertising time.

(C) establish monopolies over particular segments of the broadcasting business.

(D) prevent labor unions from increasing their cost of doing business through higher salaries.

(E) control the content of the television news programs they broadcast.

14. Today, more Americans than ever are covered by health insurance plans that provide full or partial coverage of the costs of psychotherapy. Nonetheless, the average number of psychotherapy sessions attended by the typical patient last year fell to its lowest level in history.

Which of the following, if true, would best explain the phenomenon described above?

(A) The number of Americans believed to suffer from psychological problems amenable to therapy has remained constant in recent years.

(B) Last year, the number of patients attending group and family psychotherapy sessions exceeded those attending individual sessions for the first time.

(C) In recent years, increased numbers of professionals such as social workers and registered nurses have begun offering psychotherapy.

(D) The cost of a typical psychotherapy session has increased more slowly than the rate of inflation over the past five years.

(E) Although more insurance plans are covering psychotherapy, most have recently introduced strict limits on the number of sessions they will pay for.

EXERCISE 2

14 Questions

Time—25 Minutes

> **Directions:** For each question, select the best of the answer choices given.

1. Although we may be exposed to all the various types of music—classical, folk, jazz, rock, and country—over the course of a lifetime, the type of music we loved as adolescents will always be our favorite.

   Which of the following, if true, would most seriously weaken the argument above?

   (A) Some people who are exposed to folk music only late in life learn to enjoy it.

   (B) Some people who love rock as adolescents come to prefer classical music later in life.

   (C) Those who are exposed to jazz only as children never learn to appreciate it.

   (D) Those who enjoy country music as adolescents always favor it over other types of music.

   (E) Some people who are exposed to classical music as adolescents never learn to enjoy it.

2. Due to outdated marine regulations, when the supposedly "unsinkable" R.M.S. *Titanic* struck an iceberg and sank in April, 1912, there were enough lifeboats aboard to accommodate fewer than half of the passengers and crew, and more than 1,500 lives were lost. The public was shocked by the sinking and appalled at the loss of life. Shortly after the disaster, marine regulations were changed to require all passenger ships to carry enough lifeboats for everyone on board.

All of the following conclusions can properly be drawn from the statement above EXCEPT

(A) Prior to the sinking, the public was unaware of the inadequacy of the marine lifeboat regulations.

(B) Until the disaster, the public had little interest in marine regulations.

(C) The individuals responsible for marine lifeboat regulations were unaware of their inadequacy.

(D) The public's reaction to the *Titanic* disaster was a contributing factor in changing the marine lifeboat regulations.

(E) The public's reaction to the *Titanic*'s sinking was due in part to the ship's reputation as "unsinkable."

3. First editions of books by famous authors have long found a ready market among serious book collectors, some of them fetching extremely high prices. Curiously, though, first editions of books by the contemporary horror novelist Stephen King, who is not generally considered a significant literary figure, bring higher prices at auction than books by such esteemed American authors as Faulkner and Fitzgerald.

Which of the following, if true, would be most helpful in accounting for the phenomenon described above?

(A) Neither Faulkner nor Fitzgerald was as popular in his time as King is today.

(B) Most serious book collectors are not interested in the books of contemporary authors.

(C) On average, collectors of Faulkner and Fitzgerald have about as much discretionary income as collectors of King.

(D) Because of King's popularity, many more people collect first editions of his books than those of other authors.

(E) Books sold at auction today invariably bring higher prices than they did in the past.

4. Because cable television networks rely on subscribers rather than advertisers for their income and are subject to less stringent censorship, they are able to offer programs with more explicit sexual content than their broadcast counterparts. This provides cable networks with an unfair competitive advantage over broadcast networks, which should be eliminated by the Federal Communications Commission.

Knowledge of which of the following would be LEAST useful in evaluating the argument made in the passage above?

(A) The extent of the public demand for shows with explicit sexual content

(B) The difference between the censorship exerted on cable and broadcast networks

(C) The nature of the FCC's regulations, if any, regarding competition between networks

(D) The amount of programming on cable networks with explicit sexual content

(E) The extent of the influence exerted by advertisers on the contents of television programming

5. *Publishers Weekly* is the most important and widely read magazine in the book industry, providing news about trade publishing (that is, the publishing of books primarily for sale in bookstores). It is accordingly essential for all those involved in publishing, and anyone interested in the field, to read each issue as soon as it is available.

All of the following are valid criticisms of the conclusion stated above EXCEPT

(A) Those not concerned with publishing do not have to keep up with the latest news in that industry.

(B) Some publishers produce books to be sold mainly through direct mail rather than bookstores.

(C) Publishers can generally function effectively without being aware of the latest news.

(D) There are several areas of publishing that are concerned with products other than books.

(E) News about publishing is rarely so timely that a delay in reading it causes a significant disadvantage.

6. Company spokesperson: It is true that specimens of five rare or endangered animals have died within two months of the opening of our new Animal World theme park. However, the more than one thousand other animals at the park are in healthy condition, and park management has taken every reasonable precaution to ensure their continued survival and good health.

Which of the following, if true, would most strengthen the claim above?

(A) The five animals that died succumbed to infectious diseases spread through unclean drinking water.

(B) Most zoos and other facilities that house rare animals experience several fatalities within two months of opening.

(C) Over $2 million was spent by the management of Animal World on health facilities for the animals at the park.

(D) The rare or endangered animals living at Animal World were obtained through legally sanctioned conservation programs.

(E) One of the world's most famous zoo directors was hired by Animal World as a consultant on animal health.

7. Suburban home owners have more living space than city apartment dwellers; they are buying something—their homes—with the money they spend for housing, rather than merely paying rent; they save on taxes because they can deduct part of their mortgage payments from their taxable incomes; they have greater access to the outdoors; and they live in quieter surroundings. For all these reasons, owning a suburban home is always preferable to living in a city apartment.

All of the following assumptions underlie the conclusion of the passage above EXCEPT

(A) All city apartment dwellers rent rather than buy their apartments.

(B) Everyone wants to have greater access to the outdoors.

(C) City apartments dwellers prefer not having to commute to downtown jobs.

(D) Everyone prefers living in quieter surroundings.

(E) All suburban houses contain more or larger rooms than do city apartments.

8. In his book *A Moveable Feast,* Ernest Hemingway claimed that when fellow writer F. Scott Fitzgerald remarked to him, "The rich are different from you and I," Hemingway responded by saying, "Yes, they have more money."

   All of the following conclusions can be reasonably drawn from the above EXCEPT

   (A) Fitzgerald believed that there was some fundamental difference between the rich and everyone else.
   (B) Hemingway believed that the difference between those with and without money was simply financial.
   (C) Hemingway had a sardonic sense of humor.
   (D) neither of the authors had as yet achieved significant commercial success.
   (E) having at one time been wealthy, Hemingway knew firsthand that Fitzgerald was wrong in his estimation of the rich.

9. When visiting a house of worship of a faith other than your own, it is respectful to follow the customs of that faith. When attending a service in an orthodox Jewish synagogue, therefore, it would be appropriate, for example, for a non-Jewish woman to sit in the women's section and a non-Jewish man to wear a *yarmulke* (skullcap) but not a *talis* (prayer shawl).

   If the statements above are true, all of the following statements must also be true EXCEPT

   (A) men of the Jewish faith generally cover their heads during orthodox services.
   (B) men and women generally do not sit together in orthodox Jewish synagogues.
   (C) only Jewish men are supposed to wear prayer shawls in an orthodox synagogue.
   (D) only those of the Jewish faith are allowed to attend orthodox synagogue services.
   (E) it would be considered disrespectful for a man to appear bareheaded in an orthodox synagogue.

10. Beginning at the end of World War II, the enormous expenditure on arms that the Cold War forced on both the United States and the Soviet Union, although having no obvious effect on the quality of life in America, resulted in a considerable dimunition of that quality in the Soviet Union. This, in turn, led to general dissatisfaction, disappointment in the Communist system, and ultimately the dismantling of the Soviet Union.

Which of the following, if true, most seriously weakens the argument above?

(A) Although it was not obvious, the arms expenditures of the Cold War did affect the quality of life in America.

(B) The quality of life in the Soviet Union was relatively poor even prior to the end of World War II.

(C) Overall, the quality of life actually improved in America during the years after the conclusion of World War II.

(D) There was widespread political and economic dissatisfaction in the Soviet Union prior to the onset of World War II.

(E) Dissatisfaction with the quality of life was only one of many factors that contributed to the Soviet people's disillusionment with communism.

11. Collectors—whether they collect books, CDs, dolls, spoons, or anything else—would be well advised to purchase one of the various computer database programs available because any such program will enable them to create catalogues of their collections from which information can be accessed quickly and easily.

All of the following are valid objections to the argument above EXCEPT

(A) some database programs may be more appropriate for creating catalogues of collection than others.

(B) entering information into a computer database can be extremely time-consuming.

(C) not every collector has or is comfortable using a computer.

(D) not all collectors are interested in cataloguing their collections.

(E) a catalogue of a collection may be created using handwritten index cards instead of a computer.

12. Many, if not most, people find history uninteresting and are unable to see the point of making the effort to learn about it. However, in his book *Reason and Common Sense*, philosopher George Santayana argued that "Those who cannot remember the past are condemned to repeat it."

Which of the following assumptions is most pivotal to the argument above?

(A) Mistakes can be avoided by one who knows about similar mistakes made in the past.

(B) Fate determines the decisions people make, regardless of their knowledge of the past.

(C) Understanding what occurred in the past provides no real help in planning for an unpredictable future.

(D) The lessons learned by individuals in the past are not directly transferable to those living in the present.

(E) Both fortunate and unfortunate events of the past can be sources of knowledge for those who study history.

13. Which of the following best completes the passage below?

Although professional sports franchises are privately run, for-profit businesses, the expensive stadiums and arenas in which the sports are played are typically built with public funds. In defending these public expenditures for private benefit, city politicians typically point to studies showing the increased tax revenues that will result from the influx of tourist dollars produced by a sports franchise. However, _____.

(A) the projected tax revenues are usually inflated by wishful thinking, so most cities lose money when they build a stadium.

(B) many sports fans prefer to watch games on television rather than attend them in person, which reduces the revenues generated.

(C) not all fans who attend sports events in a particular stadium are tourists from outside the city or its immediate environs.

(D) because professional sports is a for-profit business, team owners are basically unconcerned about the tax revenues generated.

(E) other kinds of attractions, such as art museums and theatres, are also capable of attracting tourist dollars and increasing tax revenues.

14. The percentage of patients who die while being treated at Hospital M is almost twice as great as the percentage who die while being treated at Hospital R. Therefore, the doctors at Hospital R are more skilled than those at Hospital M.

Which of the following, if true, most seriously weakens the conclusion above?

(A) Doctors at Hospital M, on average, have as many years of experience as those at Hospital R.

(B) Hospital M employs more doctors per patient than does Hospital R.

(C) Hospital M treats a much higher percentage of acutely ill patients than does Hospital R.

(D) The county health department has cited Hospital R for more violations of the local health code than Hospital M.

(E) The length of the average stay at Hospital M is significantly longer than at Hospital R.

EXERCISE 3

14 Questions

Time—25 Minutes

> **Directions:** For each question, select the best of the answer choices given.

1. The two men who led the North and South during the Civil War were as different as they could have been. Abraham Lincoln was easy to talk to, extremely communicative, and skilled at efficiently delegating authority. Jefferson Davis, president of the southern Confederacy, was difficult to approach, kept things to himself, and insisted on being involved in every decision. It is clear, then, that Lincoln's leadership skills were the decisive factor in the North's winning the war.

    All of the following, if true, weaken the argument above EXCEPT

    (A) The number of men available for military service in the North was much greater than in the South.
    (B) Before the Civil War, Jefferson Davis had served with distinction in the U.S. Senate, a higher post than any Lincoln had held.
    (C) The North's superior manufacturing capabilities gave it a significant military advantage over the South.
    (D) The South's military officers were less skilled than those of the North.
    (E) During most of his presidency, Lincoln was strongly disliked by many citizens of the North.

2. Senator C: I oppose the use of statistical techniques by the U.S. Census Bureau to estimate how many Americans have been mistakenly omitted from the population tally and add them into the official count for each state. The clause in the U.S. Constitution that provides for a census calls for "an actual enumeration," not an estimate, so the Bureau has no right to make its guesswork part of the official count.

Senator M: Senator C's opposition is without merit. It is solely based on the fact that the political party he opposes is likely to gain seats in Congress based on the newly adjusted population figures.

Which of the following is the most serious weakness in Senator M's response?

(A)   It criticizes Senator C on personal grounds without responding to the argument he has made.

(B)   It fails to focus on the vagueness of Senator C's description of the Census Bureau's statistical techniques.

(C)   It assumes that those listening are more likely to be members of Senator M's party than of Senator C's.

(D)   It does not raise the possibility of amending the relevant clause of the U.S. Constitution.

(E)   It assumes a degree of knowledge concerning statistical methods that most listeners are unlikely to have.

3. In 1893, Arthur Conan Doyle, having wearied of writing about Sherlock Holmes, his popular fictional detective, wanted to drop the character. Fearing that his public would demand more Holmes stories, Doyle wrote "The Final Problem," a story in which Holmes and his newly invented archrival, Professor Moriarty, plunge to their deaths at the Reichenbach Falls. Doyle eventually brought Holmes back to life, in "The Empty House," and wrote 30 more Holmes stories, but critics have said that after the Reichenbach Falls, Holmes was never the same man.

All of the following may be properly concluded from the information above EXCEPT

(A)   Doyle killed Holmes because he considered this the best way to justify writing no more stories about him.

(B)   After the Reichenbach Falls, Doyle was less interested in writing about Sherlock Holmes than he had been earlier in his career.

(C)   It was egotism that led Doyle to believe that the reading public would demand that he continue to write about Holmes.

(D)   Doyle in all likelihood created the character of Professor Moriarty as a means of bringing about Holmes's death.

(E)   The reading public reacted positively to Holmes's reappearance in "The Empty House."

4. During the Renaissance, many people in western Europe apparently believed that those of the Jewish faith had horns on their heads. In fact, Michelangelo's famous statue of Moses, part of the tomb he sculpted for Pope Julius II between 1520 and 1534, depicts the Jewish patriarch with a pair of clearly discernible horns.

All of the following, if true, would help account for the information presented above EXCEPT

(A) Some of the Jews living in western Europe at the time actually had horns.

(B) A mistranslation in a passage of the Bible most commonly read in western Europe at the time suggested that Jews had horns.

(C) Anti-Jewish prejudice among non-Jews in western Europe at the time encouraged the proliferation of false beliefs about Jews.

(D) There were so few Jews living in western Europe at the time that most non-Jewish people had never met one.

(E) None of the Jews living in western Europe at the time actually had horns.

5. Although many ghost sightings have been claimed by people of questionable veracity, there have been a significant number of sightings by people who are highly intelligent, honest, and reputable. It is reasonable, therefore, to assume that there are such things as ghosts and that they do make themselves known to the living.

All of the following, if true, would serve to weaken the conclusion of the argument above EXCEPT

(A) Those who believe in ghosts are likely to interpret any ambiguous or inexplicable sight as a ghost sighting.

(B) There is no demonstrable correlation between intelligence and honesty.

(C) Highly intelligent people are often more imaginative than others.

(D) Even people who are normally honest may lie on occasion.

(E) A good reputation is no assurance of accurate eyesight.

6. Due to a misunderstanding, U.S. President Andrew Jackson married his wife Rachel before she was legally divorced from her previous husband. Although the divorce was finalized shortly after the wedding, in the presidential election of 1828, Jackson's opponents used this bigamous marriage to smear the couple. Although Jackson won the election, Rachel died before he took office, and the new president blamed his wife's death on the personal attacks she had suffered during the campaign.

Which of the following assumptions must be true if Jackson's claim about his wife's death is true?

(A) Jackson's opponents were trying to smear him through attacks on his wife.

(B) Rachel Jackson would not have died when she did had it not been for the attacks on her.

(C) The couple were attacked by Jackson's enemies despite the fact that Rachel's divorce had been finalized.

(D) Rachel's previous husband was behind the attacks on the couple.

(E) Rachel was ill during the presidential campaign and would probably have died shortly anyway.

7. In September, 1920, eight members of the Chicago White Sox baseball team were indicted on charges of accepting bribes to lose the 1919 World Series to the Cincinnati Reds. Although they were acquitted of all charges on August 2, 1921, the following day baseball commissioner Kenesaw Mountain Landis justifiably banned them from ever playing professional baseball again.

If the statements above are true, all of the following must also be true EXCEPT

(A) The baseball commissioner had the legal and moral authority to ban players from professional baseball.

(B) Despite the verdict, Landis believed that the accused players were guilty of having deliberately lost the series.

(C) If players accept bribes to lose games, they deserve to be be banned from professional baseball.

(D) An indictment, even if justified by the facts, does not guarantee a guilty verdict.

(E) Professional baseball fell into disrepute as a result of the trial and the surrounding scandal.

8. Mail is delivered every day, from Monday through Saturday, to Henry's house, and a day has never passed on which Henry received no mail. If one day Henry goes to the mailbox and finds it empty, the only possible explanation is that it is a Sunday.

Knowledge of all of the following would be helpful in evaluating the argument above EXCEPT

(A) the time of day at which Henry's mail is normally delivered.
(B) whether the mail deliverer's truck has broken down.
(C) whether Henry's neighbors received mail that day.
(D) the age of the mail deliverer.
(E) the time of day at which Henry goes to the mailbox and finds it empty.

9. Contemporary newspapers carry stories about infanticide—the murder of children—among the poor much more frequently than 19th century newspapers did. It's clear, then, that due to the fact that less value is placed on human life today, there has been a substantial increase in the incidence of infanticide.

All of the following, if true, are valid objections to the argument above EXCEPT

(A) editors of 19th century newspapers were less inclined to carry stories about infanticide than contemporary editors.
(B) there was less interest in, and less newspaper coverage of, the poor in the last century than there is today.
(C) no studies have demonstrated that less value is placed on human life today than in the 19th century.
(D) historical police records do not indicate a smaller number of infanticides in the past.
(E) studies have indicated that there was less value placed on human life in the 19th century than today.

10. Those who collect books, whether or not they actually read what they buy, generally find it almost impossible to restrain themselves from buying more books to add to their collections. However, a collector can solve this problem simply by staying away from bookstores.

Which of the following is an assumption underlying the reasoning in the argument above?

(A) Book collectors sometimes spend so much money on books that they fall into serious financial difficulties.

(B) Avid collectors find a way to buy books regardless of any impediments put in their way.

(C) Books are only available through bookstores.

(D) All people who love to read are book collectors.

(E) Some book collectors buy more books than they actually read.

11. Digital clocks are preferable to analog clocks with dials because they keep time more accurately, are much easier to read, and have no moving parts to wear out. They also enable children to grasp the concept of time, and to learn how to tell time more easily than they can with analog clocks.

All of the following assumptions underlie the conclusion of the passage above EXCEPT

(A) The moving hands of analog clocks do not help children to understand the concept of time.

(B) Digital clocks are less expensive to produce and to buy than are analog clocks.

(C) Analog clocks cannot be made to tell time as accurately as digital clocks.

(D) Even those who learned how to tell time on analog clocks find digital clocks easier to read.

(E) Analog clocks have no esthetic advantages over digital clocks.

12. It has never been easy to find a reasonably priced apartment to rent in New York City, particularly one with two or more bedrooms. The situation has, however, become even more difficult due to two recent trends: the increase in the relative number of new office buildings as compared to new apartment buildings and the increasing number of rental apartment buildings being turned into cooperatives that are sold rather than rented.

All of the following may be concluded from the above EXCEPT

(A) The demand for reasonably priced rental apartments in New York has long been greater than the supply.

(B) New York City builders currently perceive the need for offices to be greater than the need for apartments.

(C) As more apartment buildings in New York City become cooperatives, the supply of rental apartments decreases.

(D) In the past, the ratio of rental apartments to cooperatives in New York City was greater than today.

(E) The likelihood of finding an affordable one-bedroom apartment in New York City is about the same today as in the past.

13. To encourage innovation, the M3 Corporation has a goal of achieving 50 percent of its annual revenues from sales of products that are no more than 3 years old. Last year, M3 Corporation achieved this goal, despite the fact that the company introduced no new products during the year.

Which of the following, if true, best explains the results described above?

(A) Sales of many of the company's older products were discontinued during the last year.

(B) The company has introduced very few new products during the last three years.

(C) The company's single best-selling product was introduced more than 15 years ago.

(D) Company spending on research and development has increased slightly over the past five years.

(E) Scientists at the company report that they are close to breakthroughs that should result in several new products during the coming year.

14. Which of the following best completes the passage below?

A national performing arts association conducted a survey that appears to confirm the public's interest in high culture. More than 90 percent of those surveyed said that they were "somewhat interested" or "very interested" in attending performances of opera, ballet, or classical music. However, the survey results should be regarded with a degree of skepticism because _____.

(A) most of those surveyed may have reported being "somewhat interested" rather than "very interested."

(B) figures show that more people attend sporting events than performances of opera, ballet, or classical music.

(C) people often respond to surveys with answers they think will reflect highly on themselves, whether true or not.

(D) not all performances of opera, ballet, or classical music should be considered "high culture."

(E) not all those who are interested in attending performances are willing to support an arts association.

EXERCISE 4

14 Questions

Time—25 Minutes

> **Directions:** For each question, select the best of the answer choices given.

1. The Hudson River, which flows through New York State from its source in the Adirondack Mountains through New York City, was so polluted two decades ago that only the most foolhardy dared go near it. Today, however, thousands of local inhabitants and tourists engage in a wide range of water sports on the river.

   Which of the following, if true, is the most likely explanation for the facts presented above?

   (A) There has been a significant increase in tourism in the Hudson River region.

   (B) Some twenty years ago, local conservation groups mounted a major effort to clean up the waters of the Hudson.

   (C) More people today live within five miles of the banks of the Hudson River than ever before.

   (D) Surveys suggest that most local residents no longer regard pollution in the Hudson as a major problem.

   (E) More people are interested in water sports today than in the past.

2. One of the first American authors to use a typewriter was Mark Twain. This enabled him to write faster than other authors, make changes more easily, get his manuscripts to his publisher faster, see them published sooner and, consequently, become one of the most popular authors of his day.

All of the following, if true, are valid objections to the argument above EXCEPT

(A) Many of the other popular authors of Mark Twain's time also used typewriters to write their books.

(B) Using a typewriter does not necessarily enable a writer to finish a book sooner.

(C) The means by which a manuscript is delivered to a publisher is not affected by the manner in which it is written.

(D) Having books published more quickly than other authors does not ensure a writer's popularity.

(E) Making changes in a typewritten manuscript is no easier than making changes in a handwritten one.

3. Compared to older houses, new houses are sure to have newer, more efficient heating and cooling units, more modern kitchen appliances, and more contemporary-style bathroom fixtures. They also generally conform to the most up-to-date code regulations. It is accordingly always advantageous to purchase a new house rather than an old one.

Which of the following is the best criticism of the argument above?

(A) When an older house is sold, correcting any code violations is the responsibility of the seller.

(B) As a rule, older houses have more of the kind of details that lend charm to a home than do new houses.

(C) Some people prefer more traditional styles of bathroom fixtures.

(D) New equipment and fixtures are not the only factors home buyers consider when choosing a house.

(E) New houses are generally more expensive than older houses of comparable size.

4. In the closing days of the Civil War, President Abraham Lincoln was planning to graciously welcome the defeated Confederate states back into the Union. After Lincoln was assassinated, however, the "Radical Republicans" in Congress imposed martial law in the South, creating resentment that caused problems well into this century. Had Lincoln lived, the history of regional conflict in 20th century America would have been considerably different.

    All of the following assumptions underlie the argument above EXCEPT

    (A)   The imposition of martial law in the South was primarily responsible for the resentment felt in the South.
    (B)   Had he lived, Lincoln would have treated the defeated South as he had planned.
    (C)   Lincoln would have been able to prevent the Radical Republicans in Congress from imposing martial law in the South.
    (D)   Factors other than the imposition of martial law in the South affected the history of regional conflicts in 20th century America.
    (E)   Had Lincoln been able to carry out his plans, people in the southern states would have felt less resentment toward the Union.

5. Rock and roll music started in the 1950s as a young man's medium, and rock is still best performed by men in their 20s and 30s. As rock performers grow into their 40s, and even 50s, they are simply less physically capable of producing the kind of exciting music they did when they were younger.

    All of the following assumptions underlie the argument above EXCEPT

    (A)   As rock performers mature, their performances tend to become less exciting.
    (B)   Rock music is dominated by male performers.
    (C)   Women performers have always played a significant role in rock music.
    (D)   The physical demands of performing rock are better met by the young.
    (E)   Those who played rock music in its earliest days are no longer among its best performers.

6. In 1969, when the Apollo 11 spacecraft successfully landed men on the moon, the entire country was suffused with excitement. Today, after thirty more years of space exploration, space shuttle launches cause hardly a ripple in the country's consciousness.

Which of the following conclusions can be properly drawn from the information presented above?

(A) Diminished public interest in space flight poses a political threat to the continuance of the space program.

(B) There is less interest in space shuttle flights than there was in the Apollo moon landing.

(C) The Apollo 11 mission was exciting because it was the first successful flight into space.

(D) The news media should do a better job of publicizing space shuttle launches, which would help rekindle public interest in space flight.

(E) The discontinuation of the Russian space program has helped to erode public interest in space flight.

7. From the 1920s to the 1950s, when televisions became standard equipment in most American homes, at-home entertainment was provided by the family radio. Because television has both sound *and* pictures, however, it provides more quality entertainment, more opportunity for the family to be together, and a better means of helping children develop their interests and abilities.

All of the following, if true, are valid objections to the argument in the paragraph above EXCEPT

(A) Because it lacked pictures, radio helped foster the development of imagination in children.

(B) Families spend more time watching television than they used to spend listening to the radio.

(C) Because it fascinates children, television keeps them from spending time in other worthwhile endeavors.

(D) The quality of today's television programming is lower than that of yesterday's radio programming.

(E) Families are no more likely to gather around a television set than around a radio.

8. On September 12, 1919, Adolph Hitler attended a monthly meeting of the German Worker's Party—one of many political parties in Germany at the time—and electrified the attendees with a speech urging unity among Germans. He subsequently turned it into the National Socialist German Workers (or Nazi) party, took over Germany, and started the Second World War. Therefore, if Hitler had never attended that fateful meeting, World War II would never have occurred.

All of the following are valid objections to the argument above EXCEPT

(A) Hitler might have attended another of the party's regular meetings.

(B) Someone else with equally warlike intentions might have taken over the party.

(C) Hitler might have come to power through some other means.

(D) Another equally warlike party might have taken control of Germany.

(E) Hitler's speech might have had no effect on the meeting's attendees.

9. The frequently quoted Old Testament injunction, "an eye for an eye, a tooth for a tooth," has been used as an argument in many debates. In fact, it has been justifiably used in the argument that those found guilty of murder should suffer the death penalty.

Which of the following, if true, most weakens the argument above?

(A) Elsewhere in the Bible, the death penalty is explicitly recommended.

(B) At the time the Bible passage in question was written, the death penalty was commonplace.

(C) The Bible passage in question actually specifies that punishment must not exceed "an eye for an eye."

(D) Those who argue for the death penalty include many who profess no belief in the authority of the Bible.

(E) The Biblical passage in question has only recently been applied to the debate over the death penalty.

10. The Cloisters, a New York museum devoted to ecclesiastical art of the Middle Ages, is one building comprising five medieval structures brought from Europe. Although the intent was to provide the average visitor with a pleasant sense of actually touring a medieval cloister, because the five component buildings are all in different architectural styles, a visit to the museum is an unpleasant experience for most tourists.

All of the following assumptions underlie the conclusion of the argument above EXCEPT

(A) The average New York tourist is interested in experiencing a medieval cloister.

(B) The average tourist recognizes, at least unconsciously, the differences among the architectural styles.

(C) The different styles of architecture in the Cloisters clash with each other.

(D) The average visitor finds the combination of styles in the Cloisters unpleasant.

(E) It is impossible to create a harmonious building incorporating several different architectural styles.

11. A larger percentage of those who work in Chicago commute to work by train than by any other means. Even so, traffic going into the city during the morning rush hour and leaving the city at the end of the work day is so bad that what would otherwise be a one-hour car trip often takes twice as long.

All of the following conclusions can be drawn from the information above EXCEPT

(A) Commuting by train to and from Chicago is quicker than commuting by any other means.

(B) Commuting by car to Chicago is likely to be a frustrating experience.

(C) The train is the single most popular commuting method among those who work in Chicago.

(D) A sizeable percentage of Chicago commuters drive to and from the city during rush hours.

(E) Drivers can get into and out of Chicago faster during non-rush hours than during rush hours.

12. By August 1945, although the Second World War had ended in Europe, American forces were still fighting the Japanese in the Pacific. To bring the war to a quick conclusion and to save the estimated thousands of American lives that would be lost in an invasion of Japan, it was necessary for the United States to drop atomic bombs on the cities of Hiroshima and Nagasaki.

If the statements above are true, all of the following must also be true EXCEPT

(A) America's military leaders believed that the estimate of the number of American lives that would be lost in an invasion of Japan was accurate.

(B) The war would have lasted longer if the United States had not dropped the atomic bombs.

(C) Japan was on the verge of surrender by August and would probably have capitulated quickly even without the dropping of the atomic bombs.

(D) It would not have been possible to negotiate a speedy and acceptable end to the war with Japan prior to dropping the atomic bombs.

(E) President Harry Truman, who had to approve the use of atomic bombs, believed that their use was the best alternative.

Questions 13–14 are based on the following passage.

Within the advertising community, debate has long raged over the effectiveness of humorous commercials. Those who advocate using humor to sell products like to point to survey results, which show that ordinary consumers are almost twice as likely to recall a humorous commercial as they are to recall a serious commercial.

13. In their argument, the advocates of humor in advertising assume that

(A) the ordinary consumer has a sense of humor similar to that of most advertising copywriters.

(B) humorous commercials can be effective even when shown during serious television dramas.

(C) the effectiveness of humorous advertising is not affected by the nature of the product being sold.

(D) a commercial that is recalled by consumers is a more effective selling vehicle than one that is not recalled.

(E) most television viewers enjoy watching commercials as much as they enjoy the programs themselves.

14. Which of the following, if true, most weakens the argument made by the advocates of humor in advertising?

    (A) The consumers surveyed about humorous commercials included people considered unlikely to buy the particular products advertised.

    (B) According to viewer ratings, the popularity of humorous television programming has been declining in recent years.

    (C) Although most consumers surveyed were able to recall viewing humorous commercials, many said they enjoyed the serious commercials more.

    (D) For certain types of products, humorous advertising would be inappropriate and potentially offensive.

    (E) Although most consumers surveyed were able to recall viewing humorous commercials, most failed to recall the name of the product advertised.

EXERCISE 5

14 Questions

Time—25 Minutes

> **Directions:** For each question, select the best of the answer choices given.

1. When inhaled, asbestos fibers are known to significantly increase the likelihood of lung cancer and other respiratory ailments. Thousands of American buildings, including apartment houses, offices, and schools, are insulated with asbestos, and some localities have initiated massive and costly campaigns to remove this asbestos. However, the health of those who occupy the buildings may actually be better preserved by leaving the asbestos in place.

    Which of the following, if true, most strongly supports the conclusion of the argument above?

    (A) At the time the asbestos insulation was installed, the health hazards it posed were little known.
    (B) Asbestos removal is itself a hazardous operation, posing important health dangers to those who perform it.
    (C) Fewer than one person in a hundred who breathes asbestos-contaminated air is likely to contract lung cancer.
    (D) In removing the asbestos, millions of fibers are likely to be dislodged and sent into circulation in the air.
    (E) The cost of removing the asbestos from buildings across America has been estimated at over $5 billion.

2. Twenty years ago, relatively gas-efficient American-made sedans were by far the most popular type of motor vehicle in the United States. Today, however, less-efficient vans and light trucks, primarily those produced by Japanese companies, are threatening to overtake the traditional family car in popularity.

Which of the following conclusions is most strongly supported by the statements above?

(A) Americans are buying more vans and trucks today because they are having larger families.

(B) American companies produce vehicles that are inferior to those from Japanese companies.

(C) On average, vehicles on the road in the United States waste more gasoline today than twenty years ago.

(D) Japanese companies produce vehicles that are safer than those from American companies.

(E) Americans are buying more vans and trucks today because they have become status symbols.

3. In the 1930s, an undershirt was a standard item of clothing for middle-class men in America. In 1934, however, when Clark Gable removed his shirt in the film *It Happened One Night* to reveal a torso without an undershirt, sales of undershirts dropped precipitously across the country.

All of the following, if true, would help account for the above EXCEPT

(A) Clark Gable was a popular hero among middle-class American men in the 1930s.

(B) Women who bought clothing for their husbands wanted them to be more like Clark Gable.

(C) European designers, who recommended undershirts, were coming into vogue in the U.S. in the 1930s.

(D) The winter of 1934 was a particularly warm one in the U.S.

(E) *It Happened One Night* was one of the most popular films of 1934.

4. When the state of Tennessee passed a law prohibiting the teaching of the theory of evolution in its public schools, leaders of the American Civil Liberties Union (ACLU) persuaded John T. Scopes, a teacher in Dayton, Tennessee, to teach evolution in his classroom in order to test the law in court. However, because Scopes did not break the law on his own initiative, he should never have been brought to trial.

Which of the following is an assumption underlying the conclusion of the passage above?

(A) Those who commit crimes at the suggestion of others should not be held responsible for their actions.

(B) Both Scopes and the ACLU leaders should have been tried for breaking the law.

(C) The ACLU leaders, rather than Scopes, should have been brought to trial.

(D) Groups like the ACLU should not encourage criminal activities as a means of testing laws.

(E) The state of Tennessee did not have the right to make the teaching of evolution a crime.

5. In a famous letter written to a young friend in 1745, Benjamin Franklin argued that if one must take a lover outside of marriage, older women were preferable to younger ones for a number of reasons, among which were that "When women cease to be handsome, they study to be good," "There is no hazard of children," "They are more prudent and discreet," and, finally, because "They are so *grateful*."

All the following are valid objections to Franklin's arguments above EXCEPT

(A) older women do not necessarily "cease to be handsome"

(B) some women are capable of bearing children late in life

(C) older women are not necessarily more discreet than younger ones

(D) some women become less prudent as they grow older

(E) older women are less likely to engage in extramarital affairs than younger ones

6. Charles: All the wealthiest men I've ever met have dressed in expensive suits from exclusive London tailors. There must be something about wearing expensive London suits that helps men to become very wealthy.

The most serious logical weakness in Charles's argument lies in its apparent

(A) confusion of cause and effect.
(B) failure to define terms consistently.
(C) reliance on circumstantial evidence.
(D) confusion of logical categories.
(E) reliance on a questionable assumption.

7. There is a saying in Maine that has been offered to visitors to the state for as long as anyone can remember: "If you don't like the weather here, wait a minute."

Which of the following, if true, would best account for the origin of the saying mentioned above?

(A) Tourists in Maine rarely complain about the weather.
(B) The weather in Maine has historically been very changeable.
(C) The people of Maine are generally not very hospitable toward tourists.
(D) The weather is something over which no one has any control.
(E) Those who live in Maine like to boast about the local weather.

8. During the American civil rights movement of the 1960s, many television viewers, particularly those outside the South, were appalled to see news coverage in which young southern children—some of them barely able to speak—taunted civil rights marchers with racist remarks. The children, however, were really only emulating their parents.

If the statements above are true, all of the following must also be true EXCEPT

(A) The children who taunted the marchers were repeating remarks their parents had made.
(B) The parents of the children who taunted the marchers were opposed to the civil rights movement.
(C) Some of the children who taunted the marchers didn't entirely understand what they were saying.
(D) The children who taunted the marchers sincerely believed that the objectives of the civil rights movement were wrong.
(E) Racist attitudes were relatively common in the South during the 1960s.

9. According to Albert Einstein's famous theory of relativity, time travel is theoretically possible. Assuming that time travel were to be made possible through some technological breakthrough, it would be advantageous to send someone back in time to prevent the assassination of Archduke Franz Ferdinand in 1914 and thus keep World War I from ever occurring.

The argument above makes which of the following assumptions?

(A) It is not possible to alter a significant current in world history merely by changing a single event.

(B) The technology necessary for time travel is likely to be developed in the near future.

(C) If Franz Ferdinand had not been assassinated, some other catalytic event would have led to the start of World War I.

(D) The assassination of Franz Ferdinand was the crucial event that triggered the start of Word War I.

(E) If time travel were to be developed in the future, evidence of time travelers would be apparent to those living today.

10. A bedroom in which the windows face north rather than south will always be relatively dark regardless of how sunny it may be outside. Placing a skylight in such a room will not only make the room a great deal brighter but will invariably give the person inhabiting the room a happier disposition.

All of the following, if true, are valid objections to the argument above EXCEPT

(A) some people prefer relative darkness to light in their bedrooms.

(B) trees with heavy foliage overhanging the skylight would prevent sunshine from reaching the room.

(C) the amount of sunlight in a person's room does not always affect his disposition.

(D) if a taller house towers above the north-facing bedroom, little additional sunlight may reach the skylight.

(E) rooms facing east or west normally receive more light than those facing north.

11. In the film *Jurassic Park,* scientists create living dinosaurs by replicating dinosaur DNA found inside an insect that had bitten a dinosaur and was then trapped in amber. Although such a feat has not yet been accomplished, one day modern science will probably succeed in recreating prehistoric creatures in a similar manner.

All of the following assumptions underlie the conclusion of the passage above EXCEPT

(A) The genetic information in DNA is sufficient to permit the recreation of an entire animal.

(B) It will someday be possible to accurately replicate DNA in a laboratory.

(C) Enough DNA can be extracted from an insect to recreate an entire animal.

(D) Scientists will never fully understand how DNA functions.

(E) It is possible for DNA to survive for millions of years inside an insect's body.

12. In March 1917, under pressure from communist revolutionaries, Tsar Nicholas II of Russia abdicated his throne. Sixteen months later, the tsar and his immediate family, including Alexis, the heir apparent, were executed on orders of the new communist government because its leaders believed that all vestiges of the old regime had to be obliterated for the security of the new regime.

The leaders of the new communist government must have made which of the following assumptions?

(A) Executing the tsar and his heir would send a clear message to all in Russia concerning the ruthlessness of the new regime.

(B) If Nicholas or Alexis had remained alive, he could have provided a rallying point for supporters of the old regime.

(C) A communist regime could theoretically be compatible with a government ruled by a tsar.

(D) The populace of Russia would be overwhelmingly supportive of the decision to execute the tsar and his family.

(E) Nicholas had abdicated the throne because of his sincere belief that a communist government could provide better leadership for Russia.

13. Which of the following best completes the passage below?

Global competitiveness doesn't necessarily refer to a company's ability to do business anywhere in the world. Even a purely local company must meet global standards of quality because smart competitors are constantly importing the best ideas and methods from other countries and using them to gain the advantage. Thus, the manager of such a purely local business as a dry-cleaning shop _____.

(A) should aspire to the highest level of quality purely as a matter of personal ethical standards.

(B) need fear global competition only if an international chain of dry-cleaning shops were to come into existence.

(C) must be aware of business ideas from around the world, lest they be used against him by a smart competitor.

(D) should seek out opportunities to expand his operation into other localities, and, eventually, other nations.

(E) is unlikely to face international competition and therefore faces a less rigorous competitive challenge than those in global businesses.

14. In the last twenty years, the average playing time of a major-league baseball game has increased from 2 hours and 40 minutes to 3 hours and 15 minutes, causing complaints from many fans. To combat this problem, baseball officials must crack down on the use of delaying tactics by the teams, such as conferences between players and coaches.

Which of the following, if true, casts the most doubt on the effectiveness of the proposal suggested above?

(A) Despite the complaints about the increased length of games, attendance at baseball games has increased steadily in the last twenty years.

(B) Players and coaches are likely to resent any attempt by baseball officials to speed up the pace of the games.

(C) Some fans enjoy the leisurely pace of baseball games because it provides an opportunity to consider and discuss the strategy underlying play.

(D) If conferences between players and coaches are forbidden, teams will use other delaying tactics instead.

(E) Most of the increased length of baseball games may be attributed to expanded time for television commercials between innings of the games.

Answer Key

Exercise 1	Exercise 2	Exercise 3	Exercise 4	Exercise 5
1. C	1. B	1. B	1. B	1. D
2. C	2. C	2. A	2. A	2. C
3. E	3. D	3. C	3. D	3. C
4. B	4. D	4. E	4. D	4. A
5. D	5. A	5. B	5. C	5. E
6. A	6. B	6. B	6. B	6. A
7. C	7. C	7. E	7. B	7. B
8. C	8. E	8. D	8. E	8. D
9. A	9. D	9. E	9. C	9. D
10. E	10. E	10. C	10. A	10. E
11. E	11. E	11. B	11. A	11. D
12. D	12. A	12. E	12. C	12. B
13. A	13. A	13. A	13. D	13. C
14. E	14. C	14. C	14. E	14. E

Explanatory Answers

EXERCISE 1

1. **The correct answer is (C).** The last sentence of the passage draws a direct connection between the arrival of the baby-boom generation at middle age and their increasing interest in genealogy.

2. **The correct answer is (C).** Answer (C) is not relevant to explaining Selznick's success in winning the approval of the movie censors. If anything, it relates merely to Selznick's willingness to include the controversial line in the movie script despite the possibility of public disapproval. The other answer choices all suggest possible explanations as to why the censors might have been willing to make an exception to their usual rule concerning "off-color language."

3. **The correct answer is (E).** Choices (A) through (D) all offer possible explanations as to how the story of the exodus might have been preserved in writing without any current trace of that writing. Choice (E) is unrelated to this point; it merely suggests that the story of the exodus is likely to have been changed as a result of oral rather than written transmission.

4. **The correct answer is (B).** Choice (B) fails to undermine Holmes's reasoning because it ignores the fact that, according to the detective, all possibilities other than the improbable have already been eliminated. If this is so, then even the improbable is relatively likely, since it is the only remaining possibility.

5. **The correct answer is (D).** All of the other answer choices represent beliefs that the author of the passage must accept if his conclusion—that Olivier is not really a great actor—is to be sound. Choice (D) might help to explain why critics exaggerate their praise of Olivier, but it doesn't support the conclusion of the passage.

6. **The correct answer is (A).** When Dr. T. says that he "disagrees" with Dr. O.'s statement because of the fact that women find the drug effective, the strong implication is that Dr. T. has interpreted Dr. O.'s statement as meaning that only men can use Pilogro.

7. **The correct answer is (C).** Choice (A) is an effective response to the argument offered in the second sentence of the passage; choices (B), (D), and (E) are all logical responses to the points made in the first sentence. However, choice (C) merely suggests that other careers may be just as bad as book publishing, which doesn't demonstrate that book publishing is a desirable career.

8. **The correct answer is (C).** Rather than supporting Huxley's argument, the point made in choice (C) would tend to undermine it.

9. **The correct answer is (A).** The argument is supposed to demonstrate the greatness of Wright as an architect on the basis of the specific buildings mentioned—Fallingwater and the others. This argument makes sense only if the buildings referred to are in fact great works of architecture; if they are not, then Wright's reputation, based upon them, will surely suffer.

10. **The correct answer is (E).** Choices (A) through (D) all support the conclusion of the passage that every allergy sufferer can be helped by one or another antihistamine. By contrast, answer (E), if true, weakens the conclusion; it suggests that there are some allergy sufferers who cannot be helped by any antihistimine formulation.

11. **The correct answer is (E).** The phrase "due to" in the middle of the passage clearly implies that the movie and the opening of the museum played pivotal roles in making the Holocaust a topic of popular conversation among Americans.

12. **The correct answer is (D).** If the information in the passage is true, then the statement in choice (D) is probably false. The passage says that Hemingway's sexism had made him "less popular than some of his contemporaries," clearly implying that many of Hemingway's contemporaries had attitudes free of sexism—otherwise, their work would suffer from the same disfavor as Hemingway's.

13. **The correct answer is (A).** The point of the passage is to develop an analogy between the nineteenth-century robber barons and the TV networks of today. Since the passage explains how the robber barons sought to own "all the companies involved in the production and distribution of a given commodity," the conclusion of the passage must logically point to a similar desire by TV networks to own all the companies involved in producing and distributing TV programs. Hence, choice (A).

14. **The correct answer is (E).** Only choice (E) suggests a possible explanation for the phenomenon described. If insurance plans today are limiting the number of psychotherapy sessions they will pay for, it makes sense that patients would be attending fewer such sessions.

EXERCISE 2

1. **The correct answer is (B).** The statement in choice (B) directly contradicts the argument by showing that some people do *not* continue to prefer the music of their adolescence later in life.

2. **The correct answer is (C).** Each of the other answer choices is strongly implied in the passage. However, the passage offers no evidence one way or another concerning the awareness of those responsible for lifeboat regulations of their own inadequacy.

3. **The correct answer is (D).** Choices (A) and (E) are irrelevant to the question of why King first editions draw higher prices than Faulkner and Fitzgerald, when all the books in question are sold today. Choices (B) and (C) undermine potential explanations. Only choice (D) suggests a possible explanation, by showing that the potential market for King first editions is greater than that for more esteemed authors, thereby increasing the competition to buy and, consequently, the prices fetched.

4. **The correct answer is (D).** Choices (B), (C), and (E) all call into question some of the factual statements made in the passage; choice (A) challenges the author's contention that cable's freedom from sexual censorship gives it "an unfair competitive advantage." Only choice (D) bears no direct relationship to the argument being offered in the passage; whether or not cable operators take full advantage of their "competitive advantage" by showing a lot of sexy programming doesn't affect whether or not that advantage exists.

5. **The correct answer is (A).** Choice (A) is irrelevant to the conclusion of the passage, since the author claims only that "those involved in publishing" ought to read *Publishers Weekly*; he makes no assertions about anyone else.

6. **The correct answer is (B).** If the statement in choice (B) is true, it suggests that the track record of Animal World is comparable to that of other similar facilities, and therefore that the management of the park has probably been reasonably careful about its treatment of the animals. Choices (C), (D), and (E) do not in and of themselves significantly support the general claim that the park management has been responsible. For example, to evaluate the importance of choice (C), one would have to know whether $2 million is an adequate sum for such facilities. The passage doesn't tell us that.

7. **The correct answer is (C).** Each of the other answer choices states a fact that supports the arguments made in the passage. Choice (C), however, points in the opposite direction; it suggests an advantage for city apartment dwelling rather than an advantage of suburban home life.

8. **The correct answer is (E).** Choices (A) through (D) are all implied by one part of the exchange or the other. However, we can't tell from the information provided in the passage whether or not Hemingway had ever been rich, so choice (E) is the best answer.

9. **The correct answer is (D).** This is the only *false* answer choice; the passage is based on the assumption that non-Jews may attend orthodox Jewish services, which choice (D) contradicts.

10. **The correct answer is (E).** The passage states that one and only one cause—the costs of the arms race—produced the collapse of the Soviet system. Choice (E) points out the weakness of this argument by suggesting what is probably true—that so massive an effect was probably the result of a combination of factors rather than just one.

11. **The correct answer is (E).** Choices (B) through (D) all suggest reasons why a collector might not want to use a computer to create a catalogue. Choice (A) undermines the author's point that "any such program" can be used. Only choice (E) is beside the point; the author does not assert that *only* a computer is capable of creating a catalogue, merely that a computer database is a quick and easy way of doing so.

12. **The correct answer is (A).** This statement accurately summarizes the point of the famous Santayana quotation. Choices (B), (C), and (D) run counter to Santayana's point, and choice (E) makes a fundamentally irrelevant point.

13. **The correct answer is (A).** The word *however*, which introduces the (missing) conclusion of the passage, suggests that the sentence to be inserted should strongly contradict or call into question the idea that "increased tax revenues . . . will result from the influx of tourist dollars produced by a sports franchise." Choice (A) does this by saying that, in fact, the tax revenues produced aren't sufficient to cover costs.

14. **The correct answer is (C).** Choice (C) weakens the conclusion drawn by suggesting an alternative explanation for the higher death rate at Hospital M: the fact that the patients at that hospital are much sicker, on average, than those at Hospital R. Thus, even the most highly skilled doctors might not be able to save them.

EXERCISE 3

1. **The correct answer is (B).** The other answer choices all weaken the point that Lincoln's leadership skills were the decisive factor in the North's victory—choices (A), (C), and (D) by suggesting other factors, choice (E) by undermining the contention that Lincoln was a popular leader. Choice (B) is irrelevant because in itself the fact that Davis had served in the Senate does not demonstrate that he was an effective leader.

2. **The correct answer is (A).** Whether or not one agrees with Senator C, he makes an argument based on the language of the Constitution that deserves a response. However, rather than offer a response, Senator M merely attacks Senator C's motivations, a logical weakness that choice (A) reveals.

3. **The correct answer is (C).** The passage does not suggest that Doyle's belief in the popularity of Holmes was egotistical—if anything, the opposite, since there was evidently sufficient demand for stories about Holmes to justify Doyle's writing of thirty such stories after the character's supposed death.

4. **The correct answer is (E).** Choices (A) through (D) all suggest possible reasons why the weird belief described in the passage might have been held by some Europeans. (Choice A, of course, is clearly very improbable; however, "if true," as specified in the question stem, it *would* help to explain the belief.) Choice (E) merely underscores the irrationality of the belief; it doesn't help to explain it.

5. **The correct answer is (B).** Each of the other answer choices help to show why people who are "intelligent, honest, and reputable" may nonetheless believe in something as apparently unlikely as ghosts. Choice (B) is irrelevant, since the passage doesn't assume any connection between intelligence and honesty; it merely bases its conclusion on the testimony of people who happen to exhibit both qualities.

6. **The correct answer is (B).** If Jackson blamed his wife's death on the personal attacks she suffered, then he must have believed the statement given in choice (B)—that she died because of those attacks rather than because of more "natural" causes.

7. **The correct answer is (E).** The other answer choices all derive either from the sequence of events described in the passage or from the author's use of the word "justifiably," which means that Landis did the morally right thing in banning the White Sox players. Choice (E), however, can't be inferred from the passage; if you agree with it, it must be on the basis of outside knowledge rather than by inference from the statements in the passage itself.

8. **The correct answer is (D).** Each of the other choices is relevant to possible counter-explanations of the emptiness of Henry's mailbox (the possibility, for example, that the mail deliverer has simply not arrived yet). The age of the letter carrier, however, is irrelevant.

9. **The correct answer is (E).** Whereas each of the other answer choices weakens the argument, choice (E) strengthens it by providing support for one of the author's contentions.

10. **The correct answer is (C).** This states an assumption underlying the author's conclusion since, if books are actually available through channels other than bookstores (as of course they are), then merely avoiding bookstores is no guarantee that the addicted collector will stop buying books.

11. **The correct answer is (B).** The argument does not cite relative cost as an advantage of digital clocks, so the information mentioned in choice (B) is irrelevant to the conclusion drawn.

12. **The correct answer is (E).** Unlike the other choices, choice (E) is not supported by the information in the passage; in fact, it is contradicted by it.

13. **The correct answer is (A).** Choice (A) helps to explain last year's sales results by suggesting that sales of products three years old and older could have fallen sharply during the year. Thus, the proportion of sales produced by newer products could have grown, even without an influx of popular new products.

14. **The correct answer is (C).** The most significant weakness of the argument lies in its willingness to accept at face value the statements made by those polled, despite the likelihood of dissembling when such a value-laden topic is under discussion. Choice (C) points this out effectively. Choice (B) is wrong because the mere fact that sports is more popular than high culture (if true) doesn't mean that high culture is not of significant interest to the public.

EXERCISE 4

1. **The correct answer is (B).** The new found popularity of water sports on the Hudson is best explained by this answer because it suggests how the pollution of the river might have been alleviated in recent years. Choice (D) merely asserts in another form the fact that local residents now enjoy the cleanliness of the Hudson; it doesn't help to explain how that came to be.

2. **The correct answer is (A).** If true, choice (A) doesn't weaken the conclusion of the argument; it merely states that other writers of Twain's time enjoyed the same relative advantage he did in using the typewriter. The other choices weaken the conclusion by suggesting that the advantages asserted in the passage are more illusory than real.

3. **The correct answer is (D).** The passage draws the general conclusion that home buyers should "always" buy a new house based on a couple of specific advantages that new houses offer. Choice (D) is the best criticism of the argument because it suggests that these factors are not necessarily the only factors, or the most important ones, in the home buying decision.

4. **The correct answer is (D).** The author of the passage emphasizes the importance of the imposition of martial law in the South as an influence on later U.S. history. Therefore, choice (D), which tends to minimize that importance, is not an assumption made by the author.

5. **The correct answer is (C).** Although the passage uses the (slightly sexist) term "young man" to describe the typical early performer of rock and roll, the author is not concerned with gender but with age. Therefore, the prevalence of women among rock and roll performers is irrelevant to the argument and neither underlies it not weakens it.

6. **The correct answer is (B).** Of the five statements offered, only the one in choice (B) can be inferred from the passage. You might agree or disagree with one of the other statements, but it would have to be on the basis of outside knowledge, not on what appears in the passage itself.

7. **The correct answer is (B).** Each of the other answer choices undermines the assertion that TV is a better source of entertainment and family togetherness than the radio. Choice (B) does not; if anything, it somewhat strengthens the argument by suggesting that TV is more enjoyable than radio was.

8. **The correct answer is (E).** Choices (A) through (D) all weaken the argument by suggesting that history might have developed along much the same lines even if Hitler had not attended the meeting on September 12, 1919. However, choice (E) makes a counterfactual assertion—that Hitler's speech might not have "electrified" the crowd, as it actually did. Since it merely denies what really happened, this is not an effective objection to the conclusion drawn in the passage.

9. **The correct answer is (C).** This weakens the argument because it suggests that the "eye for an eye" standard was originally intended to set an *upper limit* to the revenge exacted for crime rather than a *floor*.

10. **The correct answer is (A).** Whether or not the average New York tourist would want to visit the Cloisters is irrelevant to the question of whether the experience of touring the building is an esthetically pleasing one. Choices (B) through (E) all name assumptions that must be true if the author's conclusion—that a visit to the Cloisters is esthetically unpleasing—is correct.

11. **The correct answer is (A).** From the information in the passage, we can't draw any conclusions as to the relative speed to commuting by train into Chicago and the speed of auto or other alternative forms of travel.

12. **The correct answer is (C).** Rather than supporting the conclusion of the passage—that "it was necessary for the United States to drop atomic bombs"—choice (C) weakens the conclusion by suggesting that the war would soon have ended even without the use of the bombs.

13. **The correct answer is (D).** Since the advocates of humor use a high rate of recall as evidence of the "effectiveness" of humor as a selling tool, they must assume that effectiveness and memorability are one and the same—as stated in choice (D).

14. **The correct answer is (E).** This statement weakens the argument of the humor advocates by exposing a disconnect in their logic: it may well be that a memorable ad is an ineffective selling tool.

EXERCISE 5

1. **The correct answer is (D).** This answer supports the conclusion by suggesting that the removal of the asbestos could endanger people by sending the dangerous fibers into circulation in the atmosphere.

2. **The correct answer is (C).** If it is true, as stated in the passage, that less-gas-efficient vehicles are more popular today than they were twenty years ago, then it must be true, as stated in choice (C), that the average gas efficiency of today's cars must be less than that of cars two decades ago.

3. **The correct answer is (C).** The other answer choices help to explain why many men, influenced in part by the example set by Gable, would have shunned undershirts in 1934. Choice (C) does not; if anything, it suggests a counterinfluence that one would think might have increased rather than decreased their popularity.

4. **The correct answer is (A).** Reread the last sentence of the passage. The author contends that Scopes should not have been tried for his "crime" because he "did not break the law on his own initiative." The obvious implication is that a person whose crime is originally suggested by another should not be held responsible for that crime.

5. **The correct answer is (E).** Choices (A) through (D) all call into question one or another of Franklin's assertions. Choice (E), however, merely implies that finding a willing older woman for an extramarital affair is likely to be more difficult than finding a willing younger woman—not that Franklin was wrong in recommending that course of action.

6. **The correct answer is (A).** It's clearly more logical to assume that the wealthy men Charles has met wear expensive London suits *because* they are rich and can afford them, rather than the opposite—that the expensive suits somehow bring riches to those who wear them.

7. **The correct answer is (B).** The point of the saying, of course, is that the weather in Maine changes so frequently that one is likely to notice a difference every minute or so. (Literally an exaggeration, of course.)

8. **The correct answer is (D).** Choice (D) is the one answer that need not be true based on the information in the passage. In fact, the passage tends to imply that the statement in choice (D) is false; that the children who taunted the marchers were "emulating their parents" without necessarily having any sincere (or even well thought out) opinions concerning the validity of the civil rights movement.

9. **The correct answer is (D).** Since the author states that preventing the assassination of Franz Ferdinand would "keep World War I from ever occurring," he must believe what choice (D) states—that the assassination was critical in triggering the war.

10. **The correct answer is (E).** The passage is making a point concerning the relative lack of light in a north-facing room as compared to a south-facing room. The fact that rooms facing east and west are also relatively sunnier than a north-facing room doesn't weaken the argument; perhaps, if anything, it strengthens it.

11. **The correct answer is (D).** Choice (D) is not an assumption underlying the passage; in fact, if it is true, then the conclusion of the passage (that recreation of the dinosaurs from their DNA will one day be possible) is almost certainly false.

12. **The correct answer is (B).** The passage states that the communists believed that the execution of the tsar and his heir was necessary "for the security of the new regime." The implication is that, had the tsar or his heir survived, his popularity would have endangered the communists. This is the point stated explicitly in choice (B).

13. **The correct answer is (C).** The passage says that local companies must meet "global standards of quality" because of the risk that competitors will import good business techniques from other countries. To exemplify this in the dry-cleaning business, we must imagine a dry cleaner who imports a smart business idea from another country and uses it to gain a competitive edge, as suggested in choice (C).

14. **The correct answer is (E).** The original argument assumes that the use of delaying tactics by the teams is the major reason baseball games are growing longer. Choice (E) undermines the logic of the proposed solution by suggesting that other factors are more important.

Chapter 7

Problem Solving

Get the Scoop On . . .

- Proven strategies for tackling problem-solving items
- How rounding off and guesstimating can save you time and help you avoid errors
- How to work backwards to untangle challenging questions
- How to find answers in the diagrams provided by the test makers
- How to master the numerical data buried in charts and graphs

THE TEST CAPSULE

What's the Big Idea?

Problem-solving questions are designed to test your knowledge of the basic math facts and skills most students learn in high school. You'll be given a varied mixture of problem types, including some word problems, problems that involve reading and interpreting graphs and charts, geometry problems with and without diagrams, and a few straightforward arithmetic and algebra problems. For each question, five answer choices are provided; you just have to pick the right one.

How Many?

Your GMAT CAT will probably have 22 problem-solving questions out of 37 total Quantitative questions.

How Much Do They Count?

Problem-solving questions are 22 out of 37 total quantitative questions. They count as 59 percent of your overall quantitative score.

How Much Time Should They Take?

Plan to answer problem-solving items at an average rate of 90 seconds per question.

What's the Best Strategy?

When in doubt, try something. The problem itself will often suggest a procedure you often used in high school (or college) math class. If so, use it, even if you can't see how it will lead to the answer you want. Quite often, this sort of "tinkering with the numbers" will quickly lead you toward the solution.

What's the Worst Pitfall?

It's a mistake to get bogged down in lengthy or complex calculations. Most GMAT CAT math questions are deliberately designed to make complicated calculations unnecessary: The test makers are more interested in seeing whether you understand the basic structure of the problem than whether you can correctly complete a series of computations. If you find yourself starting a complicated set of calculations, stop; you're probably overlooking a simple shortcut.

THE OFFICIAL DESCRIPTION

What They Are

Problem-solving items are designed to test your ability to "reason quantitatively," which is your ability to use knowledge of specific math facts, formulas, techniques, and methods to solve problems. Basic information about the procedures of math is needed, but the questions focus more on the underlying concepts than on the procedures themselves.

Where They Are

In the typical computerized GMAT CAT, you'll have a 75-minute Quantitative section with a total of 37 questions. Problem solving is one of the two types of questions that will appear in this section, intermingled in a seemingly random sequence. Reminder: The test makers claim the right to change the format at any time! However, the typical format we just described is what you're most likely to encounter.

What They Measure

To score high, it's important to be very comfortable with the basic operations of arithmetic—not only addition, subtraction, multiplication, and division, but also such procedures as working with fractions and decimals, figuring out averages, and the like. You'll also need to be skilled at the basic operations of algebra, including solving equations, using negative numbers and square roots, and factoring. Finally, many of the basic principles of geometry are tested, including such concepts as the properties of triangles, circles, and quadrilaterals and determining the areas and volumes of simple figures.

What They Cover

The math areas tested on the GMAT CAT are those studied by virtually every high school student: arithmetic, basic algebra, and plane and coordinate geometry. Many advanced and specialized math topics are *not* covered on the GMAT CAT, including trigonometry and calculus. See Appendix B, The Insider's GMAT CAT Math Review, for a detailed review of the math concepts most frequently tested on the exam.

The Directions

Directions: Solve the problem and indicate the best of the answer choices given.

Numbers: All numbers used are real numbers.

Figures: A figure accompanying a problem-solving question is intended to provide information useful in solving the problem. Figures are drawn as accurately as possible EXCEPT when it is stated in a specific problem that its figure is not drawn to scale. Straight lines may sometimes appear jagged. All figures lie in a plane unless otherwise indicated.

THE INSIDER'S REPORT: STRATEGIES THAT REALLY WORK

Focus on What's Actually Being Asked

FYI

Don't overlook the little words in the question, which can make a huge difference in what's being asked. "Which of the following may be true?" has a very different meaning from "Which of the following must be true?" Both, of course, are very different from "Which of the following may not be true?" So don't skim; read every word carefully.

Read the question carefully and make sure you know the answer being sought. Most GMAT CAT math problems will include a series of interrelated facts. The kinds of facts will vary depending on the kind of question.

In a word problem, these facts might include the speed of a train, the distance between two cities, and the time when the train leaves the station.

In a geometry problem, the facts might include the degree measures of two angles in a triangle, the length of one side of the triangle, and the diameter of a circle in which the triangle is inscribed.

In a graph-reading problem, the facts might include an entire series of numbers as depicted in the graph—monthly inches of rainfall in a particular county over a one-year period, for example.

One key to tackling any of these kinds of problems is to make sure you know which fact is being asked about and what form the answer should take. If you read hastily, you may *assume* a particular question when, in fact, the test makers want to focus on a different one. Rather than ask about when the train will arrive at City B, they may ask when the train will reach the one-third point of the trip. Rather than ask about the area of either the triangle or the circle, they may ask instead about the area of the odd-shaped shaded region that falls between them. Rather than ask about the amount of rainfall in any particular month, they may ask about the *difference* among two of the months—a number that doesn't appear directly on the graph itself.

When in Doubt, Try Something

Occasionally, you'll find yourself staring at a problem without knowing how to begin solving it. If you're at a loss, try something. Often, the numbers stated in the problem will suggest a starting point by reminding you of operations and procedures you often used in high school (or college) math class.

If fractions are involved, for example, try reducing them to the lowest terms or multiplying them out to change them into whole numbers. Or change them into decimals or percentages if they lend themselves easily to that process (for example, $\frac{1}{10} = 10\%$).

If a geometry diagram appears, work from what you know (such as the degree measures of certain angles) to fill in other information you don't know: the complementary angle alongside the angle that's marked, for example, or the angle on the other side of the transversal that must be equal to the angle you know.

If you're given a problem involving probability or permutations (varying combinations of things), just start listing all the possibilities.

Quite often, seemingly random experimenting like this will lead you quickly toward the right answer. Why? It's because of the peculiar way in which GMAT CAT math problems are designed. The test makers want to test you on a wide array of math topics in a short period of time. That means they want to ask you a lot of questions that you can do quickly—in just one to two minutes each. Therefore, the questions are written so that the numbers themselves are generally "obvious." What's tricky is the underlying connection among the numbers. As soon as you "see" that connection, the math is usually simple.

As a result, GMAT CAT math tends to reward students who are willing to "mess around" with the numbers in the problem until an insight into the solution emerges. Once that "Aha!" moment happens, the answer is usually close at hand.

Round Off and "Guesstimate" Freely

FYI

Be guided in your guesstimating by the answer choices. If the answers are all close together, you need a fairly precise answer. If they are far apart, feel free to work with approximate numbers. You'll probably come up with a result that's close enough to pick the right answer.

It's not always necessary to work with exact numbers in solving the math problems in the GMAT CAT. Sometimes the fastest and even the most accurate way to an answer is to guesstimate. Here's an example, using a real math problem from a past exam:

A total of 60 advertisements were sold for a school yearbook. If 20 percent of the first 20 sold were in color, 40 percent of the next 30 sold were in color, and 80 percent of the last 10 sold were in color, what percent of the 60 advertisements were in color?

(A)   30%

(B) $33\frac{1}{3}$%

(C)   40%

(D) $46\frac{2}{3}$%

(E)   60%

Obviously, you can solve this problem precisely with a few calculations. If you're adept with percentages, you may be able to work it out in your head rather quickly; if you're not, but you have plenty of time, you can handle it slowly and carefully and come up with the exact answer after a minute or so.

However, if you're short on time and don't have the facility with numbers to figure it quickly in your head, here's a simple way to "see" the answer using approximations only. Look back at the facts in the problem. Of the first 20 ads, 20% were in color; of the next 30, 40% were in color. Obviously, the overall average for these two groups will be between 20% and 40%. Now, the size of the two groups isn't the same, so we can't just average 20% and 40% to come up with the overall average—but we can see that the overall average for the first 50 ads will be fairly close to 30%, and a little higher (because there are more ads in the 40% group than in the 20% group).

That just leaves the last 10 ads, of which 80% were in color. All you need to realize about this is two things. First, because the percentage for this group is 80%, which is higher than 30%, it will raise the overall average somewhat. Second, this is a small group—just ten ads—so it won't affect the overall average very much.

Without doing any calculations, we can guesstimate that the correct answer will be a percentage somewhat higher than 30%—but not too much higher. This immediately eliminates choices (A) and (E), and it makes choices (B) and (D) look a little low and a little high, respectively.

It so happens that the correct answer, if you work it out in detail, is choice (C) 40%—pretty much what we figured, based on sheer guesstimating.

Rounding off and guesstimating aren't necessary on most GMAT CAT items; in many cases, the numbers used are so few and so simple that you might as well work with them directly. But the chances are that you'll encounter several problems on every exam that will be easier and quicker to solve by guesstimating.

If Stymied, Plug in an Answer and Work Backward

FYI

When plugging in a number, start with choice (C). The answer choices are normally in size order, so choice (C) will be the middle-size choice. If it is wrong, you can usually tell whether the correct answer is probably larger or smaller—so you've already narrowed the possibilities to just two remaining answers.

On some questions, a quick route to the answer will jump out at you within a few seconds. In other cases, experimenting in some obvious way with the numbers will quickly direct you toward a solution. If neither of these works, try grabbing an answer from the five multiple-choice options and plugging it into the question. This will often lead you to the right answer quickly.

Here's an example, based on a question from an actual exam.

A ball is dropped from 192 inches above level ground, and after the third bounce, it rises to a height of 24 inches. If the height to which the ball rises after each bounce is always the same fraction of the height reached on its previous bounce, what is this fraction?

(A) $\dfrac{1}{8}$

(B) $\dfrac{1}{4}$

(C) $\dfrac{1}{3}$

(D) $\dfrac{1}{2}$

(E) $\dfrac{2}{3}$

It helps if you can picture what's happening here. Think of a handball or a tennis ball, repeatedly bouncing, but each time rising less high until at last it settles on the ground, motionless. The problem suggests that, on each bounce, the ball will rise to a height that is some particular fraction of the previous bounce. The question is what is that fraction; is it $\dfrac{1}{8}, \dfrac{1}{4}$, or what?

The fastest way to a solution is to plug in an answer. Try choice (C), and see what happens. If the ball bounces up one third as high as it started, then after the first bounce it will rise up one third as high as 192 inches. If you're fast with numbers, you'll know that this is 64 inches. (A precise number isn't essential; if you can tell it's "around 60," you're close enough.)

After the second bounce, it'll rise one third as high as that, which is $21\frac{1}{3}$ inches (or, if you're guesstimating, "around 20"). *Stop!* The problem says that the ball rises to 24 inches after the *third* bounce. Obviously, if the ball rises less than that after *two* bounces, it'll be way too low after three! So choice (C) cannot be the answer.

We can see that the ball must be bouncing higher than one third of the way; so the correct answer must be a larger fraction, meaning either choice (D) or choice (E). If you're pressed for time, choose one and move on (you have a 50 percent chance of being right). If you have time, plug in either and see whether it works. If you do, you'll see that choice (D) is right.

Would it be possible to develop a formula to answer this question? Probably—some physicist has done it, I'll bet. But it would be crazy to try to devise a formula for the exam. Remember the unique advantage of a test like the GMAT CAT: *All the correct answers have been provided.* When it's not obvious which one is correct, pick one and try it. Even if the one you pick first is wrong, this method will usually let you home in on the best choice fairly quickly.

THE INSIDER'S REPORT: THE BEST TIPS

For Word Problems, Build an Equation That Will Yield the Answer You Want

FYI

When creating an equation for a word problem, use obvious letter symbols (T for Ted's age, H for hours worked, P for price, and so on) rather than "textbook" letters such as x, y, or z. They're easier to remember and less likely to cause you confusion.

For some students, word problems pose the toughest math challenge. You know the kind: They deal with planes traveling at a certain speed, pipes filling vats with liquid at a particular rate, workers painting walls at so many square feet per hour, and so on.

Curiously enough, in most word problems, the math itself is not difficult. You may have a couple of fractions to multiply or divide or a simple equation to solve, but the computations will be easy. What's tricky is setting up the math in the first place—in other words, turning the words into numbers and symbols. Here are some pointers that will help.

- Let the unknown quantity equal what you want to solve for. If the question asks "What fraction of the entire job will be completed after three hours?" begin writing your equation with $J =$, where J represents that fraction of the job. Conversely, if the question asks, "How many hours will it take to do $\frac{3}{7}$ of the entire job?" then begin your equation with H, which should equal the hours of work needed. This way, once you've solved the equation, you automatically have your answer, with no further conversions needed.

- Break the problem down into phrases, and translate each into a numerical expression. Word problems can be intimidating because of their length and complexity. Your strategy: Divide and conquer. Break the problem down into its component parts, and give each an appropriate number or symbol. Then, devise an equation or formula that describes the relationship among these parts, and go ahead with the math.

Here's an example, using one typical kind of word problem—an age problem:

Paul is eight years older than Sarah. Four years ago, Sarah was half the age Paul is now. How old is Sarah now?

First, notice that what you're looking for is Sarah's age now. Set up your equation making S (Sarah's age now) the unknown for which you will solve. The only other letter we'll need is P, which stands for Paul's age now.

Now create a couple of simple equations that state in symbols and numbers what the sentences in the problem say.

"Paul is eight years older than Sarah" becomes: $P - 8 = S$.

"Four years ago, Sarah was half the age Paul is now" becomes $S - 4 = \frac{P}{2}$.

To get rid of the fraction (usually a good idea), multiply this equation through by 2: $2S - 8 = P$.

Now you can solve for S by substituting the expression $2S - 8$ for P in the first equation:

$$(2S - 8) - 8 = S$$
$$2S - 16 = S$$
$$-16 = -S$$
$$S = 16$$

So Sarah's age today is 16 (Paul is 24).

Check out Table 7.1. It gives you some of the most common translations of words and phrases into mathematical operations. Learn the list; it'll work as a kind of "foreign phrasebook" for turning English into numbers on the exam.

Table 7.1
Words and Phrases with Mathematical Translations

Equals	is, amounts to, is the same as
Addition	and, with, along with, added to, in addition to, increased by, more than, greater than, larger than
Subtraction	less than, fewer than, without, take away, difference, decreased by, reduced by, smaller than
Multiplication	times, each, per, by, of, product
Division	divided by, part of, fraction, piece, portion

Convert All Quantities Into Units That Are Easier to Work With

Don't feel locked into the numbers presented in the problem. If you can see that a different number that you can easily get to will be simpler to work with, go for it by changing the units of measurement.

In particular, when you can, look for opportunities to convert working units into the units in which the answer is wanted. For example, if you see that the answers are all stated in terms of square feet, whereas one of the numbers in the problem is in square yards, change it to square feet before beginning your work. (One square yard equals nine square feet.)

On Geometry Problems: Mine the Diagram for Clues to the Answer

Most geometry problems on the GMAT CAT are accompanied by diagrams. They are there for a reason. You can usually leap from what you know—the facts you are given—to what you need to know simply by using the parts of the diagram as "stepping stones." Here's an example:

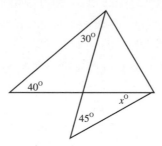

In the figure above, what is the value of x?

(A) 65
(B) 45
(C) 40
(D) 30
(E) 25

The diagram gives you three explicit facts: the degree measures of the angles that are marked as 30°, 40°, and 45°. However, a host of implicit facts are also contained there. If you recall some basic facts about geometric figures, they'll fall into your lap one by one. Quickly, as you'll see, they'll lead you to the answer.

First, you should remember that the number of degrees in the three (interior) angles of a triangle will always sum to 180°. This allows us to calculate the size of the third, unmarked angle in the upper-right triangle; it must measure 110°.

Next, you should recall that, when two straight lines intersect (cross), the opposite angles formed are equal. (This is easy to remember; the angles in such a figure *look* equal.) Based on this, we can see that the "top" angle in the bottom triangle must also measure 110°, like its twin.

From this fact, we can now figure out the size of the angle in question. Because 110° + 45° = 155°, there are just 25° left for the third angle of the triangle; the right answer is choice (E).

Solving a geometry problem like this one is easy. Just fill in the blank parts of the diagram using what you can deduce from the information you're given. (You'll need to quickly replicate the diagram on a piece of scrap paper and mark in the new information as you deduce it.) Once you get to the fact being asked about, you're home free.

In some geometry questions, studying the diagram can make "math" totally unnecessary:

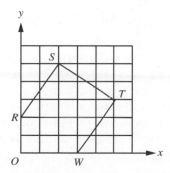

In the figure above, which two sides of polygon *ORSTW* have the same slope?

(A) *OR* and *OW*
(B) *OW* and *ST*
(C) *RS* and *ST*
(D) *RS* and *WT*
(E) *ST* and *WT*

When you studied coordinate geometry in high school, you learned that the slope of a line is often expressed as a fraction. You also learned a formula for calculating the slope of a line from its end points. It's possible you may need to use that formula for one question on the GMAT CAT. (If you've forgotten it, don't worry; you can refresh your memory with Appendix B, The Insider's GMAT CAT Math Review.)

However, *the formula is totally unnecessary for this problem—and so are any numbers whatsoever.* You can tell which two sides have the same slope just by looking at the diagram and deciding which two sides of the polygon "go in the same direction." It's easy; the only possibility is choice (D), sides *RS* and *WT*, which are obviously parallel to one another.

As long as you have even a vague idea as to what the word *slope* means, you can scarcely get this question wrong. The diagram does all the work for you.

If No Diagram Is Given, Sketch One

Sometimes, a question without a diagram simply cries out for one. That's what your pencil is for—and that's also why the test makers give you scrap paper. Draw your own diagram and read the answer right off it.

Here's an example:

Five distinct points lie in a plane such that 3 of the points are on line l and 3 of the points are on a different line, *m*. What is the total number of lines that can be drawn so that each line passes through exactly 2 of these 5 points?

(A)   Two
(B)   Four
(C)   Five
(D)   Six
(E)   Ten

Can you picture this in your mind's eye? Me neither. Grab your pencil and start sketching. The only tricky thing to notice is the discussion of the number of points involved. You're told that three points line on one line and three points line on another line—and that the total number of points is five. $3 + 3 = 6$, not 5; obviously, something funny is going on here. What's the solution?

The answer is that one of the points must line on *both* lines, as shown in Figure 7.3.

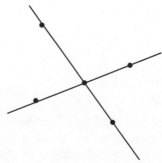

Now, how did we know how to draw these lines—the angle at which they cross, for example—and where to place the other four points? We didn't know; we just took a guess. Notice that the question strongly implies that *it doesn't matter* exactly how these details are drawn; there is one and only one answer, no matter what the sketch looks like.

(If several answers were possible, the question would have to say something like, "Which of the following *is a possible number of lines* . . . ?" or "What is the *the greatest possible number of lines* . . . ?" But it doesn't say that. It just says, "What is the number . . . ?" so you can tell that there's only one possible answer.)

Now that we have our basic drawing, we just have to figure out how many lines can be drawn that pass through two of the five points. Don't agonize over it; just start drawing. In a flash, you'll have your answer. (The lines in question are the *dotted* lines in the figure that follows.)

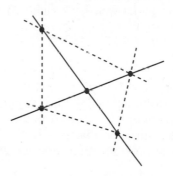

I can't think of any other way to fit in more lines here; can you? So the answer is choice (B), four. (Don't get confused and pick choice (D), six. The original two lines don't count—because they pass through three dots each, not two.)

This question is considered fairly hard by GMAT CAT standards. That's true only because many students allow the wording to confuse them and don't think to make a picture. Once you do, the answer almost jumps off the page.

On "Weird Operation" Questions, Just Plug in Numbers

Perhaps the most intimidating GMAT CAT math problems of all are what we call "weird operation" problems, in which the test makers create some new way of manipulating or mangling numbers and ask you to imitate it.

Like many GMAT CAT math problems, these are really tests of your reasoning ability, not your number skills. If you calmly and methodically plug in the simple numbers they give you, you'll usually find these problems laughably easy. Here's an example:

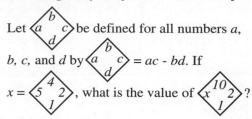

Let $\langle a \overset{b}{\underset{d}{}} c \rangle$ be defined for all numbers a, b, c, and d by $\langle a \overset{b}{\underset{d}{}} c \rangle = ac - bd$. If $x = \langle 5 \overset{4}{\underset{1}{}} 2 \rangle$, what is the value of $\langle x \overset{10}{\underset{1}{}} 2 \rangle$?

(A) 1
(B) 2
(C) 18
(D) 38
(E) 178

This looks weird, all right. Arranging letters or numbers in a diamond and then treating this as a math computation? You never learned *this* back in tenth grade!

Nonetheless, don't get nervous. The test makers tell you precisely what to do, although in slightly cryptic style. When they "define" the diamond-shaped figure as "$ac - bd$," what they are saying is that, whenever you see four numbers in a diamond like this, you should plug them into the mathematical expression shown in the order given. The question itself then requires you to perform this simple task twice.

First, let's figure out the value of x. If x is the diamond labeled as x, then $a = 5$, $b = 4$, $c = 2$, and $d = 1$. Now, we plug those numbers into the simple math computation:

$x = (5 \times 2) - (4 \times 1)$
$x = 10 - 4$
$x = 6$

There, that wasn't so bad, was it? Now, we tackle the second step. Having figured out the value of x, we can plug it into our second diamond, where $a = 6$ (our old friend x, that is), $b = 10$, $c = 2$, and $d = 1$. Again, plug in the numbers:

$(6 \times 2) - (10 \times 1)$
$12 - 10$
2

The answer is choice (B), 2. *Notice how ridiculously easy the math itself is.* You could have done these calculations when you were seven years old! The only "trick" is understanding what the test makers are doing, which is "defining" a new math operation and then patiently plugging in the numbers.

With a little practice, you'll never get a "weird operation" problem wrong.

On Graph Interpretation Problems, Spend 30 Seconds Analyzing the Graphs Before Tackling the Questions

The structural features of the graph—the labels on the axes, the units of measurement, and any information in the key—are more important than the data presented. If you understand the structure of the graph, you'll understand the kind of information it presents and the nature of the questions that the graph is designed to answer. Once you know these things, the specific details provided by the data—the answers to the questions, in effect—are easy to look up when you need them.

Some GMAT CAT problems are designed to test your ability to understand and use information presented in a table or graph. Again, the math involved is usually not hard. The key is knowing how to find the relevant information and separating it from the mass of other information in which it is embedded.

Think of these problem sets as resembling reading comprehension questions. Spend 30 seconds "reading" the graphs first, noting their structure and basic contents. Then, turn to the questions, referring back to the details—the specific data in the graphs—as often as necessary.

There are many different types of graphs. Three kinds commonly appear on the GMAT CAT: *bar graphs, line graphs,* and *circle graphs.*

Bar Graphs

- Bar graphs are good for making simple comparisons, such as comparing a single set of statistics (birth rates, for example) for different countries or different years. Figure 7.6 shows an example.

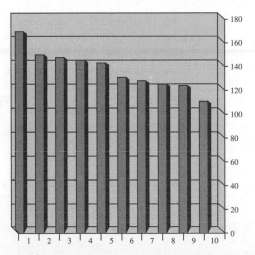

In this graph, each bar represents the annual sales of a different major industrial corporation. This type of graph makes the differences in size from one corporation to another very clear. However, if the data were more complex, this graph would be more difficult to look at and understand. (You wouldn't use a bar graph, for example, to show the sales of the entire *Fortune* 500, for example!) A bar graph also has limitations when it comes to spotting trends.

Line Graphs

■ Line graphs, by contrast, can be both precise and intricate. Large numbers of data points can be shown in one or more lines on a graph, and trends of increase or decrease can be easily and quickly "read" on a line graph. For these reasons, line graphs are the kinds of graphs most often used by scientists and statisticians.

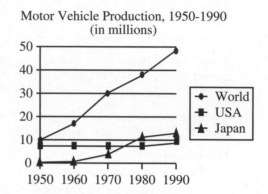

Motor Vehicle Production, 1950-1990
(in millions)

Both bar and line graphs have certain features in common:

All bar and line graphs have two *axes*, the *horizontal* (or *x*) *axis* and the *vertical* (or *y*) *axis*. By convention, the independent variable in an experiment or a statistical study is usually placed on the horizontal axis, and the dependent variable on the vertical axis. For example, if a chemist were studying the effect of temperature on the solubility of a substance, the independent variable would be temperature, and the dependent variable would be solubility. When the experiment was documented later, a graph of the data would have temperature along the horizontal axis and solubility on the vertical axis.

Circle Graphs

■ Circle graphs are used to show the breakdown of some large quantity into smaller quantities. The larger the relative size of a particular "slice of the pie," the larger the fraction of the overall quantity represented by that sector of the circle. Typical uses of a circle graph would include the division of the budget of a nation, business, or family into portions representing either different sources of income or different types of spending and the division of a general population into particular categories (by age, religion, or occupation, for example).

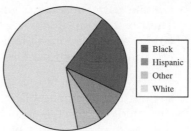

- All properly designed graphs are clearly labeled with the names of the variables being studied and the units of measurement (degrees, centimeters, percent, and so on). The divisions along the axes should be clearly numbered. All graphs should also have a title. Many graphs have a *key* that provides additional information about the graph or the data. The key is usually found in one corner of the graph or outside the limits of the graph altogether. A key is most often used when more than one line (or bar, or set of points) is plotted on one graph. Because it would be otherwise impossible for the viewer to know what is meant by the data in such a case, different sets of data are distinguished from each other by using different shadings or patterns for each line, bar, or set of points. The key explains to the viewer what each of the colors or patterns represents. You should always be sure to examine all of these features carefully whenever you encounter a graph on the GMAT CAT.

THE INSIDER'S REPORT: THE MOST IMPORTANT WARNINGS

Avoid lengthy calculations and working with big numbers. We've already seen examples of how straightforward the mathematical computations on the GMAT CAT generally are. You can count on this. In fact, if you find yourself getting involved in long, complicated, or tricky calculations— especially ones using big numbers—stop work! You've probably overlooked a shortcut or trick that would make the calculations unnecessary.

Here's an example:

The tip of a blade of an electric fan is 1.5 feet from the axis of rotation. If the fan spins at a full rate of 1,760 revolutions per minute, how many miles will a point at the tip of a blade travel in one hour? (1 mile = 5,280 feet)

(A) 30π
(B) 40π
(C) 45π
(D) 48π
(E) 60π

If you're doubtful where to begin, glance at the answer choices. The presence of π should remind you that the blades of a fan travel in a circular path (because π gets involved only when circles are involved). The point we are following is going round and round, ticking off 1,760 circles every minute. Thus, the relevant geometric formula is the equation for the circumference of a circle: $C = 2\pi r$.

What is the radius of this circle? The "axis of rotation" is a fancy way of saying "the point the blade spins around"—or, in even simpler words, the middle of the fan. The 1.5-foot measurement casually mentioned is the same as the radius of the circle. This makes it easy to figure the circumference: $C = 2\pi(1.5) = 3\pi$.

Every time the blade goes around once, it travels 3π feet. How many miles will it travel in an hour? Your instinct may be to grab your calculator and start working out the number of feet it will travel in an hour and then divide that by the number of feet in a mile (which the test makers have kindly provided) . . . but stop! Remember our warning: Don't get bogged down with big numbers. Instead, look for a shortcut.

Here's where it's hiding. The curious number 1,760 for the number of revolutions per minute wasn't chosen at random. (Curious numbers never are on the GMAT CAT.) It happens to be exactly one third the number of feet in a mile. Remember, the tip of the blade travels 3π feet for every revolution. Because $3 \times 1,760$ equals the number of feet in a mile, we can see that the blade tip will travel $\pi \times$ one mile every minute.

Now, just multiply this by 60 minutes to get the total distance traveled in an hour: 60π miles.

If you'd worked this out the long way—figuring out, to start with, that the tip traveled 316,800 feet per hour—you could have gotten the right answer, but it would have taken longer. And working with big numbers raises the risk of careless, easy-to-overlook math errors.

The lesson: avoid long calculations, and especially shun working with big numbers. The test makers usually don't want you to mess with them.

JUST THE FACTS

- On GMAT CAT problem-solving items, guesstimate and look for shortcuts; most questions have them.

- Break word problems into simple phrases that you can translate into numbers or symbols.

- Mine geometry diagrams for answer clues—and sketch your own when necessary.

- On "weird operation" problems, just plug in numbers and work out the solutions carefully.

- On graph interpretation questions, spend 30 seconds examining the graphs before tackling the questions.

PRACTICE, PRACTICE, PRACTICE: PROBLEM-SOLVING EXERCISES

Instructions

The following exercises will give you a chance to practice the skills and strategies you've just learned for tackling problem-solving items. As with all practice exercises, work under true testing conditions. Complete each exercise in a single sitting. Eliminate distractions (TV, music) and clear away notes and reference materials. Time yourself with a stopwatch or kitchen timer, or have someone else time you.

If you run out of time before answering all the questions, stop and draw a line under the last question you finished. Then, go ahead and tackle the remaining questions. When you are done, score yourself based only on the questions you finished in the allotted time.

Understanding Your Scores

0–2 correct: A poor performance. Study this chapter again, as well as The Insider's GMAT CAT Math Review (Appendix B).

3–4 correct: A below-average score. Study this chapter again, as well as all portions of The Insider's GMAT CAT Math Review (Appendix B) that cover topics you find unfamiliar or difficult.

5–6 correct: An average score. You may want to study this chapter again. Also be sure you are managing your time wisely (as explained in Chapter 3) and avoiding errors due to haste or carelessness.

7–8 correct: An above-average score. Depending on your personal target score and your strength on the other quantitative question type, you may or may not want to devote additional time to problem solving.

9–10 correct: An excellent score. You are probably ready to perform well on GMAT CAT problem-solving questions.

EXERCISE 1

10 Questions

Time—15 Minutes

> **Directions:** Solve the problem and indicate the best of the answer choices given.
>
> *Numbers:* All numbers used are real numbers.
>
> *Figures:* A figure accompanying a problem-solving question is intended to provide information useful in solving the problem. Figures are drawn as accurately as possible EXCEPT when it is stated in a specific problem that its figure is not drawn to scale. Straight lines may sometimes appear jagged. All figures lie in a plane unless otherwise indicated.

1. On the number line shown, which point corresponds to the number 2.27?

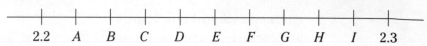

   (A) *I*
   (B) *H*
   (C) *G*
   (D) *F*
   (E) Not a labeled point

2. If $m = 121 - 5k$ is divisible by 3, which of the following may be true?

   I.   *m* is odd
   II.   *m* is even
   III. *k* is divisible by 3

   (A) I only
   (B) II only
   (C) II and III only
   (D) I and II only
   (E) I, II, and III

3. The cost of 4 rolls, 6 muffins, and 3 loaves of bread is $9.10. The cost of 2 rolls, 3 muffins, and a loaf of bread is $3.90. What is the cost of a loaf of bread?

   (A) $1.05
   (B) $1.10
   (C) $1.20
   (D) $1.25
   (E) $1.30

4. If $3x + 4y$ is an odd number, which of the following CANNOT be true?

   I. x is odd and y is odd
   II. x is even and y is even
   III. x is even and y is odd

   (A) I only
   (B) I and II only
   (C) II only
   (D) III only
   (E) II and III only

5. The ratio of Democrats to Republicans in a certain state legislature is 5:7. If the legislature has 156 members, all of whom are either Democrats or Republicans (but not both), what is the difference between the number of Republicans and the number of Democrats?

   (A) 14
   (B) 26
   (C) 35
   (D) 37
   (E) 46

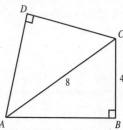

6. The area of the region shown above is

(A) $16 + 8\sqrt{3}$

(B) $8 + 8\sqrt{3}$

(C) $12 + 4\sqrt{3}$

(D) 16

(E) $8\sqrt{3}$

7. If $A < 2 - 4B$, which of the following is true?

(A) $\dfrac{2 - A}{4} > B$

(B) $\dfrac{2 - A}{4} < B$

(C) $B > 4A + 2$

(D) $B < 4A + 2$

(E) None of the above

8. A box contains five blocks numbered 1, 2, 3, 4, and 5. Johnnie picks a block and replaces it. Lisa then picks a block. What is the probability that the sum of the numbers they picked is even?

(A) $\dfrac{9}{25}$

(B) $\dfrac{2}{5}$

(C) $\dfrac{1}{2}$

(D) $\dfrac{13}{25}$

(E) $\dfrac{3}{5}$

9. If a fleet of m buses uses g gallons of gasoline every two days, how many gallons of gasoline will be used by 4 buses every 5 days?

(A) $\dfrac{10g}{m}$

(B) $10gm$

(C) $\dfrac{10m}{g}$

(D) $\dfrac{20g}{m}$

(E) $\dfrac{5g}{4m}$

10. If x and y are positive integers and $x + y = 10$, what is the value of $x^3 - y^3$ when $x^2 + y^2$ is as small as possible?

(A) 8
(B) 6
(C) 4
(D) 2
(E) 0

EXERCISE 2

10 Questions

Time—15 Minutes

> **Directions:** Solve the problem and indicate the best of the answer choices given.
>
> *Numbers:* All numbers used are real numbers.
>
> *Figures:* A figure accompanying a problem-solving question is intended to provide information useful in solving the problem. Figures are drawn as accurately as possible EXCEPT when it is stated in a specific problem that its figure is not drawn to scale. Straight lines may sometimes appear jagged. All figures lie in a plane unless otherwise indicated.

1. On the number line shown, where is the number that is less than D and half as far from D as D is from G?

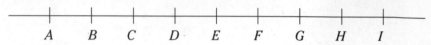

(A) A
(B) B
(C) C
(D) D
(E) Not a labeled point

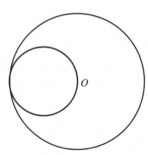

2. In the figure above, the larger circle shown has an area of 36π. What is the circumference of the smaller circle?

   (A) 2π
   (B) 4π
   (C) 6π
   (D) 8π
   (E) 12π

3. A faucet is dripping at a constant rate. If, at noon on Sunday, 3 ounces of water have dripped from the faucet into a holding tank and, at 5 p.m. on Sunday, a total of 7 ounces have dripped into the tank, how many ounces will have dripped into the tank by 2:00 a.m. on Monday?

    (A) 10

    (B) $\dfrac{51}{5}$

    (C) 12

    (D) $\dfrac{71}{5}$

    (E) $\dfrac{81}{5}$

4. If A and B are positive integers and $24AB$ is a perfect square, then which of the following CANNOT be possible?

    I.   Both A and B are odd.
    II. AB is a perfect square.
    III. Both A and B are divisible by 6.

    (A) I only
    (B) II only
    (C) III only
    (D) I and II only
    (E) I, II, and III

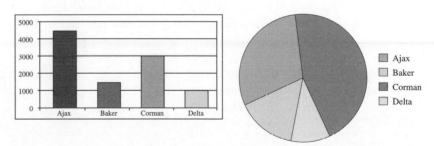

5. The two graphs above show the payments made by XYZ Corporation on contracts to four different suppliers last month. What is the degree measure of the angle marking the sector of the circle graph representing payments to Corman?

    (A) 36
    (B) 60
    (C) 100
    (D) 108
    (E) 120

6. If $r = -2$, then $r^4 + 2r^3 + 3r^2 + r =$

   (A) -8
   (B) -4
   (C) 0
   (D) 6
   (E) 10

7. $[3(a^2b^3)^2]^3 =$

   (A) $27a^{12}b^{18}$
   (B) $729a^{12}b^{18}$
   (C) $27a^7b^8$
   (D) $3a^8b^{12}$
   (E) $3a^{12}b^{18}$

$$\begin{array}{r} 7x \\ xy \\ \underline{xx} \\ 117 \end{array}$$

8. Shown above is a correct problem in addition, with x and y representing certain digits. What is the value of y?

   (A) 1
   (B) 2
   (C) 3
   (D) 4
   (E) 5

9. How many liters of 50% antifreeze must be mixed with 80 liters of 20% antifreeze to get a mixture that is 40% antifreeze?

   (A) 160
   (B) 140
   (C) 120
   (D) 100
   (E) 80

10. Horace averaged 70 on his first m exams. After taking n more exams, he had an overall average of 75 for the year. In terms of n and m, his average for his last n exams was

(A) $\dfrac{5m + 75}{n}$

(B) $\dfrac{5m}{n} + 75$

(C) $\dfrac{5n}{m} + 75$

(D) $\dfrac{70m + 75n}{m + n}$

(E) 80

EXERCISE 3

10 Questions

Time—15 Minutes

Directions: Solve the problem and indicate the best of the answer choices given.

Numbers: All numbers used are real numbers.

Figures: A figure accompanying a problem-solving question is intended to provide information useful in solving the problem. Figures are drawn as accurately as possible EXCEPT when it is stated in a specific problem that its figure is not drawn to scale. Straight lines may sometimes appear jagged. All figures lie in a plane unless otherwise indicated.

1. Which of the following numbers is evenly divisible by 3, 4, and 5, but not by 9?
   - (A) 15,840
   - (B) 20,085
   - (C) 23,096
   - (D) 53,700
   - (E) 79,130

2. If $a = -1$ and $b = -2$, what is the value of $(2 - ab^2)^3$?
   - (A) 343
   - (B) 216
   - (C) 125
   - (D) 64
   - (E) 27

3. Which of the following expressions is equivalent in value to $9y - \dfrac{6y^3}{2y^2}$?
   - (A) $\dfrac{3y}{4}$
   - (B) $\dfrac{3}{y}$
   - (C) $3y$
   - (D) $6y$
   - (E) $-6y$

4. If x and y are positive integers, and $x - 2y = 5$, which of the
    following could be the value of $x^2 - 4y^2$?

    (A) -3
    (B) 0
    (C) 14
    (D) 45
    (E) 51

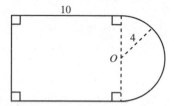

5. Find the area of the region shown in the figure above. Note: The
    curved side is a semicircle.

    (A) $20 + 4\pi$
    (B) $20 + 6\pi$
    (C) $40 + 6\pi$
    (D) $60 + 8\pi$
    (E) $80 + 8\pi$

6. If the result of squaring a number n is less than twice the number,
    then the value of n must be

    (A) negative
    (B) positive
    (C) between -1 and $+1$
    (D) greater than 1
    (E) between 0 and 2

Questions 7 and 8 are based on the following definition:

$$n^\wedge = \frac{2n}{n-1}$$

7. If $n = p + 1$, what is the value of $n^\wedge$?
    (A) 2
    (B) $\dfrac{2p}{p-1}$
    (C) $\dfrac{2p+1}{p-1}$
    (D) $2 + \dfrac{1}{p}$
    (E) $2 + \dfrac{2}{p}$

8. For which non-zero value of n is $n^\wedge = n$?
    (A) 1
    (B) 2
    (C) 3
    (D) 4
    (E) 5

9. You roll a fair six-sided die twice. What is the probability that the die will land with the same side facing up both times?
    (A) $\dfrac{1}{6}$
    (B) $\dfrac{1}{12}$
    (C) $\dfrac{2}{36}$
    (D) $\dfrac{1}{36}$
    (E) 0

10. The ratio of the arithmetic mean of two numbers to one of the numbers is 3:5. What is the ratio of the smaller number to the larger?
    (A) 1:5
    (B) 1:4
    (C) 1:3
    (D) 1:2
    (E) 2:3

EXERCISE 4

10 Questions

Time—15 Minutes

> **Directions:** Solve the problem and indicate the best of the answer choices given.
>
> *Numbers:* All numbers used are real numbers.
>
> *Figures:* A figure accompanying a problem-solving question is intended to provide information useful in solving the problem. Figures are drawn as accurately as possible EXCEPT when it is stated in a specific problem that its figure is not drawn to scale. Straight lines may sometimes appear jagged. All figures lie in a plane unless otherwise indicated.

1. The advertised price of potatoes is 35¢ per pound. If a 3-pound bag actually weighs 3 pounds, what is the closest approximation in cents to the actual price per pound for that bag?

   (A) 36
   (B) 35
   (C) 34
   (D) 33
   (E) 32

2. If $\left(\dfrac{-2}{5}\right)^3$ is equal to N thousandths, what is N

   (A) -100
   (B) -64
   (C) -32
   (D) 32
   (E) 64

3. In the figure above, the centers of all three circles lie on the same line. The medium-sized circle has twice the radius of the smallest circle. The smallest circle has radius 1. What is the length of the boundary of the shaded region?

    (A) 12π
    (B) 6π
    (C) 12
    (D) 3π
    (E) 6

4. What is the perimeter of a rectangle that is twice as long as it is wide and has the same area as a circle of diameter 8?

    (A) $8\sqrt{\pi}$

    (B) $8\sqrt{2\pi}$

    (C) 8π

    (D) $12\sqrt{2\pi}$

    (E) 12π

5. If the negative of the sum of two consecutive odd numbers is less than -35, which of the following may be one of the numbers?

    (A) 18
    (B) 16
    (C) 15
    (D) 13
    (E) 11

6. How many gallons of milk that is 2% butterfat must be mixed with milk that is 3.5% butterfat to get 10 gallons that are 3% butterfat?

(A) 3

(B) $\dfrac{10}{3}$

(C) $\dfrac{7}{2}$

(D) $\dfrac{11}{3}$

(E) 4

7. If the arithmetic mean of x and y is m, and $z = 2m$, then the arithmetic mean of x, y, and z is

(A) m

(B) $\dfrac{2m}{3}$

(C) $\dfrac{4m}{3}$

(D) $\dfrac{3m}{4}$

(E) $\dfrac{3}{4m}$

8. Which of the following is a common factor of both $x^2 - 4x - 5$ and $x^2 - 6x - 7$?

(A) $x - 5$
(B) $x - 7$
(C) $x - 1$
(D) $x + 5$
(E) $x + 1$

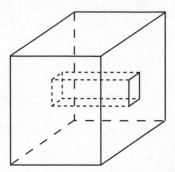

9. The figure above shows a cube 3 units on a side with a 1 × 1 square hole cut through it. How many square units is the total surface area of the resulting solid figure?

    (A) 66
    (B) 64
    (C) 60
    (D) 54
    (E) 52

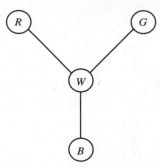

10. In a certain computer game, a light starts at the center (white) at time zero and moves once every second in the following pattern: from white to blue, back to white, then to green, back to white, then to red, in a clockwise direction. If the light continues to move in this way, what will be the color sequence at times 208–209?

    (A) white to green
    (B) white to blue
    (C) white to red
    (D) red to white
    (E) green to white

EXERCISE 5

10 Questions

Time—15 Minutes

> **Directions:** Solve the problem and indicate the best of the answer choices given.
>
> *Numbers:* All numbers used are real numbers.
>
> *Figures:* A figure accompanying a problem-solving question is intended to provide information useful in solving the problem. Figures are drawn as accurately as possible EXCEPT when it is stated in a specific problem that its figure is not drawn to scale. Straight lines may sometimes appear jagged. All figures lie in a plane unless otherwise indicated.

1. For which n is the remainder largest when the number 817,380 is divided by n?

   (A) 4
   (B) 5
   (C) 6
   (D) 8
   (E) 9

2. The towns of Andover and Diggstown are 840 miles apart. On a certain map, this distance is represented by 14 inches. The towns of Lincoln and Charleston are 630 miles apart. On the same map, the distance between them in inches is

   (A) $9\frac{1}{2}$

   (B) 10

   (C) $10\frac{1}{2}$

   (D) 11

   (E) $11\frac{1}{2}$

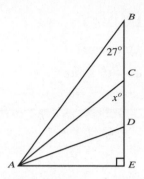

3. In the figure above, lines *AC* and *AD* trisect ∠A. What is the value of *x*?

    (A) 21
    (B) 27
    (C) 42
    (D) 48
    (E) 60

4. If the radius of a cylinder is tripled while its height is halved, its volume will be

    (A) halved
    (B) unchanged
    (C) doubled
    (D) increased by 350%
    (E) four times as large

5. Through how many degrees does the minute hand of a clock turn from 3:50 p.m. to 4:15 p.m. on the same day?

    (A) 25
    (B) 45
    (C) 90
    (D) 120
    (E) 150

6. Harvey paid $400 for a used car that travels 28 miles per gallon on the highway and 20 miles per gallon in the city. If he drove twice as many highway as city miles last month while using 34 gallons of gasoline, how many miles did he drive altogether?

    (A) 1,000
    (B) 840
    (C) 400
    (D) 340
    (E) 280

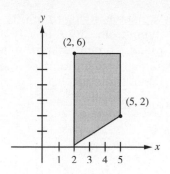

7. The area of the shaded region in the figure above is

(A)   15
(B)   16
(C)   17
(D)   18
(E)   20

8. What is the perimeter of a rectangle that is three times as long as it is wide and has the same area as a circle of circumference 6?

(A) $8\sqrt{3\pi}$

(B) $8\sqrt{\pi}$

(C) $4\sqrt{3\pi}$

(D) $\dfrac{8\sqrt{3}}{\sqrt{\pi}}$

(E) $\dfrac{8}{\sqrt{3\pi}}$

9. A plane is flying from City A to City B at m mph. Another plane flying from City B to City A travels 50 mph faster than the first plane. The cities are R miles apart. If both planes depart at the same time, in terms of R and m, how far are they from City A when they pass?

(A) $\dfrac{R}{m} + 50$

(B) $\dfrac{Rm}{2m} - 50$

(C) $\dfrac{Rm}{2m + 50}$

(D) $\dfrac{R + 50}{m + 50}$

(E) $\dfrac{m + 50}{R}$

10. P percent of $20\sqrt{3}$ is 3. $P =$

(A) $\sqrt{3}$

(B) 3

(C) $5\sqrt{3}$

(D) $10\sqrt{3}$

(E) 20

Answer Key

Exercise 1	Exercise 2	Exercise 3	Exercise 4	Exercise 5
1. C	1. E	1. D	1. E	1. D
2. D	2. C	2. B	2. B	2. C
3. E	3. D	3. D	3. B	3. D
4. E	4. D	4. D	4. D	4. D
5. B	5. D	5. E	5. C	5. E
6. A	6. E	6. E	6. B	6. B
7. A	7. A	7. E	7. C	7. A
8. D	8. C	8. C	8. E	8. D
9. A	9. A	9. A	9. B	9. C
10. E	10. B	10. A	10. C	10. C

Explanatory Answers

EXERCISE 1

1. **The correct answer is (C).** Because the labeled end points are 2.2 and 2.3, the ten intervals between must each be one tenth of the difference. Hence the "tick marks" must represent hundredths. That is, $A = 2.21$, $B = 2.22$, and so on. Thus, we know that $G = 2.27$.

2. **The correct answer is (D).** The fact that a number is divisible by 3 does not make it odd. (Think of 6 or 12.) Therefore, $121 - 5k$ could be either odd or even. However, k cannot be divisible by 3 because 121 is not. Hence, only I or II is possible.

3. **The correct answer is (E).** Let r, m, and b be the prices in cents of rolls, muffins, and bread, respectively. This yields two equations:

$$4r + 6m + 3b = 910$$

and

$$2r + 3m + b = 390$$

If we multiply the second equation by -2 and add the two together, we have

the first equation:	$4r + 6m + 3b = 910$
-2 times the second equation:	$-4r - 6m - 2b = -780$
	$b = 130$

Hence, the price of a loaf of bread is \$1.30, which is choice (E).

4. **The correct answer is (E).** $4y$ must be even, so for the sum of $3x$ and $4y$ to be odd, $3x$ must be odd. Because 3 is odd, $3x$ will be odd only if x is odd. Hence, x is odd and y can be anything. So II and III cannot be true.

5. **The correct answer is (B).** Let the number of Democrats be $5m$ and the number of Republicans be $7m$ so that D : R :: $5m : 7m = 5 : 7$. The total is $5m + 7m = 12m$, which must be 156. Therefore, $12m = 156$, and $m = 13$. Of course, the difference is $7m - 5m = 2m = 2(13) = 26$. Hence, the answer is choice (B).

6. **The correct answer is (A).** Because $BC = 4$ and $AC = 8$, we know that $\triangle ABC$ is a 30°-60°-90° right triangle. Hence, we know that $AB = 4\sqrt{3}$, and taking one half the product of the legs, the triangle has area $\frac{1}{2}(4)(4\sqrt{3}) = 8\sqrt{3}$. Because $\triangle ADC$ is an isosceles right triangle with hypotenuse 8, each leg must be $\frac{8}{\sqrt{2}}$. Again, taking one half the product of the legs, the triangle has area $\frac{1}{2}\left(\frac{8}{\sqrt{2}}\right)\left(\frac{8}{\sqrt{2}}\right) = \frac{64}{4} = 16$. Adding the two areas, we have $16 + 8\sqrt{3}$.

7. **The correct answer is (A).** Add -2 to both sides:

$$A < 2 - 4B$$
$$\underline{-2 = -2}$$
$$A - 2 < -4B$$

Divide by -4, remembering to reverse the inequality, thus $\frac{A - 2}{-4} > b$—that is, $\frac{2 - A}{4} > B$, which is choice (A).

8. **The correct answer is (D).** Because each person had 5 choices, there are 25 possible pairs of numbers. The only way the sum could be odd is if one person picked an odd number and the other picked an even number. Suppose that Johnnie chose the odd number and Lisa the even one. Johnnie had 3 possible even numbers to select from, and for each of these, Lisa had 2 possible choices, for a total of $(3)(2) = 6$ possibilities. However, you could have had Johnnie pick an even number and Lisa pick an odd one, and there are also 6 ways to do that. Hence, out of 25 possibilities, 12 have an odd total, and 13 have an even total. The probability of an even total, then, is (D), $\frac{13}{25}$.

9. **The correct answer is (A).** Running m buses for 2 days is the same as running one bus for $2m$ days. If we use g gallons of gasoline, each bus uses gallons each day. If you multiply the number of gallons per day used by each bus by the number of buses and the number of days, you should get total gasoline usage. That is, $\frac{g}{2m} \times (4)(5) = \frac{10g}{m}$.

10. **The correct answer is (E).** If $x = 5$ and $y = 5$, $x^2 + y^2 = 50$. For any other choice, say 6 and 4, the sum is larger. Hence, $x^2 + y^2$ is at a minimum when $x = y$ and $x^3 - y^3 = 0$.

EXERCISE 2

1. **The correct answer is (E).** Any number less than D must lie to the left of D. The distance from D to G is 3 units. Thus, the point we want must be 1 unit to the left of D, that is, halfway between B and C. Because this is not a labeled point, the correct choice is (E).

2. **The correct answer is (C).** The larger circle has area $AL = \pi(r)^2 = 36\pi$. That means that $r^2 = 36$ and $r = 6$. The diameter of the smaller circle equals the radius of the larger one, so its radius is $\frac{1}{2}(6) = 3$. Its circumference must be $CS = 2\pi(3) = 6\pi$, choice (C).

3. **The correct answer is (D).** In 5 hours, 4 ounces $(7 - 3)$ have dripped. Therefore, the "drip rate" is of an ounce per hour. From 5:00 p.m. on Sunday until 2:00 a.m. on Monday is 9 hours, causing the total to be

$$7 + \frac{4}{5} \times 9 = 7 + \frac{36}{5} = \frac{71}{5}$$

4. **The correct answer is (D).** The prime factorization of 24 is $2^3 3$, hence, if $24AB$ is a perfect square, then AB must have a factor of 2 and a factor of 3. This means, first of all, that both A and B cannot be odd. So I cannot be possible. II also cannot be possible because if AB were a perfect square and $24AB$ were also a perfect square, then 24 would be a perfect square, which it is not. Of course, if, for example, A were 6 and B were 36, $24AB$ would be a perfect square with both A and B divisible by 6, so III is possible. Hence, the correct choice is (D).

5. **The correct answer is (D).** Totaling the payments made to all four suppliers, you have $4,500 + 1,500 + 3,000 + 1,000 = 10,000$. Of this total, $3,000$ was paid to Corman—that is, 30% of the total. Hence, the sector representing Corman must be 30% of $360° = 108°$.

6. **The correct answer is (E).** Substituting: $(-2)^4 + 2(-2)^3 + 3(-2)^2 + (-2) = 16 - 16 + 12 - 2 = 10$.

7. **The correct answer is (A).** Working outward from the inner parentheses, $[3(a^2b^3)^2]^3 = [3a^4b^6]^3 = 27a^{12}b^{18}$

8. **The correct answer is (C).** The only way that $7 + x + x$ in the left column can total 11 is if x is 2, because if there were a "carry" of 1, x would not be a whole number, and if you try for a "carry" of 2, x would be 1, and $x + y + x$ in the right column would be at most 11, with a carry of only 1. Because $x = 2$, the only way $2x + y$ could have a units digit of 7 is if $y = 3$. In other words, the original addition must have been $72 + 23 + 22$.

9. **The correct answer is (A).** Let x be the unknown number of liters of 50% antifreeze. Now, the final mixture will have $(x + 80)$ liters, and the amount of antifreeze will be

$$0.50x + 0.20(80) = 0.40(x + 80)$$
$$0.5x + 16 = 0.4x + 32$$
$$0.1x = 16$$
$$x = 160$$

10. **The correct answer is (B).** Because Horace's average overall was 75, he had a total overall of $75(m + n) = 75m + 75n$ on $n + m$ exams. Because he averaged 70 on m exams, he had total of $70m$ on the first m. That means that his total on the last n exams was $75m + 75n - 70m = 5m + 75n$, and his average was $(5m + 75n) \div n = \dfrac{5m}{n} + 75$.

EXERCISE 3

1. **The correct answer is (D).** The easiest thing to look for is divisibility by 5. Does the number end in 5 or 0? By inspection, we eliminate 23,096, which ends in 6. We want the number to be divisible by 4, which means it must be even, and its last two digits must form a number divisible by 4. That knocks out the one ending in 5 (which is odd) and also 79,130 because 30 is not divisible by 4. This leaves 15,840 and 53,700. The digits of 15,840 add up to 18, whereas those of 53,700 total 15. Both are divisible by 3, but 15,840 is also divisible by 9. Therefore, only choice (D) 53,700 meets all the conditions.

2. **The correct answer is (B).** Substituting: $[2 - (-1)(-2)^2]^3 = [2 - (-4)]^3 = 6^3 = 216$.

3. **The correct answer is (D).** The fraction reduces to $3y$, and $9y - 3y = 6y$.

4. **The correct answer is (D).** Because $x^2 - 4y^2 = (x - 2y)(x + 2y) = 5(x + 2y)$, $x^2 - 4y^2$ must be divisible by 5. Therefore, -3, 14, and 51 are not possible. If the result is to be zero, $x + 2y = 0$, which means $y = -2x$, so that both numbers cannot be positive. Hence, the expression must equal 45, which you get for $x = 7$ and $y = 1$.

5. **The correct answer is (E).** The dotted line divides the region into a rectangle and a semicircle. Because the radius of the circular arc is 4, the diameter is 8, and that is the width of the rectangle. The length is 10. Hence, its area is 80. The area of the whole circle would be $\pi r^2 = \pi(4^2) = 16\pi$. Hence, the area of the semicircle is half of that, or 8π. Therefore, the total area is choice (E) $80 + 8\pi$.

6. **The correct answer is (E).** If $n^2 < 2n$, that means that $n^2 - 2n < 0$, or $n(n - 2) > 0$. Clearly, if n is any positive number less than 2, then n is positive and $(n - 2)$ is negative, making the result true.

7. **The correct answer is (E).** Substituting $(p + 1)$ for n, we have
$$n\hat{\ } = \frac{2(p + 1)}{(p + 1) - 1} = \frac{2p + 2}{p} = 2 + \frac{2}{p}$$

8. **The correct answer is (C).** It is easiest to plug in the values offered. You'll find that for $n = 3$, $n\hat{\ } = \dfrac{2(3)}{3 - 1} = \dfrac{6}{2} = 3$.

9. **The correct answer is (A).** It really doesn't matter what number you roll on the first roll; the chance of matching it the next time is always $\dfrac{1}{6}$.

10. **The correct answer is (A).** Calling the numbers x and y, $\dfrac{x+y}{2}:x = \dfrac{3}{5}$. That is,

$\dfrac{x+y}{2x} = \dfrac{3}{5}$. Cross-multiplying: $5x + 5y = 6x$; $5y = x$. Hence, one number is five times as large as the other, so their ratio is 1:5.

EXERCISE 4

1. **The correct answer is (E).** At 35¢ per pound, the 3-pound bag will be marked $1.05 or 105¢. Dividing this by the weight of the bag, we have $105 \div 3.25$. Hence, choice (E), 32, is the closest.

2. **The correct answer is (B).** Cubing, $\left(\dfrac{-2}{5}\right)^3 = \dfrac{-8}{125}$. To convert this fraction to thousandths, multiply both the numerator and the denominator by 8 to get $\dfrac{-64}{1000}$. Hence, $N = -64$.

3. **The correct answer is (B).** Because the smallest circle has a radius of 1, the medium circle has radius 2, and the diameter of the large circle must be 6, which makes its radius 3. The length of a semicircle is half that of a circle, that is, πr. So the length of the boundary of the shaded region is the sum of the lengths of the three semicircles: $\pi + 2\pi + 3\pi = 6\pi$.

4. **The correct answer is (D).** The area of a circle of diameter 8 is $\pi 4^2 = 16\pi$ because its radius is 4. Let the width of the rectangle be w. Its length is $2w$ and its area is $2w^2$, which must equal 16π. Thus:

$$2w^2 = 16\pi$$
$$w^2 = 8\pi \text{ and } w = \sqrt{8\pi} = 2\sqrt{2\pi}$$

Thus, $L = 4\sqrt{2\pi}$.

The perimeter is $2W + 2L = 8\sqrt{2\pi} + 4\sqrt{2\pi} = 12\sqrt{2\pi}$.

5. **The correct answer is (C).** Calling the numbers x and $(x + 2)$, the negative of the sum is $-[x + (x + 2)]$, and this should be less than -35. That is, $-[2x + 2] < -35$. Solving the inequality:

$$-2x - 2 < -35$$
$$-2x < -33$$

Dividing by -2 reverses the inequality:

$$x > 16.5$$

Looking at the choices, 18 and 16 are both even, and we need an odd number. $x = 15$ will work because $(x + 2) = 17 > 16.5$.

6. **The correct answer is (B).** Let g be the number of gallons that are 2% butterfat. Then, $10 - g$ will be the amount that is 3.5% butterfat. The total amount of butterfat is

$$0.02g + 0.035(10 - g) = 0.03(10)$$
$$0.02g + 0.35 - 0.035g = 0.3$$

Let's multiply by 1000 to clear out the decimals:

$$20g + 350 - 35g = 300$$
$$-15g = -50$$
$$g = \frac{10}{3}$$

7. **The correct answer is (C).** The arithmetic mean of x and y is $\frac{x + y}{2} = m$, which means that $x + y = 2m$ and $x + y + z = 4m$. Dividing by 3 to get the arithmetic mean of x, y, and z, we get $\frac{x + y + z}{3} = \frac{4m}{3}$.

8. **The correct answer is (E).** $x^2 - 4x - 5 = (x - 5)(x + 1)$, and $x^2 - 6x - 7 = (x - 7)(x + 1)$. The common factor is $x + 1$.

9. **The correct answer is (B).** Each side of the cube has an area of $3 \times 3 = 9$. Because there are 6 sides, the original cube had a surface area of 54 square units. Two 1×1 squares are missing, making the outside area 52. The "hole" has four 3×1 rectangular sides with a total area of 12, giving us a final total of 64.

10. **The correct answer is (C).** The sequence is

    0 1 2 3 4 5 6 7 8 9 10 11 12
    W B W G W R W B W G W   R   W

Every time you reach a time divisible by 6, the sequence starts over with W and proceeds: $WBWGWR$. 204 is divisible by 6; hence, we must have the sequence:

    204   205   206   207   208   209
     W   B   W   G   W   R

Times 208–209 are $W-R$.

EXERCISE 5

1. **The correct answer is (D).** 817,380 is divisible by all the numbers in the list except 8. Hence, 8 must give the largest remainder because it is the only one that is not zero. To start, 7,380 is divisible by 5 because it ends in 0. It is divisible by 2 because it is even and by 4 because 80 is divisible by 4. However, it is not divisible by 8 because 380 isn't. In addition, the sum of its digits is 27, which is divisible by 3 and by 9. Because it is divisible by both 2 and 3, it is also divisible by 6.

2. **The correct answer is (C).** The actual distance and the distance on the map must be in the same proportion. That is, $630:840 = x:14$, where x is the unknown distance. In fractions:

$$\frac{630}{480} = \frac{x}{14}; \frac{3}{4} = \frac{x}{14}$$

Cross-multiplying: $4x = 42$; $x = 10.5$.

3. **The correct answer is (D).** Looking first at $\triangle ABE$, we have a right triangle with one angle 90° and one 27°. Thus, $\angle A$ must be 63°. Hence, $\angle BAC$ is one third of that, or 21°. So looking at $\triangle ADC$, $\angle BCA$ must be $180° - 21° - 27° = 132°$. Because x is the supplement to that angle, $x = 48$.

4. **The correct answer is (D).** The volume is $V = \pi r^2 h$. Replacing r by $3r$ and h by $\frac{1}{2}h$, we have $V = \pi(3r)^2\left(\frac{1}{2}h\right) = \frac{9}{2}\pi r^2 h$. That is, it is 4.5 times as large, which means it's 350% larger than it was.

5. **The correct answer is (E).** The clock hand has moved through 25 minutes, which is $\frac{25}{60} = \frac{5}{12}$ of the full circle. Thus, in degrees: $\frac{5}{12}(360) = 150$.

6. **The correct answer is (B).** Let x be the number of city miles Harvey drove, and let $2x$ be the number of highway miles. Miles divided by miles per gallon should give the number of gallons of gas used:

$$\frac{x}{20} + \frac{2x}{28} = 34$$

$$\frac{x}{20} + \frac{x}{14} = 34$$

Multiply the equation by the *LCD* 140 to get:

$$7x + 10x = 4760$$
$$17x = 4760$$
$$x = 280$$

Because Harvey drove a total of $3x$ miles, the correct choice is $3(280) = 840$.

7. **The correct answer is (A).** If we drop a perpendicular from the point (5,2) to the *x*-axis, it will hit the axis at (5,0), and we will have a rectangle that is 3 units wide and 6 units high (because it goes from the *x*-axis, where $y = 0$, to the height of (2,6), which is 6 units). The area of this rectangle is 18 square units. Subtracting the area of the missing triangle, which is $(2)(3) = 3$, we see that the area of the shaded portion is 15.

8. **The correct answer is (D).** If the circle has a circumference of 6, its radius is given by $6 = 2\pi r$ so that $r = \dfrac{3}{\pi}$. The area of a circle of radius $\dfrac{3}{\pi}$ is $\pi\left(\dfrac{3}{\pi}\right)^2 = \dfrac{9}{\pi}$. Let the width of the rectangle be w. Its length is $3w$, and its area is $3w^2$, which must equal $\dfrac{9}{\pi}$. Thus:

$$3w^2 = \frac{9}{\pi}$$

$$w^2 = \frac{3}{\pi}$$

and

$$w = \sqrt{\frac{3}{\pi}} = \frac{\sqrt{3}}{\sqrt{\pi}}$$

The perimeter is $2L + 2W = 6W + 2W = 8W = \dfrac{8\sqrt{3}}{\sqrt{\pi}}$.

9. **The correct answer is (C).** The planes pass at the time when the sum of the distances traveled by both is R. Call this time t. The first plane, going m miles per hour, has traveled mt miles. The second plane, going $(m + 50)$ miles per hour, has traveled $(m + 50)t$ miles. The two sum to R. Thus:

$$R = mt + mt + 50t$$
$$R = (2m + 50)t$$

Thus:

$$t = \frac{R}{2m + 50}$$

Hence, the planes' distance from City A is m times this time, or

$$mt = \frac{Rm}{2m + 50}$$

10. **The correct answer is (C).** P percent means $\dfrac{P}{100}$. Hence, $\dfrac{P}{100} \times 20\sqrt{3} = 3$ must be solved for P. Thus, $\dfrac{P\sqrt{3}}{5} = 3$. Multiply by $\dfrac{5}{\sqrt{3}}$, and notice that $\dfrac{3}{\sqrt{3}} = \sqrt{3}$ gives $P = 5\sqrt{3}$.

Chapter 8

Data Sufficiency

Get the Scoop On . . .

- Crucial techniques for understanding and answering data sufficiency items
- The three-stage system that makes tackling data sufficiency questions simple
- How to save time by stopping your calculations *before* you solve the problem
- The most important data relationships you should know from arithmetic, algebra, geometry, and more
- How to avoid the tempting assumptions that produce wrong answers

THE TEST CAPSULE

What's the Big Idea?

Data sufficiency questions test your knowledge of basic math facts and skills along with reasoning, analytical, and problem-solving abilities not unlike those you may be called upon to use in business. Each data sufficiency item presents you with a question which you do *not* have to answer; instead, your challenge is to decide whether or not the information presented along with the question would be sufficient to allow you to answer the question. A special array of five answer choices is provided, each of which categorizes in a different way the relationship between the question and the information provided. You must select the answer choice that describes this relationship accurately.

How Many?

Your GMAT CAT will probably have 15 data sufficiency questions out of 37 total Quantitative questions.

How Much Do They Count?

Data sufficiency questions are 15 out of 37 total quantitative questions. They count as 41 percent of your overall quantitative score.

How Much Time Should They Take?

You should be able to answer data sufficiency items at an average rate of 90 seconds per question.

What's the Best Strategy?

Tackle each item using the three-stage system. (1) Examine the question, (2) consider the information provided by each statement individually, and

(3) *only if necessary,* combine the two statements. At each stage in this process, you'll eliminate one or more wrong answers. Thus, if you run out of time or are stymied by a tricky calculation, you can guess from among the remaining possible answers with a fair chance of choosing correctly.

What's the Worst Pitfall?

The worst pitfall is making any assumption not explicitly stated in the question or either of the two numbered statements. Many seemingly "common-sense" assumptions may be false and, if relied upon, will produce incorrect answer choices. In addition, the accuracy of geometry diagrams provided by the test makers may or may not be reliable. Measure the appearance of the diagram against the hard data provided in words and numbers, and give the data preference when it contradicts the diagram.

THE OFFICIAL DESCRIPTION

What They Are

Data sufficiency items are designed to test your ability to "reason quantitatively," which in this case refers to your ability to use knowledge of specific math facts, formulas, techniques, and methods to analyze the relationship between the question and the information provided, which may or may not enable you to answer the question. In some cases, you will need to perform calculations so as to actually answer the question; in other cases, you simply need to recognize whether or not it is *possible* to answer the question based on the information presented.

Where They Are

In the typical computerized GMAT CAT, you'll have a 75-minute quantitative section with a total of 37 questions. Data sufficiency is one of the two types of questions that will appear in this section, intermingled in a seemingly random sequence. Reminder: the test-makers claim the right to change the format at any time! However, the typical format we just described is what you're most likely to encounter.

What They Measure

To score high, it's important to be very comfortable with the basic operations of arithmetic—not only addition, subtraction, multiplication, and division, but also such procedures as working with fractions and decimals and figuring out averages. You'll also need to be skilled at the basic operations of algebra, including solving equations, using negative numbers and square roots, and factoring. Finally, many of the basic principles of geometry are tested, including such concepts as the properties of triangles, circles, and quadrilaterals and determining the areas and volumes of simple figures.

What They Cover

The math areas that are tested on the GMAT CAT are those studied by virtually every high school student: arithmetic, basic algebra, and plane and coordinate geometry. Many advanced and specialized math topics are *not* covered on the GMAT CAT, including trigonometry and calculus. See Appendix B for a detailed review of the math concepts most frequently tested on the exam.

The Directions

Directions (Data Sufficiency): This data sufficiency problem consists of a question and two statements, labeled (1) and (2), in which certain data are given. You have to decide whether the data given in the statements are *sufficient* for answering the question. Using the data given in the statements *plus* your knowledge of mathematics and everyday facts (such as the number of days in July or the meaning of *counterclockwise*), you must indicate whether

- statement (1) ALONE is sufficient, but statement (2) alone is not sufficient to answer the question asked;
- statement (2) ALONE is sufficient, but statement (1) alone is not sufficient to answer the question asked;
- BOTH statements (1) and (2) TOGETHER are sufficient to answer the question asked; but NEITHER statement ALONE is sufficient;
- EACH statement ALONE is sufficient to answer the question asked;
- statements (1) and (2) TOGETHER are NOT sufficient to answer the question asked, and additional data specific to the problem are needed.

Numbers: All numbers used are real numbers.

Figures: A figure accompanying a data sufficiency problem will conform to the information given in the question, but will not necessarily conform to the additional information given in statements (1) and (2).

Lines shown as straight can be assumed to be straight and lines that appear jagged can also be assumed to be straight.

You may assume that the positions of points, angles, regions, etc., exist in the order shown and that angle measures are greater than zero.

All figures lie in a plane unless otherwise indicated.

Note: In data sufficiency problems that ask for the value of a quantity, the data given in the statements are sufficient only when it is possible to determine exactly one numerical value for the quantity.

THE INSIDER'S REPORT: STRATEGIES THAT REALLY WORK

Learn the Directions Backwards and Forwards

Although, on the CAT, the answer choices for each question do not have letter labels, for our convenience we'll refer to them as if they do. Thus, the first answer choice will be called choice (A), the second answer choice will be called choice (B), and so on. The test makers will not change the sequence of answer choices, so it's perfectly safe to think of them as choices (A), (B), (C), (D), and (E).

As you've already perceived, data sufficiency is what you might call a "weird" question type. It ranks with analytical reasoning as one of the test makers' most diabolical conceptions, because it probably bears little resemblance to any type of question you tackled in a classroom math test during high school or college.

However, in defense of the test makers (listen closely: we rarely use those words!), data sufficiency *does* bear some relationship to a skill you use every day, perhaps without fully realizing it. Whenever you must make a decision, you mentally determine what information is needed to make that decision and whether or not you possess it.

For example, suppose you are planning a spur-of-the moment trip to (say) Seattle and need to decide which airline to take. There are probably two or three relevant and necessary pieces of information: the times and dates of flights to Seattle on each airline, the availability of seats on those flights, and the price of the available tickets. Once you have those pieces of information, you have the data you need to answer your question (Which airline should I take?). Other pieces of information, such as the kind of snack served on the flight or the way in which the planes are painted may be interesting but are ultimately irrelevant to answering the question.

Data sufficiency on the GMAT CAT is a little like this. Each item presents you with a question to be answered. Your job is to decide how two pieces of information ("statements" in GMAT CAT parlance) relate to the question. The correct answer choice for the item depends on the nature of the relationship between the two statements and the question. ETS has devised an elaborate system for the answer choices that reflects the different possible relationships, which is important for you to master.

First, make sure that you understand the meaning of each of the answer options:

- If the first piece of information provided—statement (1), in GMAT CAT-speak—is by itself enough to enable you to answer the question, but the second piece of information—statement (2)—is not enough, then the correct answer is choice (A).

- Choice (B) means that the reverse is true: statement (1) is not enough by itself to answer the question, but statement (2) is enough.

- Choice (C) is correct if you must *combine* the information from the two statements in order to answer the question.

- Choice (D) means that either statement by itself provides enough information to answer the question.

- Finally, if you can't answer the question even when you combine the information in both statements, then the correct answer is choice (E).

You might think of the answer choices, in shorthand, this way:

> (A)—(1).
> (B)—(2).
> (C)—Both.
> (D)—Either.
> (E)—Neither.

Get the idea? Don't worry if this answer system isn't yet crystal-clear to you; after you finish this chapter and try your hand at a few sample items, it will make more sense. But it's important that you know the answer choices extremely well before the day of the exam. You shouldn't have to spend time during the test figuring out, reviewing, or referring back to the five answer choices (although they will appear on the computer screen alongside every data sufficiency item). Instead, you should know the meaning of choices (A) through (E) so well that picking the right oval should come to you almost automatically.

Tackle Each Item in Three Stages

Because data sufficiency is such a weird and unfamiliar question type, most students find it helpful—even comforting—to have a system for approaching the questions. This helps eliminate the sense of floundering that can lead to confusion, loss of time, and wrong answers.

The following is a system that many students have found helpful. Try it, especially when you first begin practicing data sufficiency items. Eventually, you may find that you can tackle some questions without consciously going through the three stages we describe, but even the most skilled GMAT CAT test taker finds the system helpful on the more difficult items.

Stage One: Examine the Question

Before looking at the two numbered statements, take 20 to 30 seconds to consider the question by itself.

Figure out what is being asked. There are generally two possibilities: a specific number may be sought ("What is the value of x?" "How many gallons of water are in the tank?"), or a true/false answer may be needed ("Is it true that $a > 7$?" "Is n a prime number?"). Make sure you understand exactly what the question is asking.

Then, consider what information would be needed to answer the question. This will depend on the type of question, of course. If it is a geometry question, the information needed will be based on rules you've learned about how one geometric fact can be deduced from another. For example, to determine the area of a circle, you need to know either its radius, its diameter, or its circumference. To determine the length of the hypotenuse of a right triangle, you need to know the length of the other two sides.

On the other hand, if it is a percentage question, different rules come into play. To determine what percentage X is of Y, for example, you need to know the value of X and the value of Y. When a change from one value to another is involved—the increase in value of an investment, for example—you need to know both the old value and the percentage by which it has increased if you want to calculate the new value.

As these examples suggest, the data sufficiency question format allows the test makers to measure your knowledge of a wide array of mathematical topics. Later in this chapter, we'll provide reference charts for the math areas that are most commonly tested on the GMAT CAT, which will help solidify your knowledge of which facts are needed to answer which kinds of questions. In addition, Appendix B can help refresh your knowledge of all the basic math facts, skills, formulas, and concepts that appear on the exam. Use it to improve your grasp of any topic mentioned in this chapter on which you feel a little shaky.

FYI

Notice that every decision you make eliminates one or more answer choices. *This means that if you run out of time or are stymied by a calculation or a math topic you can't handle, you can at least use the decisions you* have *completed to eliminate answer choices and guess from among those that remain. Such educated guessing is* always *worth doing and will generally boost your score.*

Stage Two: Consider Each Numbered Statement Individually

Having figured out the nature of the question and decided, in a general way, what information is needed to answer it, look at each of the two numbered statements provided. Consider them one at a time, without reference to each other.

First, look at statement (1). Does it provide, all by itself, enough information to answer the question? If so, you've already narrowed the possible answer choices to just two: choices (A) and (D). If not, three answer choices are possible: (B), (C), and (E).

Then look at statement (2). Does it provide, all by itself, enough information to answer the question? If so, only choices (B) and (D) are possible. If not, only choices (A), (C), and (E) are possible.

Having gotten this far, you may already be able to pick the right answer. If either statement by itself provides enough information to answer the question, you can pick from choices (A), (B), and (D), depending on which statement is sufficient or whether either statement will do.

If neither statement by itself is sufficient to answer the question, go on to the third stage:

Stage Three: Combine the Two Statements

Third, *if necessary,* combine the two statements. If neither statement by itself is sufficient to answer the question, consider whether or not you can answer the question by combining the information in both statements. If so, the answer is choice (C); if not, the answer is choice (E).

The following flow chart summarizes the questions you need to ask yourself as you use the three-stage system. It's a handy way to review and refresh your understanding of this method.

The Three-Stage System for Data Sufficiency Items

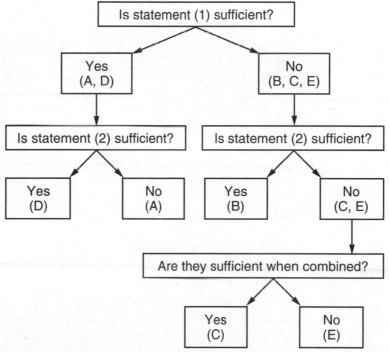

To illustrate this process, let's look at a sample question much like those you'll encounter on the real GMAT CAT.

1. What percentage of the sales of the National Motor Company in 1998 were represented by sales of the Cobra sedan?

    (1) In 1998, sales of the Cobra sedan amounted to $35.7 billion.
    (2) National Motor Company's sales in 1998 increased by 10.6% over sales in 1997.

Go through the stages in order. First, examine the question. What is being asked? You're being asked to determine what percentage (that is, what part) of the overall National Motor Company sales in 1998 were sales of the Cobra sedan.

What would you need to know to figure this out? In general, to answer a percentage question like this, you would need to know two things: the amount of the company's overall sales, and the amount of sales of the Cobra sedan. So we'll be examining the two numbered statements in search of those pieces of data.

Next, we consider each statement individually. First, consider statement (1). Does this statement by itself give us what we need to know to answer the question? No—it gives us half of the information we need (sales of the Cobra sedan), but not the other half (overall company sales). Since statement (1) is not sufficient, the answer must be choice (B), (C), or (E).

Next, consider statement (2). Does this statement by itself allow us to answer the question? No. It tells us the size of the increase in overall company sales from 1997 to 1998, but it doesn't give us any dollar amount or any other way of figuring out the actual value of those sales. Without a real number, the percentage of the increase is irrelevant. Since statement (2) is not sufficient, the answer must be either choice (C) or (E), and we have to go on to the last stage in the process.

Can we answer the question by combining the two statements? No! We know the part (sales of the Cobra sedan), but not the whole (overall company sales), so we can't compute the percentage that one is of the other. The correct answer is (E)—statements (1) and (2) together are NOT sufficient.

Try another example:

2. If n is a prime number between 10 and 20, what is the value of n?

   (1) $n > 12$
   (2) $n < 17$

In this question, we're being asked to determine the value of n. This means the *exact* value that n represents. One and only one number is an acceptable answer to a question so phrased.

What would we need to know to determine this? If you know the definition of a prime number (an integer that can be evenly divided only by itself and 1), then you can quickly figure out that there are four prime numbers between 10 and 20: 11, 13, 17, and 19. To answer the question, we'd have to narrow the field from four candidates to one. Let's consider the two statements and see whether either or both give us the information we need to do that.

What about statement (1)? It tells us that n is greater than 12, which does not enable us to answer the question. It still leaves three possible answers (13, 17, and 19). Since statement (1) is not sufficient, the answer must be either choice (B), (C), or (E).

FYI

It's easy to be tricked into selecting choice (B) for this item by inadvertently assuming the information from statement (1) when you consider statement (2). "Oh," you may say, "If n is less than 17, and we already know that n is greater than 12, then it's possible to answer the question." Wrong! When you look at statement (2), forget the information in statement (1); it no longer applies.

Statement (2) by itself is also not sufficient. If *n* is less than 17, there are still two possible answer choices (11 and 13). This eliminates possible answer choice (B) and narrows the choices to (C) and (E).

Finally, you must ask: can the question be answered if we combine the two statements? The answer is Yes: if we know that *n* is greater than 12 *and* that *n* is less than 17, only one possible number fits: 13. The correct answer for this item is choice (C).

Stop Work As Soon As You Know Whether the Data Are Sufficient— Even Before Solving the Problem

In the heat of battle, it's easy to forget that *you don't have to answer the question asked* in a data sufficiency item. All you need to determine is whether or not it would be possible to answer the question. As soon as you can tell that an answer would be obtainable, you can *stop work*.

Here's an illustration of how this principle works and how it can save you time on the exam:

3. What is the average weight of the five starting players on the defensive line of the Mammoths football team?
    (1) The three heaviest players on the line have an average weight of 340 pounds.
    (2) The two lightest players on the line weigh 275 and 290 pounds, respectively.

To calculate the average of a group of numbers, you need just two pieces of information: the total of the numbers and the number of numbers. In this case, the only missing piece of information is the total weight of the Mammoths defensive line. (You already know the number of numbers involved—five, since there are five players on the line.)

Neither numbered statement alone gives you the players' total weight, but if you combine statements (1) and (2), you can determine it. You'd multiply 340 by 3 (to get the combined weight of the three heaviest players) and add 275 and 290 (the weights of the two lightest players). But whatever you do, *don't actually perform these steps. It's not necessary.* All that matters is that you can tell that it would be *theoretically* possible to make these calculations and so determine the average. This is enough to pick the correct answer, choice (C).

Another illustration:

4. What is the value of $j + k$?
    (1) $3j = 4k - 2$
    (2) $3k - 3 = 2j$

You should know from your algebra studies that, in general, two independent equations will suffice to determine the value of two unknowns. (There are a couple of methods for working with simultaneous equations that will permit you do to this; they are reviewed in Appendix B.) Therefore, a glance at this problem should tell you that the most likely answer is (C): using the two equations provided in statement (1) and statement (2) should enable you to find the value of j and the value of k, and therefore to find their sum.

If the clock is running down, you can pick choice (C) and move on. However, if you have a little time to spare, you can begin the process of solving for j and k, just to make sure that no special tricks or roadblocks have been built into the question. (Occasionally, that's the case.)

A possible approach is to solve one of the equations for j in terms of k, then plug this definition into the other equation, like this:

As explained in Chapter 3, your timing strategy should change as you work your way through the GMAT CAT. Work slowly and thoroughly during the first several questions of the section, since these have the greatest impact on your final score. Later in the section, you can shortcut steps freely, since each question is worth fewer points and your primary objective is to complete as many items as possible.

Step 1: $3j = 4k - 2$

$$j = \frac{(4k - 2)}{3}$$

Step 2: Plug this definition of j into statement (2):

$3k - 3 = 2j$

$3k - 3 = 2 \times \dfrac{(4k - 2)}{3}$

$3k - 3 = \dfrac{(8k - 4)}{3}$

Step 3: Multiply both sides by 3 to remove the fraction, then solve for k:

$9k - 9 = 8k - 4$

$9k - 8k = -4 + 9$

$k = 5$

Step 4: By plugging this value for k into either equation, you can quickly determine that $j = 6$; so the sum of $j + k = 11$. The answer is choice (C): combining both statements enables you to answer the question.

Now, how much of this work should you actually do when tackling this problem on the exam? The answer depends on your overall timing status. If you have ample time for the item, you can perform the whole process. If you need to move more quickly, you might stop after step 2 or even step 1. Either is probably enough to tell you that the problem is soluble—which is all you really need to know.

THE INSIDER'S REPORT: THE BEST TIPS

Use Elimination to Narrow Your Answer Choices, Then Guess

As you've already seen, every stage in the process of analyzing a data sufficiency item involves decisions that eliminate possible answer choices. Therefore, it should never be necessary for you to select an answer based on a purely random guess. Instead, you should virtually always be able to eliminate one, two, or three answer choices and guess from among those that remain.

Table 8.1 contains a data sufficiency guessing guide which will help to clarify and organize your guessing strategy. Memorize the information it contains.

Round Off, Guesstimate, and Plug in Numbers to Save Time

You learned in Chapter 7 about how and why GMAT CAT math rewards rounding off, guesstimating, and other techniques for taking shortcuts or eliminating lengthy calculations. All of the same methods also apply to data sufficiency questions. If anything, they are doubly applicable, since the questions don't require you to calculate precise answers or (in some cases) any answer at all. Review the discussion of those techniques in Chapter 7 and apply them liberally as you practice data sufficiency questions between now and the day of the exam.

Know and Apply the Basic Data Relationships from Each Area of Math

Any familiar math formula can be applied to data sufficiency items in such a way as to make it obvious, with few or no calculations, whether or not the data supplied are enough to answer the question.

Table 8.1
Data Sufficiency Guessing Guide

- IF you know that statement (1) is sufficient but are unsure about statement (2), GUESS (A) or (D).

- IF you know that statement (1) is NOT sufficient but are unsure about statement (2), GUESS (B), (C), or (E).

- IF you know that statement (2) is sufficient but are unsure about statement (1), GUESS (B) or (D).

- IF you know that statement (2) is NOT sufficient but are unsure about statement (1), GUESS (A), (C), or (E).

- IF you know that neither statement (1) nor statement (2) alone is sufficient but are unsure about whether the combination is sufficient, GUESS (C) or (E).

Table 8.2
Basic Data Relationships for GMAT CAT Math Areas

Arithmetic and Algebra

- **Averages:** If you know any two of the following—the sum of a group of numbers, the number of numbers in the group, or the average of the group of numbers—you can find the third.

- **Percentages and Fractions:** If you know any two of the following—a quantity, the percentage or fraction of that quantity represented by a part, or the size of the part itself—you can find the third.

- **Proportions:** If you know any three terms from a proportion, you can find the fourth term.

- **Finding An Unknown Value:** In general, you can find the value of an unknown quantity if you have as many independent equations as there are unknowns. That is, with one equation you can solve for one unknown; with two equations you can solve for two unknowns, etc.

- **Travel Problems:** If you know any two of the following—the rate of travel, the time traveled, or the distance traveled—you can find the third.

Number Properties and Probability

- **Odd and Even:** If you know whether two numbers are odd or even, you can find whether their sum, difference, or product is odd or even.

- **Positive and Negative:** If you know whether two numbers are positive or negative, you can find whether their product is positive or negative.

- **Probability:** If you know the number of possible outcomes, you can find the probability of any single outcome.

- **Random Combinations:** If you know the number of items to be combined, you can find the number of possible combinations.

Table 8.2 (above) covers each of the major math areas commonly tested on the GMAT CAT and lists for each the basic data relationships in that area. Review this table carefully. If you find that you're uncertain about which formula to use to solve a given problem, refer to Appendix B, The Insider's GMAT CAT Math Review. All the important formulas and facts you need for the exam are explained in detail there.

Table 8.2—*Continued*

Geometry

- **Angles:** If you know the degree measure of either of two supplementary or complementary angles, you can find the other. If you know the degree measure of any one angle formed where two lines cross, you can find the other three.

- **Triangle:** If you know any two of the following—the height, base, or area of a triangle—you can find the third. If you know the sum of any two angles of a triangle, you can find the third. If you know the lengths of any two sides of a triangle, you can find the maximum and minimum lengths of the third.

- **Right Triangle:** If you know the lengths of any two sides of a right triangle, you can find the length of the third.

- **Circle:** If you know any one of the following—the radius, the diameter, the circumference, or the area of a circle—you can find any of the others.

- **Parallelogram:** If you know the degree measure of any interior angle of a parallelogram, you can find the other three.

- **Rectangle:** If you know the length and width of a rectangle, you can find its area and perimeter. If you know its area or perimeter and the ratio between the length and the width, you can find the length and the width.

- **Square:** If you know any one of the following—the side, the area, or the perimeter of a square—you can find any of the others.

- **Rectangular Solid:** If you know the length, width, and height of a rectangular solid, you can find its volume and surface area.

- **Cylinder:** If you know the height and the area of the base (or its radius), you can find the volume and surface area of a cylinder.

- **Midpoint and Slope:** If you know the coordinates of any two points on a grid, you can find the midpoint and the slope of the line that connects them.

THE INSIDER'S REPORT: THE MOST IMPORTANT WARNINGS

When Plugging in Numbers, Don't Forget Negatives, Fractions, Zero, and One

Many data sufficiency items include one or more unknown quantities—x, n, a, and so forth. Just as with multiple-choice problems (as discussed in Chapter 7), there may be times when the easiest and quickest way to tackle such an item is by plugging a possible value into the equation or statement and then working backward.

When you do this, don't forget to take into account the kind of "oddball" values often overlooked: negative numbers, fractions, zero, and 1. Unless these are explicitly ruled out, they are possible values for the unknown, and the variations they introduce can turn an "answerable" question into an "unanswerable" one.

Here's an example:

5. If x and y are integers, what is the value of x?

   (1) $xy = 7$
   (2) $y < 4$

It's probably clear that neither statement alone gives enough information to answer the question. However, you might be tempted to select choice (C), reasoning as follows: "Statement (1) tells us that the product of x and y equals 7, and since 7 is a prime number, the only two numbers we can multiply together to get 7 are 1 and 7. Then statement (2) tells us that y is less than 4. Combining these two facts, we conclude that y must equal 1, making x equal to 7."

Not so! The possibility overlooked here is that x and y might both be *negative* integers—specifically, -1 and -7. When multiplied together, these two integers have a product of $+7$, just as statement (1) says. And *both* have a value less than 4, in accordance with statement (2). Therefore, even when we combine the two numbered statements, we cannot determine with certainty the value of x, which could equal either 1, -1, or -7. Thus, the correct answer is choice (E).

Don't Assume Any Information Not Stated in the Problem

One of the logical skills that the test makers are measuring is your ability to distinguish "true facts" stated in the problem from unsupported assumptions made out of carelessness or inattention. It's likely that several data sufficiency items on your GMAT CAT will test this ability. Here are a couple of examples.

6. What percentage of the students in a certain history class are majoring in economics?

   (1)   64% of the male students in the class are majoring in economics.
   (2)   42% of the female students in the class are majoring in economics.

The question would be solvable, and easily so, if the number of male and female students in the class was equal (or, for that matter, if we knew the

---

FYI

The test makers are especially fond of testing this "uncertainty principle" when using exponents. Remember that, unless otherwise specified, all even exponents have two possible roots, one positive and one negative. For example, if you're told that $x^2 = 9$, x may equal either 3 or -3. By contrast, when the square root sign is used, by convention only the positive root is meant. Thus, $\sqrt{9} = +3$ only.

proportion of male to female students). However, we can't assume that the number of males and the number of females is equal, so the answer is choice (E).

7. In what year did Rajiv move to Denver?

   (1)   Rajiv moved to Denver 22 months after Peter.
   (2)   Peter moved to Denver in 1991.

Twenty two months is *almost* two years, so the obvious assumption is that Rajiv moved to Denver in 1993. However, suppose Peter moved to Denver in January, 1991. In that case, Rajiv moved to Denver in November, 1992, not 1993 at all. It's *probable* that Rajiv moved to Denver in 1993, but not certain; so the answer for this question is also choice (E).

8. In triangle *ABC*, what is the length of side *AC*?

   (1)   Triangle *ABC* is a right triangle.
   (2)   The length of *AB* is 4 and the length of *BC* is 3.

Eager to use your knowledge of the Pythagorean Theorem and the famous "Pythagorean triple" triangles, you may assume that this is a 3-4-5 right triangle, with side *AC* being the hypotenuse. However, we can't actually tell that from the information given. It's possible that the triangle might look something like this:

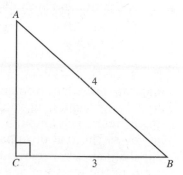

In this case, with side *AC* being the shorter leg rather than the hypotenuse, the Pythagorean Theorem tells us that side AC would have a length of $\sqrt{7}$, equal to about 2.65 units. Since there is more than one possible solution, this question, too, should be answered with choice (E).

Don't Assume That Any Diagrams Provided Are Accurate

The test makers go out of their way to warn you about their diagrams. There are a couple of specific considerations to bear in mind.

First, any diagram provided will agree with the information stated in the question, but *not* necessarily with the information provided in either of the numbered statements.

Second, the diagram may or may not be drawn to scale. You can safely assume that lines do, in fact, touch where they appear to touch; you can also assume that lines that appear straight are straight. But you can't make any assumptions about things like the size of angles, the length of lines, and the regularity of figures.

Here's an example of what to watch for when examining diagrams on the GMAT CAT:

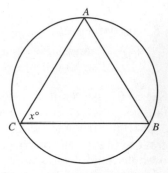

9. Is the triangle in the figure above equilateral?

   (1)   Arc *AB* has a degree measure of 120°.
   (2)   *x* = 60

The triangle inscribed in the circle certainly *looks* equilateral in the diagram provided. You might even be able to measure its sides, if crudely, by fashioning a ruler from a piece of scrap paper and holding it up against the computer monitor. That would be a waste of time, however. The real or apparent dimensions of the triangle as shown in the diagram are irrelevant to answering the question. Only the facts given in the question and the two numbered statements can be taken seriously.

In this case, we have another choice (E) answer—the two statements taken together are *not* sufficient. Both statement (1) and statement (2) tell us the same thing: that angle *C* has a measure of 60°—as it would if the triangle *were* equilateral. But without further information, we can't tell that angles *A* and *B* are also 60° angles. It's possible that angle *A* measures 59° while angle *B* measures 61°, in which case this is *not* an equilateral triangle. Since we can't know for sure, the answer must be choice (E).

The lesson is clear: never base an answer on the looks of a diagram. It may be helpful to you in picturing the figures described, but take its appearance with a very large grain of salt.

JUST THE FACTS

- Learn the data sufficiency directions backwards and forwards, so you don't need to review them on test day.

- Use the three-stage system to tackle each item, eliminating wrong answers at every step.

- Master the crucial data relationships from each GMAT CAT math area, so you'll know which facts can be deduced from which kinds of data.

- Don't make any assumptions not stated in the question or the numbered statements.

- Don't assume the accuracy of any diagram provided by the test makers.

PRACTICE, PRACTICE, PRACTICE: DATA SUFFICIENCY EXERCISES

Instructions

The following exercises will give you a chance to practice the skills and strategies you've just learned for tackling data sufficiency items. As with all practice exercises, work under true testing conditions. Complete each exercise in a single sitting. Eliminate distractions (TV, music) and clear away notes and reference materials. Time yourself with a stopwatch or kitchen timer, or have someone else time you.

If you run out of time before answering all the questions, stop and draw a line under the last question you finished. Then go ahead and tackle the remaining questions. When you are done, score yourself based only on the questions you finished in the allotted time.

Record your answers by writing the letter of your answer choice—(A), (B), (C), (D), or (E)—next to each question.

Understanding Your Scores

0–5 correct: A poor performance. Study this chapter again, as well as the Insider's GMAT CAT Math Review (Appendix B).

6–9 correct: A below-average score. Study this chapter again, as well as all portions of the Insider's GMAT CAT Math Review (Appendix B) that cover topics you find unfamiliar or difficult.

10–13 correct: An average score. You may want to study this chapter again. Also be sure you are managing your time wisely (as explained in Chapter 3) and avoiding errors due to haste or carelessness.

14–16 correct: An above-average score. Depending on your personal target score and your strength on the other quantitative question type, you may or may not want to devote additional time to data sufficiency.

17–20 correct: An excellent score. You are probably ready to perform well on GMAT CAT data-sufficiency questions.

EXERCISE 1

20 Questions

Time—15 Minutes

Directions (Data Sufficiency): This data sufficiency problem consists of a question and two statements, labeled (1) and (2), in which certain data are given. You have to decide whether the data given in the statements are *sufficient* for answering the question. Using the data given in the statements *plus* your knowledge of mathematics and everyday facts (such as the number of days in July or the meaning of *counterclockwise*), you must indicate whether

- statement (1) ALONE is sufficient, but statement (2) alone is not sufficient to answer the question asked;
- statement (2) ALONE is sufficient, but statement (1) alone is not sufficient to answer the question asked;
- BOTH statements (1) and (2) TOGETHER are sufficient to answer the question asked; but NEITHER statement ALONE is sufficient;
- EACH statement ALONE is sufficient to answer the question asked;
- statements (1) and (2) TOGETHER are NOT sufficient to answer the question asked, and additional data specific to the problem are needed.

Numbers: All numbers used are real numbers.

Figures: A figure accompanying a data sufficiency problem will conform to the information given in the question, but will not necessarily conform to the additional information given in statements (1) and (2).

Lines shown as straight can be assumed to be straight and lines that appear jagged can also be assumed to be straight.

You may assume that the positions of points, angles, regions, etc., exist in the order shown and that angle measures are greater than zero.

All figures lie in a plane unless otherwise indicated.

Note: In data sufficiency problems that ask for the value of a quantity, the data given in the statements are sufficient only when it is possible to determine exactly one numerical value for the quantity.

1. If $\dfrac{0.56}{1.26} = \dfrac{a}{b}$, where a and b are positive whole numbers, what is the value of b?

    (1) $a = 4$

    (2) $\dfrac{a}{b}$ has been reduced to lowest terms.

2. The number of compact disks owned by Pedro is what fraction of the number of compact disks owned by Marcia?

    (1) Pedro owns half as many compact disks as Andrea.

    (2) Marcia owns $\dfrac{3}{5}$ as many compact disks as Andrea.

3. To earn a grade of B in her French class, Erica must have an average score of 80 on her exams. She has taken four exams so far. What score must she get on the fifth exam to have an 80 average?

    (1) She averaged 76 on her first four exams.

    (2) If she gets an 86 on the fifth exam, her average will be 78.

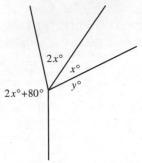

4. What is the value of y in the figure above?

    (1) $y = 3x$

    (2) $2x + y = 175$

5. A rectangular garden is 20 yards long and 10 yards wide. What is the total cost in dollars of seeding the garden and putting up a hedge around it?

    (1) It costs 80¢ per square yard to seed the lawn.

    (2) It costs $7.00 per running yard to put up a hedge.

6. Is $5m + 25$ divisible by 50?

> (1) m is divisible by 5.
> (2) m is divisible by 10.

7. What is the value of x?

> (1) $2x - 5y = -3$
> (2) $-6x + 15y = 9$

8. Mark has some nickels and some pennies in his pocket. How many pennies does he have?

> (1)   The coins in Mark's pocket have a total value of 32¢.
> (2)   Mark has more nickels than pennies in his pocket.

9. What is the value of $\dfrac{-A - (-B)}{B}$ if $B \neq 0$?

> (1) $A = B$
> (2) $B = 6$

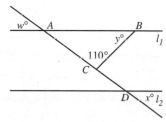

10. In the figure above, $x = 47$. What is the value of y?

> (1) $x = w$
> (2) $l_1 \parallel l_2$

11. On Bring Your Daughters to Work Day, some workers at the Ajax Corporation brought one child to work, while others brought two. No worker brought more than two. What percent of the workers who brought children brought two?

> (1)   A total of 350 children were brought to work.
> (2)   150 workers brought a single child.

12. A carton of books weighs 70 pounds. A truck carrying cartons of books loses 30% of its contents in an accident. How many cartons were on the truck before the accident?

> (1)   The weight of the cartons left on the truck is $2\dfrac{1}{3}$ times the weight of those that were lost.
> (2)   The difference between the weight of those that remained on the truck and those that were lost is 3,360 pounds.

13. If u and v are integers, is u divisible by 7?

    (1) uv is divisible by 14.

    (2) v is divisible by 2.

14. If $\dfrac{x}{y} = \dfrac{2}{3}$ what is the value of $3x + 2y$?

    (1) $3x - 2y = 0$

    (2) $x + y = 30$

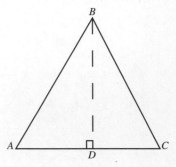

15. In the figure above, if $BD = 5$, what is the area of $\triangle ABC$?

    (1) $\angle BAC = \angle BCA = 45°$

    (2) BD bisects $\angle ABC$.

16. An urn contains red discs, white discs, and blue discs. A disc is selected at random. What is the probability that it is blue?

    (1)   The probability of picking a white disc is twice as great as the probability of picking a red disc.

    (2)   The ratio of red to white to blue discs in the urn is 1:2:4.

17. AB and CB are two-digit numbers. What digit is represented by A?

    (1) $AB + CB = 104$

    (2) $AB - CB = 30$

18. If $x > 1$, is $y^2 > 5$?

    (1) $1 < xy < 3$

    (2) $x + y = 3$

19. The *range* of a group of numbers is the value of the largest number minus the value of the smallest. For example, the range of 1,3,4,5,7 is $7 - 1 = 6$. If the arithmetic mean of 5 numbers is 60, what is the range of the numbers?

   (1)   The arithmetic mean of the 4 largest numbers is 72.
   (2)   The arithmetic mean of the 4 smallest numbers is 44.

20. What is the ratio of $(x + y)$ to xy?

   (1) $\dfrac{1}{x} + \dfrac{2}{y} = \dfrac{2}{3}$

   (2) $\dfrac{x}{y} = \dfrac{2}{2}$

EXERCISE 2

20 Questions

Time—15 Minutes

Directions (Data Sufficiency): This data sufficiency problem consists of a question and two statements, labeled (1) and (2), in which certain data are given. You have to decide whether the data given in the statements are *sufficient* for answering the question. Using the data given in the statements *plus* your knowledge of mathematics and everyday facts (such as the number of days in July or the meaning of *counterclockwise*), you must indicate whether

- statement (1) ALONE is sufficient, but statement (2) alone is not sufficient to answer the question asked;
- statement (2) ALONE is sufficient, but statement (1) alone is not sufficient to answer the question asked;
- BOTH statements (1) and (2) TOGETHER are sufficient to answer the question asked; but NEITHER statement ALONE is sufficient;
- EACH statement ALONE is sufficient to answer the question asked;
- statements (1) and (2) TOGETHER are NOT sufficient to answer the question asked, and additional data specific to the problem are needed.

Numbers: All numbers used are real numbers.

Figures: A figure accompanying a data sufficiency problem will conform to the information given in the question, but will not necessarily conform to the additional information given in statements (1) and (2).

Lines shown as straight can be assumed to be straight and lines that appear jagged can also be assumed to be straight.

You may assume that the positions of points, angles, regions, etc., exist in the order shown and that angle measures are greater than zero.

All figures lie in a plane unless otherwise indicated.

Note: In data sufficiency problems that ask for the value of a quantity, the data given in the statements are sufficient only when it is possible to determine exactly one numerical value for the quantity.

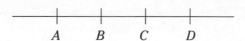

1. On the number line above, if *BC:AD* = 1:3 and *AC:AD* = 1:2, what is the value of *B*?

    (1) *A* = 6
    (2) *D* = 8

2. Is at least one of the three numbers *F* < *G* < *H* divisible by 3?

    (1) *F*, *G*, and *H* are consecutive even numbers.
    (2) *H* − *F* = 4

3. What were Albert's average weekly earnings for the first five weeks of the year?

    (1) Albert earned an average of $435 per week for the first six weeks of the year.
    (2) Albert earned an average of $450 per week for the first four weeks of the year.

4. How fast did Andrew have to drive to get from Zalesville to Aurora in 80 minutes?

    (1) It took Andrew $1\frac{2}{2}$ hours to drive from Aurora to Zalesville.
    (2) Andrew averaged 52 miles per hour on the trip from Aurora to Zalesville.

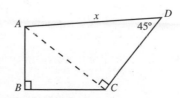

5. In the figure above, what is value of *x*?

    (1) *AB* = 6
    (2) *BC* = 8

6. What percent of a group of English majors and history majors have taken a college-level math course?

    (1) There are 20 English majors and 30 history majors in the group.
    (2) 50% of the English majors in the group have not taken a college-level math course.

7. Three consecutive odd integers are written in increasing order. What is the second number?

   (1) The sum of the first and the third integers is 22.
   (2) The sum of the first and second integers and twice the third integer is 46.

8. What is the sum of two negative numbers?

   (1) One number is 5 more than the other.
   (2) The product of the two numbers is 23 more than their sum.

9. Maria came home from the mall with one third of the amount of money she took to the mall. How much money did she take to the mall?

   (1) She bought a sweater with half of her money and spent $16 on food.
   (2) She spent three times as much to buy a sweater as she spent on food.

10. If x and y are both nonzero numbers, what is the value of $R = \dfrac{x^2 - y^2}{x^2 + y^2}$?

   (1) $x = 2y$
   (2) $y = 3$

11. If $x \neq 0$, what is the value of $\left(\dfrac{x^m}{x^n}\right)^p$?

   (1) $p = 1$
   (2) $m = n$

12. Of 120 fliers, how many made stopovers in both Chicago and St. Louis?

   (1) 87 fliers made stopovers in Chicago.
   (2) 96 fliers made stopovers in St. Louis.

13. What is the price in dollars of one roll?

   (1) A bakery order for three loaves of bread and twelve rolls costs $8.10.
   (2) A bakery order for two loaves of bread and five rolls costs $4.35.

14. What is the absolute value of the sum of two numbers?

   (1) The product of the two numbers is 6.
   (2) One number is 5 less than the other.

15. The total revenue at Hal's Haberdashery from sales of x shirts at price p per item is xp. What is the percent decrease in revenue if the price per shirt is lowered by 10%?

    (1) Decreasing the price of shirts by 10% causes a 5% increase in the number of shirts sold.
    (2) Last month, Hal's sold 100 shirts at $30 per shirt.

16. A recipe calls for $\frac{2}{3}$ of a cup of butter to make a batch of cookies. How big is a batch?

    (1) If six people each wanted to eat five cookies, $\frac{5}{3}$ of a cup of butter would be necessary.
    (2) Three batches would require 2 cups of butter.

17. What is the value of the smaller of two consecutive odd integers?

    (1) The sum of the two numbers is greater than 24.
    (2) The sum of the two numbers is less than 34.

18. What is the value of $x + 3y$?

    (1) The slope of the line passing through $Q(x,y)$ and $R(2,5)$ is 1.
    (2) $R(2,5)$ is the midpoint between $P(-1,2)$ and $Q(x,y)$.

19. What is the value of u?

    (1) The distance from $P(6,9)$ to $Q(1,u)$ is 13.
    (2) The slope of the line through points P and Q is $-\frac{12}{5}$.

20. What is the value of the integer N?

    (1) One third of the square of N is a perfect square.
    (2) One third of the cube of N is a perfect square.

EXERCISE 3

20 Questions

Time—15 Minutes

Directions (Data Sufficiency): This data sufficiency problem consists of a question and two statements, labeled (1) and (2), in which certain data are given. You have to decide whether the data given in the statements are *sufficient* for answering the question. Using the data given in the statements *plus* your knowledge of mathematics and everyday facts (such as the number of days in July or the meaning of *counterclockwise*), you must indicate whether

- statement (1) ALONE is sufficient, but statement (2) alone is not sufficient to answer the question asked;
- statement (2) ALONE is sufficient, but statement (1) alone is not sufficient to answer the question asked;
- BOTH statements (1) and (2) TOGETHER are sufficient to answer the question asked; but NEITHER statement ALONE is sufficient;
- EACH statement ALONE is sufficient to answer the question asked;
- statements (1) and (2) TOGETHER are NOT sufficient to answer the question asked, and additional data specific to the problem are needed.

Numbers: All numbers used are real numbers.

Figures: A figure accompanying a data sufficiency problem will conform to the information given in the question, but will not necessarily conform to the additional information given in statements (1) and (2).

Lines shown as straight can be assumed to be straight and lines that appear jagged can also be assumed to be straight.

You may assume that the positions of points, angles, regions, etc., exist in the order shown and that angle measures are greater than zero.

All figures lie in a plane unless otherwise indicated.

Note: In data sufficiency problems that ask for the value of a quantity, the data given in the statements are sufficient only when it is possible to determine exactly one numerical value for the quantity.

---

1. What is the ratio of Robert's salary to Timothy's salary?

    (1) If Robert's pay were cut by 25% and Timothy's pay were raised by 25%, they would earn the same amount.
    (2) Robert earns $100 more per week than Timothy.

2. How many quarts of oil will a car burn during a 3,600-mile trip?

    (1) The car burns half a quart of oil every 1,000 miles.
    (2) At $1.50 a quart, the car uses $2.70 worth of oil during the trip.

3. Kyra borrowed $800 at 8% simple interest. She put part of the money in one investment and part in another. After one year, she had a net profit of $16.50. What rate did Kyra earn on her better investment?

    (1) She invested $500 of the money at the lower rate.
    (2) She invested $300 of the money at the higher rate.

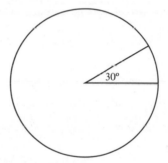

4. In the figure above, what is the diameter of the circle?

    (1) The area of the largest section of the circle is 33π.
    (2) The length of the arc on the unshaded portion of the circle is π.

5. What is the value of z?

    (1) $z - x + 2y = 11$
    (2) $4y - 2x + 8 = 0$

6. How old is Sally?

    (1) Sally is 6 years older than Manuel.
    (2) Three years ago, Sally was twice as old as Manuel.

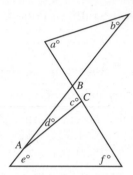

7. In the figure above, what is the value of $(c + d)$?

   (1) $b + f = 80$
   (2) $a + b = 110$

8. What is the value of $x^2 - 4y^2$?

   (1) $x - 2y = 0$
   (2) $x + 2y = 0$

9. Is it true that $x > y$?

   (1) $3x > 3y$
   (2) $3 - x < 3 - y$

10. What was the cost, before tax or delivery charge, on an item for which the total bill with tax and delivery charge was $92.35? (Assume that there is no tax on delivery charges.)

   (1) The sales tax rate is 8%.
   (2) The delivery charge was $3.25.

11. In a scale drawing of a rectangular playground, the scale is 1 inch equals 2 feet. What is the actual area of the playground in square feet?

   (1) In the drawing, the perimeter of the playground is 194 inches.
   (2) In the drawing, the width of the playground is 22 inches.

12. Alicia lost 60% of her matches during her first year of playing competitive handball. If she played no tie matches, what was her overall winning percentage for her first two years?

   (1) She won 73% of her matches in her second year.
   (2) She played twice as many matches in her second year as she played in her first.

13. The operation # is defined by $M \# N = MN + N^2$. What is the value of y?

    (1) $1 \# y = 2y$
    (2) $y \# 1 = 1$

14. Helena and Sergei between them applied to 16 different colleges. How many colleges did both Helena and Sergei apply to?

    (1)   Helena applied to 12 colleges.
    (2)   Sergei applied to 10 colleges.

15. How many degrees are there in the smallest angle in a triangle?

    (1)   The largest angle is 105°.
    (2)   The angles in the triangle are in the ratio of 2:3:7.

16. Point $(t, -1)$ lies on a circle with a radius of 5. What is the value of t?

    (1)   The center of the circle is at (4,2).
    (2) t is an integer.

17. A group of students are lined up randomly for a photograph. What is the chance that they will line up in order of height from shortest to tallest, left to right?

    (1)   There are four students in the group.
    (2)   Three of the students in the group are girls.

18. N is an integer greater than 2. Is N a prime number?

    (1) $N + 1$ is divisible by 4.
    (2) $N + 2$ is divisible by 3.

19. Is n an even number?

    (1)   The average of n consecutive integers is zero.
    (2)   The sum of the first n perfect squares $1^2 + 2^2 + \ldots + n^2 = 55$.

20. If x and y are integers not equal to 1, what is the value of y?

    (1) $x \div y = 36$
    (2) $2xy = 24$

EXERCISE 4

20 Questions

Time—15 Minutes

Directions (Data Sufficiency): This data sufficiency problem consists of a question and two statements, labeled (1) and (2), in which certain data are given. You have to decide whether the data given in the statements are *sufficient* for answering the question. Using the data given in the statements *plus* your knowledge of mathematics and everyday facts (such as the number of days in July or the meaning of *counterclockwise*), you must indicate whether

- statement (1) ALONE is sufficient, but statement (2) alone is not sufficient to answer the question asked;
- statement (2) ALONE is sufficient, but statement (1) alone is not sufficient to answer the question asked;
- BOTH statements (1) and (2) TOGETHER are sufficient to answer the question asked; but NEITHER statement ALONE is sufficient;
- EACH statement ALONE is sufficient to answer the question asked;
- statements (1) and (2) TOGETHER are NOT sufficient to answer the question asked, and additional data specific to the problem are needed.

Numbers: All numbers used are real numbers.

Figures: A figure accompanying a data sufficiency problem will conform to the information given in the question, but will not necessarily conform to the additional information given in statements (1) and (2).

Lines shown as straight can be assumed to be straight and lines that appear jagged can also be assumed to be straight.

You may assume that the positions of points, angles, regions, etc., exist in the order shown and that angle measures are greater than zero.

All figures lie in a plane unless otherwise indicated.

Note: In data sufficiency problems that ask for the value of a quantity, the data given in the statements are sufficient only when it is possible to determine exactly one numerical value for the quantity.

---

1. What is Robert's weekly salary?

    (1)   If Robert's pay were cut 25% and Timothy's pay were raised 25%, they would make the same amount.
    (2)   Robert earns $100 more per week than Timothy.

2. What is the total profit on sales of seven dozen washers?

    (1)   Washers are bought for 45¢ per dozen and sold at 4 for 18¢.
    (2)   The markup on washers is 20%.

3. Working together, how many hours will it take John and Armando to vacuum all of the rooms on one floor of a hotel?

    (1)   John can vacuum a room in 20 minutes.
    (2)   Armando can vacuum a room in 15 minutes.

4. James and Grant scored 72 points between them in two basketball games. How many points did Grant score?

    (1)   James scored twice as many points as Grant.
    (2)   James scored as many points in the first game as Grant did in both games combined.

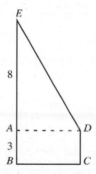

5. What is the perimeter of *BCDE* in the figure above?

    (1)   The perimeter of rectangle *ABCD* is 18.
    (2)   The area of rectangle *ABCD* is 18.

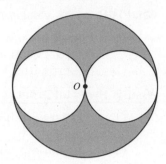

6. What is the radius of the circle with center O in the figure above?

    (1)   The area of the shaded region is 8π.

    (2)   The circumference of one of the smaller circles is 4π.

7. x is equal to one of the following numbers: $\dfrac{1}{3}, \dfrac{2}{7}, \dfrac{3}{14}$. What is the value of $\dfrac{1}{x}$?

    (1) $2.5 < \dfrac{1}{x} < 3.7$

    (2) $2.8 < \dfrac{1}{x} < 3.9$

8. What is the value of $A^2 - B^2$?

    (1) $4(A - 1) = 3B - (4 - B)$

    (2) $3A = 15 - 5B$

9. Myra borrowed \$1,500 for one year at 8% simple interest. She invested part at $9\dfrac{1}{2}\%$. The balance she used to buy stocks. By what percent did the value of her stocks increase?

    (1)   Her net profit for the year was \$128.

    (2)   The amount she invested at $9\dfrac{1}{2}\%$ was \$800.

10. Six people want to share the rent on a summer cottage. What is the total rent?

    (1)   If two people drop out, each person will have to pay \$200 more.

    (2)   If two more people join the group, each person will have to pay \$100 less.

11. What is the arithmetic mean of a, b, and c?

    (1)   The arithmetic mean of a and b is 5.

    (2)   The arithmetic mean of a and c is 9.

12. What is the value of the positive integer n?

    (1)   One third of n is a perfect square.

    (2) n minus three times its reciprocal equals 2.

13. If $x < y < z$ are odd integers, are they consecutive odd integers?

    (1) $z - x = 4$

    (2) y is the numerical average of x and z.

14. The retail price of commodity A is 20% more than the wholesale price. The discounted price of commodity B is 20% less than the retail price of commodity B. What percent of the discounted price of B is the retail price of A?

    (1)   The retail price of B is twice the retail price of A.

    (2)   The discounted price of B is 60% more than the wholesale price of A.

15. If x is an odd integer, is y an odd integer?

    (1)   The average of x and y is odd.

    (2)   The average of x, y, and $(y + 1)$ is an integer.

16. Water barrel A is filled to 50% of capacity, and water barrel B is filled to 80% of capacity. Which barrel is larger?

    (1)   Pouring water from A into B until B is full would leave A $\frac{5}{6}$ empty.

    (2)   Pouring water from B into A until A is full would leave B half full.

17. Is $x > 1$?

    (1) $\frac{1}{x} < 1$

    (2) $x^3 > 1$

18. From a group of 18 people, one third of whom are men, a person is selected at random. What is the probability the person selected is a man who is a college graduate?

    (1)   The probability that a person selected at random is a college graduate is $\frac{5}{18}$.

    (2)   The probability that a woman selected at random is a college graduate is $\frac{1}{3}$.

19. If the cold water tap and hot water tap running together could fill a bathtub in 30 minutes, how long would it take the hot water tap alone to fill the tub?

(1)   The cold water tap alone could fill the tub in 45 minutes.
(2)   The hot water tap can fill a 10-gallon tank in 10 minutes.

20. If x and y are integers not equal to 1, what is the value of y?

(1) $|x^2 y| = 36$
(2) $2xy = 24$

EXERCISE 5

20 Questions

Time—15 Minutes

Directions (Data Sufficiency): This data sufficiency problem consists of a question and two statements, labeled (1) and (2), in which certain data are given. You have to decide whether the data given in the statements are *sufficient* for answering the question. Using the data given in the statements *plus* your knowledge of mathematics and everyday facts (such as the number of days in July or the meaning of *counterclockwise*), you must indicate whether

- statement (1) ALONE is sufficient, but statement (2) alone is not sufficient to answer the question asked;
- statement (2) ALONE is sufficient, but statement (1) alone is not sufficient to answer the question asked;
- BOTH statements (1) and (2) TOGETHER are sufficient to answer the question asked; but NEITHER statement ALONE is sufficient;
- EACH statement ALONE is sufficient to answer the question asked;
- statements (1) and (2) TOGETHER are NOT sufficient to answer the question asked, and additional data specific to the problem are needed.

Numbers: All numbers used are real numbers.

Figures: A figure accompanying a data sufficiency problem will conform to the information given in the question, but will not necessarily conform to the additional information given in statements (1) and (2).

Lines shown as straight can be assumed to be straight and lines that appear jagged can also be assumed to be straight.

You may assume that the positions of points, angles, regions, etc., exist in the order shown and that angle measures are greater than zero.

All figures lie in a plane unless otherwise indicated.

Note: In data sufficiency problems that ask for the value of a quantity, the data given in the statements are sufficient only when it is possible to determine exactly one numerical value for the quantity.

1. Which costs more, a can of corn or a can of beets?

    (1)   Canned corn sells at three cans for a dollar.
    (2)   Canned beets have been marked down 10%.

2. John received a $140 fine for speeding. What was the greatest speed he could have been driving?

    (1)   The fine was $65 for the first 5 miles per hour by which he exceeded the limit plus an additional $25 for each additional 5 miles per hour or part.
    (2)   John drove from Baltimore to New York, a distance of 180 miles, in less than three hours.

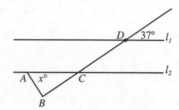

3. In the figure above, is $\angle ABC$ a right angle?

    (1) l_1 is parallel to l_2.
    (2) $x = 53°$

4. How many apples did Victor pick?

    (1)   Victor ate half the apples plus half an apple and had 7 apples left over.
    (2)   Picking at a rate of 6 apples every half hour, it took Victor 1 hour and 15 minutes to pick the apples.

5. What is the area of $\triangle ABC$?

    (1) $AC = 16$, $BC = 12$, and $AB = 20$.
    (2) $AB = 20$, and the perpendicular distance from C to AB is 9.6.

6. The ratio of Marjorie's weekly salary to Sylvester's weekly salary is 2:3. What is Marjorie's salary?

    (1)   Sylvester earns $200 more per week than Marjorie.
    (2)   Between them, Sylvester and Marjorie earn $1,000 per week.

7. Is $5x$ an integer?

    (1) $10x$ and $15x$ are integers.
    (2) $\dfrac{1}{2} + \dfrac{1}{3} = \dfrac{6}{x}$

8. What is the value of x?

    (1) $x^2 - 4x + 3 = 0$
    (2) $x^2 - 2x + 1 = 0$

9. In a certain calculus class, did more than $\frac{1}{5}$ of the class get grades of A?

    (1) Exactly 60% of the boys got grades of B or better, and $\frac{1}{3}$ of those grades were A.
    (2) Exactly 5 girls got As.

10. Is x between 1 and 2?

    (1) x^2 is greater than 1 and less than 4.
    (2) x^2 is greater than x and less than $2x$.

11. Is x greater than 3.5?

    (1) $2x$ is greater than 7.2.
    (2) $3x$ is less than 10.9.

12. If $x \neq 0$, what is the ratio of x to $(x + y)$?

    (1) $\dfrac{2x - y}{2x + y} = 0$
    (2) $x + y = 3$

13. Is $z > 0$?

    (1) $\dfrac{x}{y} < 0$ and $\dfrac{z}{y} > 0$
    (2) $x < 0$

14. Maryanne has $2.05 in quarters and dimes. How many quarters does she have?

    (1) She has more quarters than dimes.
    (2) She has a total of ten coins.

15. $\triangle ABC$ is a right triangle with hypotenuse $AB = 10$. What is the perpendicular distance from C to AB?

    (1) $AC = 6$
    (2) The area of the triangle is 24 square units.

16. Point $P(4,t)$ is equidistant from Q and R. What is the value of t?

    (1) The coordinates of point Q are $(1,1)$.
    (2) The coordinates of point R are $(5,3)$.

17. What is the absolute value of the sum of x and y?

   (1) The product of x and y is 30.
   (2) y is 7 more than x.

18. If x and y are integers, is $x + 2y$ divisible by 6?

   (1) x is divisible by 6.
   (2) y is an odd number

19. x is an even number. What is x?

   (1) The square of x is 4 more than 10 times the next larger even number.
   (2) x is positive.

20. What is the value of the ratio of $(a + c)$:c?

   (1) The ratio of a:b = 1:5.
   (2) The ratio of b:c = 3:2.

Answer Key

Exercise 1	Exercise 2	Exercise 3	Exercise 4	Exercise 5
1. D	1. C	1. A	1. C	1. E
2. C	2. A	2. D	2. A	2. E
3. D	3. E	3. E	3. E	3. C
4. D	4. C	4. D	4. A	4. D
5. C	5. C	5. C	5. D	5. D
6. B	6. E	6. C	6. D	6. D
7. E	7. D	7. B	7. E	7. D
8. C	8. C	8. D	8. A	8. B
9. A	9. A	9. D	9. C	9. E
10. D	10. A	10. C	10. D	10. B
11. C	11. B	11. C	11. E	11. A
12. B	12. C	12. C	12. B	12. A
13. E	13. C	13. B	13. A	13. B
14. B	14. C	14. C	14. D	14. C
15. A	15. A	15. B	15. A	15. D
16. B	16. A	16. E	16. D	16. C
17. C	17. E	17. A	17. B	17. C
18. C	18. B	18. E	18. C	18. E
19. C	19. B	19. D	19. A	19. C
20. C	20. A	20. C	20. E	20. C

Explanatory Answers

EXERCISE 1

1. **The correct answer is (D).** Using statement (1), we have an equation $\frac{0.56}{1.26} = \frac{4}{b}$. Cross multiplying, $0.56b = 4(1.26)$ or $0.56b = 5.04$. Dividing both sides by 0.56 yields $b = 9$. The options are choices (A) or (D). From statement (2): Rewriting both numerator and denominator as their fractional equivalents, $0.56 = \frac{56}{100} = \frac{14}{25}$ and $1.26 = 1 + \frac{26}{100} = 1\frac{13}{50} = \frac{63}{50}$. We now accomplish the division by inverting and multiplying by the denominator. Thus, $\left(\frac{14}{25}\right)\left(\frac{50}{63}\right) = \frac{4}{9}$ and $b = 9$.

2. **The correct answer is (C).** Using P, A, and M to stand for the number of CDs each owns respectively, we have from statement (1) $P = \frac{1}{2}A$, which gives us no information about Marcia. The options are choices (B), (C), and (E). From statement (2), we have $M = \frac{3}{5}A$, which tells us nothing about Pedro. The options are choices (C) or (E). However, combining the two,

$$\frac{P}{M} = \frac{\frac{1}{2}A}{\frac{3}{5}A} = \frac{1}{2} \cdot \frac{5}{3} = \frac{5}{6}.$$ Thus, Pedro has as many CDs as Marcia.

3. **The correct answer is (D).** From statement (1), her average is 76 on four exams, so she must have a total of $(4)(76) = 304$. In order to average 80 on five exams, her total must be $(5)(80) = 400$. Therefore, she must score $400 - 304 = 96$ on her last exam. Choices (A) or (D) are possible. From statement (2), letting her present total be T, we know that $\frac{T + 86}{5} = 78$. That is, $T + 86 = 390$. Thus, we know that $T = 304$, and we can proceed just as we did before.

4. **The correct answer is (D).** Since the sum of the angles around a point must be $360°$, we have $x + 2x + (2x + 80) + y = 360$. Using statement (1) alone, we can replace y by $3x$ and get $8x + 80 = 360$, which can be solved for x: $8x = 280$; $x = 35$. Hence, $y = 3(35) = 105$. Choices (A) and (D) are possible. Using statement (2) alone, we can replace y by $175 - 2x$ and get $x + 2x + 2x + 80 + 175 - 2x = 360$. That is, $3x + 255 = 360$, which can again be solved for x, yielding $x = 35$ and $y = 105$.

5. **The correct answer is (C).** Statement (1) alone tells us nothing about the cost of the hedge, and statement (2) alone tells us nothing about the cost of seeding. The options are choices (C) and (E). Using both, the area of the garden is $(20)(10) = 200$ square yards. At 80¢ per square yard, the cost of seeding is $(200)(0.80) = \$16$. The perimeter of the garden is $2(20) + 2(10) = 60$ running yards. At \$7 per yard, the cost of the hedge is $7(60) = \$420$. The total cost is $420 + 16 = 436$.

6. **The correct answer is (B).** Using statement (1) alone, since m is divisible by 5, $5m$ can be divided by 25. Therefore, the sum $5m + 25$ can be divided by 25, but it can only be divided by 50 if it is also divisible by 2; that is, only if m is odd, so that $5m + 25$ becomes even. Choices (B), (C), and (E) are possible. From statement (2), we know that m is even and, hence, that $5m + 25$ is odd and *not* divisible by 50.

7. **The correct answer is (E).** One linear equation in two unknowns cannot usually tell you the value of one unknown, and this case is no exception. That is, neither statement (1) nor statement (2) alone is sufficient. The options are choices (C) or (E). You can try to solve a system of two equations in two unknowns. Here, if we try multiplying the first equation by 3 in order to add it to the second equation and eliminate x, we see that one equation is just the negative of the other, so the two are really the same equation. Hence both together will not answer the question.

8. **The correct answer is (C).** Using the obvious notation, statement (1) tells us that $5n + p = 32$. This single equation has several solutions, such as $n = 6, p = 2; n = 5, p = 7; n = 4, p = 12$; etc. Statement (2) alone is not very informative. For only one possibility from statement (1) is n greater than p. Thus, statement (1) and statement (2) together answer the question. That is, $n = 5, p = 2$.

9. **The correct answer is (A).** The numerator of the fraction is $-A + B$. Thus, from statement (1) alone, the numerator is $-A + A = 0$ and the fraction must be 0. Choices (A) or (D) are possible. From statement (2) alone, $B = 6$ gives us the fraction $\dfrac{-A + (6)}{6}$, which we cannot evaluate without knowing A.

10. **The correct answer is (D).** Using statement (1) alone, we see that $\angle BAC = w° = x° = 47°$. Hence, in $\triangle ABC$, $47 + y + 110 = 180$, and $y = 33$. Using statement (2) alone, we can see that $\angle BAC = x°$ by the properties of corresponding angles. Hence statement (2) alone also allows you to answer the question.

11. **The correct answer is (C).** From statement (1), we know how many children there were but not the breakdown. From statement (2), we know that there were 150 workers who brought a single child, but not how many brought two. Hence, neither statement alone is sufficient. That leaves choices (C) and (E). Using both statements together, we know that there were 200 children in pairs; that is, 100 workers brought two children and 150 brought one. Hence, 100 out of 250 or 40% brought two children.

12. **The correct answer is (B).** Let W be the weight of all of the cartons. Now $0.3W$ is the weight of those lost, and 0.7 is the weight of those that remained. From statement (1), $0.7W = 2\frac{1}{3}(0.3W) = \frac{7}{3}(0.3W) = 0.7W.$. That is true for any W, and, therefore, will not answer the question. That leaves choices (B), (C), or (E). From statement (2) alone, $0.7W - 0.3W = 3360$; $0.4W = 3360$. Dividing by 0.4, $W = 8400$. Thus, the total weight was 8,400 pounds, which at 70 pounds per carton is the weight of 120 cartons.

13. **The correct answer is (E).** Knowing statement (1) alone tells us only that the product of u and v is divisible by 14. It could be that v is divisible by 14, and u could be any number whatsoever. That leaves choices (B), (C), or (E). Knowing statement (2) tells us nothing about u. Now, only choices (C) or (E) are possible. Knowing both statement (1) and (2) still does not answer the question, because it could be that v is divisible by 14 and u could still be any number.

14. **The correct answer is (B).** Cross-multiplying in the given equation, we have $3x = 2y$, that is, $3x - 2y = 0$. Thus, statement (1) is just a restatement of the equation given, adding no information. That leaves choices (B), (C), and (E). Combining $3x = 2y$ with (2) $x + y = 30$, we can rewrite the latter equation as $2x + 2y = 60$ and substitute $3x$ for $2y$. This gives $5x = 60$; $x = 12$. Using $x = 12$, we have $2y = 36$; $y = 18$. Knowing both x and y, it is no trick to calculate $3x + 2y = 72$.

15. **The correct answer is (A).** From statement (1) alone, we see that $\triangle BDC$ is a $45°$–$45°$–$90°$ right triangle with one leg 5. Thus, the other leg is also 5 and the area is $\frac{1}{2}(5)(5)$. But this is exactly half of $\triangle ABC$. Hence, the area of $\triangle ABC$ is 25. That leaves choices (A) and (D). Statement (2) alone tells us nothing about the length of the base of $\triangle ABC$, and knowing only its altitude is not sufficient to find its area.

16. **The correct answer is (B).** The probability of choosing any given color is given by the number of discs of that color divided by the total number of discs. Statement (1) alone tells us only that there are twice as many white as red discs, but the total number in the urn could be anything. For example, you could have 10 discs with 1 red and 2 whites, or 1,000 discs with 3 red and 6 whites. Statement (2) is much more informative. If we let r = the number of red discs, then $2r$ = the number of white discs and $4r$ = the number of blue discs. The total number of discs is $r + 2r + 4r = 7r$. Thus, the probability of a blue is $\frac{4r}{7r} = \frac{4}{7}$.

17. **The correct answer is (C).** From statement (1), we can tell that B is either 2 or 7. If it is 2, then $A + C = 10$, and if it is 7, then $A + C = 9$. That leaves choices (B), (C), or (E). From statement (2), we can see that $A - C = 3$. That narrows it down to choices (C) or (E). Combining the two pieces of information, we can see that if $A + C = 9$ and $A - C = 3$, then $A = 6$ and $C = 3$. If $A + C = 10$ and $A - C = 3$, then A is not a whole number. Hence, the only possibility is $A = 6$.

18. **The correct answer is (C).** Using only the inequality in statement (1), we can only say that $\frac{1}{x} < y < \frac{3}{x}$. Since x could be very close to 1 or as large as we wish, all we can say is that y is positive and less than 3. Thus, y^2 could be almost 0 or almost 9. That leaves choices (B), (C), and (E). The equation in statement (2) tells us that $y = 3 - x$, and since $x > 1$, $y < 2$. If we knew y to be positive, this would assure us that y^2 is less than 4 and answer the question. However, y could be a large negative number. That further narrows the options to choice (C) or choice (E). Using both pieces of information, we know that $x > 1$ and therefore positive, which implies that y is positive, and thus, $y^2 < 5$.

19. **The correct answer is (C).** Since the average of the 5 numbers is 60, they must total 300. Statement (1) informs us that the sum of the 4 largest numbers is $4(72) = 288$. That means that the fifth (the smallest) number is $300 - 288 = 12$, but that does not fix the upper end. Statement (2) tells us that the sum of the four smallest numbers is $4(44) = 176$, which implies that the largest number is $300 - 176 = 124$, but that also does not fix the lower end. That eliminates choices (A), (B), and (D). The combination of the two makes it easy: $124 - 12 = 112$, choice (C).

20. **The correct answer is (C).** We can rewrite the ratio: $\dfrac{x+y}{xy} = \dfrac{1}{x} + \dfrac{1}{y}$. This is pretty close to $\dfrac{1}{x} + \dfrac{2}{y} + \dfrac{2}{3}$, but not close enough to tell us the value. That narrows the options to choices (B), (C), or (E). Cross-multiplying the ratio in statement (2) gives us $2x = y$. Substituting $2x$ for y in the ratio, we get $\dfrac{x+2x}{x(2x)} = \dfrac{3x}{2x^2} = \dfrac{3}{2x}$. Since we do not know x, this is also not sufficient. The decision is now between choices (C) and (E). However, substituting $y = 2x$ into $\dfrac{1}{x} + \dfrac{2}{y} - \dfrac{2}{3}$ gives us $\dfrac{1}{x} + \dfrac{2}{2x} = \dfrac{2}{3}$, that is, $\dfrac{1}{x} + \dfrac{1}{x} = \dfrac{2}{3}$. Thus, $\dfrac{2}{x} = \dfrac{2}{3}$, and $x = 3$. Knowing $x = 3$, it is not hard to see that the desired ratio is $\dfrac{3}{6} = \dfrac{1}{2}$.

EXERCISE 2

1. **The correct answer is (C).** From the information given, we know that the length of AC is $\dfrac{1}{2}$ the length of AD, and the length of BC is $\dfrac{1}{3}$ the length of AD. By subtraction, AB is $\dfrac{1}{6}$ the length of AD. Thus, we need the length of AD to answer the question. Knowing only A or only D is not sufficient; that is, neither statement (1) nor statement (2) alone is sufficient. Choices (C) and (E) are left. Of course, taken together, statement (1) and statement (2) tell us that AD is of length 2, and thus, $B = 6 + \left(\dfrac{1}{6}\right)2 = 6\dfrac{1}{3} = \dfrac{19}{3}$.

2. **The correct answer is (A).** From statement (1) alone, we know that at least one of the three is divisible by 3. Try any set of three consecutive even numbers, such as 12, 14, 16 or 4, 6, 8 to convince yourself. It can be proved formally as follows. If the first number is divisible by 3, you are done. If not, then the remainder when you divide by 3 is either 1 or 2. Hence, it is either of the form $3p + 1$ or $3p + 2$. If it is $3p + 1$, then the next number is $3p + 3$, which is divisible by 3. If it is $3p + 2$, then the third number is $3p + 6$, divisible by 3. This leaves choices (A) and (D). Statement (2) alone is not sufficient. Consider the two possibilities 4, 5, 8 and 4, 6, 8. Both satisfy the condition, but for one the answer is yes and for the other it is no. So the best answer is chioce (A).

3. **The correct answer is (E).** Statement (1) tells us that Albert averaged $435 for 6 weeks, so he must have earned a total of (6)(435) = $2,610 for six weeks. Since we do not know what he earned in the sixth week, we cannot know his total (or average) for the first five weeks. Choices (B), (C), and (E) are the remaining possibilities. Statement (2) tells us that he averaged $450 for 4 weeks, so he must have earned a total of (4)(450) = $1,800 for four weeks. Since we do not know what he earned in the fifth week, we cannot know his total (or average) for the first five weeks. The field is now narrowed to choices (C) or (E). Combining the two, we know that his total for weeks five and six was $2,610 − $1,800 = $810, but we have no way of knowing how much he earned in week five. Thus, even together, statement (1) and statement (2) are not sufficient.

4. **The correct answer is (C).** Using statement (1) alone, we know how long it took Andrew to drive from A to Z, but we do not know the distance or his speed. Choices (B), (C), and (E) are left. Using statement (2) alone, we know how fast he drove, but not the distance or time. Choices (C) and (E) are left. Combining both pieces of information, the distance from Aurora to Zalesville must be given by $d = rt = (52)(1.5) = 78$ miles. Since 80 minutes is 1 hour and 20 minutes or $1 = \dfrac{1}{3} = \dfrac{4}{3}$ hours, we must solve $78 = \dfrac{4}{3}r$. Multiplying by 3, we have $234 = 4r$, and dividing by 4, $r = 58.5$ mph.

5. **The correct answer is (C).** Statement (1) alone gives no information about $\triangle ACD$ and, hence, no information about x. Choices (B), (C), or (E) remain. Statement (2) alone gives no information about $\triangle ACD$ and, hence, no information about x. Choices (C) and (E) remain. Using both statement (1) and statement (2) and the Pythagorean Theorem in $\triangle ABD$, $AC^2 = 6^2 + 8^2 = 100$. Thus, $AC = 10$. $\triangle ACD$ is a $45°-45°-90°$ right triangle with one leg 10, and so the hypotenuse $x = 10\sqrt{2}$.

6. **The correct answer is (E).** Statement (1) alone gives no information about math courses taken. This leaves choices (B), (C), and (E). Statement (2) alone gives no information about history majors. Choices (C) and (E) are left. Using both statement (1) and statement (2) and starting with English majors, 50% of 20 $= (0.50)(20) = 10$ have taken and 10 have not taken a math course. For history majors, we have no information as to how many may have taken a math course. Thus, we cannot know the percent of the total.

7. **The correct answer is (D).** Calling the smallest number x, the second is $(x + 2)$ and the third is $(x + 4)$. From statement (1) alone, we know that $x + (x + 4) = 22$. That is, $2x + 4 = 22$; $2x = 18$; and $x = 9$. That makes the middle number 11. Choices (A) and (D) are left. From statement (2) alone, $x + (x + 2) + 2(x + 4) = 46$. That is, $x + x + 2 + 2x + 8 = 46$; $4x + 10 = 46$; $4x = 36$; $x = 9$. Hence, the middle number is 11.

8. **The correct answer is (C).** Calling one number x and the other y, statement (1) alone tells us that the second number can be written as $y = x + 5$ but gives no information about their sum. Choices (B), (C), and (E) are still possible. Statement (2) tells us that $xy = x + y + 23$ gives no information about their sum, so choices (C) and (E) are left. Using both statement (1) and statement (2) and substituting $x + 5$ for y yields:

$$x(x + 5) = x + (x + 5) + 23$$
$$x^2 + 5x = 2x + 28$$
$$x^2 + 3x - 28 = 0$$

This factors as:

$$(x + 7)(x - 4) = 0$$
$$x + 7 = 0 \text{ or } x - 4 = 0$$

Hence, $x = -7$ or $x = 4$. We must choose the negative value, -7, giving $x + 5 = -2$, with sum -9.

9. **The correct answer is (A).** Let M be the amount she started with. She must have used $\frac{2}{3}M$ at the mall. From statement (1) alone, we have $\frac{2}{3}M = \frac{1}{2}M + 16$. Multiplying by 6: $4M = 3M + 96$; $M = 96$. The possible answer is choice (A) or choice (D). From statement (2), we know only that the $\frac{2}{3}M$ she had was divided between the sweater and food in the ratio of 3:1.

10. **The correct answer is (A).** Substituting $x = 2y$, statement (1) alone gives us $R = \frac{4y^2 - y^2}{4y^2 + y^2} = \frac{3y^2}{5y^2} = \frac{3}{5}$, which leaves choice (A) or choice (D). Statement (2) alone gives us R in terms of x, but that is not enough to find the value of R.

11. **The correct answer is (B).** From statement (1) alone, we can tell only that $\left(\frac{x^m}{x^n}\right)^p = \frac{x^m}{x^n}$, which leaves choices (B), (C), and (E). From statement (2) alone, we know that $\frac{x^m}{x^n} = 1$. Hence, $\left(\frac{x^m}{x^n}\right)^p = 1^p = 1$.

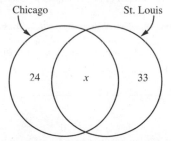

12. **The correct answer is (C).** Statement (1) tells us that $120 - 87 = 33$ people made stopovers in St. Louis but not Chicago. But since it doesn't tell us the total number who made stopovers in St. Louis, the choices are narrowed to choice (B), (C), or (E). Statement (2) tells us that $120 - 96 = 24$ people made stopovers in Chicago but not St. Louis. But since it doesn't tell us the total number who made stopovers in Chicago, the options are choices (C) and (E). Using both statements, however, we can display the information in a Venn diagram, as shown above. We see that the sum $33 + x + 24 = 120$; $x = 63$.

13. **The correct answer is (C).** Using b and r for the unknown prices and expressing all prices in cents, we have from statement (1), $3b + 12r = 810$. Of course, one equation in two unknowns is not solvable and therefore not sufficient, leaving choices (B), (C), and (E). From statement (2), we have $2b + 5r = 435$, and, again, one equation in two unknowns is not sufficient. Now, choice (C) or (E) is possible. Using both equations, we may divide the first equation by 3, to get $b + 4r = 270$; $b = 270 - 4r$. Substituting into the other equation: $2(270 - 4r) + 5r = 435$; $540 - 8r + 5r = 435$; $-3r = -105$; $r = 35¢ = \$.35$.

14. **The correct answer is (C).** Calling one number x and the other y, statement (1) tells us that $xy = 6$ but gives no information about their sum, narrowing the options to choice (B), (C), or (E). Statement (2) alone tells us that the second number can be written as $y = x - 5$ but gives no information about their sum. The choice is (C) or (E). Using both statement (1) and statement (2) and substituting $x - 5$ for y yields:

$$x(x - 5) = 6$$
$$x^2 - 5x - 6 = 0$$

This factors as:

$$(x - 6)(x + 1) = 0$$
$$x - 6 = 0$$

or $x + 1 = 0$

Hence, $x = 6$ and $x - 5 = 1$, with sum 7, or $x = -1$ and $x - 5 = -6$ with sum -7. Either way, the absolute value of the sum is 7.

15. **The correct answer is (A).** Using statement (1) alone, the total revenue would change from $r_{old} = xp$ to $r_{new} = (1.05x)(0.9p) = 0.945xp = 94.5\%$ of r_{old}; that is a 5.5% decrease. The options are now choices (A) and (D). Using statement (2) alone tells us only the original revenue but not the new revenue. Hence, statement (2) alone is not sufficient.

16. **The correct answer is (A).** Let the size of a batch be B. If 6 people each eat 5 cookies, you will need 30 cookies. To find the size of a batch, use the ratio $B{:}30 = \dfrac{2}{3}{:}\dfrac{5}{3}$. That is, $\dfrac{B}{30} = \dfrac{\frac{2}{3}}{\frac{5}{3}}$, or $\dfrac{B}{30} = \dfrac{2}{5}$. Multiplying by 30, $B = 12$, leaves choice (A) or (D). Statement (2) alone tells us nothing we did not already know. It merely says that tripling the desired output is achieved by tripling the quantity of each ingredient; that is, $3\left(\dfrac{2}{3}\right) = 2$.

17. **The correct answer is (E).** Calling the smaller number n, the larger will be $n + 2$. Thus, statement (1) tells us that $24 < n + (n + 2)$; $24 < 2n + 2$; $22 < 2n$; $11 < n$. Hence, n could be 13 or 15 or . . . The best selection is either choice (B), (C), or (E). Similarly, statement (2) alone tells us that $2n + 2 < 34$; $2n < 32$; $n < 16$. Thus, n could be 15 or 13 or . . . The best selections is now either choice (C) or (E). Statement (1) and statement (2) together limit the choice of n to 13 or 15, but that is not sufficient to answer the question. The best answer is choice (E).

18. **The correct answer is (B).** From the slope formula, statement (1) tells us that $\dfrac{y - 5}{x - 2} = 1$. Multiplying by $(x - 2)$, we have $y - 5 = x - 2$ or $y = x + 3$. Thus, $x + 3y = x + 3(x + 3) = 4x + 3$; but, not knowing x, we can go no further, thus, choices (B), (C), and (E) are left. Using the fact that the coordinates of the midpoint are the averages of the coordinates of the end points, statement (2) alone tells us that 2 is the average of -1 and x, so $x = 5$. And 5 is the average of 2 and y, so $y = 8$. Thus, $x + 3y = 5 + 3(8) = 29$.

19. **The correct answer is (B).** Using statement (1) and the distance formula:

$$\sqrt{(6-1)^2 + (9-u)^2} = \sqrt{(5)^2 + (9-u)^2} = 13$$

Squaring both sides:

$$25 + 81 - 18u + u^2 = 169$$

Moving everything to the left hand side and combining like terms:

$$u^2 - 18u - 63 = 0$$
$$(u - 21)(u + 3) = 0$$
$$u - 21 = 0 \ \text{ or } u + 3 = 0$$
$$u = 21 \text{ or } u = -3$$

With two choices, we must conclude that the answer is choice (B), (C), or (E). From statement (2) alone and the slope formula, we have $m = \dfrac{u-9}{1-6} = \dfrac{-12}{5}$. $\dfrac{u-0}{-5} = \dfrac{-12}{5}$. Multiplying by -5: $u - 9 = 12$ and $u = 21$.

20. **The correct answer is (A).** From statement (1), we know that $\dfrac{1}{3}N^2 = M^2$; that is, $N^2 = 3M^2$ for some M. This can be true only if $N = M = 0$, which leaves choices (A) and (D). From statement (2), $\dfrac{1}{3}N^3 = K^2$ for some K. This could be true for $K = 0$, which gives $N = 0$, or for $K = 3$ and $N = 3$.

EXERCISE 3

1. **The correct answer is (A).** Letting R be Robert's weekly salary and T be Timothy's weekly salary, statement (1) says that $0.75R = 1.25T$. That is, $\dfrac{3}{4}R = \dfrac{5}{4}T$, or $3R = 5T$. Dividing by $3T$, $\dfrac{R}{T} = \dfrac{5}{3}$. The decision in between choice (A) or (D). Statement (2) alone tells us the difference between their salaries, but not the ratio.

2. **The correct answer is (D).** In thousands, $3{,}600 = 3.6$. Hence, from statement (1) alone we know that the car burns $(3.6)\left(\dfrac{1}{2}\right) = 1.8$ quarts, leaving choices (A) and (D). Letting $q = $ the number of quarts of oil, statement (2) tells us $1.5q = 2.7$. Dividing by 1.5, $q = 1.8$.

3. **The correct answer is (E).** $\$800$ at 8% costs Kyra $(0.08)(\$800) = \$64$ in interest. Calling the lower rate r and the higher rate R, statement (1) tells us that she earned $500r + 300R$ on the two investments, for a profit of $\$16.50$. That is, $500r + 300R - 64 = 16.50$; $500r + 300R = 80.50$. We cannot solve this one equation in two unknowns, leaving choices (B), (C), and (E). Trying statement (2) alone, we get the identical equation. Choices (C) and (E) are now the only options. Since the two equations are identical, using both at once is no more help than using one alone.

4. **The correct answer is (D).** The unshaded region is a sector with a $30°$ central angle, which is $\frac{1}{12}$ of the circle. Hence, from statement (1) alone, the shaded portion must be $\pi r^2 = 33\pi$. Dividing by 11π and multiplying by 12, we have $r^2 = 36$. Hence, $r = 6$, and the diameter is 12. From statement (2), the length of the arc must be $\frac{1}{12}$ of the circumference of the circle. That is, $\pi = \left(\frac{1}{12}\right)(2\pi r)$. Multiplying by 12 and dividing by 2π, $r = 6$, and the diameter is 12. The best answer is choice (D).

5. **The correct answer is (C).** Certainly, one equation in three unknowns will not answer the question, therefore, choice (C) or choice (E) is the answer. Usually, you need three equations in order to solve for three unknowns. In this case, however, statement (2) tells us that $-2x + 4y = -8$, and dividing by 2, $-x + 2y = -4$. Thus, using statement (1) and statement (2), $z - (-4) = 11$, and $z = 7$.

6. **The correct answer is (C).** If S is Sally's age and M is Manuel's, statement (1) tells us that $S = M + 6$. Since M could be almost anything, this is not sufficient, so the answer must be choice (B), (C), or (E). Using statement (2), three years ago, Sally was $S - 3$, and Manuel was $M - 3$. So:

$$S - 3 = 2(M - 3) \text{ or } S - 3 = 2M - 6$$

That is, $S = 2M - 3$. Again, this alone is not sufficient. Combining the two equations, we substitute $S = M + 6$ into the second equation, yielding $M + 6 = 2M - 3$. This we solve for M, getting $M = 9$, which means Sally is $9 + 6 = 15$. The best answer is choice (C).

7. **The correct answer is (B).** From statement (1), we know what $b + f$ is, but the individual values could be almost anything, and it tells us very little about the other angles, so the answer is choice (B), (C), or (E). Using statement (2), we know that the sum of the angles in any triangle is $180°$. Letting the measure of $\angle ABC$ be m, using the property of vertical angles being equal, we have in the upper triangle $a + b + m = 180$; $110 + m = 180$; $m = 70$. Similarly, looking at $\triangle ABC$, we know that $c + d + 70 = 180$, and $c + d = 110$.

8. **The correct answer is (D).** Since $x^2 - 4y^2 = (x - 2y)(x + 2y)$, if either factor is zero, the product is zero. Hence, either statement (1) or statement (2) alone is sufficient.

9. **The correct answer is (D).** From statement (1) alone, we can divide both sides of an inequality by a positive number, in this case 3, without changing it. Thus, $x > y$ and the answer is either choice (A) or choice (D). From statement (2) alone, we can add -3 to both sides of the inequality without changing it, yielding $-x < -y$. Multiplying now by -1 reverses the inequality to give $x > y$.

10. **The correct answer is (C).** Statement (1) tells us nothing about the delivery charge, so choices (A) and (D) are eliminated. Similarly, statement (2) tells us nothing about the tax rate, so the answer is choice (C) or (E). Together, subtracting the delivery charge, we have $\$92.35 - \$3.25 = \$89.10$ as the price including sales tax. Calling the base price b, we get $1.08b = \$89.10$. Dividing by 1.08, $b = \$82.50$.

11. **The correct answer is (C).** Using statement (1) alone, since $P = 2L + 2W$ and on the drawing $P = 194$, we know that on the drawing $L + W = 97$. However, that alone is not sufficient, leaving choices (B), (C), and (E). Statement (2) tells us that on the drawing $W = 22$, but gives no indication of L. Using both pieces of data, $L + 22 = 97$; $L = 75$. Since each inch represents 2 feet, the actual dimensions are 44 by 150, for an area of 6,600 square feet.

12. **The correct answer is (C).** Using statement (1) alone, we know that she won 40% of her matches in the first year and 73% in her second year, but we do not know how many matches she played, so we cannot calculate her overall winning percentage. The options are choices (B), (C), and (E). Statement (2) alone gives us no information about her winning percentage in the second year. Clearly, the answer is choice (C) or choice (E). Even with both pieces of data, we do not know how many matches she played in each year. But does it matter? Suppose in the first year she played N matches. She won 40% or $0.4N$. The second year, she played $2N$ matches and won 73% of them, or $1.46N$. Hence, she won $1.86N$ matches out of $3N$, for a winning rate of $1.86N \div 3.00N = 0.62 = 62\%$.

13. **The correct answer is (B).** From statement (1) alone, we have $1 \# y = (1)(y) + y^2$. Thus, $y + y^2 = 2y$; $y^2 - y = 0$; $y(y - 1) = 0$, and $y = 0$ or $y = 1$. Thus, statement (1) alone is not sufficient. You are left with choices (B), (C), and (E). From statement (2), we have $y \# 1 = (y)(1) + 1$. Thus, $y + 1 = 1$, and $y = 0$.

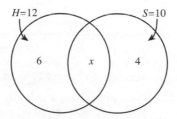

14. **The correct answer is (C).** Let H be the set of colleges to which Helena applied and S be those to which Sergei applied. Statement (1) tells us that there were $16 - 12 - 4$ colleges to which only Sergei applied. But since it doesn't tell us the number to which only Helena applied, choices (B), (C), and (E) are left. Statement (2) tells us there were $16 - 10 = 6$ to which only Helena applied. But since it doesn't tell us the number to which only Sergei applied, only choices (C) and (E) are still possible. Using both, however, we can display the information in a Venn diagram as shown above. We see that the sum $6 + x + 4 = 16$; $x = 6$.

15. **The correct answer is (B).** From statement (1) alone, you know only that the other two angles must sum to 75°. Choices (A) and (D) are eliminated. Using statement (2) alone, we let the number of degrees in the smallest angle be $2k$. Now the other two are $3k$ and $7k$. Adding them, $2k + 3k + 7k = 180$; $12k = 180$; $k = 15$, and the middle angle is $3(15) = 45°$.

16. **The correct answer is (E).** Since every point on the circle must be 5 units from the center, using statement (1) we know that $(t,-1)$ must be 5 units from $(4,2)$. By the distance formula:

$$\sqrt{(4-t)^2 + (2-(-1))^2} = 5$$

$$\sqrt{(16 - 8t - t^2) + 9} = 5$$

$$\sqrt{t^2 - 8t + 25} = 5$$

Squaring both sides, we have $t^2 - 8t + 25 = 25$. We subtract 25 from both sides to yield $t^2 - 8t = 0$, which factors as $t(t - 8) = 0$ with two possibilities: $t = 0$ or $t = 8$. This narrows down the possible answer to choices (B), (C), and (E). Statement (2) alone tells us almost nothing, so choices (C) and (E) are possible. Combining the two statements, we know that t is either 0 or 8, and knowing that t is an integer does not distinguish between the two.

17. **The correct answer is (A).** Statement (1) tells us that there are 4 distinguishable people who can be arranged in $4! = 4 \times 3 \times 2 \times 1 = 24$ ways. In only one of these ways will they be in the correct order. Therefore, the chance is $\dfrac{1}{24}$. Choices (A) and (D) are left. Statement (2) alone tells us only that there are at least $3! = 6$ possible arrangements, but since there could be any number of boys, that is not sufficient. The best answer is choice (A).

18. **The correct answer is (E).** From statement (1) alone, we know that $N + 1$ is even; thus, N is odd and could be prime. For example, $N = 7$ would do the trick. However, $N = 55$ is an example of a non-prime that would also satisfy the condition, leaving choices (B), (C), and (E). Similarly, $N = 7$ and $N = 55$ would both satisfy the condition in statement (2).

19. **The correct answer is (D).** If the average of n consecutive integers is zero, then their sum is zero. Thus, the list of numbers must start with $-k$ and end at $+k$. Since the list must also include 0, statement (1) tells us that n is odd. Statement (2) alone tells us that $n = 5$ ($1^2 + 2^2 + 3^2 + 4^2 + 5^2 = 55$).

20. **The correct answer is (C).** Since x and y are integers greater than 1, it is tempting to conclude from statement (1) that $x = 2$ and $y = 9$, but it is also possible that $x = 3$ and $y = 4$, leaving choices (B), (C), and (E). From statement (2) alone, $xy = 12$, and there are several possibilities for the choice of x and y. The possibilities are narrowed to choices (C) and (E). Using both statements, we can rewrite $x^2y = 36$ as $x(xy) = 36$ and substitute $xy = 12$ to get $12x = 36$ and $x = 3$. If $x = 3$, $y = 4$.

EXERCISE 4

1. **The correct answer is (C).** Letting R be Robert's weekly salary and T be Timothy's weekly salary, statement (1) says that $0.75R = 1.25T$. That is, $\frac{3}{4}R = \frac{5}{4}T$, or $3R = 5T$. Dividing by $3T$, $\frac{R}{T} = \frac{5}{3}$. Not knowing Timothy's salary, this is not sufficient, leaving choices (B), (C), and (E). Statement (2) alone tells us that $R = 100 + T$, but it does not tell us either salary, leaving choices (C) and (E). Together, the equation $\frac{R}{T} = \frac{5}{3}$ is the same as $T = \frac{3}{5}R$, which we can substitute into $R = 100 + T$ to give us $R = 100 + \frac{3}{5}R$, which we can solve. $5R = 500 + 3R$; $2R = 500$; $R = 250$.

2. **The correct answer is (A).** From statement (1), at 4 for 18¢, you can sell one dozen washers for $3(18¢) = 54¢$, making a profit of $54 - 45 = 9¢$ per dozen. The total profit is $7(9¢) = 63¢$, so choice (A) or choice (D) are possible. From statement (2) alone, we know only that the profit will be 20%, but we do not know the base or selling price.

3. **The correct answer is (E).** Statement (1) tells us nothing about Armando's speed, so choices (B), (C), and (E) are possible. Statement (2) tells us nothing about John's speed, so the answer is choice (C) or (E). Together, since John takes 20 minutes per room, he can do 3 rooms in one hour. Armando can do 4 rooms in an hour. Thus, together they do 7 rooms in one hour. However, we are not told how many rooms there are, so the best answer is choice (E).

4. **The correct answer is (A).** Letting $G =$ the number of points that Grant scored, then from statement (1), James scored $2G$ points and their total was 72. That is, $G + 2G = 72$; $3G = 72$; $G = 24$. The possible answer is choice (A) or choice (D). Since there is no reason to suppose that James's scoring was distributed evenly over the two games, statement (2) alone is not sufficient.

5. **The correct answer is (D).** In order for rectangle $ABCD$ have perimeter 18 as given in statement (1), with one side as 3, the other must be 6. Thus, $BC = AD = 6$, and $\triangle AED$ is a 6–8–10 right triangle. Now, $BE = 11$, $ED = 10$, $DC = 3$, and $BC = 6$. The perimeter is $11 + 10 + 3 + 6 = 30$, so choices (A) and (D) are possible. Using statement (2) alone, the area of $ABCD$ is 18 and one side is 3. Thus, the other side must be 6, and we again conclude that the perimeter is $11 + 10 + 3 + 6 = 30$.

6. **The correct answer is (D).** Using statement (1) alone, we know that the area of the shaded region is equal to the area of the larger circle minus the areas of the two smaller circles. Calling the radius of the larger circle r, each of the smaller circles has radius $\frac{1}{2}r$. Since the area of a circle is πr^2, the area of the shaded region is $\pi r^2 - 2\left(\pi\left[\frac{1}{2}r\right]^2\right) = \pi r^2 - \frac{1}{2}\pi r^2$. This must equal 8π. Thus, $\frac{1}{2}\pi r^2 = 8\pi$, which means that $r^2 = 16$ and $r = 4$. Using statement (2) alone and the fact that the circumference of a circle is $2\pi r$, with the same notation we have $2\pi\left(\frac{1}{2}r\right) = 4\pi$. Thus, $r = 4$.

7. **The correct answer is (E).** The reciprocals of the three possible values of x are 3, 3.5, and 4.666 . . . Both statement (1) and statement (2) allow for the two possibilities, 3 and 3.5.

8. **The correct answer is (A).** Expanding the equation in statement (1), $4A - 4 = 3B - 4 + B$; $4A - 4 = 4B - 4$; $4A = 4B$; $A = B$. Knowing $A = B$, $A^2 - B^2 = 0$, leaving choice (A) or choice (D) as options. Statement (2) tells us only that A depends upon B, but does not give sufficient information to evaluate $A^2 - B^2$.

9. **The correct answer is (C).** She paid $(0.08)(1500) = \$120$ on her loan. Calling her net profit on the stocks S and the return on her other investment R, we have $S + R - 120 = $ net profit. Statement (1) gives us one equation in two unknowns, that is, $S + R - 120 = 128$; $S + R = 248$. Let the amount she invested at $9\frac{1}{2}\%$ be A. The balance is $1{,}500 - A$. Thus, $0.095A = R$, and $S + 0.095A = 248$, which is not sufficient to solve for S. The remaining options are choices (B), (C), and (E). Statement (2) tells us nothing about her annual profit and hence, by itself, cannot be sufficient, leaving choice (C) or choice (E). Together, statement (1) and statement (2) tell us that $A = 800$ and thus, she earned $(0.095)(\$800) = \$76$ on her first investment and $S + 76 = 248$; $S = 172$. Hence, she made a profit of 172 on 700. $172 \div 700 = 0.2457 = 24.6\%$ to the nearest tenth of a percent.

10. **The correct answer is (D).** Let the total rent be R. Using statement (1) alone, $\frac{R}{4} = \frac{R}{6} + 200$. Multiplying by 12: $3R = 2R + 2400$; $R = 2400$. Choices (A) and (D) are left. From statement (2) alone, $\frac{R}{8} = \frac{R}{6} - 100$. Multiplying by the LCD 24: $3R = 4R - 2400$; $R = 2400$.

11. **The correct answer is (E).** To find the arithmetic mean of a, b, and c, it is sufficient to find $a + b + c$. From statement (1), we know that $a + b = 10$, but know nothing about c. Choices (B), (C), and (E) remain. From statement (1), we know that $a + c = 18$, but know nothing about b. Choices (C) and (E) remain. Combining the two, we still do not have enough information. For example, we could have $a = 0$, $b = 10$, $c = 18$, with a total of 28; or $a = 10$, $b = 0$, $c = 8$ with a total of only 18.

12. **The correct answer is (B).** Statement (1) tells us only that $\frac{1}{3}n$ is a perfect square. That is, $n = 3m^2$. There are many possible values for n, such as 3, 12, 27 . . . Choices (B), (C), and (E) remain. Statement (2) gives us the equation $n - 3\left(\frac{1}{n}\right) = 2$. Multiplying by n: $n^2 - 3 = 2n$; $n^2 - 2n - 3 = 0$; $(n - 3)(n + 1) = 0$ yields $n = 3$ or $n = -1$. Since n is positive, $n = 3$.

13. **The correct answer is (A).** From statement (1) alone, we know that the answer is yes. Do you see why? Since z is 4 more than x, $z = x + 4$. And since y must be an odd integer between them, y must be $x + 2$, leaving choice (A) or (D). Statement (2) is certainly true for consecutive odd integers, but it is also true for sets like 7, 11, 15.

14. **The correct answer is (D).** Call the wholesale price of A, x, and the retail price z. Now $z = 1.2x$. Call the normal retail price of B, y, and the sales price w. Now $w = 0.8y$. Essentially, what we are trying to find is the ratio of z to w. Statement (1) tells us that $y = 2x$, so that $w = 1.6x$, and the ratio of z to w is $\dfrac{1.2}{1.6} = \dfrac{3}{4} = 0.75$, that is, 75%. Choices (A) and (D) are now possible answers. Statement (2) tells us that $w = 1.6x$. Since $z = 1.2x$, $x = \dfrac{z}{1.2}$, and $w = (1.6)\left(\dfrac{z}{1.2}\right) = \dfrac{4z}{3}$. Again, the ratio of z to w is $\dfrac{1.2}{1.6} = \dfrac{3}{4} = 0.75$, that is, 75%.

15. **The correct answer is (A).** Statement (1) alone tells us more than we need to know. Simply knowing that the average of x and y is a whole number is enough to tell us that y is odd, since the only way for the average to be a whole number is for the sum of x and y to be even. Thus, if x is odd, so is y. The answer is either choice (A) or choice (D). Statement (2) alone is not sufficient. If y is odd, then $y + 1$ is even; and if y is even, then $y + 1$ is odd. In either case, $x + y + (y + 1)$ is the sum of two odds and an even, which must be even. There are many even numbers that are divisible by 3 giving an integer for the average.

16. **The correct answer is (D).** Letting a be the capacity of barrel A in gallons and letting b be the capacity of barrel B in gallons, we know that, initially, A contains $\dfrac{a}{2}$ gallons and B contains $\dfrac{4b}{5}$ gallons. Using statement (1) alone, we know that reducing the quantity in A from $\dfrac{a}{2}$ to $\dfrac{a}{6}$ will fill B; that is, it will provide b gallons. Since $\dfrac{a}{2} - \dfrac{a}{6} = \dfrac{a}{3}$, we can deduce that $\dfrac{a}{3} = \dfrac{b}{5}$; that is, $a = \dfrac{3}{5}b$. Thus, A is smaller than B, and the answer is either choice (A) or choice (D). From statement (2) alone, we see that reducing $\dfrac{4b}{5}$ to $\dfrac{b}{2}$ will fill A. That is, $\dfrac{4b}{5} - \dfrac{b}{2} = \dfrac{a}{2}$, or $\dfrac{3b}{10} = \dfrac{a}{2}$, and once again, $a = \dfrac{3}{5}b$.

17. **The correct answer is (B).** If we knew that x was positive, then we could multiply the inequality in statement (1) by x to arrive at $x > 1$. But that inequality is also satisfied by any negative x, so the options are choices (B), (C), or (E). Statement (2) alone is sufficient. Cubing any number greater than 1 gives a result greater than 1, and cubing any number less than 1 gives a result less than 1.

18. **The correct answer is (C).** Since there are 18 people, 6 are men and 12 are women. Statement (1) tells us that there are exactly 5 college graduates, but not how many are men, leaving choices (B), (C), and (E). Statement (2) tells us that of the 12 women, 4 are college graduates, but it does not tell us how many college graduates there are altogether, so we cannot tell how many are men, leaving choices (C) and (E). Together, we know that there are 4 women college graduates out of a total of 5. Thus, there is only 1 male college graduate out of the 6 men, making the probability $\dfrac{1}{6}$.

19. **The correct answer is (A).** Let C be the capacity of the tub. In one minute, the two taps together will fill $\frac{1}{30}$ of the tub. From statement (1), the cold water tap will fill $\frac{1}{45}$ of the tub in one minute. That means that the hot water tap must be filling $\frac{1}{30} - \frac{1}{45} = \frac{1}{90}$ of the tub in one minute. In other words, it would take 90 minutes to fill the tub. This leaves choice (A) or choice (D). Statement (2) alone tells us how fast the water runs into the tub, but since we do not know its capacity, we cannot tell how long it will take to fill.

20. **The correct answer is (E).** Since x and y are integers greater than 1, it is tempting to conclude from statement (1) that $x = 2$ and $y = 9$, but it is also possible that $x = 3$ and $y = 4$, which leaves choices (B), (C), and (E). From statement (2) alone, $xy = 12$, and there are several possibilities for the choice of x and y. The options are now choices (C) and (E). Using both statements, we can rewrite $x^2y = 36$ as $x(xy) = 36$ and substitute $xy = 12$ to get $|12x| = 36$. This tells us that $x = 3$ or $x = -3$. If $x = 3$, then $y = 4$, but if $x = -3$, then $y = -4$. The best answer is choice (E).

EXERCISE 5

1. **The correct answer is (E).** From statement (1) alone, we know only the cost of corn. From statement (2) alone, we know that beets have been marked down, but from what price we do not know, so we do not know the cost of beets. Choices (C) and (E) are left. Even taken together, we only know the price of one item and cannot compare them.

2. **The correct answer is (E).** From statement (1), we can determine that he must have gone at least 20 miles per hour over the speed limit, but we do not know what the speed limit was, which eliminates choices (A) and (D). From statement (2), we know that he had to average better than 60 mph but we do not know how fast he was going at any particular time. The options are now choices (C) and (E). Combining the information from statement (1) and statement (2) will still not answer the question, because we do not know the speed limit.

3. **The correct answer is (C).** Since corresponding angles formed when two parallel lines are crossed by a transversal are equal, statement (1) tells us that $\angle DCE = 37°$, and thus, by the equality of vertical angles, $\angle ACB = 37°$. However, not knowing $\angle CAB$, we can conclude nothing about $\angle ABC$. Thus, choices (B), (C), and (E) are left. Similarly, from statement (2) alone we know only one angle in $\triangle ABC$. The decision is now between choice (C) or choice (E). Combining the two, we see that the two angles we know total 90°. Hence, the remaining angle $\angle ABC$ is also 90°.

4. **The correct answer is (D).** Let A be the number of apples. From statement (1), Victor ate $\frac{1}{2}A + \frac{1}{2}$. He had left $A - \left(\frac{1}{2}A + \frac{1}{2}\right) = \frac{1}{2}A - \frac{1}{2}$. Thus, $\frac{1}{2}A - \frac{1}{2} = 7$. Multiplying by 2, we have $A - 1 = 14$; $A = 15$. Choices (A) and (D) are the remaining options. From statement (2), we know that 6 apples picked every half hour means 3 apples picked every 15 minutes. Since 1 hour and 15 minutes is five 15-minute periods, he picked $5(3) = 15$ apples.

5. **The correct answer is (D).** Using statement (1) alone, since the sides are 12–16–20, the triangle is a disguised 3–4–5 right triangle, with AB being the hypotenuse. Hence, using the two legs as base and height, the area of the triangle must be $A = \frac{1}{2}(12)(16) = 96$. The answewer is now either choice (A) or (D). By statement (2) alone, we know that $A = \frac{1}{2}(20)(9.6) = 96$.

6. **The correct answer is (D).** Calling Marjorie's salary $2k$ and Sylvester's $3k$, we have, from statement (1), $3k - 2k = 200$. That is, $k = 200$, from which we know Marjorie's salary is \$400 per week. This narrows down the options to choice (A) or (D). From statement (2), we can write $2k + 3k = 1,000$; $5k = 1,000$; $k = 200$ again.

7. **The correct answer is (D).** From statement (1), $15x - 10x = 5x$, and the difference of two integers is an integer. Statement (2) gives an equation that can be solved by multiplying both sides by the least common denominator $6x$ to yield $3x + 2x = 36$; $5x = 36$; $x = \frac{36}{5}$, and $5x = 36$.

8. **The correct answer is (B).** Statement (1) is a factorable quadratic equation for which $(x - 3)(x - 1) = 0$, giving two possibilities, $x = 1$ or $x = 3$, which leaves choices (B), (C), and (E). Statement (2) is also a quadratic equation, but when factored, it yields $(x - 1)(x - 1) = 0$. That is, there is just one root, $x = 1$.

9. **The correct answer is (E).** From statement (1), we know that $\left(\frac{1}{3}\right)(60\%) = 20\% = \frac{1}{5}$ of the boys got an A. So if the same is true for the girls, we would know that the answer is yes. But we do not know that, so choices (B), (C), and (E) are options. From statement (2) alone, we know nothing about the boys and nothing about the fraction of girls who got an A, because we have no information about the total number of girls, leaving choices (C) and (E). From statement (1) and statement (2) together, we still cannot answer the question, because we have no information about the total number of girls.

10. **The correct answer is (B).** Statement (1) looks as if it is sufficient, but it is not, because x between -2 and -1 also satisfies the condition, so choices (B), (C), and (E) are still options. Writing statement (2) as an inequality, we have $x < x^2 < 2x$. Since $x = 0$ could not satisfy this strict inequality, we can divide by x if we consider the two possibilities, $x > 0$ and $x < 0$. Trying first $x > 0$, division keeps the direction of the inequality the same and yields $1 < x < 2$. Trying x negative, the inequalities are reversed, giving $1 > x > 2$, which is nonsense. Thus, the only solution is $1 < x < 2$; that is, x is between 1 and 2.

11. **The correct answer is (A).** We can solve the inequality in statement (1), $2x > 7.2$, by dividing by 2 to yield $x > 3.6$. This certainly means that x is greater than 3.5, so the options are choices (A) and (D). We can also solve the inequality in statement (2), $3x < 10.9$, by dividing by 3 to obtain $x < 3.6333 \ldots$, which does not resolve the question.

12. **The correct answer is (A).** Since the only way a fraction can be zero is if the numerator is zero, we know from statement (1) alone that $2x = y$. We can substitute that into the ratio $\dfrac{x}{x+y}$ to get $\dfrac{x}{x+2x} = \dfrac{x}{3x} = \dfrac{1}{3}$. Choice (A) or choice (D) are options. Knowing only that $x + y = 3$ does not tell us the value of x in the numerator of $\dfrac{x}{x+y}$, and thus will not answer the question.

13. **The correct answer is (B).** From statement (1), we can see that if $z > 0$, then $y > 0$ (because their ratio is positive), and $x < 0$. However, z could be negative, making y negative and x positive, leaving choices (B), (C), and (E). Statement (2) alone tells us nothing about z, so choice (B) is eliminated. Taken together, we see that x positive implies that y is negative, which in turn implies that z is negative.

14. **The correct answer is (C).** Letting q be the number of quarters and d be the number of dimes, we know that $25q + 10d = 205$. Dividing by 5: $5q + 2d = 41$. This equation has many solutions, but we are interested only in those for which q and d are non-negative whole numbers. We can list these (notice that q cannot be an even number because that would make d a fraction): $q = 1$, $d = 18$; $q = 3$, $d = 13$; $q = 5$, $d = 8$; $q = 7$, $d = 3$. If you try $q = 9$, d turns out to be negative. From this list, only $q = 7$, $d = 3$ is a case with more quarters than dimes, so choice (A) or choice (D) are possible. Looking at the list again, only in one case is $q + d = 10$. Thus, statement (2) alone is also sufficient.

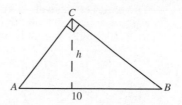

15. **The correct answer is (D).** From statement (1) alone, we recognize that the triangle is a 6–8–10 right triangle. Drawing the triangle, as shown above, we see that by using the two legs as base and height, the area of the triangle must be $A = \frac{1}{2}(6)(8) = 24$. By using the hypotenuse and the unknown altitude, the area must be $A = \frac{1}{2}(10)(h) = 5h$. Therefore, $5h = 24$, and $h = 4.8$, leaving choices (A) and (D). From statement (2) alone, we know directly that $A = \frac{1}{2}(10)(h) = 5h$. Therefore, $5h = 24$, and $h = 4.8$.

16. **The correct answer is (C).** Knowing that P is equidistant from Q and R but knowing only one of the two points does not tells us anything useful. The answer is either choice (C) or (E). From statement (1) and statement (2) together: since the distances from the two given points are the same, we use the distance formula twice and equate the results, thus,

$$\sqrt{(4-1)^2 + (t-1)^2} = \sqrt{(5-4)^2 + (3-t)^2}$$
$$\sqrt{9 + (t^2 - 2t + 1)} = \sqrt{1 + (9 - 6t + t^2)}$$
$$\sqrt{10 - 2t + t^2} = \sqrt{10 - 6t + t^2}$$

Squaring both sides:

$$10 - 2t + t^2 = 10 - 6t + t^2.$$

Subtracting $t^2 + 10$ leaves:

$$-2t = -6t$$
$$4t = 0; t = 0$$

17. **The correct answer is (C).** Knowing that $xy = 30$ tells us nothing about their sum. Thus, choices (B), (C), and (E) are possible. Knowing that $y = x + 7$ tells us their difference but not their sum, which narrows down the possibilities to choices (C) and (E). Combining both pieces of information, $x(x + 7) - 30; x^2 + 7x - 30 - 0$. This factors as $(x - 3)(x + 10) - 0; x - 3 = 0$ or $x + 10 = 0$. Hence, $x = 3$ and $x + 7 = 10$, with sum 13, or $x = -10$ and $x + 7 = -3$, with sum -13. Either way, $x + y = 13$. The best answer is choice (C).

18. **The correct answer is (E).** From statement (1) alone, we know only that x is divisible by 6. If y were divisible by 3, then we would know that $x + 2y$ is divisible by 6, but we do not know tha, so choices (B), (C), and (E) are possible. Knowing, from statement (2) alone, that y is an odd number certainly will not answer the question, so the options are choices (C) and (E). Putting both pieces of information together still is not sufficient, because not every odd number is divisible by 3.

19. **The correct answer is (C).** From statement (1) alone, saying that the square of x is 4 more than 10 times the next even number means that $x^2 - 10(x + 2) = 4$. Solving:

$$x^2 - 10x - 20 = 4$$
$$x^2 - 10x - 24 = 0$$
$$(x - 6)(x + 4) = 0$$
$$x = 6 \text{ or}$$
$$x = -4$$

Since there are two possible answers, statement (1) alone is not sufficient. Of course, just knowing that x is positive is not sufficient. The options are now choices (C) and (E). However, knowing that x is positive when combined with the information from statement (1) is sufficient to narrow down the choice to $x = 6$.

20. **The correct answer is (C).** Statement (1) does not even mention c, so it alone is surely not sufficient, which eliminates choices (A) and (D). Similarly, statement (2) alone does not mention a, so it alone is not sufficient, eliminating choice (B) and leaving choices (C) and (E). With the two data statements, we see that we need to express the fraction $\dfrac{a + c}{c}$ in terms of one letter. Of course, $\dfrac{a + c}{c} = \dfrac{a}{c} + 1$, so we need only find $\dfrac{a}{c}$ and add 1. Since $a{:}b = 1{:}5$ means $\dfrac{a}{b} = \dfrac{1}{5}$, and $b{:}c = 3{:}2$ means $\dfrac{b}{c} = \dfrac{3}{2}$, we can multiply the two, giving $\dfrac{a}{b} \times \dfrac{b}{c} = \dfrac{3}{2} \times \dfrac{1}{5}$. That is, $\dfrac{a}{c} = \dfrac{3}{10}$, and $\dfrac{a}{c} + 1 = \dfrac{13}{10}$.

Chapter 9

The Analytical Writing Assessment

Get the Scoop On . . .

- How to ace the GMAT CAT essay-writing sections
- The four-step writing process that quickly and easily budgets your time and energy
- How to come up with ideas to write about, no matter what the topic
- Professionals' proven techniques for sounding smart whenever you write
- Ways to make your essay as nearly error-free as possible

THE TEST CAPSULE

What's the Big Idea?

In the analytical writing assessment, you'll be given two essay assignments: one requiring you to develop your own point of view on a particular issue, the other asking you to critique the reasoning behind someone else's argument on an issue. For each assignment, you'll have 30 minutes in which to write an essay that is clear, well-organized, and follows the rules of standard written English.

How Many?

Your GMAT CAT will probably have two essay questions, each to be completed within 30 minutes.

How Much Do They Count?

Your essays will be graded by two readers each, using a scale ranging from 0 (worst) to 6 (best). Your final analytical writing score is an average of all four grades. This average does *not* contribute either to your overall GMAT CAT score or to your verbal score, but is reported as a separate score to be interpreted by the schools to which you're applying as they see fit.

How Much Time Should They Take?

You'll have half an hour to complete each essay. As we'll explain, however, you should plan to devote just 20 minutes to actual writing. This will leave you 5 minutes for pre-writing and 5 minutes to proofread and check your work.

What's the Best Strategy?

Use the four-step writing process to organize and budget your time: (1) Brainstorm (3 minutes); (2) Outline (2 minutes); (3) Write (20 minutes); (4)

Revise (5 minutes). You'll end up with a much better essay much more easily than if you'd just plunged in and started writing without a plan.

What's the Worst Pitfall?

The worst pitfall is getting overly complicated in your ideas or your essay's structure. The simpler your outline, the better; a simple plan will allow you to develop each idea in interesting detail and produce a clear, coherent essay in which the ideas sound well-connected and you come across as a smart, logical thinker.

THE OFFICIAL DESCRIPTION

What They Are

The test makers describe the analytical writing assessment as consisting of two 30-minute "writing tasks" designed to test "your ability to think critically and to communicate your ideas." Within the 30 minutes provided, you'll have to decide on your approach to the assigned topic, plan an essay, write your essay (using the computer's simple word-processing program), and put your essay into final form after proofreading or checking it in any way you wish.

Where They Are

In the typical computerized GMAT CAT, you'll have two 30-minute sections, each containing one essay writing assignment. These usually appear first when you take the exam. Reminder: the test-makers claim the right to change the format at any time! However, you're most likely to encounter the typical format we described.

What They Measure

The readers who grade your essays will be instructed to assign each essay a one-digit score ranging from 0 (worst) to 6 (best), considering three main factors: (1) how well you organized, developed, and expressed your ideas; (2) how well you provided relevant reasons and examples to support and explain your ideas; and (3) how correctly you followed the rules of standard written English.

What They Cover

You'll have no choice as to what topic you write about; if you fail to write on the assigned topic, you'll receive a grade of 0 for that essay. The topics deal with mildly controversial issues, some from business, some from various social, political, and ethical fields, on which almost anyone could be expected to have some opinions or ideas. No outside knowledge or background information is provided, and none is needed. You'll almost certainly have enough facts and ideas to write the required essays if you draw upon information you've gathered from your reading for school and work and the general background knowledge you derive from newspapers, magazines, and other media.

The Directions

There are two types of analytical writing assessment assignments: analysis of an issue and analysis of an argument. Each has a slightly different set of directions:

ANALYSIS OF AN ISSUE

In this section, you will need to analyze the issue presented and explain your views on it. There is no "correct" answer. Instead, you should consider various perspectives as you develop your own position on the issue.

WRITING YOUR RESPONSE: Take a few minutes to think about the issue and plan a response before you begin writing. Be sure to organize your ideas and develop them fully, but leave time to reread your response and make any revisions that you think are necessary.

EVALUATION OF YOUR RESPONSE: College and university faculty members from various subject-matter areas, including management education, will evaluate the overall quality of your thinking and writing. They will consider how well you

- organize, develop, and express your ideas about the issue presented
- provide relevant supporting reasons and examples
- control the elements of standard written English

ANALYSIS OF AN ARGUMENT

In this section, you will be asked to write a critique of the argument presented. *You are NOT being asked to present your own views on the subject.*

WRITING YOUR RESPONSE: Take a few minutes to evaluate the argument and plan a response before you begin writing. Be sure to organize your ideas and develop them fully, but leave time to reread your response and make any revisions that you think are necessary.

EVALUATION OF YOUR RESPONSE: College and university faculty members from various subject-matter areas, including management education, will evaluate the overall quality of your thinking and writing. They will consider how well you

- organize, develop, and express your ideas about the argument presented
- provide relevant supporting reasons and examples
- control the elements of standard written English

THE INSIDER'S REPORT: STRATEGIES THAT REALLY WORK

The analytical writing assessment—AWA for short—was added to the GMAT CAT at the request of the graduate business schools that sponsor the exam. They'd found that too many of their entering students—including some who scored high on the GMAT CAT—were unable to write clear and coherent English prose. True, every B-school applicant must submit a personal statement in essay form; but this doesn't necessarily reflect the applicant's own writing ability, since it's always possible to enlist outside editing and rewriting help. Forcing the applicant to write two essays within time constraints at the same time that he takes the GMAT CAT was their solution.

The AWA differs from the rest of the GMAT CAT in several ways.

- Unlike the rest of the GMAT CAT, the AWA is graded subjectively rather than objectively. Trained readers will scrutinize your essays and assign them scores based solely on their opinions of your writing. No two readers are likely to score you the same.

- Unlike the rest of the GMAT CAT, the AWA is graded "holistically" rather than item by item. The readers will assign your essay a single number based on their overall assessment of your work. By contrast, your scores in other areas of the GMAT CAT are based on a mass of detailed plusses and minuses—right and wrong answers to individual test questions.

- And, unlike the rest of the GMAT CAT, your AWA score will have only a minor impact on your B-school admission decision.

Enter the Computer

FYI

The teachers who read and score the AWA essays work under intense time pressure. On average, they have only 2 minutes to spend on each essay. As you'll learn, this constraint has a definite impact on the writing strategies that will and will not make a difference in the score you receive.

The subjectivity of the AWA represents a departure from typical ETS practice. After all, the modern testing industry was built on a foundation of "objectivity" based on standardized tests scored by machines, with (supposedly) no room for human bias or error.

Until recently, the grading of essays is one field in which even ETS had to grudgingly rely on human beings. Now that is changing. In early 1999, the test-makers announced the development of a test-scoring "robot" (really a sophisticated software program) called "E-rater," which they intended to use in grading AWA essays for the GMAT CAT.

The E-rater will not operate alone. Under the current plan, your essays will be read by one human and by the computer. Each will assign every essay a grade on the 0–6 scale. If their grades on a given essay differ by more than 1 point (say, a 2 and a 4), then a third reader—a human being—will read the essay and cast the deciding vote. (A similar tie-breaking mechanism was used before the advent of E-rater.)

Undoubtedly, ETS will follow the results of this experiment with great interest. If the scores doled out by the E-rater closely track those of the human graders, the test-makers will surely be tempted to declare a victory for artificial intelligence, claiming that they've developed software that is as capable of judging good writing as even a skilled human being. The logical next step will be to eliminate the human readers altogether. It seems likely that the grading would become, if not more accurate, at least more predictable and uniform. And ETS would certainly save a lot of money—though we won't hold our breath waiting for testing fees to be reduced.

Should you change your approach to essay writing on the exam as a result of the introduction of the E-rater? Probably not, for two main reasons. First, details about the algorithm (that is, the logical procedure) by which the software will judge your writing have not yet been released by ETS. A spokesperson for the test-makers said only, "What we look for are such things as the organization of ideas and syntactical structure." It will take some time and experience to determine exactly how this vague generality translates into specific test scores.

Second, it seems likely that the ETS computer will grade papers based on mechanical, superficial features that are susceptible to objective measurement: the use of words that suggest the logical development of ideas; whether verbs agree with their subjects; whether your paper contains more than one or two misspellings, and so on. It's a somewhat mindless way of judging a piece of writing, of course. But in truth, the scoring of the AWA essays has *always* been both mechanical and superficial.

The human readers have only about 2 minutes in which to read and grade your essay. This isn't enough time to notice, much less respond to, any profound idea, clever witticism, thoughtful analysis, or brilliant phrasing you come up with. It's only enough time for the reader to get a sense as to whether your essay is clear and logically developed and whether your writing contains a large number of errors in grammar, usage, and spelling. Your score is based on a quick determination of how you compare to other test takers in these two areas. Thus, the E-rater isn't likely to be much less sophisticated than the human readers have always been.

The essay-writing strategies we'll explain later in this chapter were designed to make it relatively easy to write an essay that sounds logical and thoughtful in just a few minutes—an essay that makes it easy for a reader to give you a score of 4, 5, or 6. The same strategies will continue to work even with the E-rater playing a role in grading you.

Don't Agonize Over the AWA

The way business schools evaluate and interpret AWA scores varies, but it's rare for an AWA score to make or break a candidate. Most schools think of the AWA as an extra way of checking the applicant's writing ability. If a student has good overall credentials and earns a high GMAT CAT score, a low AWA score (3 or less) may make a school ask: Is there some reason why this student might have trouble expressing himself in writing? Would a remedial writing course be advisable? But it's unlikely that a student who otherwise would be accepted would be rejected because of a poor AWA score. By the same token, a student with poor or marginal credentials isn't going to be accepted to B-school because of a high score on the AWA.

Therefore, we recommend that you *not* agonize over the AWA. Review the writing tips in this chapter, and practice the essay questions when you take the sample tests in this book. Beyond that, most students don't need to focus on the AWA. The other parts of the GMAT CAT are more important and deserve more attention.

Having said that, there are definite strategies you can use to improve your performance on this part of the exam. In fact, they're largely the same strategies that savvy test takers use whenever they work on an essay exam. If you've been successful on essay tests in history, English, or other college courses, you may find that the ideas in this chapter sound familiar—even if you never consciously learned them. They reflect smart essay-writing practice as used by many students over the years.

FYI

When you brainstorm, the notes you jot needn't be in any particular order, nor should they be detailed, well thought out statements. Just write a word or two about each idea that pops into your head. After all, you only need to use these notes for the next half-hour, at most; there's no need to make them complete or especially clear.

Use the Four-Step Writing Process

The thirty minutes you're allowed to write each essay isn't much time. Of course, the expectations of the readers who grade your paper will reflect that fact. Almost no one is capable of writing a profound, thoroughly developed, well-crafted, technically perfect essay in just half an hour, and you *don't* need to achieve this to earn a high score (5 or 6) on the AWA.

However, you do need to use your time wisely. It's best to have a clear game plan in mind, which will allow you to tackle each step of the essay-writing process with self-confidence and inner calm. The four-step process we're about to describe is such a game plan. Practice it between now and the day of the exam, and it'll help you feel organized and in control when you tackle the AWA.

Brainstorm (3 minutes)

For each of the two essay topics, you'll need to come up with some things to write about.

For the Analysis of an Issue essay, you'll probably be asked to agree or disagree with someone's opinion. This opinion (we'll call it the *stimulus*, since it serves to stimulate your own writing) will be stated in such broad, general terms that almost anyone can find some facets of the opinion with which to quibble or to agree.

For the Analysis of an Argument essay, the assignment is slightly different: you'll be asked to evaluate the strength or weakness of someone's argument regarding a particular, mildly controversial topic. Again, the stimulus you must respond to will be so general in scope that almost anyone can come up with something to say about it.

Your first step in developing your essay is to brainstorm ideas about what to say. There's no magic formula for this process. Just take about 3 minutes to jot down on a piece of scrap paper a handful of ideas that are relevant to the topic.

You may begin with a clear idea as to whether you agree or disagree with the stimulus. (Perhaps as soon as you read the opinion in the question, you'll have a strongly positive or negative reaction.) If so, that's fine. Just spend your three minutes imagining all the points you could raise to support your point of view. List them as they occur to you, without evaluating how "good" or "bad" they are. Brainstorming is a nonjudgmental activity.

If you begin without clearly feeling any agreement or disagreement with the stimulus, that's okay too. Just start jotting down ideas on *either* side of the argument as they come to you. You'll probably find that you think of more ideas on one side than the other. Bingo!—that's your opinion. Since there's truly no "right" or "wrong" opinion, just pick whichever opinion you have the most things to say about and run with it.

Here's an example of a typical Analysis of an Issue topic like those you'll find on the real GMAT CAT:

> "Schools should be responsible only for teaching academic skills and not for teaching ethical and social values."
>
> Discuss the extent to which you agree or disagree with the opinion expressed above. Support your point of view with reasons and/or examples from your own experiences, observations, or reading.

Notice how broad the stimulus is. You can define "schools," "academic skills," and "ethical and social values" any way you like. You could write about teaching kindergarten kids to get along with one another, whether high school students should be allowed to have organized prayer in public schools, "speech codes" on college campuses, or any of several dozen other possible variations. The AWA topics are deliberately designed so that any halfway conscious person can probably think of something to say about them.

Notice, too, that the instructions that follow the stimulus are designed to jog your thinking about ideas to discuss. Refer to those instructions if you find yourself at a loss. They suggest that you provide "reasons and/or examples from your own experiences, observations, or reading." Again, a very wide net is being cast—deliberately. You can come up with things to say based upon:

- classroom discussions
- things you learned in school
- movies or TV shows
- books, essays, or other writings
- the lives of famous people
- your own experiences
- stories people have told you
- current events
- episodes from history

. . . and so on. Again, almost anyone can come up with a few things to mention by simply drawing on one or more of these sources.

Here's an example of what a student's brainstorming notes for the topic above might look like:

```
Whose values?
     Amish
     suburbanites
     yuppies
     Southern Baptists
pluralism
schools need focus
sex education
classroom cooperation vs. competition
teachers set examples—indirectly
drugs & violence
```

The first several lines reflect one train of thought: if schools were to teach ethical values, *whose* values would they teach? Those of the

Amish? Suburban values (family togetherness, peace and harmony, leisure)? Yuppie values (greed, ambition)? Those of Southern Baptists (tradition, piety, respect for authority)? Because America is pluralistic, it may be impractical for schools to teach values; they need to focus on academics.

The other notes reflect other random ideas:

> Should sex education be academic in focus (the biology of sex) or values-based?

> Most schools encourage classroom competition rather than cooperation (if you look at a neighbor's test paper, you're "cheating"); is that ethically proper?

> Teachers set ethical examples every day by what they do and say.

> Finally, would the problems of drugs and violence in schools be less serious if ethics were deliberately taught?

The notes, obviously, are somewhat of a hodgepodge. *That's all right.* The point of brainstorming is just to generate a bunch of ideas. There'll be time in a moment to narrow and organize them.

Naturally, no two people will write notes that look alike. The point is to keep this first step in the writing process simple and straightforward: generate raw material for your essay by writing down whatever comes to mind in a matter of 3 minutes or less. It'll almost certainly provide plenty of fodder for the remaining steps and for the essay that's your ultimate goal.

Outline (2 minutes)

Now spend 2 minutes organizing the raw, random notes you created by brainstorming into a simple outline for your essay.

This can be done quite quickly. Here's how.

First, if you haven't already, decide on a point of view (pro or con) you want to defend in your essay.

Then, look at your notes and pick the three or four ideas you like best. They should be ideas that you think (1) make sense, (2) relate to the topic, (3) support your point of view reasonably well, and (4) you know enough about to write a few sentences on. Put a check or other mark next to those ideas. You'll use these in your essay.

If there aren't enough good ideas that fit these criteria, take one or two of the ideas you like and elaborate on them. Think of related ideas, add details or examples, and use these to fill out your list.

Finally, decide on a sequence for the ideas. This can be done in several ways. Occasionally, a sequence will be obvious: one idea may be the cause of all the others and, therefore, should clearly come first. The ideas may all reflect historic events that took place in a definite time sequence that it would be natural to follow. If there's an obvious sequence, use it.

If there is no obvious sequence, decide which idea you like *best*. It may be the idea you find most interesting; it may be the idea you consider most convincing; it may be an idea you were recently talking about with a friend, or wrote a paper about for school, so you happen to know a lot about it. Whatever the reason, put your favorite idea *first*. Then, put your second favorite idea *last,* and then stick the remaining idea(s) in between, in an arbitrary order.

What's the rationale for this strategy? The most emphatic parts of any essay—the parts the reader is most likely to remember—are the beginning and the end. What appears in the middle is most likely to be half forgotten. Therefore, your best material ought to come either at the start or the end of your essay. It'll have the greatest positive effect on your grade in those locations.

Once you've decided on a sequence for your ideas, just mark the items with numbers in the appropriate sequence, right there on your notes: 1, 2, 3, 4. That's your outline. Simple, no?

Here's an example of how the brainstorming notes from above might be turned into a simple outline:

> 2. ✔ <u>Whose values?</u>
>   Amish
>   suburbanites
>   yuppies
>   Southern Baptists
>
> 1. ✔ pluralism
>
> 3. ✔ schools need focus
>   sex education
>   classroom cooperation vs. competition
>   teachers set examples-indirectly
>   drugs & violence
>
> 4, ✔ U.S. Schools lag

The test taker who produced the original notes decided that (for the purposes of the AWA) he would agree with the argument presented—

that schools should teach academics only, not ethical values. (Why did he decide that? Maybe that's his sincere belief. More important, he has a few good notes he can use to defend that point of view! That's all that really matters when tackling the AWA.)

Having decided this, he scanned his notes and found that the first three points listed all seemed to fit nicely into his argument. He also thought of a fourth idea that might make a good ending, so he jotted this at the end: "U.S. schools lag." (The idea here is that American schools are already behind most other countries in academic standards—at least, so people say—so why take precious teaching time away from academic subjects to teach ethics? This seems like a reasonably effective argument to close with.) He marked all four ideas with a check.

Finally he decided, somewhat arbitrarily, on a logical order for the four ideas. He'll start with the idea that America is pluralistic. From that, it makes sense to ask, "Whose values would be taught in schools?" and use the Amish/suburban/etc. examples. This leads nicely into the point about focusing on academics and, finally, the argument about how American students lag behind others. Wham, bam, we're done.

Again, no two students will produce the same outline based on any given topic. It doesn't matter. All that matters is that you come up with a few ideas you feel able to write about and put them into a more-or-less logical sequence.

Now you're ready to do some actual writing.

Write (20 minutes)

Five minutes have passed, and you haven't yet typed a single word of your essay. Don't get nervous! The time you've spent getting organized is about to pay dividends. Writing your essay will go much more smoothly than it otherwise would because you've invested a few minutes in picking the best ideas to write about and in coming up with a logical sequence for them.

Go ahead and begin writing your essay. You'll be typing it on the test center computer, of course. The test makers have equipped your machine with a simple word-processing program able to handle most of the basic maneuvers found in other such programs. You can move from place to place in the essay using the arrow keys; you can delete, insert, and move text; you can use the mouse to jump to a particular word, etc.

As you write, follow the simple outline you created a moment ago, with these two added elements:

- Begin the essay with a brief introductory paragraph that sets forth your point of view and, if you like, suggests the nature of the ideas you'll be using to defend it.

FYI

"Tell 'em what you're going to tell 'em; then tell 'em; then tell 'em what you told 'em."—Old maxim for writers. This traditional advice isn't always best because it produces formulaic writing—but on the AWA, a handy formula is exactly what you want. Try it!

- End the essay with a brief concluding paragraph that summarizes your point of view in a clear, concise, forceful way.

Use the paragraph as your structural unit. That is, think of each idea as occupying a single, fully developed paragraph, three to six sentences long. This isn't a rigid rule: a "big" idea may develop into two paragraphs, and two simple ideas may nestle comfortably in a single longish paragraph. But, in general, the simplest and clearest structure for writing is to start a new paragraph each time you begin a new idea. This makes your writing easy to follow and makes you sound clearheaded—something the weary, harried readers of your AWA essay will appreciate.

Here's how the notes from above might be turned into a first-draft essay. (The numbers at the start of each paragraph are included for our ease in discussing the essay.)

FYI

As you read this essay, compare it to the brainstorming notes and outline that appeared earlier. See how the notes and outline became the basis for the essay?

[1] Schools, especially in a pluralistic nation like America, should stick to teaching academic subjects and leave ethics for the home and the church, temple, or synagogue. To do otherwise is to invite trouble, as this essay will show.

[2] The most important question to be answered, if our schools are to teach values, is whose values would they teach? After all, not all ethical values are the same. The Amish have a way of life that stresses simplicity and austerity; they avoid modern conveniences and even shun dancing. By contrast, the typical young urban family—"yuppies," as they're sometimes called—enjoys buying the latest electronic gadgets and going on expensive vacations. Either group might be offended by the values of the other.

[3] True, Amish and yuppie children aren't likely to attend the same schools; but what about Jewish kids and fundamentalist Christians? These two groups may live in the same town or neighborhood, and either one would be incensed to have the other group's moral teachings imposed on them.

[4] The only way to avoid the inevitable conflicts that teaching ethics would bring to our schools is by allowing teachers to focus on what they're paid to do: to teach academics. We send children to school to learn math, English, history, and science. How would we feel if our kids came home ignorant about geometry but filled with someone else's religious or ethical ideas? Justly annoyed, I think.

[5] Given the fact that American schoolchildren lag behind those in most other nations in academic achievement, it would be foolish for us to divert precious classroom time to teaching morality.

[6] Ironically, the most ethical thing our schools can do for our children is to avoid getting entangled in ethical issues. Stick to academics, and let families teach morality in their own way and on their own time.

Notice a few features of this essay:

- Paragraphs 1 and 6 succinctly summarize the writer's point of view. They make the argument clear and easy to follow and give the essay a forthright tone that suggests a clear, self-confident mind.

- Paragraphs 2 through 5 reflect the numbered points from the outline. Each time the writer completes an idea from the outline, he starts a new paragraph. The result is a logical sequence of paragraphs, laying out the points of the essay in easy-to-follow fashion.

- The writer adapted his outline slightly as he wrote, using new ideas and new approaches as they occured to him. For example, point 2 in the outline ("whose values?") became the basis for two paragraphs in the final essay, not just one (paragraphs 2 and 3). Furthermore, after writing about the Amish and the yuppies in paragraph 2, the writer seemed to realize that the contrast between these two groups was a little exaggerated; hence, paragraph 3 offers a more down-to-earth pairing, which strengthens the argument. The suburbanites got left out altogther, since they seemed unnecessary.

Is this essay a masterful piece of writing, worthy of standing beside Thoreau or George Orwell in an anthology of fine English prose? Not really. But it's a clear, workmanlike, reasonably wellûthought out defense of the writer's point of view, and as such it's likely to earn a high score on the AWA. Mission accomplished.

Revise (5 minutes)

The last of the four writing steps is revision—literally, a "re-seeing" of your work. After you finish writing your first draft, pause for a moment; shut your eyes, lean back in your chair, stretch your arms, take a deep breath, and relax. Then scroll back up to the top of your essay and spend the last 5 minutes rereading it, finding and fixing as many errors and imperfections as possible.

A little later in this chapter, we offer some tips and warnings that will help you polish the style and mechanics of your essay. For now, these general suggestions:

- Reread your essay slowly, line by line, to make sure you spot any places where you accidentally left out words, garbled phrases, or made typographical errors.

- Try to read the essay with fresh eyes, as though you'd never seen it before. Make sure you've really said what you intended to say: as the classic writing guide, *The Elements of Style*, puts it, "Your chances of having said it are only fair."

- Don't get drawn into drastic rewriting. Your essay is what it is; you don't have time to rethink it substantially. Tinker around the edges, but don't try to rebuild the house.

Keep Your Essay Simple

Throughout this chapter, we've emphasized the need to avoid getting complicated. The point is worth stressing. In a half hour, you have time to write an essay of only 250 to 400 words. That means, at most, five or six paragraphs expressing three or four ideas. Trying to get more complicated will lead you into trouble in several ways: it may cause you to run out of time before finishing your essay; it may cause you, or your reader, to lose track of your point of view, producing confusion and a sense of incompetence; it may force you to streamline your discussion of each point so drastically as to make it seem simple to the point of inanity.

A few ideas, each one developed in a few interesting sentences: that's the formula for a winning AWA essay.

Make Sure Your Point of View Comes Through Clearly

Surprisingly often, student essays (on the AWA and elsewhere) fail to clearly express a strong and distinctive point of view. True, the GMAT CAT readers don't particularly care about your point of view; there's no right or wrong opinion that you can express about any of the topics, and one can write a technically correct essay without expressing a forceful opinion. But *an essay with a clear point of view sounds smarter.* When you write as if you know what you're talking about and have the facts to back up what you believe, your writing carries conviction and authority; and such writing is apt to earn a higher score from your readers.

So lean toward an opinionated rather than a wishy-washy tone in your essay; it's more interesting and more impressive.

THE INSIDER'S REPORT: THE BEST TIPS

So far, we've focused mainly on *what* to say in your essay: how to come up with ideas to write about and how to organize those ideas. Now, let's consider *how* to say it: specifically, how to tailor your writing style for the most positive effect on your readers.

The writing challenge on the AWA is actually a simple one: *to sound smart.* As we've mentioned, each AWA essay is read and graded in about 2 minutes. This means that your reader will never notice or appreciate any subtle irony your essay may contain, any clever metaphor you use, any profound observation you make, or any moving self-revelation you share. There's no time for that. About all the reader has time to notice is whether you sound smart or dumb. Your score is a snap judgment about that point.

But not to worry. You can use several proven techniques to make sure you sound smart, even when writing under the gun. These are techniques developed and used by professional writers—craftsmen who must sound at least reasonably smart even when cranking out reams of prose (for newspapers, magazines, TV broadcasts, what have you) on deadline. The same techniques will work for you.

Here are a few to try. In particular, as you revise your essays, look for ways to incorporate these writing techniques. You'll find that making just a few changes in your essay in accordance with these ideas can make a big difference in its overall effectiveness.

Guide the Reader Using Signpost Words

Signpost words are words that draw connections among the ideas in your essay. There are many examples. An illustrative story may be introduced by signpost words such as *For instance* or *For example.* A series of three arguments might be introduced by the words, *First . . . Second . . . Finally.* When two ideas contrast with one another, signpost words such as *On the other hand* or *However* can be used.

Signpost words are valuable in many ways. They help the reader follow your argument more easily. They make the purpose of each detail, fact, story, or example you use more obvious. Most important, they make your essay sound well organized. By emphasizing the structure of your argument, they prove that you've thought through the argument; rather than rambling aimlessly from one idea to another, you've got a plan and you are following it intelligently.

Look for opportunities to use these four kinds of signpost words in your essays:

- Words that show a contrast or change in idea: *although, but, by contrast, despite, however, nevertheless, nonetheless, on the other hand, unlike, yet*

FYI

Historic events (preferably with dates); allusions to famous books or authors; favorite quotations—all of these will help boost your essay's smartness quotient. But don't overdo it, one or two relevant, accurate references will be more effective than a frantic scramble to squeeze in several, some of which may be erroneous.

- Words that show a similarity or the continuation of an idea: *also, as well, equally, in the same way, likewise, parallel, similarly, so, thus, too*

- Words that show a time sequence: *after, before, earlier, later, next, previous, prior, subsequently, then*

- Words that show a cause-and-effect relationship: *as a result, because, consequently, due to, led to, produced, resulted in, since, therefore*

The more blatant your essay's logical structure, the more logical you'll sound—and that's a good thing.

Be Specific

Most writers—especially when writing hastily—tend to be vague. They fail to make it really clear what they are talking about. The result is prose that sounds poorly thought out, or even devoid of ideas.

To sound smart, make a deliberate effort to express each of your ideas in as specific and detailed a way as possible. Here are a couple of illustrations of what we mean. Suppose you wanted to refer to the contributions of Arab cultures to western civilization (a point that could be relevant to any number of essay topics). Here's a vague way of doing so, which is typical of many quickly written student essays:

> Many important ideas in science and other areas were brought to the western world from other regions during the years following the Middle Ages.

Here's a more specific way, using a couple of details to make the point much more vivid and interesting:

> Such vital scientific principles as the concept of zero and the geographical teachings of Ptolemy were imported to western Europe from Arabic culture during the fourteenth and fifteenth centuries.

Another example of the vague:

> Some people in the nineteenth century felt that modern science had called into question basic concepts concerning the relationship between human beings and God.

As compared to the specific:

> The writings of authors such as Matthew Arnold and Alfred Tennyson reflected the feeling that Darwin's theory of evolution had weakened belief in Christian doctrines about the creation of humans by God.

True, you need to know and use some actual facts in order to write specifically rather than vaguely. But it's not as hard as it looks. Consider the first example above, about Arabic science. It contains just two examples—the concept of zero and the geography of Ptolemy—which may be all the student happens to remember from a semester-long course in the History of Science; and since he's unclear about his dates, he carefully fudges by referring to "the fourteenth and fifteenth centuries." Sounds impressive, though, doesn't it?

Anyway, no one is going to check your facts; remember, your poor reader has just 2 minutes to spend. The important thing is that you *sound* as though you know something. Grab a fact or two that you do know and insert them in your essay. The result will sound much smarter than if you merely generalize.

Vary the Length of Your Sentences

There's nothing really *wrong* with an essay in which all the sentences are about the same length. Most readers won't consciously notice. But the effect is monotonous, and the result is often an essay that sounds dull, lifeless, and uninteresting.

Instead, consciously try to vary the length of your sentences. Make some of your sentences fairly long and complicated in grammatical form, as we've done with the sentence you're reading now. Keep others short, like this one. The changing rhythms of your writing will help keep your reader alert and interested and give your prose a snappy, intelligent tone.

In particular, use short sentences for emphasis. A great way to highlight a significant idea is to express it in a sentence of only five to eight words. It's especially effective when the short sentence appears among several longer ones. The bluntness of the short sentence stands out.

Here's an example of how this works. Notice how the short sentence in the middle of this paragraph draws your attention:

> In the nineteenth century, when the science of psychology was founded, its methods were generally, by modern standards, unscientific. Rather than considering only evidence that could be objectively verified or data drawn from experiments that could be repeated by other scientists, psychologists often based their theories on evidence that was highly subjective. Today, this has largely changed. Psychologists are now learning to restrict themselves to studying phenomena that can be directly observed and objectively analyzed.

This is an easy trick to use whenever you write, even when the time pressures of an exam force you to work quickly. Just write a short sentence every now and then. The result is a crisp, smart-sounding style.

Make Concessions as Needed

A final way of sounding smart is to show that you recognize the limitations of your own arguments. We attribute intelligence to the judicious person—one who weighs arguments thoughtfully, seeing shades of gray rather than mere black-and-white truths. Make a point of introducing this tone into your essays by making a least one or two concessions to the oppposing point of view.

You can insert a concession almost anywhere in an essay, except at the end. (In that spot, it will make your essay sound unresolved, as though you're not sure *what* you believe.) Here's an example of how our earlier essay, about teaching ethics, could *begin* with a concession:

> Sometimes it seems as if our society is at the brink of ethical chaos. Violence is all too common on our streets and even in our schools; politicians and business people seem to get away with deceit and crime. Under the circumstances, it's understandable that many people would like our schools to fill the moral gap. Teach ethics in schools, they say, and the next generation will have a better moral grounding. It's an appealing idea, but one that would hurt our society more than it would help.

Notice how this paragraph, presenting the opposing point of view in a sympathetic, understanding way, actually *strengthens* the writer's position by making him sound eminently reasonable. Try this technique. It really works.

THE INSIDER'S REPORT: THE MOST IMPORTANT WARNINGS

Take Steps to Eliminate Errors in Spelling, Grammar, and Usage

Theoretically, the AWA is not a test of writing mechanics. Rather it's intended to focus on your ability to structure and develop a well-organized, intelligent essay. Thus, you might assume that minor details such as spelling, grammar, and word usage "don't count." They don't—in the sense that your reader is not keeping a running tally of technical errors and then deducting (for example) one grade for every five mistakes. AWA scoring doesn't work that way.

On the other hand, the teachers who read and grade the AWA essays have their biases, like anyone else. And most teachers share the assumption that errors in spelling, grammar, and usage suggest ignorance, laziness, or both. Consciously or unconsciously, they can't help being influenced by this when they read and score your paper.

Therefore, when you revise your essay, follow these tips:

■ Catch and fix as many spelling errors as possible. (No, the GMAT CAT software doesn't include a spell-check program—sorry.)

- If in doubt about a word's proper spelling, pick instead a word you *do* know, even if its meaning is a trifle less apt.

- Catch and fix as many grammar and usage errors as you can. Appendix C, The Insider's GMAT CAT Writer's Manual, is a handy way to review the errors in grammar and usage that bedevil most writers. Learn the rules it teaches, and apply them to your own writing.

- When in doubt about the grammatical structure of a sentence, simplify it: break one long, unwieldy sentence into two, or trim away extra phrases until you're sure the remaining structure is sound.

Perfection isn't the goal; almost no one can write a perfectly error-free essay in half an hour, and your work will be judged against that of other students laboring under the same time pressure. But an essay that's relatively free of grammar and spelling bugs will—even subconsciously—provoke a more respectful response, and a higher score, from your reader.

JUST THE FACTS

- Use the four-step writing process on the AWA to manage your time and effort effectively.

- Keep your essay simple and make sure your point of view comes through clearly.

- To sound smart, use guidepost words, be specific, vary sentence length, and make concessions where needed.

- Although mechanical errors "don't count," they really do; find them, fix them, or avoid them.

Part III

The Insider's GMAT CAT

Chapter 10

The Insider's GMAT CAT Sample Test

Instructions

The following Insider's GMAT CAT Sample Test will give you a chance to practice the skills and strategies you've learned throughout this book.

This test is about the same length as the real GMAT CAT. Take it under true testing conditions. Complete the entire test in a single sitting. Eliminate distractions (TV, music) and clear away notes and reference materials.

Time each section of the test separately with a stopwatch or kitchen timer, or have someone else time you. If you run out of time before answering all the questions, stop and draw a line under the last question you finished. Then go on to the next test section. When you are done, score yourself based only on the questions you finished in the allotted time. Later, for practice purposes, you should answer the questions you were unable to complete in time.

The answer key, explanatory answers, and information about interpreting your test results appear at the end of the test, beginning on page 388.

SECTION 1

ANALYTICAL WRITING 1

Time—30 Minutes

ANALYSIS OF AN ISSUE

In this section, you will need to analyze the issue presented and explain your views on it. There is no "correct" answer. Instead, you should consider various perspectives as you develop your own position on the issue.

WRITING YOUR RESPONSE

Take a few minutes to think about the issue and plan a response before you begin writing. Be sure to organize your ideas and develop them fully, but leave time to reread your response and make any revisions that you think are necessary.

EVALUATION OF YOUR RESPONSE

College and university faculty members from various subject-matter areas, including management education, will evaluate the overall quality of your thinking and writing. They will consider how well you

- organize, develop, and express your ideas about the issue presented
- provide relevant supporting reasons and examples
- control the elements of standard written English

Directions: Read the statement and the instructions that follow it, and then make any notes that will help you plan your response. Write your response on scrap paper or type it on a word processor.

"People often complain that the introduction of new labor-saving machines costs workers their jobs. However, most new technologies actually create more jobs than they destroy."

To what extent do you agree or disagree with the opinion expressed above? Support your views with reasons and examples drawn from your own experiences, observations, or reading.

SECTION 2

ANALYTICAL WRITING 2

Time—30 Minutes

ANALYSIS OF AN ARGUMENT

In this section, you will be asked to write a critique of the argument presented. *You are NOT being asked to present your own views on the subject.*

WRITING YOUR RESPONSE

Take a few minutes to evaluate the argument and plan a response before you begin writing. Be sure to organize your ideas and develop them fully, but leave time to reread your response and make any revisions that you think are necessary.

EVALUATION OF YOUR RESPONSE

College and university faculty members from various subject-matter areas, including management education, will evaluate the overall quality of your thinking and writing. They will consider how well you

- organize, develop, and express your ideas about the argument presented
- provide relevant supporting reasons and examples
- control the elements of standard written English

Directions: Read the statement and the instructions that follow it, and then make any notes that will help you plan your response. Write your response on scrap paper or type it on a word processor.

The following appeared as part of a plan proposed by an executive of the Stan Doncé Magazine Group to the company's president.

"Our need for printing services varies from month to month, depending on the size of our magazines and variations in scheduling. Working with outside printers has necessitated a constant scramble for adequate press time at reasonable prices. If we were to buy and operate our own printing operation, we would be better able to control both the availability and the cost of printing our magazines, which would have a favorable impact on the efficiency and profitability of our business."

Discuss how well reasoned you find this argument. In your discussion, be sure to analyze the line of reasoning and the use of evidence in the argument. For example, you may need to consider what questionable assumptions underlie the thinking and what alternative explanations or counterexamples might weaken the conclusion. You can also discuss what sort of evidence would strengthen or refute the argument, what changes in the argument would make it more logically sound, and what, if anything, would help you better evaluate its conclusion.

SECTION 3

QUANTITATIVE

37 Questions

Time—75 Minutes

Directions (Data Sufficiency): This data sufficiency problem consists of a question and two statements, labeled (1) and (2), in which certain data are given. You have to decide whether the data given in the statements are *sufficient* for answering the question. Using the data given in the statements *plus* your knowledge of mathematics and everyday facts (such as the number of days in July or the meaning of *counterclockwise*), you must indicate whether

- statement (1) ALONE is sufficient, but statement (2) alone is not sufficient to answer the question asked;
- statement (2) ALONE is sufficient, but statement (1) alone is not sufficient to answer the question asked;
- BOTH statements (1) and (2) TOGETHER are sufficient to answer the question asked; but NEITHER statement ALONE is sufficient;
- EACH statement ALONE is sufficient to answer the question asked;
- statements (1) and (2) TOGETHER are NOT sufficient to answer the question asked, and additional data specific to the problem are needed.

Numbers: All numbers used are real numbers.

Figures: A figure accompanying a data sufficiency problem will conform to the information given in the question, but will not necessarily conform to the additional information given in statements (1) and (2).

Lines shown as straight can be assumed to be straight and lines that appear jagged can also be assumed to be straight.

You may assume that the positions of points, angles, regions, etc., exist in the order shown and that angle measures are greater than zero.

All figures lie in a plane unless otherwise indicated.

Note: In data sufficiency problems that ask for the value of a quantity, the data given in the statements are sufficient only when it is possible to determine exactly one numerical value for the quantity.

Directions (Problem Solving): Solve the problem and indicate the best of the answer choices given.

Numbers: All numbers used are real numbers.

Figures: A figure accompanying a problem solving question is intended to provide information useful in solving the problem. Figures are drawn as accurately as possible EXCEPT when it is stated in a specific problem that its figure is not drawn to scale. Straight lines may sometimes appear jagged. All figures lie in a plane unless otherwise indicated.

1. A group of 85 people took a trip to Atlantic City. How many played both blackjack and slot machines?

   (1)   34 played blackjack.
   (2)   71 played slot machines.

   (A)   Statement (1) ALONE is sufficient, but statement (2) alone is not sufficient.
   (B)   Statement (2) ALONE is sufficient, but statement (1) alone is not sufficient.
   (C)   BOTH statements (1) and (2) TOGETHER are sufficient, but NEITHER statement ALONE is sufficient.
   (D)   EACH statement ALONE is sufficient.
   (E)   Statements (1) and (2) TOGETHER are NOT sufficient.

2. Which of the following numbers is evenly divisible by 3 and 5 but not by 4 or 9?

   (A)   16,840
   (B)   20,085
   (C)   23,094
   (D)   56,790
   (E)   79,260

3. What fraction of a reprogramming job could Angelo and Mario get done by both working on it for seven days?

    (1) Mario figures that he could finish the job in twenty days.
    (2) Angelo figures that he could finish the job in twenty-five days.

(A) Statement (1) ALONE is sufficient, but statement (2) alone is not sufficient.
(B) Statement (2) ALONE is sufficient, but statement (1) alone is not sufficient.
(C) BOTH statements (1) and (2) TOGETHER are sufficient, but NEITHER statement ALONE is sufficient.
(D) EACH statement ALONE is sufficient.
(E) Statements (1) and (2) TOGETHER are NOT sufficient.

4. Mrs. Green and her three children went to the local movie. The total cost of their admission tickets was $14. What was the cost of one child's ticket?

    (1) Mr. and Mrs. Arkwright and their five children had to pay $25.
    (2) Mr. and Mrs. Wilson and their six children had to pay $28.

(A) Statement (1) ALONE is sufficient, but statement (2) alone is not sufficient.
(B) Statement (2) ALONE is sufficient, but statement (1) alone is not sufficient.
(C) BOTH statements (1) and (2) TOGETHER are sufficient, but NEITHER statement ALONE is sufficient.
(D) EACH statement ALONE is sufficient.
(E) Statements (1) and (2) TOGETHER are NOT sufficient.

5. When 3 times a certain number k is subtracted from 14, the result is 2 more than k. Which of the following equations expresses the value of k?

(A) $3k - 14 = k + 2$
(B) $3k + 14 = 2 - k$
(C) $14 - 3k = k + 2$
(D) $14 - 3k = 2k$
(E) $(k + 3) - 14 = (k + 2)$

6. A man buys $12 worth of groceries. He presents $2.50 worth of coupons, which are deducted from the price of the groceries, and then receives a 10% senior citizen reduction on the balance. How much change will the man receive if he pays with a $20 bill?

   (A) $11.70
   (B) $11.45
   (C) $9.55
   (D) $8.55
   (E) $8.00

7. If $(x - 6)(x - m) = x^2 + rx + k$, what is the value of m?

   (1) $k = 18$
   (2) $r = -9$

   (A) Statement (1) ALONE is sufficient, but statement (2) alone is not sufficient.
   (B) Statement (2) ALONE is sufficient, but statement (1) alone is not sufficient.
   (C) BOTH statements (1) and (2) TOGETHER are sufficient, but NEITHER statement ALONE is sufficient.
   (D) EACH statement ALONE is sufficient.
   (E) Statements (1) and (2) TOGETHER are NOT sufficient.

8. If x is one of the numbers from the set {1,3,5} and y is one of the numbers from the set {2,3,6}, how many different values are there for the number $|x - y|$?

   (A) 5
   (B) 6
   (C) 7
   (D) 8
   (E) 9

9. A triangle has sides with lengths of x, y, and z. If x, y, and z are all integers, what is the difference between the maximum and minimum possible perimeters of the triangle?

   (1) $x = 9$
   (2) $y = 14$

   (A) Statement (1) ALONE is sufficient, but statement (2) alone is not sufficient.
   (B) Statement (2) ALONE is sufficient, but statement (1) alone is not sufficient.
   (C) BOTH statements (1) and (2) TOGETHER are sufficient, but NEITHER statement ALONE is sufficient.
   (D) EACH statement ALONE is sufficient.
   (E) Statements (1) and (2) TOGETHER are NOT sufficient.

10. 20% of what number is equal to $\frac{2}{3}$ of 90?

    (A)   30
    (B)   60
    (C)   120
    (D)   150
    (E)   300

11. 150 people were surveyed to determine their favorite soft drinks. The results of the survey in order from most to least popular are shown in the table below.

Brand	Number
A	55
B	43
C	x
D	y
E	12

If each brand was selected by a different number of individuals, what is the maximum possible value of x?

    (A)   40
    (B)   32
    (C)   27
    (D)   22
    (E)   18

12. The midpoint between (3,4) and (R,S) is (x_M, y_M). What is the value of y_M?

    (1) $R = 2$
    (2) $S = -2$

    (A)   Statement (1) ALONE is sufficient, but statement (2) alone is not sufficient.
    (B)   Statement (2) ALONE is sufficient, but statement (1) alone is not sufficient.
    (C)   BOTH statements (1) and (2) TOGETHER are sufficient, but NEITHER statement ALONE is sufficient.
    (D)   EACH statement ALONE is sufficient.
    (E)   Statements (1) and (2) TOGETHER are NOT sufficient.

13. If H and K are real numbers, what is the largest possible value of B?

    (1) $H = \sqrt{B-1}$
    (2) $K = \sqrt{3-B}$

    (A) Statement (1) ALONE is sufficient, but statement (2) alone is not sufficient.
    (B) Statement (2) ALONE is sufficient, but statement (1) alone is not sufficient.
    (C) BOTH statements (1) and (2) TOGETHER are sufficient, but NEITHER statement ALONE is sufficient.
    (D) EACH statement ALONE is sufficient.
    (E) Statements (1) and (2) TOGETHER are NOT sufficient.

14. If $2(y - 3) = 4 + 3y$, then $y = $?

    (A) -10
    (B) -7
    (C) 2
    (D) 7
    (E) 10

15. In a group of 20 singers and 40 dancers, 20% of the singers are under 25 years old, and 40% of the entire group are under 25 years old. What percent of the dancers are under 25 years old?

    (A) 20%
    (B) 40%
    (C) 50%
    (D) 60%
    (E) 80%

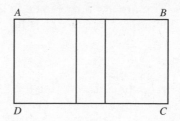

16. In rectangle *ABCD* above, the vertical lines divide the region into two squares and a center rectangle. If the area of each square is 25 and the area of the center rectangle is 15, what is the perimeter of *ABCD*?

    (A) 20
    (B) 26
    (C) 30
    (D) 36
    (E) 50

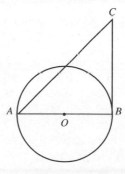

17. In the figure above, *CB* is tangent to the circle. What is the area of △*ABC*?

    (1) The circumference of the circle is 12π.
    (2) *AC* = 15, and the area of the circle is 36π.

(A) Statement (1) ALONE is sufficient, but statement (2) alone is not sufficient.
(B) Statement (2) ALONE is sufficient, but statement (1) alone is not sufficient.
(C) BOTH statements (1) and (2) TOGETHER are sufficient, but NEITHER statement ALONE is sufficient.
(D) EACH statement ALONE is sufficient.
(E) Statements (1) and (2) TOGETHER are NOT sufficient.

18. The area of a rectangle is 60 and its perimeter is 32. What is the length of its shorter side?

(A) 3
(B) 6
(C) 10
(D) 12
(E) 15

19. If $y > x$, what is the value of x?

(1) x and y are consecutive integers.
(2)   The square of the smaller minus 8 times the larger is 25.

(A)   Statement (1) ALONE is sufficient, but statement (2) alone is not sufficient.
(B)   Statement (2) ALONE is sufficient, but statement (1) alone is not sufficient.
(C)   BOTH statements (1) and (2) TOGETHER are sufficient, but NEITHER statement ALONE is sufficient.
(D)   EACH statement ALONE is sufficient.
(E)   Statements (1) and (2) TOGETHER are NOT sufficient.

20. A taxicab charges $3.00 for the first one fifth of a mile traveled and 30¢ for each additional one fifth of a mile, or part thereof. There is also a charge of 20¢ for every 30 seconds of time spent waiting in traffic but not moving. Angela took a cab from her hotel to the airport. She spent 4 minutes waiting in traffic, and the entire cab bill was $22. Which of the following could have been the distance to the airport in miles?

(A) 8.4
(B) 9.2
(C) 10.9
(D) 11.5
(E) 11.7

21. Three consecutive odd integers are written in increasing order. If the sum of the first and second integers and twice the third integer is 46, what is the second integer?

(A) 17
(B) 15
(C) 13
(D) 11
(E) 9

22. What is the slope of the line passing through (6,4) and (r,s)?

    (1)   (r,s) = (3,−1)
    (2)   The line has a y-intercept of −6.

    (A)   Statement (1) ALONE is sufficient, but statement (2) alone is not sufficient.
    (B)   Statement (2) ALONE is sufficient, but statement (1) alone is not sufficient.
    (C)   BOTH statements (1) and (2) TOGETHER are sufficient, but NEITHER statement ALONE is sufficient.
    (D)   EACH statement ALONE is sufficient.
    (E)   Statements (1) and (2) TOGETHER are NOT sufficient.

23. If $\blacklozenge x \blacklozenge = \dfrac{x + \sqrt{x}}{2}$, which of the following is an even number?

    (A) $\blacklozenge 1 \blacklozenge$
    (B) $\blacklozenge 4 \blacklozenge$
    (C) $\blacklozenge 9 \blacklozenge$
    (D) $\blacklozenge 25 \blacklozenge$
    (E) $\blacklozenge 36 \blacklozenge$

24. A jar contains five blocks, each painted entirely in one color. Hal picks a block, records the color, and then picks a second block. How many possible different pairs of colors can Hal pick if the order in which the colors are selected counts?

    (1)   The blocks are all painted different colors.
    (2)   The second block is chosen without replacing the first.

    (A)   Statement (1) ALONE is sufficient, but statement (2) alone is not sufficient.
    (B)   Statement (2) ALONE is sufficient, but statement (1) alone is not sufficient.
    (C)   BOTH statements (1) and (2) TOGETHER are sufficient, but NEITHER statement ALONE is sufficient.
    (D)   EACH statement ALONE is sufficient.
    (E)   Statements (1) and (2) TOGETHER are NOT sufficient.

25. If p is an integer, and $(x - 3)(x + p) = x^2 + x - m$, what is the value of $m - p$?

    (A)   8
    (B)   4
    (C)   0
    (D)   −4
    (E)   −8

26. Marla earns d dollars per hour plus tips working in a restaurant. On Monday she worked m hours, and on Wednesday she worked w hours. If she received t dollars in tips and gave one fifth of her tips to the busboy, in terms of d, m, w, and t, the amount she kept was

   (A) $\dfrac{d + m + w + t}{5}$

   (B) $\dfrac{d(m + w) + t}{5}$

   (C) $d(m + w) + \dfrac{t}{5}$

   (D) $d(m + w) + \dfrac{4t}{5}$

   (E) $\dfrac{4[d(m + w) + t]}{5}$

27. What is the numerical value of $6x - 8y$?

   (1) $3x - 4y + z = 45$
   (2) $3x - 4y - 2z = 36$

   (A) Statement (1) ALONE is sufficient, but statement (2) alone is not sufficient.
   (B) Statement (2) ALONE is sufficient, but statement (1) alone is not sufficient.
   (C) BOTH statements (1) and (2) TOGETHER are sufficient, but NEITHER statement ALONE is sufficient.
   (D) EACH statement ALONE is sufficient.
   (E) Statements (1) and (2) TOGETHER are NOT sufficient.

28. If $\dfrac{r}{s} = \sqrt{t}$, what is the value of s?

   (1) $\dfrac{t}{r^2} = 9$

   (2) $t = 36$ and $r = 2$

   (A) Statement (1) ALONE is sufficient, but statement (2) alone is not sufficient.
   (B) Statement (2) ALONE is sufficient, but statement (1) alone is not sufficient.
   (C) BOTH statements (1) and (2) TOGETHER are sufficient, but NEITHER statement ALONE is sufficient.
   (D) EACH statement ALONE is sufficient.
   (E) Statements (1) and (2) TOGETHER are NOT sufficient.

29. Points $(-1,-1)$, $(3,11)$, and $(1,t)$ lie on the same line. What is the value of t?

    (A) 8
    (B) 5
    (C) 2
    (D) -5
    (E) -8

30. If a and b are whole numbers and $3a = 2b$, which of the following statements must be true?

    I. a is divisible by 2
    II. b is divisible by 2
    III. b is divisible by 3

    (A) I only
    (B) II only
    (C) III only
    (D) I and II only
    (E) I and III only

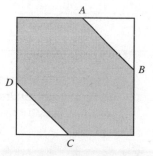

31. The figure above is a square of area 4. If the points A, B, C, D are the midpoints of the four sides, what is the perimeter of the shaded region?

    (A) $2 + \sqrt{2}$
    (B) 4
    (C) $4 + \sqrt{2}$
    (D) $4 + 2\sqrt{2}$
    (E) $4 + 4\sqrt{2}$

32. $\dfrac{n}{m}$ is defined to be $\dfrac{2n - m}{2n + m}$. What is the value of n?

    (1) $n//0 = 1$
    (2) $n//2n = 0$

(A) Statement (1) ALONE is sufficient, but statement (2) alone is not sufficient.
(B) Statement (2) ALONE is sufficient, but statement (1) alone is not sufficient.
(C) BOTH statements (1) and (2) TOGETHER are sufficient, but NEITHER statement ALONE is sufficient.
(D) EACH statement ALONE is sufficient.
(E) Statements (1) and (2) TOGETHER are NOT sufficient.

33. If $\dfrac{x}{y} + \dfrac{2}{z} = \dfrac{1}{2}$, and $\dfrac{y}{x} + z = 0$, what is the value of z?

(A) 3
(B) 2
(C) $\dfrac{3}{2}$
(D) $\dfrac{2}{3}$
(E) It cannot be determined from the information given.

34. A rectangle is inscribed in a circle of radius 2. The diagonals of the rectangle are diameters of the circle that cross at an angle of $60°$. What is the area of the rectangle?

(A) $4\sqrt{3}$
(B) $2 + 2\sqrt{3}$
(C) $2 + 2\sqrt{2}$
(D) 4
(E) $2\sqrt{3}$

35. If x, y, and r are all nonzero numbers, what is the value of $r = \dfrac{x - y}{2x + y}$?

    (1) $|x| = |y|$
    (2) $x = -3$

(A) Statement (1) ALONE is sufficient, but statement (2) alone is not sufficient.
(B) Statement (2) ALONE is sufficient, but statement (1) alone is not sufficient.
(C) BOTH statements (1) and (2) TOGETHER are sufficient, but NEITHER statement ALONE is sufficient.
(D) EACH statement ALONE is sufficient.
(E) Statements (1) and (2) TOGETHER are NOT sufficient.

36. If x and y are positive integers, and $y^2 = x^2 + 7$, then $y =$

(A) 4
(B) 3
(C) 2
(D) 1
(E) It cannot be determined from the information given.

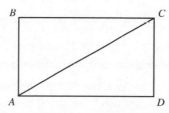

37. In a certain computer game illustrated above, a red square moves around rectangle *ABCD* in a counterclockwise direction, changing position once every second. At the same time, a green dot moves around △*ABC* in a clockwise direction, changing position once every second. The values (R,G) represent the position of the red square and the green dot, respectively. If at time zero, their position is (A,A), which pair describes their position at time 415 seconds?

(A) (A,A)
(B) (A,B)
(C) (B,C)
(D) (C,B)
(E) (B,B)

SECTION 4

VERBAL

41 questions

Time—75 Minutes

Directions (Reading Comprehension): The questions in this group are based on the content of a passage. After reading the passage, choose the best answer to each question. Answer all questions following the passage on the basis of what is *stated* or *implied* in the passage.

Directions (Critical Reasoning): For this question, select the best of the answer choices given.

Directions (Sentence Correction): The following questions present a sentence, part of which or all of which is underlined. Beneath the sentence you will find five ways of phrasing the underlined part. The first of these repeats the original; the other four are different. If you think the original is best, choose the first answer; otherwise choose one of the others.

---

1. The high level of violence in children's television programming today has often been cited as an explanation for the increased violence in our society as a whole. And, in fact, some recent studies show that the level of TV violence has increased considerably over the past twenty years. However, other studies indicate that the level, while high, is only slightly greater than it was twenty years ago.

    All of the following, if true, would be useful in explaining the above EXCEPT

    (A) Numerous studies of TV violence have been conducted in the past twenty years, and their results were not always in agreement.
    (B) All of those involved in conducting the studies cited had the same perception of what constitutes "violence" in TV programming.
    (C) Despite their best efforts at impartiality, those who conduct studies of TV violence sometimes allow their preconceived ideas to affect their findings.
    (D) Many factors other than TV violence have a significant effect on the level of violence in society.
    (E) The methodology generally used in studies of TV violence has changed considerably over the past twenty years.

2. Abraham Lincoln was unquestionably a profound thinker as well as a great president, but it's unfortunately true that the same can't be <u>said for any of the more recent holders</u> of that office.

   (A)   said for any of the more recent holders
   (B)   said of none of the more recent holders
   (C)   said for none of those who are more recent holders
   (D)   said of anyone who are recent holders
   (E)   said for one of the most recent holders

3. Cordless phones send radio waves through the air, so when you have more than one in your home, you have to <u>make sure that it doesn't interfere with each other.</u>

   (A)   make sure that it doesn't interfere with each other.
   (B)   be sure that each doesn't interfere with the other one.
   (C)   ensure against their interfering with each other.
   (D)   make sure that they don't interfere with each other.
   (E)   ensure that it don't interfere with the other one.

Questions 4–7 are based on the following passage.

(The article from which this passage is excerpted was written in 1986.)

Line   Methods for typing blood were developed around the turn of the century, about the same time that fingerprints were first used for identification. Only in the last ten years, however, have scientists begun to believe that genetic markers in blood and other body fluids may someday prove as useful in crime detection as
(5)   fingerprints.
        The standard ABO blood typing has long been used as a form of negative identification. Added sophistication came with the discovery of additional subgroups of genetic markers in blood and with the discovery that genetic markers are present not only in blood but in other body fluids, such as
(10)   perspiration and saliva.
        These discoveries were of little use in crime detection, however, because of the circumstances in which police scientists must work. Rather than a plentiful sample of blood freshly drawn from a patient, the crime laboratory is likely to receive only a tiny fleck of dried blood of unknown age from an
(15)   unknown "donor" on a shirt or a scrap of rag that has spent hours or days exposed to air, high temperature, and other contaminants.
        British scientists found a method for identifying genetic markers more precisely in small samples. In this process, called electrophoresis, a sample is placed on a tray that contains a gel through which an electrical current is then
(20)   passed. A trained analyst reads the resulting patterns in the gel to determine the presence of various chemical markers.
        Electrophoresis made it possible to identify several thousand subgroups of blood types rather than the twelve known before. However, the equipment and special training required were expensive. In addition, the process could lead
(25)   to the destruction of evidence. For example, repeated tests of a blood-flecked shirt—one for each marker—led to increasing deterioration of the evidence and the cost of a week or more of laboratory time.

It remained for another British researcher, Brian Wrexall, to demonstrate that simultaneous analyses, using inexpensive equipment, could test for ten (30) different genetic markers within a 24-hour period. This development made the study of blood and fluid samples an even more valuable tool for crime detection.

4. It can be inferred from the passage that electrophoresis resembles fingerprinting in that both

(A) provide a form of negative identification in crime detection.
(B) were first developed by British scientists.
(C) may be used to help identify those who were present at the time of a crime.
(D) were developed by scientists at around the same time.
(E) must be employed almost immediately after a crime to be effective.

5. The passage implies that electrophoresis may help scientists determine

(A) whether or not a sample of blood could have come from a particular person.
(B) the age and condition of a dried specimen of blood or other body fluid.
(C) when and where a crime was probably committed.
(D) the means by which the victim of a violent crime was probably attacked.
(E) the age, gender, and ethnic background of an unknown criminal suspect.

6. According to the passage, Wrexall's refinement of electrophoresis led to

(A) more accurate test results.
(B) easier availability of fluid samples.
(C) wider applicability of the tests.
(D) increased costs of testing.
(E) more rapid testing.

7. According to the passage, all of the following may reduce the usefulness of a fluid sample for crime detection EXCEPT

(A) the passage of time.
(B) discoloration or staining.
(C) exposure to heat.
(D) the small size of the sample.
(E) exposure to contaminants.

8. The United States, which was founded mainly by people who had
    emigrated from northern Europe, had an essentially open-door
    immigration policy for the first 100 years of its existence. But
    starting in the 1880s and continuing through the 1920s, Congress
    passed a series of restrictive laws that led, ultimately, to a quota
    system for immigration based on the number of individuals of
    each national origin reported in the 1890 census.

    All of the following, if true, would help account for the above
    EXCEPT

    (A)   The American economy was weak in the 1880s, and many
          Americans were afraid that new immigrants would further
          weaken it.
    (B)   Political upheavals in Europe in the late 19th century
          encouraged many left-wing radicals to emigrate to America.
    (C)   Most of those emigrating to America in the 1880s were
          central and eastern Europeans, against whom many Ameri-
          cans were prejudiced.
    (D)   Throughout American history, most Americans have been
          sympathetic toward those living under repressive regimes in
          Europe and seeking refuge abroad.
    (E)   Most of the U.S. population in the 1880s were members of
          Protestant churches, while many of the new immigrants were
          Catholics and Jews.

9. Prior to the development of the "horseless carriage" around the
    start of the twentieth century, horses in our cities left tons of
    unsightly, messy, and malodorous manure on our streets. Based
    on this fact alone, there is no question that by any measure, the
    automobile has been a boon to humankind.

    Which of the following, if true, most seriously weakens the
    argument above?

    (A)   Air pollution caused by automobile exhaust is less deleteri-
          ous to health than that caused by horse manure.
    (B)   In the nineteenth century, almost as many people were killed
          each year by horse-drawn conveyances as are killed today by
          automobiles.
    (C)   In many cities, automobile traffic has been banned from large
          downtown areas to provide room for pedestrian malls.
    (D)   Compared to horse-drawn carriages, automobiles are less
          efficient in terms of the energy required to operate them.
    (E)   Automobiles enable people to travel greater distances in less
          time than did horse-drawn conveyances.

10. Before the invention of modern clocks, the day was not divided into twenty-four hours but <u>rather into various number</u> of equal, and sometimes unequal, time spans.

 (A) rather into various number
 (B) instead into some various numbers
 (C) rather into various numbers
 (D) rather into a various number
 (E) into various number

11. *Charlotte's Web* is now considered one of the classics of children's literature, but it <u>weren't very well received</u> when it was first published.

 (A) weren't very well received
 (B) wasn't very well received
 (C) weren't so well liked
 (D) hadn't been so well received
 (E) wasn't received as well

12. A recent study showed that parents whose children under the age of ten go to bed by nine o'clock in the evening have sexual relations an average of three times a week, while those whose children under ten do not go to bed until ten o'clock do so only once a week on average. Clearly, then, there is a cause-and-effect relationship between childrens' bedtimes and their parents' level of sexual activity.

 Knowledge of which of the following would be LEAST useful in evaluating the claim made in the passage above?

 (A) The number of families that participated in the study
 (B) Whether the study differentiated between parents in their twenties, thirties, and forties
 (C) The parents' level of sexual activity prior to the birth of their children
 (D) Whether any of the parents in the study had additional children over ten years of age
 (E) Whether the study differentiated between those parents who had to get up early in the morning and those who could sleep late

13. He bought several books a week, which piled up to such an extent that he <u>realized he would never be able to read it.</u>

(A) realized he would never be able to read it.

(B) had to admit his inability to read it.

(C) realized he would never be able to read them.

(D) came to realize that he would not ever be able to read them.

(E) realized he was unable to read the books.

Questions 14–16 refer to the following passage.

Line   A story from an economist's life can sketch the poetics of economics at work. Shortly after the Second World War, the agricultural economist Theodore Schultz, later to win a Nobel prize for the work, spent a term based at Auburn University in Alabama, interviewing farmers in the neighborhood. One day he
(5)   interviewed an old and poor farm couple and was struck by how contented they seemed. Why are you so contented, he asked, though very poor? They answered: You're wrong, Professor. We're not poor. We've used up our farm to educate four children through college, remaking fertile land and well-stocked pens into knowledge of law and Latin. We are rich.
(10)   The parents had told Schultz that the *physical* capital, which economists think they understand, is in some sense just like the *human* capital of education. The children now owned it, and so the parents did, too. Once it had been rail fences and hog pens and mules. Now it was in the children's brains, this human capital. The farm couple *was* rich.
(15)   The average economist was willing to accept the discovery of human capital as soon as he understood it, which is in fact how many scientific and scholarly discoveries are received. It was an argument in a metaphor (or if you like: an analogy, a simile, a model). A hog pen, Schultz would say to another economist, is "just like" Latin 101.
(20)   The other economist would have to admit that there was something to it. Both the hog pen and the Latin instruction are paid for by saving. Both are valuable assets for earning income, understanding "income" to mean, as economists put it, "a stream of satisfaction." Year after year the hog pen and the Latin cause satisfaction to stream out like water from a dam. Both last a long
(25)   time but finally wear out when the pen falls down and the Latin-learned brain dies.
        And the one piece of "capital" can be made into the other. An educated farmer, because of his degree in agriculture from Auburn, can get a bank loan to build a hog pen; when his children grow up he can sell off the part of the farm
(30)   with the hog pen to pay for another term for Junior and Sis up at Auburn, too.

14. According to the passage, the farm couple interviewed by Schultz were "rich" in the sense that

   (A) the farmer had earned a degree in agriculture from Auburn University.
   (B) they were able to obtain ready credit as needed from the local bank.
   (C) their children's minds had been well-stocked with knowledge.
   (D) their children were supporting them in a comfortable style of life.
   (E) their fields and animal pens were fertile and highly productive.

15. The author most probably places the words "just like" within quotation marks (line 19) primarily to suggest that the words

   (A) are quoted from a scholarly paper by Schultz.
   (B) reflect Schultz's unique and idiosyncratic way of speaking.
   (C) are quoted from a comment by the farm couple interviewed by Schultz.
   (D) are technical jargon likely to be used only by a professional economist.
   (E) should be understood figuratively rather than literally.

16. Which of the following offers the best additional illustration of the point made in the last paragraph of the passage?

   (A) Sis can deposit money that she has saved in the same bank that gave her father a loan.
   (B) A successful farmer can sell his farm and use the proceeds to support himself in retirement.
   (C) Like a hog pen, a college building lasts a long time, producing a stream of satisfaction as long as it exists.
   (D) Junior can use his knowledge of law to earn money with which to buy a farm of his own.
   (E) A college education produces a stream of personal satisfaction regardless of its monetary value.

17. A thesaurus can be a useful tool for writers, providing he knows how to use it correctly.

   (A) writers, providing he knows how to use it
   (B) a writer, providing they know how to use them
   (C) a writer, provided they know how to use it
   (D) writers, providing they know how to use it
   (E) a writer, provided he knows how to use such a book

18. Under current U.S. tax laws, while those with higher incomes theoretically pay a higher percentage of their earnings to the federal government, loopholes in the law often make it possible for the wealthy to pay *less* taxes than those with lower incomes. If the government created a flat tax, under which every citizen's income was taxed at the same rate and eliminated the loopholes, everyone would pay his fair share and the government would receive ample revenues.

If the statements above are true, which of the following must be true?

(A)   Under a flat tax, all of the wealthy would pay higher taxes than they do at present.

(B)   Under a flat tax, every wage earner would pay the same amount in taxes.

(C)   Under a flat tax, the wealthy would not be able to use loopholes to avoid paying their share of taxes.

(D)   Under a flat tax, the wealthy would bear a larger share of the government's expenses than the middle class.

(E)   Under a flat tax, lower-income wage earners would pay less in income taxes than they do now.

19. Frank Lloyd Wright was the preeminent American architect of the 20th century, and there have been many less talented people who, both in the past and today, have imitated his style.

(A)   there have been many less talented people who, both in the past and today, have

(B)   many less talented people, both in the past and today, have

(C)   a great number of less talented people of today, as well as in the past, have

(D)   there have been many less talented people, both today and in the past, who

(E)   many of the less talented people, both in the past and today, have

20. Smokers used to be able to light up wherever they wanted to, but with the increased restrictions on smoking in public places it's becoming more difficult for those who do smoke to find places where smoking is allowed.

(A)   those who do smoke to find places where smoking

(B)   them to find places where it

(C)   those of us who like to smoke to find places where it

(D)   many of those who do smoke to find places where smoking

(E)   smokers to find places in which to smoke

21. At the end of the nineteenth century, most Americans lived in houses in rural areas, and dogs were by far the most popular type of pet. Today, however, the majority of Americans live in urban apartments, and more people keep cats than any other animal.

Which of the following conclusions is most strongly supported by the statements above?

(A) City life is more congenial than country life for people and their pets.

(B) Cats are more appropriate as pets for apartment dwellers than are dogs.

(C) More people prefer having cats as pets rather than dogs today than they did in the past.

(D) Dogs who live in city apartments are often unhealthy and unhappy.

(E) Dogs have decreased in popularity due to city ordinances restricting the maintenance of pets in apartments.

22. There are more lawyers per capita in the United States than in any other country in the world. The best possible explanation of this is that our legal system is more complicated than those of many other countries, and we are accordingly in greater need of professional help in dealing with it.

All of the following, if true, weaken the argument above EXCEPT

(A) Great Britain has a much simpler legal system but almost as many lawyers per capita as the U.S.

(B) The law is a very lucrative profession and is accordingly attractive to many people.

(C) France has a more complicated legal system but has many fewer lawyers per capita than the U.S.

(D) The number of lawyers in the United States, both in absolute terms and as a percentage of the population, has grown steadily over the past twenty years.

(E) Americans are by nature litigious, so that more lawsuits are brought against individuals in the U.S. than in any other nation.

Questions 23–25 refer to the following passage.

Line   When the framers of the Constitution set to work devising the structure of the
United States government, it was natural for them to consider the forms already
existing in the several states. The three most basic patterns may be referred to
as the Virginia, Pennsylvania, and Massachusetts models.

(5)   The Virginia model borrowed its central principal, legislative supremacy,
from the thinking of the English philosopher John Locke. Locke had favored
making the legislature the dominant focus of government power, and he stressed
the importance of preventing a monarch, governor, or other executive from
usurping that power. In line with Locke's doctrine, Virginia's constitution

(10)   provided that the governor be chosen by the assembly rather than by the
people directly, as were the members of a special governor's council. The
approval of this council was necessary for any action by the governor.

Also derived from Locke was Virginia's bicameral legislature, in which
both chambers must concur to pass a bill. Thus dividing the legislative power

(15)   was supposed to prevent its domination by any single faction—the so-called
"division of powers," which later became an important feature of the national
constitution.

Pennsylvania's constitution was probably the most democratic of any in
the former colonies. Pennsylvania extended the right to vote to most adult

(20)   males. (With the exception of Vermont, the other states allowed only property
owners to vote; New Jersey alone extended the privilege to women.)

Pennsylvanians elected the members of a single-house legislature, as well
as an executive council. These bodies jointly selected the council president,
who served as the state's chief executive officer; there was no governor. Neither

(25)   legislators nor council members could remain in office more than four years out
of seven.

The most conservative of the models was found in Massachusetts. The
legislature here included two chambers. In the house of representatives, the
number of legislators for a given district was based on population; in the

(30)   "aristocratic" senate, representation was based on taxable wealth. The governor
could veto legislature, he appointed most state officials, and he was elected
independently on the legislature.

23. The state governments described in the passage varied in all of
the following respects EXCEPT

(A)   the number of chambers in the legislature.
(B)   the existence of the office of governor.
(C)   restrictions on tenure in state offices.
(D)   whether the members of the legislature were chosen directly
by the people.
(E)   restrictions on the eligibility of citizens to vote.

24. According to the passage, the principal purpose of the "division of powers" in the Virginia model was to

   (A) allow citizens of every social class to participate fully in government.
   (B) prevent any one group from controlling the legislative power.
   (C) ensure the independence of the executive from legislative manipulation.
   (D) discourage the concentration of power in the hands of the governor.
   (E) disperse elective offices among as many propertied citizens as possible.

25. It can be inferred from the passage that those who favored a democratic system of government would most strongly support

   (A) apportioning seats in the legislature on the basis of taxable wealth.
   (B) concentration of power in the hands of the executive.
   (C) limitation on the number of terms in office served by legislators.
   (D) establishment of a bicameral legislature.
   (E) granting the power to veto legislation to a popularly elected executive.

26. In the 1964 presidential campaign, Lyndon Johnson, campaigning on a promise not to escalate the then-small war in Vietnam, ran against Barry Goldwater, who was widely portrayed as a war hawk, and defeated him soundly. Despite his promises, as president, Johnson did escalate the war, and by 1968 public protests over this action forced him to decide against running for president again.

   All of the following are assumptions underlying the conclusion of the passage above EXCEPT

   (A) Johnson would probably have run for president in 1968 if there had been no protests against his conduct of the war.
   (B) The war in Vietnam was a major campaign issue in both the 1964 and 1968 elections.
   (C) If the war in Vietnam had been won by 1968, Johnson would probably have run for president again.
   (D) The portrayal of Goldwater as a war hawk was an accurate one.
   (E) Johnson was either unable or unwilling to keep his campaign promise concerning the war in Vietnam.

27. Unquantifiable risk due to currency fluctuations, political upheavals, and recurrent economic crises <u>have led many investors to avoid</u> businesses, even promising ones, that are based in the developing nations.

 (A) have led many investors to avoid
 (B) has led many investors to avoid
 (C) has been leading many investors toward avoidance of
 (D) have led many investors in avoiding
 (E) leads many investors into avoidance of

28. Although the framers of the United States Constitution provided for the direct election of members of the House of Representatives, U.S. senators were originally elected by state legislatures, and to this day the president is elected not directly by the people but by the Electoral College. It appears that the framers believed that democracy is a good thing, but that you can have too much of a good thing.

 If the statements above are true, all of the following must be true EXCEPT

 (A) The framers did not believe in direct election of the president by the people.
 (B) The framers did not believe in direct election of the members of the Senate by the people.
 (C) Today, U.S. senators are no longer elected by state legislatures.
 (D) The framers believed in direct election of members of the House of Representatives by the people.
 (E) The framers believed that direct election of representatives by the people would represent an excess of democracy.

29. Recognizing the need for drastic improvements in the manufacturing process, <u>quality circles were instituted by the workers at the plant</u>.

 (A) quality circles were instituted by the workers at the plant.
 (B) the workers instituted at the plant quality circles.
 (C) quality circles at the plant were instituted by the workers.
 (D) the workers at the plant instituted quality circles.
 (E) at the plant were instituted quality circles by the workers.

30. In the past, business people were generally content to use the U.S. Postal Service (USPS) to deliver written communications. However, due to the institution of overnight delivery by private carriers, and the subsequent development of facsimile machines and electronic mail, most business people now feel their communications must be delivered as quickly as possible, if not instantly, neatly illustrating the economic adage that "Supply creates demand."

All of the following are valid objections to the conclusion drawn above EXCEPT

(A) Many changes in the business environment have led business people to feel they need information more quickly than in the past.

(B) A decline in the quality of service provided by the USPS has led business people to seek other means of communication.

(C) In many fields of business, there has always been a real need to have communications delivered instantly.

(D) Most businesses do not actually require immediate delivery of written communications to operate efficiently.

(E) The vast majority of business communications today are delivered by the USPS and other traditional, low-speed carriers.

31. Although, in the past, President Abraham Lincoln was generally portrayed as a country bumpkin who was able to steer the United States through the harrowing Civil War only because of his native intelligence, today he is seen as an extremely accomplished politician who was able to skillfully conduct the war against the rebelling Southern states while holding together numerous quarrelsome factions in the North.

All of the following, if true, would help account for the facts described above EXCEPT

(A) Historians have only recently uncovered writings by Lincoln that document his high level of political sophistication.

(B) It was previously believed that the northern states were generally united in their efforts to defeat the South.

(C) Unlike most politicians of his day (or our own), Lincoln had almost no formal education.

(D) Most historians in the past were academicians who tended to be disdainful of those with little education.

(E) Lincoln often used unsophisticated language and spoke with a strong Midwestern accent.

32. Gates was one of the first entrepreneurs to realize that the greatest fortunes of the computer age would be made not in the production of hardware <u>but the development of software.</u>

    (A)   but the development of software
    (B)   so much as in software
    (C)   but in developing software
    (D)   as rather in the development of software
    (E)   but in the development of software

Questions 33–36 refer to the following passage.

Line   The ability of certain plants and animals to emit light has long been a source of fascination to humans, and the manifestations of bioluminescence are as diverse as they are elegant. Yet virtually all of the known or proposed ways in which bioluminescence functions may be classed under three major rubrics: assisting
(5)   predation, helping escape from predators, and communicating.

    Many examples of the first two uses can be observed in the ocean's midwaters, a zone that extends from about 100 meters deep to a few kilometers below the surface. Almost all of the animals that inhabit the murky depths where sunlight barely penetrates are capable of producing light in one way or another.
(10)   Certain animals, when feeding, are attracted to a spot of light as a possible food source. Hence, other animals use their own luminescence to attract them. Just in front of the angler fish's mouth is a dangling luminescent ball suspended from a structure attached to its head. What unwitting marine creatures see as food is really a bait to lure them into the angler fish's gaping maw.

(15)   The uses of luminescence to elude prey are just as sophisticated and various. Some creatures take advantage of the scant sunlight in their realm by using bioluminescence as a form of camouflage. The glow generated by photophores, light producing organs, on the undersides of some fishes and squids acts to hide them through a phenomenon known as countershading: the
(20)   weak downward lighting created by the photophores effectively erases the animals' shadows when viewed from below against the (relatively) lighted waters above.

    Bioluminescence clearly functions to help certain species ensure their survival. Yet, when we look at the larger evolutionary picture, bioluminescence
(25)   as such is generally considered a "nonessential" characteristic. After all, closely related species and even strains of the same species may have both luminous and nonluminous members, and the nonluminous ones appear just as viable and vigorous as their glowing counterparts. For instance, while many of the small marine organisms known as dinoflagellates are luminous, many are not.

(30)   Yet, on closer inspection, we find that the nonluminous dinoflagellates may benefit from the diversionary flashing tactics of the luminous ones. When the sea is disturbed and light flashes create phosphorescence, the species which flash may provide enough light to serve the entire population. Thus, selection pressure for the development or maintenance of luminescence in
(35)   additional species is not great if light generated by a part of the population serves the entire community.

33. The angler fish's use of bioluminescence in predation is most nearly analogous to

    (A) a deer hunter's use of a flashlight to find his way in a dark and overgrown forest.
    (B) an exterminator's use of insecticide to poison the insects that have infested a home.
    (C) a duck hunter's use of a reed-shielded blind as a hiding place from which to shoot at ducks.
    (D) a trout fisherman's use of a lure designed to resemble an insect that trout love to eat.
    (E) a police detective's use of a bright lamp to blind and so intimidate a suspect during questioning.

34. Each of the following statements about the use of bioluminescence in countershading is true EXCEPT

    (A) The light given off by photophores underneath certain fish and squid makes the animals appear to blend in with the sunlit waters above them.
    (B) Bioluminescence allows the parts of an animal normally in shadow to appear lighter.
    (C) Countershading is one of several ways in which bioluminescence is used to avoid predation.
    (D) Countershading is used most effectively in regions of relatively weak sunlight.
    (E) Bioluminescent animals use countershading as a way to elude predators that lurk in the sunlit waters above them.

35. The author mentions the behavior of bioluminescent and nonluminous dionoflagellates (lines 30–33) primarily in order to illustrate

    (A) why bioluminescence is generally considered an unnecessary function in dinoflagellates.
    (B) why the ocean waters sometimes sparkle when there is a physical disturbance.
    (C) one of the functions of bioluminescence in the ocean's midwaters.
    (D) why more species have not evolved with bioluminescence.
    (E) how nonluminous animals may benefit from proximity to luminous ones.

36. The passage implies that, if bioluminescence were NOT a nonessential characteristic, which of the following would be true?

   (A) Luminous species would be seen to thrive more successfully than closely related nonluminous ones.
   (B) Nonluminous species would enjoy a reproductive advantage by comparison to luminous ones.
   (C) Nonluminous species would benefit from the light-producing capabilities of luminous ones.
   (D) Luminous species would gradually die out and be replaced by closely related nonluminous ones.
   (E) Luminous and nonluminous species would not be observed living in close proximity to one another.

37. Compared to the salaries of lower-level employees, the compensation of chief executive officers in American corporations is proportionately much higher than that of their counterparts in other countries. As a result, there is considerably more resentment toward CEOs in American companies than exists in other nations.

   All of the following are assumptions underlying the conclusion of the passage above EXCEPT

   (A) The proportionate difference between the compensation of American and foreign CEOs is substantial.
   (B) Compensation is among the most important work-related issues among American employees.
   (C) Differences in compensation are a major cause of resentment among American employees.
   (D) Work-related issues other than compensation are of equal importance to employees outside America.
   (E) In general, American workers are no more likely to be resentful about their jobs than their foreign counterparts.

38. Owners of professional baseball teams who are concerned about sagging attendance figures have one easy option for improving their sport's popularity. If they change the rules to permit players to use the new aluminum bats in place of the traditional wooden ones, more home runs will be hit and games will be higher scoring, attracting millions of new fans to the stadiums.

The conclusion of the argument above cannot be true unless which of the following is true?

(A) Aluminum bats are no more expensive to purchase than wooden bats.
(B) Professional baseball teams derive most of their revenues from ticket purchases.
(C) Every professsional baseball team is suffering from poor attendance.
(D) Baseball fans tend to be traditional in their tastes and opposed to changes in the game's rules.
(E) More fans would be attracted to higher scoring baseball games.

39. By the time a commercial pilot steps aboard his first jet airliner, <u>he has flown</u> over 300 hours' worth of training flights and experienced countless simulated emergencies.

(A) he has flown
(B) he flies
(C) his flying includes
(D) he will fly
(E) he had flown

40. Under current regulations, licensed television broadcasters <u>are under requirement to provide</u> a certain numbers of hours of community service programming each week.

(A) are under requirement to provide
(B) have the requirement of providing
(C) must be required to provide
(D) are required to provide
(E) are to provide, as required,

41. Which of the following best completes the passage below?

Pablo Picasso is generally regarded as the quintessential modern artist, the genius who instigated the greatest revolutions in painting of the twentieth century. Yet undoubtedly the most significant revolution in modern art was the invention in the 1930s of the non-representational, purely abstract painting. And in all of Picasso's long and varied career, . . .

(A) he employed an amazing range of styles and forms.
(B) he never painted a single abstract painting.
(C) new artistic techniques were continually developed.
(D) no single painting may be chosen as his greatest work.
(E) the quest for abstraction was a constant theme.

Answer Key

SECTIONS 1 AND 2—ANALYTICAL WRITING

On the real GMAT CAT, your essays will be graded on a scale of 0 (lowest) to 6 (highest) by the "holistic" method—that is, a single score will be assigned to each essay based on the overall impression it makes on the reader. See chapter 9 for more information on the holistic scoring system and how to evaluate your own writing in the light of the GMAT CAT scoring criteria.

<table>
<tr><td colspan="4" align="center">Section 3
Quantitative</td><td colspan="4" align="center">Section 4
Verbal</td></tr>
<tr><td>1. E</td><td>11. C</td><td>21. D</td><td>31. D</td><td>1. B</td><td>12. D</td><td>23. D</td><td>34. E</td></tr>
<tr><td>2. B</td><td>12. B</td><td>22. D</td><td>32. E</td><td>2. A</td><td>13. C</td><td>24. B</td><td>35. E</td></tr>
<tr><td>3. C</td><td>13. B</td><td>23. C</td><td>33. B</td><td>3. D</td><td>14. C</td><td>25. C</td><td>36. A</td></tr>
<tr><td>4. A</td><td>14. A</td><td>24. C</td><td>34. A</td><td>4. C</td><td>15. E</td><td>26. D</td><td>37. D</td></tr>
<tr><td>5. C</td><td>15. C</td><td>25. A</td><td>35. A</td><td>5. A</td><td>16. D</td><td>27. B</td><td>38. E</td></tr>
<tr><td>6. B</td><td>16. D</td><td>26. D</td><td>36. A</td><td>6. E</td><td>17. D</td><td>28. E</td><td>39. A</td></tr>
<tr><td>7. D</td><td>17. B</td><td>27. C</td><td>37. E</td><td>7. B</td><td>18. C</td><td>29. D</td><td>40. D</td></tr>
<tr><td>8. A</td><td>18. B</td><td>28. B</td><td></td><td>8. D</td><td>19. B</td><td>30. D</td><td>41. B</td></tr>
<tr><td>9. C</td><td>19. E</td><td>29. B</td><td></td><td>9. D</td><td>20. B</td><td>31. B</td><td></td></tr>
<tr><td>10. E</td><td>20. E</td><td>30. E</td><td></td><td>10. C</td><td>21. C</td><td>32. E</td><td></td></tr>
<tr><td></td><td></td><td></td><td></td><td>11. B</td><td>22. D</td><td>33. D</td><td></td></tr>
</table>

Scoring Guide

COMPUTING YOUR QUANTITATIVE SCALED SCORE

Step 1. Count the number of correct answers you chose for the questions in Section 3. Write the total here: _____

Step 2. Count the number of incorrect answers you chose for the questions in Section 3. (Do not count questions you did not answer.) Write the total here: _____

Step 3. Divide the total from Step 2 by 4. (The result may include a fraction.) Write the result here: _____

Step 4. Subtract the result from Step 3 from the total in Step 1. Write the result here: _____

Step 5. Round off the result from Step 4 to the nearest whole number. Round a number ending in $\frac{1}{2}$ *down*; for example, $\frac{1}{2}$ 28 rounds to 28. Write the result here: _____ This is your Quantitative Raw Score.

Step 6. Look up your Quantitative Raw Score on the Score Conversion Table (page XXX). Find the corresponding Quantitative Scaled Score and write it here: _____

COMPUTING YOUR VERBAL SCALED SCORE

Step 1. Count the number of correct answers you chose for the questions in Section 4. Write the total here: _____

Step 2. Count the number of incorrect answers you chose for the questions in Section 4. (Do not count questions you did not answer.) Write the total here: _____

Step 3. Divide the total from Step 2 by 4. (The result may include a fraction.) Write the result here: _____

Step 4. Subtract the result from Step 3 from the total in Step 1. Write the result here: _____

Step 5. Round off the result from Step 4 to the nearest whole number. Round a number ending in $\frac{1}{2}$ *down*; for example, $\frac{1}{2}$ 28 rounds to 28. Write the result here: _____ This is your Verbal Raw Score.

Step 6. Look up your Verbal Raw Score on the Score Conversion Table (page 340). Find the corresponding Verbal Scaled Score and write it here: _____

Score Conversion Table

Insider's GMAT CAT Sample Test

Raw Score	Verbal Scaled Score	Quantitative Scaled Score
41	50	
40	50	
39	49	
38	48	
37	47	50
36	46	49
35	45	48
34	44	47
33	43	46
32	42	45
31	41	44
30	40	43
29	40	42
28	39	41
27	38	40
26	37	40
25	36	39
24	36	38
23	35	37
22	34	36
21	33	35
20	32	34
19	31	34
18	30	33
17	30	32
16	29	31
15	28	30
14	28	30
13	27	29
12	26	28
11	25	27
10	24	26
9	23	25
8	22	24
7	21	23
6	20	22
5	20	21
4	18	20
3	16	17
2	14	14
1	12	12
0 or less	10	10

Computing Your Total Scaled Score

Add your Quantitative Raw Score and your Verbal Raw Score from Step 5. The result is your Total Raw Score. Find this number on the Total Score Conversion Table to determine the corresponding Total Scaled Score.

**Total Score Conversion Table
Insider's GMAT CAT Sample Test**

Total Raw Score	Total Scaled Score	Total Raw Score	Total Scaled Score
78	800	64	690
77	780	63	680
76	770	62	680
75	760	61	670
74	750	60	660
73	750	59	660
72	740	58	650
71	730	57	650
70	730	56	640
69	720	55	640
68	710	54	630
67	710	53	630
66	700	52	620
65	690	51	620
50	610	24	460
49	600	23	460
48	600	22	450
47	590	21	450
46	590	20	440
45	580	19	440
44	580	18	430
43	570	17	430
42	570	16	420
41	560	15	410
40	560	14	400
39	550	13	390
38	550	12	390
37	540	11	380
36	540	10	370

Total Raw Score	Total Scaled Score	Total Raw Score	Total Scaled Score
35	530	9	360
34	520	8	350
33	510	7	340
32	500	6	330
31	500	5	310
30	490	4	300
29	490	3	280
28	480	2	250
27	480	1	220
26	470	0	200
25	47		

Explanatory Answers

SECTION 3—QUANTITATIVE

1. **The correct answer is (E).** Knowing the number who played each game separately does not tell you how many may have played both. Hence, statements (1) or (2) alone are not sufficient, so the answer is either choice (C) or choice (E). If everyone played at least one of the two games, statement (1) and statement (2) together could tell you the number who played both. But it is possible that some people did not play either game. Hence, the best answer is choice (E).

2. **The correct answer is (B).** The easiest thing to look for is divisibility by 5. Does the number end in 5 or 0? By inspection, we eliminate 23,094, which ends in 4. We want the number not to be divisible by 4, which means its last two digits must not form a number divisible by 4. That knocks out 16,840 and 79,260. This leaves 20,085 and 56,790. The digits of 20,085 add up to 15, while those of 56,790 total 27. Both are divisible by 3, but 56,790 is also divisible by 9. Therefore, only choice (B), 20,085, meets all the conditions.

3. **The correct answer is (C).** Knowing only information about one worker cannot tell you how much they can get done working together. Hence, statement (1) or statement (2) alone is not sufficient. Thus, the only possibilities are choice (C) and choice (E). Using both statement (1) and statement (2), we see that in 7 days, Mario would do $\frac{7}{20}$ of the entire task. In the same week, Angelo would do $\frac{7}{25}$ of the entire task. Therefore, together they do $\frac{7}{20} + \frac{7}{25}$. Find the LCD, which is 100. Then, $\frac{7}{25} + \frac{7}{20} = \frac{28}{100} + \frac{35}{100} + \frac{63}{100} = 0.63$. The best answer is choice (C).

4. **The correct answer is (A).** Using statement (1) alone and expressing all amounts in dollars, let x = cost of an adult ticket, and let y = cost of a child's ticket.

   For the Greens: $x + 3y = 14$.

   For the Arkwrights: $2x + 5y = 25$.

   Solve the first equation for x, because that is the simplest unknown to isolate: $x = 14 - 3y$. Substitute this into the second equation: $2(14 - 3y) + 5y = 25$.

   This gives us one equation in one unknown that we can solve:

   $$28 - 6y + 5y = 25$$
   $$-y = -3; y = 3$$

   That is, the cost of a child's ticket was $3.00. Thus, statement (1) alone is sufficient, and the answer is either choice (A) or choice (D). Using the same unknowns, statement (2) tells us:

   For the Greens: $x + 3y = 14$.

   For the Wilsons: $2x + 6y = 28$.

   This is simply twice the first equation, so we cannot solve them simultaneously and get a unique solution. The best answer is choice (A).

5. **The correct answer is (C).** 3 times k subtracted from 14 means $14 - 3k$. 2 more than k means $k + 2$. Thus, $14 - 3k = k + 2$.

6. **The correct answer is (B).** From the $12.00 total bill, subtract the $2.50 worth of coupons, leaving a bill of $9.50. 10% of $9.50 is 95¢ or $0.95, which we subtract from $9.50, leaving only $8.55 to be paid. The change from a $20 bill is $20.00 - 8.55 = 11.45, which is choice (B).

7. **The correct answer is (D).** From statement (1), the product of the last terms, $6m$, must be 18. Therefore, $m = 3$. The options are choice (A) or choice (D). From statement (2), the sum of the outer and inner products, becomes $-6x - mx = -9x$. Hence, $-6 - m = -9$, and $m = 3$. The best answer is choice (D).

8. **The correct answer is (A).** There are nine possible ways to form the difference $x - y$, but they do not all give different values, especially when you take the absolute values, so that numbers with the same magnitude but different signs give the same value. We can list the possibilities in a little table of $|x - y|$:

y/x	1	3	5
2	1	1	3
3	2	0	2
6	5	3	1

Now you can see that there are only 5 possible numbers: 0, 1, 2, 3, and 5.

9. **The correct answer is (C).** Knowing the length of only one side tells us almost nothing about the perimeter. Hence, neither statement (1) nor statement (2) is sufficient. The answer is either choice (C) or choice (E). Combining the two, however, we see that whenever we form a triangle, the sum of any two sides must exceed the third. Hence, $9 + 14 > z$. Therefore, z must be less than 23. The greatest integer less than 23 is 22. Hence, the maximum possible perimeter is $9 + 14 + 22 = 45$. Similarly, $z + 9 > 14$, which means that $z > 5$. The smallest integer greater than 5 is 6, and so the minimum possible perimeter is $9 + 14 + 6 = 29$. The difference between the two is $45 - 29 = 16$. The best answer is choice (C).

10. **The correct answer is (E).** Calling the unknown N, $\dfrac{2}{3}$ of 90 means $\dfrac{2}{3} \times 90 = 60$.

    We want 20% or $\dfrac{1}{5}$ of N to equal 60. That is, $N = 60$ or $N = 300$, which is choice (E).

11. **The correct answer is (C).** Since the numbers in the table must total 150, we have $55 + 43 + x + y + 12 = 150$. That is, $x + y = 40$. Since y must be a whole number greater than 12, y must be at least 13. Therefore, x can be at most 27.

12. **The correct answer is (B).** Statement (1), $R = 2$, tells us that $x_M = \dfrac{3 + 2}{2} = \dfrac{5}{2}$ but nothing about y_M. The options are choice (B), choice (C), or choice (E). From statement (2), $y_M = \dfrac{4 + (-2)}{2} = \dfrac{2}{2} = 1$. The best answer is choice (B).

13. **The correct answer is (B).** From statement (1): In order that H be real, we must have $B - 1 \geq 0$, that is, $B \geq 1$. This tells us that the smallest possible value of B is 1, but tells us nothing about the largest possibility, so the options are choice (B), choice (C), or choice (E). From statement (2): In order that K be real, we must have $3 - B \leq 0$, that is $3 \leq B$. The largest possible value of B is 3. The best answer is choice (B).

14. **The correct answer is (A).** Using the distributive law on the left-hand side gives us:

$$2y - 6 = 4 + 3y$$

To solve, we add $-2y - 4$ to both sides, thus:

$$\begin{array}{r} 2y - 6 = 4 + 3y \\ -2y - 4 = -2y - 4 \\ \hline -10 = y \end{array}$$

15. **The correct answer is (C).** Of the whole group of 60, 40% are under 25. 40% of 60 is $(0.4)(60) = 24$. For the singers, 20% of $20 = (0.2)(20) = 4$ are under 25. Hence, the remaining "25 or unders" must be dancers. That is, 20 dancers, or one half of all the dancers, fall into this category. Since one half is 50%, the correct choice is choice (C).

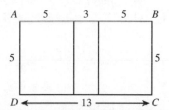

16. **The correct answer is (D).** If each square has an area of 25, each has a side of 5. Since that is also the side of the small central rectangle, which has area 15, the short side of the small rectangle must be 3 (see the figure above). Hence, the dimensions of the whole rectangle $ABCD$ are 5×13. The perimeter is $2(5) + 2(13) = 36$.

17. **The correct answer is (B).** From statement (1) alone, we know that $12\pi = 2\pi r$. That is, $r = 6$. Hence, we know one leg of the triangle but not the other. Using statement (2) alone, the area of the circle is $\pi r^2 = 36\pi$, which makes the radius 6. Hence, $AB = 12$, and since the tangent to the circle is perpendicular to the radius, $\triangle ABC$ is a right triangle with one side 12 and the hypotenuse 15, making the third side 9. The area of the triangle is $\frac{1}{2}bh = \frac{1}{2}(9)(12) = 54$. The best answer is choice (B).

18. **The correct answer is (B).** Calling the dimensions L and W, we have $LW = 60$ and $2L + 2W = 32$. Dividing by 2, $L + W = 16$. Therefore, $L = 16 - W$, which we substitute in $LW = 60$, giving us:

$$(16 - W)W = 60$$
$$16W - W^2 = 60$$

Grouping everything on the right-hand side, we have:

$$0 = W^2 - 16W + 60$$

Factoring:

$$0 = (W - 10)(W - 6)$$

yields:

$$W = 10 \text{ or } W = 6$$

Of course, if $W = 6$, then $L = 10$, and if $W = 10$, then $L = 6$. So the dimensions are 6×10 and the shorter side is 6.

19. **The correct answer is (E).** Statement (1) alone tells us that $y = x + 1$, but it tells us nothing else about x. Statement (2) alone tells us that $x^2 - 8y = 25$, but one equation in two unknowns allows for many possibilities. For example, $y = 0$, $x = -5$ or $y = 3$, $x = -7$. The possibilities are choice (C) or choice (E). Combining statement (1) and statement (2) and substituting $(x + 1)$ for y:

$$x^2 - 8(x + 1) = 25$$
$$x^2 - 8x - 8 = 25$$
$$x^2 - 8x - 33 = 0$$

This factors as:

$$(x + 3)(x - 11) = 0$$
$$x + 3 = 0 \text{ or}$$
$$x - 11 = 0$$

Hence, $x = -3$ or $x = 11$. Thus, we still do not know x uniquely. The best answer is choice (E).

20. **The correct answer is (E).** From the total bill of $22, subtract the cost of waiting in traffic, which was 4 minutes, or 8 times 30 seconds. That cost 8 times 20¢, or $1.60. Thus, the bill for mileage was $22 − $1.60 = $20.40. $3.00 for the first one-fifth mile leaves $17.40 unaccounted for. Dividing by 30¢ per one-fifth mile we have $(17.4) \div (0.3) = 58$ fifths of a mile, or 11.6 miles. Adding back the first fifth, we have 11.8 miles. Of course, 11.7 costs the same as 11.8, so choice (E) is correct.

21. **The correct answer is (D).** Calling the smallest number x, the second is $(x + 2)$, and the third is $(x + 4)$. Therefore:

$$x + (x + 2) + 2(x + 4) = 46$$
$$x + x + 2 + 2x + 8 = 46$$
$$4x + 10 = 46$$
$$4x = 36; x = 9$$

Hence the middle number is $9 + 2 = 11$.

22. **The correct answer is (D).** Using statement (1) and the slope formula, $m = \dfrac{4 - (-1)}{6 - 3} = \dfrac{5}{3}$. The answer is either choice (A) or choice (D). Using statement (2) alone, we have $y = mx - 6$. Since the line passes through $(6,4)$, those coordinates must satisfy the equation. That is, $4 = 6m - 6$. We solve this for m. $6m = 10$; $m = \dfrac{5}{3}$. The best answer is choice (D).

23. **The correct answer is (C).** Try each of the choices: choice (A) $\blacklozenge 1 \blacklozenge = \dfrac{1 + \sqrt{1}}{2} = \dfrac{2}{2} = 1$. Similarly, choice (B) $\blacklozenge 4 \blacklozenge = 3$; choice (C) $\blacklozenge 9 \blacklozenge = 6$; choice (D) $\blacklozenge 25 \blacklozenge = 15$; choice (C) $\blacklozenge 36 \blacklozenge = 21$. Only choice (C), 6, is even.

24. **The correct answer is (C).** Statement (1) alone is not sufficient, because we do not know if the second block is chosen with or without replacement. Statement (2) alone is not sufficient, because we do not know how many blocks of each color are present. Thus choice (C) and choice (E) are possibilities. The two combined tell us that we have five color choices for the first block, and for each of these there are four choices for the second. Hence, the number of ordered color combinations is $(5)(4) = 20$. The best answer is choice (C).

25. **The correct answer is (A).** Using the FOIL method for multiplying the binomials, we see that the middle term should be $-3x + px = x$, which means that $-3 + p = 1$, or $p = 4$. The constant term is $-3p = -m$. That is, $m = 3p$, $m = 12$. Hence, $m - p = 12 - 4 = 8$.

26. **The correct answer is (D).** The total hourly wages Marla took in was the total number of hours, $m + w$, times the pay per hour; thus, $d(m + w)$. In addition, she kept $\dfrac{4}{5}$ of her tips, or $\dfrac{4}{5} \times t = \dfrac{4t}{5}$, which we add to the hourly wages to end up with $d(m + w) + \dfrac{4t}{5}$.

27. **The correct answer is (C).** From statement (1), we have $3x - 4y = 45 - z$. We can double this to get $6x - 8y = 90 - 2z$, but not knowing z, we can go no further. Similarly, from statement (2) alone, we have $3x - 4y = 36 + 2z$ or $6x - 8y = 72 + 4z$, and again, not knowing z, we can go no further, so choice (C) and choice (E) are possible. Using both pieces of information, $90 - 2z = 72 + 4z$; $18 = 6z$; dividing by 6, $z = 3$. Now, since $6x - 8y = 90 - 2z$, we have $6x - 8y = 84$. The best answer is choice (C).

28. **The correct answer is (B).** We can square both sides to get $\dfrac{r^2}{s^2} = t$. Multiplying by s^2 and dividing by t, $s^2 = \dfrac{r^2}{t}$, which is the reciprocal of $\dfrac{t}{r^2}$. Now, using statement (1) alone, $s^2 = \dfrac{1}{9}$ and $s = \pm\dfrac{1}{3}$. The options are choice (B), choice (C), or choice (E). From statement (2) alone, $\dfrac{t}{r^2} = 9$ and $s^2 = \dfrac{1}{9}$ and $s = \pm\dfrac{1}{3}$, but now we can reject the possibility that $s = -\dfrac{1}{3}$. Why? We know that $\sqrt{x}$ is positive (by definition), so if s were negative, then r would also be negative; but we know that r is positive ($r = 2$). The best answer is choice (B).

29. **The correct answer is (B).** Since the slope of a line is the same for any two points on the line, and $m = \dfrac{y_1 - y_2}{x_1 - x_2}$, using $(-1,-1)$ and $(3,11)$, we must have $m = \dfrac{11 - (-1)}{3 - (-1)} = \dfrac{12}{4} = 3$. Now, using the pair $(-1,-1)$ and $(1,t)$, $3 = \dfrac{t - (-1)}{1 - (-1)} = \dfrac{t + 1}{2}$. Multiplying by 2, $6 = t + 1$, and $t = 5$.

30. **The correct answer is (E).** If $3a$ equals $2b$, then $3a$ must be divisible by 2, which means a must be divisible by 2, since 3 is not. Similarly, $2b$ must be divisible by 3, which means b must be divisible by 3, since 2 is not. Thus, the correct choice is choice (E); both I and III must be true. Notice that II need not be true, since $b = 3$, $a = 2$ is a perfectly satisfactory solution.

31. **The correct answer is (D).** Knowing that the area is 4, we know that each side is of length 2. Therefore, half of each side is 1, and the unshaded triangles are each isosceles right triangles with legs of length 1 and a hypotenuse of length $\sqrt{2}$. Hence, the shaded region has 4 sides of length 1 and two of length $\sqrt{2}$, for a total of $4 + 2\sqrt{2}$.

32. **The correct answer is (E).** Using statement (1), we have $\dfrac{2n - 0}{2n + 0} = 1$. This is true for any n except $n = 0$. From statement (2), we have $\dfrac{2n - 2n}{2n + 2n} = \dfrac{0}{4n}$ except for $n = 0$. The options are choice (C) or choice (E). Even when we combine the two statements, we know only that n is not zero. The best answer is choice (E).

33. **The correct answer is (B).** From the second equation, we have $\dfrac{y}{x} = -z$, so that $\dfrac{x}{y} = -\dfrac{1}{z}$, which we can substitute into the first equation. This gives us $-\dfrac{1}{z} + \dfrac{2}{z} = \dfrac{1}{2}$, that is, $\dfrac{1}{z} = \dfrac{1}{2}$ or $z = 2$, which is choice (B). Of course, this can also be solved by trying the various choices to see which one satisfies both equations.

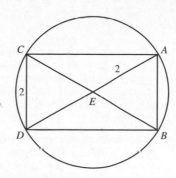

34. **The correct answer is (A).** If the diagonals of the rectangle meet at an angle of 60° (see the figure above), then ΔECD and ΔAEB are both equilateral triangles with sides equal to the radius, 2. Hence, the length of CD is 2, which is the width of the rectangle. Further, since $\angle ECD$ is 60°, $\angle CBD$ is 30°, making ΔBCD a 30°–60°–90° triangle with shorter leg 2. That makes the longer leg $BD = 2\sqrt{3}$, which is the length of the rectangle. So its area $A = LW = 2(2\sqrt{3}) = 4$, which is choice (A).

35. **The correct answer is (A).** Since $r \neq 0$, we know that $x \neq y$. Thus, statement (1) alone tells us that $x = -y$. Substituting $-y$ for x in the fraction, we have $r = \dfrac{-y - y}{-2y + y} = \dfrac{-2y}{-y}$. The options are choice (A) or choice (D). Knowing that $x = -3$ without knowing y does not help us to evaluate r. The best answer is choice (A).

36. **The correct answer is (A).** If we rewrite the equation as $y^2 - x^2 = 7$ and factor, we have $(y - x)(y + x) = 7$. Thus, 7 must be the product of the two whole numbers, $(y - x)$ and $(y + x)$. But 7 is a prime number that can only be factored as 7 times 1. Hence,

$$y + x = 7$$

and

$$y - x = 1$$

Adding the two equations gives us

$$2y = 8; y = 4$$

Of course, $x = 3$, but you weren't asked that.

37. **The correct answer is (E).** The square is moving A-D-C-B-A-D-C-B- . . . Thus, every time the number of seconds is divisible by 4, the red square is back at A. Hence, you can find its location by looking at the remainder when the time is divided by 4. 415 ÷ 4 leaves a remainder of 3, so the square has gone three steps beyond A and is at B. Similarly, the dot's location is given by the remainder when 415 is divided by 3. The remainder is 1, so the dot has reached one location beyond A, but it is moving A-B-C-A-B-C- . . . Hence, it, too, has reached B.

SECTION 4—VERBAL

1. **The correct answer is (B)** Each of the other answer statements could help to explain either the discrepancy between the various studies of TV violence or the apparent cause-and-effect relationship between TV violence and real-life violence. Only choice (B) does neither; instead, it sharpens the apparent contradiction among the various studies without helping to explain it.

2. **The correct answer is (A).** The original phrasing is both idiomatic and clear. Choices (B) and (C) are wrong because using "none" along with "can't" creates a double negative, something that's considered incorrect. Choice (D) uses a plural verb, "are," with a singular subject, "anyone who." And choice (E) changes the meaning of the sentence.

3. **The correct answer is (D).** There are two possible correct phrasings for the idea here: you can make sure that "each one doesn't interfere with the other" or that "they don't interfere with each other." Only choice (D) forms one of these correctly.

4. **The correct answer is (C).** Both fingerprinting and electrophoresis can be used as a means of identifying the person who produced a given sample of blood, from which their presence at a crime scene may be inferred. Choice (A) is wrong because only fingerprinting is referred to in the passage as a "negative" form of identification (see the second paragraph of the passage).

5. **The correct answer is (A).** The fifth paragraph of the passage suggests this idea. The fact that electrophoresis can identify thousands of blood subgroups suggests that this method is capable of narrowing down the identity of a blood "donor" quite specifically.

6. **The correct answer is (E).** The last paragraph explains that Wrexall showed how "simultaneous analyses" could produce useful results within 24 hours—in other words, "more rapid testing."

7. **The correct answer is (B).** All of the answer choices except choice (B) are explicitly mentioned somewhere in the passage.

8. **The correct answer is (D).** Answer choices (A), (B), (C), and (E) all help to account for the restrictions on immigration that were put in place starting in the 1880s. Choice (D) does not; in fact, it suggests that these restrictions were an anomaly in need of some explanation not provided in the passage.

9. **The correct answer is (D).** Choice (D) is the only answer that clearly suggests a drawback to our reliance on automobiles rather than horses for transportation.

10. **The correct answer is (C).** The sentence is explaining the fact that, prior to the invention of modern clocks, the day was divided in many different ways. Therefore, the plural phrase "various numbers" is necessary. Choice (C) is the answer that phrases this idiomatically.

11. **The correct answer is (B).** The singular past-tense verb "wasn't" is necessary with the singular pronoun "it" in this sentence. Choice (E) also uses this verb, but the phrase "as well" seems to imply a comparison (to some other book, perhaps?) that is never completed and so is confusing.

12. **The correct answer is (D).** It seems irrelevant whether or not additional, older children are part of the same family. All of the other answer choices, however, raise issues that could be relevant to determining whether or not the study's conclusion is valid.

13. **The correct answer is (C).** The sentence can't end with *it,* since the antecedent of the pronoun is the plural *books*; the plural pronoun *them* must be used instead.

14. **The correct answer is (C).** The ideas of the farm couple are summarized in the final sentences of the first paragraph. In their judgment, they were "rich" because of the education their children had received, which they (and economist Schultz) regarded as a form of capital comparable to a piece of valuable farm equipment.

15. **The correct answer is (E).** The words "just like" are in quotation marks because they are to be taken figuratively. There are obviously many differences between a hog pen and Latin 101; in a way, it's very surprising that anyone should think of comparing the two. Schultz says they are "just like" one another because both can be considered sources of "streams of satisfaction," despite the fact that they are clearly very different kinds of things.

16. **The correct answer is (D).** The point of the last paragraph is that physical capital (like a piece of the farm) can be turned into intellectual capital (like a college education), and vice versa. Choice (D) gives another example of this: Junior can turn his knowledge of the law into a new farm, which is a form of physical capital.

17. **The correct answer is (D).** The plural antecedent *writers* must be referred to by the plural pronoun *they*; the singular antecedent *thesaurus* must be referred to by the singular pronoun *it.* Choice (E), like choice (D), is technically correct, but it is awkward by comparison.

18. **The correct answer is (C).** Only this statement *must* be true given the information presented. Choice (D) is wrong because the truth of the statement would depend, in part, on how many wealthy people there are compared to middle-class people.

19. **The correct answer is (B).** This is the most graceful and least wordy of the five answer choices.

20. **The correct answer is (B).** Choices (A), (B), and (C) are all technically correct; however, choice (B) is the least wordy and awkward of the three. Choice (D) changes the meaning of the sentence by introducing the qualifier "*many of those* who do smoke."

21. **The correct answer is (C).** The exact nature of the relationship between the shift from rural to urban living and the change in Americans' choice of pets can't be determined based simply on the information given. All we can tell is that, in fact, more Americans are choosing cats as pets than dogs.

22. **The correct answer is (D).** All of the other answer choices either suggest reasons other than the complications of our legal system for the proliferation of lawyers in the U.S. or else undermine the argument by showing that the same cause-and-effect relationship doesn't seem to hold up elsewhere

23. **The correct answer is (D).** All of the variations mentioned in the other answer choices are noted somewhere in the passage; however, none of the state governments discussed is said to involve a legislature that is not popularly elected.

24. **The correct answer is (B).** The second sentence of the third paragraph makes this point.

25. **The correct answer is (C).** The fourth and fifth paragraphs describe the government of Pennsylvania, which is said to be the "most democratic" among the former colonies. Of the answer choices, only choice (C) describes a feature of this state's government.

26. **The correct answer is (D).** Whether or not Goldwater was really a "war hawk" is irrelevant to the conclusion of the passage, which is that Johnson's withdrawal from the 1968 election was prompted by the controversy over the war in Vietnam.

27. **The correct answer is (B).** The subject of the verb is *risk,* which is singular; therefore, the singular verb *has led* must be used, rather than the plural *have led. To avoid* is more idiomatic and natural sounding than using the word *avoidance* in a sentence like this.

28. **The correct answer is (E).** Only this answer choice is false, since the framers clearly intended for representatives to be chosen directly by the people.

29. **The correct answer is (D).** The first half of the sentence is a modifying phrase that clearly describes and refers to the workers at the plant. (They are the ones who were "recognizing the need" described.) Therefore, the words "the workers at the plant" must be placed as close as possible to that phrase, which choice (D) does. Otherwise, the modifier is misplaced.

30. **The correct answer is (D).** The conclusion drawn in the passage is that business people today demand speedy delivery merely because it is available. All of the answer choices except choice (D) challenge this conclusion in one way or another, whereas choice (D) strengthens it.

31. **The correct answer is (B).** The other answer choices either help to explain why Lincoln was once considered a "country bumpkin" or why respect for his political acumen has grown. Choice (B) suggests that the understanding of the difficulties Lincoln faced as president has recently improved, which doesn't actually affect either element of the conclusion.

32. **The correct answer is (E).** For the sake of parallelism, the preposition *in* needs to be repeated: "not in A but *in* B." Choice (C) spoils the parallelism in another way, by pairing the noun *production* with the gerund *developing* rather than with the matching noun *development.*

33. **The correct answer is (D).** Just as the angler fish uses a fake piece of food as bait to capture a hungry prey, so does the trout fisherman when he lures a trout with a tasty-looking fake insect.

34. **The correct answer is (E).** Countershading is described in the third paragraph, where it is stated that this effect protects fish from predators *below* them, not above.

35. **The correct answer is (E).** This point is made in the first sentence of the fifth paragraph.

36. **The correct answer is (A).** The fourth paragraph says that bioluminescence is considered nonessential because nonluminous species seem to thrive as well as luminous ones. From this, we can conclude that if bioluminescence were essential, the opposite would be true—luminous species would do better than nonluminous ones.

37. **The correct answer is (D).** The factors that influence the attitudes of non-American employees toward their CEOs aren't directly relevant to the present argument, which focuses completely on explaining the resentment of American employees toward their bosses.

38. **The correct answer is (E).** The author of the passage is arguing that aluminum bats will lead to higher scoring games, which in turn will improve baseball attendance. This conclusion is true, obviously, only if it's true that high-scoring games lead to greater fan interest and attendance, as choice (E) states.

39. **The correct answer is (A).** The present perfect verb *has flown* is the correct tense to use when describing an event that immediately precedes a present-tense event (described in this sentence by the present-tense verb *steps*). Choice (C) is awkward and nonidiomatic.

40. **The correct answer is (D).** The normal idiom is to say that people "are required to do something."

41. **The correct answer is (B).** The word "Yet" in the middle of the passage suggests a contradiction. This tells us that the author wants to explain some way in which Picasso, the supposedly revolutionary artist, did *not* participate in the art revolutions of the century. Since the passage says that abstract painting was the century's greatest revolution, the contradiction is best carried out by choice (B), which states that Picasso did not create abstract paintings.

Part IV

Making It Official

Chapter 11

Scheduling and Taking the Test

Get the Scoop On . . .

- Choosing the test date and location that's best for you
- Saving time and money when you register for the exam
- Obtaining any special test accommodations you may need to do your best
- Which ETS services are worth buying—and which ones to skip
- How to ensure you'll feel good and perform well the day of the exam

---

DECIDING HOW AND WHEN TO TAKE THE GMAT CAT

The GMAT CAT CAT is administered year round, Monday through Saturday, at about 400 Sylvan Learning Centers throughout the United States and Canada as well as at a few other locations (including some universities and ETS offices). So to begin with, you have a lot of flexibility in picking your test date. But when you start factoring in B-school application deadlines and other considerations, your options rapidly begin to narrow. Here are some of the main points to consider in choosing a test date.

FYI

If you are interested in applying for scholarships, fellowships, or other special programs, an earlier deadline may apply. Don't forget to take that into consideration.

- **Check the application deadlines for your program(s) of choice.** Most schools set a single date by which they want to receive all the supporting data they need—not only test scores but also college transcripts, your personal statement, letters of recommendation, etc. Determine which program you are applying to sets the *earliest* deadline, and count back six weeks from that date. (This allows enough time for your score report to be received. ETS aims to send reports out within three weeks of the test, but four to five weeks is more common.) The date you count back to should be your *latest* date for taking the GMAT CAT.

- **Allow yourself the option of retaking the GMAT CAT.** Suppose that, working backwards from your earliest B-school deadline, you determine that you must take the GMAT CAT no later than early November. Don't simply apply for that test date. Instead, if you can, we recommend that you take the exam at least two months earlier. That means applying for an early September test or, better still, a test in April or May of the previous year.

Why the hurry? In the event your GMAT CAT scores don't hit the targets you've set, you'll want to have the opportunity to take the exam at least once more before your application deadline hits.

Most students find that their test scores rise the second time they take the GMAT CAT, and if you prepare in a focused and disciplined way before your second exam, you'll have the opportunity to achieve a significant score increase. (For more information about whether and how to plan on retaking the exam, see chapter 12.) But this will be impossible if you schedule your exam during the final pre-deadline window.

- If you are a non-native speaker of English, you will probably be required to take the Test of English as Foreign Language (TOEFL). Information and registration forms are available at most colleges, or you can call ETS.

REGISTERING FOR THE EXAM

FYI

If you take the GMAT CAT in October, it'll be possible to retake the exam in November—but just barely. ETS allows you to take the CAT only once during any calendar month. Plan ahead, and check the current policy by calling ETS or checking the GMAT CAT Web page at www.gmat.org.

ETS supplies colleges with plentiful stacks of GMAT CAT bulletins and registration forms, so one easy way to get the forms you need is to stop by the guidance office and ask for them. If you prefer, you can call ETS and have them send you the materials.

When you register by mail, you'll fill in a fairly lengthy computerized form. Take your time filling out the form; it's easier than a tax return, but not much. Be especially careful when looking up and transferring the code numbers for the universities you're listing to receive your test scores. Mistakes are easy to make.

You can also register for the GMAT CAT by phone, using a credit card to pay the fee. Dial 1-800-GMAT-NOW, and you'll be connected to Sylvan Learning Centers, the private organization that administers the GMAT CAT on behalf of ETS.

In any case, you'll need to register well in advance of your chosen test date. Regular registration deadlines are about four weeks prior to the exam. You can register late for an extra fee, but this only gives you a few more days. So don't put off registration.

Once you've registered, you can use the phone to do things like register for subsequent tests, request a change in your test center, or add universities to your score report list. Expect a fee for each service you request.

THE INSIDER'S REPORT: KNOW YOUR OPTIONS

FYI

If you take the GMAT CAT with any nonstandard procedures, your score reports will contain the nota-tion "Nonstandard Administration," and the nature of the accommoda-tion will be ex-plained. Presum-ably, your disability will be known to the uni-versities you're applying to, so this notation should come as no sur-prise and have no negative impact on the evaluation of your scores.

Choosing the Best Location

You'll probably want to schedule a test-taking appointment at the Sylvan Learning Center nearest to you. However, the conditions at these centers vary. Some are more spacious, less noisy, cleaner, and better organized than others. If two or more centers are located reasonably close to you, consider visiting them both before you select your test location. Or ask a classmate about her experience in taking the GMAT CAT.

Special Testing Arrangements

Some students need special accommodations when they take the GMAT CAT. For example, a student in a wheelchair or a student whose sight or hearing is impaired may need special seating arrangements, the use of a Braille or large-print test booklet, or a sign-language interpreter.

In addition, if you have a learning disability or any physical or psychological condition that would make it impossible or unfair for you to have to complete the GMAT CAT under the same time limits as other students, you may be able to take the test with special extended timing.

If you fall into a category like these, speak to a counselor at the office of your college that provides services for students with disabilities or to a human resources officer at the company where you work. You'll need him to complete a form called the Documentation Certification for Nonstandard Testing Accommodations. There's another form, the Examinee's Eligibility Questionnaire for Nonstandard Testing Accommo-dations, that you'll fill out; it appears in the GMAT CAT Bulletin.

If for any reason you can't get a certification form from your college or company, you'll need a letter from the physician or other professional involved in treating your condition. The letter must describe the accommodation needed, explain the reason for it, and document the need through diagnostic test results or other medical records. You'll enclose this letter with your regular test registration form.

ETS is strict about demanding authentication of your need for special testing arrangements. If your need is real, stick to your guns! Just be sure to begin the registration process early, so that any letters, forms, or documents ETS requires can be submitted in plenty of time.

Score Reporting

When you register for the GMAT CAT, you'll be allowed to pick five business schools to receive reports of your scores. Even if you're not yet completely sure to which schools you'll be applying, take advantage of

FYI

If you requested any special test accommodations, try to arrive early. You may need to find or be directed to a different room or building from your fellow test-takers, and the test administrators may have to do some last-minute scrambling to get all the details in place.

this opportunity to name five of your most likely choices. There is an additional charge for extra schools (currently $15.00 per school).

There are two ways you can add to the list of programs that will receive your scores.

- Space for up to four additional reports is provided on the test registration form. The $15.00 fee will be charged for each college listed here, of course.

- You can fill out and mail an Additional Score Report Request form, which you'll receive with your test admission.

See Chapter 12 for more information about your score reports.

Selecting Other Services

At the time you register for the GMAT CAT, you'll have the opportunity to select other ETS services. Here's a rundown of your options, with our explanation and recommendation concerning each one.

- **Graduate Management Admission Search Service.** Unless you choose to opt out of this service, your name and personal profile, based on the information you provide in the questionnaire that is part of your registration form, will be given to interested universities. As a result, they may add you to their mailing lists to receive brochures and ads about their programs. Our recommendation: participate. There's no fee, and you may find it interesting to hear from business schools whose programs you may not have considered.

- **GMAC Publications.** You'll have the option of ordering several GMAC publications, including their test preparation software packages, and books containing actual past GMAT CAT questions. Appendix D of the book you're now reading lists these and other useful resource guides you may want to own; the GMAC books are fine, but there are competing books you may like better. (The fact that the Graduate Management Admission Council is an "official," university-sponsored organization makes their publications a little less revealing and more stodgy than other books, we think.) Our recommendation: check out the GMAC books in a bookstore first. If you like them, go ahead and order them.

- **MBA Forums®.** Each fall, the GMAC sponsors a series of day-long meetings in cities around the U.S. about graduate business education. These are the MBA Forums. In recent years, they've been held in Washington, D.C.; San Francisco; New York; Cleveland; Houston; and Chicago. The Forums feature booths manned by representatives of various universities and workshops on admissions, financial aid, GMAT CAT preparation, and other topics. An MBA Forum is worth attending if it's conveniently located; we wouldn't travel any great distance to attend one. The registration fee is modest (currently $5), so sign up if you're interested.

WHEN TEST TIME COMES

FYI

Here's a relaxation routine to use during the test breaks. Close your eyes. Sit back. Begin taking deep, slow, cleansing breaths, filling your lungs completely. Then deliberately tense and release the muscles in each part of your body, one region at a time, from feet and legs to torso, arms, and head. When done, take a final deep breath and open your eyes, ready to return to work.

See Appendix D, "The Insider's Stress-Buster's Guide," for more tips on managing fatigue and anxiety at test time.

The big day is here. You're about to face one of the important challenges of your academic and business life, comparable to the final exam of a crucial course or your presentation of a business plan to prospective investors. If you've used this book (and other resources) effectively, you can be confident that you're well prepared for the GMAT CAT. Here are some last-minute reminders and suggestions that will help you handle the stress of "game time" gracefully.

The Night Before

- Don't cram. Last-minute study isn't likely to make much difference in your skills or knowledge, but it can needlessly elevate your levels of anxiety and fatigue.

- Put out everything you'll want to bring with you to the test center. This includes: your official admission ticket; a photo ID (driver's license, passport, etc.); a pen and pencil; and a small snack, like a granola bar or a piece of fruit.

- If the weather is cool, lay out a sweater or two—dressing in layers will let you adjust to conditions in the test room. If you're traveling to an unfamiliar test site, put out the map or directions you'll be following.

- Set your clock, and if possible have a backup system in place to wake you if the clock fails. (The best such system is a truly reliable roommate, friend, or relative.) You need to arrive at the test center half an hour early for the CAT, so plan accordingly.

- Get to sleep early. Remember that the GMAT CAT—three-and-a-half to four-and-a-half hours long—is a physical as well as a mental challenge.

The Morning of the Test

- Wake up early and have your usual breakfast. If you normally skip breakfast, consider having something light this day—cereal or fruit. You'll be needing more energy than usual.

- Leave plenty of time for travel, so you can arrive early and relaxed, not late and frazzled.

■ Don't listen to the predictions and advice of the students around you. If you've prepared with the help of this book, you know exactly what to expect—probably better than your fellow test takers. Last-minute speculation can only fuel needless worry.

During the Test

■ Make sure your accommodations are appropriate and comfortable. You should have a comfortable chair, an adequate writing surface, plenty of light, and a space that is reasonably quiet, well-heated or cooled, and pollution-free. If any of these conditions are lacking, ask for help.

■ As you begin the GMAT CAT, work through the tutorial material patiently and make sure you are completely comfortable with the software before tackling the real test questions. Make sure your computer, monitor, and mouse are all functioning properly. Above all, use the GMAT CAT strategies explained in Chapter 3, especially taking the time you need with the earliest questions to start each section with a bang.

■ You'll have two short (5-minute) breaks during the test. Use these to eat your snack and to relax. A 3-minute relaxation routine will help you feel refreshed before you tackle the next test section.

After the Test

■ If you encountered any problems with the test or the testing procedures—a mistake by the proctor, incorrect timing, a disruptive environment, a computer malfunction, or any other distraction—make detailed notes about it immediately after the test. A letter of complaint should be faxed to ETS no later than seven days after your test. Use this fax number: 609-883-4349.

■ If you're convinced that you bombed on the exam, consider cancelling your scores *before seeing them on screen*. See Chapter 12 for details on how this works and how to decide whether this option is right for you.

■ If you think you encountered an erroneous or flawed test question, consider mounting an official challenge to the item. Chapter 12 tells how.

■ Now go party. You've earned it.

JUST THE FACTS

■ Pick a testing date based on your B-school application deadlines, but leave yourself a chance to retake the test if needed.

■ Find a test center that's comfortable and close to home.

- Be sure to request any test-taking accommodations you need and deserve.

- Some—not all—of the products and services offered by ETS and GMAC are worthwhile investments.

- Manage your energies the day of the exam to minimize anxiety and maximize performance.

Chapter 12

Understanding Your Scores

Get the Scoop On . . .

- What your score report really means
- How business schools interpret your GMAT CAT scores
- How and when to consider cancelling your scores
- What to do if you think your score is wrong or the test was flawed
- How to decide whether to retake the GMAT CAT

You've taken the GMAT CAT . . . congratulations! Getting this far hasn't been easy. We hope you found that your study-and-practice program prepared you well for the challenge of the exam, and that you're feeling reasonably confident about how you did.

While you await your scores, don't agonize over the test, and don't assume that the way you feel is any indication of your real performance. Students who think they did poorly often get surprisingly high scores. (This happens more often than the reverse.) Here's why: When you took the exam, you spent more time puzzling over the hardest questions—the ones you may have gotten wrong—than over the easy ones, which you whizzed through. So when you think about the test later, your main memory is of struggling to figure out the toughest problems. That selective recall isn't necessarily an accurate gauge of how you did overall.

Even after you receive your scores, however, your "GMAT CAT work" may not be done. It's time now to analyze your scores and what they mean, which may be a little more complicated that you realize. And you may have some important decisions to make—especially about whether to take the exam again. In this chapter, we'll explain what you need to know to win this phase of the great GMAT CAT game.

YOUR GMAT CAT SCORE REPORT

Understanding Your Score Report

As soon as you complete the CAT, you'll have the option of seeing your scores, both on-screen and in the form of a simple printout that the test proctor can give you. Your Analytical Writing scores, of course, are not included. Go ahead and see your scores, *unless* you want to cancel them (see below).

Despite ETS's use of computers to score their exams, it has always taken quite a while for students to receive their official score reports in the mail. Three weeks is what ETS predicts, but students say that four to five weeks is more common, and even longer delays are not unusual. The wait can be inconvenient, so be sure to take the exam early enough to get score reports to all the schools that need them.

The printed score report you'll eventually get in the mail offers more information than you'll get at the test center. However, even savvy test-takers don't always find it clear. Here's a point-by-point description and explanation of what your score report will tell you.

- **Your Verbal, Quantitative, and Total Scores.** The Verbal and Quantitative scores are two-digit scores, ranging from 0 (low) to 60 (high). Almost no one scores below 10 or above 46. Average or mean scores vary from year to year and even from test to test. However, in recent years, the average Verbal score has been around 28, while Quantitative scores have averaged around 32.

  Your total score combines your performance of the Verbal and Quantitative sections into a single, three-digit score. The range is 200 (low) to 800 (high), with the recent average hovering around 510.

- **Your Analytical Writing Assessment Score.** Your Analytical Writing essays will be scored on a two-digit scale ranging from 0.0 (low) to 6.0 (high), in increments of 0.5. The recent average is between 3.5 and 4.0; a score of 5.0 or higher puts you in the top fifth of all test takers.

- **Your Percentile Scores.** You'll also receive four percentile scores—Verbal, Quantitative, Analytical Writing, and Total. These compare your performance to that of all students who took the exam during the last three years. The percentile score indicates what percentage of these students scored *lower* than you on the test. So if you have a Verbal percentile score of 70 (for instance), it means that 70 percent of students scored lower than you. Obviously, the higher your percentile scores, the better.

- **Your Scores on Past GMAT CATs.** Your score report will also list your scores on past GMAT CATs, up to five years old. ETS will also report older scores if you request them, but they caution business schools that older scores may not accurately reflect your current level of ability. Thus, the schools to which you're applying may require you to retake the exam.

HOW BUSINESS SCHOOLS INTERPRET GMAT CAT SCORES

FYI

Students are often surprised to learn what the GMAT CAT is supposed to show. The "psychometricians" (test experts) at ETS tell universities that GMAT CAT scores—in combination with college grades— are supposed to help predict the performance of students in first-year business school classes. That's all. The GMAT CAT cannot predict who will successfully complete the graduate degree— let alone who will achieve success in later life.

The schools to which you ask ETS to send your scores will receive reports containing all the information from your own score report. What do they look for in reading your score report? Naturally, it varies from school to school. However, here are some general observations that apply to most programs.

■ Business schools look to GMAT CAT scores to amplify their picture of you. In combination with your college grades, GMAT CAT scores are supposed to help B-schools measure your academic abilities and achievements. Did you pursue a challenging college program and earn grades that were good but not great? Or were your classroom grades hampered by difficult personal circumstances—loss of a parent, for instance, or the need to work throughout college? In cases like these, good GMAT CAT scores could help confirm that you are brighter than your grades alone suggest.

■ Universities generally focus on your *best* GMAT CAT scores. If you take the exam twice or more, most schools will evaluate you on the basis of your highest score. A sizeable minority—up to 40 percent—will even combine your highest Verbal, Quantitative, and Total scores if those occurred on different days. Just a few insist on considering only your most recent scores—even if those were lower than some earlier scores. The school will generally tell you their policy.

■ Universities evaluate you against this year's pool of applicants. Your B-school application—not only your test scores but all your credentials—will never be considered in a vacuum. You are always being measured against the other students who've applied to a particular program. As the size and quality of this applicant pool rises and falls from one year to the next, a particular set of credentials may look better or worse by comparison.

Luck and fashion play a huge role in this process. For reasons that are often hard to fathom, some schools get "hot" at particular times; everybody and their brother decides to apply to University X, and the happy faculty members there get a chance, for a time, to skim off the very best students. An applicant who might have waltzed through the door two years earlier may not make the cut now. And the opposite happens when a school falls out of vogue. Bear this in mind if you're tempted to apply to this year's fashionable program: although the education probably hasn't improved, getting in has gotten a lot harder.

THE INSIDER'S REPORT: KNOW YOUR OPTIONS

Now you know how universities look at your GMAT CAT scores. What can you do about it all? Are there ways of managing the post-test part of the GMAT CAT process to make it work better for you?

Absolutely yes. Let's look at some of the options you have *after* your exam to minimize the damage from a bad day in the testing arena and to maximize your chances of getting your best possible scores.

Cancelling Your Scores

FYI

If you merely feel you may have done poorly on the exam, you should probably go ahead and allow the test to be graded. Then examine your scores to determine which areas need most work and which ones are fairly strong. This will help you a lot in preparing to do better next time—and it's an option that's not available if you cancel your scores.

Occasionally, a student knows on the day of the test that he has truly bombed. Most often, the problem is physical: people do get ill, sometimes unexpectedly, and the stress of a 4-hour exam can worsen the early symptoms of a flu bug or stomach virus. Once in a great while, a student simply freezes up and is psychologically or emotionally unable to finish the test. And sometimes an ill-prepared student realizes, in despair, that he really should have studied and practiced before sitting down on test day. (If you've read the previous chapters in the book you're holding, you're not a candidate for this problem.)

If any of these calamities befalls you, there is an option—score cancellation. ETS will wipe clear your score slate for a particular day at your request; your test won't be graded, and neither you nor any school will know how well (or poorly) you did.

However, these caveats:

- You must request score cancellation immediately. A screen is provided for this purpose on the CAT. Once you've viewed your scores, cancellation is no longer an option, so think carefully before you make this choice.

- The request is irrevocable. Once you cancel your scores, they can never be reinstated. And you can't cancel just your Verbal or just your Quantitative score: the entire test must be wiped out.

- You won't receive any refund of your testing fee.

Obviously, cancelling your scores is a fairly serious step. Probably most significantly, it will put you in a position where you must retake the exam several weeks or months later, by which time application deadlines may be looming. The sense of pressure you feel on this subsequent test date may be even greater than before.

Therefore, you should cancel your scores only if you really must—illness being the most likely culprit.

If Your Scores Are Delayed

On rare occasions, a student's official GMAT CAT score reports are delayed. A simple glitch in mail delivery may be to blame. We suggest that, if you haven't received an official report of your scores by six weeks after the test date, you call the admissions offices of the universities to which you are applying and ask whether they've received your score report. If they have, the problem on your end is with the mails. Send a fax to ETS at 609-883-4349 to request a duplicate of your score report.

If neither you nor your universities have received a report by six weeks after the test date, try to find out whether other students are experiencing delays. Once in a while, computer or other problems at ETS cause general delays for all students who took a particular test. It's rare but frustrating, and there's not much you can do except sit tight.

Finally, if it appears that the score delay involves you alone (or only a handful of other students), it's possible that ETS may be investigating an apparent testing irregularity or a test security problem.

A *testing irregularity* means a problem with the way the test was administered. It could be due to a proctor's error (test-takers were given incorrect instructions), an ETS error (faulty test items were used), or circumstances beyond anyone's control (a test center is disrupted by fire or flood, or a computer malfunctions).

A *test security problem* means, quite specifically, a suspicion that students had access to the test beforehand; used books, calculators, or other forbidden aids during the exam; took the test under false names; passed answers to one another; or otherwise cheated.

If you fall under suspicion of cheating, you'll be in for an unpleasant experience, whether or not you are guilty. Although ETS makes an effort at "due process," the adjudication of such cases is basically an internal process controlled by the test makers.

This doesn't mean, however, that you are helpless, much less that you should meekly accept a "guilty" verdict if you are really innocent. Here is some advice as to what to do if you find yourself accused of misconduct on the GMAT CAT.

- Insist on understanding the accusation and the process. When an investigation is started, you should receive a copy of the ETS booklet *Why and How Educational Testing Service Questions Test*

Scores. Read it thoroughly. Then make sure that the test makers inform you as to exactly what misconduct is supposed to have occurred, so that you can marshal evidence in your defense.

■ Enlist the help and advice of a college counselor, professor, business mentor, or other trusted adviser. This is an important problem that can seriously affect your future academic and career prospects, and the bureaucracy at ETS can be intimidating. Don't try to handle it alone.

■ Communicate with ETS clearly and in writing. Use registered mail and keep copies of all your communications with the test makers. Make sure that you "admit" nothing that is not completely true.

■ As soon as you can, make detailed notes of everything you remember about your test-preparation and test-taking experience. In particular, if you remember anything "odd" that happened on the day of the exam, jot it down. (A mistake by a proctor, for example, may innocently explain some discrepancy ETS thinks is sinister.) Be sure to be as complete and accurate as possible. The sooner you make these notes, the clearer and more convincing your memory of events is likely to be.

■ Provide the test makers with any facts that could help to clear you. If you know why you're suspected of wrongdoing, you may be able to resolve the dispute by responding with information. For example, if you're suspected of cheating because you left the test room several times during the exam, you may want to ask your doctor to provide a letter confirming that you were suffering from a stomach complaint on the day of the test (if that was the case).

Sometimes, ETS will investigate a test-taker solely because of a dramatic score increase—200 points or more over a previous test. If you're in this category, be prepared to explain (and document, if possible) how you prepared for your second test. Describe your use of coaching, tutoring, books, software, and any other test-prep tools, and estimate the number of hours you devoted to study before the exam. A convincing account of your significant test-prep effort can go a long way toward showing that your score increase was produced not by trickery but by good old-fashioned hard work.

■ Consider enlisting legal help. In America, of course, the final recourse in disputes between groups and individuals is the law. Most wrangles with ETS don't require the help of a lawyer, but you may want to consider this option if you've been unjustly accused, if the test makers refuse to resolve the dispute quickly and fairly, and if the cost is not a major problem for you.

■ If the dispute is not resolved within a reasonable time (say, four to six weeks), insist on your right to retake the exam as soon as possible, at no charge to you. ETS is supposed to provide this service to give an innocent test taker the chance to demonstrate his abilities again without penalty and free from any cloud of suspicion.

If You Think Your Scores Are Wrong

On rare occasions, a student becomes convinced that one or more of her test scores are inaccurate. Here's what to do if this happens to you.

FYI

Test-question challenges have been much more effective in regard to math questions than to verbal ones—not because the verbal questions are "better," but because it's far easier to demonstrate actual errors on math questions. A degree of ambiguity and subjectivity is almost impossible to eliminate from verbal questions, making it almost impossible to prove that the test-maker's chosen answer is truly "wrong."

■ **Requesting rescoring of your Analytical Writing Assessment.** Sometimes, a student feels that the scoring of his or her essays is inaccurate or unfair. This is hardly unlikely; as we explained in Chapter 9, the holistic grading system used by ETS puts a premium on speedy judgments, not detailed or authoritative ones. It's entirely possible that a good essay could be misinterpreted by a hasty or exhausted reader.

Your best option in this case is to request rescoring of your essays. You can do this up to six months after taking the exam by either fax or phone. (As you probably guessed, there's a fee for this service—currently $45.) You'll get a new score report within three to five weeks. If it's found that your test *was* misgraded, ETS will send a notification letter to all of your universities. Note, however, that the revised scores will stand—whether they are higher or lower!

■ **Challenging a test question or procedure.** A more complicated problem arises if you become convinced that you were harmed either by some unfair procedure on the day of the test or by an inaccurate and flawed test question. There's a system for appealing such problems, but be prepared for a fairly lengthy process.

If you feel burned by a test procedure or question, write down all the details you can remember as soon as possible. Your complaint must be received no more than seven days after you take the test. Then send a registered letter to the test-makers at this address:

GMAT
Distribution and Receiving Center
225 Phillips Blvd.
Ewing, New Jersey 08628-7435

Include your name, address, phone number, birth date, social security number, and test registration number, and mention the name of the test you took, the date, and the name, number, and address of the test center you used. In your letter, explain what happened and why you think it was unfair.

ETS will investigate and respond. In most cases, they will defend their procedure or test question (and often they are right to do so). If you aren't satisfied, there are several further levels of appeal you can request, culminating in a formal review by an independent panel. It's up to you to decide how significant your complaint is, how strongly you feel about it, and how much time and effort you want to invest in this process.

ETS is obviously not perfect. Over the years, they have been forced to admit errors in over a dozen test questions, increasing the scores of hundreds of thousands of students.

So don't hesitate to challenge the test makers if you're convinced it's appropriate. The only way powerful institutions like ETS can be kept responsive to human concerns is if individuals hold them accountable for their actions, right and wrong.

FairTest, the nonprofit organization dedicated to fair and open testing, may be able to help you with information and referrals if you have a complaint or dispute about the GMAT CAT. Contact them at:

FairTest
342 Broadway
Cambridge, Massachusetts 02139-1802
Phone: 617-864-4810
Fax: 617-497-2224
E-mail: fairtest@aol.com

The Decision to Retest

Should you retake the GMAT CAT if you're not satisfied with your scores? In many cases, the answer is yes. Here are some of the factors to consider in making this decision.

- How do the scores you've already received match the credentials wanted by the business school(s) of your choice? Remember that you need to establish target GMAT CAT scores based on the admission requirements of the schools you want to attend, as well as the other credentials you bring to the table—your college grades, etc. If the test scores you've already earned fall outside the range in which most students at your ideal school score—or if they are at the lower end of that range—you should strongly consider retaking the test.

- How often have you already been tested? If you've taken the GMAT CAT twice or more previously—and especially if you prepared beforehand—you may have already tapped most of your potential for improvement. However, if you've been tested

FYI

ETS confirms that most students who take the GMAT CAT a second time enjoy at least a modest score increase, due to sheer familiarity with the exam. If you retake the test following a serious preparation program tailored to the weaknesses revealed by your first score report, the effects of that preparation, combined with the "familiarity effect," should give you a great shot at a significant score increase."

just once before—and especially if your preparation in the past was superficial—there's every reason to believe your score can go up, perhaps a lot.

- Can you identify test areas with potential for improvement? You're an especially strong candidate to retake the exam if your practice tests reveal specific areas of weakness. For example, if you generally perform well on all the Verbal areas except sentence corrections, a targeted practice program focusing on grammar, usage, and sentence correction strategies can boost your overall score significantly. Similarly, if a particular math area gave you trouble the first time around, work with a review book, teacher, or tutor to master that topic, and the chances are good that your Quantitative score will rise on test number two.

- Do you have time to invest in preparing for another test? Look realistically at your plans for school, work, and other activities. Before you schedule another exam, make sure you can block out hours during the prior weeks for study and practice. If you take the second test cold, without any real preparation or warm-up, you may wind up spinning your wheels, earning scores no higher than your first scores.

A final tip about retaking the exam: Don't forget to review *every* test area, at least briefly, before your second or later GMAT CAT. Although you may need to focus the bulk of your study on algebra (for example), it's important to keep your verbal skills and your knowledge of other math areas sharp, too. You don't want to gain points on one end while losing them on the other.

JUST THE FACTS

- Study your score report carefully, and make sure you understand what each number means.

- Evaluate your performance as universities will—against the credentials of their pool of applicants.

- If you think you completely bombed on the exam, consider cancelling your scores.

- If you think your GMAT CAT was unfair for any reason, you have ways to complain and be heard.

- Consider retaking the exam if your scores fall below the targets you need to achieve.

- If you do retake the test, focus your preparation on areas where you need the most improvement.

Chapter 13

The Insider's Tip Sheet

Get The Scoop On . . .

■ The most important test-taking strategies to review just before taking the GMAT CAT

I t's the night before you'll be taking the GMAT CAT—or maybe the very morning of the exam. You've been studying, practicing, and preparing for days, weeks, or even months, and you're about as ready to take the test as you'll ever be.

Trouble is, the strategies, techniques, and methods you've learned from this book feel as if they're lodged in dozens of separate compartments scattered throughout your overloaded brain. A few weeks may have passed since you last tried your hand at a particular question type; you've probably become a little fuzzy about exactly how to tackle it. But you don't have time now—hours before the test—to review hundreds of pages covering strategies for nine separate question types. If you try, you may just intensify that gnawing sense of anxiety in the pit of your stomach—and maybe even develop a full-blown case of panic.

That's where this chapter comes in. It's a concise recap of the most important tips, strategies, warnings, and techniques from the entire book, organized for easy study during the final day before your exam. For a true last-minute review, you may want to tear these pages out of the book and carry them with you in the car, bus, or train that takes you to the test center. It's even better to read them the night before—that way, if any one or two ideas don't ring a bell, you can look them up in the relevant chapters and refresh your memory.

OVERALL STRATEGIES FOR THE GMAT CAT

■ Work your way patiently through the tutorial materials at the start of the exam. Don't begin work on the real test until you're sure you're comfortable with all of the mechanics of the computerized test. Time spent mastering the computer tutorials does *not* affect your test-taking time.

- Remember, answering the first five questions in each test section correctly is crucially important. Take your time! Read and reread the questions, double-check your work, and consider every answer choice carefully. Getting these questions right will have a disproportionate effect on your overall scores.

- The question types will be interspersed, seemingly at random, throughout a given test section: A critical reasoning item may be followed by a sentence correction or a reading comprehension passage, unpredictably. Be prepared to adjust frequently from one type of question to another.

- After spending as much time as you need to on the first five questions, speed up slightly. The GMAT CAT is fairly generous with time, but you shouldn't dawdle or get bogged down on a single, unusually tough question. If you work at a steady pace, you should have ample time to answer every question.

- Use scrap paper freely—to perform computations, outline reading passages, and outline your essays. If you run out of paper, don't be shy about asking for more.

- Guess selectively. Use what you know to eliminate answers that are clearly wrong, then pick the best answer from among those that remain. Chances are you'll gain points by following this method.

- Each test section will include a few questions that will not be scored for experimental or research purposes. Since these questions are not labeled as experimental, every question should be taken seriously. But if you encounter a handful of "weird" questions of a type you've never seen before, don't fret about it—they are almost certainly experimental and will not affect your score.

VERBAL STRATEGIES

On All Verbal Questions

- Read every answer choice. In the Verbal section, there are degrees of right and wrong; the first answer may be partially correct, while the second answer is a little better, and the third answer is better still. Don't jump to select the first answer that appears tempting.

Reading Comprehension

- Use the three-stage method (previewing, reading, reviewing) to get the most out of each reading passage.

- Focus on the big ideas in each passage, not the small details.

- Look for the connections among the ideas in each passage.

- Review the passage as often as necessary to locate the answer for a specific question.

- Don't pick an answer just because it sounds familiar, seems to be true, or reflects information that actually appears in the passage—the answer must also accurately respond to the question being asked.

Sentence Corrections

- Start by reading the sentence carefully, "listening" for the error (if any). In most cases, the word or phrase that contains an error in grammar or usage will *sound* wrong.

- If no error is apparent, look for the four most common types of errors tested on the GMAT CAT: errors in the relationship between the verb and its subject, pronoun errors, sentence structure errors, and awkwardness, verbosity, and incorrect use of idioms.

- Once you spot the error, think of how you'd revise the sentence to correct it, and scan the answer choices, looking for the one(s) that fix the error. Then pick an answer that corrects the error without introducing any new error.

- Expect three or four sentences to be correct as originally written. For these, the first answer choice is correct.

- If you can't decide which of two answer choices is best, prefer the shorter of the two.

Critical Reasoning

- Start by looking for the key elements of any argument (the conclusion, the evidence, the hidden assumptions)—most of the questions will turn on the relationship among them.

- Then look for any fallacy (a logical flaw or weakness) contained in the argument.

- Always read all the answer choices before selecting the best one—there are "degrees of correctness" in critical reasoning.

QUANTITATIVE STRATEGIES

On All Quantitative Items

- As soon as you've found the right answer, mark it and move on—there are no "degrees of rightness" to be considered.

Multiple-Choice Problems

- The questions are designed to focus primarily on the underlying relationships among the numbers presented, not your ability to perform calculations. Therefore, if you find yourself spending too much time doing figuring, you've probably overlooked a simple shortcut.

- Feel free to round off and guesstimate, using approximate values.

- When in doubt about how to get started on a problem, try something—anything! This will often lead you toward a solution.

Data Sufficiency

- Tackle each item using the three-stage system: examine the question; consider the information provided by each statement individually; then, only if necessary, combine the two statements. At each stage, eliminate one or more wrong answers.

- Stop work as soon as you know whether the data are sufficient—it's not necessary to actually solve the problem.

- When plugging in numbers for unknown quantities, don't forget to consider negative numbers, fractions, zero, and 1.

- Don't assume any information not provided in the question or the statements, and don't assume the accuracy of any diagram provided by the test makers.

STRATEGIES FOR THE ANALYTICAL WRITING ASSESSMENT

- Use the four-step writing process to organize your work— brainstorm (3 minutes), outline (2 minutes), write (20 minutes), revise (5 minutes). Use the scrap paper provided to brainstorm and outline, then write and revise on the computer.

- Keep your outline simple, and use the paragraph as the unit of organization—one big idea, fully developed, to each paragraph you write.

- Use signpost words (nonetheless, similarly, next, consequently) to guide your reader through the essay.

- Be as specific as possible when offering examples or evidence to back up your ideas.

- Vary the length of your sentences, using short sentences to state ideas you want to emphasize.

- Proofread carefully, looking for errors in spelling, grammar, and word choice. When in doubt, rephrase to make the sentence correct.

Part V

Appendices

The Insider's GMAT CAT Word List

WHY STUDY VOCABULARY?

If you're a native speaker of English, you already know thousands of words. (The average person has a working vocabulary of more than 10,000 words—and is probably capable of at least recognizing thousands more.) After four years of college, you probably have an extensive vocabulary of words drawn from many fields of study, to say nothing of the words you hear, see, and use in everyday life. Is it really necessary for you to study vocabulary in preparation for the GMAT CAT?

For most people, the answer is Yes.

The test makers consider vocabulary so important that they test it in several ways on the GMAT CAT.

Your ability to fully understand reading comprehension passages will often turn on your knowledge of vocabulary. The broader, more varied, and more accurate your vocabulary knowledge, the better your chances of answering the questions that cover these passages quickly and correctly.

The better your vocabulary knowledge, the easier you'll find it to understand both the sentence correction items and the critical reading passages (which are, in effect, mini-reading passages focused on logic). Even an occasional math item is made a little more complicated by the use of a challenging vocabulary word.

So vocabulary knowledge makes a clear and significant difference in your performance on the GMAT CAT. Fortunately, the kinds of words that regularly appear on the GMAT CAT—as with so much else on the exam—fall into definite patterns.

The GMAT CAT is basically a test of "book learning." It's written and edited by bookish people for the benefit of the other bookish people who run university business schools. It's designed to test your ability to handle the kinds of bookish tasks graduate business students usually have to master, such as reading textbooks, finding information in reference books and company documents, deciphering scholarly journals, studying research abstracts, and writing impressive-sounding papers and reports.

So the hard words on the GMAT CAT are hard words of a particular sort: bookish hard words that deal, broadly speaking, with the manipulation and communication of *ideas*—words like *ambiguous, amplify, arbitrary,* and *arcane.* The better you master this sort of vocabulary, the better you'll do on the exam. (Note that the technical language of business—words like *securitize, capitalization, arbitrage,* and *bull market*—are not specifically tested on the GMAT CAT.)

Happily, you don't need to uncover GMAT CAT vocabulary on your own. We've done the spadework for you. By examining actual GMAT CATS from the last several years, we've been able to list the words most commonly used in reading passages, sentence corrections, and critical reasoning passages, including both the question stems and the answer choices. This list became the basis of the

Insider's GMAT CAT Word List. It includes about 500 primary words that are most likely to appear in one form or another on your GMAT CAT. It also includes hundreds of related words—words that are either variants of the primary words (*abrasion* as a variant of *abrade*, for example) or that share a common word root (like *ample, amplify,* and *amplitude*).

If you acquaint yourself with all the words in the Insider's GMAT CAT Word List, you will absolutely learn a number of new words that will appear on your GMAT CAT. You'll earn extra points as a result.

THE SIX BEST INSIDER'S VOCABULARY-BUILDING TIPS FOR THE GMAT CAT

Study Vocabulary Daily

There are some topics you can easily cram. Vocabulary isn't one of them. Words generally stick in the mind not the first or second time you learn them but the fourth or fifth time. Try to begin your vocabulary study several weeks before the exam. Take fifteen or twenty minutes a day to learn new words. Periodically review all the words you've previously studied; quiz yourself, or have a friend quiz you. This simple regimen can enable you to learn several hundred new words before you take the GMAT CAT.

Learn a Few Words at a Time

Don't try to gobble dozens of words in one sitting. They're likely to blur into an indistinguishable mass. Instead, pick a reasonable quantity—say, ten to fifteen words—and study them in some depth. Learn the definition of each word; examine the sample sentence provided in the word list; learn the related words; and try writing a couple of sentences of your own that include the word. Refer to your own dictionary for further information if you like.

Learn Words in Families

Language is a living thing. Words are used by humans, innately creative beings who constantly twist, reshape, invent, and recombine words. (Think of the jargon of your favorite sport or hobby, or the new language currently blossoming in cyberspace, for some examples.) As a result, most words belong to families, in which related ideas are expressed through related words. This makes it possible to learn several words each time you learn one.

In the Insider's GMAT CAT Word List, we've provided some of the family linkages to help you. For example, you'll find the adjective *anachronistic* in the word list. It means "out of the proper time," as illustrated by the sample sentence: *The reference in Shakespeare's* Julius Caesar *to "the clock striking twelve" is anachronistic, since there were no striking timepieces in ancient Rome.*

When you meet this word, you should also get to know its close kinfolk. The noun *anachronism* means something that is out of its proper time. The clock in *Julius Caesar,* for example, is an anachronism; in another way, so are the knickers worn by modern baseball players, which reflect a style in men's fashions that went out of date generations ago. When you learn the adjective, learn the noun (and/or verb) That goes with it at the same time.

Become a Word Root Explorer

The two words we just discussed—*anachronistic* and *anachronism*—are like brother and sister. Slightly more distant relatives can be located and learned through the Word Origin feature you'll find near many of the words in the list. The Word Origin for *anachronistic* connects this word to its origin in a source from another language: the Greek word *chronos* = time. Ultimately, this is the root from which the English word *anachronistic* grows.

As you explore the Word Origin, you'll find that many words—especially bookish GMAT CAT words—come from roots in Latin and Greek. There are complicated (and interesting) historical reasons for this, but the nub is that, for several centuries, learned people in England and America knew ancient Latin and Greek and deliberately imported words from those languages into English.

They rarely imported just one word from a given root. Thus, many word roots can enable you to learn several English words at once. The Word Origin for *anachronistic* tells you that *chronos* is also the source of the English words *chronic, chronicle, chronograph, chronology, synchronize.* All have to do with the concept of time:

> *chronic* = lasting a long time
> *chronicle* = a record of events over a period of time
> *chronograph* = a clock or watch
> *chronology* = a timeline
> *synchronize* = to make two things happen at the same time

Learning the word root *chronos* can help you in several ways. It will make it easier to learn all the words in the *chronos* family, as opposed to trying to learn them one at a time. It will help you to remember the meanings of *chronos* words if they turn up on the exam. And it may even help you to guess the meaning of an entirely new *chronos* word when you encounter it.

Use the Words You Learn

Make a deliberate effort to include the new words you're learning in your daily speech and writing. It will impress people (professors, bosses, friends, and enemies), and it will help solidify your memory of the words and their meanings. Maybe you've heard this tip about meeting new people: if you use a new acquaintance's name several times, you're likely never to forget it. The same is true with new words: use them, and you won't lose them.

Create Your Own Word List

Get into the habit of reading a little every day with your dictionary nearby. When you encounter a new word in a newspaper, magazine, or book, look it up. Then jot down the new word, its definition, and the sentence in which you encountered it in a notebook set aside for this purpose. Review your vocabulary notebook periodically—say, once a week. Use the words you learn this way. It's a great way to supplement our Insider's GMAT CAT Word List, because it's personally tailored—your notebook will reflect the kinds of things you read and the kinds of words you find most difficult. And the fact that you've taken the time and made the effort to write down the words and their meanings will help to fix them in your memory. Chances are good that you'll encounter a few words from your vocabulary notebook on the exam.

THE WORD LIST

Word Origin

Latin brevis = short. Also found in English brevity.

abbreviate (verb)   To make briefer, to shorten. *Because time was running out, the speaker was forced to abbreviate his remarks.* abbreviation (noun).

aberration (noun)   A deviation from what is normal or natural, an abnormality. *Jack's extravagant lunch at Lutece was an aberration from his usual meal, a peanut butter sandwich and a diet soda.* aberrant (adjective).

abeyance (noun)   A temporary lapse in activity; suspension. *In the aftermath of the bombing, all normal activities were held in abeyance.*

abjure (verb)   To renounce or reject; to officially disclaim. *While being tried by the inquisition in 1633, Galileo abjured all his writings holding that the Earth and other planets revolved around the sun.*

Word Origin

Latin abradare = to scrape. Also found in English abrasive.

abrade (verb)   To irritate by rubbing; to wear down in spirit. *Olga's "conditioning facial" abraded Sabrina's skin so severely that she vowed never to let anyone's hands touch her face again.* abrasion (noun)

abridge (verb)   To shorten, to reduce. *The Bill of Rights is designed to prevent Congress from abridging the rights of Americans.* abridgment (noun).

abrogate (verb)   To nullify, to abolish. *During World War II, the United States abrogated the rights of Japanese Americans by detaining them in internment camps.* abrogation (noun).

abscond (verb)   To make a secret departure, to elope. *Theresa will never forgive her daughter, Elena, for absconding to Miami with Philip when they were only seventeen.*

accretion (noun)   A gradual build-up or enlargement. *My mother's house is a mess due to her steady accretion of bric-a-brac and her inability to throw anything away.*

activism (noun)   A belief or practice based on direct action. *The young man's interest in activism led him to participate in numerous protest marches against the war.*

adjunct (noun)   Something added to another thing, but not a part of it; an associate or assistant. *While Felix and Fritz were adjuncts to Professor Himmelman during his experiments in electrodynamics, they did not receive credit when the results were published.*

adulterate (verb)   To corrupt, to make impure. *Unlike the chickens from the large poultry companies, Murray's free-roaming chickens have not been adulterated with hormones and other additives.*

Word Origin

Latin vertere = to turn. Also found in English adversary, adverse, reverse, vertical, vertigo.

adversary (noun)   An enemy or opponent. *When the former Soviet Union became an American ally, the United States lost its last major international adversary.* adverse (adjective).

advocate (noun)   One who pleads on another's behalf. *The woman's attorney served as an excellent advocate during her trial.*

affability (noun)   The quality of being easy to talk to and gracious. *Affability is a much-desired trait in any profession that involves dealing with many people on a daily basis.* affable (adjective).

affected (adjective)   False, artificial. *At one time, Japanese women were taught to speak in an affected high-pitched voice, which was thought girlishly attractive.* affect (verb), affectation (noun).

affiliation (noun)   Connection, association. *The close affiliation among the members of the team enabled them to outplay all their opponents.*

affinity (noun)   A feeling of shared attraction, kinship; a similarity. *When they first fell in love, Andrew and Tanya marveled over their affinity for bluegrass music, obscure French poetry, and beer taken with a squirt of lemon juice. People often say there is a striking affinity between dogs and their owners ('but please don't tell Clara that she and her basset hound are starting to resemble each other).*

aggrandize (verb)   To make bigger or greater; to inflate. *When he was mayor of New York City, Ed Koch was renowned for aggrandizing his accomplishments and strolling through city events shouting, "How'm I doing?"* aggrandizement (noun).

aggression (noun)   Forceful action or procedure. *Mohandas K. Ghandi argued that aggression on the part of one's oppressors was best met with passive resistance.* aggressive (adjective).

agitation (noun)   A disturbance; a disturbing feeling of upheaval and excitement. *After the CEO announced the coming layoffs, the employees' agitation was evident as they remained in the auditorium talking excitedly among themselves.* agitated (adjective), agitate (verb).

alignment (noun)   The proper positioning of parts in relation to each other. *If the wheels of an automobile are not in alignment, the car will not function properly.* align (verb).

allocate (verb)   To apportion for a specific purpose; to distribute. *The President talked about the importance of education and health care in his State of the Union address, but, in the end, the administration did not allocate enough resources for these pressing concerns.* allocation (noun).

alluded (verb)   Made indirect reference to. *Without actually threatening to fire his employee, the manager alluded to the possibility of his being terminated.*

amalgamate (verb)   To blend thoroughly. *The tendency of grains to sort when they should mix makes it difficult for manufacturers to create powders that are amalgamated.* amalgamation (noun).

ameliorate (verb)   To make something better or more tolerable. *The living conditions of the tenants were certainly ameliorated when the landlord finally installed washing machines and dryers in the basement.* amelioration (noun).

amortize (verb)   To pay off or reduce a debt gradually through periodic payments. *If you don't need to take a lump sum tax deduction, it's best to amortize large business expenditures by spreading the cost out over several years.*

Word Origin

Latin amplus = *full. Also found in English* ample, amplitude.

amplify (verb)   To enlarge, expand, or increase. *Uncertain as to whether they understood, the students asked the teacher to amplify his explanation.* amplification (noun).

anachronistic (adjective)   Out of the proper time. *The reference in Shakespeare's Julius Caesar to "the clock striking twelve" is anachronistic, since there were no striking timepieces in ancient Rome.* anachronism (noun).

analogous (adjective)   Having a likeness or similarity. *The student pilot quickly learned that flying a plane was only slightly analogous to driving an automobile.* analogue (noun).

analytical (adjective)   Separating something into its component parts. *The mathematician's analytical ability enabled him to determine the correct answer to the problem.* analyze (verb).

anarchy (noun)   Absence of law or order. *For several months after the Nazi government was destroyed, there was no effective government in parts of Germany, and anarchy ruled.* anarchic (adjective).

Word Origin

Latin anima = *mind, spirit. Also found in English* animate, magnanimous, pusillanimous, unanimous.

animosity (noun)   Hostility, resentment. *During the last debate, the candidates could no longer disguise their animosity and began to trade accusations and insults.*

anomaly (noun)   Something different or irregular. *The tiny planet Pluto, orbiting next to the giants Jupiter, Saturn, and Neptune, has long appeared to be an anomaly.* anomalous (adjective).

antagonism (noun)   Hostility, conflict, opposition. *As more and more reporters investigated the Watergate scandal, antagonism between the Nixon administration and the press increased.* antagonistic (adjective), antagonize (verb).

antipathy (noun)   A long-held feeling of dislike or aversion. *When asked why he didn't call for help immediately after his wife fell into a coma, the defendant emphasized his wife's utter antipathy to doctors.*

apprehension (noun)   A feeling of fear or foreboding; an arrest. *The peculiar feeling of apprehension that Harold Pinter creates in his plays derives as much from the long silences between speeches as from the speeches themselves. The policewoman's dramatic apprehension of the gunman took place in full view of the midtown lunch crowd.* apprehend (verb).

appropriate (verb)   Take possession of. *Because he wanted to play with it, the little boy appropriated his sister's new doll.*

Word Origin

Latin arbiter = *judge. Also found in English* arbiter, arbitrage, arbitrate.

arbitrary (adjective)   Based on random or merely personal preference. *Both computers cost the same and had the same features, so in the end I made an arbitrary decision about which one to buy.*

archaic (adjective)   Old fashioned, obsolete. *Those who believe in "open marriage" often declare that they will not be bound by archaic laws and religious rituals, but state instead that love alone should bring two people together.* archaism (noun).

argumentation (noun)   Forming reasons, drawing conclusions, and applying them to a discussion. *A discussion of the merits and demerits of grass and artificial turf in ballparks provides an excellent opportunity for argumentation.* argumentative (adjective).

arid (adjective)   Very dry; boring and meaningless. *The arid climate of Arizona makes farming difficult. Some find the law a fascinating topic, but for me it is an arid discipline.* aridity (noun).

Word Origin

Latin articulus =
*joint, division.
Also found in
English* arthritis,
article, inarticu-
late.

articulate (adjective)   To express oneself clearly and effectively. *Compared to George Bush, with his stammering and his frequently incomplete sentences, Bill Clinton was considered a highly articulate president.*

asperity (noun)   Harshness, severity. *Total silence at the dinner table, baths in icy water, prayers five times a day—these practices all contributed to the asperity of life in the monastery.*

assail (verb)   To attack with blows or words. *When the President's cabinet members rose to justify the case for military intervention in Iraq, they were assailed by many audience members who were critical of U.S. policy.* assailant (noun).

assay (verb)   To analyze for particular components; to determine weight, quality, etc. *The jeweler assayed the stone pendant Gwyneth inherited from her mother and found it to contain a topaz of high quality.*

assertion (noun)   A positive statement or declaration. *If he had not sincerely believed that he was the best person for the job he would not have made that assertion.* assert (verb).

assessment (noun)   An appraisal. *The woman's assessment of the situation led her to believe that it was an appropriate time to take some action.* assess (verb).

assimilate (verb)   To absorb into a system or culture. *New York City has assimilated one group of immigrants after another, from the Jewish, German, and Irish immigrants who arrived at the turn of the last century to the waves of Mexican and Latin American immigrants who arrived in the 1980s.* assimilated (adjective). *Unlike her sister, Sook Lee is thoroughly assimilated to Southern California; she speaks more like a valley girl than a Korean and dismisses such traditional notions as respect for one's elders as "boring."*

assuage (verb)   To ease, to pacify. *Knowing that the pilot's record was perfect did little to assuage Linnet's fear of flying in the two-seater airplane.*

attainment (noun)   The act of achieving a goal, or the goal itself. *Had the company's vice president not already reached a certain level of attainment she would never have been considered for the presidency.*

audacious (adjective)   Bold, daring, adventurous. *Her plan to cross the Atlantic single-handed in a twelve-foot sailboat was an audacious, if not reckless, one.* audacity (noun).

authoritarian (adjective)   Favoring or demanding blind obedience to leaders. *Despite most Americans' strong belief in democracy, the American government has sometimes supported authoritarian regimes in other countries.* authoritarianism (noun).

authoritative (adjective)   Official, conclusive. *For over five decades, American parents regarded Doctor Benjamin Spock as the most authoritative voice on baby and child care.* authority (noun), authorize (verb).

autonomy (noun)   The quality of being self-governing. *Only in the most progressive companies are managers given the autonomy they really need to effectively do their jobs.*

aver (verb)   To claim to be true; to avouch. *The fact that the key witness averred the defendant's innocence was what ultimately swayed the jury to deliver a "not guilty" verdict.*

avow (verb)   To declare boldly. *Immediately after Cyrus avowed his atheism at our church fund-raiser, there was a long, uncomfortable silence.* avowal (noun), avowed (adjective).

belligerent (adjective)   Quarrelsome, combative. *Mrs. Juniper was so belligerent toward the clerks at the local stores that they cringed when they saw her coming.* belligerent (noun) An opposing army, a party waging war. *The Union and Confederate forces were the belligerents in the American Civil War.*

benevolent (adjective)   Wishing or doing good. *In old age, Carnegie used his wealth for benevolent purposes, donating large sums to found libraries and schools around the country.* benevolence (noun).

Word Origin

Latin bene = *well. Also found in English* benediction, benefactor, beneficent, beneficial, benefit, benign.

boggle (verb)   To overwhelm with amazement. *The ability of physicists to isolate the most infinitesimal particles of matter truly boggles the mind.*

bogus (adjective)   Phony, a sham. *Senior citizens are often the target of telemarketing scams pushing bogus investment opportunities.*

bombastic (adjective)   Inflated or pompous in style. *Old-fashioned bombastic political speeches don't work on television, which demands a more intimate, personal style of communication.* bombast (noun).

brazenly (adverb)   Acting with disrespectful boldness. *Some say that the former White House intern brazenly threw herself at the President, but the American public will probably never know the full truth.* brazen (adjective).

broach (verb)   To bring up an issue for discussion, to propose. *Knowing my father's strictness about adhering to a budget, I just can't seem to broach the subject of my massive credit-card debt.*

burgeon (verb)   To bloom, literally or figuratively. *Due to the extremely mild winter, the forsythia burgeoned as early as March. The story of two prison inmates in Manuel Puig's play* The Kiss of The Spiderwoman *is testimony that tenderness can burgeon in the most unlikely places.*

burnish (verb)   To shine by polishing, literally or figuratively. *After stripping seven layers of old paint off the antique door, the carpenter stained the wood and burnished it to a rich hue. When Bill Gates, the wealthiest man in the country, decided to endorse the Big Bertha line of Golf Clubs, many suggested that he was trying to burnish his image as a "regular guy."*

buttress (noun)   Something that supports or strengthens. *The endorsement of the American Medical Association is a powerful buttress for the claims made on behalf of this new medicine.* buttress (verb).

cacophony (noun)   Discordant sounds; dissonance. *In the minutes before classes start, the high school's halls are filled with a cacophony of shrieks, shouts, banging locker doors, and pounding feet.* cacophonous (adjective)

calibrate (verb)   To determine or mark graduations (of a measuring instrument); to adjust or finely tune. *We tried to calibrate the heating to Rufus's liking, but he still ended up shivering in our living room.* calibration (noun).

caste (noun)   A division of society based on differences of wealth, rank, or occupation. *While the inhabitants of India, for example, are divided into castes, in theory no such division exists in the United States.*

castigate (verb)   To chastise; to punish severely. *The editor castigated Bob for repeatedly failing to meet his deadlines.* castigation (noun).

catalytic (adjective)   Bringing about, causing, or producing some result. *The conditions for revolution existed in America by 1765; the disputes about taxation that arose during the following decade were the catalytic events that sparked the rebellion.* catalyze (verb).

causal (adjective)   Indicating a reason for an action or condition. *The continuing threat of rain was a causal factor in the canceling of the annual school picnic.*

caustic (adjective)   Burning, corrosive. *No pretensions were safe when the famous satirist H. L. Mencken unleashed his caustic wit.*

cessation (noun)   A temporary or final stopping. *Due to the cessation of the major project he was working on, the architect found himself with a considerable amount of time on his hands.* cease (verb).

chaos (noun)   Disorder, confusion, chance. *The first few moments after the explosion were pure chaos: no one was sure what had happened, and the area was filled with people running and yelling.* chaotic (adjective).

chary (adjective)   Slow to accept, cautious. *Yuan was chary about going out with Xinhua, since she had been badly hurt in her previous relationship.*

chronology (noun)   An arrangement of events by order of occurrence, a list of dates; the science of time. *If you ask Susan about her two-year-old son, she will give you a chronology of his accomplishments and childhood illnesses, from the day he was born to the present. The village of Copan was where Mayan astronomical learning, as applied to chronology, achieved its most accurate expression in the famous Mayan calendar.* chronological (adjective).

circumspect (adjective)   Prudent, cautious. *After he had been acquitted of the sexual harassment charge, the sergeant realized he would have to be more circumspect in his dealings with the female cadets.* circumspection (noun).

cleave (verb)   A tricky verb that can mean either to stick closely together or to split apart. (Pay attention to context.) *The more abusive his father became, the more Timothy cleaved to his mother and refused to let her out of his sight. Sometimes a few words carelessly spoken are enough to cleave a married couple and leave the relationship in shambles.* cleavage (noun).

coagulant (noun)   Any material that causes another to thicken or clot. *Hemophilia is characterized by excessive bleeding from even the slightest cut and is caused by a lack of one of the coagulants necessary for blood clotting.* coagulate (verb).

coalesce (verb)   To fuse, to unite. *The music we know as jazz coalesced from diverse elements from many musical cultures, including those of West Africa, America, and Europe.* coalescence (noun).

coerce (verb)   To force someone either to do something or to refrain from doing something. *The Miranda ruling prevents police from coercing a confession by forcing them to read criminals their rights.* coercion (noun).

Word Origin

Greek kaustikos = *burning. Also found in English* holocaust.

Word Origin

Latin circus = *circle. Also found in English* circumference, circumnavigate, circumscribe, circumvent.

Word Origin

Latin mensura = *to measure. Also found in English* measure, immeasurable, immense, mensuration.

cogent (adjective) Forceful and convincing. *The committee members were won over to the project by the cogent arguments of the chairman.* cogency (noun).

commensurate (adjective) Aligned with, proportional. *Many Ph.D.s in the humanities do not feel their paltry salaries are commensurate with their abilities, their experience, or the heavy workload they are asked to bear.*

commingle (verb) To blend, to mix. *Just as he had when he was only five years old, Elmer did not allow any of the foods on his plate to commingle: the beans must not merge with the rice nor the chicken rub shoulders with the broccoli!*

companionate (adjective) Suitably or harmoniously accompanying. *Even though the two women had never traveled together before, they found each other to be extremely companionate.*

compensate (verb) To counterbalance or make appropriate payment to. *Although the man received a considerable salary for all his hard work and long hours, he did not feel it was enough to compensate him for the time taken away from his family.* compensation (noun).

complaisant (adjective) Tending to bow to others' wishes; amiable. *Of the two Dashwood sisters, Elinor was the more complaisant, often putting the strictures of society and family above her own desires.* complaisance (noun).

complement (noun) Something that completes, fills up, or makes perfect. *Red wine serves as an excellent complement to a steak dinner.* complementary (adjective).

compound (verb) To intensify, to exacerbate. *When you make a faux pas, my father advised me, don't compound the problem by apologizing profusely; just say you're sorry and get on with life!*

compulsory (adjective) Mandatory, required. *Prior to the establishment of a volunteer army, military service was compulsory for young men in the United States.*

conceivable (adjective) Possible, imaginable. *It's possible to find people with every conceivable interest by surfing the World Wide Web—from fans of minor film stars to those who study the mating habits of crustaceans.* conception (noun).

conclusive (adjective) Putting an end to debate, question, or uncertainty. *The district attorney was able to provide conclusive proof of the defendant's guilt.* conclude (verb).

concur (verb) To agree, to approve. *We concur that a toddler functions best on a fairly reliable schedule; however, my husband tends to be a bit more rigid than I am.* concurrence (noun).

condensation (noun) A reduction to a denser form (from steam to water); an abridgment of a literary work. *The condensation of humidity on the car's windshield made it difficult for me to see the road. It seems as though every beach house I've ever rented features a shelf full of* Reader's Digest *condensations of b-grade novels.* condense (verb).

condescending (adjective) Having an attitude of superiority toward another; patronizing. *"What a cute little car!" she remarked in a condescending fashion. "I suppose it's the nicest one someone like you could afford!"* condescension (noun).

condone (verb)   To overlook, to permit to happen. *Schools with Zero Tolerance policies do not condone alcohol, drugs, vandalism, or violence on school grounds.*

conglomerate (verb)   To form into a mass or coherent whole. *When one company buys another, the two conglomerate into a single larger entity.*

congruent (adjective)   Coinciding; harmonious. *Fortunately, the two employees who had been asked to organize the department had congruent views on the budget.* congruence (noun).

Word Origin

Latin jungere = *to join. Also found in English* injunction, junction, juncture.

conjunction (noun)   The occurrence of two or more events together in time or space; in astronomy, the point at which two celestial bodies have the least separation. *Low inflation, occurring in conjunction with low unemployment and relatively low interest rates, has enabled the United States to enjoy a long period of sustained economic growth. The moon is in conjunction with the sun when it is new; if the conjunction is perfect, an eclipse of the sun will occur.* conjoin (verb).

consolation (noun)   Relief or comfort in sorrow or suffering. *Although we miss our dog very much, it is a consolation to know that she died quickly, without much suffering.* console (verb).

consternation (noun)   Shock, amazement, dismay. *When a voice in the back of the church shouted out, "I know why they should not be married!" the entire gathering was thrown into consternation.*

contention (noun)   A point made in an argument or debate. *Despite evidence to the contrary, it had always been the president's contention that he was not guilty of any crimes or misdemeanors.* contentious (adjective).

contingency (noun)   An event that is possible but unlikely to occur. *When making plans for the future, it is always wise to prepare for any contingency that may occur.* contingent (adjective).

convergence (noun)   The act of coming together in unity or similarity. *A remarkable example of evolutionary convergence can be seen in the shark and the dolphin, two sea creatures that developed from different origins to become very similar in form and appearance.* converge (verb).

Word Origin

Latin vivere = *to live. Also found in English* revive, vital, vivid, vivisection.

conviviality (noun)   Fond of good company and eating and drinking. *The conviviality of my fellow employees seemed to turn every staff meeting into a party, complete with snacks, drinks, and lots of hearty laughter.* convivial (adjective).

convoluted (adjective)   Twisting, complicated, intricate. *Income tax law has become so convoluted that it's easy for people to violate it completely by accident.* convolute (verb), convolution (noun).

corrective (noun)   Something that removes errors or mistakes. *A safe driving course can serve as a corrective for dangerous driving habits.* correctively (adverb).

correlation (noun)   A correspondence between two comparable entities. *Whether or not there should be, there is not necessarily a correlation between the amount of work people do and the compensation they receive for it.* correlate (verb).

corroborating (adjective)   Supporting with evidence; confirming. *A passerby who had witnessed the crime gave corroborating testimony about the presence of the accused person.* corroborate (verb), corroboration (noun).

corrosive (adjective)   Eating away, gnawing, or destroying. *Years of poverty and hard work had a corrosive effect on her strength and beauty.* corrode (verb), corrosion (noun).

cosmopolitanism (noun)   International sophistication; worldliness. *Budapest is known for its cosmopolitanism, perhaps because it was the first Eastern European city to be more open to capitalism and influences from the West.* cosmopolitan (adjective).

counterargument (noun)   A point made in a discussion contrary to an already stated point. *The lack of proof that the death penalty has historically served as a deterrent to potential murderers is a good counterargument to those who contend that it will do so in the future.*

countering (verb)   Offering something opposite or contrary. *Because they were so close to agreeing on a price, the seller believed that countering the buyer's offer would result in their reaching an agreement.* counter (noun).

covert (adjective)   Secret, clandestine. *The CIA has often been criticized for its covert operations in the domestic policies of foreign countries, such as the failed Bay of Pigs operation in Cuba.*

covetous (adjective)   Envious, particularly of another's possessions. *Benita would never admit to being covetous of my new sable jacket, but I found it odd that she couldn't refrain from trying it on each time we met.* covet (verb).

craven (adjective)   Cowardly. *Local gay and lesbian activists were outraged by the craven behavior of a policeman who refused to come to the aid of an HIV-positive accident victim.*

credulous (adjective)   Ready to believe; gullible. *Elaine was not very credulous of the explanation Serge gave for his acquisition of the Matisse lithograph.* credulity (noun).

cryptic (adjective)   Puzzling, ambiguous. *I was puzzled by the cryptic message left on my answering machine about "a shipment of pomegranates from an anonymous donor."*

culmination (noun)   The climax. *The Los Angeles riots, in the aftermath of the Rodney King verdict, were the culmination of long-standing racial tensions between the residents of South Central L.A. and the police.* culminate (verb).

culpable (adjective)   Deserving blame, guilty. *Although he committed the crime, because he was mentally ill he should not be considered culpable for his actions.* culpability (noun).

cursory (adjective)   Hasty and superficial. *Detective Martinez was rebuked by his superior officer for drawing conclusions about the murder after only a cursory examination of the crime scene.*

cyclic (adjective)   Relating to a regularly repeated event or sequence of events. *Since autumn follows summer each year, and is in turn always followed by winter and spring, the year is said to be cyclic.* cyclically (adverb).

debilitating (adjective)   Weakening; sapping the strength of. *One can't help but marvel at the courage Steven Hawking displays in the face of such a debilitating disease as ALS.* debilitate (verb).

Word Origin

Latin celer = *swift. Also found in English* accelerate, celerity.

decelerate (verb)   To slow down. *Randall didn't decelerate enough on the winding roads, and he ended up smashing his new sports utility vehicle into a guard rail.* deceleration (noun).

decimation (noun)   Almost complete destruction. *Michael Moore's documentary, "Roger and Me," chronicles the decimation of the economy of Flint, Michigan, after the closing of a General Motors factory.* decimate (verb).

decry (verb)   To criticize or condemn. *Cigarette ads aimed at youngsters have led many to decry the unfair marketing tactics of the tobacco industry.*

defamation (noun)   Act of harming someone by libel or slander. *When the article in the* National Enquirer *implied that she was somehow responsible for her husband's untimely death, Renata instructed her lawyer to sue the paper for defamation of character.* defame (verb).

defer (verb)   To graciously submit to another's will; to delegate. *In all matters relating to the children's religious education, Joy deferred to her husband. since he clearly cared more about giving them a solid grounding in Judaism.* deference (noun).

deliberate (verb)   To think about an issue before reaching a decision. *The legal pundits covering the O.J. Simpson trial were shocked by the short time the jury took to deliberate after a trial that lasted months.* deliberation (noun).

demagogue (noun)   A leader who plays dishonestly on the prejudices and emotions of his followers. *Senator Joseph McCarthy was a demagogue who used the paranoia and biases of the anti-communist 1950s as a way of seizing fame and considerable power in Washington.* demagoguery (noun).

Word Origin

Greek demos = *people. Also found in English* democracy, demographic, endemic.

demographic (adjective)   Relating to the statistical study of population. *Three demographic groups have been the intense focus of marketing strategy: baby boomers, born between 1946 and 1964; baby busters, or the youth market, born between 1965 and 1976; and a group referred to as tweens, those born between 1977 and 1983.* demography (noun), demographics (noun).

deprecate (verb)   To express disapproval of. *Even if you disagree with an individual on a given subject, it is not necessary—nor even advisable—to personally deprecate him or her.*

derisive (adjective)   Expressing ridicule or scorn. *Many women's groups were derisive of Avon's choice of a male CEO, since the company derives its $5.1 billion in sales from an army of female salespeople.* derision (noun).

derivative (adjective)   Imitating or borrowed from a particular source. *When a person first writes poetry, her poems are apt to be derivative of whatever poetry she most enjoys reading.* derivation (noun), derive (verb).

desiccate (verb)   To dry out, to wither; to drain of vitality. *The long drought thoroughly desiccated our garden; what was once a glorious Eden was now a scorched and hellish wasteland. A recent spate of books has debunked the myth that menopause desiccates women and affirmed, instead, that women often reach heights of creativity in their later years.* desiccant (noun), desiccation (noun).

despotic (adjective)   Oppressive and tyrannical. *During the despotic reign of Idi Amin in the 1970s, an estimated 200,000 Ugandans were killed.* despot (noun).

desultory (adjective)   Disconnected, aimless. *Tina's few desultory stabs at conversation fell flat as Guy just sat there, stony-faced; it was a disastrous first date.*

deteriorated (verb)   Made inferior in character, quality, or value. *As a result of having been driven more than 150,000 miles, the salesman's car had deteriorated to the point that it had to be replaced.* deterioration (noun).

determinant (noun)   An element that identifies the nature of something or fixes an outcome. *Location is a determinant—one of many—in making a decision about buying a home.* determinantal (adjective).

deviate (verb)   To depart from a standard or norm. *Having agreed upon a spending budget for the company, we mustn't deviate from it; if we do, we may run out of money before the year ends.* deviation (noun).

diatribe (noun)   Abusive or bitter speech or writing. *While angry conservatives dismissed Susan Faludi's* Backlash *as a feminist diatribe, it is actually a meticulously researched book.*

differentiate (verb)   To show the difference in or between. *When considering two offers, a job applicant must clearly differentiate between them to determine which is the best.*

diffident (adjective)   Hesitant, reserved, shy. *Someone with a diffident personality is most likely to succeed in a career that involves little public contact.* diffidence (noun).

digress (verb)   To wander from the main path or the main topic. *My high school biology teacher loved to digress from science into personal anecdotes about his college adventures.* digression (noun), digressive (adjective).

disabuse (verb)   To correct a fallacy, to clarify. *I hated to disabuse Filbert, who is a passionate collector of musical trivia, but I had to tell him that the Monkees had hardly sung a note and had lip-synched their way through almost all of their albums.*

disburse (verb)   To pay out or distribute (funds or property). *Jaime was flabbergasted when his father's will disbursed all of the old man's financial assets to Raymundo and left him with only a few sticks of furniture.* disbursement (noun).

discern (verb)   To detect, notice, or observe. *With difficulty, I could discern the shape of a whale off the starboard bow, but it was too far away to determine its size or species.* discernment (noun).

discordant (adjective)   Characterized by conflict. *Stories and films about discordant relationships that resolve themselves happily are always more interesting than stories about content couples who simply stay content.* discordance (noun).

discourse (noun)   Formal and orderly exchange of ideas, a discussion. *In the late twentieth-century, cloning and other feats of genetic engineering became popular topics of public discourse.* discursive (adjective).

Word Origin

Latin credere =
to believe. Also
found in English
credential,
credible, credit,
credo, credulous,
incredible.

discredit (verb)   To cause disbelief in the accuracy of some statement or the reliability of a person. *Although many people still believe in UFOs, among scientists the reports of "alien encounters" have been thoroughly discredited.*

discreet (adjective)   Showing good judgment in speech and behavior. *Be discreet when discussing confidential business matters—don't talk among strangers on the elevator, for example.* discretion (noun).

discrete (adjective)   Separate, unconnected. *Canadians get peeved when people can't seem to distinguish between Canada and the United States, forgetting that Canada has its own discrete heritage and culture.*

disparity (noun)   Difference in quality or kind. *There is often a disparity between the kind of serious, high-quality television people say they want and the low-brow programs they actually watch.* disparate (adjective).

dissemble (verb)   To pretend, to simulate. *When the police asked whether Nancy knew anything about the crime, she dissembled innocence.*

dissemination (noun)   Spreading abroad or dispersing. *The dissemination of information is the most important aspect of a public relations person's job.*

dissipate (verb)   To spread out or scatter. *The windows and doors were opened, allowing the smoke that had filled the room to dissipate.* dissipation (noun).

Word Origin

Latin sonare = to
sound. Also found
in English
consonance,
sonar, sonic,
sonorous.

dissonance (noun)   Lack of music harmony; lack of agreement between ideas. *Most modern music is characterized by dissonance, which many listeners find hard to enjoy. There is a noticeable dissonance between two common beliefs of most conservatives: their faith in unfettered free markets and their preference for traditional social values.* dissonant (adjective).

distillation (noun)   Something distilled, an essence or extract. In chemistry, a process that drives gas or vapor from liquids or solids. *Sharon Olds' poems are powerful distillations of motherhood and other primal experiences. In Mrs. Hornmeister's chemistry class, our first experiment was to create a distillation of carbon gas from wood.* distill (verb).

diverge (verb)   To move in different directions. *Frost's poem "The Road Less Traveled," tells of the choice he made when "Two roads diverged in a yellow wood."* divergence (noun), divergent (adjective).

diversify (verb)   To balance by adding variety. *Any financial manager will recommend that you diversify your stock portfolio by holding some less-volatile blue-chip stocks along with more growth-oriented technology issues.* diversification (noun), diversified (adjective).

divest (verb)   To rid (oneself) or be freed of property, authority, or title. *In order to turn around its ailing company and concentrate on imaging, Eastmann Kodak divested itself of peripheral businesses in the areas of household products, clinical diagnostics, and pharmaceuticals.* divestiture (noun).

divulge (verb)   To reveal. *The people who count the votes for the Oscar awards are under strict orders not to divulge the names of the winners.*

dogmatic (adjective)   Holding firmly to a particular set of beliefs with little or no basis. *Believers in Marxist doctrine tend to be dogmatic, ignoring evidence that contradicts their beliefs or explaining it away.* dogma (noun), dogmatism (noun).

Word Origin

Latin dormire =
to sleep. Also
found in English
dormitory.

dormant (adjective) Temporarily inactive, as if asleep. *An eruption of Mt. Rainier, a dormant volcano in Washington state, would cause massive, life-threatening mud slides in the surrounding area. Bill preferred to think that his sex drive was dormant rather than extinct.* dormancy (noun)

dross (noun) Something that is trivial or inferior; an impurity. *As a reader for the* Paris Review, *Julia spent most of her time sifting through piles of manuscripts to separate the extraordinary poems from the dross.*

dubious (adjective) Doubtful, uncertain. *Despite the chairman's attempts to convince the committee members that his plan would succeed, most of them remained dubious.* dubiety (noun).

dupe (noun) Someone who is easily cheated. *My cousin Ravi is such a dupe; he actually gets excited when he receives those envelopes saying "Ravi Murtugudde, you may have won a million dollars," and he even goes so far as to try claiming his prize.*

eccentricity (noun) Odd or whimsical behavior. *Rock star Michael Jackson is now better known for his offstage eccentricities—such as sleeping in an oxygen tank, wearing a surgical mask, and building his own theme park—than for his on-stage performances.* eccentric (adjective).

edifying (adjective) Instructive, enlightening. *Ariel would never admit it to her high-brow friends, but she found the latest self-help best seller edifying and actually helpful.* edification (noun), edify (verb).

Word Origin

Latin facere = to
do. Also found in
English facility,
factor, facsimile,
faculty.

efficacy (noun) The power to produce the desired effect. *While teams have been enormously popular in the workplace, there are some who now question their efficacy and say that "one head is better than ten."* efficacious (noun).

effrontery (noun) Shameless boldness. *The sports world was shocked when a pro basketball player had the effrontery to choke the head coach of his team during a practice session.*

elaborate (verb) To expand upon something; develop. *One characteristic of the best essayists is their ability to elaborate ideas through examples, lists, similes, small variations, and even exaggerations.* elaborate (adjective), elaboration (noun).

emanating (verb) Coming from a source. *The less than pleasant odor emanating from the frightened skunk was enough to send the campers in search of another campsite.* emanation (noun).

embellish (verb) To enhance or exaggerate; to decorate. *The long-married couple told their stories in tandem, with the husband outlining the plot and the wife embellishing it with colorful details.* embellished (adjective). *Both Salman Rushdie, of India, and Patrick Chamoiseau, of Martinique, emerged from colonized countries and created embellished versions of their colonizers' languages in their novels.*

embezzle (verb) To steal money property that has been entrusted to your care. *The church treasurer was found to have embezzled thousands of dollars by writing phony checks on the church bank account.* embezzlement (noun).

emollient (noun) Something that softens or soothes. *She used a hand cream as an emollient on her dry, work-roughened hands.* emollient (adjective).

empirical (adjective)   Based on experience or personal observation. *Although many people believe in ESP, scientists have found no empirical evidence of its existence.* empiricism (noun).

emulate (verb)   To imitate or copy. *The British band Oasis is quite open about their desire to emulate their idols, the Beatles.* emulation (noun).

enervate (verb)   To reduce the energy or strength of someone or something. *The stress of the operation left her feeling enervated for about two weeks.* enervation (noun).

engender (verb)   To produce, to cause. *Countless disagreements over the proper use of national forests and parklands have engendered feelings of hostility between ranchers and environmentalists.*

enhance (verb)   To improve in value or quality. *New kitchen appliances will enhance your house and increase the amount of money you'll make when you sell it.* enhancement (noun).

enigmatic (adjective)   Puzzling, mysterious. *Alain Resnais' enigmatic film Last Year at Marienbad sets up a puzzle that is never resolved: a man meets a woman at a hotel and believes he once had an affair with her—or did he?* enigma (noun).

enmity (noun)   Hatred, hostility, ill will. *Long-standing enmity, like that between the Protestants and Catholics in Northern Ireland, is difficult to overcome.*

ensure (verb)   To make certain; to guarantee. *In order to ensure a sufficient crop of programmers and engineers for the future, the United States needs to raise the quality of its math and science schooling.*

enumerate (verb)   To count off or name one by one. *In order to convince his parents that he was choosing the right college, the high school senior felt it would be advisable to enumerate all the reasons for his decision.* enumeration (noun).

epithet (noun)   Term or words used to characterize a person or thing, often in a disparaging way. *In her recorded phone conversations with Linda Tripp, Monica Lewinsky is said to have referred to President Clinton by a number of epithets including "The Creep," and "The Big He."* epithetical (adjective).

Word Origin

Latin aequus = equal. *Also found in English* equality, equanimity, equation.

equable (adjective)   Steady, uniform. *While many people can't see how Helena could possibly be attracted to "Boring Bruno," his equable nature is the perfect complement to her volatile personality.*

equity (noun)   The state of being impartial and fair. *Although our legal system is designed to provide equity, it does not always provide justice.*

equivocate (verb)   To use misleading or intentionally confusing language. *When Pedro pressed Renee for an answer to his marriage proposal, she equivocated by saying, "I've just got to know when your Mercedes will be out of the shop!"* equivocal (adjective), equivocation (noun).

Word Origin

Latin radix = root. *Also found in English* radical.

eradicate (verb)   To destroy completely. *American society has failed to eradicate racism, although some of its worst effects have been reduced.* eradication (noun).

erosion (noun)   The process of being worn away by degrees. *The process by which the elements reduce mountains to hills over time is an excellent example of erosion.* erode (verb).

erudition (noun) Extensive knowledge, usually acquired from books. *When Dorothea first saw Mr. Casaubon's voluminous library she was awed, but after their marriage she quickly realized that erudition is no substitute for originality.* erudite (adjective).

esoterica (noun) Items of interest to a select group. *The fish symposium at St. Antony's College in Oxford explored all manner of esoterica relating to fish, as is evidenced in presentations such as "The Buoyant Slippery Lipids of the Escolar and Orange Roughy" and "Food on Board Whale Ships—from the Inedible to the Incredible."* esoteric (adjective).

espouse (verb) To take up as a cause; to adopt. *No politician in American today will openly espouse racism, although some behave and speak in racially prejudiced ways.*

estimable (adjective) Worthy of esteem and admiration. *After a tragic fire raged through Malden Mills, the estimable mill owner, Aaron Feuerstein, restarted operations and rebuilt the company within just one month.* esteem (noun).

ethnology (noun) A science dealing with the division of mankind into races and their origins. *The anthropologist Margaret Mead is best known for her study of the ethnology of the natives of New Guinea.* ethnologic (adjective).

euphemism (noun) An agreeable expression that is substituted for an offensive one. *Some of the more creative euphemisms for "layoffs" in current use are: "release of resources," "involuntary severance," "strengthening global effectiveness," and "career transition program."* euphemistic (adjective).

Word Origin

Latin acer = *sharp. Also found in English* acerbity, acrid, acrimonious.

exacerbate (verb) To make worse or more severe. *The roads in our town already have too much traffic; building a new shopping mall will exacerbate the problem.*

excoriation (noun) The act of condemning someone with harsh words. *In the small office we shared, it was painful to hear my boss's constant excoriation of his assistant for the smallest faults—a misdirected letter, an unclear phone message, or even a tepid cup of coffee.* excoriate (verb).

exculpate (verb) To free from blame or guilt. *When someone else confessed to the crime, the previous suspect was exculpated.* exculpation (noun), exculpatory (adjective).

executor (noun) The person appointed to execute someone's will. *As the executor of his Aunt Ida's will, Phil must deal with squabbling relatives, conniving lawyers, and the ruinous state of Ida's house.*

exigent (adjective) Urgent, requiring immediate attention. *A two-year-old is likely to behave as if her every demand is exigent, even if it involves simply retrieving a beloved stuffed hedgehog from under the couch.* exigency (noun).

expedient (adjective) Providing an immediate advantage or serving one's immediate self-interest. *When the passenger next to her was strafed by a bullet, Sharon chose the most expedient means to stop the bleeding; she whipped off her pantyhose and made an impromptu, but effective, tourniquet.* expediency (noun).

explicitly (adverb) Clearly, unambiguously. *Using a profit- and loss-statement, the company's accountant explicitly explained the company's dire financial situation.* explicit (adjective).

extant (adjective)   Currently in existence. *Of the seven ancient "Wonders of the World," only the pyramids of Egypt are still extant.*

Word Origin

Latin tenere = *to hold. Also found in English* retain, tenable, tenant, tenet, tenure.

extenuate (verb)   To make less serious. *Karen's guilt is extenuated by the fact that she was only 12 when she committed the theft.* extenuating (adjective), extenuation (noun).

extol (verb)   To greatly praise. *At the party convention, one speaker after another took to the podium to extol the virtues of their candidate for the presidency.*

extraneous (adjective)   Irrelevant, nonessential. *One review of the new Chekhov biography said the author had bogged down the book with far too many extraneous details, such as the dates of Chekhov's bouts of diarrhea.*

extrapolate (verb)   To deduce from something known, to infer. *Meteorologists were able to use old weather records to extrapolate backward and compile lists of El Niño years and their effects over the last century.* extrapolation (noun).

extricate (verb)   To free from a difficult or complicated situation. *Much of the humor in the TV show "I Love Lucy" comes in watching Lucy try to extricate herself from the problems she creates by fibbing or trickery.* extricable (adjective).

facetious (adjective)   Humorous in a mocking way; not serious. *French composer Erik Satie often concealed his serious artistic intent by giving his works facetious titles such as "Three Pieces in the Shape of a Pear."*

facilitate (verb)   To make easier or to moderate. *When the issue of racism reared its ugly head, the company brought in a consultant to facilitate a discussion of diversity in the workplace.* facile (adjective), facility (noun).

fallacy (noun)   An error in fact or logic. *It's a fallacy to think that "natural" means "healthful"; after all, the deadly poison arsenic is completely natural.* fallacious (adjective).

fatuous (adjective)   Inanely foolish; silly. *Once backstage, Elizabeth showered the opera singer with fatuous praise and embarrassing confessions, which he clearly had no interest in hearing.*

feint (noun)   A bluff; a mock blow. *It didn't take us long to realize that Gaby's tears and stomachaches were all a feint, since they appeared so regularly at her bedtime.*

ferret (verb)   To bring to light by an extensive search. *With his repeated probing and questions, Fritz was able to ferret out the location of Myrna's safe deposit box.*

finesse (noun)   Skillful maneuvering; delicate workmanship. *With her usual finesse, Charmaine gently persuaded the Duncans not to install a motorized Santa and sleigh on their front lawn.*

florid (adjective)   Flowery, fancy; reddish. *The grand ballroom was decorated in a florid style. Years of heavy drinking had given him a florid complexion.*

flourish (noun)   An extraneous embellishment; a dramatic gesture. *The napkin rings made out of intertwined ferns and flowers were just the kind of flourish one would expect from Carol, a slavish follower of Martha Stewart.*

Word Origin

Latin fluere = *to flow. Also found in English* affluent, effluvia, fluid, influx.

fluctuation (noun) A shifting back and forth. *Investment analysts predict fluctuations in the Dow Jones Industrial Average due to the instability of the value of the dollar.* fluctuate (verb).

foil (verb) To thwart or frustrate. *I was certain that Jerry's tendency to insert himself into everyone's conversations would foil my chances to have a private word with Helen.*

foment (verb) To rouse or incite. *The petty tyrannies and indignities inflicted on the workers by upper management helped foment the walkout at the meat-processing plant.*

forestall (verb) To hinder or prevent by taking action in advance. *The pilot's calm, levelheaded demeanor during the attempted highjacking forestalled any hysteria among the passengers of Flight 268.*

fortuitous (adjective) Lucky, fortunate. *Although the mayor claimed credit for the falling crime rate, it was really caused by a series of fortuitous accidents.*

foster (verb) To nurture or encourage. *The whitewater rafting trip was supposed to foster creative problem solving and teamwork between the account executives and the creative staff at Apex Advertising Agency.*

functionary (noun) Someone holding office in a political party or government. *The man shaking hands with the Governor was a low-ranking Democratic Party functionary who had worked to garner the Hispanic vote.*

gainsay (verb) To contradict or oppose; deny, dispute. *Dot would gainsay her married sister's efforts to introduce her to eligible men by refusing to either leave her ailing canary or give up her thrice-weekly bingo nights.*

garrulous (adjective) Annoyingly talkative. *Claude pretended to be asleep so he could avoid his garrulous seatmate, a self-proclaimed expert on bonsai cultivation.*

Word Origin

Latin genus = *type or kind; birth. Also found in English* congenital, genetic, genital, genre, genuine, genus.

generic (adjective) General; having no brand name. *Connie tried to reduce her grocery bills by religiously clipping coupons and buying generic brands of most products.*

gist (noun) The main point, the essence. *Although they felt sympathy for the victim's family, the jurors were won over by the gist of the defense's argument; there was insufficient evidence to convict.*

guile (noun) Deceit, duplicity. *In Margaret Mitchell's* Gone with the Wind, *Scarlett O'Hara uses her guile to manipulate two men and then is matched for wits by a third: Rhett Butler.* guileful (adjective).

gullible (adjective) Easily fooled. *Terry was so gullible she actually believed Robert's stories of his connections to the Czar and Czarina.* gullibility (noun).

habitat (noun) The place where a plant or animal normally lives and grows. *Even though frogs do occasionally come up onto land, their natural habitat is water.*

hackneyed (adjective) Without originality, trite. *When someone invented the phrase, "No pain, no gain," it was clever and witty, but now it is so commonly heard that it seems hackneyed.*

haughty (adjective)   Overly proud. *The fashion model strode down the runway, her hips thrust forward and a haughty expression, something like a sneer, on her face.* haughtiness (noun).

hesitance (noun)   Holding back in doubt or indecision. *The young woman was thrilled that her boyfriend had proposed to her but had some hesitance about marrying him because of his dysfunctional family.* hesitantly (adverb).

hierarchy (noun)   A ranking of people, things, or ideas from highest to lowest. *A cabinet secretary ranks just below the president and vice president in the hierarchy of the government's executive branch.* hierarchical (adjective).

Word Origin

Greek homos = same. Also found in English homologous, homonym, homosexual.

homogeneous (adjective)   Uniform, made entirely of one thing. *It's hard to think of a more homogenous group than those eerie children in "Village of the Damned," who all had perfect features, white-blond hair, and silver, penetrating eyes.*

hone (verb)   To improve and make more acute or effective. *While she was a receptionist, Norma honed her skills as a stand-up comic by trying out jokes on the tense crowd in the waiting room.*

hoodwink (verb)   To deceive by trickery or false appearances; to dupe. *That was my cousin Ravi calling to say that he's been hoodwinked again, this time by some outfit offering time shares on a desolate tract of land in central Florida.*

humanitarian (noun)   One who promotes human welfare and social reform. *In providing millions of dollars to build libraries around the country, Andrew Carnegie showed himself to be a true humanitarian.*

hypothesized (verb)   Theorized. *As part of his famous Theory of Relativity, Albert Einstein hypothesized that time travel was a real possibility.* hypothesis (noun).

iconoclast (noun)   Someone who attacks traditional beliefs or institutions. *Comedian Dennis Miller relishes his reputation as an iconoclast, though people in power often resent his satirical jabs.* iconoclasm (noun), iconoclastic (adjective).

idealization (noun)   Bringing something to perfection. *Marrying Prince Charming was the idealization of Cinderella's dreams.* idealize (verb).

ideology (noun)   A body of ideas or beliefs. *Thomas Jefferson's ideology was based on the assumption, as he put it, that "all men are created equal."* ideological (adjective).

idolatry (noun)   The worship of a person, thing, or institution as a god. *In communist China, admiration for Mao resembled idolatry; his picture was displayed everywhere, and millions of Chinese memorized his sayings and repeated them endlessly.* idolatrous (adjective).

idyll (noun)   A rustic, romantic interlude; poetry or prose that celebrates simple pastoral life. *Her picnic with Max at Fahnstock Lake was not the serene idyll she had envisioned; instead, they were surrounded by hundreds of other picnickers blaring music from their boom boxes and cracking open soda cans.* idyllic (adjective).

illicit (adjective)   Illegal, wrongful. *When Janet caught her thirteen-year-old son and his friend downloading illicit pornographic photos from the World Wide Web, she promptly pulled the plug on his computer.*

illuminate (verb)   To brighten with light; to enlighten or elucidate; to decorate (a manuscript). *The frosted-glass sconces in the dressing rooms at Le Cirque not only illuminate the rooms but make everyone look like a movie star. Alice Munro is a writer who can illuminate an entire character with a few deft sentences.*

immaculate (adjective)   Totally unblemished, spotlessly clean. *The cream-colored upholstery in my new Porsche was immaculate—that is, until a raccoon came in through the window and tracked mud across the seats.*

immaterial (adjective)   Of no consequence, unimportant. *"The fact that your travel agent is your best friend's son should be immaterial," I told Rosa; "If he keeps putting you on hold and acting nasty, just take your business elsewhere."*

immunity (noun)   Being free of or exempt from something. *Polio vaccinations provide children with immunity to the polio virus and thus keep them from contracting the disease.*

Word Origin

Latin mutare = *to change. Also found in English* immutable, mutant, mutation.

immutable (adjective)   Incapable of change. *Does there ever come an age when we realize that our parents' personalities are immutable, when we can relax and stop trying to make them change?*

impartial (adjective)   Fair, equal, unbiased. *If a judge is not impartial, then all of her rulings are questionable.* impartiality (noun).

impassivity (noun)   Apathy, unresponsiveness. *Dot truly thinks that Mr. Right will magically show up on her door step, and her utter impassivity regarding her social life makes me want to shake her!* impassive (adjective).

imperceptible (adjective)   Impossible to perceive, inaudible or incomprehensible. *The sound of footsteps was almost imperceptible, but Donald's paranoia had reached such a pitch that he immediately assumed he was being followed.*

imperturbable (adjective)   Cannot be disconcerted, disturbed, or excited. *The proper English butler in Kazuo Ishiguro's novel* Remains of the Day *appears completely imperturbable even when his father dies or when his own heart is breaking.*

impetuous (adjective)   Acting hastily or impulsively. *Ben's resignation was an impetuous act; he did it without thinking, and he soon regretted it.* impetuosity (noun).

Word Origin

Latin placare = *to please. Also found in English* complacent, placate, placid.

implacable (adjective)   Unbending, resolute. *The state of Israel is implacable in its policy of never negotiating with terrorists.*

implement (verb)   To carry out. *The entrepreneur had to have all his financing in place before he could implement his plans for expanding the company.* implementation (noun).

implosion (noun)   To collapse inward from outside pressure. *While it is difficult to know what is going on in North Korea, no one can rule out a violent implosion of the North Korean regime and a subsequent flood of refugees across its borders.* implode (verb).

incessant (adjective)   Unceasing. *The incessant blaring of the neighbor's car alarm made it impossible for me to concentrate on my upcoming Bar exam.*

inchoate (adjective)   Only partly formed or formulated. *At editorial meetings, Nancy had a habit of presenting her inchoate book ideas before she had a chance to fully determine their feasibility.*

Word Origin

Latin caedere = *to cut. Also found in English* concise, decide, excise, incision, precise.*"*

incise (verb)   To carve into, to engrave. *My wife felt nostalgic about the old elm tree since we had incised our initials in it when we were both in high school.* incisive (adjective) Admirably direct and decisive. *Ted Koppel's incisive questions have made many politicians squirm and stammer.*

incongruous (adjective)   Unlikely. *Art makes incongruous alliances, as when punk-rockers, Tibetan folk musicians, gospel singers, and beat poets shared the stage at the Tibet House benefit concert.* incongruity (noun).

incorrigible (adjective)   Impossible to manage or reform. *Lou is an incorrigible trickster, constantly playing practical jokes no matter how much his friends complain.*

incur (verb)   To become liable or subject to. *When you have a difficult boss, it's wise to avoid anything that might incur his or her wrath.*

incursion (noun)   A hostile entrance into a territory; a foray into an activity or venture. *It is a little-known fact that the Central Intelligence Agency organized military incursions into China during the 1950s. The ComicCon was Barbara's first incursion into the world of comic strip artists.*

indefatigable (adjective)   Tireless. *Eleanor Roosevelt's indefatigable dedication to the cause of human welfare won her affection and honor throughout the world.* indefatigability (noun).

indigenous (adjective)   Native. *It's much easier for a gardener to cultivate indigenous plants than those which are native to other climates.* indigenously (adverb).

individualistic (adjective)   Asserting independence of thought and action. *The woman's insistence on going against the tide of popular opinion was only one aspect of her individualistic nature.* individualist (noun).

inducement (noun)   A consideration leading one to action. *In order to compete effectively, some automobile companies offer inducements to potential customers, such as special features at no additional cost.* induce (verb).

inequities (noun)   Injustice, unfairness. *Sometimes it takes a person many years to accept the fact that life is full of inequities, and some people simply refuse ever to recognize the basic unfairness of life.*

inevitable (adjective)   Unable to be avoided. *Once the Japanese attacked Pearl Harbor, U.S. involvement in World War II was inevitable.* inevitability (noun).

inextricably (adverb)   Incapable of being disentangled. *When a man and woman have lived together for many years, particularly if they've raised children together, their lives become inextricably intertwined.* inextricable (adjective).

infer (verb)   To conclude, to deduce. *Can I infer from your hostile tone of voice that you are still angry about yesterday's incident?* inference (noun).

influx (noun)   Flowing in. *The influx of immigrants from the former Soviet Union was so great that it overwhelmed the immigration authorities.*

informant (noun)   One who apprises, acquaints, or notifies. *In order for police officers to maintain an awareness of the criminal world, it's often necessary for them to have relationships with an informant or two.*

inhibiting (verb)   Restraining, holding back. *The boxer's fear of doing serious damage was an inhibiting factor in his attack on his opponent.* inhibition (noun), inhibitory (adjective).

inimical (adjective)   Unfriendly, hostile; adverse or difficult. *Relations between Greece and Turkey have been inimical for centuries.*

inimitable (adjective)   Incapable of being imitated, matchless. *John F. Kennedy's administration dazzled the public, partly because of the inimitable style and elegance of his wife, Jacqueline.*

inopportune (adjective)   Awkward, untimely. *When Gus heard raised voices and the crash of breaking china behind the kitchen door, he realized that he'd picked an inopportune moment to visit the Fairlights.*

inscrutability (noun)   Quality of being extremely difficult to interpret or understand, mysteriousness. *I am still puzzling over the inscrutability of the package I received yesterday, which contained twenty pomegranates and a note that said simply, "Yours."* inscrutable (adjective).

insensible (adjective)   Unaware, incognizant; unconscious, out cold. *It's a good thing that Marty was insensible to the titters and laughter that greeted his arrival in the ballroom. In the latest episode of police brutality, an innocent young black man was beaten insensible after two cops stormed his apartment.*

insinuate (verb)   Hint or intimate; to creep in. *During an extremely unusual broadcast, the anchor man insinuated that the Washington bureau chief was having a nervous breakdown. Marla managed to insinuate herself into the Duchess of York's conversation during the "Weight Watchers" promotion event.* insinuation (noun).

insipid (adjective)   Flavorless, uninteresting. *Most TV shows are so insipid that you can watch them while reading or chatting without missing a thing.* insipidity (noun).

insolence (noun)   An attitude or behavior that is bold and disrespectful. *Some feel that news reporters who shout accusatory questions at the president are behaving with insolence towards his high office.* insolent (adjective).

insoluble (adjective)   Unable to be solved, irresolvable; indissoluble. *Fermat's last theorum remained insoluble for more than 300 years until a young mathematician from Princeton solved it in 1995. If you are a gum chewer, you probably wouldn't like to know that insoluble plastics are a common ingredient of most popular gums.*

instigate (verb)   To goad or urge on. *It's never a good idea to instigate a fight between other people, because you might get caught in the middle of it.* instigation (noun).

insular (adjective)   Narrow or isolated in attitude or viewpoint. *New Yorkers are famous for their insular attitudes; they seem to think that nothing important has ever happened outside of their city.* insularity (noun).

intangible (adjective)   Incapable of being perceived by the senses. *Having a child's love is one of the intangible benefits of being a parent.*

intercede (verb)   To step in, to moderate; to mediate or negotiate on behalf of someone else. *After their rejection by the co-op board, Kevin and Sol asked Rachel, another tenant, to intercede for them at the next board meeting.* intercession (noun).

interception (noun)   The act of stopping or interrupting an intended course. *Interception of drugs coming over the border is one of the means federal authorities use in their efforts to combat the drug trade.* intercept (verb).

intermediary (noun)   One who acts as an agent between persons or things. *When the policemen's union has to discuss a new contract with the city, they often find it necessary to use an intermediary during the negotiations.*

interpolate (verb)   To interject. *The director's decision to interpolate topical political jokes into his production of Shakespeare's* Twelfth Night *was not viewed kindly by the critics.* interpolation (noun).

interrelated (verb)   Mutually connected or associated. *If all the parts of an automobile engine were not interrelated, the engine would not function properly.* interrelation (noun).

interspersed (verb)   Distributed among other things at intervals. *In the library, all the historical biographies were interspersed among the general history books.*

interval (noun)   A period of time between events. *Because they wanted to be married quickly, the interval between the couple's engagement and their wedding was an extremely busy one.*

intransigent (adjective) Unwilling to compromise. *Despite the mediator's attempts to suggest a fair solution to the disagreement, the two parties were intransigent, forcing a showdown.* intransigence (noun).

intricate (adjective)   Complicated. *Because of the many elements to be included in the company's logo, creating the design was an intricate process.* intricately (adverb).

intrinsically (adverb) Essentially, inherently. *There is nothing intrinsically difficult about upgrading a computer's microprocessor, yet Al was afraid to even open up the hard drive.* intrinsic (adjective).

Word Origin

Latin unda = *wave. Also found in English* undulate.

inundate (verb)   To overwhelm; to flood. *When America Online first announced its flat-rate pricing, the company was inundated with new customers, and thus began the annoying delays in service.* inundation (noun).

invective (noun)   Insulting, abusive language. *I remained unscathed by his blistering invective, because in my heart I knew I had done the right thing.*

invigorate (verb)   To give energy to, to stimulate. *As her car climbed the mountain road, Lucinda felt herself invigorated by the clear air and the cool breezes.* invigoration (noun).

irascible (adjective)   Easily provoked into anger, hot-headed. *Soup chef Al Yeganah, the model for Seinfeld's "Soup Nazi," is an irascible man who flies into a temper if his customers don't follow his rigid procedure for purchasing soup.* irascibility (noun).

irreconcilable (adjective)   Impossible to settle or resolve. *The two sides were so far apart in the negotiations that they had to admit their differences were irreconcilable.*

irreversibly (adverb)   Incapable of being turned backward. *The car was moving at such a fast rate when the collision took place that it was irreversibly damaged.* irreversible (adjective).

jeopardize (verb)   To put in danger. *Terrorist attacks on civilians jeopardize the fragile peace in the Middle East.* jeopardy (noun).

labyrinthine (adjective)   Extremely intricate or involved; circuitous. *Was I the only one who couldn't follow the labyrinthine plot of the movie L.A. Confidential? I was so confused I had to watch it twice to see "who did it."*

laconic (adjective)   Concise to the point of terseness; taciturn. *Tall, handsome, and laconic, the actor Gary Cooper came to personify the strong, silent American, a man of action and few words.*

Word Origin

Latin laus = *praise. Also found in English* applaud, laud, laudatory, plaudit.

laudable (adjective)   Commendable, praiseworthy. *The Hunt's Point nonprofit organization has embarked on a serious of laudable ventures pairing businesses and disadvantaged youth.*

leery (adverb)   Distrustful or suspicious. *Whether deserved or not, car salesmen have a reputation for being dishonest, so many people are leery of whatever they say.*

legitimizing (verb)   Making lawful or conforming to accepted rules. *Establishing the man's familial relationship to the deceased was an essential aspect of legitimizing his claim to the woman's substantial estate.* legitimate (adjective).

lethargic (adjective)   Lacking energy; sluggish. *Visitors to the zoo are surprised that the lions appear so lethargic, but, in the wild, lions sleep up to 18 hours a day.* lethargy (noun).

levy (verb)   To demand payment or collection of a tax or fee. *The environmental activists pushed Congress to levy higher taxes on gasoline, but the auto makers' lobbyists quashed their plans.*

lien (noun)   A claim against a property for the satisfaction of a debt. *Nat was in such financial straits when he died that his Fishkill property had several liens against it, and all of his furniture was being repossessed.*

Word Origin

Latin loqui = *to speak. Also found in English* colloquial, colloquy, eloquent, grandiloquent, locution.

loquacity (noun)   Talkativeness, wordiness. *While some people deride his loquacity and his tendency to use outrageous rhymes, no one can doubt that Jesse Jackson is a powerful orator.* loquacious (adjective).

lucid (adjective)   Clear and understandable. *Hawking's A Brief History of the Universe is a lucid explanation of a difficult topic: modern scientific theories of the origin of the universe.* lucidity (noun).

magnanimous (adjective)   Noble, generous. *When media titan Ted Turner pledged a gift of $1 billion to the United Nations, he challenged other wealthy people to be equally magnanimous.* magnanimity (noun).

maladroit (adjective) Inept, awkward. *It was painful to watch the young congressman's maladroit delivery of the nominating speech.*

malinger (verb) To pretend illness to avoid work. *During the labor dispute, hundreds of employees malingered, forcing the company to slow production and costing it millions in profits.*

malleable (adjective) Able to be changed, shaped, or formed by outside pressures. *Gold is a very useful metal because it is so malleable. A child's personality is malleable and is often deeply influenced by things her parents say and do.* malleability (noun).

mandate (noun) Order, command. *The new policy on gays in the military went into effect as soon as the president issued his mandate about it.* mandate (verb), mandatory (adjective).

marginal (adjective) At the outer edge or fringe; of minimal quality or acceptability. *In spite of the trend toward greater paternal involvement in child rearing, most fathers still have a marginal role in their children's lives. Jerry's GMAT CAT scores were so marginal that he didn't get accepted into the graduate schools of his choice.*

marginalize (verb) To push toward the fringes; to make less consequential. *Hannah argued that the designation of a certain month as "Black History Month" or "Gay and Lesbian Book Month" actually does a disservice to minorities by marginalizing them.*

martial (adjective) Of, relating to, or suited to military life. *My old teacher, Miss Woody, had such a martial demeanor that you'd think she was running a boot camp instead of teaching fifth grade. The military seized control of Myanmar in 1988, and this embattled country has been ruled by martial law since then.*

Word Origin

Latin medius = middle. Also found in English intermediate, media, medium.

mediate (verb) To reconcile differences between two parties. *During the baseball strike, both the players and the club owners expressed willingness to have the president mediate the dispute.* mediation (noun).

mercenary (adjective) Doing something only for pay or for personal advantage. *People have criticized the U.S. motives in the Persian Gulf War as mercenary, pointing out that the U.S. would not have come to Kuwait's defense had it grown carrots rather than produced oil.* mercenary (noun).

mercurial (adjective) Changing quickly and unpredictably. *The mercurial personality of Robin Williams, with his many voices and styles, made him a natural choice to play the part of the ever-changing genie in* Aladdin.

metamorphose (verb) To undergo a striking transformation. *In just a century, book publishers have metamorphosed from independent, exclusively literary businesses to minor divisions in multimedia entertainment conglomerates.* metamorphosis (noun).

methodology (noun) A procedure or set of procedures. *Because the methodology the scientist employed was an unconventional one, the results of his study were questioned by others in the field.* methodical (adjective).

meticulous (adjective) Very careful with details. *Watch repair calls for a craftsperson who is patient and meticulous.*

Word Origin

Greek anthropos
= *human. Also
found in English*
anthropology,
anthropoid,
anthropomor-
phic, philan-
thropy.

mimicry (noun)   Imitation, aping. *The continued popularity of Elvis Presley has given rise to a class of entertainers who make a living through mimicry of "The King."* mimic (noun and verb).

misanthrope (noun)   Someone who hates or distrusts all people. *In the beloved Christmas classic, It's a Wonderful Life, Lionel Barrymore plays Potter, the wealthy misanthrope who is determined to make life miserable for everyone, and particularly for the young, idealistic George Bailey.* misanthropic (adjective), misanthropy (noun).

miscreant (adjective)   Unbelieving, heretical; evil, villainous. *After a one-year run playing Iago in Othello, and then two years playing Bill Sikes in Oliver, Sean was tired of being typecast in miscreant roles.* miscreant (noun).

mitigate (verb)   To make less severe; to relieve. *There's no doubt that Wallace committed the assault, but the verbal abuse Wallace had received helps to explain his behavior and somewhat mitigates his guilt.* mitigation (noun).

moderated (verb)   Arbitrated, mediated. *The professor moderated the debate between the advocates of open enrollment and those who were opposed to it.* moderator (noun).

monitoring (verb)   Watching or observing for a purpose. *Court-appointed parole officers are responsible for monitoring the behavior of criminals who have been released from prison.*

monopoly (noun)   A condition in which there is only one seller of a certain commodity. *Wary of Microsoft's seeming monopoly of the computer operating–system business, rivals are asking for government intervention.* monopolistic (adjective). *Renowned consumer advocate Ralph Nader once quipped, "The only difference between John D. Rockefeller and Bill Gates is that Gates recognizes no boundaries to his monopolistic drive."*

monotonous (adjective)   Tediously uniform, unchanging. *Brian Eno's "Music for Airports" is characterized by minimal melodies, subtle textures, and variable repetition, which I find rather bland and monotonous.* monotony (noun).

moorings (noun)   Elements providing security or stability. *When her best friend moved to another city, the young woman felt that to a great extent she had lost her moorings.*

morose (adjective)   Gloomy, sullen. *After Chuck's girlfriend dumped him, he lay around the house for a couple of days, refusing to come to the phone and feeling morose.*

mutation (noun)   A significant change; in biology, a permanent change in hereditary material. *Most genetic mutations are not beneficial, since any change in the delicate balance of an organism tends to be disruptive.* mutate (verb).

nadir (noun)   Lowest point. *Pedro and Renee's marriage reached a new nadir last Christmas Eve when Pedro locked Renee out of the house upon her return from the supposed "business trip."*

nascent (adjective)   Newly born, just beginning. *While her artistry is still nascent, it was 15-year-old Tara Lipinski's technical wizardry that enabled her to win a gold medal in the 1998 Winter Olympics.* nascence (noun).

necessitated (verb) Required. *The college senior's desire to attend graduate school necessitated his taking the Graduate Management Admission Test.* necessity (noun).

negligence (noun) The state of being careless or casual. *The author's negligence in checking his spelling resulted in his editor having to do more work than she had anticipated.* negligent (adjective).

neutrality (noun) The state of being unallied with either side in a disagreement. *Switzerland's neutrality during the Second World War was the reason it was not attacked by either the Axis or the Allied powers.* neutral (adjective).

noisome (adjective) Putrid, fetid, noxious. *We were convinced that the noisome odor infiltrating every corner of our building was evidence of a moldering corpse.*

notorious (adjective) Famous, especially for evil actions or qualities. *Warner Brothers produced a series of movies about notorious gangsters such as John Dillinger and Al Capone.* notoriety (noun).

Word Origin

Latin durus = hard. Also found in English *durable, endure.*

obdurate (adjective) Unwilling to change; stubborn, inflexible. *Despite the many pleas he received, the governor was obdurate in his refusal to grant clemency to the convicted murderer.*

oblivious (adjective) Unaware, unconscious. *Karen practiced her oboe solo with complete concentration, oblivious to the noise and activity around her.* oblivion (noun), obviousness (noun).

obscure (adjective) Little known; hard to understand. *Mendel was an obscure monk until decades after his death, when his scientific work was finally discovered. Most people find the writings of James Joyce obscure; hence the popularity of books that explain the many odd references and tricks of language in his work.* obscure (verb), obscurity (noun).

obsolete (adjective) No longer current; old-fashioned. *W. H. Auden said that his ideal landscape would contain water wheels, grain mills, and other forms of obsolete machinery.* obsolescence (noun).

obstinate (adjective) Stubborn, unyielding. *Despite years of government effort, the problem of drug abuse remains obstinate.* obstinacy (noun).

obtuse (adjective) Dull witted, insensitive; incomprehensible, unclear, or imprecise. *Amy was so obtuse she didn't realize that Alexi had proposed marriage to her. French psychoanalyst Jacques Lacan's collection of papers, Ecrits, is notoriously obtuse, yet it has still been highly influential in linguistics, film theory, and literary criticism.*

obviate (verb) Preclude, make unnecessary. *Truman Capote's meticulous accuracy and total recall obviated the need for note-taking when he wrote his account of a 1959 murder, In Cold Blood.*

odium (noun) Intense feeling of hatred, abhorrence. *When the neighbors learned that a convicted sex offender was now living in their midst, they could not restrain their odium and began harassing the man whenever he left his house.* odious (adjective).

opprobrium (noun) Dishonor, disapproval. *Switzerland recently came under public opprobrium when it was revealed that Swiss bankers had hoarded the gold the Nazis had confiscated from their victims.* opprobrious (adjective).

orthodox (adjective) In religion, conforming to a certain doctrine; conventional. *George Eliot's relationship with George Lewes, a married journalist, offended the sensibilities of her more orthodox peers.* orthodoxy (noun).

ossified (adjective) In biology, to turn into bone; to become rigidly conventional and opposed to change. *His harsh view of coeducation had ossified over the years, so that he was now the only teacher who sought to bar girls from the venerable boys' school.* ossification (noun).

ostentatious (adjective) Overly showy, pretentious. *To show off his new wealth, the financier threw an ostentatious party featuring a full orchestra, a famous singer, and tens of thousands of dollars' worth of food.* ostentation (noun).

ostracize (verb) To exclude from a group. *In Biblical times, those who suffered from the disease of leprosy were ostracized and forced to live alone.* ostracism (noun).

pantheon (noun) A group of illustrious people. *It seems unlikely that any of our recent presidents are likely to join the pantheon of American statesmen.*

parse (verb) To break a sentence down into grammatical components; to analyze bit by bit. *In the wake of the sex scandal, journalists parsed every utterance by administration officials regarding the President's alleged promiscuity. At $1.25 million a day, Titanic is the most expensive movie ever made, but director James Cameron refused to parse the film's enormous budget for inquisitive reporters.*

partisan (adjective) Reflecting strong allegiance to a particular party or cause. *The vote on the president's budget was strictly partisan: every member of the president's party voted yes, and all others voted no.* partisan (noun).

patriarchal (adjective) Relating to a man who is a father or founder. *When children take over businesses from their fathers, they often find it difficult to meet patriarchal expectations.*

peccadillo (noun) A minor offense, a lapse. *What Dr. Sykes saw as a major offense—being addressed as Marge rather than Doctor—Tina saw as a mere peccadillo and one that certainly should not have lost her the job.*

pedantic (adjective) Academic, bookish. *The men Hillary met through personal ads in the* New York Review of Books *were invariably pasty-skinned pedantic types who dropped the names of nineteenth-century writers in every sentence.* pedantry (noun).

pedestrian (adjective) Unimaginative, ordinary. *The new Italian restaurant received a bad review due to its reliance on pedestrian dishes such as pasta with marinara sauce and chicken parmigiana.*

Word Origin

Latin fides = faith. *Also found in English* confide, confidence, fidelity, infidel.

perfidious (adjective) Disloyal, treacherous. *Although he was one of the most talented generals of the American Revolution, Benedict Arnold is remembered today as a perfidious betrayer of the patriot cause.* perfidy (noun).

peripatetic (adjective) Moving or traveling from place to place; always on the go. *In Barbara Wilson's* Trouble in Transylvania, *peripatetic translator Cassandra Reilly is on the road again, this time to China by way of Budapest, where she plans to catch the TransMongolian Express.*

permeate (verb) To spread through or penetrate. *Little by little, the smell of gas from the broken pipe permeated the house.*

personification (noun)   The embodiment of a thing or an abstract idea in human form. *Many people view Theodore Kaczynski, the killer known as the Unabomber, as the very personification of evil.* personify (verb).

perturbed (verb)   Made uneasy or anxious. *Because she expected her mother to be at home, the woman was extremely perturbed when she called and the phone just rang and rang.* perturbation (noun).

pervasive (adjective)   Spreading throughout. *As news of the disaster reached the town, a pervasive sense of gloom could be felt everywhere.* pervade (verb).

phenomenon (noun)   An unusual and significant occurrence or person. *Johann Sebastian Bach's extraordinary talent would have made him a phenomenon in his own or any other century.* phenomena (plural).

pith (noun)   The core, the essential part; in biology, the central strand of tissue in the stems of most vascular plants. *After spending seventeen years in psychoanalysis, Frieda had finally come face to face with the pith of her deep-seated anxiety.* pithy (adjective).

placate (verb)   To soothe or appease. *The waiter tried to placate the angry customer with the offer of a free dessert.* placatory (adjective).

placid (adjective)   Unmarked by disturbance; complacent. *Dr. Kahn was convinced that the placid exterior presented by Frieda in her early analysis sessions masked a deeply disturbed psyche.* placidity (noun).

plaintive (adjective)   Expressing suffering or melancholy. *In the beloved children's book* The Secret Garden, *Mary is disturbed by plaintive cries echoing in the corridors of gloomy Misselthwaite Manor.*

plastic (adjective)   Able to be molded or reshaped. *Because it is highly plastic, clay is an easy material for beginning sculptors to use.* plasticity (noun).

platitude (noun)   A trite remark or saying; a cliché. *How typical of June to send a sympathy card filled with mindless platitudes like "One day at a time," rather than calling the grieving widow.* platitudinous (adjective).

plausible (adjective)   Apparently believable. *The idea that a widespread conspiracy to kill the president has been kept secret by all the participants for more than thirty years hardly seems plausible.* plausibility (noun).

plummet (verb)   To dive or plunge. *On October 27, 1997, the stock market plummeted by 554 points and left us all wondering if the bull market was finally over.*

polarize (adjective)   To separate into opposing groups or forces. *For years, the abortion debate polarized the American people, with many people voicing views at either extreme and few people trying to find a middle ground.* polarization (noun).

ponderous (adjective)   Unwieldy and bulky; oppressively dull. *Unfortunately, the film director weighed the movie down with a ponderous voice-over narrated by the protagonist as an old man.*

posit (verb)   To put forward as a fact. *It is possible, if ill advised, to posit an argument even if you have little or no evidence to support it.*

positivism (noun)   A philosophy that denies speculation and assumes that the only knowledge is scientific knowledge. *David Hume carried his positivism to an extreme when he argued that our expectation that the sun will rise tomorrow has no basis in reason and is purely a matter of belief.* positivistic (adjective).

posterity (noun)   Future generations. *Even if a man has no wealth to pass onto his children, he can bequeath his ideals and beliefs to posterity.*

practitioners (noun)   Those who engage in a profession or technique. *Those who hold black belts in karate are the most proficient practitioners of the martial arts.*

pragmatism (noun)   A belief in approaching problems through practical rather than theoretical means. *Roosevelt's attitude toward the economic troubles of the Depression was based on pragmatism: "Try something," he said; "If it doesn't work, try something else."* pragmatic (adjective).

precedent (noun)   An earlier occurrence that serves as an example for a decision. *In a legal system that reveres precedent, even defining the nature of a completely new type of dispute can seem impossible.* precede (verb).

precept (noun)   A general principle or law. *One of the central precepts of Tai Chi Ch'uan is the necessity of allowing ki (cosmic energy) to flow through one's body in slow, graceful movements.*

precipitate (verb)   To spur or activate. *In the summer of 1997, the selling off of the Thai baht precipitated a currency crisis that spread throughout Asia.*

Word Origin

Latin claudere = *to close. Also found in English* conclude, include, recluse, seclude.

preclude (verb)   To prevent, to hinder. *Unfortunately, Jasmine's appointment at the New Age Expo precluded her attendance at our weekend Workshop for Shamans and Psychics.* preclusive (adjective), preclusion (noun).

precursor (noun)   A forerunner, a predecessor. *The Kodak Brownie camera, a small boxy camera made of jute board and wood, was the precursor to today's sleek 35mm cameras.* precursory (adjective).

prefigured (verb)   Showed or suggested by an antecedent form or model. *The stream of consciousness style of James Joyce's* Ulysses *was prefigured to some extent by the nonsense verse of Edward Lear.* prefigurement (noun).

preponderance (noun)   A superiority in weight, size, or quantity; a majority. *In Seattle, there is a great preponderance of seasonal affective disorder, or SAD, a malady brought on by light starvation during the dark winter.* preponderate (verb)

presage (verb)   To foretell, to anticipate. *According to folklore, a red sky at dawn presages a day of stormy weather.*

prescience (noun)   Foreknowledge or foresight. *When she saw the characteristic, eerie, yellowish-black light in the sky, Dorothy had the prescience to seek shelter in the storm cellar.* prescient (adjective).

presumptuous (adjective)   Going beyond the limits of courtesy or appropriateness. *The senator winced when the presumptuous young staffer addressed him as "Ted."* presume (verb), presumption (noun).

prevaricate (verb)   To lie, to equivocate. *When it became clear to the FBI that the mobster had threatened the 12-year-old witness, they could well understand why he had prevaricated during the hearing.*

Word Origin

Latin primus =
*first. Also found in
English* primate,
primitive,
primogeniture,
primordial.

primacy (noun)   State of being the utmost in importance; preeminence. *The anthropologist Ruth Benedict was an inspiration to Margaret Mead for her emphasis on the primacy of culture in the formation of an individual's personality.* primal (adjective).

pristine (adjective)   Pure, undefiled. *As climbers who have scaled Mt. Everest can attest, the trails to the summit are hardly in pristine condition and are actually strewn with trash.*

probity (noun)   Goodness, integrity. *The vicious editorial attacked the moral probity of the senatorial candidate, saying he had profited handsomely from his pet project, the senior-citizen housing project.*

procreative (adjective)   Capable of reproducing. *If a species were for some reason to lose its procreative ability, it would die out with the current generation.* procreation (noun).

procure (verb)   To obtain by using particular care and effort. *Through partnerships with a large number of specialty wholesalers, W. W. Grainger is able to procure a startling array of products for its customers, from bear repellent for Alaska pipeline workers to fork-lift trucks and toilet paper.* procurement (noun).

prodigality (noun)   The condition of being wastefully extravagant. *Richard was ashamed of the prodigality of his bride's parents when he realized that the cost of the wedding reception alone was more than his father earned in one year.* prodigal (adjective).

proliferate (verb)   To increase or multiply. *Over the past fifteen years, high-tech companies have proliferated in northern California, Massachusetts, and other regions.* proliferation (noun).

prolixity (noun)   A diffuseness; a rambling and verbose quality. *The prolixity of Sarah's dissertation on Ottoman history defied even her adviser's attempts to read it.* prolix (adjective).

pronounced (adjective)   Distinct or strongly marked. *As a result of a leg injury he received during the war, the man walked with a pronounced limp.*

propagandistic (adjective)   Relating to the spread of ideas or information designed to help or injure a cause, institution, or individual. *Margaret Sanger's propagandistic efforts to foster the use of birth control was instrumental in making the public aware of its possibilities.* propaganda (noun).

propagate (verb)   To cause to grow; to foster. *John Smithson's will left his fortune for the founding of an institution to propagate knowledge, leaving open whether that meant a university, a library, or a museum.* propagation (noun).

prophetic (adjective)   Auspicious, predictive of what's to come. *We often look at every event leading up to a new love affair as prophetic—the flat tire that caused us to be late for work, the chance meeting in the elevator, the horoscope that augured "a new beginning."* prophecy (noun), prophesy (verb).

propitiating (adjective)   Conciliatory, mollifying, or appeasing. *Management's offer of a 5-percent raise was meant as a propitiating gesture, yet the striking workers were unimpressed.* propitiate (verb).

propitious (adjective)   Favorably disposed. *She had learned as a little girl that when her father was in a good mood it was a propitious time to ask for something he might not otherwise have been willing to give her.* propitiously (adverb).

propriety (noun)   Appropriateness. *Some people expressed doubts about the propriety of Clinton's discussing his underwear on MTV.*

Word Origin

Latin proprius = *own. Also found in English* appropriate, property, proprietary, proprietor.

prospective (adjective)   Likely to happen. *The young man's prospective in-laws were more than happy to involve him in planning for the wedding.* prospectively (adverb).

proximity (noun)   Closeness, nearness. *Neighborhood residents were angry over the proximity of the proposed sewage plant to the local elementary school.* proximate (adjective).

pundit (noun)   Someone who offers opinions in an authoritative style. *The Sunday afternoon talk shows are filled with pundits, each with his or her own theory about week's political news.*

Word Origin

Latin pungere = *to jab, to prick. Also found in English* pugilist, punctuate, puncture, pungent.

pungency (noun)   Marked by having a sharp, biting quality. *Unfortunately, the pungency of the fresh cilantro overwhelmed the delicate flavor of the poached turbot.* pungent (adjective).

purify (verb)   To make pure, clean, or perfect. *The new water-treatment plant is supposed to purify the drinking water provided to everyone in the nearby towns.* purification (noun).

quiescent (adjective)   In a state of rest or inactivity; latent. *Polly's ulcer has been quiescent ever since her mother-in-law moved out of the condo, which was well over a year ago.* quiescence (noun).

quixotic (adjective)   Foolishly romantic, idealistic to an impractical degree. *In the novel* Shoeless Joe, *Ray Kinsella carries out a quixotic plan to build a baseball field in the hopes that past baseball greats will come to play there.*

quotidian (adjective)   Occurring every day; commonplace and ordinary. *Most of the time, we long to escape from quotidian concerns, but in the midst of a crisis we want nothing more than to be plagued by such simple problems as a leaky faucet or a whining child.*

rancorous (adjective)   Marked by deeply embedded bitterness or animosity. *While Ralph and Kishu have been separated for three years, their relationship is so rancorous that they had to hire a professional mediator just to discuss divorce arrangements.* rancor (noun).

rapacious (adjective)   Excessively grasping or greedy. *Some see global currency speculators like George Soros as rapacious parasites who destroy economies and then line their pockets with the profits.* rapacity (noun).

rarefied (adjective)   Of interest or relating to a small, refined circle; less dense, thinner. *Those whose names dot the society pages live in a rarefied world where it's entirely normal to dine on caviar for breakfast or order a $2,000 bottle of wine at Le Cirque. When she reached the summit of Mt. McKinley, Deborah could hardly breath in the rarefied air.*

receptivity (noun)   Willingness or ability to take or acquire something. *The student's receptivity to constructive criticism from his teachers helped him improve his grade average substantially.* receptive (adverb).

reclusive (adjective)   Withdrawn from society. *During the last years of her life, Garbo led a reclusive existence, rarely appearing in public.* recluse (noun).

recompense (noun)   Compensation for a service rendered or to pay for damages. *The 5 percent of the estate that Phil received as executor of his Aunt Ida's will is small recompense for the headaches he endured in settling her affairs.* recompense (verb).

reconcile (verb)   To make consistent or harmonious. *Roosevelt's greatness as a leader can be seen in his ability to reconcile the differing demands and values of the varied groups that supported him.* reconciliation (noun).

recondite (adjective)   Profound, deep, abstruse. *Professor Miyaki's recondite knowledge of seventeenth-century Flemish painters made him a prized—if barely understood—member of the art history department.*

redemptive (adjective)   Liberating and reforming. *While she doesn't attend formal church services, Carrie is a firm believer in the redemptive power of prayer.* redeem (verb), redemption (noun).

Word Origin

Latin frangere = *to break. Also found in English* fraction, fractious, fracture, frangible, infraction, refract.*"*

refractory (adjective)   Stubbornly resisting control or authority. *Like a refractory child, Jill stomped out of the car, slammed the door, and said she would walk home, even though her house was 10 miles away.*

regulatory (adjective)   Related to controlling or directing according to a rule. *The Federal Communications Commission is the regulatory agency charged with ensuring the broadcast industry's compliance with government rules.* regulate (verb).

reinforced (verb)   Strengthened. *His mother's agreement with his father's position reinforced the teenagers belief that, despite what they said, she was making the right decision.* reinforceable (adjective).

relentless (adjective)   Unyielding. *After weeks of relentless attacks by the class bully, the boy finally complained to their teacher.* relentlessness (noun).

relevance (noun)   Connection to the matter at hand; pertinence. *Testimony in a criminal trial may only be admitted to the extent that it has clear relevance to the question of guilt or innocence.* relevant (adjective).

reparation (noun)   The act of making amends; payment of damages by a defeated nation to the victors. *The Treaty of Versailles, signed in 1919, formally asserted Germany's war guilt and ordered it to pay reparations to the allies.*

replicate (verb)   Duplicate, copy. *Authors whose first books are very successful often find it difficult to replicate that success with their second efforts.* replication (noun).

reproof (noun)   A reprimand, a reproach, or castigation. *Joe thought being grounded for one month was a harsh reproof for coming home late only once.* reprove (verb).

repudiate (verb)   To reject, to renounce. *After it became known that Duke had been a leader of the Ku Klux Klan, most Republican leaders repudiated him.* repudiation (noun).

repugnant (adjective)   Causing dislike or disgust. *After the news broke about Mad Cow Disease, much of the beef-loving British public began to find the thought of a Sunday roast repugnant.*

resilient (adjective)   Able to recover from difficulty. *A pro athlete must be mentally resilient, able to lose a game one day and come back the next with renewed enthusiasm and confidence.* resilience (noun).

resolution (noun)   The act of deciding to do something. *Around New Year's Day, it's not unusual for people hoping to attain some goal to make a resolution or two about the upcoming year.* resolve (verb).

resonant (adjective)   Full of special import or meaning. *I found the speaker's words particularly resonant because I, too, had served in Vietnam and felt the same mixture of shame and pride.* resonance (noun).

rumination (noun)   The act of engaging in contemplation. *Marcel Proust's semi-autobiographical novel cycle,* Remembrance of Things Past, *is less a narrative than an extended rumination on the nature of memory.* ruminate (verb).

Word Origin

Latin salus = *health. Also found in English* salubrious, salutation, salute.

salutary (adjective)   Restorative, healthful. *I find a short dip in an icy stream to be extremely salutary, although the health benefits of my bracing swims are, as yet, unclear.*

sanction (verb)   Support or authorize. *Even after a bomb exploded on the front porch of his home, the Reverend Martin Luther King refused to sanction any violent response and urged his angry followers to love their enemies.* sanctify (verb), sanction (noun).

satiate (verb)   To fulfill to or beyond capacity. *Judging by the current crop of films featuring serial killers, rape, ritual murder, gun-slinging, and plain old-fashioned slugfests, the public appetite for violence has not yet been satiated.* satiation (noun), satiety (noun).

saturate (verb)   To drench or suffuse with liquid or anything that permeates or invades. *The hostess' furious dabbing at the tablecloth was in vain, since the spilt wine had already saturated the damask cloth.* saturation (noun), saturated (adjective)

scrutinize (verb)   To study closely. *The lawyer scrutinized the contract, searching for any detail that could pose a risk for her client.* scrutiny (noun).

sedulous (adjective)   Diligent, industrious. *Those who are most sedulous about studying this vocabulary list are likely to breeze through the antonyms sections of their GMAT CAT.*

Word Origin

Latin sequi = *to follow. Also found in English* consequence, sequel, subsequent.

sequential (adjective)   Arranged in an order or series. *The courses required for the chemistry major are sequential; you must take them in the prescribed order, since each course builds on the previous ones.* sequence (noun).

signatory (noun)   Someone who signs an official document or petition along with others. *Alex urged me to join the other signatories and add my name to the petition against toxic sludge in organic foods, but I simply did not care enough about the issue. The signatories of the Declaration of Independence included John Adams, Benjamin Franklin, John Hancock, and Thomas Jefferson.*

sinuous (noun)   Winding, circuitous, serpentine. *Frank Gehry's sinuous design for the Guggenheim Museum in Bilbao, Spain, has led people to hail the museum as the first great building of the twenty-first century.* sinuosity (noun).

skepticism (noun)   A doubting or questioning attitude. *When someone is making what seem to be grandiose promises, it's always a good idea to maintain a certain level of skepticism.* skeptical (adjective).

specious (adjective)   Deceptively plausible or attractive. *The infomercial for Fat-Away offered mainly specious arguments for a product that is, essentially, a heavy-duty girdle.*

spontaneous (adjective)   Happening without plan or outside cause. *When the news of Kennedy's assassination hit the airwaves, people everywhere gathered in a spontaneous effort to express their shock and grief.* spontaneity (noun).

sporadically (adverb)   Appearing occasionally. *Although the girl's father had left her and her mother years before, he sporadically turned up at the door to ask for money or other favors.* sporadic (adjective).

spurious (adjective)   False, fake. *The so-called Piltdown Man, supposed to be the fossil of a primitive human, turned out to be spurious, though who created the hoax is still uncertain.*

squander (verb)   To use up carelessly, to waste. *Those who had made donations to the charity were outraged to learn that its director had squandered millions on fancy dinners, first-class travel, and an expensive apartment for entertaining.*

stanch (verb)   To stop the flow. *When Edison began to bleed profusely, Dr. Munger stanched the blood flow by applying direct pressure to the wound.*

stint (verb)   To limit, to restrain. *The British bed and breakfast certainly did not stint on the breakfast part of the equation; they provided us with fried tomatoes, fried sausages, fried eggs, smoked kippers, fried bread, fried mushrooms, and bowls of a cereal called Wheatabix (which tasted like cardboard).* stinting (adjective).

stipulate (verb)   To specify as a condition of an agreement. *When the computer company president sold his operation to another firm, he was required to stipulate that he would not start a competing company for at least five years.* stipulation (noun).

stolid (adjective)   Impassive, unemotional. *The popular animated television series* King of the Hill *chronicles the woes of a stolid, conservative Texan confronting changing times.* stolidity (noun).

stringent (adjective)   Severe, rigid. *Because their father was stringent about their behavior, the children were always careful to behave well in his presence.* stringency (noun).

subordination (noun)   The state of being subservient or treated as less valuable. *Heather left the naval academy because she could no longer stand the subordination of every personal whim or desire to the rigorous demands of military life.* subordinate (verb).

Word Origin

Latin poena = *pain. Also found in English* impunity, penal, penalty, punishment.

subpoena (noun)   An order of a court, legislation, or grand jury that compels a witness to be present at a trial or hearing. *The young man's lawyer asked the judge to subpoena a boa constrictor into court on the grounds that the police had used the snake as an "instrument of terror" to coerce his confession.*

subside (verb)   To settle or die down. *The celebrated lecturer had to wait 10 minutes for the applause to subside before he began his speech.*

subsidization (noun)   The state of being financed by a grant from a government or other agency. *Without subsidization, the nation's passenger rail system would probably go bankrupt.* subsidize (verb).

substantiated (adjective)   Verified or supported by evidence. *The charge that Nixon had helped to cover up crimes was substantiated by his comments about it on a series of audio tapes.* substantiate (verb), substantiation (noun).

subsume (verb)   To encompass or engulf within something larger. *In Alan Dershowitz's* Reversal of Fortune, *he makes it clear that his work as a lawyer subsumes his personal life.*

subterranean (adjective)   Under the surface of the earth. *Subterranean testing of nuclear weapons was permitted under the Nuclear Test Ban Treaty of 1963.*

summarily (adverb)   Quickly and concisely. *No sooner had I voiced my concerns about the new ad campaign than my boss put her hand on my elbow and summarily ushered me out of her office.*

superficial (adjective)   On the surface only; without depth or substance. *Her wound was only superficial and required no treatment except a light bandage. His superficial attractiveness hides the fact that his personality is lifeless and his mind is dull.* superficiality (noun).

superimpose (verb)   To place or lay over or above something. *The artist stirred controversy by superimposing portraits of certain contemporary politicians over images of such reviled historical figures as Hitler and Stalin.*

supersede (verb)   To displace, to substitute or supplant. *"I'm sorry," the principal announced, "but today's afternoon classes will be superseded by an assembly on drug and alcohol abuse."*

supposition (noun)   Assumption, conjecture. *While most climate researchers believe that increasing levels of greenhouse gases will warm the planet, skeptics claim that this theory is mere supposition.* suppose (verb).

synthesis (noun)   The combination of separate elements to form a whole. *Large multinational corporations are frequently the result of the synthesis of several smaller companies from several different countries.* synthesize (verb).

tactical (adjective)   Regarding a means for achieving an end. *In the early Indian Wars, since the U.S. Cavalry had repeating rifles and the Native Americans had only bows and arrows, the soldiers had a distinct tactical advantage.* tactic (noun).

Word Origin

Latin tangere = to touch. Also found in English contact, contiguous, tactile, tangent, tangible.

tangential (adjective)   Touching lightly; only slightly connected or related. *Having enrolled in a class on African-American history, the students found the teacher's stories about his travels in South America only of tangential interest.* tangent (noun).

tedium (noun)   Boredom. *For most people, watching even a 15-minute broadcast of the Earth as seen from space would be an exercise in sheer tedium.* tedious (adjective).

temperance (noun)   Moderation or restraint in feelings and behavior. *Most professional athletes practice temperance in their personal habits; too much eating or drinking and too many late nights, they know, can harm their performance.*

temperate (adjective)   Moderate, calm. *The warm gulf streams are largely responsible for the temperate climate of the British Isles.*

tenuous (adjective)   Lacking in substance; weak, flimsy, very thin. *His tenuous grasp of the Spanish language was evident when he addressed Señor Chavez as "Señora."*

terrestrial (adjective)   Of the Earth. *The movie Close Encounters tells the story of the first contact between beings from outer space and terrestrial creatures.*

tirade (noun)   A long, harshly critical speech. *Reformed smokers, like Bruce, are prone to delivering tirades on the evils of smoking.*

torpor (noun)   Apathy, sluggishness. *Stranded in an airless hotel room in Madras after a twenty-seven-hour train ride, I felt such overwhelming torpor that I doubted I would make it to Bangalore, the next leg of my journey.* torpid (adjective).

Word Origin

Latin tractare = *to handle. Also found in English* intractable, tractate, traction.

tractable (adjective)   Obedient, manageable. *When he turned 3, Harrison suddenly became a tractable, well-mannered little boy after being, quite frankly, an unruly little monster!*

tranquillity (noun)   Freedom from disturbance or turmoil; calm. *She moved from New York City to rural Vermont seeking the tranquillity of country life.* tranquil (adjective).

transgress (verb)   To go past limits; to violate. *If Iraq has developed biological weapons, then it has transgressed the UN's rules against manufacturing weapons of mass destruction.* transgression (noun).

transmute (verb)   To change in form or substance. *Practitioners of alchemy, a forebear of modern chemistry, tried to discover ways to transmute metals such as iron into gold.* transmutation (noun).

treacherous (adjective)   Untrustworthy or disloyal; dangerous or unreliable. *Nazi Germany proved to be a treacherous ally, first signing a peace pact with the Soviet Union, then invading. Be careful crossing the rope bridge; parts of the span are badly frayed and treacherous.* treachery (noun).

tremor (noun)   An involuntary shaking or trembling. *Katherine Hepburn still manages to appear regal despite the tremors caused by Parkinson's disease. Brooke felt the first tremors of the 1989 San Francisco earthquake while she was sitting in Candlestick Park watching a Giants baseball game.*

trenchant (adjective)   Caustic and incisive. *Essayist H. L. Mencken was known for his trenchant wit and was famed for mercilessly puncturing the American middle class (which he called the "booboisie").*

Word Origin

Latin trepidus = *alarmed. Also found in English* intrepid.

trepidation (noun)   Fear and anxiety. *After the tragedy of TWA Flight 800, many previously fearless flyers were filled with trepidation whenever they stepped into an airplane.*

Word Origin

Latin turba = *confusion. Also found in English* disturb, perturb, turbid.

turbulent (adjective)   Agitated or disturbed. *The night before the championship match, Martina was unable to sleep, her mind turbulent with fears and hopes.* turbulence (noun).

turpitude (noun)   Depravity, wickedness. *Radical feminists who contrast women's essential goodness with men's moral turpitude can be likened to religious fundamentalists who make a clear distinction between the saved and the damned.*

typify (verb)   To serve as a representative example. *Due in large part to post–Civil War minstrel shows, the smiling, shuffling, lazy black man came to unjustifiably typify the African American male.*

tyro (noun)   Novice, amateur. *For an absolute tyro on the ski slopes, Gina was surprisingly agile at taking the moguls.*

ubiquitous (adjective)   Being or seeming to be everywhere at one time. *The proliferation of chain-owned bookstores in malls across the country have made them a ubiquitous feature of American retailing.* ubiquitously (adverb).

unalloyed (adjective)   Unqualified, pure. *Holding his newborn son for the first time, Malik felt an unalloyed happiness that was unlike anything he had ever experienced in his 45 years.*

unconventional (adjective)   Out of the ordinary. *The manager's unconventional methods for inspiring his staff—such as providing additional vacation days for good work—pleased those who worked for him but dismayed his superiors.* unconventionally (adverb).

undermine (verb)   To excavate beneath; to subvert, to weaken. *Dot continued to undermine my efforts to find her a date by showing up at our dinner parties in her ratty old sweat suit.*

unfeigned (adjective)   Genuine, sincere. *Lashawn responded with such unfeigned astonishment when we all leapt out of the kitchen that I think she had had no inkling of the surprise party.*

univocal (adjective)   With a single voice. *While they came from different backgrounds and classes, the employees were univocal in their demands that the corrupt CEO resign immediately.*

unstinting (adjective)   Giving with unrestrained generosity. *Few people will be able to match the unstinting dedication and care that Mother Theresa lavished on the poor people of Calcutta.*

upsurge (noun)   A rapid or sudden rise. *Since no one could explain why it had occurred, the tremendous upsurge in sales in the shoe department was a source of amazement for everyone.*

Word Origin

Latin urbs = *city. Also found in English* suburb, urban.

urbanity (noun)   Sophistication, suaveness, and polish. *Part of the fun in a Cary Grant movie lies in seeing whether the star can be made to lose his urbanity and elegance in the midst of chaotic or kooky situations.* urbane (adjective).

usurious (adjective)   Lending money at an unconscionably high interest rate. *Some people feel that Shakespeare's portrayal of the Jew, Shylock, the usurious money lender in* The Merchant of Venice, *has enflamed prejudice against the Jews.* usury (adjective).

Word Origin

Latin validus =
*strong. Also found
in English* invalid,
invaluable,
prevail, value.

validate (verb)   To officially approve or confirm. *The election of the president is formally validated when the members of the Electoral College meet to confirm the verdict of the voters.* valid (adjective), validity (noun).

vapid (adjective)   Flat, flavorless. *Whenever I have insomnia, I just tune the clock radio to Lite FM, and soon those vapid songs from the seventies have me floating away to dreamland.* vapidity (noun).

variables (noun)   Things that are able or apt to have different attributes or characteristics. *When you are considering the purchase of a car, it's necessary to take all the variables—price, size, reliability, etc.—into account in making your decision.* variably (adverb).

venal (adjective)   Corrupt, mercenary. *Sese Seko Mobuto was the venal dictator of Zaire who reportedly diverted millions of dollars in foreign aid to his own personal fortune.* venality (noun).

venerate (verb)   To admire or honor. *In Communist China, Mao Tse-Tung is venerated as an almost god-like figure.* venerable (adjective), veneration (noun).

Word Origin

Latin verus =
*true. Also found in
English* verisimili-
tude, veritable,
verity."

veracious (adjective)   Truthful, earnest. *Many people still feel that Anita Hill was entirely veracious in her allegations of sexual harassment during the Clarence Thomas confirmation hearings.* veracity (noun).

verify (verb)   To prove to be true. *The contents of Robert L. Ripley's syndicated "Believe it or Not" cartoons could not be verified, yet the public still thrilled to reports of "the man with two pupils in each eye," "the human unicorn," and other amazing oddities.* verification (noun).

veritable (adjective)   Authentic. *A French antiques dealer recently claimed that a fifteenth-century child-sized suit of armor that he purchased in 1994 is the veritable suit of armor worn by heroine Joan of Arc.*

victimizing (verb)   Subjecting to swindle or fraud. *On the streets of New York City, as well as on those of other large cities, three-card monte players are extremely adept at victimizing gullible tourists.* victim (noun).

vindictive (adjective)   Spiteful. *Paula embarked on a string of petty, vindictive acts against her philandering boyfriend, such as mixing dry cat food with his cereal and snipping the blooms off his prize African violets.*

viscid (adjective)   Sticky. *The 3M company's "Post-It," a simple piece of paper with one viscid side, has become as commonplace—and as indispensable—as the paper clip.*

viscous (adjective)   Having a gelatinous or gooey quality. *I put too much liquid in the batter, so my Black Forest cake turned out to be a viscous, inedible mass.*

vitiate (verb)   To pollute, to impair. *When they voted to ban smoking from all bars in California, the public affirmed their belief that smoking vitiates the health of all people, not just smokers.*

vituperative (adjective)   Verbally abusive, insulting. *Elizabeth Taylor should have won an award for her harrowing portrayal of Martha, the bitter, vituperative wife of a college professor in Edward Albee's* Who's Afraid of Virginia Woolf? vituperate (verb).

volatile (adjective)   Quickly changing; fleeting, transitory; prone to violence. *Public opinion is notoriously volatile; a politician who is very popular one month may be voted out of office the next.* volatility (noun).

volubility (noun)   Quality of being overly talkative, glib. *As Lorraine's anxiety increased, her volubility increased in direct proportion, so during her job interview the poor interviewer couldn't get a word in edgewise.* voluble (adjective).

Word Origin

Latin vorare = *to eat. Also found in English* carnivorous, devour, omnivorous.

voracious (adjective)   Gluttonous, ravenous. *"Are all your appetites so voracious?" Wesley asked Nina as he watched her finish off seven miniature sandwiches and two lamb kabob skewers in a matter of minutes.* voracity (noun).

warrant (noun)   Authorization or certification. *The judge provided the police officer with a warrant for the alleged criminal's arrest.* warranted (verb).

xenophobia (noun)   Fear of foreigners or outsiders. *Slobodan Milosevic's nationalistic talk played on the deep xenophobia of the Serbs, who, after 500 years of brutal Ottoman occupation, had come to distrust all outsiders.*

zenith (noun)   Highest point. *Compiling the vocabulary list for the* Insider's Guide to the GMAT CAT *was the zenith of my literary career: after this, there was nowhere to go but downhill.*

The Insider's GMAT CAT Math Review

Perhaps more than any other subject, math creates a gulf between classes of students. Generally speaking, some students who think of themselves as "good at math" do well in all the usual math subjects and often take advanced classes in high school and college. Then, the others, more numerous, are a little afraid of math. They take only those math classes they are required to take and breathe a sigh of relief when they pass.

Here's the good news. The test makers know that the GMAT CAT will be taken by hundreds of thousands of students in both classes. *They've deliberately designed the exam to be fair to both.* As a result, many of the math topics that students find most intimidating—such as trigonometry and calculus—do not appear on the test. Because many students are never exposed to these subjects, the test makers wouldn't consider it fair to test them. Instead, they restrict their questions to topics that virtually all high school students study in the ninth and tenth grades.

This doesn't mean that all the GMAT CAT math questions are easy. But it does mean that it's highly unlikely that you'll be tested on any topic you never learned in high school.

In the Insider's GMAT CAT Math Review, we've selected the fifty math topics that are most frequently tested on the exam. For each, we've created a mini-lesson reviewing the basic facts, formulas, and concepts you need to know. We've also provided an example or two of how these concepts might be turned into test questions.

You'll probably find that you are comfortable with many of the topics included in the "Nifty Fifty" that follow. If so, great. Make a note of the other topics—the ones you find confusing, tricky, or difficult. Perhaps you never quite mastered those concepts when they were presented in high school, or you've forgotten the details in the intervening years. In your study between now and the day of the GMAT CAT, concentrate on reviewing and practicing these topics. You can boost your GMAT CAT math score significantly by mastering as many of your personal "math demons" as possible.

FYI

When a number line is shown on the exam, you can safely assume that the line is drawn to scale (unless otherwise indicated) and that numbers between the markings are at appropriate locations. Thus, 1.5 is halfway from 1 to 2, and −2.4 is four tenths of the way from −2 to −3 (closer to −2). However, be sure to check the scale, because the tick marks do not have to be at unit intervals!

ARITHMETIC

Topic 1. Numbers and the Number Line

The real numbers can be represented as points on a line. Usually, we think about a horizontal line, with one point chosen to represent zero. All the positive numbers are to the right of zero, and all the negative numbers are to the left. The numbers get larger as you go from left to right.

The further you get from zero, the larger the *absolute value* of a number is. Numbers far to the left are negative numbers with large absolute values.

Example 1

On the number line shown below, where is the number that is less than *E* and half as far from *E* as *E* is from *H*?

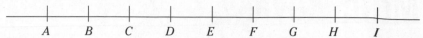

Solution

First, any number less than *E* must lie to the left of *E*. (Get it? Left = less!) The distance from *E* to *H* is 3 units. Thus, the point we want must be $1\frac{1}{2}$ units to the left of *E*. Hence, it is halfway between *C* and *D*.

Example 2

On the number line shown below, which point corresponds to the number 1.26?

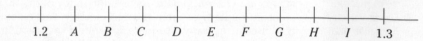

Solution

Because the labeled end points are 1.2 and 1.3, the ten intervals between must each represent one-tenth of the difference. Hence, the tick marks must represent hundredths. That is, $A = 1.21$, $B = 1.22$, and so on. Thus, we know that $F = 1.26$.

Topic 2. Laws of Arithmetic and Order of Operations

In carrying out arithmetic or algebraic operations, you should follow the famous mnemonic (memory) device Please Excuse My Dear Aunt Sally. The operations of Parentheses, Exponents, Multiplication, Division, Addition, and Subtraction should be carried out *in that order*.

If we want to indicate a change in order, we place the operation in parentheses, creating one number. In other words, calculate the number within parentheses first. Thus, $5 + 3 \times 4$ is read as $5 + 12 = 17$ because we multiply before adding. If we instead want the number $5 + 3$ to be multiplied by 4, we must write $(5 + 3) \times 4 = 8 \times 4 = 32$.

The basic laws of arithmetic were defined for whole numbers, but they carry over to all numbers. You should be very familiar with all of them from past experience:

- **The commutative law.** This says that it doesn't matter in which order you add or multiply two numbers. That is, $a + b = b + a$, and $ab = ba$.

- **The associative law** (also called *the regrouping law*). This law says that it doesn't matter how you group the numbers when you add or multiply more than two. That is, $a + (b + c) = (a + b) + c$, and $a(bc) = (ab)c$. Notice that enclosing the numbers in parentheses indicates that the operation within the parentheses should be done first.

- **The distributive law** for multiplication over addition. This law can be stated as $a(b + c) = ab + ac$. In other words, you can either add first and then multiply or multiply each term in the sum by a and then add the results. It doesn't matter; the value of the answer will be the same.

- **The properties of zero and one.** Zero times any number is zero. Zero added to any number leaves the number unchanged. One times any number leaves the number unchanged. Finally, it is very important to know that if the product of several numbers is zero, at least one of the numbers must be zero.

- **The additive inverse** (or opposite). For every number n, there is a number $-n$ such that $n + (-n) = 0$.

- **The multiplicative inverse.** For every number n, except 0, there exists a number $\frac{1}{n}$, such that $\left(\frac{1}{n}\right)(n) = 1$. Division by n is the same as multiplication by $\frac{1}{n}$. *Division by zero is never allowed.*

Example

What is the value of $\dfrac{3 + 4 \cdot 3}{6 \cdot 3 - 3A}$ if $A = 3$? What value may A not have?

Solution

The fraction bar in a fraction acts as a "grouping symbol" like parentheses, meaning we should calculate the numerator and denominator separately. Therefore, we should read this as $(3 + 4 \times 3),(6 \times 3 - 3 \times A)$. The numerator is $3 + 12 = 15$. When $A = 3$, the denominator is

$$18 - 3 \times 3 = 18 - 9 = 9$$

Therefore, the fraction is $\dfrac{15}{9} = \dfrac{5}{3}$. Because we cannot divide by zero, we cannot let $6 \times 3 - 3 \times A = 0$. In order for this to be zero, $6 \times 3 = 3 \times A$. By the commutative law, $A = 6$. Thus, the only value that A cannot have is 6.

Topic 3. Divisibility Rules

A *factor* or *divisor* of a whole number is a number that divides evenly into the given number, that is, leaving no remainder. For example, the divisors of 28 are 1, 2, 4, 7, 14, and 28 itself. A *proper divisor* is any divisor except the number itself. Thus, the proper divisors of 28 are 1, 2, 4, 7, and 14.

Several useful rules for testing for divisibility for certain small numbers are summarized in Table B.1.

For example, consider the number 7,890. It is divisible by all the numbers in the table except 4, 8, and 9. Do you see why? To start, 7,890 is divisible by 10 and 5 because it ends in 0. It is divisible by 2 because it is even—but not by 4 because 90 is not divisible by 4. Of course, it cannot be divisible by 8 unless it is already divisible by 4. In addition, the sum of its digits is 24, which is divisible by 3 but not 9. Finally, because it is divisible by both 2 and 3, it is also divisible by 6.

Example

Which numbers in the following list are divisible by 5 and 3 but not 4?

```
10,435
20,085
23,096
56,700
79,140
```

FYI

If you want to know whether k *is a divisor of* n, *simply divide* k *into* n *and see whether there is any remainder. If the remainder is zero, then* n *is divisible by* k.

Table B.1
Rules for Testing Divisibility.

Number	Divides into a Number N if . . .
2	N is even; that is, it ends in 2, 4, 6, 8, or 0.
3	The sum of the digits of N is divisible by 3.
4	The last two digits form a number divisible by 4.
5	The number ends in 5 or 0.
6	The number is divisible by 2 and 3.
8	The last three digits form a number divisible by 8.
9	The sum of the digits of N is divisible by 9.
10	The number ends in 0.

Solution

The easiest thing to look for is divisibility by 5. Just ask, does the number end in 5 or 0? By inspection, we eliminate 23,096, which ends in 6. Now, we don't want the number to be divisible by 4, so we knock out all the even numbers, leaving 10,435 and 20,085. The digits of 10,435 add up to 13, whereas those of 20,085 total 15. Therefore, only 20,085 is divisible by 3 and 5, but not by 4.

Topic 4. Divisibility in Addition, Subtraction, and Multiplication

If you add or subtract two numbers that are both divisible by some number k, then the new number formed is also divisible by k. For example, 21 and 15 are both divisible by 3. If you take their sum, 36, or their difference, 6, both numbers are also divisible by 3.

If you multiply two numbers together, any number that divides either one divides the product. That is, if j divides M and k divides N, then jk divides MN. If both have a common divisor, then the product is divisible by the square of that number. Thus, $21 \times 15 = 315$ is divisible by 7 because 7 divides 21, and by 5 because 5 divides 15. It is also divisible by $35 = 5 \times 7$ and by 9 because $9 = 3^2$ and 3 divides both 21 and 15!

Example 1

If k is divisible by 7, what is the largest number that must divide into $8k + 14$?

Solution

Because k is divisible by 7 and 8 is divisible by 2, $8k$ can be divided by 14. Therefore, the sum $8k + 14$ can be divided by 14.

Example 2

If a and b are whole numbers and $5a = 4b$, which of the following must be true?

    I. a is divisible by 4
    II. b is divisible by 4
    III. b is divisible by 5

    (A) I only
    (B) II only
    (C) III only
    (D) I and II only
    (E) I and III only

Solution

If $5a$ equals $4b$, then $5a$ must be divisible by 4, which means a must be divisible by 4 because 5 is not. Similarly, $4b$ must be divisible by 5, which means b must be divisible by 5 because 4 is not. The correct choice is (E): both I and III must be true. Notice that II need not be true; because $b = 5$, $a = 4$ is a perfectly satisfactory solution.

Topic 5. Even Numbers and Odd Numbers

Even numbers are those that are divisible by 2: 0, 2, 4, 6, . . . Odd numbers are not divisible by 2: 1, 3, 5, . . . Certain simple results follow from these definitions, and they can be very useful:

- If you add or subtract two even numbers, the result is even.

- If you add or subtract two odd numbers, the result is even.

- Only when you *add or subtract* an *odd and an even* number is the result *odd*. (Thus, $4 + 8$ is even, as is $9 - 3$. But $4 + 5$ is odd.)

- If you multiply any whole number by an even number, the result is even.

- Only when you *multiply two odd numbers* will the result be *odd*. (Again, (4)(6) and (4)(7) are both even, but (5)(7) is odd.)

Example 1

If $3k + 2c$ is an even number, is k odd or even—or can't you tell?

Solution

$2c$ must be even (because of the even factor 2), so for the sum of $3k$ and $2c$ to be even, $3k$ must also be even. But 3 is odd, so k is even.

Example 2

If $121 - 5k$ is divisible by 3, can k be odd?

Solution

The fact that a number is divisible by 3 does not make it odd. (Think of 6 or 12.) Therefore, $121 - 5k$ could be either odd or even. It will be odd when k is even and even when k is odd. (Do you see why?) Thus, k could be odd or even. For example, for $k = 2$, $121 - 5k = 111$, which is divisible by 3; for $k = 5$, $121 - 5k = 96$, which is divisible by 3.

Topic 6. Least Common Multiples

Given two numbers, M and N, any number that is divisible by both is called a *common multiple* of M and N. The *least common multiple* (LCM) of the two numbers is the *smallest* number that is divisible by both. For example, 9 and 12 both divide into 108, so 108 is a common multiple of 9 and 12—but the LCM is 36.

For small numbers, the easiest way to find the LCM is to mentally, or in writing, list the multiples of each until you find the first "common" multiple. For example, for 9 and 12, we have

9, 18, 27, 36, 45 . . .

12, 24, 36, 48, 60 . . .

We see that the first number that appears in both lists is 36.

However, the traditional method, which is really the method that translates most readily into algebra, requires that you find the *prime factorization* of the numbers. You are expected to know that every whole number is either *prime* or *composite*. A prime is a whole number greater than 1 for which the only factors (divisors) are 1 and the number itself. Any number not a prime is a composite number.

All composite numbers can be factored into primes in an essentially unique way. To find an LCM, you must find the smallest number that contains all of the prime factors of both numbers. Thus, 9 factors as (3)(3), and 12 factors as (2)(2)(3). The smallest number to use all the prime factors of both has to have factors (3)(3)(2)(2) = 36.

This definition also extends to sets of more than two numbers. Thus, the LCM of 12, 15, and 20 must contain all the prime factors of all three numbers: (2)(2)(3), (3)(5), (2)(2)(5). That is, (2)(2)(3)(5) = 60.

Example 1
Find the LCM for 36 and 30.

Solution
Using prime factorization, 36 = (2)(2)(3)(3); 30 = (2)(3)(5). Because the prime factorization of both numbers includes 2 and 3, we'll start with those. Then we need to multiply in one more 2 and one more 3 to have all the prime factors of 36 and one 5 to have all the prime factors of 30. Thus, the LCM = (2)(2)(3)(3)(5) = 180.

Example 2
If the LCM of $5k$ and 20 is 100, what is k?

Solution
Using prime factorization, 20 = (2)(2)(5) and 100 = (2)(2)(5)(5). Why are there two factors of 5 in the LCM? It must be that $5k$ has two factors of 5. That is, k must itself have a factor 5. Hence, $k = 5x$ for some x. In order to have only two 2s and two 5s in the LCM, x could only be 1, 2, or 4. That is, $k = 5$, 10, or 20.

Topic 7. Equality of Fractions

Two fractions $\frac{a}{b}$ and $\frac{c}{d}$ are defined to be equal if $ad = bc$. For example, $\frac{3}{4} = \frac{9}{12}$ because (3)(12) = (4)(9). This definition, using *cross-multiplication*, is very useful in solving algebraic equations involving fractions. However, for working with numbers, the important thing to remember is that multiplying the numerator and denominator of a fraction by the same number (other than zero) results in a fraction equal in value to the original fraction. Thus, by multiplying top and bottom by 3, we have $\frac{3}{4} = \frac{(3)(3)}{(3)(4)} = \frac{9}{12}$.

Similarly, dividing the numerator and denominator of a fraction by the same number (other than zero) results in a fraction equal in value to the original fraction. It is usual to divide the top and bottom by the greatest common factor of both numerator and denominator to "reduce the fraction to lowest terms."

Thus, by dividing top and bottom by 5, we have $\frac{15}{25} = \frac{15 \div 5}{25 \div 5} = \frac{3}{5}$.

Example 1

If b and c are both positive integers (whole numbers) greater than 1, and $\dfrac{5}{c} = \dfrac{b}{3}$, what are b and c?

Solution

Using cross-multiplication, $bc = 15$. The only ways 15 can be the product of two positive integers is as $(1)(15)$ or $(3)(5)$. Because both b and c must be greater than 1, one must be 3 and the other 5. Trying both cases, it is easy to see that the only possibility is that $b = 3$ and $c = 5$, and both fractions are equal to 1.

Example 2

If the fraction $\dfrac{60}{N}$ has been reduced to lowest terms, which of the following numbers can be a factor of N: $\{25, 27, 49, 110, 213\}$?

Solution

If the fraction has been reduced to lowest terms, N cannot have as a factor any number whose prime factorization has any numbers in common with the prime factors of 60. But $60 = (2)(2)(3)(5)$. Thus, the answer must be 49 because in this set, only $49 = (7)(7)$ has a prime factorization lacking 2, 3, and 5. Check the others for yourself.

Topic 8. Comparing Fractions

For positive numbers: If two fractions have the same denominator, the one with the larger numerator is larger. If two fractions have the same numerator, the one with the *smaller* denominator is the larger one. For example, $\dfrac{5}{19}$ is smaller than $\dfrac{8}{19}$, but $\dfrac{8}{17}$ is larger than $\dfrac{8}{19}$.

Example 1

Which is larger, $\dfrac{6}{11}$ or $\dfrac{13}{22}$?

Solution

If the two fractions had a common denominator (or numerator), it would be easy. But it's easy to get there because the denominator 11 is exactly half of the denominator 22. Just multiply the top and bottom of $\dfrac{6}{11}$ to yield $\dfrac{12}{22}$, and it is easy to see that $\dfrac{13}{22}$ is the larger fraction.

Example 2

Which is larger, $\dfrac{4}{7}$ or $\dfrac{3}{5}$?

Solution

The first fraction has a larger numerator, but it also has a larger denominator, so we rewrite both with the common denominator 35 by multiplying the top and bottom of $\frac{4}{7}$ by 5 and the top and bottom of $\frac{3}{5}$ by 7 to yield $\frac{20}{35}$ and $\frac{21}{35}$ respectively. Now, it is easy to see that $\frac{3}{5}$ is the larger fraction.

Example 3

If a must be chosen from the set $\{1,4,5\}$ and b must be chosen from $\{3,6,7\}$, what is the largest possible value of $\frac{4}{2a-b}$?

Solution

To make the fraction as large as possible, we should make the denominator the smallest possible positive number it can be. We can't let $a = 1$ because that would make the denominator negative for any of the possible bs. However, choosing $a = 4$, we see that for $b = 7$, $2a - b = 1$, which is the smallest possible whole number. Therefore, the maximum value of the fraction is $\frac{4}{1} = 4$.

Topic 9. Multiplication and Division of Fractions

When multiplying two fractions, the result is the product of the numerators divided by the product of the denominators. In symbols, $\frac{a}{b} \cdot \frac{c}{d} = \frac{ac}{bd}$. Thus, $\frac{3}{7} \cdot \frac{2}{5} = \frac{6}{35}$. Don't forget that the resulting fraction can be reduced to lowest terms by canceling out like factors in the numerator and denominator, such as $\frac{3}{5} \cdot \frac{10}{9} = \frac{2}{3}$.

Example 1

Joan earns $\frac{3}{4}$ of what Sally earns, and Sally earns $\frac{2}{3}$ of what Pedro earns. What fraction of Pedro's salary does Joan earn?

Solution

Using J, S, and P, to stand for the people's earnings respectively, we have

$$S = \frac{2}{3}P \,; J = \frac{3}{4}S$$

thus

$$J = \frac{3}{4} \cdot \frac{2}{3}P = \frac{1}{2}P$$

Hence, Joan's earnings are one half of Pedro's.

When dividing fractions, simply invert the divisor and then multiply. Remember, the divisor is the one you are dividing by (usually the second one named) or the denominator in a "built-up" fraction. In symbols,

$$\frac{a}{b} \div \frac{c}{d} = \frac{a}{b} \cdot \frac{d}{c} = \frac{ad}{bc}$$

or

$$\frac{\frac{a}{b}}{\frac{c}{d}} = \frac{a}{b} \cdot \frac{d}{c} = \frac{ad}{bc}$$

For example:

$$\frac{3}{5} \div \frac{4}{11} = \frac{3}{5} \cdot \frac{11}{4} = \frac{33}{20}$$

Example 2

Patty has half as many pairs of jeans as Alfred has, and Marco has as many pairs of jeans as Alfred. What fraction of Marco's number of pairs does Patty have?

Solution

Using P, A, and M to stand for the number of jeans each person owns, we have

$$P = \frac{1}{2}A; M = \frac{3}{5}A$$

thus

$$\frac{P}{M} \div \frac{\frac{1}{2}A}{\frac{3}{5}A} = \frac{1}{2} \cdot \frac{5}{3} = \frac{5}{6}$$

Thus, Patty has $\frac{5}{6}$ as many pairs as Marco.

Topic 10. Addition and Subtraction of Fractions

To add (or subtract) fractions with the same denominator, simply add (or subtract) the numerators. For example, $\frac{5}{17} + \frac{3}{17} = \frac{8}{17}$ and $\frac{5}{17} - \frac{3}{17} = \frac{2}{17}$.

However, if the denominators are different, you must first rewrite the fractions so they will have the same denominator. Most books stress that you should use the *least common denominator* (LCD), which is the least common multiple (LCM) of the original denominators. This will keep the numbers smaller. However, any common denominator will do! For example, to add $\frac{5}{12} + \frac{3}{8}$, the LCM of 12 and 8 is 24. You should write $\frac{5}{12} = \frac{10}{24}$ and $\frac{3}{8} = \frac{9}{24}$ so that $\frac{5}{12} + \frac{3}{8} = \frac{10}{24} + \frac{9}{24} = \frac{19}{24}$.

However, if you are rushed, you can always find a common denominator by just taking the product of the two denominators, that is, $12 \times 8 = 96$. Thus,

$$\frac{5}{12} + \frac{3}{8} = \frac{5 \cdot 8}{12 \cdot 8} + \frac{3 \cdot 12}{8 \cdot 12} = \frac{40}{96} + \frac{36}{96} = \frac{76}{96}$$

Now, you can divide numerator and denominator by 4 to reduce the fraction to its lowest terms, that is, $\frac{76}{96} = \frac{19}{24}$. Maybe not as efficient—but guaranteed to work!

Example

Mark figures that, working every day, he could finish a certain task in 30 days. Alfonso figures that he could finish the same task in 20 days. What fraction of the task could they get done by working on it together for a week?

Solution

In one week (7 days), Mark would do $\frac{7}{30}$ of the entire task. In the same week, Alfonso would do $\frac{7}{20}$ of the entire task. Therefore, together they do $\frac{7}{30} + \frac{7}{20}$.

Now, we have to add two fractions that have the same numerator. Can we add them directly by just summing the denominators? No! To add directly, it is the bottoms that must be the same. We must find a common denominator.

First, find the LCD, which is 60. Thus, $\frac{7}{30} + \frac{7}{20} = \frac{14}{60} + \frac{21}{60} = \frac{35}{60}$, which reduces to $\frac{7}{12}$.

Topic 11. Fractions and Decimals

FYI

To convert a number given as a percent to decimal form, simply move the decimal point two places to the left. *To convert decimals to percent, reverse the process; that is, move the decimal point two places to the right. To avoid confusion, keep in mind the fact that, written as a percent, the number should look bigger. Thus, the "large" number 45% is 0.45, and the "small" number 0.73 is 73%.*

Every fraction can be expressed as a decimal, which can be found by division. Those fractions for which the prime factorization of the denominator involves only 2s and 5s will have terminating decimal expansions. All others will have repeating decimal expansions. For example, $\frac{3}{20} = 0.15$ and $\frac{3}{11} = 0.272727\ldots$

To convert a decimal given to a fixed number of decimal places into a fraction, you must know what the decimal means. In general, the decimal represents a fraction with denominator 10, or 100, or 1000, and so on, where the number of zeros is equal to the number of digits to the right of the decimal point. Thus, for example,

$$0.4 \text{ means } \frac{4}{10} = \frac{2}{5}$$
$$0.52 \text{ means } \frac{52}{100} = \frac{13}{25}$$
$$0.103 \text{ means } \frac{103}{1000}$$

Decimals of the form 2.15 are equivalent to mixed numbers. Thus, $2.15 = 2 + \frac{15}{100} = 2 + \frac{3}{20} = 2\frac{3}{20}$. For purposes of addition and subtraction, mixed numbers can be useful. But for purposes of multiplication or division, it is usually better to convert a mixed number to an *improper fraction* (one whose numerator is larger than its denominator). That is, $2\frac{3}{20} = \frac{43}{20}$.

How did we figure that? Formally, we realize that $2 = \frac{2}{1}$, and we add the two fractions $\frac{2}{1}$ and $\frac{3}{20}$ using the common denominator 20. More simply, we multiply the whole number part (2) by the common denominator (20), and add the numerator of the fraction (3) to get the numerator of the resulting improper fraction. That is, $(2)(20) + 3 = 43$.

Example

If $\dfrac{0.56}{1.26}$ reduced to lowest terms is $\dfrac{a}{b}$, where a and b are positive whole numbers, what is b?

Solution

Rewriting both numerator and denominator as their fractional equivalents, $0.56 = \dfrac{56}{100} = \dfrac{14}{25}$ and $1.26 = 1 + \dfrac{26}{100} = 1\dfrac{13}{50} = \dfrac{63}{50}$. We now accomplish the division by inverting and multiplying by the denominator. Thus, $\left(\dfrac{14}{25}\right)\left(\dfrac{50}{63}\right) = \dfrac{4}{9}$ and $b = 9$.

Of course, you could also do this example by changing the numerator and denominator of the original fraction to whole numbers. That is, multiply the top and bottom by 100 to move both decimal points two places to the right, thus $\dfrac{0.56}{1.26} = \dfrac{56}{126}$. Now you can divide out the common factor of 14 in the numerator and the denominator to reduce the fraction to $\dfrac{4}{9}$.

Notice that by using long division or dividing on a calculator, you will find that $\dfrac{0.56}{1.26} = 0.4444444\ldots$, which you might recognize as $\dfrac{4}{9}$.

Topic 12. Decimals and Percents

Remember, per*cent* means per *hundred*. (The word comes from the Latin *centum*, which means hundred.) For example, 30% means 30 per hundred, or as a fraction, $\dfrac{30}{100}$; as a decimal, 0.30.

Example

In a group of 30 doctors and 20 lawyers, 20% of the doctors and 40% of the lawyers wear contact lenses. What percent of the entire group wears contact lenses?

Solution

Start with the doctors. Because 20% = 0.20, 20% of 30 = (0.20)(30) = 6 doctors wear contacts. For the lawyers, 40% = 0.40; 40% of 20 = (0.40)(20) = 8 lawyers wear contacts. Hence, a total of 14 out of 50 people in the group wear contacts.

The fraction of contact wearers is $\dfrac{14}{50} = 0.28 = 28\%$.

ALGEBRA

Topic 13. Addition and Subtraction of Signed Numbers

To add two numbers of the same sign, just add them and attach their common sign. So $7 + 9 = 16$, and $(-7) + (-9) = -16$. (Of course, you could drop the parentheses and instead of $(-7) + (-9)$, you could write $-7 - 9$, which means the same thing.)

When adding numbers of opposite signs, temporarily ignore the signs, subtract the smaller from the larger, and attach to the result the sign of the number with the larger absolute value. Thus, $9 + (-3) = 6$, but $(-9) + 3 = -6$. (Again, we could have written $9 + (-3) = 9 - 3 = 6$ and $(-9) + 3 = -9 + 3 = -6$.)

When subtracting, change the sign of the "second" number (the *subtrahend*) and then use the rules for addition. Thus, $7 - (-3) = 7 + 3 = 10$, and $-7 - 3 = -7 + (-3) = -10$.

Example
What is the value of $A - (-B)$ when $A = -5$ and $B = -6$?

Solution
All the minus signs can be confusing. However, if you remember that "minus a minus is a plus," you can do this in two ways. The first is to realize that if $B = -6$, then $-B = +6$. Thus, $A - (-B) = A - 6 = -5 - 6 = -11$. Alternatively, you can work with the letters first: $A - (-B) = A + B = -5 - (-6) = -5 + 6 = 1$.

Topic 14. Multiplication and Division of Signed Numbers

If you multiply two numbers with the same sign, the result is positive. If you multiply two numbers with opposite signs, the result is negative. Thus, $(-4)(-3) = +12$, and $(-4)(3) = -12$.

Furthermore, the exact same rule holds true for division. For division, it doesn't matter which number is negative and which is positive, thus $(-6) \div (2) = -3$ and $(6) \div (-2) = -3$, but $(-6) \div (-2) = +3$.

Example 1
If $A = (234,906 - 457,219)(35)(-618)$, and $B = (-2,356)(-89,021)(-3,125)$, which is larger, A or B?

Solution
Don't actually do the arithmetic! 457,219 is greater than 234,906, so the difference is a negative number. Now, you see that A is the product of two negative numbers and one positive number, which makes the result positive. B is the product of three negative numbers, so it must be negative. Every positive number is greater than any negative number, and so A is greater than B.

Example 2
If $\dfrac{AB}{MN}$ is a negative number and N is negative, which of the following are possible?

  I. A is positive, but B and M are negative.
  II. A, B, and M are all negative.
  III. A, B, and M are positive.

  (A) I only
  (B) II only
  (C) I and II only
  (D) I and III only
  (E) II and III only

Solution
To determine the sign of the fraction, just think of A, B, M, and N as four factors. Knowing that N is negative, the product of the other three must be positive in order for the result to be negative. The only possibilities are that all three are

positive or that one is positive and the other two are negative. This corresponds to cases I and III. Thus, the answer is choice (D).

Topic 15. Laws of Exponents

FYI

Commit to memory small powers of small numbers that come up in many questions. For example: The powers of 2: 2, 4, 8, 16, 32, . . . ; the powers of 3: 3, 9, 27, 81, . . . ; and so on.

In an expression of the form b^n, b is called the *base* and n is called the *exponent* or *power*. We say, "b is raised to the power n." Notice, $b^1 = b$, so the power 1 is usually omitted.

If n is any positive integer, then b^n is the product of n bs. For example, 4^3 is the product of three 4s—that is, $4^3 = 4 \times 4 \times 4 = 64$. Certain rules for operations with exponents are forced upon us by this definition:

- $b^m \times b^n = b^{m+n}$. When multiplying powers of the same base, keep the base and add the exponents.

  Thus, $3^2 \times 3^3 = 3^{2+3} = 3^5 = 243$.

- $(ab)^n = a^n b^n$, and $\left(\dfrac{a}{b}\right)^x = \dfrac{a^x}{b^x}$.

  To raise a product or a quotient to a power, raise each factor to that power, whether that factor is in the numerator or denominator (top or bottom). Thus,

  $$(2x)^3 = 2^3 x^3 = 8x^3$$

  and

  $$\left(\frac{2}{x}\right)^3 = \frac{2^3}{x^3} = \frac{8}{x^3}$$

- $(b^m)^n = b^{nm}$. To raise to a power to a power, multiply exponents. Thus, $(2^3)^2 = 2^6 = 64$.

- $\dfrac{b^n}{b^m} = b^{n-m}$ if $n > m$, and $\dfrac{b^n}{b^m} = \dfrac{1}{b^{m-n}}$ if $n < m$.

  To divide powers with the same base, retain the base and subtract exponents. For example,

  $$\frac{4^5}{4^2} = 4^3 = 64$$

  and

  $$\frac{4^2}{4^5} = \frac{1}{4^3} = \frac{1}{64}$$

For various technical reasons, $x^0 = 1$ for all x except $x = 0$, in which case it is undefined.

Topic 16. Even Powers and Odd Powers

Even powers of real numbers cannot be negative. Thus, x^2 is positive, except for $x = 0$, when it is zero. Note that -3^2 means $-(3^2) = -9$. If you want the square of -3, which equals $+9$, you must write it $(-3)^2$.

Odd powers are either positive or negative, depending upon whether the base is positive or negative. Thus, $2^3 = 8$, but $(-2)^3 = -8$. Zero to any power is zero, except zero to the zero, which is undefined.

Example 1

If $x < 0$ and $y > 0$, what is the sign of $-4x^4y^3$?

Solution

x^4 is positive because it has an even power. y^3 is positive because y is positive, and -4 is obviously negative. The product of two positives and a negative is negative. Thus, $-4x^4y^3$ is negative.

Example 2

If $x^4 + 3y^2 = 0$, what is the sign of $2x - 6y + 1$?

Solution

Because neither x^4 nor $3y^2$ can be negative, the only way their sum can be zero is if both x and y are zero. Therefore, $2x - 6y + 1 = +1$, which is positive.

Topic 17. Averages

The *average* or *arithmetic mean* of a collection of numbers is simply the sum of the numbers divided by the number of numbers in the collection. In symbols, $A = \dfrac{T}{n}$. So, for example, if your grades on four math exams are 92, 86, 67, and 91, your average in math is $(92 + 86 + 67 + 91) \div 4 = 326 \div 4 = 81.5$.

Example 1

Arnold picked six bags of apples. His average bag weighed 12 pounds. Frank picked four bags of apples. His average bag weighed 16 pounds. What was the overall average of the ten bags?

Solution

You can't just say the answer is 14, the average of 12 and 16, because we do not have the same number of bags in each group. We need to know the total weight of all ten bags. Because Arnold's six bags averaged 12 pounds, the total weight of the six bags was 72. ($12 = \dfrac{T}{6}$ means $T = (6)(12) = 72$). In the same way, Frank's four bags must have weighed 64 pounds in order to average 16 per bag. Therefore, we have a total of ten bags weighing $72 + 64 = 136$, and the average is $\dfrac{136}{10} = 13.6$.

Example 2

Margaret earns an average of 88 on her first four calculus exams. To get an A for the course, she must have a 90 average. What grade must she earn on the next exam to bring her average to 90?

Solution

If her average is 88 on four exams, she must have a total of $(4)(88) = 352$. To average 90 on five exams, her total must be $(5)(90) = 450$. Therefore, she must score $450 - 352 = 98$ on her last exam. Study hard, Margaret!

Two other quantities are sometimes used in ways similar to averages. They are the *median*, which is the middle number when the numbers are arranged in

FYI

When people analyze statistics, they sometimes speak as if the mean, median, and mode are interchangeable— but as you can see, they are not. Be careful to keep in mind the differences among these three terms.

order of size, and the *mode*, the most common number. Thus, for the set of nine integers {1, 2, 2, 2, 3, 5, 6, 7, 8} the median (middle number) is 3, the mode is 2 (because there are more 2s in the set than any other number), and the mean is

$$(1 + 2 + 2 + 2 + 3 + 5 + 6 + 7 + 8) \div 9 = 4.$$

Topic 18. Ratio and Proportion

The ratio of two quantities defines a fractional relationship between the quantities. This can be expressed as a fraction, in the form of $\frac{b}{a}$ or in the form $b : a$, (read "*b* is to *a*").

A proportion is a statement that two ratios are equal. To say, for example, that the ratio of passing to failing students in a class is 5:2 means that if we set up the fraction $\frac{P}{F}$, it should reduce to $\frac{5}{2}$. If we write this statement as *P*:*F*::5:2, we read it as "*P* is to *F* as 5 is to 2," and it means $\frac{P}{F} = \frac{5}{2}$.

Very frequently, a good way to handle ratios is to write the actual numbers as multiples of the same number.

Example

The ratio of passing to failing students in a certain class is 5:2. Which of the following could be the number of students in the class?

- (A)　12
- (B)　15
- (C)　21
- (D)　30
- (E)　34

Solution

Because *P*:*F* = 5:2, we let *P* = 5*k* and *F* = 2*k*. But the total number in the class must be *P* + *F* = 5*k* + 2*k* = 7*k*. Clearly, choice (C) 21, will work because 21 is evenly divisible by 7; in this instance, *k* = 3. If you try the other possibilities, *k* will be a fraction for which neither 5*k* nor 2*k* will be a whole number. Of course, you can't have a fractional number of students (there's no such thing as one third of a student), so the answer must be choice (C).

Topic 19. Solving Linear Equations

There are two keys to solving linear equations:

- If you add or subtract the same quantity from both sides of an equation, the equation is still true.

- If you multiply or divide both sides of an equation by any number *except zero*, the equation is still true.

The idea when solving most equations is to use these two properties in order to isolate the unknown quantity on one side of the equation, leaving only known quantities on the other side.

Example 1

If $A = 3x - 1$, and $A = \frac{1}{2}x + 4$, what is the numerical value of *A*?

Solution

Because things that are equal to the same thing are also equal to each other, we can equate the two expressions in x that are both equal to A. That is,

$$3x - 1 = \frac{1}{2}x + 4$$

As a general rule, when an equation involves one or more fractional coefficients, it pays to multiply by a common denominator to clear (eliminate) the fractions. We multiply by 2 to get rid of the $\frac{1}{2}$. (Be careful when you multiply by 2: be sure to use the distributive law and multiply every term on both sides by 2.) You should now have

$$6x - 2 = x + 8$$

Because we want to have x (the unknown) on one side of the equation and only known quantities on the other, we first add $-x + 2$ to both sides:

$$6x - 2 = x + 8$$
$$\underline{-x + 2 = -x + 2}$$
$$5x = 10$$

Now we can divide both sides by 5:

$$\frac{5x}{5} = \frac{10}{5}; x = 2$$

Of course, the question asked for A, not x. We substitute $x = 2$ into $A = 3x - 1$ and get $A = 3(2) - 1 = 5$.

Example 2

If $3x + 7 = b$ and $y = 2x + 5$, find an expression for y in terms of b.

Solution

How do we do this? We realize that if we knew what x was in terms of b, we could substitute that expression for x into $y = 2x - 5$ and have y in terms of b. In other words, we want to solve $3x + 7 = b$ for x. To do so, we start by adding -7 to both sides of the equation:

$$3x + 7 = b$$
$$\underline{-7 = -7}$$
$$3x = b - 7$$

Now divide by 3:

$$\frac{3x}{3} = \frac{(b - 7)}{3}$$

$$x = \frac{(b - 7)}{3}$$

The Insider's GMAT CAT Math Review

Substituting:

$$y = 2\left(\frac{b-7}{3}\right) + 5$$

$$y = \frac{2b - 14}{3} + \frac{15}{3} = \frac{2b + 1}{3}$$

Combining fractions with the common denominator 3.

Topic 20. Solving Linear Inequalities

To say that one number, M, is less than another number, N, is to say that $N - M$ is positive. That is, when you subtract a smaller number from a larger number, the result is positive. We say that M is less than N and write $M < N$ (read as "M is less than N") or $N > M$ ("N is greater than M").

Graphically, we think M lies to the left of N on the number line. This means, in particular, that any negative number is less than any positive number. It also implies that for negative numbers, the one with the larger absolute value is the smaller number.

There are three keys to solving *linear inequalities* (or *inequations*):

- If you add or subtract the same quantity from both sides of an inequation, the inequality remains in the same order.

  Thus, $14 > 7$ and $14 - 5 > 7 - 5$.

- If you multiply or divide both sides of an inequation by the same positive number, the inequality remains in the same order.

  Thus, $3 < 8$ and $(6)(3) < (6)(8)$.

- If you multiply or divide both sides of an equation by the same *negative* number, the inequality remains, but the order is *reversed*. Thus, $4 < 9$, but if you multiply by (-2), you get $-8 > -18$. Remember, for negative numbers, the one with the larger absolute value is the smaller number.

The idea in solving most inequalities is to use these three properties to isolate the unknown quantity on one side of the inequality, leaving only known quantities on the other side. Notice that these rules hold whether you are working with $<$ and $>$ or $\leq$ (is less than or equal to) and $\geq$ (is greater than or equal to).

Example 1

For what values of x is $2x - 5 = 4x + 3$?

Solution

We solve this just like an equation. Start by adding the like quantity $(-2x - 3)$ to both sides in order to group the x terms on one side and the constants on the other; thus,

$$
\begin{array}{r}
2x - 5 = 4x + 3 \\
-2x - 3 = -2x - 3 \\
\hline
-8 = 2x
\end{array}
$$

Now divide both sides by 2, which does not change the sense of the inequality, yielding

$$-4 = x$$

Hence, the inequality will be true for any number less than or equal to -4 and false for any number greater than -4. For example, for $x = 3$, $2x - 5 = 1$, $4x + 3 = 15$, and the inequality is *not* satisfied.

Example 2

If $A < 1 - 3B$, can you tell how large B is in terms of A? Can you tell how small B is?

Solution

We are really being asked to solve the inequality for B. To start, we add -1 to both sides, thus:

$$\begin{array}{rl} A & < 1 - 3B \\ -1 &= -1 \\ \hline A - 1 &< -3B \end{array}$$

Next divide by -3, remembering to reverse the inequality, thus:

$$\frac{A - 1}{-3} > B; \; = \frac{1 - A}{3} > B$$

Notice that to change the denominator on the left-hand side from -3 to $+3$, we multiplied top and bottom by -1 and, of course, $(-1)(A - 1) = (1 - A)$. This tells us what B is less than but tells us nothing about what B might be greater than. For example, if A were 7, then $B < -2$, but B could be -100 or -1000 or anything "more negative."

Topic 21. Solving Two Linear Equations in Two Unknowns

Many word problems lead to equations in two unknowns. Usually, one needs two equations to solve for both unknowns, although there are exceptions. There are two generally used methods to solve two equations in two unknowns. They are the method of *substitution* and the method of *elimination by addition and subtraction*.

We'll illustrate both methods via example. Here is one that uses the method of substitution.

Example 1

Mr. Green took his four children to the local craft fair. The total cost of their admission tickets was $14. Mr. and Mrs. Molina and their six children had to pay $23. What was the cost of an adult ticket to the craft fair, and what was the cost of a child's ticket?

Solution

Expressing all amounts in dollars, let x = cost of an adult ticket and let y = cost of a child's ticket.

For the Greens:

$$x + 4y = 14$$

For the Molinas:

$$2x + 6y = 23$$

The idea of the method of substitution is to solve one equation for one variable in terms of the other and then substitute that solution into the second equation. We solve the first equation for x because that is the simplest one to isolate:

$$x = 14 - 4y$$

and substitute into the second equation:

$$2(14 - 4y) + 6y = 23$$

This gives us one equation in one unknown that we can solve:

$$28 - 8y + 6y = 23$$

$$-2y = -5; y = 2.5$$

Now that we know $y = 2.5$, we substitute this into $x = 14 - 4y$ to get

$$x = 14 - 4(2.5) = 4$$

Thus, the adult tickets were $4.00 each, and the children's tickets were $2.50 each.

Here is an example using the method of elimination.

Example 2
Paul and Denise both have after-school jobs. Two weeks ago, Paul worked 6 hours, Denise worked 3 hours, and they earned a total of $39. Last week, Paul worked 12 hours, Denise worked 5 hours, and they earned a total of $75. What is each one's hourly wage?

Solution
Again, let us express all amounts in dollars. Let $x =$ Paul's hourly wage, and let $y =$ Denise's hourly wage.

For the first week:

$$6x + 3y = 39$$

For the second week:

$$12x + 5y = 75$$

The idea of the method of elimination is that adding equal quantities to equal quantities gives a true result. So we want to add some multiple of one equation to the other one so that *if we add the two equations together,* one variable will be eliminated. In this case, it is not hard to see that if we multiply the first equation by -2, the coefficient of x will become -12. Now when we add the two equations, x will drop out.

-2 times the first equation is:	$-12x - 6y = -78$
the second equation is:	$12x + 5y = 75$
adding them:	$-y = -3$

Thus, $y = 3$. We now substitute this into either of the two equations. Let's use the first:

$6x + (3)(3) = 39; x = 5$

Thus, Denise makes only \$3 per hour, whereas Paul gets \$5.

Topic 22. Word Problems in One or Two Unknowns

Word problems can be broken down into a number of categories. To do *consecutive integer* problems, you need to remember that consecutive integers differ by 1, so a string of such numbers can be represented as $n, n + 1, n + 2, \ldots$

Consecutive even integers differ by 2, so a string of such numbers can be represented as $n, n + 2, n + 4, \ldots$ Consecutive odd integers also differ by 2! A string of such numbers can also be represented as $n, n + 2, n + 4, \ldots$ *Rate-time-distance* problems require you to know the formula $d = rt$. That is, distance equals rate times time.

Here are some examples of several types of word problems.

Example 1

Sibyl is 5 years older than Moira. Three years ago, Sibyl was twice as old as Moira. How old is Sibyl?

Solution

If you have trouble setting up the equations, use numbers. Suppose that Moira is 11. If Sibyl is 5 years older than Moira, how old is Sibyl? She is 16. You got from 11 to 16 by *adding* 5. If S is Sibyl's age and M is Moira's age, $S = M + 5$. Three years ago, Sibyl was $S - 3$, and Moira was $M - 3$. From the second sentence, $S - 3 = 2(M - 3)$ or $S - 3 = 2M - 6$, or adding 3 to both sides,

$$S = 2M - 3$$

Now, substituting $S = M + 5$,

$$M + 5 = 2M - 3$$
$$M = 8$$

which means Sybil is $8 + 5 = 13$.

Example 2

Three consecutive integers are written in increasing order. If the sum of the first and second and twice the third is 93, what is the second number?

Solution

Calling the smallest number x, the second is $x + 1$, and the third is $x + 2$. Therefore,

$$x + (x + 1) + 2(x + 2) = 93$$
$$x + x + 1 + 2x + 4 = 93$$
$$4x + 5 = 93$$
$$4x = 88$$
$$x = 22.$$

Hence the middle number is $22 + 1 = 23$.

Example 3

It took Andrew 15 minutes to drive downtown at 28 miles per hour to get a pizza. How fast did he have to drive back in order to be home in 10 minutes?

Solution

15 minutes is $\frac{1}{4}$ of an hour. Hence, going 28 miles per hour, the distance to the Pizza Parlor can be computed using the formula $d = rt$; $d = (28)\left(\frac{1}{4}\right) = 7$ miles. Because 10 minutes is $\frac{1}{6}$ of an hour, we have the equation $7 = r\left(\frac{1}{6}\right)$ and multiplying by 6, $r = 42$ mph.

Topic 23. Monomials and Polynomials

When we add a collection of expressions together, each expression is called a *term*. *Monomial* means one term. For example, we might say that $2x + 3y^2 + 7$ is the sum of three terms or three monomials. When we talk about a monomial, we generally mean a term that is just the product of constants and variables, possibly raised to various powers. Examples are 7, $2x$, $-3y^2$, and $4x^2z^5$. The constant factor is called the *coefficient* of the variable factor. Thus, in $-3y^2$, -3 is the coefficient of y^2.

If we restrict our attention to monomials of the form Ax^n, the sums of such terms are called *polynomials* (in one variable). Expressions such as $3x + 5$, $2x^2 - 5x + 8$, and $x^4 - 7x^5 - 11$ are all examples of polynomials. The highest power of the variable that appears is called the *degree* of the polynomial. The three examples just given are of degree 1, 2, and 5 respectively.

In evaluating monomials and polynomials for negative values of the variable, the greatest pitfall is keeping track of the minus signs. Always remember that in an expression such as $-x^2$, the power 2 is applied to the x, and the minus sign in front should be thought of as (-1) times the expression. If you want to have the power apply to $-x$, you must write $(-x)^2$.

Example
Find the value of $3x - x^3 - x^2$, when $x = -2$.

Solution
Substitute -2 every place you see an x, thus:

$$3(-2) - (-2)^3 - (-2)^2 = -6 - (-8) - (+4) = -6 + 8 - 4 = -2.$$

Topic 24. Combining Monomials

Monomials with identical variable factors can be added together by adding their coefficients. So $3x^2 + 4x^2 = 7x^2$. Of course, subtraction is handled the same way, thus

$$3x^4 - 9x^4 = -6x^4$$

Monomials are multiplied by taking the product of their coefficients and taking the product of the variable part by adding exponents of factors with like bases. So $(3xy^2)(2xy^3) = 6x^2y^5$.

Monomial fractions can be reduced to lowest terms by dividing out common factors of the coefficients and then using the usual rules for subtraction of exponents in division. An example might be

$$\frac{6x^3y^5}{2x^4y^3} = \frac{3y^2}{x}$$

Example

Combine into a single monomial $\frac{8x^3}{4x^2} - 6x$.

Solution

The fraction reduces to $2x$, and $2x - 6x = -4x$.

Topic 25. Combining Polynomials and Monomials

Polynomials are added or subtracted by combining like monomial terms in the appropriate manner:

$$(3x^2 - 3x - 4) + (2x^2 + 5x - 11)$$

is summed by removing the parentheses and combining like terms to yield

$$5x^2 + 2x - 15$$

In subtraction, when you remove the parentheses with a minus sign in front, be careful to change the signs of *all* the terms within the parentheses:

$$(3x^2 - 3x - 4) - (2x^2 + 5x - 11) = 3x^2 - 3x - 4 - 2x^2 - 5x + 11$$
$$= x^2 - 8x + 7$$

(Did you notice that $3x^2 - 2x^2 = 1x^2$ but the "1" is not shown?)

To multiply a polynomial by a monomial, use the distributive law to multiply each term in the polynomial by the monomial factor. For example, $2x(2x^2 + 5x - 11) = 4x^3 + 10x^2 - 22x$.

When multiplying a polynomial by a polynomial, you are actually repeatedly applying the distributive law to form all possible products of the terms in the first polynomial with the terms in the second polynomial. The most common use of this is in multiplying two *binomials* (polynomials with two terms), such as $(x + 3)(x - 5)$. In this case, there are four terms in the result, $x \times x = x^2$; $x(-5) = -5x$; $3 \times x = 3x$; and $3 \times (-5) = -15$; but the two middle terms are added together to give $-2x$. Thus, the product is $x^2 - 2x - 15$.

This process is usually remembered as the FOIL method. That is, form the products of First, Outer, Inner, Last, as shown in the figure below.

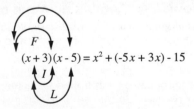

$$(x+3)(x-5) = x^2 + (-5x + 3x) - 15$$

Example

If d is an integer, and $(x + 2)(x + d) = x^2 - kx - 10$, what is the value of $k + d$?

Solution

The product of the two last terms, $2d$, must be -10. Therefore, $d = -5$. If $d = -5$, then the sum of the outer and inner products becomes $-5x + 2x = -3x$, which equals $-kx$. Hence, $k = 3$, and $k + d = 3 + (-5) = -2$.

Topic 26. Factoring Monomials

Factoring a monomial simply involves reversing the distributive law. For example, if you are looking at $4x^2 + 12xy$, you should see that $4x$ is a factor of both terms. Hence, you could just as well write this as $4x(x + 3y)$. Multiplication using the distributive law will restore the original formulation.

Example

If $3x - 4y = -2$, what is the value of $9x - 12y$?

Solution

Although you seem to have one equation in two unknowns, you can still solve the problem because you do not need to know the values of the individual variables. Just rewrite $9x - 12y = 3(3x - 4y)$. Because $3x - 4y = -2$, $9x - 12y$ is 3 times -2, or -6.

Topic 27. Trinomial Factoring and Quadratic Equations

FYI

Notice that, in working with any equation, you can move a term from one side of the equal sign to the other by simply changing its sign.

When you multiply two binomials $(x + r)(x + s)$ using the FOIL method, the result is a *trinomial* (a polynomial with three terms) of the form $x^2 + bx + c$, where b, the coefficient of x, is the sum of the constants r and s, and the constant term c is their product.

Trinomial factoring is the process of reversing this multiplication. For example, to find the binomial factors of $x^2 - 4x - 5$, we need to find two numbers whose product is -5 and whose sum is -4. Because the product is negative, one of the numbers must be negative and the other positive. The only possible factors of 5 are 1 and 5. For the sum to be -4, we must choose -5 and $+1$. Thus,

$$x^2 - 4x - 5 = (x - 5)(x + 1)$$

One major use of this skill is in solving *quadratic equations*. If you have an equation such as

$$x^2 - 6x + 8 = 0$$

you can factor the trinomial. You need two numbers whose product is 8 and whose sum is -6. Because the product is positive, both numbers must have the same sign, and because the sum is negative, they must both be negative. It is not hard to see that -2 and -4 are the correct options. Thus, the equation becomes

$$(x - 2)(x - 4) = 0$$

The only way a product of numbers can be zero is for one of the numbers to be zero. Thus, either

$$x - 2 = 0 \text{ or } x - 4 = 0$$

Therefore,

$$x = 2 \text{ or } x = 4$$

It's common for this kind of problem to yield two possible solutions.

Example

The area of a rectangle is 28 and its perimeter is 22. What are its dimensions?

Solution

As you probably know, the area of a rectangle is calculated by multiplying the length by the width (see Topic 36). Calling the dimensions L and W, we have

$LW = 28$ and $2L + 2W = 22$. Dividing by 2, $L + W = 11$. Therefore, $L = 11 - W$, which we substitute in $LW = 28$, giving

$$(11 - W)W = 28$$
$$11W - W^2 = 28$$

Grouping everything on the right hand side, we have

$$0 = W^2 - 11W + 28$$

Now, factoring

$$0 = (W - 7)(W - 4)$$

yields

$$W = 7 \text{ or } W = 4$$

Of course, if $W = 4$, $L = 7$, and if $W = 7$, $L = 4$. So the dimensions of the rectangle are 4×7.

Topic 28. The Difference and the Sum of Two Squares

The difference of two squares $A^2 - B^2 = (A - B)(A + B)$. For example, $x^2 - 9$ can be thought of as $x^2 - 3^2 = (x - 3)(x + 3)$

If your calculator were broken, you could still find $101^2 - 99^2$ as $(101 - 99)(101 + 99) = 2(200) = 400$. However, binomials such as $x^2 + 16$, which is the *sum* of two squares, cannot be factored.

Example 1
If x and y are positive integers, and $2x + y = 7$, which of the following is the value of $4x^2 - y^2$?

   (A)   0
   (B)   16
   (C)   35

Solution
Because $4x^2 - y^2 = (2x - y)(2x + y) = 7(2x - y)$, $4x^2 - y^2$ must be divisible by 7. Therefore, 16 is not a possible value. If the result is to be zero, $2x - y = 0$, which means $y = 2x$, so that $2x + 2x = 4x = 7$, which is also impossible (remembering that x is an integer). Hence the result must be 35, which you get for $x = 3$ and $y = 1$.

Example 2
If x and y are positive integers and $y^2 = x^2 + 11$, find the value of y.

Solution
If we rewrite the equation as $y^2 - x^2 = 11$ and factor, we have $(y - x)(y + x) = 11$. Thus, 11 must be the product of the two whole numbers $(y - x)$ and $(y + x)$. But 11 is a prime number, which can only be factored as 11 times 1. Because $y + x$ must be larger than $y - x$, we know that

$$y + x = 11$$

and

$$y - x = 1$$

Adding the two equations gives us

$$2y = 12; y = 6$$

(Of course, $x = 5$, but we weren't asked that.)

Topic 29. Operations with Radicals

The *square root* of a number N, written $\sqrt{N}$, is a number that, when squared, produces N. Thus, $\sqrt{4} = 2$, $\sqrt{9} = 3$, $\sqrt{16} = 4$, and so on. You should be aware that $\sqrt{0} = 0$ and $\sqrt{1} = 1$. Square roots of negative numbers are not real numbers.

The symbol $\sqrt{}$ is called a *radical*, and many people refer to $\sqrt{N}$ as "radical N." When we write $\sqrt{N}$, it is understood to be a positive number. When you are faced with an algebraic equation such as $x^2 = 4$, where you must allow for both positive and negative solutions, you must write $x = \pm\sqrt{4} = \pm 2$, where, as you know, $\pm$ is read "plus or minus."

All positive numbers have square roots, but most are *irrational numbers*. Only numbers that are *perfect squares* such as 4, 9, 16, 25, 36, . . . have integer square roots.

If you assume that you are working with non-negative numbers, you can use certain properties of the square root to simplify radical expressions. The most important of these rules is $\sqrt{AB} = \sqrt{A} \cdot \sqrt{B}$.

This rule can be used to advantage in either direction. Reading it from right to left, we may write $\sqrt{3} \cdot \sqrt{12} = \sqrt{36} = 6$. But you should also know how to use this rule to simplify radicals by extracting perfect squares from "under" the radical. Thus,

$$\sqrt{18} = \sqrt{9 \cdot 2} = \sqrt{9} \cdot \sqrt{2} = 3\sqrt{2}$$

The key to using this technique is to recognize the perfect squares in order to factor them out in a sensible manner. Thus, it would do you little good to factor 18 as 3×6 in the preceding example because neither 3 nor 6 is a perfect square.

Example

If $\sqrt{5} \cdot \sqrt{x} = 10$, which is larger, $\sqrt{x}$ or $2\sqrt{5}$?

Solution

Because $10 = \sqrt{100}$ and $\sqrt{5} \cdot \sqrt{x} = \sqrt{5x}$, we know that $5x = 100$ and $x = 20$. But $20 = 4 \times 5$, so $\sqrt{20} = 2\sqrt{5}$. Hence the two quantities are equal.

GEOMETRY

Topic 30. Angles, Complements, and Supplements

When two *rays* originate from the same point, they form an *angle*. Angles are usually measured in *degrees* or *radians*. For our purposes, we shall use degree measure, as is customary on the GMAT CAT.

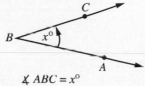

$$\angle ABC = x°$$

It's useful to be familiar with the following terminology. The terminology itself is not tested on the exam, but the geometry problems will require you to rapidly use and manipulate all these concepts, so the more comfortable you are with them, the better.

The measure of a *straight angle* is 180°. Any two angles that sum to a straight angle are called *supplementary*. Thus, angles measuring 70° and 110° are supplementary. Two equal supplementary angles are 90° each, and a 90° angle is called a *right angle*.

Two angles that sum to a right angle are called *complementary*. Thus, angles measuring 30° and 60° are complementary. Angles less than 90° are called *acute*, and angles between 90° and 180° are called *obtuse*. The sum of all the angles around a given point must equal 360°.

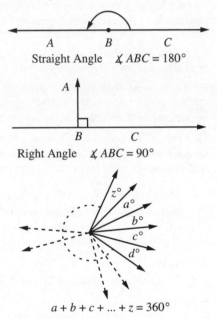

Example 1
Find the value of x in the figure below.

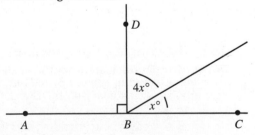

Solution
Because angle ABD is a right angle, so is angle DBC. Thus, $x + 4x = 90$, $5x = 90$, and $x = 18$.

Example 2

Find the value of x in the figure below.

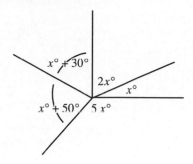

Solution

Because the sum of the angles around a point must be 360°, we have $x + 2x + (x + 30) + (x + 50) + 5x = 360$. Removing parentheses and combining like terms,

$$10x + 80 = 360; \, 10x = 280; \, x = 28$$

Topic 31. The Angles in a Triangle

The measure of a straight angle is 180°. Regardless of the shape of a triangle, the sum of its angles is always 180°. In an *equilateral* triangle, all of whose sides are equal in length, all of the angles have the same degree measure, 60°.

Example

In triangle ABC, $\angle B$ is three times $\angle A$, and $\angle C$ is 30° more than $\angle A$. How many degrees are there in the largest angle?

Solution

Calling the degree measure of $\angle A$ x, we have the following:

$$x = \text{number of degrees in } \angle A$$
$$3x = \text{number of degrees in } \angle B$$
$$x + 30 = \text{number of degrees in } \angle C$$

Summing, we have $x + 3x + (x + 30) = 180$. Removing parentheses and combining like terms:

$$5x + 30 = 180$$
$$5x = 150; \, x = 30$$

Therefore, $x = 30$, $3x = 90$, and $x + 30 = 60$. We have here an example of the 30°–60°–90° right triangle (see Topic 39), and the largest angle is 90°.

Topic 32. Isosceles and Equilateral Triangles

A triangle with exactly two sides of equal length is called an *isosceles* triangle. If all three sides are equal, it is called an *equilateral* triangle. The angles opposite the equal sides in an isosceles triangle (as shown in the next figure) are equal in degree measure, and if two angles are equal, then the triangle must be isosceles.

If all three angles are equal, the triangle is equilateral.

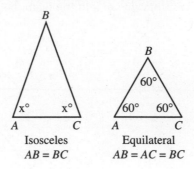

Isosceles
$AB = BC$

Equilateral
$AB = AC = BC$

Example

If, in $\triangle ABC$ as shown in the figure below, $AC = BC$ and $x = 70$, what is the greatest possible value for y?

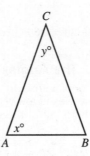

Solution

Because the sides are of equal length, the two base angles must be equal. The three angles, as always, must total $180°$. Hence, $2x + y = 180$, which means that $y = 180 - 2x$. The greatest possible value for y is achieved when x is as small as possible. That is, at $x = 70$, for which $y = 40$.

Topic 33. Other Triangle Properties

In a triangle, the sum of the lengths of any two sides must exceed the length of the third. Thus, you cannot draw a triangle with sides of lengths 3, 6, 10 because $3 + 6 < 10$. In addition, in comparing any two sides of a triangle, the longer side will be opposite the larger angle.

Example 1

A triangle has sides 5, 12, x. If x is an integer, what is maximum possible perimeter of the triangle?

Solution

Because the sum of the lengths of any two sides must exceed the length of the third $x < 5 + 12 = 17$. The largest integer less than 17 is 16. Hence, the maximum perimeter is $5 + 12 + 16 = 33$. (Bonus question: Can you see why the minimum possible perimeter must be 25?)

Example 2

In the triangle shown in the following figure, $AB = BC$. Which is longer, AC or AB?

Note: Diagram not drawn to scale.

Solution

Because the triangle is isosceles, the base angles are equal. Thus, $\angle A = \angle C = 40°$. This implies that $\angle B = 100°$ in order to reach the full 180° in the triangle. But that means that $AC > AB$ because it is the side opposite the larger angle.

Topic 34. Vertical Angles are Equal

When two lines intersect, two pairs of *vertical angles* are formed (as shown in the figure below). The "facing" pairs are equal, and, of course, each pair on one side of either line adds up to 180°.

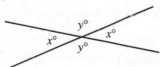

Note: $x + y = 180$. This fact can be used in a number of different ways. Try the following example.

Example

In the figure below, which is larger, $x + y$ or $c + d$?

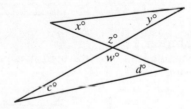

Solution

We know that the sum of the angles in any triangle is 180°. Therefore, looking at the upper triangle, we know that

$$x + y + z = 180$$

that is,

$$x + y = 180 - z$$

Similarly, looking at the lower triangle, we know that

$$c + d = 180 - w$$

But $w = z$ (vertical angles are equal). Therefore, $x + y = c + d$.

Topic 35. Parallel Lines and Transversals

Parallel lines are lines that run in the same direction. No matter how far they are extended, parallel lines will never meet. When two parallel lines are cut by a third line, called a *transversal*, several sets of equal angles are formed. In particular, the *corresponding angles*, labeled C in the figure below, and the *alternate interior angles*, labeled A in the next figure, are equal.

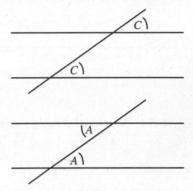

These facts are commonly combined with the properties of vertical angles and the number of degrees in a triangle in constructing problems.

Example 1

In the figure below, l_1 is parallel to l_2. Find the value of x.

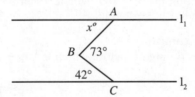

Solution

Extending the line AB until it intersects l_2 at D as shown below, we have a triangle, $\triangle BCD$.

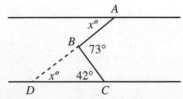

In the triangle, $\angle B$ is the supplement of $73°$, that is, $107°$. $\angle C$ is given as $42°$, and $\angle D$ is $x°$ because it is the alternate interior angle to $\angle A$. Now, the sum $107 + 42 + x = 180$, so $x = 31$.

Example 2

In the figure below, l_1 is parallel to l_2. Find the value of x.

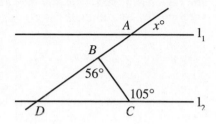

Solution

This time, in $\triangle BCD$, $\angle C$ is the supplement of $105°$, that is, $75°$. $\angle B$ is given as $56°$, and $\angle D$ is $x°$ because it is the corresponding angle to $\angle A$. Now, the sum $75 + 56 + x = 180$, so $x = 49$.

Topic 36. Rectangles and Parallelograms

A *parallelogram* is a *quadrilateral* (a four-sided figure) in which the pairs of opposite sides are parallel. The opposite angles will be equal, and the opposite sides will be of equal length (as shown in the figure below).

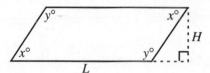

The area of a parallelogram is calculated by multiplying the length times the height. That is, $A = LH$ as labeled in the diagram.

If the angles in the parallelogram are right angles, then we have a *rectangle*. For a rectangle of length L and width W, the area is $A = LW$, and the *perimeter* (the distance around the figure) is $P = 2L + 2W$ (see figure below).

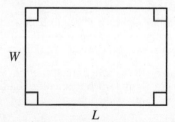

For example, to carpet a rectangular room that is 12 feet long and 9 feet wide requires $(12)(9) = 144$ square feet of carpeting. However, to put up a molding strip around the edge of the ceiling of the same room requires $2(12) + 2(9) = 42$ running feet of molding.

Example 1

The total area of the figure shown is 70 square inches. Find the total perimeter of the region *ABCDE*. (Note: You may assume that all the angles that appear to be right angles are right angles.)

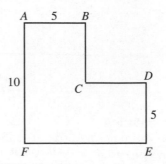

Solution

Inserting a vertical line as shown in the figure below, we see that the larger rectangle has an area of $5 \times 10 = 50$. Hence, the smaller rectangle must be 20. This tells us that the line segment *CD* must be of length 4, and *FE* must be $5 + 4 = 9$. Also $CG = DE = 5$, which means that $BC = 5$. We now find the perimeter by adding the lengths of the segments, starting at *A* and proceeding in a clockwise direction: $5 + 5 + 4 + 5 + 9 + 10 = 38$.

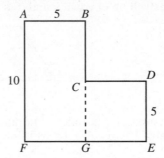

Example 2

Rectangle 1 has perimeter 36 and Rectangle 2 has perimeter 8. Which has a larger area?

Solution

We can't tell! For Rectangle 1, $2L + 2W = 36$, which means that $L + W = 18$. The area could be as large as $9 \times 9 = 81$, but it could be *virtually as small as you like*. After all, we could make it $(17.9) \times (0.1) = 1.79$.

Similarly, Rectangle 2 must have $L + W = 4$. The area could be $2 \times 2 = 4$, which is larger than 1.79 but smaller than 81. In fact, it too could be as small as you like.

Topic 37. The Pythagorean Theorem

A *right triangle* is a triangle that contains a right angle—an angle with a degree measure of 90 degrees. Right triangles figure prominently in western civilization (think of the corners found in street grids, houses, the shapes of books and windows, and so on) and in GMAT CAT geometry problems. Many of these problems are based on the *Pythagorean Theorem*.

The Pythagorean Theorem states that the square of the *hypotenuse* (the longest side) of a right triangle is equal to the sum of the squares on the other two sides. In symbols, it is depicted as shown in the following figure.

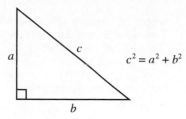

$$c^2 = a^2 + b^2$$

The Pythagorean Triples are integer solutions of the Pythagorean Theorem—that is, sets of integers that represent possible lengths of the three sides of a right triangle. However, there are other important cases that yield non-integer solutions. For example, the hypotenuse of a triangle with one leg of length 1 and the other of length 2 can be found by applying the Pythagorean Theorem: $c^2 = 1^2 + 2^2$, that is, $c^2 = 5$ and $c = \sqrt{5}$.

Example 1

In the figure below, $AB = 3$, $AD = 4$, and $BC = 12$. Find the perimeter of the quadrilateral $ABCD$.

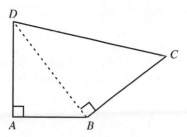

Solution

This example uses two well-known right triangles. We see that in $\triangle ABD$, one leg is 3 and one is 4, which makes the length of the hypotenuse, $BD = 5$. This tells us that $\triangle BDC$ is a 5–12–13 right triangle (another Pythagorean Triple). Thus, CD is 13, and the entire perimeter is $3 + 4 + 12 + 13 = 32$.

Example 2

A rectangle has one side 5 and area 60. What is the length of its diagonal?

Solution

Notice that the diagonal of a rectangle divides the rectangle into two identical right triangles. Hence, if you know the lengths of the sides of the rectangle, the length of its diagonal can be found by using the Pythagorean Theorem.

In this case, because the area, 60, is the product of the length and the width, and one side is 5, the other must be 12. These two sides with the diagonal form a 5-12-13 triangle. Thus, the diagonal is 13.

Topic 38. The Area of a Triangle

The area of a triangle is given by the formula

$$A = \frac{1}{2}bh$$

where b = length of the *base* of the triangle and h = the length of the *altitude*. The base is any side of the triangle (for convenience, often the side at the "bottom" of the triangle); the altitude is a line perpendicular to the base that goes through the opposite *vertex* (or point of the triangle). Although we tend to think of the altitude as inside the triangle, it can actually lie outside the triangle (as seen in the figure below).

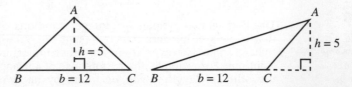

Both triangles shown have the same area: $A = \frac{1}{2}(12)(5) = 30$.

Example

In $\triangle ABC$, $AC = 6$, $BC = 8$, and $AB = 10$. Find the length of the altitude from vertex C to side AB.

Solution

Because the sides have lengths 6-8-10 (double the Pythagorean Triple 3-4-5), the triangle is a right triangle with AB being the hypotenuse. By using the two legs as base and height, the area of the triangle must be $A = \frac{1}{2}(6)(8) = 24$. By using the hypotenuse and the unknown altitude (see figure below), the area must be $A = \frac{1}{2}(10)(h) = 5h$. Therefore, $5h = 24$ and $h = 4.8$.

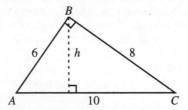

Topic 39. Other Special Triangles

In addition to the Pythagorean Triples (see Topic 37), you should be on the lookout for two other special kinds of right triangles.

The first is the 45°-45°-90° triangle. This is an isosceles triangle, so its legs are of equal length, and the hypotenuse is $\sqrt{2}$ times the length of the leg (see figure below).

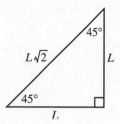

The second is the 30°-60°-90° triangle. This is half of an equilateral triangle. Hence, the shorter leg is half the hypotenuse, and the longer leg (the one opposite the 60° angle) is times the shorter leg (see figure below).

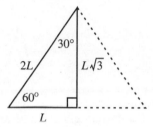

Example

Find the perimeter of the figure shown below.

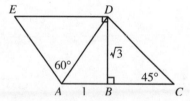

Solution

Because $BD = \sqrt{3}$ and $AB = 1$, we know that ABD is a 30°–60°–90° right triangle. Hence, we know three things: first, $AD = 2$ (twice the shorter leg); second, $\angle ADB$ is 30°; third, $\angle ADE$, which is the complement of $\angle ADB$, must be 60°. This makes $\triangle AED$ equilateral, so $AE = ED = 2$.

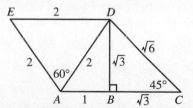

Because $\angle BCD$ is 45°, we know that $\triangle BDC$ is a 45°–45°–90° right triangle, so that $BC = BD = \sqrt{3}$ and the hypotenuse, $DC = (\sqrt{2})(\sqrt{3}) = \sqrt{6}$. Starting at A and proceeding clockwise, we add the lengths we have just found to get the perimeter $2 + 2 + \sqrt{6} + \sqrt{3} + 1 = 5 + \sqrt{6} + \sqrt{3}$.

(This is an acceptable answer. Because $\sqrt{6}$ and $\sqrt{3}$ are irrational numbers whose values cannot be precisely represented, they are conventionally expressed in this form, including on the GMAT CAT.)

Topic 40. Other Polygons

Any geometric figure with straight line segments as sides is called a *polygon*. To analyze any polygon (for example, to calculate its area), connect the vertices by line segments to divide it into triangles.

Example
Find the area of the figure *ABCDE* shown below.

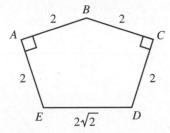

Solution
Drawing the line segments *BE* and *BD* divides the region into three triangles (see figure below).

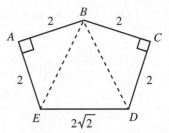

$\triangle ABE$ and $\triangle BCD$ are both 45°–45°–90° right triangles, making $BE = BD = 2\sqrt{2}$. This makes the central triangle an equilateral triangle. The area of each of the two outer triangles is $\frac{1}{2}(2)(2) = 2$, so the two together have area 4.

The center triangle has base $2\sqrt{2}$. If you draw the altitude, you get a 30°-60°-90° right triangle with shorter leg $\sqrt{2}$, which makes the height $\sqrt{3}$ times that, or $\sqrt{6}$. This gives an area of $\frac{1}{2}(2\sqrt{2})(\sqrt{6}) = \sqrt{12} = 2\sqrt{3}$. Hence, the total area of the polygon is $4 + 2\sqrt{3}$.

Topic 41. Basic Properties of Circles

Any line cutting across a circle is called a *chord*. The longest possible chord is one that goes through the center of the circle; it's called the *diameter*. The *radius* is half the diameter, and all radii are equal in length. An *arc* is a segment of the circle. Its size may be measured in degrees. The degree measure of an arc is the measure of the *central angle* subtended by it, as shown in the following figure.

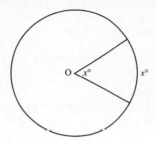

Example 1

If the arc *PS* in the figure below has a degree measure of 57°, is the chord *PS* longer or shorter than the radius?

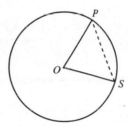

Solution

Because all radii are equal, $\triangle OPS$ is isosceles, and the angles at *P* and *S* must be equal. Suppose each has a degree measure of *x*. Now, $2x + 57 = 180$. Hence, $x = 61.5$. Therefore, *PS* is opposite the smallest angle in the triangle and must be the shortest side. That is, *PS* is shorter than a radius.

Topic 42. The Area and Circumference of a Circle

You must know two formulas for working with circles:

- The circumference of a circle is calculated by the formula $C = 2\pi r$.
- The area of a circle is calculated by the formula $A = \pi r^2$.

In both formulas, π (the Greek letter pi) is a constant, a number whose value is approximately 3.1416 (or about $\frac{22}{7}$), whereas *r* is the radius.

Example 1

Find the circumference of the region shown in the figure below. (Note: The curved side shown is a *semicircle*, an arc representing half a complete circle.)

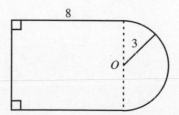

Solution

The dotted line divides the region into a rectangle and a semicircle. Because the radius of the circular arc is 3, the diameter is 6, and that is the width of the rectangle. The length is 8. Hence, the length of the three straight sides total $8 + 8 + 6 = 22$. The circumference of the whole circle is $2\pi r = 2\pi(3) = 6\pi$. Therefore, the semicircular arc must be half that length or 3π, which, added to the previous total, gives a length of $22 + 3\pi$.

Example 2

If the larger circle shown in the figure below has radius 4, find the area of the shaded region.

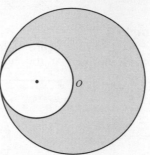

Solution

The larger circle has area $AL = \pi(4)^2 = 16\pi$. The diameter of the smaller circle equals the radius of the larger one, so its radius is $\frac{1}{2}(4)=2$. Its area must be $AS = \pi(2)^2 = 4\pi$. The shaded area is the larger area minus the smaller area, or $16\pi - 4\pi = 12\pi$.

Topic 43. Volumes

For solid figures with straight line edges and flat surfaces (known as *polyhedra*), it can sometimes be unclear whether the word *side* refers to one of the flat surfaces bounding the solid or one of the line segments bounding the surfaces. To avoid confusion, people usually refer to these as *faces* and *edges* respectively, and this is the usage followed on the GMAT CAT.

A solid also has a *surface area*, which is the sum of the areas of all its faces, and a *volume,* or capacity. Volumes are given in cubic units. You should be familiar with the following formulas for the volumes of regular figures:

- A *rectangular solid* is a polyhedron with rectangular faces at right angles to one another (see figure below). Its volume is calculated by the formula $V = LWH$; that is, volume = length × width × height.

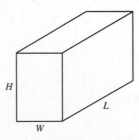

- A *cube* is a rectangular solid with all edges of equal length, s—that is, $L = W = H = s$, like one of a pair of dice. Therefore, $V = s^3$; that is, volume = side × side × side.

- A *right circular cylinder* is a figure with a circular base and a side perpendicular to that base, such as a soda can (see figure below). The volume is the area of the base times the height; that is, $V = \pi r^2 h$.

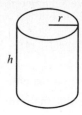

Example 1

Find the area of one face of a cube that has the same volume as a rectangular solid that is 18 inches long and has a base with one side 3 inches long and a diagonal 5 inches long.

Solution

To find the volume of the rectangular solid, we must first find the length of the third edge (see figure below).

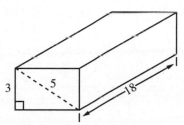

On that side, because the diagonal is 5 and one edge is 3, we must have a 3-4-5 triangle; so the other edge must be 4. Thus, the solid is $3 \times 4 \times 18$, which means its volume is $V_B = (3)(4)(18) = 216$. For the cube to have the same volume, we have $216 = s^3$. Thus, $s = 6$. The area of one side of the cube, being a square, is $6^2 = 36$.

Example 2

Arlene has a block of wood in the form of a rectangular solid that is 14 inches long with a square base that is 6 inches on a side. A right circular cylinder is drilled out of the block as shown in the following figure. Find the volume of the wood remaining to the nearest cubic inch.

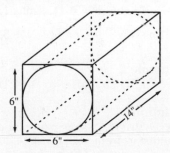

Solution

The original volume of the solid was

$$V_B = (6)(6)(14) = 504$$

Because the circle just goes from one side to the other of the square base, it must have a diameter of 6, which means its radius is 3. Hence the volume of the piece drilled out is

$$V_H = \pi(3)^2(14) = 126\pi$$

Using an approximate value for π of $\frac{22}{7}$, $126\pi = $ about 396. Therefore, to the nearest cubic inch, the volume of the remaining wood is $504 - 396 = 108$ in^3.

COORDINATE GEOMETRY

Topic 44. The Midpoint Formula

Given two points $P(x_1,y_1)$ and $Q(x_2,y_2)$, the midpoint, M, of the line segment PQ has coordinates $x_M = \frac{x_1 + x_2}{2}$, $y_M = \frac{y_1 + y_2}{2}$.

In words, this says that the coordinates of the midpoint are simply the averages of the coordinates of the end points. For example, the midpoint between (6,5) and (3,−1) is $x_M = \frac{6 + 3}{2} = \frac{9}{2}$, $y_M = \frac{5 + (-1)}{2} = \frac{4}{2} = 2$.

Hence, the midpoint is $\left(\frac{9}{2},2\right) = (4.5,2)$.

Example 1

If (5,7) is the midpoint of the line segment connecting (−1,3) to $P(x,y)$, which is larger, x or y?

Solution

We know that the average of x and −1 must be 5. That is, $5 = \frac{x + (-1)}{2}$, or $10 = x - 1$. Therefore, $x = 11$. Similarly, we know that the average of y and 3 must be 7. Thus, $7 = \frac{y + 3}{2}$, or $14 = y + 3$, $y = 11$. Therefore, $x = y$.

Example 2

If $b > 5$, is (2,b) closer to $P(-1,3)$ or $Q(5,7)$?

Solution

We see that (2,5) is the midpoint of PQ. Therefore, in the x-direction, (2,b) will be equidistant from both P and Q. However, if $b > 5$, then b must be closer to 7 than to 3. Therefore, (2,b) is closer to (5,7) than (−1,3).

Topic 45. The Distance Formula

Given two points $P(x_1, y_1)$ and $Q(x_2, y_2)$, the distance from P to Q is given by the formula:

$$d = \sqrt{(x_1 - x_2)^2 + (y_1 - y_2)^2}$$

In words, this says that the distance is the square root of the sum of the change in x squared plus the change in y squared, or $d = \sqrt{(\Delta x)^2 + (\Delta y)^2}$. For example, the distance from $(6,2)$ to $(3,-1)$ is $d = \sqrt{(6-3)^2 + (3-(-1))^2}$. Thus, $d = \sqrt{3^2 + 4^2} = \sqrt{9 + 16} = \sqrt{25} = 5$.

Example 1

The point $(a,5)$ lies on a circle of radius 10 with center at $(2,-3)$. What are the possible values of a?

Solution

Because every point on the circle must be 10 units from the center, we know that $(a,5)$ must be 10 units from $(2,-3)$. Using the distance formula

$$\sqrt{(a-2)^2 + (5-(-3))^2} = 10$$

$$\sqrt{(a^2 - 4a + 4) + 64} = 10$$

$$\sqrt{a^2 - 4a + 68} = 10$$

Squaring both sides, we have $a^2 - 4a + 68 = 100$.

We subtract 100 from both sides to yield: $a^2 - 4a - 32 = 0$, which factors as $(a - 8)(a + 4) = 0$ with two possible values for a:

$a - 8 = 0$ or $a + 4 = 0$
$a = 8$ or $a = -4$

Example 2

The point $(1,b)$ is equidistant from $(-2,3)$ and $(2,5)$. What are the possible values of b?

Solution

Because the distances from the two given points are the same, we use the distance formula twice and equate the results, thus

$$\sqrt{18 - 6b + b^2} = \sqrt{26 - 10b + b^2}$$

Squaring both sides:

$$18 - 6b + b^2 = 26 - 10b + b^2$$

The b^2 terms subtract out, leaving

$$-6b + 18 = -10b + 26$$

Adding $10b - 18$ to both sides of the equation gives us

$$4b = 8 \text{ and } b = 2$$

Topic 46. The Slope of a Line

Given two points $P(x_1, y_1)$ and $Q(x_2, y_2)$, the *slope* of the line passing through P and Q is given by the formula:

$$m = \frac{y_1 - y_2}{x_1 - x_2}$$

In words, this says that the slope is the change in y divided by the change in x, or $m = \frac{\Delta y}{\Delta x}$. For example, the slope of the line passing through (6,2) to (3,−2) is $m = \frac{2 - (-2)}{6 - 3} = \frac{4}{3}$. Notice that it doesn't matter which you consider to be the first point and which the second, as long as you are consistent in plugging in the numbers into the top and bottom of the fraction.

Example

The point $(a,5)$ lies on a line of slope $\frac{1}{3}$ that passes through (2,−3). What is the value of a?

Solution

Because $m = \frac{y_1 - y_2}{x_1 - x_2}$, we must have $\frac{1}{3} = \frac{5 - (-3)}{a - 2}$.

$$\frac{1}{3} = \frac{8}{a - 2}$$

Cross-multiplying:

$$a - 2 = 24; \ a = 26$$

COUNTING AND PROBABILITY

Topic 47. The Addition Principle for Counting

FYI

In logic, the word "or" means "either one or both"—that is, and/or.

If set A contains m objects, set B contains n objects, and there are no objects common to the two sets, then the total number of objects in the two sets combined is $m + n$. But if there are k objects common to the two sets, then the total in the combined set is $m + n - k$. That is, you must take into account the double-counting of objects common to both groups. This kind of situation is usually handled most easily by displaying the given information in a *Venn diagram*, which depicts the sets as circles that may or may not overlap.

Example 1

Of a group of students at a fast-food restaurant, 12 ate hamburgers and 9 had fries. If 4 had both hamburgers and fries, how many had either hamburgers or fries?

Solution

If we let *H* be the set of those who had hamburgers and *F* be the set of those who had fries, then the following diagram displays the data.

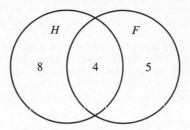

The central region holds those items that are common to both groups, and we can see that the total who had either burgers or fries is $8 + 4 + 5 = 17$.

Sometimes problems of this type can involve more than two sets.

Example 2

A survey of TV viewing habits including 50 individuals found 45 watched news shows, 38 watched mysteries, and 40 watched sitcoms. If everyone surveyed watched at least one of these types of shows and 32 watched all three types, how many watched exactly two of the three?

Solution

We draw a Venn diagram showing the given data (see figure below). Here $N =$ News, $M =$ Mystery, and $S =$ Sitcoms. The number in each region is given, with the unknowns labeled x, y, z, u, v, and w. However, we do not need to find all the unknowns, simply the sum $x + y + z$.

$$x + u + y = 13$$
$$y + z + v = 6$$
$$x + z + w = 8$$

Adding all three equations,

$$2x + 2y + 2z + u + v + w = 27$$

But,

$$x + y + z + u + v + w = 18$$

Subtracting,

$$x + y + z = 9$$

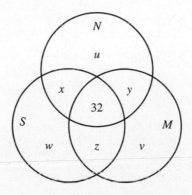

Topic 48. The Multiplication Principle for Counting

The *multiplication principle for counting* states that if an operation takes two steps and the first step can be performed in m ways, and if, for each of those ways, the second step can be performed in n ways, then the total number of ways of performing the operation is $T = mn$.

For example, suppose that a jar contains four balls numbered 1, 2, 3, and 4. If a ball is selected and the number is noted down, and then a second ball is selected without replacing the first, the number of two-digit numbers that can be formed is $(4)(3) = 12$. This process extends to more than two steps in the same way by continuing to multiply the number of options at each step.

Example 1

A class contains 4 boys and 5 girls. In how many ways can one choose a pair of one boy and one girl from this class?

Solution

You have 4 choices for a boy and 5 for a girl. By the multiplication principle, the total number of possible pairs is $4 \times 5 = 20$.

Example 2

From a club with 10 members, a slate of officers including a president, vice president, and secretary must be chosen. How many different possible slates are there if no one person can hold two offices?

Solution

By a natural extension of the principle to a three-step process, we see that we have 10 choices for president, for each of which we have 9 choices for vice president (because one person has been eliminated, having been chosen as president); for each such pair, we have 8 choices for secretary (because two people have been eliminated, having been chosen as president and vice president). Thus, the total number of possible slates is $10 \times 9 \times 8 = 720$.

Topic 49. The Number of Ways of Arranging *n* Objects in a Row

As a natural extension of the multiplication principle, it is not hard to show that the number of distinct arrangements of n distinguishable objects in a row is

$$n! = n(n - 1)(n - 2) \times \times \times 2 \times 1$$

(The expression $n!$ is called *n factorial*.)

For example, the number of ways of lining up the five starting players on the boys basketball team for a team picture is $5! = 5 \times 4 \times 3 \times 2 \times 1 = 120$.

Example 1

If four textbooks—math, English, French, and Spanish—are arranged randomly on a shelf, what is the chance that they will be in alphabetical order from left to right?

Solution

There are four distinguishable objects that can be arranged in $4! = 4 \times 3 \times 2 \times 1 = 24$ ways. In only one of these ways will they be in alphabetical order. Therefore, the chance is $\frac{1}{24}$.

Example 2

In how many ways can four textbooks—math, English, French, and Spanish—be arranged on the shelf if the Spanish and French textbooks must be next to each other?

Solution

If we "glue" the two books together, then we can think of the group as containing only 3 books, which can be arranged in $3! = 3 \times 2 \times 1 = 6$ ways. However, for each of these ways, we could have set up the "glued" books in two sequences, either French/Spanish or Spanish/French. Hence, there are really $2 \times 6 = 12$ ways altogether.

Topic 50. Probability

To find the probability of a random event, divide the number of possible outcomes favorable to the event by the total number of possible outcomes. For example, if a bag contains 12 blue marbles and 9 red marbles, the probability of randomly selecting a blue marble is $\dfrac{\textit{number of blue marbles}}{\textit{total number of marbles}} = \dfrac{12}{21} = \dfrac{4}{7}$.

Example

If six girls line up in random order to have a group picture taken, what is the probability that the tallest girl will be at the left end and the shortest girl will be at the right end?

Solution

The six girls could line up in $6! = 120$ ways. If the tallest girl must be at the left and the shortest at the right, there are $4! = 24$ ways that the other girls can line up between them. Thus, 24 line-ups are favorable to the event in question. Hence the probability is $\dfrac{24}{120} = \dfrac{1}{5}$.

The Insider's GMAT CAT Writer's Manual

Some find the study of the English language endlessly fascinating. Others, who have struggled through courses in grammar and composition, find it endlessly boring. Both agree, however, that the complications and subtleties of English make mastering it a genuine challenge—one on which serious writers may spend a lifetime.

Fortunately, preparing for the grammar and usage questions on the GMAT CAT won't take quite that long. In this area of the exam, as on all the others, the test makers are creatures of habit. English may lend itself to endless complications, but you won't find them all on the GMAT CAT. Instead, the test makers tend to focus on a handful of commonplace grammar and usage errors that the average writer typically makes. If you know the proper rules for this handful of writing situations, you'll do well on the GMAT CAT.

After examining many past GMAT CATS, we've determined that there are thirty-five key rules of grammar and usage that are most often tested on the exam. In this appendix, you'll learn those rules. Look for them when you practice for the GMAT CAT—and in your other writing as well. Chances are that you've stumbled over at least a few of these rules yourself in the past.

RULES ABOUT VERBS

As you probably know, a verb is a word that tells what someone or something *does* or *is*. Every sentence has at least one verb, and it is a crucial word in the structure of the sentence. The "someone or something" that "does or is" is called the *subject* of the verb. For example, in the sentence "George Bush was the forty-first president of the United States," *was* is the verb, and *George Bush* is the subject. Here are the rules you need to know that relate to the proper use of verbs.

Rule 1: A Verb Must Agree With Its Subject In Number

Number refers to whether the verb and its subject are *singular* or *plural*. A singular subject and verb refer to one person or thing; a plural subject and verb refer to more than one. Logically enough, the subject and verb have to match: if the subject is singular, the verb must be singular; if the subject is plural, the verb must be plural.

In most sentences, this rule is easy to follow. You can probably tell, just by the way it sounds, that it would be wrong to write, "George Bush were the president" (singular subject + plural verb). It would also be wrong to write, "He and his wife was from Texas" (plural subject + singular verb). In these two examples, the error in subject-verb agreement is easy to spot.

In some sentences, however, it's not so easy:

> Among those who played a crucial role in the Northern victory at Gettysburg were Joshua Chamberlain, a Union colonel from Maine who later enjoyed a distinguished career as an educator and politician.

In this case, the verb in the first, main clause of the sentence is *were*. Now, find the subject: ask, "Who or what were?" In this case, the answer is *Joshua Chamberlain*. Is the subject singular or plural? Singular, of course; Joshua Chamberlain was one person. Therefore, a singular verb is needed: *were* should be changed to *was*.

Subject-verb agreement is a little tricky in this sentence because the subject *follows* the verb, rather than preceding it. The sentence begins with the phrase *Among those who played a crucial role . . .* , which refers to a group of people. This could fool you into thinking the verb has a plural subject. Not so.

The next several rules deal with other cases in which subject-verb agreement can be tricky.

FYI

If you suspect that subject-verb agreement may be a problem in a sentence (it's a common error on the GMAT CAT), first find the verb; it's usually pretty easy to spot. Then, look for the subject by asking, "Who or what [insert verb]?" This process takes away the guesswork from locating the subject and verb in a sentence.

Rule 2: When Checking Agreement, Ignore Any Words or Phrases that Separate a Verb from its Subject

It's easy to compare the subject and the verb when they are next to each other. It's much harder when they are separated by many other words. Watch out for this. In particular, watch out for *prepositional phrases* that come between the subject and the verb. A *preposition* is a word that links a noun (or a pronoun) to the rest of the sentence, usually by describing a logical or place relationship of some kind. Words such as *of, by, for, with, in, on, to, through, from, against, near, under, beside,* and *above* are all prepositions—so are such phrases as *next to, along with, in place of,* and *as well as.*

A preposition is always followed by a noun (or a pronoun). The preposition, together with the noun that follows, forms a prepositional phrase. *Of the people, by accident, for fun, with my sister, in a car, on fire, to the station,* and *through the tunnel* are all examples of prepositional phrases.

The key thing to remember is that *the subject of a verb never appears in a prepositional phrase.* When you are checking a sentence for subject-verb agreement and you want to find the subject, mentally "cross out" any prepositional phrase. The subject of the verb will *not* be there. Here's an example:

> The purpose of such post-war international organizations as NATO, the World Bank, and the Organization of American States have been questioned since the demise of communism and the end of the Cold War.

This sentence contains quite a few prepositional phrases. (That's not unusual.) In looking for the subject of the verb phrase *have been questioned*, you need to mentally cross out the prepositional phrases *of such post-war international organizations* and *as NATO, the World Bank, and the Organization of American States.* The subject will not appear within either of these phrases. What remains? *The purpose,* which is the subject of the verb: The thing that people are questioning is the purpose of all those organizations. Because it is singular, the verb should also be singular; to be grammatically correct, the verb should be changed to *has been questioned*.

Rule 3: Collective Nouns Are Usually Singular

FYI

The GMAT CAT tests American English, in which the rule we've just stated applies. In British English, collective nouns are often plural: For example, BBC news reporters will say, "The government have decided . . . or "Unilever Corporation are planning. . ." This usage is correct in the U.K. but wrong in the U.S.—and wrong on the GMAT CAT.

Subject-verb agreement can be tricky when the subject is a *collective noun*—a noun that names a group of people or things rather than a single entity. Words such as *team, group, club, class, family, collection, bunch, platoon,* and *organization* are all examples of collective nouns. Even names of institutions such as *Harvard University, IBM,* and *the US Senate* may be considered collective nouns because after all, they refer to large numbers of individuals.

Despite the fact that collective nouns refer to groups, in American English they are considered singular and take singular verbs. This may strike you as logical: these nouns do look singular (i.e., they don't end in the *s* that usually marks plural nouns). However, writers sometimes make mistakes with subject-verb agreement when collective nouns are involved, as in the following example:

> The League of Women Voters, boasting members from both major parties and all positions along the political spectrum, do not formally endorse candidates in national or local elections.

In this sentence, subject-verb agreement is complicated not only by the collective noun *League* but also by the many prepositional and other phrases that divide the subject from the verb. *Of Women Voters, boasting members, from both major parties and all positions,* and *along the political spectrum* all "interrupt" the sentence and separate the subject from the verb. Despite these distractions, the subject of the verb *do* is the singular collective noun *League*, and therefore, the singular verb *does* should be used instead.

Rule 4: *The Number* is Singular; *A Number* is Plural

Distinguish these two phrases, which sound deceptively similar. Both are usually followed by prepositional phrases starting with *of*, but they play different roles in a sentence. In a sentence such as the following, the word *number* is the subject of the verb, and the usual rule about ignoring the prepositional phrase applies:

> In the wake of the latest series of airline mergers, the number of carriers serving passengers in most mid-sized cities in the eastern United States have been reduced to just three.

It is the number of carriers that has been reduced to three, so the verb should be singular, as the word *number* itself is: "The number of carriers . . . *has* been reduced to just three" is correct.

By contrast, when the phrase *a number* is used, it is generally the equivalent of a word such as *several* or *many*. Consider, for example:

> A number of scientists has testified before the Senate Armed Services Committee concerning the need for safer methods of handling nuclear wastes.

In this sentence, the entire phrase *a number of scientists* means much the same as *several scientists* or *a few scientists*. The meaning is plural, and the verb should be plural, as well. The sentence should begin, "A number of scientists *have* testified . . ."

FYI

If it's helpful, remember that these pronouns are singular by thinking of them as referring to single individuals: everybody seeking documents *means* each individual seeking documents. *This explains the underlying logic of treating the* -one, -body, *and* -thing *pronouns as singular.*

Rule 5: Pronouns Ending In *-one*, *-body*, and *-thing* Are Singular

Twelve indefinite pronouns fall in this group: someone, anyone, no one, everyone, somebody, anybody, nobody, everybody, something, nothing, anything, and everything. The rule to remember is simple: All twelve words are singular. This is true even when they refer to something that appears literally plural in meaning, as in this example:

> In the classic movie *Casablanca*, everybody seeking documents—forged or real—that will permit escape from Nazi-occupied northern Africa are forced to negotiate with black-market profiteers who make a living from others' desperation.

The subject of the verb *are forced* is *everybody seeking documents*, which clearly describes many people. Thus, it seems logical to use a plural verb. Unfortunately, logic doesn't always rule in English grammar, and this is a case in point. Because pronouns ending in *-body* are always considered singular, the singular verb *is forced* should be used instead.

Rule 6: The SANAM Pronouns—*Some, Any, None, All*, and *Most*—May Be Either Singular or Plural

Grammar is a system, designed to be logical, that seeks to explain and codify language. However, language is a form of human behavior, and we humans are rarely completely logical. Thus, most rules of grammar have exceptions, twists, and complications that arise where the logic of the rule runs up against the illogic of human behavior.

Here's an example. We explained earlier that you should ignore prepositional phrases when looking for the subject of a verb. There are exceptions, however. The chief exception involves five pronouns—*some*, *any*, *none*, *all*, and *most*—known by their initials as the SANAM pronouns. These may be either singular or plural, depending on how they are used in the sentence, and determining that generally requires you to look at the prepositional phrase beginning with *of* that usually follows the pronoun.

Consider this sentence:

> If any of the camera lenses produced by a particular worker is found to be defective, every lens he or she produced during the same shift must be double-checked for quality before it is shipped.

In this sentence, the SANAM pronoun *any* is followed by the prepositional phrase *of the camera lenses*. To decide whether *any* is singular or plural, you have to look at the object of the preposition *of*. Because that object is the plural noun *lenses*, the pronoun *any* is plural, so the verb should be the plural *are found*.

By contrast:

> If any of the wreckage are recovered, forensic scientists will examine it for clues as to the cause of the accident.

In this case, the object of the preposition *of* is the singular word *wreckage*. Therefore, the pronoun *any* is singular, and the verb should also be singular: *is recovered*.

Rule 7: Verb Tenses Must Reflect the Sequence of Events Accurately

You may never have learned about verb tenses in an English class, but if you've studied Spanish or some other foreign language, you're probably familiar with the concept. The basic purpose of verb tenses is to indicate the *time sequence* of events. On the GMAT CAT, most questions related to verb tenses will involve the misuse of tenses in such a way as to confuse the order in which events happen.

English has six main tenses. Table C.1 outlines their names and their basic appearance, using the verb *to dance* for illustrative purposes.

The past, present, and future tenses obviously are used to describe events happening in the past, present, and future. The *perfect* tenses describe events occurring *prior to* the events in the other three tenses. For example, an event described in the past perfect tense is one that happened prior to an event in the past tense:

> Before she danced with her father, the bride had danced with her husband.

An event described in the present perfect tense is one that happens prior to or up until the present:

> As a ballet student, I have danced every day this month.

An event in the future perfect tense is one that will happen prior to some other future event:

> I will dance in a recital next Thursday; by then, I will have danced thirty recitals so far this year.

(The future perfect tense probably sounds less familiar to you than any of the others; it's the rarest tense in English.)

On the GMAT CAT, tense sequence is normally tested in a sentence describing two or more events occurring in a particular, unmistakable order. Here's an example:

> Lincoln promulgated his controversial Emancipation Proclamation, which declared all slaves held in rebel territory free, only after the North would have won a significant military victory.

The two events in this sentence are Lincoln's promulgation of the Emancipation Proclamation and the North's winning a significant military victory. What is the

Table C.1
Six Main English Verb Tenses

Tense	Example
Past perfect	had danced
Past	danced
Present perfect	have danced
Present	dance
Future perfect	will have danced
Future	will dance

time sequence of these two events? The sentence makes it obvious: Lincoln promulgated the Proclamation in the past (of course), and the North's victory occurred *prior to* that. Therefore, the promulgation should be in the past tense, and the victory should be in the past perfect tense: "Lincoln *promulgated* . . . only after the North *had won*. . . ."

On the exam, watch for sentences in which two or more events are described. Make sure that the tenses are used clearly and correctly andmatch the sequence of events. If not, one of them needs to be corrected.

Rule 8: Always Use the Past Participle Form of a Verb with the Helping Verb *To Have*

Take another look at Table C.1. Notice that the past perfect, present perfect, and future perfect tenses all contain forms of the verb *to have*. Used in this way to help create tenses of other verbs, the verb *to have* is called an *auxiliary verb*, or, more casually, a *helping verb*.

The rule to remember is that when you are building a verb using the helping verb *to have*, you must be careful to use the proper form of the basic verb. The form to use is called the *past participle*. This is one of the three *principal parts* of any verb, as shown in Table C.2.

The infinitive is the basic "root" form of the verb; the past is the same as the past tense; and the past participle, as we've said, is used with the helping verb *to have* in forming the perfect tenses.

Now, with most English verbs, forming verbs isn't tricky. As with *dance*, most verbs form the past and past participle exactly the same way: by adding *-d* or *-ed* to the infinitive. This is true of all *regular* verbs.

The problem arises with *irregular* verbs: verbs that form their past and past participle forms in non-standard fashion. The verb *to fly* is an example, as shown in Table C.3.

It can be easy to confuse the past and past participle forms of an irregular verb. The most common mistake is to use the past tense form where the past participle is needed:

> By the time Lindbergh's little plane landed on an airfield outside Paris thronged with astonished well-wishers, the exhausted pilot had flew single-handedly for more than 30 hours without a break.

Because the past perfect tense is used here, the past participle should be used; the verb should read *had flown* rather than *had flew*.

To avoid this kind of error, remember the rule: when a helping verb is involved, use the past participle form, not the past tense.

Table C.2
Principal Parts of a Verb

Form	Example
Infinitive	[to] dance
Past	danced
Past participle	danced

Table C.3
Principal Parts of *Fly*

Form	Example
Infinitive	[to] fly
Past	flew
Past participle	flown

Rule 9: Use the Correct Past Tense and Past Participle Forms of Irregular Verbs

FYI

Remember, the past tense form is used by itself; the past participle form is used with a helping verb, usually a form of the verb to have.

We've already explained that the past and past participle forms of irregular verbs can be tricky and confusing. Table C.4 contains a list of some of the most commonly used, and commonly confused, irregular verbs, showing the correct forms for each of the three principle parts.

The list in Table C.4 doesn't show all irregular verbs in English, but it shows many of the most troublesome. Notice, in particular, the two verbs *lie* and *lay*. Not only is each verb irregular and confusing, but the two are quite easy to confuse with one another, leading to additional trouble. *To lie* is something one does oneself: you may *lie* on a sofa, for example. *To lay* is something one does *to* something else: you may *lay* your coat on the back of a chair, for instance.

Take a look at this sample sentence:

> Although the state constitution was amended to provide the line-item veto to the governor more than a year ago, the new provision has only took effect within the past two months.

Can you spot the problem? It's the misuse of the irregular verb *to take*. The tense used is the present perfect, which describes events happening in the past and up to the present. (The new constitutional provision's taking effect is something happening just during the past two months, up to and including today.) In the present perfect tense, with the helping verb *has*, the past participle should be used, which is *taken*, not the past tense *took*.

Table C.4
Common English Irregular Verbs

Infinitive	Past	Past Participle
do	did	done
go	went	gone
take	took	taken
rise	rose	risen
begin	began	begun
swim	swam	swum
throw	threw	thrown
break	broke	broken
burst	burst	burst
bring	brought	brought
lie	lay	lain
lay	laid	laid
get	got	got *or* gotten

Study the list of irregular verbs and their principle parts. Memorize it if necessary. Be on the lookout for other irregular verbs as they crop up in your reading and writing. Practice using them correctly, and you'll find it easy to recognize this type of error on the exam.

RULES ABOUT MODIFYING PHRASES

Rule 10: A Modifying Phrase Must Modify A Word or Phrase Appearing in the Sentence

A *modifying phrase* is a group of words that works together as a unit to modify, or give more information about, something else in the sentence. As you may recall from earlier grammar study, both adjectives and adverbs are considered modifiers; both of these parts of speech serve to modify, or give information about, other words in the sentence. Thus, modifying phrases are groups of words that act as adjectives or adverbs. Some modifying phrases work as adjectives; they modify nouns or pronouns. Others work as adverbs; they modify verbs, adjectives, or adverbs.

Got all that? If you're not sure, an example or two might help. In the sentence, "Waiting at the bus stop, Paula nervously glanced at her watch," the phrase *Waiting at the bus stop* works as an adjective; it modifies the noun *Paula*. On the other hand, in the sentence, "After 6 o'clock, buses stop here once an hour," the phrase *After 6 o'clock* acts as an adverb; it modifies the verb *stop* (by telling *when* the buses stop). Both phrases are modifying phrases, though of slightly different kinds.

So what? Well, all of this is important to you because of a grammar rule the test makers like to challenge you on—a rule stating that a modifying phrase must refer to a specific word or phrase appearing elsewhere in the same sentence. If no such word or phrase appears, the modifying phrase is called a *dangling modifier*, and it's a definite no-no. Look at this example:

> Dismayed by the news that one of the firm's top executives had suddenly decided to accept a job with a rival company, the price of the company's stock fell sharply the following day.

This sentence contains a dangling modifier—and a long one at that. The entire opening phrase (technically a *clause* because it contains a subject and a verb), beginning with the word *Dismayed* and ending with the word *company*, is designed as a modifying phrase, intended to modify or give more information about—who? Who, exactly, was *dismayed by the news*? The problem with the sentence is that we can't tell. The modifying phrase "dangles"; there is no word or phrase to which it refers.

To be correct, the sentence would have to be rewritten to name the person or people who were dismayed—maybe something like this: "Dismayed by the news (etc.) . . . , Wall Street traders drove the price of the company's stock down sharply the following day." Now the modifying phrase has a clear referent—*Wall Street traders*—naming the people it modifies.

Rule 11: A Modifying Phrase Must Be Next to What It Modifies

As you just learned, a dangling modifier lacks something clear to modify. A *misplaced modifier* has something in the sentence to modify, but the two things are separated. When the modifying phrase isn't next to what it is supposed to modify, the sentence becomes confusing—and sometimes unintentionally comic. Here's an example:

> A fabled center of monastic life during the Middle Ages, thousands of visitors travel to the island of Iona near the coast of Ireland each summer.

The phrase that begins this sentence, *A fabled center of monastic life during the Middle Ages,* is supposed to modify *the island of Iona* because that's what it describes. However, the modifying phrase is misplaced. Rather than being next to what it modifies, it is next to the words *thousands of visitors,* almost as if the visitors were *a fabled center . . .* Because that's ridiculous, we soon figure out what the writer really means to say. But the momentary confusion makes for slightly less pleasant reading and causes this sentence to be considered erroneous.

The sentence could be corrected in several ways. The misplaced modifier could simply be moved to be next to what it modifies: "Thousands of visitors travel to the island of Iona, a fabled center of monastic life during the Middle Ages near the coast of Ireland, each summer." More gracefully, *the island of Iona* could be moved to a spot next to the modifier, with the sentence rewritten accordingly: "A fabled center of monastic life during the Middle Ages, the island of Iona near the coast of Ireland is visited by thousands of travelers each summer." Either way, the misplaced modifier would be corrected.

RULES ABOUT GRAMMATICAL AND LOGICAL CONSISTENCY

Rule 12: Items In A List Must Be Grammatically Parallel

You know about parallel lines in geometry: they are lines that run in the same direction, never touching but never diverging either. In grammar, *parallelism* refers to words, phrases, or clauses that "run in the same direction": they have the same grammatical form and therefore sound and look similar—like matching bookends.

Deciding when and how to use parallelism is partly a matter of taste and judgment. But there are certain writing situations that clearly call for parallelism—situations in which phrases that *don't* match definitely sound wrong. One such situation is when two or more things or ideas are presented in the form of a list. Check out this example:

> Delegates to the conference on global climate were charged with pursuing several often contradictory goals: reducing pollution by automobiles and industry, slowing the deforestation of the third world, and the maintenance of high rates of economic growth in the developing nations.

The sentence lists three goals of the conference delegates. The first two are written in parallel grammatical form—technically speaking, in phrases that begin with *gerunds* (-ing verbs):

> *reducing* pollution by automobiles and industry

> *slowing* the deforestation of the third world

However, the third goal is written in a different grammatical form. Instead of a gerund, the phrase begins with a noun that describes the action:

the maintenance of high rates of economic growth in the developing nations

Because of the lack of parallelism, the third item in the list sounds a bit "off," as though it doesn't match. To correct the sentence, the third item should be revised to match the other two by starting with a gerund: ". . . and *maintaining* high rates of economic growth in the developing nations."

Whenever a sentence contains a list of things that play the same logical role in the sentence, make sure they are also grammatically parallel. If not, one or more of the items should be rewritten to make them consistent.

Rule 13: Two Things Being Compared Must Be Grammatically Parallel

Like items in a list, items that are compared to one another in a sentence generally need to be grammatically parallel. Otherwise, the sentence will sound a bit disjointed. Here's an example:

Because of the enormous expense of television advertising, to run for Congress today costs more than running for governor of a mid-sized state twenty years ago.

The costs of two kinds of political campaigns are being compared: a race for Congress today and a race for governor twenty years ago. Unfortunately, the sentence as written uses two different, unmatching grammatical constructions to describe the races:

to run for Congress today

running for governor of a mid-sized state twenty years ago

The first item is named in a phrase beginning with an infinitive verb (*to run*). The second is named in a phrase beginning with a gerund (*running*). It would be okay to use either an infinitive or a gerund in this sentence; the problem is with using both inconsistently. The sentence should be corrected either by using an infinitive in both phrases ("*to run* for Congress today costs more than *to run* for governor") or by using a gerund in both phrases ("*running* for Congress today costs more than *running* for governor").

Rule 14: Two Things Being Compared Must Be Logically Similar

As the saying goes, you can't compare apples and oranges. When a sentence compares two (or more) things, it should be written so that the things being compared are logically, as well as grammatically, similar and consistent.

Here's an illustration of how a comparison can go wrong:

Although the Disney Company and Murdoch's News Corporation have both built vast multimedia empires, the financial strategy being pursued by Disney is markedly different from Murdoch.

Actually, this sentence contains two comparisons. In the first half of the sentence, two companies are being compared: *the Disney Company* and *Murdoch's News Corporation*. The phrases that mention the two things being compared are logically similar: both simply name the companies.

In the second half of the sentence, however, an unclear and inconsistent comparison is made. *The financial strategy being pursued by Disney* is compared with *Murdoch*. A moment's thought reveals the problem. The first phrase mentions a company's financial strategy; the second phrase merely names the company (in the shorthand form of the name of the company's chief owner, Murdoch). You could logically compare one company's financial strategy with another company's financial strategy; you could also compare one company, as a whole, with another. But it makes no sense to compare a financial strategy with a company. They are two different types of things.

The second half of the sentence could be corrected in several ways. Here are three:

1. . . . the financial strategy being pursued by Disney is markedly different from *that being pursued by Murdoch.*

2. . . . the financial strategy being pursued by Disney is markedly different from *Murdoch's.* ("Murdoch's *strategy*" is implied.)

3. . . . Disney's financial strategy is markedly different from Murdoch's.

Each of these is correct.

Rule 15: A Subject and Its Complement Must Be Logically Consistent

The two kinds of verbs are verbs of *action* and verbs of *being*. Verbs of action tell what the subject does: *dance, type, dive, manage, eat,* and so on. Verbs of being tell what the subject is. The verb *to be* is the most obvious example, but *seem, appear, feel, sound, look, remain, become,* and many others can all be used as verbs of being.

Generally, what follows a verb of being is a *subject complement*: something that *complements* or completes the meaning of the subject. In other words, it tells us more about the subject. In the sentence "Harry seems tired," *tired* is a subject complement. In the sentence, "Renee became a firefighter," *firefighter* is a subject complement.

So far, so simple. You've been constructing sentences like these all your life with few mishaps. Problems arise with sentences like this—sentences built around verbs of being—when the subject and the subject complement are in some way mismatched. Logically, because the subject and the subject complement describe the same thing, they should be the same *kind* of thing. If they are not, then we have the same problem we saw a moment ago with unlike things being compared: what we might call the apples-and-oranges problem. Here's an example:

> The anti-democratic bias of the Electoral College has long been criticized as an anachronistic institution that has outlived the role intended for it by its founders.

The verb *to criticize* isn't always used as a verb of being, but in this case it is. What the sentence is saying is that, in the view of some people, the Electoral College *is* an anachronistic (that is, outmoded) institution. Because the sentence is telling what the subject *is* rather than what it *does*, the second half of the sentence—starting with the word *an*—is a subject complement.

The problem is that, in this sentence, the subject and the subject complement aren't logically matched. Look again at the first half of the sentence. The subject of the verb *has been criticized* isn't actually *the Electoral College*; it is actually *the anti-democratic bias*. (Remember, the subject of the verb isn't normally in a prepositional phrase—and *of the Electoral College* is a prepositional phrase.) Once you focus on this, it's obvious that the subject and the subject complement don't go together clearly. The *bias* of the Electoral College isn't *an anachronistic institution*. It's not an institution at all. The author is trying to say that the Electoral College itself is anachronistic. However, by the time he got to the second half of the sentence, he forgot exactly what he'd written in the first half—hence the confusion.

The sentence could be fixed by rewriting it to say what the author really intended: "Because of its anti-democratic bias, the Electoral College has long been criticized. . . ." Now the connection between the subject and the subject complement is logical and clear.

RULES ABOUT ADJECTIVES AND ADVERBS

Rule 16: Use Adjectives to Modify Nouns or Pronouns; Use Adverbs to Modify Verbs, Adjectives, or Adverbs

Think hard and you may remember learning the rules about adjectives and adverbs (if you weren't lucky enough to be "home sick" the day they were covered in English class). An adjective is a word that modifies (gives more information about) a noun or a pronoun; it often answers such questions as *what kind? how many? which one?* By contrast, an adverb modifies a verb, an adjective, or another adverb; it often answers such questions as *how? when? where? in what way? how often?* and *to what extent?* Adverbs often (not always) end in *-ly*.

Sometimes writers err by mistakenly using an adjective where an adverb is needed, or vice versa. Here's an example:

> From 1964 through 1968, albums recorded by the Beatles appeared consistent on the charts of best-selling popular music, not only in their native England but around the world.

The word *consistent* is an adjective; it could be used to modify a noun (*a consistent success*) or a pronoun (*she is consistent in her habits*). However, in this sentence, *consistent* is ill-chosen because the author is trying to modify the verb *appeared*. He wants to answer the question *how often did Beatles albums appear on the charts?* To answer this question, an adverb is needed.

The adverb form of the adjective *consistent* is formed like many adverbs: by adding *-ly* to the adjective. The sentence can easily be corrected by changing *consistent* to *consistently*.

Rule 17: Use A Comparative Adjective or Adverb to Compare Two Things; Use A Superlative for Three or More

The basic form of an adjective is called the *positive* form. When you want to compare two things, you use the *comparative* form, which is usually formed in one of two ways: by adding *-er* to the positive form or by putting the word *more* in front of it. (Use the second method with an adjective that is three syllables long or longer.) When comparing more than two things, use the *superlative* form, which is formed by adding *-est* to the positive form or by using the word *most*. (Again, you can generally be guided by the length of the adjective.) Thus, you would write

I am *tall*.

I am *taller* than my sister.

My brother Stan is the *tallest* person in our whole family.

With a three-syllable adjective, the words would be formed this way:

Suzy is *beautiful*.

Sharon is *more beautiful*.

Michelle Pfeiffer is the *most beautiful* woman in the galaxy.

Occasionally, errors arise when a writer gets confused about whether to use the comparative or superlative form of the adjective, as in this example:

Of the many strange creatures that inhabit the continent of Australia, the wallaby is perhaps the *more* unusual.

Because the wallaby is compared to more than one other creature, the superlative form of the adjective should be used: "The wallaby is perhaps the *most unusual*."

Comparative and superlative forms of adverbs are used in much the same way. The comparative form (made with the word *more*) is used when two things are being compared; the superlative form (made with *most*) is used when three or more things are being compared:

Jerry swims *quickly*.

Paula swims *more quickly* than Jerry.

Karen swims *most quickly* of anyone on the swim team.

Rule 18: Distinguish Among the Adjective *Good*, the Adverb *Well*, and the Adjective *Well*

This trio of words can be a bit confusing, and because they are used quite often, it's important to get the differences straight. *Good* is an adjective with a broadly positive meaning. *Well* is the adverb form of *good* (the equivalent of *goodly*, if there were such a word in modern English); it means, in effect, "in a good way." But *well* can also be an adjective meaning "healthy" or "the opposite of ill." Consider this example:

Thanks to the improved acoustics in the newly renovated Carnegie Hall, the deepest notes of the bass violins sound as well as the highest tones of the piccolos.

The verb *sound* in this sentence is a verb of being; it is used here to tell us what the deepest notes of the bass violins *are* rather than what they *do*. What follows should be a subjective complement, telling what those notes are (or, literally,

FYI

Don't be misled: Sometimes the comparative form is appropriate even in a sentence where the meaning might suggest that more than one thing is being compared. For example, if the sentence were written this way, the comparative form would be correct: "The wallaby is more unusual than any other creature in Australia." Although in a way all the creatures in Australia are being compared here, the sentence is literally comparing the wallaby to each other creature one creature at a time. Thus, only two things are (technically) being compared, and more unusual is correct.

what they sound like). In this situation, the adjective *good* is needed rather than either the adverb *well* or the adjective *well* (because the notes don't sound "healthy").

The adverb *well* would be correctly used in a sentence like this: "Carrie, the bass violinist in the Anderson Quartet, plays very *well*." (She plays "in a good way," in other words.) The adjective *well* would be correctly used in a sentence like this: "I just spoke to Carrie on the phone and she sounds *well*; I guess she has recovered from the flu." (She sounds "healthy," that is.) See the difference?

RULES ABOUT PRONOUNS

Rule 19: A Pronoun Must Have A Clear and Logical Antecedent

As you may recall, a *pronoun* refers to and takes the place of a noun. In a sentence like, "Laura said that Laura was planning to go with Laura's friends to Times Square on New Year's Eve," you'd want to use the pronouns *she* and *her* rather than repeating *Laura*. (It sounds a little boring and awkward otherwise.)

The noun that the pronoun refers to is called its *antecedent*. A problem arises when the reader can't easily tell who or what the antecedent is supposed to be—as in this example:

> Although the hospital administrators interviewed many staff members about the repeated cases of staph infections, they had no explanation for the puzzling pattern of outbreaks.

The second half of this sentence starts with the pronoun *they*. Unfortunately, we can't tell from the context who *they* are. Logically, the antecedent could be *the hospital administrators* or the *staff members*, but the sentence doesn't help us figure out which group is intended. (Some grammarians say that, in an ambiguous case such as this, the nearer antecedent applies, which would be the *staff members*, but really good writing wouldn't require the reader to puzzle over the intended meaning.)

The sentence ought to be revised. Here's one way: "Although *they* interviewed many staff members . . . , *the hospital administrators* had no explanation . . ." Notice how flip-flopping the pronoun and its antecedent makes it unmistakable who *they* are. This strategy won't work in every sentence, but it works here. In other instances, you might have to repeat the noun (or some form of it) rather than use an ambiguous pronoun. Either way, the intended meaning would at least be clear.

Rule 20: The Antecedent of a Pronoun Must Be a Noun
(or Another Pronoun)

Sometimes, rather than have two possible antecedents, a pronoun lacks an antecedent altogether. Here's an example:

> Corporate financial statements for the first three quarters of the year showed that the sales increases they had enjoyed each year of the previous decade had definitely stopped.

Who is the *they* referred to in the second half of this sentence? We can't tell. Presumably, it refers to the corporation being discussed, but the words *the corporation* or their equivalent (*the company, the firm*) don't actually appear anywhere. (In any case, *the company* is an *it*, not a *they*.) The closest thing to an antecedent here is the adjective *Corporate*, which is no good. Remember, the antecedent of a pronoun has to be a noun or another pronoun; it can't be an adjective.

The sentence must be revised, probably by replacing the pronoun *they* with a noun that makes the meaning clear: " . . . the sales increases *the company* had enjoyed . . . ."

Rule 21: A Pronoun Must Agree With Its Antecedent In Number

Just like a subject and a verb, a pronoun and its antecedent must agree in number: If the antecedent is singlular, the pronoun must also be singlular; if the antecedent is plural, the pronoun must also be plural.

Here's an example of how this can go wrong:

> A climber interested in scaling Everest must be prepared to invest a significant amount of their time and energy, as well as money, in preparing for the ordeal.

Notice the pronoun *their* in the second half of this sentence. Who does it refer to? (What is the pronoun's antecedent?) *A climber* is the answer; it is *a climber interested in scaling Everest* whose time and energy must be invested. Now you can see the problem with agreement. *A climber* is singular, but *their* is plural; it refers to two or more people only.

To correct the sentence, *their* must be changed to a singular pronoun. The choice of pronoun is a minor dilemma. One could use *his*, which, in a nonspecific context like this one, is said by many writers and grammarians (especially conservative or old-fashioned ones) to embrace either a male or a female climber; to be more scrupulously gender-neutral, one could use the phrase *his or her*. The former option has come to sound a bit sexist; the latter is a little wordy. The truth is that there's no perfect solution.

Rule 22: Use Second and Third Person Pronouns Consistently

Grammarians refer to three "persons": first person (*I, me, we*, and so on), second person (*you*), and third person (*he, she, it, they*, and so on). In most contexts, it would be difficult to confuse these persons. However, in sentences where an indefinite person is being discussed, English allows you to use either second-person or third-person constructions, and this creates the possibility of inconsistency and error. Here's an example of what we mean:

> If one lives in the northern hemisphere, on most clear winter nights you can easily see the three stars in a row that mark the belt of the hunter in the constellation Orion.

The sentence is describing how someone—anyone—can see Orion's belt in the winter sky. It starts by using the indefinite third-person pronoun *one*. (Other such words that could have been used include the pronouns *someone* and *anyone* and expressions such as *a person* or *an observer*.) However, the sentence shifts in midstream to the second person: *you can easily see* . . . This is a no-no.

The sentence could be corrected by maintaining the third person all the way through: *one can easily see.* . . . Or you could change the entire sentence to

---

FYI

People often use plural pronouns such as they, them, *and* their *in a context like this precisely to avoid the dilemma of appearing sexist. However, that strategy is still considered grammatically incorrect. On the GMAT CAT, you'll need to pick a variant that maintains proper pronoun-antecedent agreement—despite the awkwardness of the only available options.*

second person: *If you live in the northern hemisphere, . . . you can easily see . . .* Either way is consistent and correct. What's wrong is to mix and match inconsistently.

RULES ABOUT CONNECTING CLAUSES

Rule 23: Choose the Logical Conjunction

Conjunctions are connecting words. The screws and bolts of language, they clamp together words, phrases, and clauses in ways that make both logical and grammatical sense.

Conjunctions can be classified in various ways. You need to know only two categories. *Coordinating conjunctions* connect words, phrases, and clauses that are equal in grammatical importance. There are six: *and, or, for, nor, but*, and *yet*. *Subordinating conjunctions* are used especially to connect clauses (that is, groups of words that contain a subject and a verb). The clause introduced by a subordinating conjunction is called a *dependent clause*; as its name implies, it is less important than a clause without such a conjunction, which is called an *independent clause*.

A dependent clause can't stand alone as a sentence. An independent clause can. Table C.5 has a few examples of subordinating conjunctions, together with dependent clauses they might introduce.

Can you see that each of the dependent clauses in Table C.5 could *not* stand alone as a sentence? Each needs to be connected to another, independent clause. The conjunction helps to make the necessary connection.

So much for the basics of conjunctions. On the GMAT CAT, you'll have to recognize whether the proper, logical conjunction is used to connect two clauses. It depends, of course, on the meaning of the conjunction, which will either fit the context plausibly or not. Look at this example:

> Many theories as to how human beings first domesticated dogs have been proposed, and clear evidence to support any one of these theories has yet to surface.

Here, two independent clauses have been joined by the coordinating conjunction *and*. Grammatically, we're all right. The problem is with the logic of the sentence. The two clauses are actually somewhat opposed in meaning rather than complementary: *Despite the fact that* many theories exist, *no evidence supporting them* has been found. This is surprising, no? One would think that a multiplicity of theories would go hand-in-hand with an abundance of evidence. But the sentence tells us, surprisingly, that this is not so.

Table C.5
Sample Subordinating Conjunctions

Conjunction	Example
although	although it had begun to rain
when	when the plumber arrived
because	because the bicycle was broken
after	after she reached Paris

Given this near-contradiction, the conjunction *and* doesn't seem the best choice. Instead, *but* should be used. This would logically fit the opposition in meaning between the two clauses.

Watch for similar disjunctions on the GMAT CAT. No matter what conjunction is used—*and, or, but, since, before, if, unless*—make sure it makes logical sense in the context. If not, look for a correction that better fits the meaning of the sentence.

Rule 24: Use A Semicolon (;) to Connect Two Independent Clauses

We've explained that one of the six coordinating conjunctions can be used to connect two independent clauses. The other proper way to connect two independent clauses is with a semicolon (;). That's the main use of a semicolon. (The other uses are somewhat specialized; for example, you can use semicolons instead of commas to separate items within a list that contain commas. Ninety-five percent of the time, a semicolon is used between independent clauses.)

Here's an example of a semicolon gone bad:

> Adams was initially drawn into the slavery question not by the controversy over slavery itself; but by the so-called "gag rule" used by the South to stifle debates in the Senate concerning slavery.

The semicolon in the middle of this sentence is wrong because it doesn't connect two independent clauses. The semicolon should be replaced by a comma.

Rule 25: Avoid Run-on Sentences

A run-on sentence isn't necessarily a particularly long sentence. It's simply a sentence in which two (or more) independent clauses have been shoved together without either a semicolon or a coordinating conjunction to join them properly. (When a comma is erroneously used to connect them, the result is a *comma splice*—one type of run-on sentence.) Here's an example:

> Beside being a writer and lecturer, Mark Twain fancied himself an entrepreneur, he made and lost several fortunes backing various business ventures.

If this sentence were divided into two sentences after the word *entrepreneur*, either half could stand alone as a sentence. (Try it.) Therefore, it's a run-on sentence (specifically, a comma splice). It could be corrected in any of several ways:

1. You could go ahead and break it into two sentences: change the comma after *entrepreneur* into a period and capitalize *he*.

2. You could change the comma into a semicolon, which, as you just learned, is a proper punctuation mark to link two independent clauses.

3. You could add a coordinating conjunction after the comma.

4. Finally, you could change one of the clauses into a dependent clause by adding a subordinating conjunction. It would require some rewriting—

such as this, for example: "*Because* Mark Twain fancied himself an entrepreneur, beside being a writer and lecturer, he made and lost several fortunes . . ."

On the GMAT CAT, of course, you won't have to carry out all of these schemes for correcting the sentence; just recognize one of them when you see it among the answer choices.

Rule 26: Avoid Sentence Fragments

A sentence fragment is a collection of words that is punctuated as a sentence but that cannot properly stand alone as a sentence. Some sentence fragments lack either a subject or a verb, two basic elements every sentence must have. In other cases, the sentence fragment has both a subject and a verb, but it is a dependent rather than an independent clause. This usually happens because the clause begins either with a subordinating conjunction or with a particular type of pronoun, called a *relative pronoun*, which makes the clause dependent on another clause.

Got all that? Here's an example that may help make it a bit clearer:

> Carbon dating, which can be used in estimating the age of materials that are of organic origin only, because the method is based on the predictable decay of carbon-based organic compounds.

Although this collection of words is pretty long (31 words), it is a sentence fragment rather than a true sentence. Why? Not because it lacks a subject and a verb; actually, it contains *three* verbs, each with its own subject. But each of these clauses is a dependent rather than an independent clause, so none is enough to make a free-standing sentence.

The first clause here begins with the words *which can be used*. *Can be used* is the verb, and the pronoun *which* is the subject. Because *which* is a relative pronoun, it can't introduce an independent clause; instead, it connects the clause to the rest of the sentence (which hopefully includes an independent clause). You can probably "hear" the fact that a clause whose subject is *which* sounds incomplete and is therefore dependent.

The second clause begins with *that are*. *Are* is the verb and the relative pronoun *that* is the subject. Again, it's a dependent clause, which can't stand alone as a sentence.

The final clause begins with the words *because the method is based*. The verb is *is based* and the subject is *the method*. This is a dependent clause because of the subordinating conjunction *because*. Any clause beginning with this word can't stand alone. Again, you can probably tell from the way it sounds that a clause starting with *because* needs another clause to complete the thought.

To turn this into a complete sentence, you would need to add something—most likely, a verb at the end that would hook up with the words *Carbon dating* way back at the start of the sentence. Those words appear to be what the author originally intended for his subject before he got distracted and lost in the midst of those three dependent clauses. A complete sentence might read something like this: "Carbon dating, which can be used in estimating the age of materials that are of organic origin only because the method is based on the predictable decay of carbon-based organic compounds, *is useless in studying materials that are completely nonorganic*." This would give the sentence an independent clause, built around the subject and verb *Carbon dating . . . is*." Understand?

RULES ABOUT VERBOSITY

Rule 27: Avoid needless repetition

FYI

On the GMAT CAT, when you have a choice between two or more answer choices, both of which are grammatically correct and say the same thing, choose the shortest version. It is usually the best.

On the GMAT CAT, be on the lookout for sentences that are unnecessarily verbose—that is, wordy and too long. Good writing is economical and concise. The test makers will usually make their examples of verbosity fairly obvious. One form of verbosity to watch out for is sheer, needless repetition of a fact or an idea—also called *redundancy*. Here's an example:

As much as 125 years ago, the science fiction writer Jules Verne wrote predictions that foretold the future existence of such modern mechanical devices as the airplane, the submarine, and even the fax machine.

This sentence isn't grammatically "wrong"; it breaks no rules of sentence structure or usage. But it's poorly written because of the needless repetition it contains. We're told that Jules Verne wrote "predictions that foretold" something—a clear example of repetition because a prediction *by definition* foretells something. Then we learn that his predictions foretold "the future existence" of certain things. Obviously, if Verne was foretelling something, what he was foretelling *had to be* in the future.

Each of these redundancies should be eliminated, saving words and making the revised sentence much crisper in style. Other words can also be eliminated with no loss of meaning. "As much as 125 years ago, the science fiction writer Jules Verne predicted such devices as the airplane, the submarine, and even the fax machine." Compare this sentence, 25 words long, with the original version, 34 words long. Isn't the shorter version better? Apply the same kind of thinking on the exam.

Rule 28: Eliminate Words When This Can Be Done Without Sacrificing Grace, Clarity, or Meaning

Redundancy isn't the only form of wordiness. Sometimes sentences are just plain "flabby," sagging under the weight of extra words that add nothing to the meaning and can easily be eliminated. Here's an example:

Spielberg's *Amistad* is the filmmaker's second attempt to show that someone who is an unexcelled creator of funny, fast-paced action movies can also be a producer of films that try to deal in a serious fashion with weighty historical and moral themes.

This sentence can be significantly shortened without changing or obscuring its meaning. One way is by eliminating the "empty" clause *someone who is*. Clauses such as this are often injected into sentences without any real purpose; they are mere verbal tics, like the "ers" and "ahs" that people sometimes interject when they speak. Similarly, the convoluted clause *can also be a producer of films* can be radically simplified into *can also produce films*.

The improved sentence might read like this:

Spielberg's *Amistad* is the filmmaker's second attempt to show that an unexcelled creator of funny, fast-paced action movies can also produce films dealing seriously with weighty historical and moral themes.

(Note the other changes we've made here.) The sentence has been reduced from 42 words to just 30, a 29% "weight loss." More important, it now sounds more lively and vigorous, a direct result of the elimination of "verbal flab."

Rule 29: Avoid Needless Use of the Passive Construction

FYI

Be careful with sentences built around verbs of being. Fairly often, such verbs can be eliminated in favor of shorter, crisper constructions built around verbs of action.

Another way to avoid verbosity is by using active rather than passive verbs wherever possible. You remember the difference: "Sharon built the birdhouse" is active; "The birdhouse was built by Sharon" is passive. In an active construction, the subject of the verb (in this case, *Sharon*) *does* the action named. In a passive construction, the subject (*The birdhouse*) *receives* the action. The one doing the action is named, if at all, in a prepositional phrase (*by Sharon*) after the verb.

Sometimes, the passive construction is useful and appropriate. For example, when it isn't important who did the action or when it is unknown. ("We found that our summer cottage had been vandalized while we were away.") But in most sentences, the active construction sounds more vigorous and is also more concise. Consider this example:

> When the basic elements of the theory of natural selection were conceived by Darwin, it was unknown to him that most of the same ideas had already been developed by a rival naturalist, Charles Russel Wallace.

If this sentence sounds clumsy and stilted, it's largely because of the needless use of the passive construction. On reflection, it seems strange to de-emphasize the roles of Darwin and Wallace (the "doers" of the deeds being described) by relegating them to mere "by" phrases, rather than making them the subjects of the sentence. It also makes the sentence unnecessarily wordy.

Here's how the improved sentence reads when active verbs are used instead: "When Darwin conceived the basic elements of the theory of natural selection, he didn't know that Charles Russel Wallace, a rival naturalist, had already developed most of the same ideas." The sentence is shorter, crisper, and a trifle easier to understand.

Unless there is some good reason to prefer a passive verb in a particular sentence, choose active constructions instead.

RULES ABOUT IDIOMATIC USAGE

Rule 30: When Idiomatic Paired Phrases Are Used, Always Complete the Idiom

An *idiom* is a phrase that is peculiar to a particular language. Often, there is no special "logic" or "rule" behind the use of a given idiom; we explain idioms (when a child or a nonnative speaker asks for an explanation) by saying, "That's just the way you say it," and let it go at that.

If you grew up speaking English, you've been surrounded by thousands of English idioms all your life, and you've learned to use most of them flawlessly by osmosis—by hearing them used and imitating what you've heard, often unconsciously. But some idioms are tricky even for native speakers. Here's one instance.

There are certain idiomatic pairs of phrases that must always be used together. When they aren't, the resulting sentence "sounds wrong," as if something is missing. (As the saying goes, we're left waiting "for the other shoe to drop.") Look at this example:

Many historians now contend that the American Revolution was caused as much by economic factors than by political ones.

This sentence sounds slightly "off" because the idiom demands that the phrase *as much by X* be followed inexorably by *as by Y*. It seems odd to hear the word *than* where the second *as* should be.

Another illustration:

Demographers have long recognized an inverse relationship between family size and income: that is, the more a family earns, greater will be their likelihood of practicing family planning and birth control.

The proper idiom for describing this kind of cause-and-effect relationship is *the more X, the more Y*, or some close variation on that. The sentence sounds wrong because our expectation that the pair of phrases will be completed is not met. The second half of the sentence should be rewritten this way: "the more a family earns, *the greater* will be their likelihood . . ."

Keep your ear cocked for paired idioms such as these, and make sure that your sentence completes the construction by using both phrases correctly.

Rule 31: Distinguish Gerunds From Infinitives

Gerunds and infinitives are two peculiar word types that combine some of the qualities of a verb with some of the qualities of a noun. Unless you're a grammarian, you don't normally need to think about these terms and the subtleties of their usage, with one exception: It's important to know the difference between a gerund and an infinitive and to be sensitive to which one "sounds" right in a particular sentence.

A *gerund* is a noun formed by adding *-ing* to a verb. It looks the same as the present participle form of the verb—*swimming, working, enjoying*—but it's used in all the ways a noun is used: as the subject or object of a verb, as the object of a preposition, and so on. For example, in the sentence, "Swimming is my favorite exercise," *Swimming* is the subject of the verb.

An *infinitive* is the basic form of a verb, usually with *to* in front of it: *to swim, to work, to enjoy*. Like a gerund, it can also be used as a noun, either by itself or in a phrase called an *infinitive phrase*. For example, in the sentence, "To know him is to love him," the infinitive phrase *To know him* is the subject of the sentence (and *to love him* is the subject complement).

Problems arise when writers get confused about whether a gerund or an infinitive is needed in a particular type of sentence. Here's an example:

The sensitive nature of the negotiations required the company president's traveling halfway around the globe to participate personally in the final phase of the discussion.

According to idiomatic usage, the word *required* should be followed by an infinitive rather than a gerund, so the sentence should say, "required the company president *to travel* halfway around the globe. . . ."

By contrast, look at this example:

The president assured the senator that his administration had no intention to encroach on Congressional prerogatives in this matter.

Here, the infinitive sounds wrong; the sentence should say, "the administration had no intention *of encroaching* on Congressional prerogatives. . . ."

Unfortunately, you have no logical rules to follow (as is usually true with idioms). Similar meanings sometimes require opposite structures: A person *promises to do* something, but she is *committed to doing* it; she may *hesitate to do* something, but she *objects to doing* it, and so on.

Rule 32: Distinguish *Likely* From *Liable*

In casual speech, many people confuse these two words. In careful writing, however, they should be distinguished. *Likely* means "probably destined to happen"; a likely event is one you think will occur. *Liable* means "legally responsible"; if you run into another car when you're driving, you will be liable for the damages. Don't use *liable* to mean "likely," as in this example:

> Recent history suggests that many American voters are liable to deliberately split their votes, choosing a President and a member of Congress from different parties as if to limit the power of both.

The author of this sentence wants to say that vote splitting is a common practice among American voters; legal liability is not being referred to. Therefore, the word *liable* should be changed to *likely* in this sentence.

Rule 33: Distinguish *Like* From *As*

The words *like* and *as* are used in similar ways in sentences where a similarity between two things is being described. However, they should be distinguished grammatically. Here's how.

In careful writing, *like* is used as a connecting word only as a preposition, never as a conjunction. In other words, *like* should be followed by a noun or pronoun, not by a clause. By contrast, *as* is used as a subordinating conjunction; it may be followed by a clause. Look at this example:

> As the famous North Atlantic clipper ships of the nineteenth century, today's jumbo jets have revolutionized transatlantic commerce by making travel between Europe and America far faster than ever before.

What follows the word *As* in this sentence is not a clause but the noun *ships* (along with various modifying words that give more information about what kind of ships the author is talking about). Therefore, the preposition *Like* should be used instead.

As would be correct if a clause followed it—in other words, if a subject and verb appeared. You might start the same sentence this way: "*As* the famous North Atlantic clipper ships of the nineteenth century *did*, ..." Adding the word *did* turns the phrase into a clause and makes *as* the proper connecting word.

Rule 34: Distinguish Countable Quantities From Quantities That Cannot Be Counted

The word *much* is used correctly to describe quantities that cannot be counted, whereas *many* is used for quantities that can be counted. For example, you might refer to the beach as having "so *much* sand" because *sand* is not a countable substance; you don't refer to "a hundred sands," for example. By contrast, you could say that your shoe contains "so *many* grains of sand" because *grains of sand* are countable; you might count "a hundred grains of sand," for instance.

Here's another example:

> Apparently, the university administration short-sightedly overlooked the fact that an influx of much more students would naturally require much more room for housing, classrooms, and other facilities.

Much more room is fine because "room" is not a countable substance of which more is required on this particular campus. But *much more students* should be *many more students* because students are, obviously, countable.

Distinguish *fewer* (countable) and *less* (not countable) in much the same way.

Rule 35: Use the Idiomatic Preposition

Prepositions are among the most ornery and troublesome words in English. In dozens of expressions, specific prepositions are paired with other words (often verbs) to convey a particular meaning. If the wrong preposition is used, the meaning may be obscured. But even if it isn't, the resulting sentence sounds non-idiomatic—that is, wrong. Here are a couple of examples:

> Paradoxically, city planners have found that building new highways in the intention for reducing traffic congestion often increases it.

> The continuing skirmishes between Microsoft and the U.S. Justice Department suggest that antitrust law has not yet been successfully adapted regarding such new fields as the software industry.

In the first sentence, the preposition *for* should be changed to *of* because one normally speaks of an "intention *of* doing something," not *for* doing it (or anything else). In the second sentence, the offending preposition is *regarding*; it should be *to*, which is the idiomatic preposition to pair with the verb *adapt*.

Occasionally, choosing the idiomatic preposition seems illogical and arbitrary. For example, you *agree to* do something, but you *agree with* someone; two things *differ from* each other, but two people with opposite opinions *differ with* each other. Nonnative speakers find these constructions difficult to distinguish and remember.

Appendix D

The Insider's Stress-Busting Guide

by Mary-Jo D. Weber, M.S.
Psychiatric Nurse Practitioner

THE ROLE OF STRESS IN PEAK TEST PERFORMANCE

Let's face it—if you're like most people, you're not really looking forward to taking the GMAT CAT. In fact, the very thought of the test might make your stomach queasy and your neck and shoulders tight. You might become aware of your heart beating, and your hands might get clammy. You might even feel restless and be tempted to close this book right now and get a snack!

All these physical responses to the stress of test taking can work for you or against you. Conditioned by millions of years of evolution, your body has developed a complex natural reaction, sometimes called the *fight or flight* response, that comes into play whenever you feel physically or psychologically threatened. This reaction has a very real value in getting you ready to meet whatever challenge you face, whether it's a menacing stranger on a dark street, an auditorium full of people waiting to hear you deliver a speech, or a standardized exam.

The adrenaline and other hormones that are released when you are under stress can get you ready for peak performance. They arouse your senses to increased sensitivity, alert your brain cells to pay attention, sharpen your mental focus, increase the amounts of energizing oxygen delivered to all parts of your body, and raise the levels of glucose available to fuel your brain. These chemical processes account for the sense of excitement you feel when you're under stress. Some people—artists who thrill to public applause, for example, or world-class athletes—actually relish this state of physical and mental arousal, and even the average person finds it exhilarating, though perhaps scary, too.

The problem comes when these responses get out of control, freezing your thoughts and leaving you feeling uncomfortably tense or anxious. When that happens, you may develop "tunnel vision," a narrowing of perception that hampers your awareness of what's around you; you may even feel that your mind is "going blank," as if your brain is on overload and is starting to shut down.

Fortunately, you *can* manage your stress so that the natural stress response will sharpen your focus without limiting your perspective or closing off your options, making you more creative and imaginative and helping you to retrieve more of the useful information stored in your memory. This appendix will give you specific, scientifically tested techniques to use in the weeks before the exam, while you are studying, and on the very day you take the GMAT CAT. If you practice these methods, you may find yourself almost looking forward to the opportunity to tackle the test—and beat it!

PREPARING FOR PEAK PERFORMANCE

Top athletes find that mental preparation is as important to their success in competition as practicing their specific athletic skills. The field of sports psychology has taught us a lot about how you can best prepare for your test. Practicing your academic skills is something like a basketball player working on his foul shot or a swimmer perfecting her stroke: it's essential, but it's not enough. The best performers don't stop there. They also use relaxation and visualization techniques to ensure that they'll be able to apply their skills and to respond effectively and creatively to the challenges that game day will bring their way.

Similar relaxation and visualization techniques can help keep you from freezing up and allow you to efficiently handle whatever comes your way in the test-taking situation. They can also help you experience the test as a positive challenge, not a looming source of terror. You will maintain a degree of comfort and be able to manage the unpleasant symptoms of anxiety without letting them overwhelm you.

Learning to Relax

First, you'll need to learn to relax whenever you decide you want to. Yes—for most people it's a skill that must be learned. If you're like most people, you probably tend to keep going—with work, play, or just hanging around—until you're physically exhausted, and then you crash. It's not the most efficient way to harness the energy in your body and mind. Instead, if you learn to relax whenever you want to, you'll be able to modulate your stress responses so that you'll feel only the amount of anxiety you need to wake up your brain cells and perform your best.

The following exercise is a good way to start. If you're feeling any sense of tiredness or anxiety—after a couple of hours of studying, for example—this is a better way to refresh yourself than napping or taking a TV break. It takes only a few minutes and will leave you feeling energized and alert. You can either read through this suggested exercise and then try it, or, even better, get a friend with a pleasant voice to read it aloud to you while you try it. (Later, you can return the favor.) As you go through the exercise, feel free to alter it in any way that seems pertinent to your individual situation.

Relaxation Exercise

Start by sitting comfortably with both feet flat on the floor. Take some time to notice how the floor is supporting your feet. Allow the surface on which you are resting to support you completely. Take all the time you need to notice the comfort and security of this.

Next, turn your mind toward your breathing. Don't try to change it; just observe it. Observe how effortless your breathing is, realizing that, with every exhalation, the tension of the day is flowing out, and, with every inhalation, revitalizing oxygen is flowing in to nourish all parts of your body.

Turn your attention again to your feet. Notice that they are comfortably resting on the floor. Notice that feeling of comfort spreading up to your ankles, calves, and knees. Feel how securely the chair is supporting your thighs, your buttocks, your lower back, and your upper back.

Your hands may be in your lap or at your sides. Allow them to open, and as you continue to breathe comfortably and naturally, experience any tension flowing down from your shoulders to your arms and out your finger tips. You will notice that, the more relaxed you can keep your hands, the more relaxed and alert you will be.

Notice whether your eyes are open or closed. Either way is fine. Take some time now to notice the muscles around your eyes, in your cheeks, and around your mouth. Notice whatever expression you naturally have on your face, whether it's frowning, neutral, or smiling. Don't feel you need to change it. Allow these muscles to soften. Close your eyes if you wish. Feel the heaviness of your jaw, and don't try to hold it up.

As you continue to notice the comfort in your body, pay attention to your neck and scalp. If you perceive any tension there, allow it to flow out with your next breath. Scan your body now, and if you notice any areas of discomfort or tension, notice that, as you breathe, any tension or discomfort flows out with each exhalation, while energy flows in with each inhalation.

Now, as you continue to enjoy the comfort of your body securely supported by the chair and energized by your breathing, imagine that you are in a special, favorite place. It may be the beach, or the mountains, or your room, or just inside yourself. Notice how comfortable and alert you are to all the things that make that place pleasurable for you. Notice the sights, sounds, smells, and feelings that make the place so nice.

Take your time enjoying your special place. When you are ready to return to the room in which you are sitting, gently reorient yourself, experiencing your calm alertness and renewed enthusiasm for all your endeavors.

Now that you're back from your special place, notice how revitalized you feel.

With practice, this process of relaxation will become easier and quicker, but you already have noticed that, from the very first attempt, you can recharge your batteries in a way that is even better than a nap because your alertness will be increased and your focus will be sharpened. Try using this method of relaxation whenever the pressure of studying is making you feel exhausted or tense. You'll find yourself learning more—and enjoying it more, too.

Visualizing Success

The next step is to add visualization of the test-taking situation and your desired successful outcome. It's a favorite preparation strategy of many successful athletes and entertainers; they find that visualizing themselves hitting the perfect tennis stroke or playing a difficult piano concerto with fluency and ease makes it much easier to actually perform that way.

It works for test takers, too. In preparing for the GMAT CAT, it'll help if you visit the testing center beforehand, so you'll know what to expect; but you can use our visualization exercise even if you don't have a chance to make such a visit. Here's how it works.

Visualization Exercise

Repeat the relaxation exercise. This time, however, after you've imagined your special place and while you're alertly and attentively noting the sights, sounds, and feelings that you experience there, imagine that you are entering the test room. Notice the rows of cubicles and the computer monitor and keyboard at each location.

Take your seat, noting how comfortably your feet are supported by the floor, how your body is supported by the chair, and how your breathing is energizing your body and mind. You see that the computer monitor contains the directions for the GMAT CAT. You review them and you begin your work, knowing that you have prepared for this test and that you will correctly answer all the questions you need to in order to achieve your desired goal.

You experience just the right amount of anxiety you need to feel in order to achieve your peak performance. As you work, the questions appear familiar and interesting to you. You look forward to reading each question because you know you will find it to be an interesting challenge to the skills you've been learning and practicing. You work efficiently, and, when you come to the end of the test, you experience the sense of a job well done.

At this time, reorient to the room.

You may also use this exercise before going to sleep, perhaps after a strenuous study session. If you do the exercise in bed, when it's completed, simply allow yourself to drift into a refreshing sleep.

During the weeks while you are studying for your exam, you can ensure peak performance by practicing relaxation and visualization every day. The best time for many people is at night, just before sleep. This will help your learning because your mind is working even while you sleep. Thus, if you practice visualizing test-taking success before you go to sleep, your brain will probably continue to process that information while you sleep, reinforcing the positive message.

Some people find it very effective to make an audiotape of the relaxation and visualization exercises, to be played while they fall asleep.

TECHNIQUES OF POWER STUDYING

If you're an athlete, a musician, or an actor, you know how important your physical condition is to your training. What you eat or drink before practice will influence how effective your training will be. The same is true of test preparation.

Physical Conditioning for Effective Study

Everyone knows his or her own best time of the day for studying. For some people, it's early in the morning, before class or work; for others, it's late at night. Whatever time you favor, make sure you're in peak condition before you hit the books. Any alcohol intake within the past 12 to 24 hours (depending upon the amount) will decrease your mental functioning. Other mood-altering chemicals can interfere with your ability to learn and think critically for a much longer time, sometimes for as long as a month after use. A word to the wise, or to those who want to be: lay off drinking and drugs when preparing for a crucial exam.

Nutrition is just as important for studying as it is for athletic training, because thinking and learning are physical functions of your body carried out by the cells of your brain. It so happens that your brain cells work on glucose (sugar) only. That said, it would be incorrect to deduce that your diet while studying should consist of candy bars and sodas. But you do learn and think best when your brain has a steady stream of glucose.

The best way to ensure this is to eat high-protein and so-called "complex carbohydrate" foods before studying and about every 3 hours during studying. Fruit, lean meat and fish, vegetables, pasta with low-fat sauce, cereal, crackers, bread, and legumes (such as peas and beans) are the foods associated with high mental performance. These foods will keep your blood sugar steady at an optimal level.

Avoid greasy or fatty foods; the work of digesting them actually pulls oxygen-rich blood away from your brain and toward your digestive system. (So pizza, although you may love it, is really not the best study food. Wait until after the exam, and then treat yourself to a pie with your favorite toppings as a reward for the high score you've earned.)

Rest is often neglected when people are studying very hard, but this is a mistake. Research has shown that people who are in a state of chronic sleep deprivation just don't think or perform very well. When hospitals shorten the working shifts of their medical residents, the doctors suffer fewer mental lapses and make better treatment decisions. The same applies to anyone working with his or her brain. The optimal amount of sleep varies from one person to another, but few people do well on less than six hours a night over any extended period of time, and most people thrive on 7 or 8 hours a night. Don't pull an all-nighter; get the sleep you need, and you'll find yourself learning more, and more easily, the next morning.

Reducing Stress When You Study

When you sit down to study, you can improve your memory and creativity by practicing the relaxation and visualization exercises earlier in this appendix. If you don't want to spend that much time, there is a brief technique that can be used just before studying or as needed during breaks in your study sessions. It takes only a few minutes. It works best if you have already experienced the longer exercise, and the more familiar you become with the long exercise the better this short one will work.

The 3-Minute Relaxation Technique

Sit comfortably wherever you like, with your feet flat on the floor. Rest your hands on your lap or desk. Place the thumbs and index fingers of each hand together.

Close your eyes. Take a moment to notice your breathing. After a few seconds, turn your attention to the pressure of your thumbs on your index fingers. The pressure can be light or firm. Notice that pressure as you inhale and exhale several times; really notice how your fingers feel.

Then, as you exhale, release the pressure, relaxing your hands, feeling your tension and fatigue flowing out with your exhalation and melting down your arms and out your fingertips.

Continue to focus on your breathing for a few minutes. When you are ready, open your eyes and reorient yourself to your surroundings.

This quick exercise will allow you to capture a sense of calm alertness whenever you need it.

Music to Learn By

Many people enjoy listening to music while they are studying. There is nothing wrong with music as long as you like it and don't find it distracting, but there are some things to consider when you choose music for your study sessions.

Music can help you to concentrate by filtering out extraneous sounds or thoughts. For this purpose, it is helpful if the music is familiar, so listening to a selection of favorite CDs would help you to study more efficiently than listening to the radio (which will probably play both familiar and unfamiliar selections as well as interjecting a stream of chatter and commercials that may well be distracting).

Music can also set a helpful mood while you're studying. It's a very personal choice, but in certain recent studies, when research subjects listened to classical music, particularly the works of Mozart, just before and during cognitive (mental) tasks, their performance on those tasks improved. You might want to experiment with different kinds of music to see which help you to concentrate best.

STRESS-BUSTING STRATEGIES FOR TEST DAY AND TEST DAY MINUS ONE

Hopefully you're not reading these suggestions for peak performance for the first time the day before your test. Ideally you'll have used the ideas we've presented for developing your personal test-preparation plan and you will be following it, more or less closely, in the weeks leading up to the exam. In particular, repeatedly visualizing success in the weeks before the test will motivate you to study and to view the test as a challenge you can meet, not a disaster in the making.

The Night Before

On the night before the test, make sure you have your admission form, your identification, a pen and pencil, and your directions to the test site all ready and available for the morning. Make sure you know how to get to the test center and how long it will take you to get there given the expected weather conditions and traffic patterns. If you control these "petty" details, they won't inject an unnecessary note of anxiety or uncertainty on the morning of the exam.

It's really helpful if you can do something pleasant and relaxing the night before the test. Avoid alcohol and other mood-altering chemicals, and get into bed early. If you've made a tape of your relaxation and visualization exercises, have it playing as you drift off into a refreshing sleep.

However, if you're going to be worrying about that one last math rule or analogy technique while you're watching that movie—or if you're feeling that you haven't suffered enough yet to appease the testing gods so they'll allow you to get your highest score—here are some tips for last-minute studying.

Don't try to reread this book or do any kind of comprehensive review. At this point, that will only increase your anxiety and convince you, incorrectly, that all the studying you have already done was inadequate and futile. Instead, decide how long you can study while still getting a good night's sleep. If you need 9 hours to feel rested, your score will be boosted more by getting the full 9 hours than by another few hours of studying.

Then pick a few topics you can comfortably cover in the amount of time you have left. Choose topics you are good at but feel can use a little more polishing, keeping in mind that you don't need a "perfect" score or to get every question correct.

Always remember, it is really all the previous studying you've done that will determine your score; you're only reviewing the night before to appease the testing gods. When it's time to go to sleep, set your alarm clock to give you plenty of time to get ready, eat breakfast, and get to the testing site without rushing. Then practice your relaxation and visualization exercises and have pleasant dreams of test-taking victory.

The Morning of the Exam

In the morning, eat something even if you normally don't eat breakfast. Study after study has demonstrated that people perform better on tests when they have eaten about 30 to 60 minutes beforehand. The foods you should eat are the same as those recommended during studying—high protein, low fat, and complex carbohydrate. Bring a piece of fruit or a power bar to the test center to eat during the brief mid-exam break.

During the exam itself—especially during the short breaks provided between test sections—you might try using the 3-Minute Relaxation technique if you feel fatigued or stressed.

All these tips, if practiced along with the study outlined in this book, will ensure your optimal performance on the GMAT. They'll also help you attain an even higher goal: to feel balanced and sane before and after the test.

NOTES

NOTES

NOTES

NOTES

NOTES

NOTES

NOTES

NOTES

NOTES

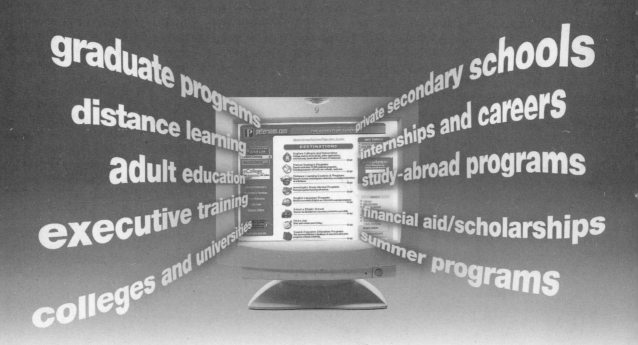